OXFORD HISTORICAL MONOGRAPHS

Marriage, Property, and Law in Late Imperial Russia

William G. Wagner

CLARENDON PRESS · OXFORD
1994

Oxford University Press, Walton Street, Oxford OX2 6DP
Oxford New York Toronto
Delhi Bombay Calcutta Madras Karachi
Kuala Lumpur Singapore Hong Kong Tokyo
Nairobi Dar es Salaam Cape Town
Melbourne Auckland Madrid
and associated companies in
Berlin Ibadan

Oxford is a trade mark of Oxford University Press

Published in the United States
by Oxford University Press Inc., New York

British Library Cataloguing in Publication Data
Data available

Library of Congress Cataloging in Publication Data
Wagner, William G.
Marriage, property, and law in late Imperial Russia / William G. Wagner.
p. cm. — (Oxford historical monographs)
Includes bibliographical references and index.
1. Husband and wife—Russia—History. 2. Marital property—Russia—History. 3. Inheritance and succession—Russia—History. 4. Law reform—Russia—History. 5. Russia—Social conditions.
I. Title. II. Series.
KLA542.W34 1994
346.4701′6—dc20 [344.70616] 94–4970
ISBN 0–19–820447–7

1 3 5 7 9 10 8 6 4 2

Typeset by Graphicraft Typesetters Ltd., Hong Kong
Printed in Great Britain
on acid-free paper by
Bookcraft Ltd., Midsomer Norton, Bath

For Linda

Acknowledgements

As the ideas expressed in this book have evolved from a tutorial essay at Oxford through a doctoral thesis and subsequent articles to their present form, they have benefited enormously from the advice and criticisms of numerous colleagues and friends. Space precludes the acknowledgement of all the people who have given generously of themselves in this way over the years, and none can be thanked adequately. I do, however, owe a special debt to several people and organizations. Particularly in the early stages of the project, my former British mentors, and now colleagues, William Butler, Bernard Rudden, Harry Shukman, and Angus Walker, offered invaluable advice and encouragement. The comments on earlier versions of the work made by Barbara Engel, Laura Engelstein, Gregory Freeze, Daniel Kaiser, and Richard Wortman contributed substantially to the development and presentation of the argument. My colleagues at Williams, in particular Gail Hershatter, Thomas Kohut, Thomas Spear, Patricia Tracy, Robert Waite, and James Wood, offered similarly helpful comments as well as giving freely of their time and expertise. Substantial assistance also was provided by several former students—Sara Beadle, Joel Hellman, Douglas Northrop, and Daniel Peris—as well as by Anne Just. Nothing could have been accomplished, of course, without the expertise and help of the staff at numerous libraries, but the librarians at the Slavonic Collection of the Helsinki University Library, who have come as close to creating a state of Nirvana for the researcher as may be possible, and my archivists at the Central State Historical Archive in what was then Leningrad, who repeatedly bent the rules for me at a time when there was some risk but no profit in doing so, deserve special thanks. Research for the project also could not have been completed without the financial support provided at various times by the International Research and Exchanges Board, the National Endowment for the Humanities, the American Council of Learned Societies, Williams College, St John's College, Oxford, and Christ Church College, Oxford. But most important of all, I could not have persevered without the encouragement, patience, and love of my wife, Linda, to whom this book is dedicated.

Contents

List of Tables

Abbreviations

AHR	*American Historical Review*
BSSU	*Biograficheskii slovar′ professorov i prepodavatelei Imp. S.-Peterburgskago Universiteta za istekshuiu tret′iu chetvert′ veka ego sushchestvovaniia, 1869–1894* (Spb., 1896, 1898)
BSUSV	*Biograficheskii slovar′ professorov i prepodavatelei Imp. Universiteta Sv. Vladimira* (1834–84) (Kiev, 1884)
BV	*Birzhevyia Vedomosti*
ChOIDR	*Chteniia v Imperatorskom Obshchestve Istorii Drevnostei Rossiiskikh pri Moskovskom Universitete*
DB	*Dukhovnaia Beseda*
des.	desiatin/a (1 desiatin = 2.7 acres)
DINU	*Dvadtsatipiatiletie Imp. Novorossiiskago Universiteta* (Odessa, 1890)
GDP	*Gosudarstvennaia Duma. Prilozheniia k stenograficheskim otchetam*
GDSO	*Gosudarstvennaia Duma. Stenograficheskii otchet*
GS 1915	*Gosudarstvennyi Sovet 1915* (Ptgd., 1915)
GSSO	*Gosudarstvennyi Sovet. Stenograficheskii otchet*
GU	*Grazhdanskoe Ulozhenie. Proekt Vysochaishe uchrezhdennoi Redaktsionnoi Kommisii po sostavleniiu Grazhdanskago Ulozheniia*
HLL	Harvard Law Library
IuG	*Iuridicheskaia Gazeta*
IuL	*Iuridicheskaia Letopis′*
IuO	*Iuridicheskoe Obozrenie*
IuV	*Iuridicheskii Vestnik*
JGO	*Jahrbücher für Geschichte Osteuropas*
KhCh	*Khristianskoe Chtenie*
Lenin.	Leningrad
Mos.	Moscow
MV	*Moskovskiia Vedomosti*
NiBG	*Novosti i Birzhevaia Gazeta*
NV	*Novoe Vremia*

ODGS	*Otchet po deloproizvodstvu Gosudarstvennago Soveta*
OGS	*Otchet po Gosudarstvennomu Sovetu*
OMIu	*Otchet Ministerstva Iustitsii*
PO	*Pravoslavnoe Obozrenie*
PS	*Pravitel'stvuiushchii Senat* (Spb., 1912)
PSob	*Pravoslavnyi Sobesednik*
PSZ	*Polnoe Sobranie Zakonov Rossiiskoi Imperii* (lst, 2nd, or 3rd series)
Ptgd.	Petrograd
RA	*Russkii Arkhiv*
RB	*Russkoe Bogatstvo*
RGKD	*Resheniia Grazhdanskago Kassatsionnago Departamenta Pravitel'stvuiushchago Senata*
RM	*Russkaia Mysl'*
ROSPKD	L. M. Rotenberg (ed.), *Polnyi svod reshenii obshchago sobraniia pervago i kassatsionnykh departamentov i kassatsionnykh departamentov Pravitel'stvuiushchago Senata*
RS	*Russkaia Starina*
RVed	*Russkie Vedomosti*
RVest	*Russkii Vestnik*
SChMIu	*Spisok chinam Pravitel'stvuiushchago Senata i Ministerstva iustitsii* (1842–1869); *Spisok chinam Pravitel'stvuiushchago Senata, Departamenta Ministerstva Iustitsii i sudebnykh mest, obrazovannykh na osnovanii sudebnykh ustavov 20-go noiabria 1864 goda* (1870, 1873); *Spisok chinam vedomstva Ministerstva iustitsii* (1877–1916)
SEER	*Slavonic and East European Review*
SG	*Sudebnaia Gazeta*
SIRIO	*Sbornik Imperatorskago Russkago Istoricheskago Obshchestva*
SKhiL	*Sel'skoe Khoziaistvo i Lesovodstvo. Zhurnal Ministerstva Zemledeliia i Gosudarstvennykh Imushchestv*
SL	*Sudebnaia Letopis'*
Spb.	St Petersburg
SR	*Slavic Review*
SRGKD	*Polnyi Svod Reshenii Grazhdanskago Kassatsionnago Departamenta Pravitel'stvuiushchago Senata, 1866–1910*
SRPS	*Sbornik reshenii Pravitel'stvuiushchago Senata*
SSSMIu	*Sbornik statisticheskikh svedenii ministerstva iustitsii*
SUst	*Sudebnye Ustavy 20 noiabria 1864 goda, s izlozheniem razsuzhdenii, na koikh oni osnovany*

SUzak	*Sobranie Uzakonenii i Rasporiazhenii Pravitel'stva*
SVed	*Sanktpeterburgskie Vedomosti*
SVest	*Sudebnyi Vestnik*
SZ	*Svod Zakonov Rossiiskoi Imperii* (year of edition)
SZPGU	*Svod zamechanii na proekt grazhdanskago ulozheniia*
TsGIA	Tsentral'nyi Gosudarstvennyi Istoricheskii Arkhiv
TsVed	*Tserkovnye Vedomosti*
TsVest	*Tserkovnyi Vestnik*
TVEO	*Trudy Imperatorskago Vol'nago Ekonomicheskago Obshchestva*
UGS	*Ustav Grazhdanskago Sudoproizvodstva*
USU	*Uchrezhdenie Sudebnykh Ustanovlenii*
UUS	*Ustav Ugolovnago Sudoproizvodstva*
VE	*Vestnik Evropy*
VOOPSS	*Izvlechenie iz otcheta Ober Prokurora Sviateishago Sinoda* (1841–52); *Izvlechenie iz otcheta po vedomstvu dukhovnykh del* (1853–8); *Izvlechenie iz otcheta po vedomstvu Pravoslavnago ispovedaniia* (1859–61); *Izvlechenie iz Vsepoddanneishago otcheta Ober-Prokurora Sviateishago Sinoda po vedomstvu Pravoslavnago ispovedaniia* (1866–83); *Vsepoddaneishii otchet Ober-Prokurora Sviateishago Sinoda po vedomstvu Pravoslavnago ispovedaniia* (1884–1914)
VP	*Vestnik Prava*
ZhD	*Zhenskoe Delo*
ZhGiUP	*Zhurnal Grazhdanskago i Ugolovnago Prava*
ZhIuOSU	*Zhurnal Iuridicheskago Obshchestva pri Imp. S.-Peterburgskom Universitete*
ZhMIu	*Zhurnal Ministerstva Iustitsii*
ZhRKGU	*Zhurnaly redaktsionnoi kommisii, vysochaishe uchrezhdennoi dlia sostavleniia proekta grazhdanskago ulozheniia*
ZNDGZ	*Zamechaniia o nedostatkakh deistvuiushchikh grazhdanskikh zakonov. Izdanie redaktsionnoi kommisii po sostavleniiu grazhdanskago ulozheniia* (Spb., 1891)
ZSL	*Za sto let. Biograficheskii slovar' professorov i prepodavatelei Imp. Kazanskago Universiteta* (1804–1904) (Kazan, 1904)

Transliteration: I have normally followed the Library of Congress system of transliteration of modern Russian with diacritical marks omitted. Proper names familiar to the reader of English, however, have been left in their commonly known form.

Introduction

Civil Law, Ideology, and Social Change

THE courtroom became 'a solemn cathedral, where the sacrament of justice, humanity, and mercy was performed', recalled a stenographer of the Kharkov District Court in the first years after the judicial reform of 1864.[1] 'What a time that was!' judge Valerian Volzhin declared from retirement. 'Strivings for the ideal and for justice were not mocked ... We, youth, at that time believed in [the reform] ... And the faith of the young was shared also by many of the older generation, who had witnessed the baptism of the judicial statutes.'[2] Such high hopes for the attainment of social justice and the perfection of public morality through judicial action were bound to be frustrated. Yet despite their disappointment with the failure of the reform to realize all their expectations, progressivist jurists like Volzhin still praised its benefits fifty years after its proclamation.[3]

Despite disagreement on the significance and subsequent fate of the judicial reform, Soviet and Western historians also generally have agreed that it improved the administration of justice in prerevolutionary Imperial Russia. But concerned primarily with the political significance of the reform, both groups of historians have concentrated on the process of reform, the position of the new courts within the tsarist governmental structure, and the role of the courts in the administration of political justice.[4] While these questions undoubtedly are important, exclusive

[1] Iul. K——n, 'Na razvalinakh glasnago suda', *VE* (1906), 7: 224.

[2] V. Volzhin, 'Iz memuarov V. A. Volzhina', *Istoricheskii Vestnik* (1912), 7: 50. The son of a noble landowner whose fortunes declined substantially after the emancipation, Volzhin studied law at Moscow University before embarking on a judicial career, largely in provincial courts. He claims to have been forced to resign for political reasons in 1910.

[3] e.g. see A. F. Koni, 'Posleslovie', in *Ottsy i deti sudebnoi reformy. K piatidesiatiletiiu sudebnykh ustavov 1864–20 noiabria 1914* (Mos., 1914), O. V. Portugalov, *Neskol'ko slov v iubileinyi venok sudebnoi reformy* (Volsk, 1914), and N. V. Davydov and N. N. Polianskii (eds.), *Sudebnaia reforma* (Mos., 1915), i, ii.

[4] For different Soviet assessments of the judicial reform, compare B. V. Vilenskii, *Sudebnaia reforma i kontrreforma v Rossii* (Saratov, 1969), P. F. Shcherbina, *Sudebnaia reforma 1864 goda na pravoberezhnoi Ukraine* (Lvov, 1974), V. A. Shuvalova, 'O sushchnosti sudebnoi

concentration on them has led both Soviet and Western historians to ignore the regular activities of the new courts and their impact on areas of the law that significantly affected the daily lives of Imperial Russian subjects. In this regard, the number of civil cases heard by the new courts far exceeded the number of political cases, including those tried before special tribunals.[5] Moreover, the decisions of the courts in the field of civil law had considerable significance given the social, economic, and cultural changes taking place in post-emancipation Imperial Russia.

By altering occupations, economic activity, and social relations and mobility, phenomena such as the abolition of serfdom in 1861, the increased commercialization of agriculture, the growth of peasant migratory labour and crafts production, rapid industrialization and urbanization, the spread of formal education, and the emergence of professional groups created pressure for corresponding changes in civil law. Of course, the complexity of the relationship between law and behaviour makes it difficult to determine the influence of legal considerations on the actions of Imperial Russian subjects during this period. In post-emancipation Imperial Russia, as elsewhere, people acted in ignorance or violation of the law or circumvented it when desirable and possible. The widespread criticism of the law expressed in contemporary sources none the less suggests that many Imperial subjects found existing legal rules to be inadequate or too constrictive in post-emancipation conditions. Activities and institutions that became common in the latter part of the nineteenth century received only scant treatment in statutory law. And even the

reformy 1864 g. v Rossii', *Sovetskoe Gosudarstvo i Pravo* (1964), 10: 121–7, N. N. Efremova, *Ministerstvo iustitsii rossiiskoi imperii 1802–1917 gg.* (Mos., 1983), N. A. Troitskii, *Tsarizm pod sudom progressivnoi obshchestvennosti, 1866–1895 gg.* (Mos., 1979), and N. V. Cherkasova, *Formirovanie i razvitie advokatury v Rossii 60–80 gody xix veka* (Mos., 1987), with P. A. Zaionchkovskii, *Rossiiskoe samoderzhavie v kontse xix stoletiia* (Mos., 1970), I. V. Orzhekhovskii, *Iz istorii vnutrennei politiki samoderzhaviia v 60–70 godakh xix veka* (Gorky, 1974), and M. G. Korotkikh, 'Sudebnaia reforma v Rossii', *Voprosy Istorii* (1987), 12: 20–34. For Western scholarship, see F. B. Kaiser, *Die Russische Justizreform von 1864: Zur Geschichte der Russischen Justiz von Katharina II bis 1916* (Leiden, 1972), S. Kucherov, *Courts, Lawyers, and Trials under the Last Three Tsars* (reprint edn., Westport, Conn., 1974), R. S. Wortman, *The Development of a Russian Legal Consciousness* (Chicago, 1976), W. G. Wagner, 'Tsarist Legal Policies at the End of the Nineteenth Century: A Study in Inconsistencies', *SEER* 54 (1976), 378–85, B. Levin-Stankevich, 'Cassation, Judicial Interpretation and the Development of Civil and Criminal Law in Russia, 1864–1917: The Institutional Consequences of the 1864 Court Reform in Russia', (Ph.D. diss., SUNY, Buffalo, 1984), and J. Baberowski, 'Das Justizwesen im späten Zarenreich 1864–1914: Zum Problem von Rechtsstaatlichkeit, politischer Justiz und Rückständigkeit in Russland', *Zeitschrift für Neuere Rechtsgeschichte*, 13 (1991), 156–72.

[5] See the statistical survey in *Sudebnye Ustavy 20 noiabria 1864 g. za piat'desiat let* (Ptgd., 1914), ii. 337–74.

pursuit of traditional socio-political goals involved the use of new forms of property or new arrangements whose legal status was unclear. To overcome these uncertainties and constraints, Imperial subjects sought clarification and revision of the law as much as its enforcement from the courts and the state.

But pressure for the revision of civil law also had ideological sources.[6] Both through the values and ideals expressed in its language and through its substantive provisions, the law reflects and supports the structure of relations, the definitions of gender, and the distribution of authority within a society. This symbolic and substantive significance often makes civil law an object of conflict between competing social, political, or ideological groups. Such conflict can become particularly acute during periods of intense social and economic change, when the disruption of relations within a society challenges the world view, or ideology, of its individual members and constituent groups.[7] Such was the case in post-emancipation Imperial Russia, where members of the educated and upper strata of society in particular responded to the changes taking place during this period by formulating different ideologies that in turn found expression in competing demands for the revision of Imperial civil law. Indeed, given the limitations imposed on political discourse and action by the tsarist regime, civil law represented an important medium for the articulation and realization of these different ideological perspectives.

Family, property, and inheritance law were particularly vulnerable to such use because of their actual and perceived role in political, social, and economic life. On the one hand, because these areas of the law at least formally define fundamental social institutions and relationships and the rules governing access to and the use of economic resources, the changes occurring in social and economic behaviour in post-emancipation Imperial Russia created practical legal problems that required a solution. On the other hand, it was widely believed among the educated and upper strata of tsarist society and proclaimed by the state and the Orthodox Church that the family constituted the foundation of the social and political order. Much as in earlier periods in Europe and America, the family therefore served as a metaphor for political authority and social

[6] I have used the term 'revision' rather than 'reform' both because conservatives as well as progressivists and similar groups sought to change the law and because, in the context of Imperial Russia, the changes demanded by the latter often had revolutionary implications.

[7] On the admittedly elusive concept of ideology, see the perceptive comments of Isaac Kramnick in *Republicanism and Bourgeois Radicalism: Political Ideology in Late Eighteenth-Century England and America* (Ithaca, NY, 1990), 29–31, and the literature cited there.

organization in general, with changes in the former thought to affect the latter.[8] In this context, attempts to provide solutions for practical legal problems arising in the interrelated areas of family, property, and inheritance law tended to become intertwined with efforts to use the law to pursue ideological goals.

Although ideological and political conflict over the law involved primarily the educated and upper strata of society, different ideological positions did not correspond neatly with particular social groups. On the contrary, all groups were divided over fundamental social values and cultural ideals and hence over how the law should be revised. These divisions reflected the growing incongruence between personal experience and the legal estates into which tsarist society continued to be classified. Some members of the educated and upper strata of society responded to this situation by consciously rejecting tradition, including the very concept of a legally ordered society, and by expressing values and attitudes that could be characterized as 'bourgeois', however much they themselves may have spurned such an identity. Others idealized traditional values and attitudes or combined them with new ones in practical, if logically inconsistent, ways. Still others adopted more radical positions, on both the left and the right. The result was the increased ideological and political fragmentation of these social strata even as the development of a national market, a national press, professional, civic, and business associations, and similar phenomena fostered their integration.[9] In this context, civil law provided

[8] On this phenomenon, see especially J. Fliegelman, *Prodigals and Pilgrims: The American Revolution Against Patriarchal Authority, 1750–1800* (Cambridge, 1982), J. F. Traer, *Marriage and the Family in Eighteenth-Century France* (Ithaca, NY, 1980), L. Hunt, *The Family Romance of the French Revolution* (Berkeley, Calif., 1992), and G. J. Schochet, *Patriarchalism and Political Thought: The Authoritarian Family and Political Speculation and Attitudes Especially in Seventeenth-Century England* (Oxford, 1975).

[9] Because they suggest an interactive process that allows for co-operation as well as conflict within and between social groups, and therefore also for ideological heterogeneity within a sociologically defined group, the concepts of a 'public sphere' or 'civil society' might usefully be applied to these developments. But the identification of these concepts with the bourgeoisie seems to me problematic, particularly because of the way it prefigures conceptualization of the interactive process. For criticisms of the traditional conception of the European bourgeoisie which stress the heterogeneity, ambiguities, and disunity of this group, see esp. P. Gay, *The Bourgeois Experience: Education of the Senses* (New York, 1984), 17–68, and W. Reddy, *Money and Liberty in Modern Europe: A Critique of Historical Understanding* (Cambridge, 1987), 1–33. On the relationship between social identity and social change in late Imperial Russia, see G. L. Freeze, 'The *Soslovie* (Estate) Paradigm and Russian Social History', *AHR* 91 (1986), 11–36, L. H. Haimson, 'The Problem of Social Identities in Early Twentieth Century Russia', *SR* 47 (1988), 1–20, and A. J. Rieber, 'The Sedimentary Society', in E. W. Clowes, S. D. Kassow, and J. L. West (eds.), *Between Tsar and People: Educated Society and the Quest for Public Identity in Late Imperial Russia* (Princeton,

not only a medium for ideological self-expression, but also an instrument for imposing social order and stability, either by limiting social change or by directing it through an appropriate legal framework.[10]

While such attempts to manage social conflict and change through civil law were common in continental Europe after the French Revolution,[11] in post-emancipation Imperial Russia they coincided with a conflict over the nature of law which threatened to undermine the existing conception of state authority. In its broadest terms, this conflict opposed a legal order defined in terms of paternalistic authority and substantive justice to one based on legality conceived as the rule of law. The former, of course, did not deny the importance of legal rules or even preclude a notion of legality, albeit understood as rule through rather than of law. Indeed, influenced by the Central European cameralist conception of law as a means of ordering and ruling society for the promotion of its general welfare, during the eighteenth century Russian autocrats had tried repeatedly to regularize administrative institutions and procedures and to codify Imperial law. Such attempts to introduce regularized norms and procedures, however, were not meant to limit, but to rationalize, and thereby to assist, autocratic rule. Legality understood as the exercise of paternalistic state authority through the medium of rational and regularized rules therefore perpetuated essential elements of the traditional tsarist legal order: an instrumentalist view of law, a higher priority on the outcome of particular cases than on the strict observance of procedural or substantive rules, and a perception of law as intrinsic to those who exercised authority. 'The Sovereign is absolute,' Catherine the Great had declared in her Instruction to the Legislative Commission convened in 1767 to codify Imperial law. And while generally a ruler should observe the laws established by her 'not to deprive the People of their natural Liberty, but to direct their Conduct in such a manner that the greatest good may be derived from all their Operations', 'there are Cases in which Power may and ought to be exerted in its full Sway'.[12] Legal rules, in other words, remained secondary to their intended ends and could be disregarded

NJ, 1991), 343–66, and on the question of the emergence of a middle class at this time, see the essays in this latter collection generally.

[10] Laura Engelstein comes to similar conclusions regarding Imperial criminal law in *The Keys to Happiness: Sex and the Search for Modernity in Fin-de-Siècle Russia* (Ithaca, NY, 1992).

[11] See in particular D. R. Kelly, *Historians and the Law in Post-Revolutionary France* (Princeton, NJ, 1984), and J. Q. Whitman, *The Legacy of Roman Law in the German Romantic Era: Historical Vision and Legal Change* (Princeton, NJ, 1990).

[12] *Catherine the Great's Instruction (Nakaz) to the Legislative Commission, 1767*, trans. and ed. P. Dukes (Newtonville, Mass., 1977), arts. 9, 13, 512.

when necessary. Such rules consequently neither stood apart from nor limited autocratic power. On the contrary, 'Russian law is the tsar's will and to act in accordance with the law is the same as doing the tsar's will . . . *Ergo* the new term "legality" . . . represents the return of Russia not only to the path of truth and justice, but also to the path of the fulfilment of the tsar's will.'[13]

The inability of the autocracy to realize even this conservative understanding of legality, however, attests to the reluctance of Russian autocrats and state officials to abandon the practice of personalized and discretionary paternalistic authority, thereby introducing a tension into tsarist governmental practices that the judicial reform increased by establishing judicial independence. Reflecting the torn loyalties that resulted, on the fiftieth anniversary of the reform the reactionary Minister of Justice, Ivan Shcheglovitov, declared:

> [j]ustice . . . presupposes that the actions of the court, which is subordinate only to the law, are free from any influence of the administration, even that of the supreme governmental power, which cannot dictate which verdicts a judge must deliver even though it has appointed him. Dependent justice will never be justice. The judge is distinguished from the administrator by independence in the administration of justice. A judge must consider only the case, the law, and his conscience. The State protects this position of the judge by granting him irremovability, exclusively in the interests of justice. On the other hand, judicial independence does not create a special state composed of judges. Above all, judges are servants of the state; they are an extremely important part of a vast state mechanism and must consider the general interests of the state. The Judicial Statutes by no means placed . . . the judicial branch in the position of some sort of independent and self-administered kingdom, having nothing above it except the open sky. The

[13] The quote is from a letter sent by one Vladimir Gol′mstrem in 1896 to Konstantin Pobedonostsev (see below), who forwarded the letter to Nicholas II. K. P. Pobedonostsev, *Pis′ma Pobedonostseva k Aleksandru III* (Mos. 1926), ii. 313. On conceptions of law in Imperial Russia, and on attempts to introduce regularized norms and procedures during the 18th c., see Wortman, *Legal Consciousness*, M. Raeff, *Understanding Imperial Russia: State and Society in the Old Regime* (New York, 1984), id., *The Well-Ordered Police State: Social and Institutional Change through Law in the Germanies and Russia, 1600–1800* (New Haven, Conn., 1983), *Absoliutizm v Rossii (xvii–xviii vv.)* (Mos., 1964), 389–459, G. L. Yaney, *The Systematization of Russian Government: Social Evolution in the Domestic Administration of Imperial Russia 1711–1905* (Urbana, Ill., 1973), A. Walicki, *Legal Philosophies of Russian Liberalism* (Oxford, 1987), N. V. Riasanovsky, *A Parting of Ways: Government and the Educated Public in Russia 1801–1855* (Oxford, 1976), Levin-Stankevich, 'Cassation', and B. A. Kistiakovskii, 'In the Defense of Law: The Intelligentsia and Legal Consciousness', in B. Shagrin and A. Todd (eds.), *Landmarks: A Collection of Essays on the Russian Intelligentsia—1909*, trans. M. Schwartz (New York, 1977), 112–37.

drafters of the Statutes considered judges to be responsible for their actions, and the judicial oath expresses the duty 'to preserve loyalty to His Imperial Majesty, the Emperor, the Autocrat of All Russia and to execute faithfully the laws of the Empire' under threat of 'answering before God at His Final Judgment'.[14]

The arch-conservative jurist and Chief Procurator of the Holy Synod, Konstantin Pobedonostsev, expressed similar views in a critique of the new judicial system in 1885. 'Experience has shown sufficiently', he argued, 'the incongruity of existing judicial institutions and procedures with the needs of the people and the conditions of their existence as well as with the general structure of state institutions in Russia.' 'Unfortunately,' he continued, 'the new judicial institutions, . . . having broadened and contained in strong forms the attributes of judicial power, incongruously constrained the freedom of action of the executive power. This produced effects that were not only not beneficial, but harmful, since with this constriction of the executive power . . . the interests of order, which are the most substantial for the people, remained entirely unsecured.' Pobedonostsev none the less maintained that the inadequacies of the post-reform system 'must be corrected while preserving so far as possible that which constitutes a substantial improvement in the new judicial structure'.[15] The solution, in his view, was to preserve the structural and functional separation of the courts from the state administration while subordinating their personnel to the Minister of Justice.

By contrast, the advocates of a legal order based on legality understood as the rule of law (which will be the meaning used in this study) stressed the integrity of legal rules and procedures. In their view, the regularity and predictability that resulted from the uniform observance of legal rules contributed to the security of individuals and their property. This security was considered both desirable in itself and necessary to promote more productive economic activity, on which national strength rested. But legality defined in terms of the observance of legal rules and procedures required toleration of any outcome produced by actions that did

[14] *Sudebnye Ustavy za 50 let*, i. 284. For similar statements by the Minister of Justice, Nikolai Muravev, see *Ministerstvo iustitsii za sto let, 1802–1902. Istoricheskii ocherk* (Spb., 1902), 224–5. Born in 1861 and the son of a wealthy noble landowner, Shcheglovitov graduated from the Imperial School of Jurisprudence in 1881 and then served chiefly as a procurator before becoming Minister of Justice, in which capacity he orchestrated the unsuccessful prosecution of the Jew Mendel Beilis for ritual murder in 1913.

[15] K. P. Pobedonostsev, *K. P. Pobedonostsev i ego korrespondenty. Pis'ma i zapiski* (Mos., Ptgd., 1923), i. (pt. 2), pp. 508, 514, and 508–15 in general. See also id., *Pis'ma*, ii. 104–6, 203–4, 311–14, and TsGIA F. 1405 op. 542 d. 124 ll. 54–5.

not violate these norms, thereby constricting the discretionary power of state administrators. The jurists who promoted this ideal of legality believed further that its realization required a specialized and independent judiciary capable of interpreting and applying legal norms uniformly and of ensuring their observance even by state officials. Structurally as well as conceptually, legal norms therefore constrained state authority and at least to this extent were perceived as extrinsic to it.[16]

Two exchanges in 1878 between the conservative Minister of Justice Count Konstantin Palen and the liberal prosecutor and judge Anatolii Koni illustrate the differences between these two conceptions of legal order. Koni was to chair the court that was to try Vera Zasulich, a young woman who had shot and wounded the governor of St Petersburg, General Fedor Trepov, in retaliation for his illegal punishment of an arrested fellow student.[17] Pressed twice by Palen to ensure a guilty verdict, Koni replied on the first occasion that '[a]ll I can assure in this case is the observance of complete impartiality and all the guarantees of correct justice' and on the second that 'the skill of the chairman [of the court] consists in the impartial observance of the law . . . My obligations and tasks are defined so clearly in the [judicial] statutes that now it is already possible to say what I will do in the [court] session.'[18] Responding agitatedly to these rebuffs, Palen declared,

[16] On the idea of legality embraced by the reformers, see Wortman, *Legal Consciousness*, 244–50, 259–61, W. B. Lincoln, *In the Vanguard of Reform: Russia's Enlightened Bureaucrats 1825–1861* (DeKalb, Ill., 1982), 58–67, 183–4, 203–4, Levin-Stankevich, 'Cassation', 63, 284–99, T. Taranovski, 'The Aborted Counter-Reform: The Murav′ev Commission and the Judicial Statutes of 1864', *JGO* 29 (1981), 163–4, and O. F. Skakun, 'Teoriia pravovogo gosudarstva v dorevoliutsionnoi Rossii', *Sovetskoe Gosudarstvo i Pravo* (1990), 2: 113–20. On the concept of legality, and on the differences between legal orders based on this principle and on personalized and/or substantive justice, see J. N. Shklar, *Legalism: Law, Morals, and Political Trials* (Cambridge, Mass., 1964), H. J. Berman, *Law and Revolution: The Formation of the Western Legal Tradition* (Cambridge, Mass., 1983), esp. 20–1, 37–41, and R. Pound, *An Introduction to the Philosophy of Law* (rev. edn., New Haven, Conn., 1954), 33–41.

[17] On this case, see Wortman, *Legal Consciousness*, 273–5, 282–3, Kucherov, *Courts*, 79–80, 214–25, 269–70, Vilenskii, *Sudebnaia reforma*, 258–64, 284–7, 322–32, P. A. Zaionchkovsky, *The Russian Autocracy in Crisis, 1878–1882*, ed. and trans. G. M. Hamburg (Gulf Breeze, Fla., 1979), 33–42, and P. I. Negretov, 'K sporam vokrug protsessa Very Zasulich', *Voprosy Istorii* (1971), 12: 183–9.

[18] A. F. Koni, *Sobranie sochinenii* (Mos., 1966–9), ii. 74, 85. Born in 1844 and the son of a writer and publicist and of a prominent actress, Koni graduated from the juridical faculty at St Petersburg University and in 1867 entered the judicial service, where he served primarily as an assistant procurator and procurator before becoming chairman of the St Petersburg District Court in 1877. He later served as Chief Procurator and then as a senator in the Criminal Cassation Department of the Senate (on the cassation departments and the reformed judicial system in general, see below, Ch. 1).

'Indeed, justice, impartiality! . . . but in this accursed affair the government has a right to expect special services from the court and from you.'

'Yes, I know—impartiality! Impartiality! So say all your "statutists" [*statisty*]. But there are cases which must be viewed . . . politically.'[19]

Palen also rejected Koni's advice to have the state prosecutor condemn the illegality of Trepov's action as a way to emphasize to the jury the equally illegal nature of Zasulich's act. Like Catherine earlier, Palen clearly believed that state interest took precedence over considerations of legality and therefore in this case legal norms should be disregarded in order to produce the desired result.[20]

Efforts to resolve the conflicts over Imperial civil law during the post-emancipation period took place primarily in two arenas: the legislative process and the courts. As several recent studies have shown, however, institutional and ideological conflicts within the tsarist government often impeded its ability to effect institutional adaptation or renovation during this period. Paradoxically, the strengthening of the central ministries during the nineteenth century contributed to this problem by transforming the government into a collection of semi-autonomous administrative entities, pursuing essentially independent policies. As the ministries became functionally more specialized and their personnel more professional, they developed interests and perspectives that both clashed with one another and limited the discretionary power of ministers themselves. The ensuing rivalries and conflicts over policies, jurisdiction, and resources led frequently to deadlock over specific legislation as well as to incoherence in the general direction of state policy. In the case of family law,

[19] Ibid. Palen used the term *Statisty* to refer derisively to officials who stressed the observance of legal and procedural rules. Born in 1833, Palen graduated from the juridical faculty at St Petersburg University in 1853 and then served chiefly in the chancellery of the State Council and the police department of the Ministry of Internal Affairs before being appointed in 1867 first as Assistant Minister of Justice and then as Minister.

[20] The jury acquitted Zasulich. Although legal systems based on the principle of legality generally provide some means of discretionary action to avoid a result deemed to be particularly unjust, such means exist only as a supplement and exception to, and therefore depend upon, the general body of legal norms (e.g. equity in English law). Referring to the English system of equity, the Minister of Justice, Nikolai Manasein, in 1893 proposed the creation of a 'supreme court of conscience' that could suspend the application of any legal rule in a particular civil case in order to achieve a result deemed more just. The proposal was successfully opposed by members of the Civil Cassation Department of the Senate and other state officials who supported the principle of legality. See TsGIA F. 1226 op. 1 d. 1 ll. 2–6, 22–33, 68–70, and F. 1405 op. 542 d. 124 ll. 192–203.

these problems were made worse by the involvement of ecclesiastical authorities, particularly of the Orthodox Church.[21]

There were few mechanisms for reconciling rival institutions, and none worked particularly effectively. Prior to 1905 individual ministers reported directly to the emperor, a relationship that underscored their independence from one another. Although it met regularly, the Committee of Ministers lacked the power either to formulate policy or to discipline its members. The interministerial committees formed on an *ad hoc* basis for specific tasks frequently were dominated by a single ministry, a situation that did not incline other ministries to accept their recommendations. Even when more evenly representative they often failed to achieve consensus over the issue being discussed. In any case, relevant institutions still had to review the proposals and could use a myriad of bureaucratic tactics to obstruct their implementation.

Charged with the review of legislation and composed of ministers and other high officials appointed by the emperor, the plenary session and various committees of the State Council provided regular forums for the discussion of general policy within the context of specific legislative proposals. But ministers used the State Council more to pursue their own interests and to check the programmes of their rivals than to co-ordinate governmental policy. In any case, the emperor was free to accept or reject the Council's advice.[22]

This structure left the emperor himself in the only position to bring coherence to state policy, a situation that suited the last Romanovs, who mistrusted central governmental institutions as potential constraints on their personal authority. Preservation of the personalized relationship between the tsar and each minister seemed to protect this authority. Yet

[21] For recent studies stressing intra-governmental conflict, see D. T. Orlovsky, *The Limits of Reform: The Ministry of Internal Affairs in Imperial Russia, 1802–1881* (Cambridge, Mass., 1981), T. S. Pearson, *Russian Officialdom in Crisis: Autocracy and Local Self-Government, 1861–1900* (Cambridge, 1989), F. W. Wcislo, *Reforming Rural Russia: State, Local Society, and National Politics, 1855–1914* (Princeton, NJ, 1990), D. A. J. Macey, *Government and Peasant in Russia 1861–1906: The Prehistory of the Stolypin Reforms* (DeKalb, Ill., 1987), T. Taranovski, 'Alexander III and his Bureaucracy: The Limitations on Autocratic Power', *Canadian Slavonic Papers*, 26 (1984), 207–19, W. C. Fuller, *Civil-Military Conflict in Imperial Russia, 1881–1914* (Princeton, NJ, 1985), G. L. Freeze, *The Parish Clergy in Nineteenth-Century Russia: Crisis, Reform, Counter-Reform* (Princeton, NJ, 1983), Yaney, *Systematization*, Zaionchkovskii, *Rossiiskoe samoderzhavie*, and V. G. Chernukha, *Vnutrenniaia politika tsarizma s serediny 50-kh do nachala 80-kh gg. xix v.* (Lenin., 1978).

[22] In addition to the works cited above in n. 21, see N. P. Eroshkin, *Istoriia gosudarstvennykh uchrezhdenii dorevoliutsionnoi Rossii* (3rd edn., Mos., 1983), and H. W. Whelan, *Alexander III and the State Council: Bureaucracy and Counter-Reform in Late Imperial Russia* (New Brunswick, NJ, 1982).

the education, training, and personal qualities of the last emperors, combined with the sheer magnitude of the task, prevented them from fulfilling this function effectively.[23]

The institutions created in the wake of the revolution of 1905 improved the governmental process only marginally while in some ways further complicating it. The revived Council of Ministers did serve briefly as an effective instrument for co-ordinating government policy, particularly under the Minister of Internal Affairs, Petr Stolypin. But Stolypin's ability to control his fellow ministers, let alone the institutions they managed, was never complete and was waning even prior to his assassination in 1911. As succeeding presidents of the Council grew progressively weaker, ministerial independence reasserted itself. The representative bodies established after 1905—the popularly elected Duma and the partially elected, partially appointed State Council—did provide a central forum for the discussion of state policy and the formulation of legislation, which Stolypin used effectively to enact several important measures. But the limited power enjoyed by these bodies, coupled with their own internal fragmentation, rendered them incapable of reconciling feuding ministries or co-ordinating state policy.[24]

Legislative revision of Imperial civil law proved extremely difficult under these conditions. Even when consensus existed over the need to change the law, proposals to do so almost invariably became mired in institutional, ideological, and professional conflicts. The importance of the courts as a medium both for adapting civil law to changing conditions and for resolving ideological and political conflict over the law consequently increased. The courts responded by changing the law. And after the judicial reform, judge-made law meant jurist-made law. The law defined by the courts therefore reflected the views, values, and perceptions existing within the juridical profession which emerged in Imperial

[23] See L. G. Zakharova, 'Krizis samoderzhaviia nakanune revoliutsii 1905 goda', *Voprosy Istorii* (1972), 8: 119–40, R. S. Wortman, 'The Russian Empress as Mother', in D. L. Ransel (ed.), *The Family in Imperial Russia: New Lines of Historical Research* (Urbana, Ill., 1978), 60–74, Zaionchkovskii, *Rossiiskoe samoderzhavie*, ch. 1, and Raeff, *Imperial Russia*, 193–201.

[24] Limited to males, after 1907 the electoral franchise for the Duma heavily favoured the landed nobility. Half the membership of the State Council consisted of state officials appointed by the tsar and half was elected through public organizations in a way that similarly favoured the nobility. Government ministers remained responsible only to the tsar. On the functioning of this system, see G. A. Hosking, *The Russian Constitutional Experiment: Government and Duma, 1907–1914* (Cambridge, 1973), and the works of A. Ia. Avrekh: *Tsarizm i tret'eiiunskaia sistema* (Mos., 1966), *Stolypin i tret'ia duma* (Mos., 1968), *Tsarizm i IV duma 1912–1914 gg.* (Mos., 1981), and *Raspad tret'eiiunskoi sistemy* (Mos., 1985).

Russia after the 1830s. But professional jurists formed a part of the educated and upper strata of society as a whole. Their views and ideological perspectives, and hence the law they made, therefore also reflected the changes and conflicts generally taking place within these strata of society. Judicial practice in post-emancipation Imperial Russia consequently combined conservatism and reformism in a way that in the context of the tsarist order had both stabilizing and destabilizing effects and revolutionary implications.

I

New Men, New Courts, and Old Laws

THE post-reform courts were able to adapt civil law to changing conditions because of the changes in both judicial personnel and judicial authority introduced by the reform, changes that were closely interrelated. As Richard Wortman has shown, the professionalization of judicial officials which began in Imperial Russia during the middle of the nineteenth century involved a reconceptualization of law that contributed significantly to the establishment of judicial independence in 1864. Changes in training, status, and occupational conditions produced a corps of jurists who viewed the law as a noble calling as well as a distinct body of knowledge and rules, with the latter requiring specialized expertise to comprehend and apply. Although in principle not incompatible with the autocracy, in practice this conception of law resulted in tension between jurists' commitment to the law and their loyalty to the autocratic order.[1] The members of other professional groups that emerged in Imperial Russia at this time experienced similar tensions as they struggled, individually and collectively, to establish their identity, status, and authority, suggesting that the autocracy had difficulty assimilating the educated élite fostered by its own policies.[2] Jurists posed a particularly difficult problem for the autocracy, however, because they dominated institutions crucial to the exercise of state power.

[1] R. S. Wortman, *The Development of a Russian Legal Consciousness* (Chicago, 1976). See also W. B. Lincoln, *In the Vanguard of Reform: Russia's Enlightened Bureaucrats 1825–1861* (Dekalb, Ill., 1982), 58–67, 183–4, 192–204.

[2] See N. M. Frieden, *Russian Physicians in an Era of Reform and Revolution, 1856–1905* (Princeton, NJ, 1981), S. J. Seregny, *Russian Teachers and Peasant Revolution: The Politics of Education in 1905* (Bloomington, Ind., 1989), the essays by H. Balzer and by C. Ruane and B. Eklof in E. W. Clowes, S. D. Kassow, and J. L. West (eds.), *Between Tsar and People: Educated Society and the Quest for Public Identity in Late Imperial Russia* (Princeton, NJ, 1991), W. C. Fuller, *Civil-Military Conflict in Imperial Russia 1881–1914* (Princeton, NJ, 1985), G. L. Freeze, *The Parish Clergy in Nineteenth-Century Russia: Crisis, Reform, Counter-Reform* (Princeton, NJ, 1983), S. D. Kassow, *Students, Professors, and the State in Tsarist Russia* (Berkeley, Calif., 1989), V. R. Leikina-Svirskaia, *Intelligentsiia v Rossii vo vtoroi polovine xix veka* (Mos., 1971), and id., *Russkaia intelligentsiia v 1900–1917 godakh* (Mos., 1981).

Professionalization and Legal Reform

Despite their common engagement in the administration of the law, the disparate backgrounds and experiences of pre-reform judicial personnel prevented the development of either a distinct professional identity or a common commitment to the integrity of the law. In most instances, judges and assessors in the provincial and district courts were elected by the local nobility, merchantry, or peasantry to represent their respective estate. Considering such service onerous, local residents generally tried to avoid it. As a result, until the 1850s the judiciary in these courts consisted primarily of noblemen of relatively modest means who lacked specialized legal training, or often any secondary or higher education at all. Nor did the prior experience of judges, especially those in the district courts, provide them with legal expertise or encourage them to view a judicial position differently from state service generally. Most judges were former military officers who had returned to their estates but still needed an income from state service.[3] The situation was not much better in the Senate departments that constituted the higher appellate courts. Although wealthier, of higher social status, and better educated than lower court judges, senators too tended to be former military officers or elderly civil officials whose appointment represented a surrogate pension. Procurators frequently were scions of prominent families being groomed for higher positions in other branches of the civil service.[4] While the generally impecunious secretaries and other chancellery officials who conducted the main work of the courts at least tended to spend their entire careers in the judicial system, they too lacked formal legal training and normally acquired their expertise while carrying out their duties. Moreover, these officials came predominantly from lower social orders than the judiciary.[5]

Nor was there a wider community of jurists which might have provided a sense of identity for judicial personnel. Until the mid-1830s, systematic training in Imperial law was not generally available. At the

[3] Wortman, *Legal Consciousness*, 72–88, and 52–95 in general. See also the works cited below in n. 38.

[4] Wortman, *Legal Consciousness*, 54–69. Established in 1722 by Peter the Great, the procuracy thereafter underwent several changes in jurisdiction, authority, and status. It generally was charged, however, with the oversight of state institutions, especially their observance of procedural rules. After the judicial reform, the procurators not only served as prosecutors in criminal cases, but also became the chief representative of the Minister of Justice, and hence also of the state administration, in the new courts.

[5] Ibid. 54–88. See also G. V. Bertgol'dt, 'Iz zapisok moskovskago advokata', *SL* (1909), 16: 1–2, and A. A. Blagoveshchenskii, 'Istoriia metod Zakonovedeniia v XVIII i XIX veke', *Zhurnal Ministerstva Narodnogo Prosveshcheniia* (1835), ch. 6, 427–31.

small number of universities, lycées, and other schools founded after the mid-eighteenth century primarily for the nobility a few individual faculty members specialized in law and lectured on natural or Roman law, the relationship between law and morals or political economy, and limited areas of Imperial law. Although juridical faculties existed at Dorpat (established 1802) and Warsaw (established 1817) Universities, they catered largely for young Baltic German and Polish noblemen respectively and concentrated on local, Roman, and Western European law. Schools for the lesser nobility and for members of other social estates sometimes provided practical training in particular areas of Imperial law. In all these cases, however, few students were involved and the objective was not to train specialized jurists but to provide either working knowledge of a limited area of the law or a generalized education, in preparation for a career in state service. The specialized practitioners who gained their livelihood by preparing legal documents and expediting cases through the courts were isolated, unorganized, and contemned socially.[6]

The scarcity of published sources of law and of specialized legal literature and the limited extent of public discourse on juridical questions likewise impeded the development of a common professional identity. Despite periodic efforts to codify the law during the eighteenth and the early nineteenth century, no comprehensive source of Imperial law existed prior to the early 1830s.[7] Few treatises on the law were available,

[6] The juridical faculty that had existed at Moscow University (founded 1755) until 1804 generally conformed to this pattern. *Moskovskii Gosudarstvennyi Universitet. Uchenye zapiski*, clxxx, *Trudy iuridicheskogo fakul'teta. Kniga 8-aia* (Mos., 1956), 6–13. In general, see Wortman, *Legal Consciousness*, 24–45, F. B. Kaiser, *Die Russische Justizreform von 1864: Zur Geschichte der Russischen Justiz von Katharina II bis 1916* (Leiden, 1972), 97–106, N. P. Druzhinin, *Obshchedostupnoe rukovodstvo k izucheniiu zakonov* (2nd edn., Spb., 1899), 74–82, E. N. Berendts, 'Proekty reformy Pravitel'stvuiushchago Senata vo vtoroi polovine xix stoletiia', in *Istoriia Pravitel'stvuiushchago Senata za dvesti let, 1711–1911 gg.* (Spb., 1911), iv. 454–9, S. Kucherov, *Courts, Lawyers, and Trials under the Last Three Tsars* (reprint edn., Westport, Conn., 1974), 107–13, N. V. Cherkasova, *Formirovanie i razvitie advokatury v Rossii 60–80 gody xix veka* (Mos., 1987), 10–19, I. V. Gessen, *Advokatura, obschchestvo i gosudarstvo. Istoriia russkoi advokatury 1864–1914* (Mos., 1914), i. 1–10, Bertgol'dt, 'Iz zapisok', 2, and Blagoveshchenskii, 'Istoriia metod Zakonovedeniia', ch. 6, pp. 427–41, and ch. 7, pp. 42–52.

[7] P. Maikov, *O svode zakonov Rossiiskoi Imperii* (Spb., 1905), 10, M. Raeff, *Michael Speransky: Statesman of Imperial Russia* (The Hague, 1957), 65–7, 322–44, Kaiser, *Russische Justizreform*, 132–6, Wortman, *Legal Consciousness*, 32–3, A. N. Kolesnikov, 'Sistematizatsiia zakonodatel'stva v Rossii v nachale XIX veka M. M. Speranskim', *Uchenye zapiski vsesoiuznogo nauchno-issledovatel'skogo instituta sovetskogo zakonodatel'stva* (Mos., 1966), viii. 189–214, and A. F. Shebanov, 'Polnoe sobranie zakonov Rossiiskoi imperii. (Iz istorii sistematizatsii zakonodatel'stva v Rossii)', *Trudy vsesoiuznogo iuridicheskogo zaochnogo instituta*, xiv (Mos., 1970), *Problemy istorii gosudarstva i prava*, 277–82.

and these often were written by jurists trained abroad, who tended to force Imperial Russian law into the system and terminology of Roman or continental Western European law.[8] Before 1859 only five specialized legal periodicals had appeared in the empire, three of which lasted less than a year; the remaining two survived for two years.[9]

Again as Wortman has demonstrated, the introduction of systematic legal training in the 1830s began to change these conditions dramatically. By the 1850s the Senate procuracy, the provincial courts, and central administrative bodies concerned with the law had come increasingly under the influence of trained jurists who believed that the law and the courts should play a crucial role in resolving the social, economic, and administrative problems facing the empire.[10] The judicial reform accelerated and expanded this process; by 1870 three-quarters of the members of the appellate and district courts established under the reform had received specialized legal training (Table 1.1). This proportion had risen to 91 per cent by 1890 and to 97 per cent by 1910. Moreover, by 1890 graduates of university juridical faculties constituted the overwhelming majority of judicial officials and had displaced graduates of the élite Imperial School of Jurisprudence even in the appellate courts (Tables 1.1–1.3). In nearly all cases, judicial officials entered service in the courts or the Ministry of Justice and devoted their entire careers to the administration of law.[11]

At the same time, the division of judicial officials into separate spheres of activity based on social background began to erode, especially in the lower courts. While in 1890 the nobility still dominated the judiciary and the procuracy in both the district and appellate courts, by 1910 it retained its dominance only in appellate courts and, barely, among full procurators of district courts. The procuracy in particular provided a bastion for the nobility as the sons of lesser officials and officers, the clergy, and urban social groups gained predominance in the district courts and moved upward in the judicial service (Tables 1.4–1.5). Regardless of their social origin, however, most judicial officials owned no land and depended on their professional expertise for their livelihood. In 1890, for example, 78 per cent of judicial officials in the appellate courts, 83 per cent of officials

[8] G. F. Shershenevich, *Nauka grazhdanskago prava v Rossii* (Kazan, 1893), 9–22, 60–1, and Blagoveshchenskii, 'Istoriia metod Zakonovedeniia', ch. 7, pp. 45–50.

[9] See the sources cited for Table 1.11.

[10] Wortman, *Legal Consciousness*, 198–234.

[11] Ibid. 237–67, Ia. K. Gorodyskii, 'Nashi sudy i sudebnye poriadki po dannym revizii 1895 g.', *ZhMIu* (1901), 2: 1–43, and *SChMIu*, for 1866, 1870, 1884, 1890, 1900, and 1910.

TABLE 1.1. *Education of judicial personnel, 1870*

	Imperial School of Jurisprudence		University juridical faculty		Alexander Lycée		Other higher juridical institute		Other higher education		Other/unknown		Total
	No.	%	No.	%	No.	%	No.	%	No.	%	No.	%	
COURTS OF APPEAL													
Judges	28	54	19	37	3	6	2	4	0	—	0	—	52
Procurators	2	50	1	25	1	25	0	—	0	—	0	—	4
Assistant procurators	6	67	2	22	1	11	0	—	0	—	0	—	9
TOTAL	36	55	22	34	5	8	2	3	0	—	0	—	65
DISTRICT COURTS													
Judges	64	21	163	54	9	3	10	3	9	3	48	16	303
Procurators	6	19	17	55	1	3	1	3	2	7	4	13	31
Assistant procurators	25	15	104	60	5	3	6	3	11	6	22	13	173
TOTAL	95	19	284	56	15	3	17	3	22	4	74	15	507
EXAMINING MAGISTRATES	17	4	292	61	21	4	26	5	21	4	106	22	483
GRAND TOTAL	148	14	598	57	41	4	45	4	43	4	180	17	1,055

Source: *SChMIu, 1870.*

TABLE 1.2. *Education of judicial personnel, 1890*

	Imperial School of Jurisprudence		University juridical faculty		Alexander Lycée		Other higher juridical institute		Other higher education		Other/unknown		Total
	No.	%	No.	%	No.	%	No.	%	No.	%	No.	%	
COURTS OF APPEAL													
Judges	31	16	139	71	9	5	6	3	2	1	9	5	196
Procurators	2	20	8	80	0	—	0	—	0	—	0	—	10
Assistant procurators	8	20	31	76	2	5	0	—	0	—	0	—	41
TOTAL	41	17	178	72	11	5	6	2	2	1	9	4	247
DISTRICT COURTS													
Judges	88	9	691	72	16	2	51	5	33	3	85	9	964
Procurators	11	13	62	76	0	—	5	6	0	—	4	5	82
Assistant procurators	51	11	346	72	8	2	58	12	7	2	10	2	480
District members of district courts	0	—	61	80	1	1	6	8	8	10	1	1	77
TOTAL	150	9	1,160	72	25	2	120	8	48	3	100	6	1,603
EXAMINING MAGISTRATES	26	2	899	72	3	0.2	232	19	36	3	61	5	1,257
GRAND TOTAL	217	7	2,237	72	39	1	358	12	86	3	170	5	3,107

Source: *SChMIu, 1890*.

TABLE 1.3. *Education of judicial personnel, 1910*

	Imperial School of Jurisprudence		University juridical faculty		Alexander Lycée		Other higher juridical institute		Other higher education		Other/unknown		Total
	No.	%	No.	%	No.	%	No.	%	No.	%	No.	%	
COURTS OF APPEAL													
Judges	32	10	256	79	7	2	23	7	2	1	6	2	326
Procurators	5	36	8	57	1	7	0	—	0	—	0	—	14
Assistant procurators	9	14	47	74	4	6	3	5	0	—	1	2	64
TOTAL	46	11	311	77	12	3	26	6	2	1	7	2	404
DISTRICT COURTS													
Judges	41	3	1,181	84	5	0.4	139	10	4	0.3	46	3	1,416
Procurators	9	9	91	86	0	—	6	6	0	—	0	—	106
Assistant procurators	50	6	794	89	2	0.2	45	5	0	—	1	0.1	892
District members of district courts	12	2	395	78	1	0.2	66	13	7	1	26	5	507
Municipal magistrates	2	0.4	399	82	2	0.4	42	9	10	2	33	7	488
TOTAL	114	3	2,860	84	10	0.3	298	9	21	1	106	3	3,409
EXAMINING MAGISTRATES	22	1	1,699	90	2	0.1	130	7	7	0.4	18	1	1,878
GRAND TOTAL	182	3	4,870	86	24	0.4	454	8	30	1	131	2	5,691

Source: *SChMIu, 1910*.

TABLE 1.4. *Social origin of judicial personnel, 1890*

	Nobility		Officers/officials		Clergy		Higher urban classes[a]		Other urban classes		Peasantry		Other/unknown		Total
	No.	%	No.	%	No.	%	No.	%	No.	%	No.	%	No.	%	
COURTS OF APPEAL															
Judges	134	68	21	11	11	6	5	3	9	5	1	1	15	8	196
Procurators	8	80	1	10	1	10	0	—	0	—	0	—	0	—	10
Assistant procurators	33	80	3	7	1	2	1	2	1	2	1	2	1	2	41
TOTAL	175	71	25	10	13	5	6	2	10	4	2	1	16	7	247
DISTRICT COURTS															
Judges	578	60	119	12	96	10	51	5	57	6	15	2	48	5	964
Procurators	57	70	8	10	5	6	5	6	6	7	0	—	1	1	82
Assistant procurators	290	60	58	12	57	12	21	4	28	6	11	2	15	3	480
District members of district courts	35	46	10	13	10	13	4	5	4	5	2	3	12	16	77
TOTAL	960	60	195	12	168	11	81	5	95	6	28	2	76	5	1,603
EXAMINING MAGISTRATES	542	43	180	14	311	25	58	5	83	7	37	3	46	4	1,257
GRAND TOTAL	1,677	54	400	13	492	16	145	5	188	6	67	2	138	4	3,107

[a] Includes honoured citizens and merchants.

Source: *SChMIu, 1890*.

TABLE 1.5. *Social origin of judicial personnel, 1910*

	Nobility		Officers/officials		Clergy		Higher urban classes[a]		Other urban classes		Peasantry		Other/unknown		Total
	No.	%	No.	%	No.	%	No.	%	No.	%	No.	%	No.	%	
COURTS OF APPEAL															
Judges	208	64	32	10	39	12	17	5	19	6	2	1	9	3	326
Procurators	12	86	2	14	0	—	0	—	0	—	0	—	0	—	14
Assistant procurators	38	59	7	11	2	3	8	13	6	9	0	—	3	5	64
TOTAL	258	64	41	10	41	10	25	6	25	6	2	1	12	3	404
DISTRICT COURTS															
Judges	645	46	228	16	217	15	101	7	115	8	53	4	57	4	1,416
Procurators	56	53	21	20	6	6	9	9	7	7	1	1	6	6	106
Assistant procurators	413	46	175	20	67	8	85	10	88	10	11	1	53	6	892
District members of district courts	229	45	74	15	86	17	33	7	45	9	18	4	22	4	507
Municipal magistrates	171	35	127	26	64	13	43	9	38	8	22	5	23	5	488
TOTAL	1,514	45	625	18	440	13	271	8	293	9	105	3	161	5	3,409
EXAMINING MAGISTRATES	585	31	497	27	257	14	147	8	194	10	70	4	128	7	1,878
GRAND TOTAL	2,357	42	1,163	20	738	13	443	8	512	9	177	3	301	5	5,691

[a] Includes honoured citizens and merchants.

Source: *SChMIu, 1910*.

in the district courts, and 92 per cent of examining magistrates were landless (Table 1.6).

With some variations, these trends also characterized the Civil Cassation Department of the Senate, the highest court of appeal for civil cases in the reformed judicial system. The dominance of the nobility continued longer and remained stronger in the Civil Cassation Department, especially among its procurators, than in the lower courts (Table 1.7). Although from the beginning most senators and procurators owned no land, the proportion was somewhat less than in the lower courts, and the proportion of those who owned substantial estates was higher (Table 1.8).[12] Moreover, it took somewhat longer for graduates of juridical institutions to gain predominance in the Civil Cassation Department, although from the outset senators were highly educated, and the dominance of graduates of élite institutions lasted longer than in the lower courts. In contrast, the procuracy consisted almost entirely of trained jurists from the start (Table 1.9). As with the judiciary in general, prior to their appointment most senators and procurators spent their careers entirely in the civil service, usually in the courts, in other Senate positions, or in the Ministry of Justice. But by 1910 a series of judgeships had replaced service in the Ministry of Justice or the general state administration as the primary route into the high court (Table 1.10).

The basis of this transformation of the judiciary lay in the provision of systematic legal training. Persuaded that the order, security, and welfare of his realm required clearer legal rules as well as specialists to apply them, in 1828 Nicholas I directed that several outstanding students be groomed for university professorships in law. Trained in Imperial Russian law under the direction of Count Mikhail Speranskii in the Second Department of the Imperial Chancellery, which at that time was attempting to codify Imperial law, and then in European and Roman law in Germany, these students played a key role in the introduction of comprehensive legal education at Imperial Russian universities during the later 1830s and the 1840s. Between 1835 and 1841 juridical faculties were established at St Petersburg, Moscow, Kharkov, Kazan, and St Vladimir (Kiev) Universities, and the teaching of law at Dorpat (Iurev) University was reorganized. To these faculties were added those at Novorossiia

[12] The widespread complaints of low salaries made by judicial officials at the end of the 19th c. also suggest the degree of their dependence on the exercise of professional expertise to earn a livelihood. See Gorodyskii, 'Nashi sudy', 9–10, 39, 41, and *Soveshchaniia starshikh predsedatelei i prokurorov sudebnykh palat po nekotorym voprosam sudebnoi praktiki v sviazi s peresmotrom zakonopolozhenii po sudebnoi chasti* (Spb., 1895) (HLL), 89–103, 244–89.

TABLE 1.6. *Landowning of judicial personnel, 1890*

	None[a]		1–200 des.		201+ des.		Unknown		Total
	No.	%	No.	%	No.	%	No.	%	
COURTS OF APPEAL									
Judges	157	80	7	4	32	16	0	—	196
Procurators	8	80	0	—	2	20	0	—	10
Assistant procurators	27	66	11	27	3	7	0	—	41
TOTAL	192	78	18	7	37	15	0	—	247
DISTRICT COURTS									
Judges	774	80	50	5	133	14	7	1	964
Procurators	71	87	2	2	9	11	0	—	82
Assistant procurators	415	87	16	3	46	10	3	1	480
District members of district courts	64	83	2	3	11	14	0	—	77
TOTAL	1,324	83	70	4	199	12	10	1	1,603
EXAMINING MAGISTRATES	1,152	92	38	3	62	5	5	0.4	1,257
GRAND TOTAL	2,668	86	126	4	298	10	15	0.5	3,107

[a] A significant number of judicial personnel—between 7% and 23% of the courts of appeal, 8% and 19% of the district courts, and 4% and 13% of the examining magistrates, including many who owned no land personally—had wives or parents who owned varying amounts of land.

Source: *SChMIu, 1890.*

TABLE 1.7. *Civil Cassation Department, 1870–1910[a]: Social origin and religion*

	No. of senators (%)			No. of Chief Procurators and Assistant Chief Procurators (%)		
	1870	1890	1910[b]	1870	1890	1910
SOCIAL ORIGIN						
Nobility	9 (90)	22 (92)	20 (67)	4 (100)	8 (89)	15 (94)
Officials/officers	1 (10)	0	5 (17)	0	0	0
Clergy	0	0	0	0	0	0
Higher urban groups[c]	0	1 (4)	1 (3)	0	1 (11)	0
Other urban groups	0	1 (4)	3 (10)	0	0	1 (6)
Peasantry	0	0	1 (3)	0	0	0
TOTALS	10 (100)	24 (100)	30 (100)	4 (100)	9 (100)	16 (100)
RELIGION						
Orthodox	6 (60)	16 (67)	22 (73)	4 (100)	5 (56)	10 (63)
Lutheran	2 (20)	7 (29)	1 (3)	0	2 (22)	4 (25)
Catholic	2 (20)	0	3 (10)	0	1 (11)	2 (13)
Other/unknown	0	1 (4)	4 (13)	0	1 (11)	0
TOTALS	10 (100)	24 (100)	30 (100)	4 (100)	9 (100)	16 (100)

[a] Court composition on 1 January of each year used to determine data.

[b] This sample includes only 30 out of 33 senators from 1910. No information was available on three senators who served only temporarily on the high court.

[c] Includes honoured citizens and merchants.

Sources: TsGIA F. 1364 op. 15, various *dela*; *SChMIu, 1870, 1890, 1910*; *PS*; *Lichnyi sostav kassatsionnykh departamentov Pravitel'stvuiushchago Senata za 1866–1891 gody* (Spb., 1891).

TABLE 1.8. *Civil Cassation Department, 1870–1910*[a]*: Landowning*

	No. of senators (%)			No. of Chief Procurators and Assistant Chief Procurators (%)		
	1870	1890	1910[b]	1870	1890	1910
None[c]	6 (60)	17 (71)	20 (67)	3 (75)	3 (33)	11 (69)
1–100 des.	0	0	1 (3)	1 (25)	1 (11)	0
101–500 des.	1 (10)	2 (8)	2 (7)	0	1 (11)	1 (6)
501+ des.	3 (30)	5 (21)	5 (17)	0	3 (33)	0
Unknown	0	0	2 (7)	0	1 (11)	4 (25)
TOTALS	10 (100)	24 (100)	30 (100)	4 (100)	9 (100)	16 (100)

[a] Court composition on 1 January of each year used to determine data.

[b] This sample includes only 30 out of 33 senators from 1910. No information was available on three senators who served only temporarily on the high court.

[c] Between 8 and 20% of senators, and between 11 and 25% of Chief Procurators and Assistant Chief Procurators, are shown as not owning any land personally, although their wives and/or parents did own varying amounts of land.

Sources: TsGIA F. 1364 op. 15, various *dela*; *SChMIu, 1870, 1890, 1910*; *PS*; *Lichnyi sostav kassatsionnykh departamentov Pravitel'stvuiushchago Senata za 1866–1891 gody* (Spb., 1891).

TABLE 1.9. *Civil Cassation Department, 1870–1910*[a]*: Education*

	No. of senators (%)			No. of Chief Procurators and Assistant Chief Procurators (%)		
	1870	1890	1910[b]	1870	1890	1910
Imperial School of Jurisprudence	2 (20)	13 (54)	4 (13)	2 (50)	3 (33)	3 (19)
University juridical faculty	1 (10)	6 (25)	22 (73)	1 (25)	4 (44)	12 (75)
Other juridical institute	0	0	0	0	1 (11)	1 (6)
Other élite	2 (20)	5 (21)	2 (7)	1 (25)	1 (11)	0
University, non-juridical faculty	4 (40)	0	2 (7)	0	0	0
Other	1 (10)	0	0	0	0	0
TOTALS	10 (100)	24 (100)	30 (100)	4 (100)	9 (100)	16 (100)

[a] Court composition on 1 January of each year used to determine data.
[b] This sample includes only 30 out of 33 senators from 1910. No information was available on three senators who served only temporarily on the high court.

Sources: TsGIA F. 1364 op. 15, various *dela*; *SChMIu, 1870, 1890, 1910*; *PS*; *Lichnyi sostav kassatsionnykh departamentov Pravitel'stvuiushchago Senata za 1866–1891 gody* (Spb., 1891).

TABLE 1.10. *Civil Cassation Department, 1870–1910*[a]*: Career patterns*

	No. of senators (%)			No. of Chief Procurators and Assistant Chief Procurators (%)		
	1870	1890	1910[b]	1870	1890	1910
Judgeships	0	6 (25)	17 (57)	0	5 (56)	9 (56)
Procuracies	2 (20)	1 (4)	3 (10)	0	1 (11)	1 (6)
Ministry of Justice/Senate	3 (30)	10 (42)	6 (20)	4 (100)	2 (22)	1 (6)
Other administration	5 (50)	4 (17)	0	0	0	0
Other	0	3 (13)	4 (13)	0	1 (11)	1 (6)
Unknown	0	0	0	0	0	4 (25)
TOTALS	10 (100)	24 (100)	30 (100)	4 (100)	9 (100)	16 (100)

[a] Court composition on 1 January of each year used to determine data.
[b] This sample includes only 30 out of 33 senators from 1910. No information was available on three senators who served only temporarily on the high court.

Sources: TsGIA F. 1364 op. 15, various *dela*; *SChMIu, 1870, 1890, 1910*; *PS*; *Lichnyi sostav kassatsionnykh departamentov Pravitel'stvuiushchago Senata za 1866–1891 gody* (Spb., 1891).

University in Odessa in 1865, Warsaw University (which had been closed in 1831) in 1869, and Tomsk University in 1898. As the teaching of law at these institutions expanded, the number of law professors increased, to 44 by 1854 and 111 by 1913. In addition, to prepare sons of the noble élite for specialized legal service in the state bureaucracy, the Imperial School of Jurisprudence was founded in 1835. The Demidov Lycée was reorganized in 1833 and again in 1868, and the Bezborodko Lycée in 1840, to provide similar training for sons of the lesser nobility as well as for members of other social estates. Opened in 1867, the Military-Juridical Academy prepared lawyers for the juridical branch of the military. Finally, after the turn of the century, several Higher Courses for Women also offered specialized study in the law.[13]

The number of graduates of these institutions increased steadily, too, after the mid-1830s and their social backgrounds grew more diverse. Between 1840 and 1863 approximately 3,650 students received law degrees from Imperial Russian universities and about 400 graduated from the Imperial School of Jurisprudence. Almost all of the latter were members of the nobility, and it is likely that over 70 per cent of the former were sons of hereditary noblemen, officers, or officials.[14] During the remainder of the century nearly 24,000 students completed legal training in Imperial universities, where by the turn of the century the proportion of the nobility and sons of officials or officers among law students appears to have declined to less than 50 per cent. Sons of unprivileged urban groups constituted the next largest group (about 25 per cent), followed by the sons of privileged urban groups, the clergy, and peasants. Between 1910 and 1913, among the 20,774 students who received law degrees from universities, the proportion of sons of the nobility, officials, and officers

[13] Wortman, *Legal Consciousness*, 44–50, 198–234, Kaiser, *Russische Justizreform*, 98–110, Druzhinin, *Obshchedostupnoe rukovodstvo*, 78–85, Shershenevich, *Nauka*, 23–86, A. Sinel, 'The Socialization of the Russian Bureaucratic Elite, 1811–1917: Life at Tsarskoe Selo Lyceum and the School of Jurisprudence', *Russian History*, 3 (1976), 1–31, G. Siuzor, *Ko dniu lxxv iubileia imperatorskago uchilishcha pravovedeniia 1835–1910 gg.* (Spb., 1910), R. G. Eimontova, *Russkie universitety na grani dvukh epokh. Ot Rossii krepostnoi k Rossii kapitalisticheskoi* (Mos., 1985), 109–10, Kassow, *Students*, 414, *Khar'kovskii gosudarstvennyi universitet im. A. M. Gor'kago za 150 let* (Kharkov, 1955), 15, 77–80, 128, 145–6, *Mos. Gos. Univ. Uch. Zap. Trudy*, 15–36, 68–76, 90–8, 112–18, 155–7, 172–9, 204–8, *Dvadtsatipiatiletie Imperatorskago Novorossiiskago Universiteta* (Odessa, 1890), 479–557, M. F. Vladimirskii-Budanov, *Istoriia imperatorskago Universiteta sv. Vladimira* (Kiev, 1884), i. 127–37, 233–8, 389–400, 443–51, *BSUSV* 455–67, S. P. Pokrovskii, *Demidovskii litsei v ego proshlom i nastoiashchem* (Iaroslavl, 1914), 119 ff., Leikina-Svirskaia, *Intelligentsiia*, 76–9, id., *Russkaia intelligentsiia*, 23–5, and Fuller, *Civil-Military Conflict*, 121–8.

[14] Berendts, 'Proekty reformy', 460. Eimontova, *Russkie universitety*, 242, provides information on the social origin of all university students from 1854–7.

had declined still further, to about 40 per cent.[15] In addition, during the post-emancipation period, nearly 8,000 students graduated from the Imperial School of Jurisprudence, the Military-Juridical Academy, and the juridical lycées.[16]

Believing in the necessity of trained jurists but also suspicious of them, the regime sought to ensure that the study of law would inculcate political loyalty while imparting the desired level of expertise. Hence the curriculum emphasized technical knowledge of Imperial Russian law, gave considerable weight to such presumedly conservative subjects as Roman law and Orthodox canon law, and paid much less attention to subjects, such as jurisprudence or European constitutional law, that might encourage speculation about the nature of law in general. At Kazan University in the 1880s, for example, students devoted over 55 per cent of their formal studies to various areas of Imperial Russian law, legal procedure, and legal history, 23 per cent to Roman law, 8 per cent to Orthodox canon law, 8 per cent to political economy and statistics, and 6 per cent to the encyclopedia of law (essentially jurisprudence). The chair in international law was vacant during this period.[17]

It is difficult to assess the effect of this pedagogical strategy. Clearly, many recipients of law degrees assimilated the values desired by the tsarist regime and adhered to traditional notions of law or passed untouched through their course of study.[18] But some teachers did manage to inspire

[15] Kassow, *Students*, 410–11, who shows that the percentage of sons of the nobility and of officials was above the average for students in all faculties.

[16] Leikina-Svirskaia, *Intelligentsiia*, 58–9, 62–4, 77–9, id., *Russkaia intelligentsiia*, 24, Kassow, *Students*, 25, 410, N. Rennenkampf, 'Sud'by privillegirovannykh i neprivillegirovannykh iuristov (k statistike iuridicheskago obrazovaniia v Rossii s 1865 g.)', *ZhGiUP* (1881), 1: 67–98, and Fuller, *Civil-Military Conflict*, 123–6.

[17] Z. D. Ivanova, 'Iuridicheskii fakul'tet Kazanskogo universiteta v period prebyvaniia na nem V. I. Lenina', *Uchenye zapiski Kazanskogo gosudarstvennogo universiteta*, cxvi, kn. 13 (1956), *Iz istorii iuridicheskoi mysli v Kazanskom universitete*, 3–17. The areas of Russian law studied were: civil law and procedure, commercial law and procedure, criminal law and procedure, history, constitutional law, police or administrative law, and financial law; forensic medicine was an optional subject. The curriculum at other institutions was comparable. See Rennenkampf, 'Sud'by privillegirovannykh', Vladimirskii-Budanov, *Istoriia*, i. 127–37, 233–8, 389–400, 443–51, *BSUSV* 455–67, *DINU* 479–80, *Mos. Gos. Univ. Uch. Zap., Trudy*, 21–5, 35–6, *Khar'kovskii gosudarstvennyi universitet*, 77–80, 128, 145–6, Siuzor, *Ko dniu lxxv iubileia*, 172–9, Pokrovskii, *Demidovskii litsei*, 187, 194–5, 206, 234–7, Sinel, 'Socialization', Wortman, *Legal Consciousness*, esp. 203–13, 223–31, and Kassow, *Students*, 30–2, 58–60, 302.

[18] D. T. Orlovsky, *The Limits of Reform: The Ministry of Internal Affairs in Imperial Russia, 1802–1881* (Cambridge, Mass., 1981), 111, 122, Kassow, *Students*, 59, Sinel, 'Socialization', and S. Iu. Vitte, *Graf S. Iu. Vitte. Vospominaniia* (reprint edn., The Hague, 1968), iii (1849–94), 57–8.

their students and to instil a belief in the autonomy and scientific nature of the law and a consciousness of the high social calling of the jurist. 'You are the high priests of justice, you are jurists,' declared Petr Redkin to his adoring students at Moscow University in the 1840s, 'Yes my lords, there is nothing higher than truth and science is its prophet. But like everything sacred and great in the world truth demands selflessness and self-renunciation.'[19] Many faculty members also taught even technical subjects from a perspective that emphasized the social and historical context of the law and encouraged a critical attitude towards Imperial law.[20] Moreover, contrary to official expectations, the considerable weight given to Roman law, and frequent references by faculty to Western European law and juridical literature, exposed students to legal institutions and concepts that clashed with the principles underlying the tsarist socio-political structure and conception of law. At the same time, these influences provided aspiring Russian jurists with both an idealized past and a contemporary role model by connecting them with the traditions of their Roman predecessors and their Western European peers.[21]

An official commentary on the influence of Konstantin Nevolin at St Vladimir University in the late 1830s and the 1840s noted, for example, that he managed to disseminate among his students the most recent currents in Western European jurisprudence despite his dry and pedantic style. Moreover, the appearance of Nevolin's *Encyclopedia of Jurisprudence* in 1839–40 'Drew us closer to the demands of Western European

[19] Cited in Wortman, *Legal Consciousness*, 224.

[20] e.g. see A. L. Borovikovskii, *Vstupitel'naia lektsiia k prakticheskomu kursu russkago grazhdanskago prava, chitannaia v Imp. Novorossiiskom universitete* (Spb., 1887), N. N. Debol'skii, *O znachenii i metode istorii russkago prava* (Spb., 1904), K. Malyshev, *Kurs obshchago grazhdanskago prava Rossii* (Spb., 1878), V. A. Iushkevich, *Rukovodiashchiia nachala k prepodavaniiu russkago grazhdanskago prava* (Iaroslavl, 1900), N. Maksimeiko, 'Sravnitel'noe izuchenie istorii prava', *Zapiski imp. Khar'kovskago Universiteta* (1898), 1: 1–14 (2nd pag.), A. N. Stoianov, 'Etiudy po vseobshchei istorii prava', ibid. (1894), 4: 1–32 (2nd pag.), id., 'Vospominanie o D. I. Kachenovskom', ibid. (1894), 1: 1–38 (4th pag.), S. A. Muromtsev, *Iz lektsii po russkomu grazhdanskomu pravu (1898–1899)* (Spb., 1899), 3–17, *Pamiati Aleksandra Dmitrievicha Gradovskago* (Spb., 1890), *Pamiati Mikhaila Vasil'evicha Dukhovskago* (Mos., 1903), *Pamiati D. I. Kachenovskago* (Kharkov, 1905), 'Pamiati zasluzhennago ordinarnago professora N. K. Nelidova', *Uchenye zapiski imp. Kazanskago Universiteta po iuridicheskomu fakul'tetu, 1888 g.* (Kazan, 1889), 1–49 (1st pag.), and M. V. Shimanovskii, *Petr Grigor'evich Redkin (Biograficheskii ocherk)* (Odessa, 1890). See also Wortman, *Legal Consciousness*, 203–13, 223–31.

[21] e.g. see the works by Iushkevich, Stoianov, and Borovikovskii cited above in n. 20. In general, see Shershenevich, *Nauka*, G. V. Shvekov, 'Sravnitel'nyi metod v russkoi istoriko-pravovoi nauke (istoricheskii obzor)', *Trudy vsesoiuznogo iuridicheskogo zaochnogo instituta*, xliii (Mos., 1977), *Problemy istorii gosudarstva i prava*, 188–223, and A. A. Tille and G. V. Shvekov, *Sravnitel'nyi metod v iuridicheskikh distsiplinakh* (Mos., 1978).

science and established a firm and fruitful basis for working out Russian law on new scientific principles'.[22] And at his inaugural lecture at the same university in 1900, A. K. Mitiukov contended that 'in [Roman law], and in the science of civil law which has grown from its soil, we find a vital and mighty source for the reforms and improvements demanded so insistently by the imperfect civil structure of our fatherland'.[23] At least for some Russian jurists, then, the science of law connected them both with a larger European juristic profession and with a body of knowledge and principles which could be used to criticize and revise Imperial Russian law.

The mixed results of specialized legal education none the less suggest that it neither imparted a uniform conception of law to Russian jurists nor by itself fostered a common identity among them. The occupational experiences of jurists and the institutional setting in which they worked proved equally important in shaping their professional ethos. In this regard, the judicial reform both elevated the status of jurists and created the most important institutional structures within which they acted and interacted professionally. It also greatly expanded the opportunities for a career in the law. In 1870 the five judicial districts reorganized on the basis of the reform contained 854 judicial personnel. This number rose to 2,386 in seven districts by 1880 and to 7,700 in all districts by 1913. In 1892 1,950 attorneys, 1,087 assistant attorneys, and 2,838 private attorneys were registered in the ten existing judicial districts; by 1914 these numbers had increased to 6,011, 5,884, and 6,955 respectively.[24] In addition, several thousand trained jurists practised their craft as notaries attached to district courts and as justices of the peace.[25]

Several other governmental and public institutions also provided jurists with opportunities for professional activity and interaction. The Ministry of Justice, various departments of the Senate, and the Second Department of the Imperial Chancellery (later the Codification Department of the State Council) employed significant numbers of lawyers for

[22] *BSUSV* 463, and 455–67 in general, which largely follows Vladimirskii-Budanov, *Istoriia*, i. 131–5.

[23] A. K. Mitiukov, *Obshchnost′ imushchestva v sem′e, kak istoricheskaia osnova nasledovaniia* (Kiev, 1900), 2. Mitiukov was a lecturer in Roman law.

[24] Leikina-Svirskaia, *Intelligentsiia*, 85–6, 90, id., *Russkaia intelligentsiia*, 36, 78, and *SSSMIu, za 1892*, 1–9, 16–38, and *za 1914*, 3–15, 18–40. On the nature and generally poor quality of private attorneys, see W. E. Pomeranz, 'Justice from Underground: The History of the Underground *Advokatura*', *Russian Review*, 52 (1993), 321–40.

[25] Leikina-Svirskaia, *Intelligentsiia*, 90, id., *Russkaia intelligentsiia*, 36, and *SSSMIu, za 1892*, 1–9, 16–38, and *za 1914*, 3–15, 18–40.

the conduct of their regular operations. Most other state agencies, the military, and institutions of local self-government also maintained legal specialists. The characteristics of these officials paralleled those of the judiciary from the 1850s onward.[26] In addition, as a result of the reform, attorneys in the cities containing an appellate court formed councils of the bar to regulate their professional life, train new attorneys, and organize legal aid for the poor.[27] Finally, to foster unity among jurists engaged in different branches of the legal profession and to encourage their co-operation in the tasks of improving Imperial law and expanding public knowledge of the law, juridical societies were established in Moscow in 1865, in St Petersburg in 1877, and in several other cities after the early 1870s. Although membership in these societies and the intensity of their activities fluctuated considerably, they succeeded in bringing governmental, private, and academic jurists together and in promoting public discussion of legal issues. Particularly after the 1880s, they also acted as lobbies for the promotion of legal reform and the professional authority of jurists.[28]

Expansion of the knowledge of Imperial law and the resulting growth in the public discussion of legal issues also served to unite Russian jurists by creating a common body of expertise as well as a shared discourse over it. A comprehensive collection of laws issued between 1649 and 1825 was finally published in 1830; subsequent volumes brought the collection up to date and maintained its currency. In 1832 a digest of current law also appeared.[29] These materials provided practitioners of law with a common source of legal rules while greatly increasing the resources available for

[26] Wortman, *Legal Consciousness*, 69–72, 218–23, N. N. Efremova, *Ministerstvo iustitsii rossiiskoi imperii 1802–1917 gg.* (Mos., 1983), 88–9, Leikina-Svirskaia, *Intelligentsiia*, 90, id., *Russkaia intelligentsiia*, 36, Fuller, *Civil-Military Conflict*, 121–8, Orlovsky, *Limits of Reform*, 80–4, 187–8, P. A. Zaionchkovskii, *Pravitel'stvennyi apparat samoderzhavnoi Rossii v xix v.* (Mos., 1978), ch. 1 *passim*, pp. 203–8, 221–4, and the references to *SChMIu* cited above in n. 11.

[27] Kucherov, *Courts*, 122–96, Gessen, *Advokatura*, and Cherkasova, *Formirovanie*. Councils of the bar were established in St Petersburg and Moscow in 1866 and in Kharkov in 1874, after which government restrictions prevented the formation of new councils until 1904, when councils were established in Novocherkassk, Kazan, Odessa, Saratov, Irkutsk, and Omsk.

[28] B. F. Adams, 'The Politics of Punishment: A History of Russia's Main Prison Administration and Related Topics from 1863 to 1917' (unpublished manuscript), 106–24, 326–43, Shershenevich, *Nauka*, 80–1, A. A. Levenstim, *Ocherk deiatel'nosti sudebnykh uchrezhdenii Khar'kovskago okruga za istekshee tridtsatipiatiletie 1867–1902 gg.* (Kharkov, 1903), 152–3, and *Iuridicheskoe obshchestvo pri Imperatorskom S.-Peterburgskom Universitete za dvadtsat' piat' let (1877–1902)* (Spb., 1902). Juridical societies also were formed in Ekaterinoslav, Iaroslavl, Kazan, Kharkov, Kiev, Kursk, Odessa, Tiflis, and Vladivostok.

[29] On these publications, see below.

the study of Imperial and earlier Russian law. As a result, in the 1840s the number of treatises and monographs (especially on the history of Russian law) began to rise and their quality improved markedly.[30] The relaxation of censorship after the late 1850s and the regular publication of judicial decisions after the judicial reform enabled the critical discussion of current law by jurists, who rightly felt that their ability to shape the law had increased enormously. Reflecting this awareness, Arnold Dumashevskii, an official in the Ministry of Justice, in 1867 called on his fellow jurists to abandon their preoccupation with historical studies and to concentrate instead on the task of adjusting Imperial law to current social conditions and needs. '[I]t is now especially necessary for our science of law to change its current orientation,' he declared, 'it is summoned to do so by the most vital, the most holy interests of our fatherland—the success of our new judicial reforms and the moral development and material welfare of our people that depend on them.'[31]

This belief in the need for critical discussion of the law and for legal education of the public contributed to the appearance of specialized legal periodicals, which provided jurists with an important public voice. Fourteen such periodicals appeared between 1859 and 1879. Most were published in St Petersburg, and only six managed to survive for more than a few years (Table 1.11). They none the less provided an important forum for the critical discussion of Imperial Russian law, judicial decisions, legal theories, and professional life, as well as a medium for disseminating knowledge of Western European law and jurisprudence. The number of such periodicals increased steadily after 1880, more of them survived for a substantial period, and their place of publication became more widespread (Table 1.11). They also became more diverse, with weekly periodicals directed at practitioners being added to the more scholarly monthly journals. Of course, it is not clear how many jurists read these periodicals regularly, although the growth in their number, stability, and place of publication suggests an expansion of readership during the late

[30] Shershenevich, *Nauka*, 26–88, and Blagoveshchenskii, 'Istoriia metod Zakonovedeniia'. e.g. compare V. G. Kukol′nik, *Nachal′nyia osnovaniia rossiiskago chastnago grazhdanskago prava dlia rukovodstva k prepodovaniiu onago na publichnykh kursakh* (Spb., 1813), with A. I. Kranikhfel′d, *Nachertanie rossiiskago grazhdanskago prava v istoricheskom ego razvitii* (Spb., 1843), or K. A. Nevolin, 'Istoriia rossiiskikh grazhdanskikh zakonov', in *Polnoe sobranie sochinenii K. A. Nevolina* (Spb., 1857), iii.

[31] A. Dumashevskii, 'Nashe pravovedenie, chto ono i chem ono dolzhno byt′', *ZhMIu* (1867), 1: 32. The son of a poor Jewish tailor from Mogilev, Dumashevskii rose to significant positions in the Ministry of Justice after studying law at St Petersburg University and in Germany.

TABLE 1.11. *Publication of legal periodicals, 1859–1916*

	St Petersburg	Moscow	Elsewhere	Total
1859–1879				
Number (%)	9 (64)	2 (14)	3 (21)	14 (100)
Published 1–5 years (%)	5 (63)	1 (13)	2 (25)	8 (100)
Published 8 or more years (%)	4 (67)	1 (17)	1 (17)	6 (100)
1880–1899				
Number (%)	8 (36)	3 (14)	11 (50)	22 (100)
Published 1–7 years (%)	3 (27)	0	8 (73)	11 (100)
Published 7 or more years (%)	5 (45)	3 (27)	3 (27)	11 (100)
1900–1916				
Number (%)	17 (52)	8 (24)	8 (24)	33 (100)
Published 1–5 years (%)	10 (56)	4 (22)	4 (22)	18[a] (100)
Published 6 or more years (%)	7 (47)	4 (27)	4 (27)	15[b] (100)

[a] Four of these periodicals were still being published in January 1917.
[b] Seven of these periodicals were still being published in January 1917.

Sources: N. M. Lisovskii, *Russkaia periodicheskaia pechat' 1703–1900 gg.* (Ptgd., 1915), A. G. Dementev, G. V. Zapadov, and M. S. Cherepakhov, *Russkaia periodicheskaia pechat' (1702–1894). Spravochnik* (Mos., 1959), M. S. Cherepakhov, *Russkaia periodicheskaia pechat' (1895–1917). Spravochnik* (Mos., 1957), and L. N. Beliaeva, M. K. Zinovieva, and M. M. Nikiforov, *Bibliografiia periodicheskikh izdanii Rossii 1901–1916* (Lenin., 1958–61), i–iv.

nineteenth and early twentieth centuries.[32] Nevertheless, such publications helped to create a public self-image for jurists and to assert an authority for their professional expertise.

Of course, there were limits to the cohesiveness engendered among lawyers by their common training, expertise, and occupational experiences. The predominance of the nobility at the highest levels of the judiciary and the dominance of members of the Orthodox faith at all levels suggest that social background and ethnicity probably continued to influence attitudes as well as appointments (Tables 1.4–1.5 and 1.8).[33] While judges resented interference in their prerogatives by jurists in the Ministry of Justice, legal scholars and attorneys criticized the judiciary either for claiming excessive power or for being too subservient to the state administration. Private attorneys envied the higher status of members of the bar, judges considered many attorneys to be unprincipled ambulance chasers, and attorneys themselves were divided by the degree of their success and resulting differences in wealth and social prominence. Through their connections, graduates of the élite Imperial School of Jurisprudence and the juridical faculty of St Petersburg University frequently received plum initial appointments in the judicial service and advanced through it more quickly than graduates of other institutions, thereby engendering animosity. Women fought for the right to enter the legal profession, while male jurists resisted the appearance of women even in lowly court positions. After the turn of the century, jurists of the older generation accused their successors of careerism and a lack of ideals.[34]

Philosophical, ideological, and political differences also divided jurists. Prior to the 1850s, the predominance among Russian jurists of legal historicism and of Hegelian idealism resulted in the production primarily

[32] In 'Iz memuarov V. A. Volzhina', *Istoricheskii Vestnik* (1912), 7: 49, Valerian Volzhin complained that his work-load during the early years of his judicial service left too little time to read legal journals, although he later contributed to several of them. See also G. L. Yaney, 'Bureaucracy and Freedom: N. M. Korkunov's Theory of the State', *AHR* 71 (1966), 485 n. 39.

[33] On religion and ethnicity, see also *SChMIu* for 1890, 1900, and 1910, and M. M. Vinaver, *Nedavnee (vospominaniia i kharakteristiki)* (Ptgd., 1917), 171–91.

[34] For examples, see *Zapiski sud'i* (3rd edn., Spb., 1912), 25–7, Shershenevich, *Nauka*, 232–43, Levenstim, *Ocherk*, 153, A. F. Koni, *Sobranie sochinenii* (Mos., 1966–9), i. 258–9, ii. 72–5, 85–6, TsGIA F. 797 op. 92 d. 51 ll. 1–2, Bertgol'dt, 'Iz zapisok', Stoianov, 'Vospominanie', 13, Rennenkampf, 'Sud'by privillegirovannykh', Volzhin, 'Iz memuarov', 7: 50, and 8: 456–7, 465, 'Vospominaniia F. N. Plevako', *SL* (1909), 5: 2–7, 6: 1–4, 7: 1–4, and 8: 1–2, and A. Luchinskaia, 'Ozhidaemyi zakon', *VE* (1913), 2: 165–77. The sources used for Tables 1.1–1.3 and 1.9 demonstrate the advantages enjoyed by graduates of St Petersburg University and the Imperial School of Jurisprudence.

of historical studies of early Russian law which generally supported existing legal and socio-political institutions, while after the 1850s jurists stressed critical ('dogmatic') analysis of current law or positivist theories of law. While advocates of legal positivism dominated Russian juridical writing and legal studies during the latter part of the century, they themselves were split between those who emphasized sociological and comparative historical methods and those who espoused a psychological conception of law. Influenced by neo-Kantian idealism, at the end of the century a new generation of Russian jurists in turn criticized legal positivism especially for its alleged inability to provide theoretical support for ethico-legal norms that could secure the dignity and well-being of the individual by limiting state power. Moreover, although proponents of positivist and neo-Kantian approaches to the law tended to be critical of Imperial law and to favour its reform, some jurists employed positivist theories and comparative historical methods to justify existing legal institutions and traditional attitudes towards the law.[35]

These philosophical and ideological differences provoked bitter conflicts among Russian jurists. Yet paradoxically, these conflicts helped to define jurists as a distinct professional group. Disputes over particular legal norms and the nature of law in general bound jurists together in a shared discourse that reinforced the ties created by common training, practice in the law, and institutional association. Regardless of their ideological orientation, all the participants in these debates agreed that the law constituted a distinct body of knowledge and an integrated system of rules that played an important role in the solution of social, political, and economic problems. It therefore required specialized learning and expertise for its proper definition, interpretation, and application. By providing this expertise, jurists considered themselves to be performing an important social function that distinguished them both from their contemporaries and from earlier Russian legal practitioners.[36]

[35] On these movements, see Shershenevich, *Nauka*, A. Walicki, *Legal Philosophies of Russian Liberalism* (Oxford, 1987), A. Vucinich, *Social Thought in Tsarist Russia: The Quest for a General Science of Society, 1861–1917* (Chicago, 1976), esp. 125–72, Yaney, 'Bureaucracy and Freedom', Shvekov, 'Sravnitel'nyi metod', Tille and Shvekov, *Sravnitel'nyi metod*, N. Ia. Kuprits, *Iz istorii gosudarstvenno-pravovoi mysli dorevoliutsionnoi Rossii* (Mos., 1980), and E. V. Kuznetsov, *Filosofiia prava v Rossii* (Mos., 1989).

[36] In their memoirs, jurists tend to focus on their professional activities and to emphasize professional criteria when judging colleagues, although they sometimes confuse ideological and professional criteria. In addition to the works cited above in n. 20 and in the Intro., n. 2, see Koni, *Sobranie sochinenii*, i, id., *Ottsy i deti sudebnoi reformy. K piatidesiatiletiiu sudebnykh ustavov 1864–20 noiabria 1914* (Mos., 1914), Vinaver, *Nedavnee*, K. K. Arsen'ev, 'Iz vospominanii', *Golos Minuvshago*, (1915), 2: 117–29, A. L. Borovikovskii, *Otchet sud'i* (posmert. izd., Spb., 1909), i–iii, and A. Kossovskii, 'Vospominaniia', *RS* (1911), 9: 427–36.

Judicial Independence and the Power of Interpretation

As they moved upward in state service, members of the emerging juridical profession added a strong voice within the government for the reform of the judicial system. And once Russian defeat in the Crimean War had created an atmosphere conducive to reform, these jurists exerted a powerful influence on the character of the new judicial system. But pressure for reform also arose from the inability of the pre-reform courts to cope with an expansion and change in character of the field of civil law and with increased commercial activity. Beginning especially in the last third of the eighteenth century, changing conditions of state service, economic considerations, and Western European cultural influences led the tsarist government gradually to uncouple important areas of civil law from state obligations and formal legal status. While still containing substantial regional, religious, ethnic, and social variation, Imperial civil law consequently became more uniform across a broader spectrum of the population than previously. By conflicting with the estate basis of the existing judicial system, this process added to the strains placed on the courts during the second quarter of the nineteenth century by a significant increase in the number of civil actions, due most likely to economic growth.[37]

But the complex structure of the pre-reform courts and the cumbersome character of civil procedure also contributed to these strains. Any of several local bodies or even police officials first heard a civil case, depending on such variables as the nature of the action, the value of a suit, and the religion, ethnicity, or social estate of those involved in the case. A case could then be reviewed on appeal or at the request of various government officials as many as eight times. The use of inquisitorial procedure only added to the time and expense required to pursue a case through this structural maze. The collection of documents, petitions, and depositions

[37] The statistics reported annually by the Minister of Justice demonstrate this increase clearly, even though the reliability of the data is uncertain and changes in categories complicate comparisons. See *OMIu* for 1835, 1840, 1845, 1850, 1855 (which showed a small decline, probably owing to the Crimean War), and 1859. On the pressure for judicial reform created by the disentanglement of private from public rights, see B. Levin-Stankevich, 'Cassation, Judicial Interpretation and the Development of Civil and Criminal Law in Russia, 1864–1917: The Institutional Consequences of the 1864 Court Reform in Russia' (Ph.D. diss., SUNY, Buffalo, 1984), 8–46, and on the history of Imperial civil law in general during this period, see the works cited below in Chs. 3 and 7. On the growth of commercial activity, see A. Kahan, *The Plow, the Hammer, and the Knout: An Economic History of Eighteenth-Century Russia* (Chicago, 1985), 1–5, 50–2, 57–9, 61–3, 77–9, 163–283, V. K. Iatsunskii, *Sotsial'no-ekonomicheskaia istoriia Rossii xviii–xix vv.* (Mos., 1973), 289–96, and B. N. Mironov, *Vnutrennii rynok Rossii vo vtoroi polovine xviii–pervoi polovine xix v.* (Lenin., 1981).

from litigants, preparation of reports by court scribes, and review of this material by several courts normally consumed many years. To expedite the resolution of their cases, litigants often resorted to bribery and engaged retired or well-connected state officials or less reputable characters as surrogate attorneys. Even with such help, however, cases not infrequently outlived the people who had initiated them.[38]

Constraints on judicial interpretation and the lack of judicial independence further complicated the judicial process. Whether appointed or (nominally) elected, any member of a court could be dismissed by superior administrative officials or the emperor, who consequently viewed the courts as merely another means of executing the Imperial will represented chiefly by them. As a result, they treated judicial personnel as their subordinates, often meddling in legal cases. Moreover, reflecting both the desire to control the judiciary and its inferior status, judges, especially in the provincial and lower courts, were constrained by formalistic rules of evidence and were required to apply the laws 'in accordance with their exact and literal meaning, without any change or expansion.' Nor could judicial decisions 'be recognized as general laws, obligatory for all, nor serve as the basis for final decisions in similar cases'.[39] Where statutory law was unclear, contradictory, or incomplete, cases were referred to the Senate and ultimately to the Minister of Justice and the State Council for resolution through the legislative process.[40]

Although the deficiencies of this system of adjudication had long been recognized even within the government, efforts at reform proved futile until the circumstances surrounding Russian defeat in the Crimean War

[38] For descriptions of the pre-reform judicial system, see Kaiser, *Russische Justizreform*, 1–89, Kucherov, *Courts*, 1–19, 107–13, Wortman, *Legal Consciousness*, 1–95, 236–42, I. A. Blinov, 'Sudebnoi stroi i sudebnye poriadki pered reformoi 1864 goda', in *Sudebnye Ustavy 20 noiabria 1864 g. za 50 let* (Ptgd., 1914), i. 3–101, V. Bochkarev, 'Doreformennoi sud', in N. V. Davydov and N. N. Polianskii (eds.), *Sudebnaia reforma* (Mos., 1915), i. 205–41, and B. V. Vilenskii, *Podgotovka sudebnoi reformy 20 noiabria 1864 goda v Rossii* (Saratov, 1963), 15–61.

[39] *SZ* (1857), i, pt. 1, *Osnov. gos. zak.*, arts. 65, 69, and in general, arts. 47, 52, 54–5, 57, 67–8, 72–3, pt. 2, *Uchrezh. pravit. sen.*, arts. 59, 61, 101–2, 225–8, and ii, pt. 1, *Obshch. gub. uchrezh.*, arts. 281, 744–6. As a practical matter, before the late 1850s judicial decisions were not circulated internally among courts and other state agencies, published regularly, or discussed publicly in the press. Nor were they mentioned in the few treatises on civil law that appeared during the first half of the 19th c. Senate decisions became available on a regular basis only in 1859 with the publication of *ZhMIu*. A selection of decisions for the first half of the 19th c. appeared in 1864–5 (*SRPS*).

[40] Created in 1711 by Peter the Great, the Senate played a variety of administrative, supervisory, judicial, and even legislative roles, although its power diminished constantly after Peter's death. By the early 19th c. it was divided into several departments that, *inter alia*, served as higher courts of appeal.

made it seem urgent. Critics now argued that the failure to institutionalize the principle of legality by separating judicial from administrative functions had contributed both to the pervasive corruption and inefficiency revealed in the state administration during the war and to the economic weakness of the empire. To overcome these administrative and economic problems, the new emperor Alexander II initiated a series of far-reaching reforms of principal governmental and social institutions. Over the next fifteen years serfdom was abolished, limited local self-government was established, universities acquired increased autonomy, censorship was relaxed, and the terms of military service were fundamentally revised. Judicial reform was expected to contribute to this policy of imperial revitalization by providing an appropriate legal environment for economic growth, by reducing corruption within the bureaucracy, and by protecting both emancipated serfs and their former owners.[41]

The imperatives and politics of the reform process, however, produced a judicial system whose principles challenged the essence of autocratic power. Of course, the officials who drafted the judicial reform had not intended this result; from their perspective, the creation of an independent judicial structure staffed by legal specialists not only was compatible with autocratic power, but in fact would strengthen it by ensuring observance of the laws promulgated by the emperor. But in practice, the Western European institutions and principles on which the reform was based conflicted irreconcilably with the paternalistic and instrumentalist conception of law that remained predominant within the state bureaucracy.[42]

Hence the reformed judicial system differed fundamentally from its predecessor. Judicial independence replaced subordination to the state administration, specialized training replaced generalist knowledge, public hearings and adversarial procedure replaced secrecy and inquisitorial formalism, broad judicial discretion replaced the prohibition against judicial interpretation of law, and equality before the law replaced the hierarchy

[41] On the judicial reform, see the references cited below in n. 42. On the reform period in general, see Lincoln, *Vanguard*, and id., *The Great Reforms: Autocracy, Bureaucracy, and the Politics of Change in Imperial Russia* (DeKalb, Ill., 1990).

[42] On the preparation and politics of the reform, see Wortman, *Legal Consciousness*, 243–67, Lincoln, *Great Reforms*, 105–17, Kaiser, *Russische Justizreform*, 149–406, Kucherov, *Courts*, 21–97, Vilenskii, *Podgotovka*, P. F. Shcherbina, *Sudebnaia reforma 1864 goda na pravoberezhnoi Ukraine* (Lvov, 1974), 74–105, M. G. Korotkikh, 'Sudebnaia reforma v Rossii', *Voprosy Istorii* (1987), 12: 20–34, G. A. Dzhanshiev, *Sbornik statei* (Mos., 1914), id., *Epokha velikikh reform: istoricheskiia spravki* (10th edn., Spb., 1907), I. V. Gessen, *Sudebnaia reforma* (Spb., 1905), Davydov and Polianskii, *Sudebnaia reforma*, *Sudebnye Ustavy za 50 let*, and Koni, *Ottsy*.

of courts and evidentiary rules based on social status. Trial by jury was introduced to determine guilt in serious criminal cases. To aid those coming before the courts, the practice of law was sanctioned and attorneys permitted to organize self-regulating associations. Admittedly, the reform allowed several exceptions to its general provisions. In the area of civil law, suits involving the government or the actions of state officials followed special procedures; ecclesiastical courts retained jurisdiction over important aspects of family life; separate courts for commercial affairs continued to operate in a few large cities. Most importantly, the peasantry was subordinated to its own courts and customs in most cases involving internal village life. But outside their own communities, peasants, too, generally fell under the jurisdiction of the new courts.[43]

To ensure the integrity as well as efficiency of the court system, the reform created two three-tiered structures that converged in a single civil or criminal court of cassation. Minor cases were to be heard by a district justice of the peace, who was required to possess either an adequate education or appropriate experience and who was elected by the newly created organs of local self-government. Decisions of these magistrates could be appealed to the district (*uezd*) congress of justices of the peace. Although the local procurator, an official subordinate to the Minister of Justice who was charged with the prosecution of criminal cases, also submitted an opinion to the district congress in civil cases, these opinions apparently carried little weight.[44] All other cases fell under the jurisdiction of the district (*okruzhnoi*) court, whose decisions could be appealed to the appropriate court of appeals (*sudebnaia palata*). Both of these courts reached their decisions collegially, again after hearing the views of a procurator. Decisions of a district congress or a court of appeals were not subject to further appeal on substantive grounds. But at the request of litigants or of a procurator (in criminal actions) they could be reviewed regarding points of law or procedure by the Civil or the Criminal Cassation Department of the Senate. Adopted from the French system of justice, these courts were to ensure that the lower courts both observed appropriate legal procedures and interpreted and applied the law uniformly. Hence they could not resolve a case on its merits but could only confirm or set aside the ruling of an appellate court, in the latter instance referring the

[43] *SUst*, pt. 1, *UGS*, pt. 2, *UUS*, and pt. 3, *USU*. These statutes were published separately under various titles until 1892 and thereafter as *SZ*, xvi, pt. 1. For detailed descriptions of the reformed judicial system, see Kucherov, *Courts*, 26–97, Vilenskii, *Sudebnaia reforma*, 163–98, and Shcherbina, *Sudebnaia reforma*, 89–105.

[44] Gorodyskii, 'Nashi sudy', 5: 141–2, and Koni, *Sobranie sochinenii*, i. 240.

case back to an appellate court for rehearing in accordance with the proper procedure or on the basis of the correct meaning of the law.[45]

The reform also sought to assure the independence of the judicial system by providing the judiciary with secure tenure and broad power to interpret the law. Although appointed by the Minister of Justice or the emperor, judicial personnel received tenure for life and could be removed only by a panel of peers for narrowly defined causes, chiefly malfeasance in office, conviction of a crime, or insolvency. The requirement that judicial personnel possess both juridical training and suitable experience further limited the control of the minister and the emperor over appointments and promotions.[46] Conversely, judges now were directed to decide cases on the basis of their conscience as well as the law. Where the law appeared unclear, contradictory, or incomplete, they were to rule in accordance with its 'general meaning' (*obshchii smysl*).[47] To prevent arbitrariness or inconsistency in the practice of lower courts, the cassation departments were empowered not only to review appellate court decisions, but also to publish for the 'guidance' (*rukovodstvo*) of lower courts those of their decisions that explained the exact meaning of the law. In addition, the cassation departments could issue warnings or reprimands to judges whose decisions involved serious procedural errors, and senators from the cassation departments composed the court that heard disciplinary actions against members of the judiciary. The judicial statutes thus placed the chief responsibility for both the definition of law and the supervision of the judiciary on the Civil and Criminal Cassation Departments of the Senate.[48]

This expansion of the power of judicial interpretation explains the ability of the post-reform judiciary to shape Imperial civil law. And the pivotal role in this process fell to the Civil Cassation Department, which exploited ambiguities in the judicial statutes regarding the strength of its decisions to assert a power of judicial law-making that was unique both in tsarist Russia and among continental European civilian legal systems. These ambiguities arose in part from a disagreement among the authors of the judicial statutes themselves over the strength of cassation decisions.

[45] *USU*, arts. 1–5, 10, 114–19, 127, 129, 137–65, 200–2, 208–11, 216–17, 219, 223, 249–52, 265–7, *UGS*, arts. 9–10, 186–8, 792–3, 805–9, 813, 815, and *UUS*, arts. 12–13, 104, 174, 927–8, 930.

[46] *USU*, arts. 216, 228–30, 243, 261–96.

[47] *UGS*, arts. 9–10, and *UUS*, arts. 12–13.

[48] *USU*, arts. 228–30, 243, 249–50, 261–96, *UGS*, art. 815, and *UUS*, art. 930. The most extensive treatment of the role and structure of the cassation departments can be found in Levin-Stankevich, 'Cassation', 98–102, 116–30, 135–98, 244–8.

Those concerned primarily with preventing injustice in individual cases believed that rulings of the cassation departments should be binding only for the case under review and therefore could provide only non-obligatory guidance for lower courts hearing similar cases. In contrast, other reformers argued that the explanations of the meaning of the law given by the cassation departments should be obligatory in all similar cases to ensure uniformity in the interpretation and application of the law.[49] The failure to resolve this question decisively resulted in both responsibilities being included in the judicial statutes. Hence the court rehearing a case on referral from a cassation department was obligated to observe the explanation of the law given by the high court in setting aside the original decision, while the cassation departments also were instructed to publish for the guidance of lower courts those of their rulings that explained the meaning of the law.[50] Controversy arose almost immediately over the meaning of the word 'guidance' and hence over the juridical strength of cassation department decisions. In this as in other such disputes, the cassation departments were able not merely to assert, but also to enforce, their point of view.

Referring primarily to its duty both to interpret the law and to ensure uniformity in the interpretation and application of the law, the Civil Cassation Department quickly developed the rule that in all cases similar to those which it already had judged, the lower courts were required to adhere to its published interpretations of the law. The high court reserved for itself the power to alter or abandon a previous interpretation. Of course, the Civil Cassation Department recognized that the lower courts had to determine the extent to which its previous rulings were applicable to a given case. But it asserted that this decision, too, was subject to its review and held that failure either to observe an appropriate

[49] See the material entitled *Sudebnaia reforma* contained in HLL (vol. nos. refer to those made by hand at Harvard): vi, no. 11, 'O kass. sud. resh.'; xii, 'Zhur. soed. depart. zak. i grazh. del Gos. sov. o preob. sud. ch. v Ros.', pp. 54–7, 105–7, 144, 287–99, 349 (arts. 1–3), 357–8 (arts. 42–5), 'Gos. sov. v obshch. sob., 27 avg. 1862 g.', pp. 22–37, 'Vyp. vys. rez.', pp. 1–2; xiv, 'Ob. zap. k proek. Uchrezh. sud. mest', pp. 50–4, 172–3, 297–9; xviii, 'Zhur. Gos. sov., No. 44', pp. 40–4; xxi, 'Svod zam. na proekt sud. grazh.', pt. 1, pp. 87 (art. 740), 122–3, pt. 2, pp. 394–400 (arts. 726, 734, 736–7, 740), 'Svod zam. na dopol. proekty . . .', pt. 1, pp. 116–23, pt. 2, pp. 143–5, 189–202; xxii, 'Zam. Min. Ius. na proekt ust. grazh. sud.', pp. 146–56; xxiii, 'ob. zap. k proek. ust. grazh. sud.', pt. 1, pp. 435–74; xxix, 'Trudy grazh. otd. kom. o sud. ref.', pp. 173–6, 180–204. See also the contrasting views expressed later by two members of the editing committee, Ia. G. Esipovich, 'O tolkovanii zakonov', *ZhMIu* (1894/5), 2: 84–112, and K. P. Pobedonostsev, *Sudebnoe rukovodstvo. Sbornik pravil, polozhenii i primerov* (Spb., 1872), 345, 349–51.

[50] *SUst*, pt. 1, *UGS*, arts. 9–10, 793, 813, 815 (with commentary) and pt. 3, *USU*, arts. 1, 114–19 (with commentary).

ruling or to interpret and apply a ruling correctly also constituted sufficient grounds for setting aside the decision of a lower court.[51] While the elaboration of this rule made its published decisions tantamount to statutory law in the resolution of legal actions, the Civil Cassation Department denied claiming such power with the fiction that it was not creating law but merely explaining the true meaning of existing law.[52]

Legal scholars divided sharply over this assertion of power. Several prominent—chiefly progressivist—jurists supported the position taken by the high court, either because they believed the resulting uniformity provided security to citizens or because they saw the courts as an important source of law as well as a legitimate medium for adapting the law to changing circumstances.[53] But most legal scholars, regardless of ideological perspective, rejected the pretensions of the high court. In their view, a decision of the Civil Cassation Department should be obligatory only for the case in which it was rendered. Otherwise, the strength of a

[51] *SRGKD/RGKD* 1867 no. 519, 1868 no. 326 (also nos. 181, 188), 1870 nos. 1598 and 1628, 1872 nos. 899 and 1217, 1874 no. 599, 1876 no. 102 (and related case 1872 no. 1188), 1878 no. 92, 1879 no. 3, 1880 no. 46, 1883 no. 49, 1893 no. 86, 1896 no. 122, 1914 no. 17 (on the obligatory force of decisions); 1868 no. 326, 1879 nos. 3 and 143, 1882 no. 166, 1914 no. 59 (on the right of lower courts to interpret decisions), and 1872 nos. 974 and 1237, 1883 no. 49, 1884 no. 47 (on the incorrect interpretation and application of decisions as grounds for cassation); 1869 no. 853, 1872 nos. 974 and 1237, 1878 no. 92, 1879 no. 3 (on the right of the Civil Cass. Dep. to review the interpretation and application of its decisions by lower courts); 1868 nos. 181, 188, and 869, 1873 no. 168, 1883 no. 49, 1884 no. 47, 1886 nos. 42, 106, and 107, 1893 no. 86, 1896 no. 122, 1899 no. 105, 1907 no. 102, 1913 no. 36, 1914 no. 59 (distinguish Cass. Dep. decisions from decisions of all other courts, including the unpublished decisions of departments within the Civil Cass. Dep.); 1880 no. 46, 1887 no. 106, and see also 1870 no. 1628, 1879 no. 143 (on the Civil Cass. Dep. altering its decision). See also *ROSPKD* 1903 no. 25, A. L. Borovikovskii, 'V sude i o sude. I. "Zakonnaia sila" kassatsionnykh reshenii', *ZhMIu* (1896), 10: 15–26, and V. L. Isachenko, *Voprosy prava i protsessa. Sbornik tsivilisticheskikh statei* (Ptgd., 1917), ii. 128, 131, 143–4. Unfortunately, the published decisions of the cassation departments do not reveal the internal disagreements within these courts over interpretations of the law. For a description of the process of decision-making within the high court, see K. P. Zmirlov, 'Zhelatel'naia reforma v nashem kassatsionnom proizvodstve i sudoustroistve', *ZhMIu* (1896), 5: 48–54.

[52] *SRGKD* 1868 nos. 181 and 188, 1873 no. 1214, and TsGIA F. 1405 op. 542 d. 124 ll. 192–203, pp. 17–18.

[53] See Borovikovskii, 'V sude', 15–26, Isachenko, *Voprosy prava*, ii. 130, 133, 139–41, 155, Esipovich, 'O tolkovanii zakonov', 84–112 (all three of whom served as senators in the Civil Cass. Dep.), G. V. Demchenko, 'Sudebnyi pretsedent', *ZhMIu* (1903), 3: 91–2, 112–13, and 4: 26–82, D. D. Grimm, 'K voprosu o poniatii i istochnike obiazatel'nosti iuridicheskikh norm', *ZhMIu* (1896), 6: 153–5, S. A. Muromtsev, 'Sud i zakon v grazhdanskom prave', *IuV* (1880), 11: 377–93, A. M. Guliaev, 'Obshchiia ucheniia sistemy grazhdanskago prava v praktike Grazhdanskago Kassatsionnago Departamenta Pravitel'stvuiushchago Senata za 50 let', *ZhMIu* (1914), 9: 333–43, and Valershtein, 'Po povodu stat'i "O sile kassatsionnykh reshenii", pomeshchennoi v "Sudebnom Zhurnale" za iul'–avgust 1873 goda', *SVest* (1873), 208: 1–2.

decision should depend solely on its merits, which were subject to criticism by lower courts and, of course, by legal scholars. In addition to relying on a narrow reading of the judicial statutes, jurists advanced several arguments in opposition to the doctrine of precedent established by the high court. Progressivists and conservatives alike charged that it violated the principle of the separation of powers and opened the door to judicial arbitrariness by transforming the Civil Cassation Department into a quasi-legislature that both created and judged legal norms. Many jurists contended that the doctrine would stifle the creativity of the lower courts and thereby inhibit their ability either to adapt the law or to develop principles of national law. Some worried that partial reform of the law through the decisions of the high court might reduce the pressure for more extensive legislative change. Virtually all authors expressed the fear, directly or indirectly, that the power claimed by the Civil Cassation Department would diminish their own role in the development of Imperial law, a role modelled chiefly on the prestige and influence enjoyed by their contemporary German counterparts.[54]

In contrast to legal scholars, the lower courts generally accepted the authority of the Civil Cassation Department and observed its precedents, albeit sometimes grudgingly.[55] They did so for a variety of reasons: respect

[54] See A. Dumashevskii, 'Iuridicheskoe obozrenie', *ZhMIu* (1868), 36: 83–6, Pobedonostsev, *Sudebnoe rukovodstvo*, 345, 349–51, 'Znachenie reshenii kassatsionnykh departamentov senata', *SVest* (1869), 165: 1–2, 'Protokoly zasedanii moskovskago iuridicheskago obshchestva, 17 ianvaria 1872 goda', *IuV* (1872), 6/7: 3–16, fon Rezon, 'O sile kassatsionnykh reshenii', *Sudebnyi Zhurnal* (1873), 4: 1–31, A. D. Gradovskii, 'O sudebnom tolkovanii zakonov po russkomu pravu', *ZhMIu* (1874), 1: 1–62, Malyshev, *Kurs*, i. 1–5, 12–20, 49–57, 63–106, 279–301, 337–55, G. Dzhanshiev, 'O starom i novom napravlenii grazhdanskoi kassatsionnoi praktiki', *IuV* (1881), 4: 747–73, Shershenevich, *Nauka*, 232–43, id., 'Primenenie norm prava', *ZhMIu* (1903), 1: 34–82, K. Chikhachev, 'O iuridicheskoi sile i prakticheskom znachenii reshenii kassatsionnykh departamentov pravitel'stvuiushchago senata', *ZhIuOSU* (1896), no. 7, pt. ii., pp. 40–56, K. N. Annenkov, *Sistema russkago grazhdanskago prava* (2nd edn., Spb., 1912), i. 2–37, E. V. Vas'kovskii, 'Sudeiskoe usmotrenie pri tolkovanii zakonov', *Pravo* (1901), 50, cols. 2215–25, and L. A. Kasso, *Istochniki russkago grazhdanskago prava* (Mos., 1900), 9–15. On the judicial role of German academic jurists, see J. Q. Whitman, *The Legacy of Roman Law in the German Romantic Era: Historical Vision and Legal Change* (Princeton, NJ, 1990), and R. C. van Caenegem, *Judges, Legislators and Professors: Chapters in European Legal History* (Cambridge, 1987).

[55] Dumashevskii, 'Iuridicheskoe obozrenie', 83–6, Gorodyskii, 'Nashi sudy', 2: 21, and 6: 91, Druzhinin, *Obshchedostupnoe rukovodstvo*, 128–9, 131–2, Shershenevich, *Nauka*, 232–43, Chikhachev, 'O iuridicheskoi sile', 40–2, 55–6, Demchenko, 'Sudebnyi pretsedent', 3: 112–13, Grimm, 'K voprosu', 153–5, Borovikovskii, 'V sude', 15–26, Isachenko, *Voprosy prava*, ii. 130, 133, 139–41, 155, and V. Nazar'ev, 'Sovremennaia glush'. Iz vospominanii mirovogo sud'i', *VE* (1879), 5: 136, 139–40, 165. For an example, see *SRGKD* 1872 no. 1188 and 1876 no. 102. For contrary arguments by lower courts, see 1887 no. 106 and A. Kh. Gol'msten, 'Praktika grazhdanskago suda', *ZhGiUP*, 1881 no. 2, pt. 2, pp. 29, 34. See also Levin-Stankevich, 'Cassation', 143–6, 254–8.

for the Civil Cassation Department as the highest court of appeal; belief in the need for, and justice of, having the law interpreted and applied uniformly; awareness of the disciplinary power exercised by the high court; and fear of having a decision set aside and reheard, especially given the already overburdened state of the courts. Moreover, given the shortcomings of statutory civil law, the guidance provided by the decisions of the high court proved genuinely helpful to heavily burdened judges. Generally, if a lower court disagreed with a precedent of the Civil Cassation Department or wished to avoid its effects in a specific case, it would not directly challenge the authority of the high court. Instead it would define the juridical facts of the case to circumvent the ruling of the high court and thereby avoid a particular outcome.[56]

This interaction between the Civil Cassation Department and the lower courts transformed the Imperial legal system into a hybrid of the civilian and common law systems and allowed the precedents established by the high court to influence civil law as much as, or in some cases even more than, statutory law did. This was an unprecedented situation for tsarist Russia. There now existed not only a reasonably successful system for interpreting and enforcing civil law uniformly throughout the empire, but also an agency capable of creating law in an important area of civil affairs which was independent of the direct control of the autocrat. While the extent of formal power claimed by the Civil Cassation Department made it unique among continental European civilian jurisdictions, its position also differed significantly from that of Anglo-American courts. In building and refining doctrine from case to case, the high court still had to argue primarily from statutes and general legal propositions, and it did not consider itself bound by its own previous decisions.[57] Such reasoning and freedom from its own precedents in some ways gave the Civil Cassation Department even greater power and flexibility than that enjoyed by Anglo-American courts.

[56] Gorodyskii, 'Nashi sudy', 6: 91. See also *SRGKD* 1869 no. 675, 1870 nos. 330 and 451, 1872 nos. 534 and 899, 1873 no. 1214, 1875 no. 969, 1882 nos. 46 and 166. In 1867 12% of the decisions of courts of appeal and 2.7% of the decisions of congresses of justices of the peace were appealed to the Civil Cass. Dept.; for the period 1909–12, these figures were 11% and 3.4% respectively. For the latter period, the high court upheld 69% of the decisions of courts of appeal and 66% of the decisions of congresses of justices of the peace. *Sudebnye ustavy za 50 let*, ii. 344, 370–1, 373.

[57] In other continental civilian jurisdictions, decisions of the equivalent court bound only the lower court actually rehearing the case (if even then), and only in that case, although these decisions in fact had wider influence. See Caenegem, *Judges, Legislators and Professors*, H. J. Abraham, *The Judicial Process: An Introductory Analysis of the Courts of the United States, England, and France* (4th edn., New York, 1980), and W. Friedmann, *Law in a Changing Society* (abr. edn., London, 1972).

The wide dissemination of its decisions further enhanced the influence of the Civil Cassation Department. Rulings of the high court were published and discussed regularly in official organs such as *The Government Herald* (*Pravitel'stvennyi Vestnik*) and the *Journal of the Ministry of Justice* (*Zhurnal Ministerstva Iustitsii*) as well as in the specialized legal journals that began to appear after the late 1850s. The general press, too, commented frequently on decisions of the high court, with most newspapers containing a section devoted to cases heard before the cassation departments as well as before the local courts. Official and unofficial collections of the decisions of the Civil Cassation Department likewise were published regularly, as were unofficial editions of parts of the *Digest of Laws*, annotated with relevant rulings of the high court. The textbooks and treatises on Imperial civil law that appeared in increasing numbers after the 1880s also invariably discussed the precedents set by the high court, even when denying their obligatory force. As a result, the rulings of the Civil Cassation Department were widely known, especially among judicial personnel and legal practitioners. Although certainly exaggerating the effect of the influence gained by the high court, the eminent legal scholar and liberal Gavriil Shershenevich underscored its extent when he complained in 1893 that

> [t]he legal practitioner slavishly catches each comment of the Cassation Department and tries to conform his action with the view of the Senate. This mass of decisions, growing stronger and stronger each year, entangles our court, which, like a lion ensnared in nets, helplessly submits to its fate, refrains from struggle, and lives by the reason of the highest judicial instance. At the present time the whole task of the practitioner consists in finding a cassation decision for the given situation. . . . The authority of cassation decisions has weaned our practitioners away from independent thought and their own juridical analysis. The mind has grown lazy, and the hand involuntarily reaches for the Borovikovskii [an edition of the *Digest* annotated with high court decisions] laying on the table as soon as a case not directly decided by statutory law comes before one's eyes.[58]

The senators in the Civil Cassation Department characterized the influence of the high court rather differently in a memorandum prepared a year later in response to changes in the Senate proposed by the Minister of Justice, Nikolai Manasein.[59] In the view of its members, the high court represented an essential medium for overcoming the legal backwardness of Imperial Russia. According to the senators, the deficiencies of statutory

[58] Shershenevich, *Nauka*, 236–7.

[59] TsGIA F. 1405 op. 542 d. 124 ll. 192–203. On this proposal, see above, Intro., n. 20.

civil law and the nascency of both the legal profession and juridical science in the Russian empire required the high court to assume more responsibility than its continental European counterparts for the development of the law. In these circumstances the Civil Cassation Department had not only to clarify and reconcile vaguely expressed and contradictory statutes and apply them to situations unforeseen by the legislators, but also

> to fill gaps in the laws regarding the character and consequences of whole groups of legal relationships that, despite their prevalence, had not been given normative definition by the legislative power, to introduce into judicial practice general propositions that, although not expressed in statutory law, are inherent in the concept of civil rights and obligations, and to establish the means for and limits to the application of these general propositions.[60]

Clearly, the senators in the Civil Cassation Department had come to conceive of their power to shape Imperial civil law in broad terms and believed their influence on the law, and on the social and economic relationships defined by it, to be a positive one.

Resistance to such judicial authority within the state bureaucracy, coupled with practical difficulties and fiscal constraints, caused the judicial reform to be implemented only gradually. None the less, by the turn of the century the only area of the empire unaffected by the reform was the Grand Duchy of Finland, which retained its own judicial structure. The Civil and Criminal Cassation Departments of the Senate and the courts within the St Petersburg and Moscow judicial districts began to operate in 1866. Over the next five years the new judicial system was extended to the remainder of European Russia, Western Siberia, the Caucasus, and much of the Ukraine with the establishment of the Kharkov, Tiflis, Odessa, Kazan, and Saratov judicial districts. The reform was introduced into Poland in 1876, the Western Provinces between 1880 and 1883, and the Baltic region in 1889. It reached Eastern Siberia and Central Asia between 1897 and 1899 with the establishment of the Irkutsk, Omsk, and Tashkent judicial districts.[61]

[60] TsGIA F. 1405 op. 542 d. 124 ll. 192–203, p. 11.

[61] As it was introduced into new territories, especially non-Russian or sparsely settled areas, the judicial system sometimes was modified, for political as well as for practical reasons. On these changes, and generally on the implementation of the reform, see Kaiser, *Russische Justizreform*, 465–74, Wortman, *Legal Consciousness*, 262, 271–89, Kucherov, *Courts*, *passim*, J. Baberowski, 'Das Justizwesen im späten Zarenreich 1864–1914. Zum Problem von Rechtsstaatlichkeit, politischer Justiz und Rückständigkeit in Russland', *Zeitschrift für Neuere Rechtsgeschichte*, 13 (1991), 156–72, Vilenskii, *Sudebnaia reforma*, 199–219, Shcherbina,

As the reform was implemented, the number of civil cases submitted to the new courts increased rapidly, frequently outpacing the growth of population within judicial districts. In the seven districts operating in 1871, 60,800 cases were submitted to the district courts and approximately 3,200 to the courts of appeal. Justices of the peace received 581,307 cases and rendered approximately 441,800 decisions, while the Civil Cassation Department issued 2,907 rulings.[62] By 1914 the number of civil actions received and resolved by justices of the peace and equivalent magistrates in all areas apart from Poland had risen to 2,507,086 and 2,465,519, respectively.[63] Tables 1.12–1.14 indicate similar sharp increases for the Civil Cassation Department and for the district courts and the courts of appeal in the European part of the empire (excluding Poland and the Caucasus). Despite the steady expansion of the judiciary, moreover, the per capita work-load of judges in these courts rose, especially after the turn of the century (Tables 1.12–1.14). Between 1871 and 1912 the average number of cases heard annually by each justice of the peace also grew, from 391 to 1,438.[64]

The Civil Cassation Department suffered particularly severely from this increase. To relieve the strain, the high court expanded and underwent structural alteration. Between its introduction in 1866 and 1914, the department grew from four to forty-nine senators, and from one assistant chief procurator to fifteen assistants.[65] Where initially all four senators

Sudebnaia reforma, 106–29, Gessen, *Sudebnaia reforma*, 122–9, *Ministerstvo iustitsii za sto let, 1802–1902. Istoricheskii ocherk* (Spb., 1902), 150–64, 175–210, 217–55, and Levenstim, *Ocherk*, esp. 85–7.

[62] *Sudebnye Ustavy za 50 let*, ii. 342–4, 363, 370–1, 373, and N. Sh. [Shreiber], 'K 35-letiiu deiatel'nosti kassatsionnykh departamentov Pravitel'stvuiushchago Senata', *ZhMIu* (1901), 8, table after p. 216. I have found no published information on the number of decisions rendered by district courts and courts of appeal in 1871. Although differences in structure and procedure make comparisons with the pre-reform system difficult, it appears that from their inception the new courts handled more cases than their predecessors. In 1859, for example, the department and chancellery of the Ministry of Justice resolved 2,147 civil cases, the combined departments of the Senate 332, individual Senate departments 14,470, provincial civil chambers 77,351, and lower courts 59,547 (in the latter two instances, a substantial proportion of these decisions represented essentially notarial acts that after 1865 were handled by separate notary offices). *OMIu, za 1859*, pt. I., pp. 2, 10–13, 17, 21.

[63] *SSSMIus, za 1914*, 372–3, 384–5, 406–15, 426–33.

[64] In addition, in 1912 each municipal magistrate heard on average 916 cases and each district member of the district court on average 297 cases. *Sudebnye Ustavy za 50 let*, ii. 342. On these judicial positions, see below.

[65] V. A. Gagen, 'Organizatsiia Pravitel'stvuiushchago Senata', in *Istoriia Pravitel'stvuiushchago Senata*, iv. 27–38, 47–8, 57–9, Berendts, 'Proekty reformy', 478–9, Levin-Stankevich, 'Cassation', 308–17, and Sh. [Shreiber], 'K 35-letiiu', 214–16, 218–19.

TABLE 1.12 *Civil cases heard by district courts, 1886–1914*

	1886[a]	1892[a]	1899[a]	1905[b]	1910[b]	1914[b]
No. of courts	62	64	70	72	74	76
No. of judges	705	748	827	948	1,107	1,309
No. of cases submitted	121,050	140,603	155,030	186,958	249,537	277,443
% change	—	+16.2	+10.3	+20.6	+33.5	+11.2
No. of cases per judge	171.7	188.0	187.5	197.2	225.4	212.0
No. of cases decided	120,828	138,248	145,726	179,706	237,936	299,112
No. of cases per judge	171.4	184.8	176.2	189.6	214.9	228.5
Total population within judicial districts (1,000s)	n/d	76,600	94,800	97,700	121,200	133,900
% change	—	—	+23.8	+3.1	+24.1	+10.5
Population per judge (1,000s)	—	102.4	114.6	103.1	109.5	102.3
% change in case load above population change	—	—	−13.5	+17.5	+9.4	+0.7

[a] Includes the St Petersburg, Moscow, Kharkov, Odessa, Kazan, Saratov, Kiev, and Vilnius Judicial Districts; excludes Warsaw and Tiflis Judicial Districts.

[b] Also includes Novocherkassk Judicial District (formed from district courts formerly in the Kharkov and Tiflis Judicial Districts); also excludes Irkutsk, Omsk, and Tashkent Judicial Districts.

Source: *SSSMIu. chast′ 1. Za 1886*, 3–11, 60–1, *Za 1892*, 1–9, 16–38, 68–9, *Za 1899*, 46–7, 82–3, *Za 1905*, 48–9, 92–3, *Za 1910*, 3–15, 18–52, 146–7, 158–9, *Za 1914*, 3–15, 18–52, 154–5, 166–7.

TABLE 1.13. *Civil cases heard by courts of appeal, 1886–1914*

	1886[a]	1892[a]	1899[a]	1905[b]	1910[b]	1914[b]
No. of courts	8	8	8	9	9	9
No. of judges	123	148	173	190	233	243
No. of cases submitted	9,334	11,176	13,837	18,799	26,956	31,194
% change	—	+19.7	+23.8	+35.9	+43.4	+15.7
No. of cases per judge	75.9	75.5	80.0	98.9	115.7	128.4
No. of cases decided	8,840	10,321	13,214	15,711	25,479	30,993
No. of cases per judge	71.9	69.7	76.3	82.7	109.4	127.5
Total population within judicial districts (1,000s)	n/d	76,600	94,800	97,700	121,200	133,900
% change	—	—	+23.8	+3.1	+24.1	+10.5
Population per judge (1,000s)	—	517.6	548.0	514.2	520.2	551.0
% change in case load above population change	—	—	0.0	+32.8	+19.3	+5.2

[a] Includes the St Petersburg, Moscow, Kharkov, Odessa, Kazan, Saratov, Kiev, and Vilnius Judicial Districts; excludes Warsaw and Tiflis Judicial Districts.

[b] Also includes Novocherkassk Judicial District (formed from district courts formerly in the Kharkov and Tiflis Judicial Districts); also excludes Irkutsk, Omsk, and Tashkent Judicial Districts.

Source: *SSSMIu. chast' 1. Za 1886*, 3–11, 44, *Za 1892*, 1–9, 16–38, 50, *Za 1899*, 46–7, 60, *Za 1905*, 48–9, 62, *Za 1910*, 3–15, 18–52, 104–7, *Za 1914*, 3–15, 112–15.

TABLE 1.14. *Cases heard by the Civil Cassation Department of the Senate, 1867–1914*

	No. of senators	No. of cases submitted	% change	Cases per senator	No. of cases decided	Cases per senator	No. of decisions published for guidance
1867	6	n/d	—	—	792	132.0	531
1871	12	n/d	—	—	2,907	242.3	1,284
1876	15	n/d	—	—	3,264	217.6	597
1881	25	5,792	—	231.7	5,594	223.8	193
1889	25	7,903	+36.4	316.1	8,273	330.9	132
1891	25	6,868[a]	−13.1	274.7	6,864	274.6	114
1895	25	7,494	+9.1	299.8	6,262	250.5	131
1899	26	9,056	+20.8	348.3	7,904	304.0	116
1905	33	8,585	−5.2	260.2	10,276	311.4	115
1910	33	12,935	+50.7	392.0	12,164	368.6	115
1914	49	16,188	+25.2	330.4	18,969	387.1	88

[a] Decrease reflects the elimination of many justices of the peace with the introduction of *zemskie nachal′niki* in 1889.

Sources: *SSSMIu. chast′ 1. Za 1881–1885*, 30, *Za 1889*, 42, *Za 1891*, 44, *Za 1895*, 48, *Za 1899*, 54, *Za 1905*, 56, *Za 1910*, 64–5, *Za 1914*, 64–5; *SChMIu, 1910, 1914*; N. Sh., 'K 35-letiiu deiatel′nosti kassatsionnykh departamentov Pravitel′stvuiushchago Senata', *ZhMIu* (1901), 8: 211–48; *Sudebnye Ustavy 20 noiabra 1864 g. za piat′desiat let* (Ptgd., 1914), ii. 371–4; RGKD, 1905, 1910, 1914.

had reviewed each case, after 1877 the department was divided into several benches consisting of at least three members. Cases not requiring a new ruling on the meaning of the law were assigned to these benches, whose decisions were not published for the guidance of lower courts. The responsibility for resolving questions of law and explaining its meaning to the lower courts now rested with the full departmental bench, which included the chairman of the department and at least six other senators. As a result of these changes, the number of rulings issued by the Civil Cassation Department for the guidance of lower courts declined, from an average of 1,235 annually between 1868 and 1876 to 375 in 1877 and to somewhat over 100 annually after the early 1880s (Table 1.14).[66] But despite the changes, the work-load of senators continued to increase (Table 1.14), so that in practice many cases were decided by an individual justice or even by an assistant chief procurator rather than by a collegial tribunal.[67]

Such practical problems as the delays caused by overburdened courts persuaded even its supporters that some modification of the reformed judicial system might be desirable. But opponents of the reformed courts often seized on these problems as a pretext for modifying the new judicial system for other reasons: state administrators sought to restore the primacy of administrative authority; conservatives wished to eliminate the threat to traditional political relationships and values posed by the principles embodied in the judicial reform; and ministers of justice felt pressure to assert control over the courts and their personnel. As a result, beginning as early as 1866, exceptions to the regular judicial procedures were expanded and changes in the reformed judicial system were introduced in order to limit the influence of the new courts in instances considered to be politically sensitive or of special concern to the state. For example, press laws were enforced extra-judicially; the category of criminal cases defined as political and therefore excluded from the competence of a jury and subordinated to special tribunals expanded steadily; jurisdiction over such cases could be transferred to military courts. After the assassination of Alexander II in 1881 an area could be declared in a 'state of emergency', which enabled the Minister of Internal Affairs, governor-general, or provincial governor to impose special administrative regulations

[66] Between 1868 and 1876 the actual number of decisions published for guidance fluctuated between 597 and 1,955. Ibid., table after p. 216.

[67] Zmirlov, 'Zhelatel'naia reforma', esp. 48–54. In general, see Gagen, 'Organizatsiia Pravitel'stvuiushchago Senata', 16–66, Berendts, 'Proekty reformy', 463–79, Sh. [Shreiber], 'K 35-letiiu', 211–21, and N. M. Reinke, 'Kassatsionnaia instantsiia', in *Sudebnye Ustavy za 50 let*, ii. 281–326. The legislation modifying the structure and procedures of the Civil Cassation Department is contained in *2PSZ* liii (1877), no. 5741, pp. 722–4.

and to undertake extra-judicial measures in order to maintain public order.[68] Ministers of justice sought to use their powers of appointment, promotion, and the granting of service awards to influence the judiciary, and in 1885 their supervisory power over judges was enhanced. While enabling ministers of justice to intimidate members of the judiciary in individual instances, however, these powers left the irremovability and thus independence of judges intact. In particular, impeachment still was possible only for specified causes, with the final decision being made by a tribunal dominated by judges.[69] In the areas where they retained unencumbered jurisdiction, the reformed courts therefore continued to act independently of the state administration. And with respect to civil law, the jurisdiction of the courts expanded constantly during the later nineteenth century, to include both new areas of the law and the additional territories into which the judicial reform was introduced.[70]

Only the introduction of district land captains in most of European

[68] On these measures, see Kucherov, *Courts*, 65–9, 79–80, 86–7, 202–25, 269–71, Wortman, *Legal Consciousness*, 273–5, 282–3, Fuller, *Civil-Military Conflict*, 111–28, D. Rawson, 'The Death Penalty in Late Tsarist Russia: An Investigation of Judicial Procedures', *Russian History*, 11 (1984), 29–52, Baberowski, 'Das Justizwesen', 167–8, W. G. Wagner, 'Tsarist Legal Policies at the End of the Nineteenth Century: A Study in Inconsistencies', *SEER* 54 (1976), 378–85, B. V. Vilenskii, *Sudebnaia reforma i kontrreforma v Rossii* (Saratov, 1969), 258–64, 284–7, 305–34, P. A. Zaionchkovsky, *The Russian Autocracy in Crisis, 1878–1882*, ed. and trans. G. M. Hamburg (Gulf Breeze, Fla., 1979), 33–42, 254–63, Zaionchkovskii, *Rossiiskoe samoderzhavie*, 160–8, N. A. Troitskii, *Tsarizm pod sudom progressivnoi obshchestvennosti, 1866–1895 gg.* (Mos., 1979), 46–76, and Gessen, *Sudebnaia reforma*, 63–5, 118 ff., 134–5, 160 ff., 192–202. See also *Zapiski sud'i*, 29–33.

[69] Zaionchkovskii, *Rossiiskoe samoderzhavie*, 246–7, Lincoln, *Great Reforms*, 188–9, Baberowski, 'Das Justizwesen', 167–8, and Levin-Stankevich, 'Cassation', 195–8, 296–9, 333–5, come to similar conclusions. On the efforts of ministers of justice to gain influence over the judiciary, their relationship to the judiciary in general, and the 1885 law, see A. V. Shavrov, 'Nadzor i distsiplinarnaia otvetstvennost′ v sudebnom vedomstve poreformennoi Rossii (1864–1917 gg.)', *Sovetskoe Gosudarstvo i Pravo* (1985), 12: 100–5, Zaionchkovskii, *Rossiiskoe samoderzhavie*, 240–7, Vilenskii, *Sudebnaia reforma*, 338–44, Efremova, *Ministerstvo iustitsii*, 68–86, 109–26, 135–6, Wortman, *Legal Consciousness*, 277–8, 287, Levin-Stankevich, 'Cassation', 155–6, 164–98, 308–17, T. Taranovski, 'The Aborted Counter-Reform: The Murav′ev Commission and the Judicial Statutes of 1864', *JGO* 29 (1981), 161–84, Wagner, 'Tsarist Legal Policies', 375–7, 388–9, *Ministerstvo iustitsii*, 160–2, 215–16, 224–8, 231–2, Gagen, 'Organizatsiia Pravitel′stvuiushchago Senata', 36–9, 56–7, Berendts, 'Proekty reformy', 478–9, Zmirlov, 'Zhelatel′naia reforma', 59–82, *Vysochaishe uchrezhdennaia kommisiia dlia peresmotra zakonopolozhenii po sudebnoi chasti, Trudy* (Spb., 1899), vii. 277–81, and TsGIA F. 1226 op. 1 d. 1 ll. 2–6, 22–50, 68–70, F. 1587 op. 1 d. 1 ll. 4–35 (pp. 59–60), and F. 1405 op. 515 d. 179 ll. 8–103, 145–51, and op. 542 d. 124 ll. 192–203. For individual cases of intimidation, see Volzhin, 'Iz memuarov', 8: 451–3, 457–60, 466, 472–3, *Zapiski sud'i*, 43–58, Gessen, *Sudebnaia reforma*, 181–2, and *VE* (1912), 6: 424–9.

[70] On the expansion of the courts' jurisdiction over additional areas of civil law, see V. S. Mal′chenko, 'Obshchii ocherk dvizheniia grazhdansko-protsessual′nago zakonodatel′stva posle 1864 goda', in Davydov and Polianskii, *Sudebnaia reforma*, ii. 72, 78–9.

Russia in 1889 significantly constricted the administration of civil law by the new courts. Intended to improve government administration in the countryside and state tutelage over the peasantry, the post combined administrative and judicial functions. Its introduction therefore was opposed not only by state officials who supported the judicial reform, but also by conservatives such as Pobedonostsev who believed that these functions should remain separate. Although this combined opposition proved sufficient to defeat the proposal by a substantial margin in the State Council, Alexander III none the less approved a version of the project under which peasant courts and land captains replaced justices of the peace for the adjudication of most minor cases in rural areas. In most cities and towns, these cases henceforward were to be heard by a municipal judge, a new magistrate with juridical training appointed by the Minister of Justice. Since appeals of the judicial decisions of both new officials were to district and provincial boards composed predominantly of administrators under the Minister of Internal Affairs, the new law largely subordinated the administration of justice at the local level to the state administration. Nor did the new officials enjoy security of tenure. The Minister of Internal Affairs appointed and dismissed the land captains, who were to be chosen from the local nobility; the Minister of Justice similarly could dismiss municipal judges.[71] Until restored in 1912, the system of justices of the peace remained only in a few major cities such as St Petersburg, Moscow, and Odessa. In addition, in other areas a narrow category of minor cases came under the jurisdiction of yet another new magistrate, the district member of the district court, who was a jurist appointed by the Minister of Justice but subordinate to the district court.[72]

While making significant inroads into the new judicial system, these

[71] On the reform, see T. S. Pearson, *Russian Officialdom in Crisis: Autocracy and Local Self-Government, 1861–1900* (Cambridge, 1989), 175–204, F. W. Wcislo, *Reforming Rural Russia: State, Local Society, and National Politics, 1855–1914* (Princeton, NJ, 1990), 83–118, Zaionchkovskii, *Rossiiskoe samoderzhavie*, 257, 366–401, Vilenskii, *Sudebnaia reforma*, 287–95, 301–3, C. A. Frierson, 'Rural Justice in Public Opinion: The Volost′ Court Debate 1861–1912', *SEER* 64 (1986), 538–44, Wagner, 'Tsarist Legal Policies', 385–9, and *OGS, za 1889*, 1–39. The legislation is contained in *3PSZ* ix (1889), nos. 6195–6, 6483, pp. 507–35, 685–714. In 'Crime and Punishment in the Russian Village: Rural Concepts of Criminality at the End of the Nineteenth Century', *SR* 46 (1987), 57, Cathy Frierson notes that by the end of the century peasant volost′ courts none the less increasingly were applying general Imperial law in civil cases.

[72] *3PSZ* ix (1889), no. 6196, v, arts. 48–50, and 'Pravila ob ust. sud. ch.', arts. 25–36. On the restoration of justices of the peace, see *SUzak* 1912 (27 June), no. 118, pt. 1, pp. 2113–91, and G. A. Hosking, *The Russian Constitutional Experiment: Government and Duma, 1907–1914* (Cambridge, 1973), 171–7.

measures still failed to subvert the independence of the regular courts. This failure led to a comprehensive review of the judicial system between 1894 and 1905 which, however, likewise failed to achieve conservative objectives.[73] The inability of conservatives to dismantle the new judicial system had several causes. The technical complexity and integrated character of the judicial process made partial reform difficult, while conservatives lacked a comprehensive programme for reform that would have achieved their goals while still preserving the perceived benefits of the new court system.[74] In this regard, the relative effectiveness of the courts strengthened the position of those officials, jurists, and other members of the educated strata of society who opposed counter-reform for ideological or professional reasons. Conversely, the exclusion from the purview of the courts of cases involving state security and the extension of the special procedural rules governing the actions of state officials reduced the urgency of further counter-reform. This bifurcation in the system of justice reflected a fundamental dichotomy in governmental policies during the late Imperial period. While the regular courts worked to create a legal environment that supported state efforts to promote economic development, the state administration resorted increasingly to extra-judicial means to contain the social dislocation and discontent that resulted from such development.[75]

Equally importantly, divisions within the government over the function of law combined with the structural organization of the government to block most efforts at counter-reform. Supporters of the judicial reform within the government generally proved able to protect it from 'regressive' modifications, even when these seemed justified by such practical needs as a reduction in the work-load of the cassation departments. The renowned criminologist and senator in the Criminal Cassation Department Ivan Foinitskii typified the attitude of such men when, reacting to the proposals of the last commission to review the new courts, he declared in 1905 that 'the sacred obligation of every Russian jurist henceforward is clear: it is to preserve the principles of the judicial statutes in their original purity and to defend their life-creating spirit and internal meaning from any distortions and alterations.'[76] This reverential view of the judicial statutes was matched by the equally intense hostility of conservatives, leaving little room for compromise. As a result, two competing

[73] On this review, see esp. Taranovski, 'Aborted Counter-Reform'.

[74] See Korotkikh, 'Sudebnaia reforma', 28, and Taranovski, 'Aborted Counter-Reform'.

[75] See Wagner, 'Tsarist Legal Policies', and Baberowski, 'Das Justizwesen'.

[76] Cited in N. V., 'K sorokaletiiu sudebnykh ustavov 1864 g.', *RM* (1905), 1: 96.

conceptions of law, and the institutions that promoted them, coexisted uneasily in the last decades of the tsarist empire.

The Character and Sources of Imperial Civil Law

If the judicial reform gave the new courts broad power to shape Imperial civil law, the character of statutory law offered them considerable scope to exercise this power. Despite substantial changes in the law since the eighteenth century, mid-nineteenth-century Imperial civil law continued to reflect the needs of a predominantly agrarian society based on unequal ascriptive status and serfdom. In addition to defining the formal relationship and obligations of different social, ethnic, and religious groups to the state, the law devoted much space to preserving the patriarchal and hierarchical relationships that existed within as well as between these groups and to regulating access to and use of various resources, including serf labour. By contrast, areas of the law that involved the mobility of resources and people, for example contract, commercial, and corporate law, remained weakly developed. Consequently, after the 1860s, as commercial activity expanded, more sophisticated economic institutions appeared, and urban society grew more complex, the courts were confronted with situations that were provided for only poorly or not at all by existing statutory law.

The method of compilation and the form of expression of statutory law added to the problem. Civil law was contained primarily in volumes ix–xii, especially part one of volume x, of the *Digest of Laws of the Russian Empire* (*Svod Zakonov Rossiiskoi Imperii*), a compendium of current law first published in 1832. Updated through regular supplements to incorporate recent legislation, the *Digest* was reissued periodically in whole or in part.[77] Although its initial publication was a significant achievement, the *Digest* none the less suffered from important flaws. It lacked the completeness, unity, and systematic exposition of both general principles and specific norms provided by contemporary Western European legal codes, even though it was arranged and expressed in this format. In theory, although not in fact, the *Digest* included all legislative and other

[77] For the publication history of the *Digest*, see N. Korevo, *Ob izdaniiakh zakonov Rossiiskoi Imperii. 1830–1899. Sbornik svedenii ob izdaniiakh Svoda zakonov i Prodolzhenii k nemu, Polnago Sobraniia Zakonov, Svodov Voennykh i Morskikh Postanovlenii, a takzhe ob izdaniiakh mestnykh zakonov* (Spb., 1900), and P. A. Zaionchkovskii, *Spravochniki po istorii dorevoliutsionnoi Rossii. Bibliograficheskii ukazatel′* (2nd edn., Mos., 1978), 25–36. For accounts of the compilation, nature, and deficiencies of the *Digest*, see M. A. Lozina-Lozinskii, *Kodifikatsiia zakonov po russkomu gosudarstvennomu pravu* (Spb., 1897), S. V. Pakhman, *Istoriia kodifikatsii grazhdanskago prava* (Spb., 1876), ii, and the references cited above in n. 7.

normative acts promulgated since the Law Code of 1649 which had not been abrogated or superseded by any subsequent act. Hence statutes, decrees, ministerial directives, decisions in particular judicial cases, and a variety of other sources, issued at different times and for divergent purposes, were chopped up, amalgamated, and rearranged to fit the system adopted for the *Digest*, a system that was influenced strongly by European civilian jurisprudence. This approach resulted in an absence of any uniform legal terminology and a casuistic character that often left the meaning of the law vague and contradictory and its coverage incomplete and uneven. The pretension of the *Digest* to completeness and to exclusivity as the source of civil law (apart from recent enactments that had not yet been included in it), however, impeded the development of a body of supplementary case law that could have compensated for its shortcomings.[78] Prior to the judicial reform, Imperial civil law thus lacked the mechanism employed by either civilian or common law legal systems to attain comprehensiveness of coverage and to articulate general norms and relied instead on a cumbersome semi-legislative process.

The diversity of the Russian empire also increased the uncertainty of the law. Although Imperial civil law applied generally to all subjects of the empire, numerous exceptions were made for nationality, ethnicity, region, religion, or social status. The Baltic provinces, the Grand Duchy of Finland, and the former Kingdom of Poland, for example, came under the jurisdiction of local laws or the Napoleonic Code. For Georgia, Bessarabia, and parts of the Ukraine, the law specified special provisions that reflected their local customs and conditions or previous political status. Cossacks, German settlers, the nomadic peoples of Siberia and Central Asia, and peasants were subject to their own laws or customs to a greater or lesser extent, as were Muslims and Jews. The ecclesiastical authorities of different religious faiths defined and administered important aspects of family law. Hence merely determining the law applicable to a given case, let alone its meaning, could prove difficult.[79] This

[78] *2PSZ* viii (1833), pt. 1, no. 5947, pp. 68–9, and ix (1834), pt. 2, no. 7654, pp. 258–9. On the debate among Russian jurists over the relative strength of the *Digest* and of the original acts incorporated into it, see Maikov, *O svode zakonov*, 137–44, 262–76, N. M. Korkunov, *Sbornik statei N. M. Korkunova, 1877–97* (Spb., 1898), 77–97, N. I. Lazarevskii, 'Zakon i svod', *Pravo* (1899), 39, cols. 1681–91, I. V. Gessen, 'Obnovlennyi stroi i kodifikatsiia', *Pravo* (1909), 10, cols. 605–19, and 12, cols. 781–7, A. I. Kaminka, 'Sila svoda zakonov', *Pravo* (1908), 1, cols. 6–19, and id., 'Novyia izdaniia svoda zakonov', *Pravo* (1908), 10, cols. 547–52.

[79] Korevo, *Ob izdaniiakh*, 83–104, M. M. Al′tman, 'Iz istorii kodifikatsii musal′manskogo prava v zakavkaz′e v XIX veke', *Uchenye zapiski Azerbaidzhanskogo gosudarstvennogo universiteta. Seriia iuridicheskikh nauk* (1974), 1: 24–31, and A. E. Nol′de, *Ocherki po istorii kodifikatsii mestnykh grazhdanskikh zakonov pri grafe Speranskom. Vypusk 2. Kodifikatsiia*

problem grew worse during the late Imperial period as centralized state agencies, including the new courts, challenged the authority of local customs and laws.

This welter of statutory material and custom provided the initial reservoir of formal legal sources available to the post-reform courts for the resolution of disputes regarding the family, property, and inheritance. The Civil Cassation Department worked within these sources to develop the law in ways that, while often cautious and modest, also had revolutionary implications for the tsarist regime. In the course of resolving particular cases the high court began to redefine legal relationships in accordance with the ideals of legality, civil equality, and affective relations within the family. In doing so, the court also reflected the desire of moderate conservative and progressivist jurists generally to use the law as an instrument for ensuring the orderly transformation of society. In this sense, senators and jurists alike preserved more than a trace of tsarist paternalism and the traditional instrumentalist conception of law. But at the same time, they challenged the patriarchal ethos which underlay the tsarist socio-political order, the claims of the state administration to hegemonic power, the authority of the Orthodox Church over family life, and the social predominance of traditional élites, especially the landed nobility.

mestnago prava pribaltiiskikh gubernii (Spb., 1914). On the problems arising from this situation, see id., 'Kolliziia raznomestnykh zakonov o nasledovanii v dvizhimostiakh po russkomu pravu', *VP* (1900), 7: 1–42, and Levenstim, *Ocherk*, 43–6.

PART I

Redefining the Family

2

Traditional Law: The Patriarchal Family and Pressures for Change

ONE fine summer day in 1902 Feona Sharapova hurled herself from a second-storey window of the Kaluga District Court building. Her action was precipitated by the court's ruling that she was legally obligated to live with her husband. When disconcerted officials reached the severely injured woman, they discovered a vial of poison concealed in her dress.[1]

Although providing few details, the short description of the case that appeared in the liberal journal *Law* (*Pravo*) reflects the intensification and convergence in early twentieth-century Imperial Russia of two sources of pressure for the revision of Imperial family law. Since the late 1850s members of the educated and upper strata of tsarist society had been demanding changes in the law considered just and necessary to meet new social conditions and needs. Because these changes tended to promote the ideals of their proponents, such demands formed part of the larger processes of social and ideological redefinition which divided these strata during this period. At the same time, but especially after the early 1890s, the number of people—particularly women of all social strata—who sought formal release from their marital bonds increased substantially. For educated advocates of legal reform, this increased incidence of formal marital dissolution constituted compelling evidence that Imperial family law urgently required revision in accordance with their own ideals and perceptions.

The Patriarchal Family

Educated critics of Imperial family law focused particularly on the principles of patriarchal authority, unequal status, patrilineal kinship, and broad ecclesiastical jurisdiction which underlay existing statutory law. Although long established, these principles had undergone significant

[1] *Pravo* (1902), 33, col. 1495.

reformulation during the eighteenth century in response to such diverse influences as the revision and then elimination of the service obligation of the nobility, changes in state taxation and recruitment policies, the administrative restructuring of the Orthodox Church, and the intrusion of Western European ideas and culture. In some cases, this reformulation of the law had mitigated, at least formally, the exercise of patriarchal authority within marriage and the family.[2] Despite such modifications, however, the basic principles of traditional law retained their strength in statutory law until the collapse of the empire in 1917.

Reflecting the autocratic socio-political order generally, the Imperial *Digest of Laws* defined family relations in terms of authority, obedience, filial duty, and paternalistic obligation. Conversely, the concept of personal rights for individual family members received only weak recognition. Although not consistently, the law also tended to divide male and female spheres of activity into the public administrative and socio-economic versus the domestic, a division that reflected the conditions and attitudes of the privileged élite who controlled its formulation. Hence articles 107 and 177 of the civil laws (*Digest*, x, pt. 1)[3] declared that

> [a] wife is obligated to obey her husband as the head of the family, to live with him in love, respect, and unlimited obedience, and to render him all pleasure and affection as mistress of the household.

> Children are obligated to render their parents sincere respect, obedience, submission, and love; to serve them in fact, to answer them with respect, and to endure parental admonitions and punishments patiently and without complaint. The respect of children for the memory of their parents must extend even beyond the death of the parents.

As the latter statement suggests, parental authority continued legally in some form for the entire lifetime of the parents and children. Hence article 179 of the civil laws proclaimed that

[2] e.g. see K. A. Nevolin, *Polnoe sobranie sochinenii K. A. Nevolina* (Spb., 1857, 1858), iii. 78–81.

[3] The following analysis is based primarily on the 1857 edn. of the *Digest of Laws*, although earlier and later edns. of all vols. cited also were used. Family law is contained principally in x, pt. 1. No definitive source of the law existed prior to the publication of the *Digest*, although the commission formed under Alexander I to codify Imperial law did produce a compendium of legislation still in force: *Sistematicheskii svod sushchestvuiushchikh zakonov Rossiiskoi Imperii, s osnovaniiami prav iz onykh izvlechennymi. Izdavaemyi Kommisieiu sostavleniia zakonov. Pravo grazhdanskoe* (Spb., 1818–22). For early 19th-c. statements of family law, see V. G. Kukol'nik, *Nachal'nyia osnovaniia rossiiskago chastnago grazhdanskago prava dlia rukovodstva k prepodovaniiu onago na publichnykh kursakh* (Spb., 1813), and I. Vasil'ev, 'O grazhdanskom sostaianii zhenskago pola v Rossii', *VE* (1826), 18: 102–8; 19/20: 210–17; and 21/2: 65–73.

[p]ersonal parental power is not terminated but only limited by . . . the entry of children [normally male] into [state] service, when . . . upon receiving new obligations they can no longer remain in [their] former direct dependence on [their] parents, [and] by the marriage of daughters, in so far as one person cannot satisfy completely two such unlimited powers as that of the parents and of the husband.

Although article 108 stated further that 'a wife is obligated primarily to submit to the will of her husband', the relative authority of husband and parents remained poorly delineated, as did that of parents with respect to a son who had left their household. Despite such unclarity, however, the basic premiss of the law was clear: within the family, as in the state and society generally, individuals were defined in terms of their position in sometimes overlapping structures of authority that assigned priority on the basis of seniority and sex.

To support their broad general authority, Imperial law granted husbands and parents specific powers to control the activities of their wives and children. For example, the law obligated a wife to reside with her husband in all circumstances except his exile to Siberia and to obtain the consent of her husband to enter employment, undertake higher education, execute a bill of exchange, or receive her own passport, which normally was necessary for residence and often for employment.[4] Children who had not separated from their parents similarly could not obtain their own passports and required parental permission to enter employment, and the failure of even a separated child to obtain parental consent for his or her marriage could result in disinheritance as well as in criminal punishment. Parents also could have their children confined in a correctional institution without judicial process and could bring formal criminal actions against them for disobedience or disrespectful behaviour; children who failed to support parents in need could be subjected to criminal penalties. Conversely, children were barred from bringing legal actions against their parents except in the narrowly defined circumstances noted below.[5]

The legal obligations of husbands and parents, by contrast, tended to be less substantive and therefore difficult to enforce. Article 106 of the civil laws stated that

[4] *SZ* (1857), x, pt. 1, arts. 100–18, 2202; xi, pt. 2, *Ust. torg.*, art. 546; and xiv, *Ust. o pas.*, arts. 40, 57, 63, 106–9, 124, 171, 176, 238–57, 267 (*Prod.* 1895, *Ust. o vid. na zhit.*, arts. 1, 3, 8–11). The husband also transmitted his name and formal social status to his wife, unless in the latter instance she belonged to a higher estate than her husband. ibid. x, pt. 1, art. 100; and ix (1833), *Zak. sost.*, arts. 5, 10, 284–5 (1876 edn., arts. 5, 11, 539–40).

[5] *SZ* (1857), x, pt. 1, arts. 1, 6–7, 164–95, 226, 229–30, 294–5, 995, 2203; xv (1845), *Ulozh. o nak.*, arts. 2040, 2057, 2064, 2084–6 (1885 edn., arts. 1549, 1566, 1572, 1592). See also the references to *Ust. o pas.* cited above in n. 4.

> [a] husband is obligated to love his wife as his own body, to live with her in harmony, to respect and defend her, and to forgive her insufficiencies and ease her infirmities. He is obligated to provide his wife with sustenance and support commensurate with his social status and capabilities.

Clearly, only the latter obligation was enforceable even in principle, let alone in practice. Similarly, Imperial law obligated parents to support their children materially, to provide them with 'a good and honourable upbringing', and to prepare daughters for marriage and sons for either state service or an appropriate trade, the latter admonition being largely irrelevant for the peasant majority of the population.[6] Again, the enforceability even in principle of all but the first obligation appears problematic.

While defining the authority of husbands and parents broadly and their obligations vaguely, Imperial law imposed few constraints on the exercise of matrimonial or parental authority. By requiring the consent of a wife to her employment, and of children to marriage, the law appeared to accept the principle that the individual rights of wives and children placed limitations on the authority of husbands and parents. These limitations, however, owed more to the conception of contracts as being voluntary in nature and to the Orthodox conception of marriage as a voluntary act than to any doctrine of individual rights.[7] After all, the will of a wife in the case of employment or of a child in the case of marriage still could not override that of a husband or of parents, respectively. Parents could be held accountable for the separate property of their children, although here the law was meant originally to protect the interests of the kin-group of the donor of the property as much as those of the child.[8] The law also held a husband to be liable criminally for severely injuring or murdering his wife, intentionally involving her in a criminal act, or pandering her sexual services, and parents were similarly liable for severely injuring or murdering their children, involving them in a criminal act, or encouraging them to engage in immoral sexual behaviour. But, again, the purpose of the law was more to preserve social order and to

[6] *SZ* (1857), x, pt. 1, arts. 172–6; quote from art. 172.

[7] Ibid., arts. 12, 2202–3 (1528–53 contain general provisions defining contracts); and xv (1845), *Ulozh. o nak.*, art. 2078 (1885 edn., art. 1586). In addition to the literature cited below and in Ch. 4, on Russian Orthodox canon law with respect to marriage see N. S. Suvorov, *Uchebnik tserkovnago prava* (Mos., 1912), 349–90, A. S. Pavlov, *Kurs tserkovnago prava* (Sviato-troitskaia Sergieva Lavra, 1902), 317–90, and E. Levin, *Sex and Society in the World of the Orthodox Slavs, 900–1700* (Ithaca, NY, 1989), 95–101.

[8] *SZ* (1857), x, pt. 1, arts, 180–95, 226, 229–30, 294–5; and xv (1845), *Ulozh. o nak.*, art. 2080 (1885 edn., art. 1590).

enforce officially sanctioned religious and public morals than to protect individual wives and children. Indeed, Imperial law condoned the use of corporal punishment in the family and provided little redress for its abuse or for that of a husband's or parent's authority in general.[9] Hence virtually the only legal remedy available for mistreatment by a husband or a parent was a criminal action for severe injury. Few wives, let alone children, appeared able or willing to initiate such actions. Apart from the costs and procedural difficulties involved, conviction of the husband would deprive the family of critical labour and material support. Moreover, a wife would still be obligated legally to live with her husband after his return from prison or exile.[10]

In seeking to reinforce the authority of husbands and fathers, Imperial law of course did not differ from Western European or American law during the nineteenth century.[11] Moreover, the lack of specificity in Imperial Russian law sometimes appeared to give married women greater formal rights than those enjoyed by their Western European or American counterparts, especially those subject to the French civil code or its derivatives. French law assigned parental authority exclusively to the father, for example, so that even the relations between a widowed mother and her children were subject to the control of the family of her deceased husband.[12] By contrast, Imperial Russian law did not discriminate between

[9] *SZ* (1857), x, pt. 1, arts. 165–70; and xv (1845), *Ulozh. o nak.*, arts. 1296–7, 1922, 2075–6, 2078–86 (1885 edn., arts. 998–9, 1451, 1583–4, 1586–92). See also L. Engelstein, *The Keys to Happiness: Sex and the Search for Modernity in Fin-de-Siècle Russia* (Ithaca, NY, 1992), chs. 1–3.

[10] I. Orshanskii, 'Lichnyia i imushchestvennyia otnosheniia suprugov', in *Izsledovaniia po russkomu pravu semeinomu i nasledstvennomu* (Spb., 1877), 19–21, 52–65, 184, 188–91, M. I. Kulisher, *Razvod i polozhenie zhenshchin* (Spb., 1896), 148–53, 178–83, and B——, 'Supruzheskoe pravo', *SG* (1895), 24: 2–4.

[11] On the legal authority of husbands in Western Europe and the United States during this period, see R. Phillips, *Putting Asunder: A History of Divorce in Western Society* (Cambridge, 1988), 185–6, 324–32, 405–11, 494–5, K. Zweigert and H. Kötz, *An Introduction to Comparative Law*, trans. T. Weir (Amsterdam, 1977), i. 79–80, 86, 90–101, 123–4, 137–8, 151–2, 163, 171, J. F. Traer, *Marriage and the Family in Eighteenth-Century France* (Ithaca, NY, 1980), 166–91, T. Zeldin, *France 1848–1945: Ambition and Love* (Oxford, 1979), 287–91, 343–4, 356–8, C. G. Moses, *French Feminism in the Nineteenth Century* (Albany, NY, 1984), 18–20, 229–30, 243–5, L. Holcombe, *Wives and Property: Reform of the Married Women's Property Law in Nineteenth-Century England* (Toronto, 1983), 11–47, 208–10, M. Ostrogorski, *The Rights of Women: A Comparative Study in History and Legislation* (London, 1891), 184–9, 208–32, N. Basch, *In the Eyes of the Law: Women, Marriage and Property in Nineteenth-Century New York* (Ithaca, NY, 1982), 22–8, 38–41, 56–69, 116, 126–34, 137, 224–32, and M. Grossberg, *Governing the Hearth: Law and the Family in Nineteenth-Century America* (Chapel Hill, NC, 1985), 4–11, 18–24.

[12] See the references to Ostrogorski, Traer, Zeldin, Moses, and Zweigert and Kötz cited above in n. 11.

parents, even though the superiority of the father could be—and generally was—inferred from the general subordination of a wife to her husband.

Perhaps the most important legal advantage enjoyed by married women in Imperial Russia in comparison with their Western European and American counterparts, however, was their right to control their own property, including their dowries. The origin of this right in tsarist Russia is disputed, and its extent fluctuated significantly over time, regionally, and by type of property and social group. But it appears to have become firmly established during the eighteenth century, at least for women from privileged social groups.[13] Such proprietary power could provide wives with a counterweight to their complete personal subordination to their husbands. Except in limited circumstances, by contrast, married women in most Western European countries and American states did not acquire comparable proprietary independence until the mid-nineteenth century or later.[14]

While significant, the superior property rights of married women under Imperial law none the less need to be viewed within a broader cultural and institutional context. Particularly prior to the judicial reform of 1864, legal norms were accorded little intrinsic value by either state officials or society generally and in any case appear often to have been poorly known, unevenly enforced, and frequently subordinated to considerations of state policy. Under such conditions, broad statutory sanction for the unlimited authority of husbands and parents merely mirrored and reinforced the practice of arbitrary personalized authority that dominated tsarist social and administrative institutions and that constituted a fundamental principle of the autocratic political system. For much of the population, especially the peasantry, moreover, the general provisions of Imperial civil law were superseded partially or fully by special regulations that granted wide discretionary authority to state administrators, serf-owners, or peasant communal bodies. The degree to which the rights formally enjoyed by married women under Imperial law were observed in practice therefore remains uncertain, as does the frequency with which wives resorted to formal legal remedies in the event of mistreatment or marital conflict.

[13] *SZ* (1857), x, pt. 1, arts. 109–18; x, pt. 2, *Zak. sud. grazh.*, arts. 2270–4; xi, pt. 2, *Ust. torg.*, arts. 1932–7; and ix (1876), *Zak. sost.*, art. 539. See also *SZ* (1835), v, pt. 1, art. 426 (1857 edn., *Prod.* 1868, *Ust. o posh.*, arts. 20, 43, and 67 of pril. to art. 464), and xi, pt. 2 (1836), *Uch. i ust. torg.*, art. 13. This issue is discussed below in Chs. 6–9.

[14] Zeldin, *France*, 287–91, 356–7, Moses, *French Feminism*, 229–30, Holcombe, *Wives*, *passim*, Basch, *In the Eyes*, *passim*, Ostrogorski, *Rights*, 208–32, C. Shammas, M. Salmon, and M. Dahlin, *Inheritance in America from Colonial Times to the Present* (New Brunswick, NJ, 1987), 83–101, and Zweigert and Kötz, *Introduction*, i. 74–111, 144–53, 157–65.

Nor did formal marital dissolution offer wives protection from mistreatment by their husbands or provide a means of relief from marital breakdown in general. Reflecting the strong institutional as well as ideological influence of the Orthodox Church on Imperial family law, especially with respect to marriage, the law defined marriage as a religious institution. Hence the appropriate ecclesiastical authority of each officially recognized faith established and administered the specific rules that governed the conclusion and dissolution of marriages for its adherents, subject to general Imperial laws that prohibited polygamy (except in the case of Muslims), restricted inter-faith marriage, and required the consent, attainment of a minimum age, and mental competency of those entering a marriage and the approval of their parents.[15]

Most of the population, of course, came under the jurisdiction of the Orthodox Church.[16] Holding that 'marriage is a sacrament established by God Himself from time immemorial, confirmed by the divine teaching of Christ the Saviour, and piously preserved in all Christian religions', the leadership of the church made formal marital dissolution extremely difficult.[17] Hence the church annulled marriages for procedural or similar defects only very rarely, and it permitted divorce only for adultery, prolonged disappearance, sexual incapacity, and exile to Siberia after conviction for a felony. By making the process cumbersome, complex, and costly, moreover, the church discouraged divorce even when valid causes existed. For example, without several eyewitnesses to an adulterous act itself, divorce on such grounds was difficult to obtain. Divorce on the grounds of disappearance could be requested only after a spouse had been absent unaccountably for at least five years and then it required a lengthy investigation. And in cases of sexual incapacity, the cause had to be physical and to have arisen prior to marriage, persisted for at least three

[15] *SZ* (1857), x, pt. 1, arts. 1–99. The approval of superiors also was required for people in state service. See the literature cited below in Ch. 3 and Pavlov, *Kurs*, 317–90, Suvorov, *Uchebnik*, 349–90, S. V. Kalashnikov, *Sbornik dukhovnykh i grazhdanskikh zakonov po delam brachnym i o zakonnosti rozhdeniia* (Kharkov, 1891), and V. Ia. Maksimov, *Zakony o razvode pravoslavnago i nepravoslavnago ispovedanii i o razdel'nom zhitel'stve suprugov, s raz"iasneniiami Pravitel'stvuiushchago Senata i tsirkuliarnymi i separatnymi ukazami Sviateishago Synoda* (Mos., 1909). For the non-Orthodox population, see also *SZ* xi, pt. 1, *Ust. dukh. del inost. ispo.*

[16] According to the 1897 census, 70% of the population of the empire was Orthodox, although this figure includes an unknown number of Old Believers. Given the nature of Imperial expansion during the 19th c., the percentage of Orthodox believers in the population probably was higher at the beginning of the century.

[17] *Polnoe sobranie postanovlenii i rasporizahenii po vedomstvu pravoslavnago ispovedaniia Rossiiskoi Imperii. Tsarstvovanie Gosudaria Imperatora Pavla Pervago, 6 noiabria 1796 g.-11 marta 1801 g.* (Ptgd., 1915), 618 (no. 504).

years, and been verified by state medical authorities; if the husband was the afflicted party, the wife had to have retained her virginity. As a further disincentive, as well as a punishment for what was perceived as a marital offence, remarriage was prohibited for a spouse found to be sexually incapable or, until 1904, guilty of adultery.[18]

The Orthodox hierarchy relaxed its stringent policy only when the actions of one spouse appeared to threaten the faith of the other. Fearing that otherwise she and her children would succumb both to heresy and to the degenerate sexual behaviour allegedly practised by the *dukhobors*, for example, in 1827 the Holy Synod granted a divorce with permission to remarry to a woman whose husband had joined this sect.[19] Advocating an identical resolution in a similar case in 1856, the influential Metropolitan Filaret (Drozdov) of Moscow argued that

> [o]n the one hand, respect for the sanctity of a marriage concluded in the Orthodox Church demands that, so far as possible, the dissolution of [this marriage] be avoided. On the other hand, it would be unjust to deprive an Orthodox wife whose husband has been exiled for unyielding adherence to *molokanstvo* of the right of marriage forever or for a lengthy period, because she is an innocent person, and the innocent must not suffer deprivation or burden for the sake of the guilty. Moreover, this would not be without danger, as is evident from the example of Matrona, who, if not permitted to remarry, will attempt to rejoin her exiled husband and, in all probability, will become polluted by *molokanstvo*.[20]

[18] *SZ* (1857), x, pt. 1, arts. 45–60. For procedural and other rules, see Maksimov, *Zakony*, 45–111, 427–8, Kalashnikov, *Sbornik*, 10–68, 97–133, S. P. Grigorovskii, *Prichiny i posledstviia razvoda i brakorazvodnyi protsess na sude dukhovnom* (Spb., 1898), and N. N. Mazurenko, *Rastorzhenie braka i zakon 28 maia* (Spb., 1905). Local diocesan authorities and the local bishop investigated and acted on petitions for divorce, with all positive decisions being subject to review and confirmation by the Holy Synod. The decisions for numerous individual cases can be found in *Polnoe sobranie postanovlenii i rasporiazhenii po vedomstvu pravoslavnago ispovedaniia Rossiiskoi Imperii*, particularly the vols. for the 19th c. For an analysis of church practice, see G. Freeze, 'Bringing Order to the Russian Family: Marriage and Divorce in Imperial Russia, 1760–1860', *Journal of Modern Hostory*, 62 (1990), 709–46. An offended spouse also could bring criminal charges against an adulterous partner, but doing so precluded an action for divorce, and the couple would be obligated legally to live together after the guilty spouse had completed a brief term in prison. Apparently few such criminal cases were heard as a result. *SZ* (1845), xv, *Ulozh. o nak.*, art. 2077 (1885 edn., art. 1585), *SUst., UUS*, art. 1016, K. A. Dvorzhitskii, 'Preliubodeianie (grekh i prestuplenie)', *SG* (1895), 43: 8–9, and M. Levitskii, 'Po povodu 1016 st. ust. ugol. sud.', *ZhIuOSU* (1894), 2: 40–58.

[19] *Polnoe sobranie postanovlenii i rasporiazhenii po vedomstvu pravoslavnago ispovedaniia Rossiiskoi Imperii. Tsarstvovanie Gosudaria Imperatora Nikolaia I* (Ptgd., 1915), i. 164–5 (no. 121). The *dukhobory* were a communitarian Christian sect that appeared in Imperial Russia during the 18th c.

[20] Mitropolit Filaret, *Sobranie mnenii i otzyvov Filareta, mitropolita moskovskago i kolomenskago, po uchebnym i tserkovno-gosudarstvennym voprosam* (Mos., 1885–8), iv. 167 (no.

Instances of such flexibility remained rare, however, with the result that during the pre-emancipation period the Holy Synod denied the overwhelming majority of petitions for divorce.[21] Hence, with the exception of 1841, in the two decades prior to the emancipation of the serfs the Synod approved only eleven to thirty-five divorces per year for all causes other than the penal exile of a spouse. Despite a sharp increase in the number of divorces granted after the mid-1860s, especially for disappearance, the number of spouses obtaining a divorce remained relatively small until after the turn of the century (Table 2.1).[22]

As Gregory Freeze has shown, both the restrictiveness and the effectiveness of this policy on marital dissolution diverged from the practices of the Orthodox Church prior to the 1760s.[23] But the policy of the church also ran counter to the dominant trends at this time in Western Europe and the United States, where secular authorities increased their control over divorce law and in most countries the grounds for divorce began steadily to expand.[24] Both the increased restrictiveness of church policy and the ability of the church to maintain its control over marriage and divorce law until the collapse of the autocracy stemmed largely from a shift in the relationship between the Orthodox Church and the tsarist state during the eighteenth century and from a conjuncture of church and state interests with respect to the family. While curtailing the influence of the Orthodox Church in many areas during the eighteenth century, the

422). The *molokane* were a Christian sect that emerged in the 18th c. as an offshoot of the *dukhobory*.

[21] According to Freeze, 70% of such petitions were denied during the period 1848–50, and the percentage remained high at the end of the century. Freeze, 'Bringing Order', 738, 745 n. 131. On the Holy Synod, see below, Ch. 4 n. 1.

[22] According to TsGIA F. 1405 op. 542 d. 666 ll. 74–144, p. 41 n. 1, between 1837 and 1860 the number of divorces for adultery averaged 2–4 per year. It is likely that the character of the household economy, limited alternatives to marriage, community pressure, and, in the case of serfs, seigneurial power constituted the strongest disincentives to divorce, especially among such social groups as the peasantry. The incidence of divorce in 19th-c. Imperial Russia remained far below that in the United States and in most Western European countries during the same period and comparable with the very low number of divorces in colonial America and 18th-c. Western Europe. See Phillips, *Putting Asunder*, 230–1, 243, 250, 257, 259, 404, 421–9, 516–25, and Freeze, 'Bringing Order', 734 n. 80.

[23] Freeze, 'Bringing Order'. See also A. I. Zagorovskii, *O razvode po russkomu pravu* (Kharkov, 1884), 88–362, A. D. Sposobin, *O razvode v Rossii* (Mos., 1881), 18–79, 139, 149–52, and N. Klimov, 'Stranitsa iz tserkovnago zakonodatel'stva Imperatritsy Ekateriny II', *KhCh* (1900), 1: 100–28.

[24] Phillips, *Putting Asunder*, 132–5, 154–60, 176–276, 403–78, and Holcombe, *Wives*, 50–7, 88–109. With the exception of England, divorce tended to be more accessible legally in Protestant than in Catholic countries. But where divorce was limited, formal marital separation and flexible policies on annulment often provided alternatives.

TABLE 2.1. *Divorces granted by the Orthodox Church and number of divorces per 1,000 marriages, 1841–1914* [a]

	Adultery		Disappearance		Sexual incapacity		Subtotal		Exile		Total divorces	Total marriages	No. of divorces per 1,000 marriages
	No.	%	No.	%	No.	%	No.	%	No.	%			
1841	7	6.5	74	69.2	2	1.9	83	77.6	24	22.4	107	N/A	—
1848	3	9.7	7	22.6	1	3.2	11	35.5	20	64.5	31	595,426	0.05
1853	1	1.8	14	25.0	2	3.6	17	30.4	39	69.6	56	523,593	0.11
1858	4	7.4	16	29.6	3	5.6	23	42.6	31	57.4	54	563,599	0.10
1860	7	9.9	24	33.8	4	5.6	35	49.3	36	50.7	71	563,773	0.13
1866	11	1.4	633	79.6	6	0.8	650	81.8	145	18.2	795	554,860	1.43
1870	47	6.8	523	75.1	8	1.1	578	83.0	118	17.0	696	602,278	1.16
1875	62	6.5	661	69.8	6	0.6	729	77.0	218	23.0	947	601,502	1.57
1880	121	13.8	482	54.8	17	1.9	620	70.5	259	29.5	879	654,496	1.34
1885	167	14.3	688	58.8	23	2.0	878	75.0	292	25.0	1,170	621,693	1.88
1890	190	21.6	342	38.9	21	2.4	553	62.9	326	37.1	879	659,836	1.33
1895	241	25.1	239	24.9	21	2.2	501	52.1	460	47.9	961	792,892	1.21
1900	474	40.5	380	32.5	35	3.0	889	75.9	282	24.1	1,171	835,265	1.40
1905	1,216	91.1	22	1.6	33	2.5	1,271	95.2	64	4.8	1,335	794,226	1.68
1906	1,469	89.6	2	0.1	22	1.3	1,493	91.1	146	8.9	1,639	1,029,159	1.59
1907	1,868	90.3	3	0.1	48	2.3	1,919	92.8	149	7.2	2,068	992,427	2.08
1908	2,841	91.9	—	—	56	1.8	2,897	93.7	196	6.3	3,093	942,104	3.28
1909	3,252	92.2	1	0.0	53	1.5	3,306	93.8	220	6.2	3,526	926,255	3.81
1911	2,132	88.3	2	0.1	58	2.4	2,192	90.8	222	9.2	2,414	994,524	2.43
1912	3,430	89.6	4	0.1	98	2.6	3,532	92.3	295	7.7	3,827	976,890	3.92
1914	2,902	78.1	421	11.3	81	2.2	3,404	91.7	310	8.3	3,714	884,476	4.20

[a] Information for 1910 and 1913 not available.

Sources: *VOOPSS* for 1841, 1848, 1853, 1858, 1860, 1866, 1870, 1875, 1880, 1885, 1890, 1895, 1900, 1905–9, 1911, 1912, 1914; TsGIA F. 1405 op. 542 d. 666 ll. 47–71, 90–134 (pp. 41 n. 1, 88 n. 2), d. 668 ll. 9–58 (pp. 56–7 n. 1), and d. 670 l. 101 (p. 106 n. 1); *GU. Kn. 2-aia*, i. 284–5.

tsarist state confirmed the authority of the church over the 'spiritual domain', which included the family. In response, the church attempted to consolidate its control over this area in order both to promote its religious ideals and to insulate itself from further state intrusion.[25] Hence, during the first half of the nineteenth century church leaders successfully resisted state attempts to relax divorce law or to introduce secular authority into divorce proceedings.[26] Russian autocrats and high state officials appeared to defer to the church in this area not only because they, too, considered the family to lie within the ecclesiastical domain, but also because—especially after the French Revolution—they relied on ecclesiastical authority to help preserve political stability through reinforcement of the patriarchal family.

The resulting influence of the Orthodox Church on Imperial law is illustrated by a decision of the State Council in 1819 which prohibited marital separation except where sanctioned specifically by the Catholic and, later, the Evangelical Lutheran Church. In resolving a dispute between a Captain Shelkovnikov and his wife, both the St Petersburg Civil Chambers and the Senate accepted the validity of an agreement by which Shelkovnikov would support his wife as long as she lived anywhere other than in St Petersburg. Reviewing this case at the insistence of the Holy Synod, however, the State Council accepted the argument of the Synod—supported by the commission on the compilation of laws—that the agreement represented the wilful dissolution of the disputants' marriage and therefore contravened both canon and state law. Also agreeing that such acts in general undermined the institution of marriage, the State Council decreed that henceforward state authorities were not to consider valid any agreement or act that resulted in spouses living apart.[27]

Although this ruling obviously did not prevent spouses from agreeing informally to separate, it left a wife who lived apart from her husband

[25] Freeze, 'Bringing Order', 709–19, 745–6, and id., 'Handmaiden of the State? The Church in Imperial Russia Reconsidered', *Journal of Ecclesiastical History*, 36 (1985), 82–102.

[26] See *Trudy kommisii sostavleniia zakonov*, tom ii, *Proekt Grazhdanskago Ulozheniia* (2nd edn., Spb., 1822), 44–9, S. V. Pakhman, *Istoriia kodifikatsii grazhdanskago prava* (Spb., 1876), i. 399–416, 464–9, 'Razskazy kniazia A. N. Golitsyna. Iz zapisok Iu. N. Barteneva', *RA* (1886), 2: 69–86, 101–2, N. Zaozerskii, *Zlonamerennoe ostavlenie odnim suprugom drugago kak osnovanie rastorzheniia braka* (Sviato-Troistkaia Sergieva Lavra, 1904), 34–42, *GU. Kn. 2-aia*, i. 311–13, and TsGIA F. 832 op. 1 d. 42 ll. 24–34, 43–6.

[27] *1PSZ* xxxvi (1819), no. 27737, pp. 114–16; *SZ* (1857), x, pt. 1, art. 46. See also Freeze, 'Bringing Order', 743–4, and the sources cited below in Ch. 4. Formed in 1804, the commission on the compilation of laws was charged with the task of codifying Imperial law. Although it failed to achieve this objective, it laid the groundwork for the future *Digest of Laws*.

with no legal right to support, while her husband could impede her ability to support herself through his control over her access to a passport or employment.[28] Recognizing such problems, even the state administration eventually found a complete ban on marital separation to be too restrictive. Hence after its formation in 1826 the Third Department of the Imperial Chancellery, or gendarmerie, issued separate passports to wives in cases of exceptional mistreatment by a husband.[29]

A combination of religious considerations and the desire to reinforce the existing social and political order likewise contributed to the severe treatment of illegitimate children under Imperial law, although here the law also sought to protect the property interests of the patrilineal kin-group. By defining as legitimate only children who had issued from a valid marriage, i.e. one accepted by an officially recognized church, Imperial law not only strengthened ecclesiastical control over marriage and attempted to enforce religious norms of sexual behaviour, but also protected ties of kinship. All other children were considered illegitimate, even if they were born in a marriage that was annulled only after their birth.[30] In contrast to Western European law, which in most instances established mutual legal rights between illegitimate children and their mother and, occasionally, their father, Imperial law accorded such children no rights with respect to either parent.[31] Nor could parents adopt,

[28] Peasant women and women from non-privileged urban estates apparently could enter employment within their district of official residence without their own passport, but their husbands often tried to claim their wages. B. A. Engel, *Between the Fields and the City: Women, Work, and Family in Russia, 1861–1914* (Cambridge, forthcoming), chs. 1, 3.

[29] This issue is discussed below in Ch. 4; see the references cited there.

[30] These rules created problems especially for Old Believers, who did not accept the authority of the official Orthodox Church or observe its rituals. Beginning in 1874, the government allowed civil registration of marriages and births in such cases. On illegitimacy, see Levin, *Sex*, 65–7, 84–5, 110, 193–5, 244–5, D. L. Ransel, *Mothers of Misery: Child Abandonment in Russia* (Princeton, NJ, 1988), esp. 9–19, 63, and the literature cited below in Chs. 3 and 4. Under Alexander I, petitions to legitimize illegitimate children born to parents who subsequently married apparently were approved regularly, whereas under Nicholas I they generally were denied. N. Martynov, *Uzakonenie i usynovlenie detei (zakon 12 marta 1891 goda), s zakonodatel'nymi motivami, raz"iasneniiami Senata i obraztsami bumag* (4th edn., Spb., 1902), 1–2.

[31] *SZ* (1857), x, pt. 1, arts. 119–44, 1119. For the period prior to the publication of the *Digest of Laws*, see Vasil'ev, 'O grazhdanskom sostaianii', 19/20: 214–17. Imperial law did grant an unmarried mother of an illegitimate child the right to bring a criminal action against the father to obtain support, provided that the father also was unmarried. See *SZ* (1845), xv, *Ulozh. o nak.*, art. 1289 (1857 edn., art. 1344; 1866, 1885 edns., art. 994), and Engelstein, *Keys to Happiness*, 53–5. On Western European and US law, see Zweigert and Kötz, *Introduction*, i. 123–32, 151–2, Traer, *Marriage*, 178–9, 189–90, Holcombe, *Wives*, 33, Grossberg, *Governing the Hearth*, 196–233, 268–80, and Shammas *et al.*, *Inheritance*, 83, 86, 95–6, 224–58.

legally recognize, or legitimize their illegitimate children except by special Imperial consent, although rules introduced by the state for fiscal reasons appear to have enabled peasants and members of unprivileged urban estates to circumvent these restrictions.[32] Again, attempts by state officials to relax the law even modestly during the first half of the nineteenth century were resisted by Orthodox prelates such as Filaret.[33]

Throughout this period the patriarchal family also found strong support in Orthodox religious and secular juridical literature. In both instances, this family order was portrayed as an essential foundation for social and political stability. 'The family is a representation of the State!', contended Ilarion Vasilev, an instructor in Imperial law at the Moscow Commercial School, in an article on family law in 1827. 'If calm, tranquility, and peace reign in the depths of families, then throughout the State hostilities and revolts fall silent and security dwells.' Asserting that '[t]he father is the monarch, his wife and children are his subjects', Vasilev declared '[l]et one try to introduce a republican order into the family, and one will realize how ruinous it would be'.[34] An instructional essay on the family published in *Addenda to the Works of the Holy Fathers* (*Pribavleniia k Tvoreniiam Sviatykh Ottsov*) in 1844 claimed similarly that 'good marriages constitute the root of state prosperity by preparing useful and necessary members for all the social estates of the great state family. And the well-ordered life of spouses is a guarantee of their faithfulness and zeal in social affairs.' And 'although a wife is not a servant but a true helpmate of her husband, in the management of the household she none the less must submit completely to her husband as the head of the family. Otherwise there will not be unity, order, and peace in the domestic community.'[35] Filaret expressed the same thought more succinctly in a memorandum in 1861, stating that '[t]he state consists of families. Disorder in the constituent parts causes disorder in the whole.'[36]

[32] *SZ* (1857), x, pt. 1, arts. 144–63, 1119; and ix, *Zak. sost.*, arts. 491, 643–4.

[33] TsGIA F. 832 op. 1 d. 42 ll. 24–34; see also Pakhman, *Istoriia*, i. 418.

[34] I. Vasil'ev, 'Nechto o semeistvennykh obiazannostiakh v otnoshenii k dolzhnostiam i obiazannostiam obshchestvennym', *Damskii Zhurnal* (1827), 17: 199, 200. See also Kukol'nik, *Nachal'nyia osnovaniia*, 58–66, and A. I. Kranikhfel'd, *Nachertanie rossiiskago grazhdanskago prava v istoricheskom ego razvitii* (Spb., 1843), 10–11, 19. Vasilev appeared to be advocating formal education for women in order to strengthen their ability to perform their maternal role. Having received a degree in moral and political sciences from Moscow University, Vasilev was appointed instructor in Russian law at the Moscow Commercial School in 1824 and also at Moscow University in 1828.

[35] 'O semeinykh obiazannostiakh', *Pribavleniia k Tvoreniiam Sviatykh Ottsov, v Russkom Perevode* (1844), ch. 2, pp. 412, 429.

[36] Filaret, *Sobranie mnenii*, v. 70 (no. 588).

While emphasizing the necessity of patriarchal authority, however, both Orthodox religious and secular juridical literature also stressed the importance of affective ties between family members for ensuring tranquil and well-ordered domestic relations. In religious writing, in particular, the relationship between spouses underwent significant modification after the mid-eighteenth century in response to Enlightenment emphasis on the contractual nature of marriage and on the role of mothers in inculcating patriotism and other virtues in their children.[37] To be sure, there was also substantial continuity. Instructional writing continued to stress the potential sinfulness of human sexuality, the preferability of celibacy, and the role of marriage in controlling sexual passion. Taboos and ritualistic prohibitions relating to the 'uncleanliness' of women also remained in place. And church literature still placed parents and children within a divinely ordained hierarchy of authority that extended from God, Christ, and the church through the tsar, state officials, and teachers to masters and servants.[38]

[37] On Western European contractual conceptions of marriage, see Phillips, *Putting Asunder*, 165–72, 202–21, and J. Rendall, *The Origins of Modern Feminism: Women in Britain, France, and the United States, 1780–1860* (New York, 1984), 8–12 (7–32 in general); on the likely influence of these ideas on 18th-c. Orthodox conceptions of marriage, see Freeze, 'Bringing Order', 720–2. See also J. L. Black, 'Educating Women in Eighteenth-Century Russia: Myths and Realities', *Canadian Slavonic Papers*, 20 (1978), 23–43, C. S. Nash, 'Educating New Mothers: Women and the Enlightenment in Russia', *History of Education Quarterly*, 21 (1981), 301–16, Ransel, *Mothers*, 22–30, 59–60, and J. Tovrov, 'Action and Affect in the Russian Noble Family from the Late Eighteenth Century through the Reform Period' (Ph.D. diss., University of Chicago, 1980), on changing conceptions of women and their maternal role during this period. For earlier Orthodox depictions of women and marriage, see Levin, *Sex*, G. Fedotov, *The Russian Religious Mind* (reprint edn., Belmont, Mass., 1975), i. 189–94, ii. 71–8, and D. I. Azarevich, 'Russkii brak', *ZhGiUP* (1880), 5: 123–32.

[38] 'O semeinykh obiazannostiakh', *passim*, Tikhon (Episkop Voronezhskago), *Nastavlenie o sobstvennykh vsiakago khristianina dolzhnostiakh* (46th edn., Mos., 1860), 180–93, *Prostrannyi khristianskii katikhizis, pravoslavnyia kafolicheskiia vostochnyia greko-rossiiskiia tserkvi, Razsmatrivannyi i odobrennyi Sviateishim Pravitel'stvuiushchim Sinodom, i izdannyi dlia prepodavaniia v uchilishchakh, po Vysochaishemu Ego Imperatorskago Velichestva Poveleniiu* (22nd edn., Mos., 1833), 73, 110–15, 118–21, I. Ch., 'Blagochestivyia materi-khristianki. Ocherki iz istorii khristianskoi zhizni', *DB* (1858), 12: 37–9, S. Mikhailovskili, 'Obiazannosti suprugi-khristianki', *DB* (1858), 41: 55–74, Arkhimandrit Fotii, 'Vzaimnyia khristianskiia otnosheniia suprugov', *Strannik* (1861), no. 8, pt. ii, pp. 63–9, N. N., *Domashniia nastavleniia pastyria* (Mos., 1862), i. 198–221, Kh., 'Khristianskoe vozzrenie na brak i sovremennye tolki o semeinom i obshchestvennom polozhenii zhenshchin', *KhCh* (1867), no. 7, pt. 2, pp. 3–39, Protoierei N. Favorov, 'O khristianskoi nravstvennosti', *Trudy Kievskoi Dukhovnoi Akademii* (1880), 1: 108–13, V. A. Pliashkevich, 'O brake, kak tainstve v drevnei khristianskoi tserkvi', *PO* (1883), 2: 199–237, and 3: 674–725, Arkhiepiskop Nikanor, *Protiv grafa L'va Tolstago. Vosem' besed vysokopreosviachennago Nikanora arkhiepiskopa Khersonskago i Odesskago* (3rd edn., Odessa, 1894), esp. 170–89, *O semeinoi zhizni* (Mos., 1906), 5–54, and Arkhiepiskop Evdokim, *Po tserkovno-obshchestvennym voprosam* (Sergiev Posad, 1914), ii. 221–6, 248. On the 'uncleanliness' of women, see Levin, *Sex*, 45–57, 169–72, 274–5, and Fedotov, *Religious Mind*, i. 189–94.

Significantly, however, the relationship between a husband and wife remained outside this hierarchy. Attempting to define this relationship, nineteenth-century Orthodox writers drew on the potentially contradictory principles of patriarchy, mutuality, and complementarity. As noted above, such writers believed that the pre-eminent authority of a husband was necessary to ensure both family and social order. But conversely, husband and wife were portrayed as voluntary partners who comforted one another, who helped each other control base passions and strive for moral perfection, and who played equally worthy and important family roles. While this ideal again preserved significant continuity with the past, its stress on the joint effort of spouses resulted in increased emphasis on common personal qualities and mutual obligations. 'Piety in both the husband and the wife is the most important condition for marital happiness,' asserted the essay in *Addenda* quoted above. '[F]rom this [follows] the true friendship, mutual respect, and loving Christian assistance of one member of this union for the other, the prudent management of the home, and the good upbringing of children.'[39] Hence Orthodox writers counselled spouses to be equally respectful, tolerant, and forgiving of one another, to be equally faithful, and to co-operate in reaching decisions on family matters.[40]

But if equal in some respects, a husband and wife remained different by nature in the eyes of Orthodox writers. 'The appointed place of a male is in the life both of the family and of society beyond the family circle,' Filaret declared in 1854 in a memorandum on parish schools, 'and therefore a family and a social upbringing and formal schooling befit him. The appointed place of a female is in the life of the family, and therefore a family upbringing befits her. . . . Any good mother can, without science, teach her children obedience, good behaviour, modesty, piety, and familial love.'[41] Accordingly, Orthodox catechistic and instructional literature

[39] 'O semeinykh obiazannostiakh', 417.

[40] See the references cited above in n. 38; for an earlier period, see N. L. Pushkareva, 'Women in the Medieval Russian Family of the Tenth through Fifteenth Centuries', in B. E. Clements, B. A. Engel, and C. D. Worobec (eds.) *Russia's Women: Accommodation, Resistance, Transformation* (Berkeley, Calif., 1991), 37–40, 43. It is difficult to know, of course, how closely the teachings and actions of parish priests conformed with official ideals.

[41] Filaret, *Sobranie mnenii*, iii. 572 (no. 399). See also 'Mysli sviatykh ottsev i drevnikh uchitelei sviatoi tserkvi o vospitanii detei', *DB* (1858), 7: 268–91. On girls' schools for members of the clerical estate, see *2PSZ* xviii (1843), pt. 1, no. 17116, pp. 528–31; and xliii (1868), pt. 2, no. 46271, pp. 254–61, G. L. Freeze, *The Parish Clergy in Nineteenth-Century Russia: Crisis, Reform, and Counter-Reform* (Princeton, NJ, 1983), 133–9, 178–9, B. A. Engel, *Mothers and Daughters: Women of the Intelligentsia in Nineteenth-Century Russia* (Cambridge, 1983), 23–7, and E. Likhacheva, *Materialy dlia istorii zhenskago obrazovaniia v Rossii* (Spb., 1890–5), iii. 147–63, 172–3.

defined the role of a wife to be the upbringing of children, the management of the domestic affairs of the household, and the provision of a shelter from the conflicts of the social world for her husband and of moral bearings for the family as a whole, whereas the role of a husband was to provide materially for the family and to act for it publicly.[42] Particularly after the 1860s, Orthodox writers contended that by elevating wives to such prominence within the family Christianity had liberated them from the slavish conditions they had endured in heathen societies, a claim that itself reflected an improvement in the image of women in Orthodox literature.[43] None the less, wives were portrayed as performing essentially an auxiliary role that left them dependent on their husbands, thereby reinforcing the authority of the latter.

Recognizing the potential conflict between the ideals of patriarchal authority and mutuality, Orthodox instructional literature attempted to resolve it through admonition and inner moral restraint. 'Do not always limit your wife in her desires, even though they sometimes are superfluous,' advised an instructional manual published in 1862, 'and do not always insistently demand the fulfilment of your own desires, because for all [her] submission to you and dependence on you, [your wife] is not your slave but your friend and consort. . . . [R]emember . . . that even though you received power over her, it was by her will.'[44] Conversely, the manual advised a wife to defend her views and to try to improve the behaviour of her husband, but with patience, tact, and prayer.[45] When such tactics failed, mediation by the clergy was encouraged. But a wife in no case should resist even the most abusive treatment by her husband, and in the end '[t]here remains only to suffer in an unhappy marriage, praying and hoping for Divine mercy'.[46] The personal welfare and rights of those

[42] In addition to the references cited above in nn. 38 and 41, see *Rechi, proiznesennyia zakonouchiteliami moskovskikh zhenskikh gimnazii, okonchivshim kurs vospitannitsam onykh* (Mos., 1892), esp. 31–8, 50–9, 86–93, 133–41, 151–62, 169–74, 188–93.

[43] A. Nadezhdin, 'Novozavetnyia zheny', *Strannik* (1872), 10: 41–86, id., 'Zhenshchiny v istorii khristianskoi tserkvi', *Strannik* (1872), 11: 141–86, id., *Prava i znachenie zhenshchiny v khristianstve* (Spb., 1873), 'Slovo, proiznesennoe Ego Vysokopreosviashchenstvom, Chlenom Sviateishago Sinoda, Vysokopreosviashchenneishim Pavlom, Arkhiepiskopom Kazanskim i Sviiazhskim, v den′ kazanskiia ikony Bozhiei Materi, 22 oktiabria 1888 goda v Kazanskom Bogoroditskom zhenskom monastyre', *PSob* (1890), 10: 1–16 (1st pag.), D. Vyshelesskii, 'Borb′a drevnerusskoi tserkvi s ostavkami iazychestva v stroe semeinom i obshchestvennom', *KhCh* (1896), 1: 93–117, and 3: 647–78, and I. Galakhov, 'Zhenskii vopros, ego prichiny i otsenka s khristianskoi tochki zreniia', *KhCh* (1903), 6: 923–35, 7: 94–107, and 8: 217–34. This line of argument may have been a response both to secular critics of ecclesiastical jurisdiction over marriage and divorce and to radical critics of marriage and the family.

[44] N. N., *Domashniia nastavleniia*, 211. [45] Ibid. 215.

[46] Ibid. 217. Similarly, Filaret asserted that '[t]o whomever an unhappy marriage befell due to an inscrutable Divine fate, that person must suffer it as a trial from God; and to

subject to patriarchal authority thus ultimately gave way to the need to maintain the social order through such authority.

A comparable tension can be seen in the few analyses of Imperial family law published during the pre-emancipation period. But tension also stemmed from an attempt to explain the law in terms of the antagonistic ideas derived from German legal historicism and Hegelian philosophy. According to the principal spirit behind the former, Karl Friedrich von Savigny, law developed from the customs and consciousness of particular nations and therefore could be understood only through historical study of the actual laws as articulated initially through custom and then through judicial decisions and juristic explication. The systematization and further development of the laws in any society consequently should remain consistent with the basic principles and traditions of national law. Hegel, by contrast, distinguished between the laws operative in a society at any given time and law as a product and instrument of the absolute ideal that he contended both manifested itself in and guided a universal process of historical development. Through philosophical analysis both the process of development and its animating ideal could be comprehended, thereby enabling legal institutions and norms to be redefined rationally. Significantly for Russian jurists, however, both the particularist and historicist conception of legal evolution advanced by Savigny and the universalist and rationalist conception advanced by Hegel entailed the gradual disencumberment of the individual, particularly with respect to property, and the establishment of secure legal rights for the individual.[47]

Patriarchy, affective ties within the family, security for individual family members, and historicist and Hegelian evolutionary conceptions of law were reconciled in pre-emancipation Russian juridical writing through the ideal of civilization. In their treatises on Imperial civil law published

whomever [such a marriage befell] because of an unreasoning choice, that person must suffer it as a punishment for his foolishness'. *Sobranie mnenii*, v. 71 (no. 588).

[47] By the end of the 1850s several Russian law professors and jurists in other areas of state service had studied in Berlin, where they were exposed to the ideas of both Savigny and Hegel. On these ideas, particularly with respect to property, see J. Q. Whitman, *The Legacy of Roman Law in the German Romantic Period: Historical Vision and Legal Change* (Princeton, NJ, 1990), 151–99, A. Ryan, *Property and Political Theory* (Oxford, 1984), 118–41, D. R. Kelly, *The Human Measure: Social Thought in the Western Legal Tradition* (Cambridge, Mass., 1990), 243–73, P. Stein, *Legal Evolution: The Story of an Idea* (Cambridge, 1980), 56–78, L. Krieger, *The German Idea of Freedom: History of a Political Tradition* (Chicago, 1972), 125–38, and M. John, *Politics and the Law in Late Nineteenth-Century Germany: The Origins of the Civil Code* (Oxford, 1989), 3–5, 23–41, 243–4. On the influence of these ideas in pre-emancipation Imperial Russia, see G. F. Shershenevich, *Nauka grazhdanskago prava v Rossii* (Kazan, 1893), 22–78, and P. I. Novgorodtsev, *Istoricheskaia shkola iuristov, eia proiskhozhdenie i sub'ba* (Mos., 1896).

in 1843 and 1851 respectively, for example, St Petersburg University law professors Aleksandr Kranikhfeld and Konstantin Nevolin depicted the development of tsarist family law as a civilizing process whose principal motive force had initially been the Orthodox Church.[48] Indeed, Nevolin contended that '[f]amily relations as defined by canon law were so different from the family relations that existed among the Russians on the basis of their customs that the transformation of Russian life . . . was necessarily a matter of religion which could be entrusted only to the clergy'.[49] According to Kranikhfeld and Nevolin, a professed Hegelian and historicist respectively, through its moral teachings the church had limited the previously unconstrained exercise of authority by husbands and parents, thereby allowing feelings of affection to develop within the family as well as providing security for individual family members. While derived partly from legal constraints, this security rested primarily on the self-restraint alleged to stem from affection and from Christian morality. Nevolin considered such inner restraint to be essential because family relations by their nature lay largely beyond the reach of legal regulation.[50] Hence both he and Kranikhfeld considered ecclesiastical jurisdiction over family matters to be legitimate, especially with respect to marriage.

Under the influence of Hegelian ideas, perhaps as reinforced by their own *déclassé* experiences, Kranikhfeld and Nevolin also argued that ties of kinship were weakening in Imperial Russia as the state arrogated to itself functions performed previously by the kin-group and as a civil society consequently emerged. Both authors none the less considered the kin-group to be a natural entity that created legitimate juridical relations between its members and that therefore retained social significance.[51] Despite their different philosophical orientations, both Kranikhfeld and Nevolin thus affirmed the legitimacy of the social structure defined by the

[48] Kranikhfel'd, *Nachertanie*, 10–14, 19, 28–40, and Nevolin, *Polnoe sobranie sochinenii*, iii. 45–87, 92–151, 246–63, 303–86. Kranikhfeld and Nevolin in many ways exemplify the early generation of Russian jurists. Both were born into the clerical estate and were plucked from ecclesiastical academies by Speranskii in the late 1820s to prepare for careers in law. After studying Imperial and Roman law in St Petersburg, they were sent to Berlin, where their legal studies were directed by Savigny and they attended lectures by Hegel. After their return to Imperial Russia, Kranikhfeld taught law at St Petersburg University and the Imperial School of Jurisprudence while Nevolin did so first at St Vladimir University and then at St Petersburg University and the Imperial School of Jurisprudence. See Shershenevich, *Nauka*, 25, 29, 31–2, 49–59, 64–6, M. F. Vladimirskii-Budanov, *Istoriia imperatorskago Universiteta sv. Vladimira* (Kiev, 1884), i. 131–5, *BSUSV* 455–67, and G. Siuzor, *Ko dniu lxxv iubileia imperatorskago uchilishcha pravovedeniia 1835–1910 gg.* (Spb., 1910), 308–9.

[49] Nevolin, *Polnoe sobranie sochinenii*, iii. 48. [50] Ibid. 45.

[51] Ibid. 386–90, and Kranikhfel'd, *Nachertanie*, 38–40, 51–5.

Digest of Laws, and they believed that existing law properly balanced both the interests of the kin-group with those of the conjugal family and the authority of husbands and parents with the security of wives and subordinate family members.

Perhaps more significant because of his more critical approach to Imperial law were the views of Dmitrii Meier, professor of civil law at Kazan University. In his classic textbook on Imperial civil law, published posthumously in 1858, Meier described the law as the juridical rules that arose from the nature, and corresponded to the purpose, of a given institution or relationship.[52] Hence he displayed more concern than had either Kranikhfeld or Nevolin with the application of the law to contemporary social conditions, and he did not hesitate to criticize those laws that he considered outdated or unsuited for their social purpose: for example, serfdom, the system of legal estates, and patrimonial property.

Yet with respect to the family, Meier expressed views very similar to those of Kranikhfeld and Nevolin. Like them, he believed that Christianity and the Orthodox Church had exerted a progressive influence on family relationships and thus on social relationships generally. At the same time, however, he considered the moral values of the church to have reinforced those arising from natural affection. '[Marriage] is a union of two people of different sexes which is based on a feeling of love,' he contended, 'a union which has as its purpose to complete the personality of an individual person, which in itself is incomplete, by the personality of a person of the other sex.'[53] Meier therefore concluded, like Nevolin, that 'it is not possible in the field of law to give a full definition of the marital union, and the conception of [this union] is established outside the field of law, in the areas of religion and morality'.[54] He argued similarly with respect to the relations between parents and children that

> [t]hese relations are based primarily on the love of parents for [their] children, a love which is voluntary and unconscious . . . In the same way, in accordance with

[52] D. I. Meier, *Russkoe grazhdanskoe pravo, chteniia D. I. Meiera, izdannyia po zapiskam slushatelei pod redaktsieiu A. Vitsyna* (2nd edn., Spb., 1862). Born in 1819 and the son of a court musician, Meier studied law and philosophy at Berlin University after graduating from the Main Pedagogical Institute in St Petersburg in 1840. His study of civil law appeared in numerous edns. and was still used as a standard text by university students in the early 20th c. See G. S. Pevzner, 'D. I. Meier—vydaiushchiisia russkii tsivilist', *Uchenye zapiski Kazanskogo gosudarstvennogo universiteta*, cxvi, kn. 16 (1956), *Iz istorii iuridicheskoi mysli v Kazanskom universitete*, 19–31, Shershenevich, *Nauka*, 25, 39, 67–77, 87–8, R. S. Wortman, *The Development of a Russian Legal Consciousness* (Chicago, 1976), 229–31, and Siuzor, *Ko dniu lxxv iubileia*, 309–10.

[53] Meier, *Russkoe grazhdanskoe pravo*, 500, and 499–562 on family law in general.

[54] Ibid. 499.

the law of nature children love their parents and in accordance with moral law recognize themselves to be obligated to [their parents] for the innumerable and unrecompensable benefits given them by [their] parents.[55]

Such views led Meier, too, to accept the legitimacy of ecclesiastical jurisdiction over family matters, although not to the exclusion of the state.

Equally importantly, his conception of the family led Meier—like Kranikhfeld, Nevolin, and the authors of Orthodox instructional literature—to rely more on self-restraint than law to limit the exercise of what he considered to be natural authority. Asserting that '[t]he personal relations of spouses are subordinated to the influence of religious and moral rules to such a degree that there is already very little place here for juridical definitions', Meier acknowledged that the law none the less had to define the basic rules determining the legal relationship between spouses. 'The essence of these rules', he continued, 'consists in the right of the authority of a husband over the person of [his] wife . . . [by which] a husband can demand the submission of his wife to those of his orders that do not transgress the boundaries of the law.' Recognizing the potential conflict between this nearly unlimited degree of power and the moral and affective nature of the relationship he had outlined, Meier added quickly that at least among the educated members of society 'this right of the authority of the husband manifests itself rather mildly, under the influence of contemporary ideas of the high importance of a woman [and] her equality with a man'.[56] Hence Meier, too, resolved the tension between patriarchal authority, mutual affection, and individual security through largely informal means that left the authority of a husband intact and a wife with few formal means of redress.

In trying to resolve this dichotomy, Orthodox instructional and secular juridical literature merely echoed Imperial law, which itself included unenforceable admonitions about mutual love and respect among its substantive rules reinforcing the patriarchal family. Ironically, these admonitions derived from the code of police regulations enacted in 1782, which combined paternalistic efforts to reorder and 'enlighten' the urban population with bureaucratic provisions for controlling it.[57] Such origins

[55] Ibid. 537–8.

[56] Ibid. 520, and 520–1 542, 551–2 in general. See also pp. 537–9, 542–4, on the relationship between parents and children, which Meier was more willing to subject to formal legal constraints.

[57] *1PSZ* xxi (1782), no. 15379, pp. 461–88, art. 41, rules viii–xi. See also Nevolin, *Polnoe sobranie sochinenii*, iii. 75. For different interpretations of this statute, see J. P. LeDonne, *Ruling Russia: Politics and Administration in the Age of Absolutism 1762–1796* (Princeton, NJ, 1984), 114–15 (and 85–141 in general), and J. T. Alexander, *Catherine the Great: Life and Legend* (New York, 1989), 191–3.

raise questions about how broadly these ideals actually were accepted in tsarist society during this period and how extensively they affected behaviour and family relations among different social groups. Even among the groups most likely to have been influenced, those that participated in the growing literary culture of Imperial Russia, patriarchal family relations apparently remained relatively undisturbed, parental arrangement of marriages persisted, and economic and similar considerations continued to outweigh emotional affinity in the selection of a prospective spouse.[58] Even when given greater weight, emotional affinity was perceived to be complementary to, rather than incompatible with, the principle of personalized authority that underlay both the patriarchal family and the autocratic political system.

Pressures for Change

When in the late 1850s members of the educated strata of society began to criticize Imperial family law, they challenged precisely this perception. Critics of the law now contended that patriarchal authority not only was incompatible with mutual affection between family members but undermined such affection. Although provoked by the circumstances of the reform era, this criticism had its roots in educational and occupational changes and cultural and intellectual movements during the first half of the nineteenth century which had fostered a new sense of individuality and ultimately also a critical attitude towards personalized authority.

Foremost among these changes were the expansion and diversification of a system of formal education derived from Western European models, particularly at the higher and secondary levels. In 1808, for example, only 975 students were enrolled in the five universities that existed in the empire, three of which were newly founded. By 1824 six universities enrolled 2,618 students, and by 1855 this figure had risen to 3,659. To these numbers must be added the several hundred students who studied each year at specialized institutes such as the Military-Medical School, the St Petersburg Forestry Institute, the Moscow Commercial School, the St Petersburg Technological Institute, and the Imperial School of Jurisprudence, all of which were created after 1799.[59] Similarly, enrolment

[58] On the family life of such groups, see Engel, *Mothers and Daughters*, 6–42, Tovrov, 'Action', *passim*, Freeze, *Parish Clergy*, 57–8, 171–8, 278–9, 310–13, A. J. Rieber, *Merchants and Entrepreneurs in Imperial Russia* (Chapel Hill, NC, 1982), 24–31, 120–9, and the essays by Tovrov, Engel, and Freeze in D. L. Ransel (ed.), *The Family in Imperial Russia: New Lines of Historical Research* (Urbana, Ill., 1978), 15–59, 124–50.

[59] W. H. E. Johnson, *Russia's Educational Heritage* (Pittsburgh, 1950), 270, 287.

in the national network of secondary schools established in 1803 reached approximately 7,700 by 1825 and 19,500 by 1856.[60] The small number of secondary schools for girls also grew modestly during this period, particularly after the introduction in 1843 of schools for girls of the clerical estate.[61]

This expansion of the educational system significantly increased the exposure of Imperial subjects to Western European ideas, even though the number of people receiving a secondary or higher education remained small relative to the total population.[62] The training received, moreover, particularly in higher specialized institutes, unconsciously emphasized personal judgement by stressing the rational solution of problems by those with technical expertise. In certain fields this training also drew on a body of Western European specialist knowledge that accented the individual and the concept of individual rights. The familiarity of Nevolin, Kranikhfeld, and Meier with Western European law, jurisprudence, and philosophy clearly increased their sensitivity to the question of individual security. Occasionally this sensitivity led to a favourable comparison of Imperial Russian with Western European law, for example with respect to the property rights of married women,[63] but especially after the late 1850s such comparisons most often were unfavourable and supported demands for legal reform.[64]

[60] D. R. Brower, *Training the Nihilists: Education and Radicalism in Tsarist Russia* (Ithaca, NY, 1975), 83; see also Johnson, *Russia's Educational Heritage*, 270. Although the trend was upward, there was considerable fluctuation in the number of students enrolled annually in secondary and higher educational institutions. The importance of education at home by private tutors, particularly for children of the noble élite during the first part of the 19th c., also should be noted.

[61] In addition to the references cited above in n. 41, see R. Stites, *The Women's Liberation Movement in Russia: Feminism, Nihilism and Bolshevism, 1860–1930* (Princeton, NJ, 1978), 3–6.

[62] See J. C. McClelland, *Autocrats and Academics: Education, Culture, and Society in Tsarist Russia* (Chicago, 1979), 49–54, and N. V. Riasanovsky, *A Parting of Ways: Government and the Educated Public in Russia 1801–1855* (Oxford, 1976), 61–6, 269–83.

[63] See Meier, *Russkoe grazhdanskoe pravo*, 523–4, and K. Zaborovskii, 'O vzaimnykh otnosheniiakh suprugov po imushchestvu', *Zhurnal Ministerstva Narodnago Prosveshcheniia* (1849), ch. 63, pt. 2, pp. 186–200.

[64] See below, Chs. 3 and 7. After the late 1820s Russian jurists frequently studied abroad, chiefly in Germany. On the influence of specific Western European—mostly German—authors on courses taught at St Vladimir University during the 1840s–1850s, see Vladimirskii-Budanov, *Istoriia*, i. 443–51. On the dissemination of Western European juridical ideas in Imperial Russia during this period, see *BSUSV* 462–4, and Shershenevich, *Nauka*, 22–78. The specialized legal periodicals that began to appear in the 1860s also reviewed Western European juridical literature, and articles and monographs by Russian jurists on particular aspects of Imperial civil law frequently included a survey of Roman and Western European law and juristic views.

Aware of the potentially subversive effects of education, the tsarist government attempted to avoid them through manipulation of the curriculum and the social composition of the student body, as well as through various forms of control over faculty and students. Orthodox religious studies were included in curricula and classical studies stressed, for example, partly to inculcate the virtues of obedience, respect for authority, patriotism, and personal loyalty to the tsar. Students sometimes were isolated to maximize the influence of the values being promoted officially and to minimize contact with undesirable ideas. The curricula of girls' secondary schools reinforced the subordinate position and domestic role of women. Typical was the revised statute of 1827 for the school founded by the Women's Patriotic Society, which stated that

> [t]he goal of the education of the students consists in their training to become good wives, caring mothers, exemplary teachers for children, and mistresses of the household who through their capable labours and their acquired skills will be able to provide a means of existence for both themselves and their families.[65]

Yet in the end such measures could not prevent the emergence of critical views and competing ideological perspectives even among tsarist officials, let alone among educated members of society as a whole.[66]

The expansion of secondary and higher education also intensified processes that already in the eighteenth century had increased the relative weight accorded personal ability in the determination of rank and status and thereby begun to erode reliance on family and kin ties. Especially after the early nineteenth century, the prolonged attendance of children at boarding schools tended to weaken family ties while forging new bonds with schoolmates, particularly among those at élite institutions.[67] The skills

[65] *2PSZ* ii (1827), no. 1012, pp. 338–40, arts. 5, 6. The curriculum included 'divine law' (chiefly Orthodox catechism and church history), Russian, French, and German grammar and composition, Russian and world history and geography, arithmetic, drawing, music, dancing, and handicrafts. For similar statutes, see *2PSZ* xxx (1855), pt. 1, no. 29625, pp. 564–82, and pt. 2, pp. 270–1; xxxv (1860), pt. 1, no. 35780, pp. 532–5; and xxxvii (1862), pt. 1, no. 37849, pp. 20–4, where the stated educational objective and curriculum remained unchanged, apart from the addition of natural sciences, geometry, and pedagogy.

[66] On state efforts to control the effects of education during this period, see McClelland, *Autocrats*, P. Alston, *Education and the State in Tsarist Russia* (Stanford, Calif., 1969), A. Sinel, *The Classroom and the Chancellory: State Educational Reform under Count Dmitry Tolstoi* (Cambridge, Mass., 1973), id., 'The Socialization of the Russian Bureaucratic Elite, 1811–1917: Life at Tsarskoe Selo Lyceum and the School of Jurisprudence', *Russian History*, 3 (1976), 1–31, and R. G. Eimontova, *Russkie universitety na grani dvukh epokh. Ot Rossii krepostnoi k Rossii kapitalisticheskoi* (Mos., 1985).

[67] On the 18th c., see M. M. Shtrange, *Demokraticheskaia intelligentsiia Rossii v xviii veka* (Mos., 1965), and M. Raeff, *Origins of the Russian Intelligentsia: The Eighteenth-Century*

and expertise acquired through formal education became more important for the pursuit of careers in state service, while more careers outside state service became available for recipients of such education. Both the increased social diversity of state officials and the educated and cultural élite and the growing number of officials in the middle and upper levels of the bureaucracy who owned neither land nor serfs but who had received secondary or higher education reflected and furthered these trends.[68] Although educated women were largely excluded from these developments, a few occupational opportunities emerged even for them after the early 1830s.[69]

Family ties and resources and formal socio-legal status remained important, of course, not least by providing favoured access to educational institutions and to desirable service appointments. Throughout the pre-emancipation period, too, the nobility retained its social dominance and hegemony over élite culture. But the nobility itself hardly constituted a homogeneous social group. And as the careers of Nevolin, Kranikhfeld, and Meier suggest, already during this period educational and occupational change had begun to weaken traditional social relationships and identities by creating new associations between individuals and by adding dimensions to their identities. This process intensified after the late 1850s as the educated strata of society continued to expand, to grow socially more diverse, and to include an increasing number of women and as occupational change and professionalization accelerated. The abandonment of their land by many noble families after the abolition of serfdom,

Nobility (New York, 1966), esp. 41, 81–4, 128–9, 140, 146–7, 150–2, 159, 161; but cf. M. Confino, 'Histoire et psychologie: A propos de la noblesse russe au xviiie siècle', *Annales: Économies, Sociétés, Civilisations*, 22 (1967), 1163–205, and J. LeDonne, 'Ruling Families in the Russian Political Order, 1689–1825', *Cahiers du monde Russe et Soviétique*, 28 (1987), 233–322. Key developments appear to have been changes in the system of service rank and the payment of salaries and pensions to state servitors. On the former, see H. A. Bennett, 'Evolution of the Meanings of Chin: An Introduction to the Russian Institution of Rank Ordering and Niche Assignment from the Time of Peter the Great's Table of Ranks to the Bolshevik Revolution', *California Slavic Studies*, 10 (1977), 1–43. On the early 19th c., see Raeff, *Origins*, and on the close ties among members of the élite Imperial School of Jurisprudence, See Sinel, 'Socialization', and Wortman, *Legal Consciousness*, 203–20.

68 In addition to Raeff, *Origins*, see W. M. Pintner and D. K. Rowney (eds.), *Russian Officialdom: The Bureaucratization of Russian Society from the Seventeenth to the Twentieth Century* (Chapel Hill, NC, 1980), chs. 7–10, W. B. Lincoln, *In the Vanguard of Reform: Russia's Enlightened Bureaucrats 1825–1861* (DeKalb, Ill., 1982), D. T. Orlovsky, *The Limits of Reform: The Ministry of Internal Affairs in Imperial Russia, 1802–1881* (Cambridge, Mass., 1981), P. A. Zaionchkovskii, *Pravitel'stvennyi apparat samoderzhavnoi Rossii v xix v.* (Mos., 1978), Wortman, *Legal Consciousness*, and N. M. Frieden, *Russian Physicians in an Era of Reform and Revolution, 1856–1905* (Princeton, NJ, 1981), chs. 1–2.

69 Likhacheva, *Materialy*, iii. 174–6.

rapid urban growth, and the emergence after the mid-1870s of a more complex civic culture in expanding cities had a similar effect.[70]

In this context of shifting relationships, several cultural and intellectual movements during the first half of the nineteenth century helped to focus attention on the individual and to revise attitudes towards women and the family, in some cases despite a conservative orientation. Both sentimentalism and romanticism, for example, stressed individual emotions, feelings, and self-fulfilment. Both likewise emphasized the priority of affective ties and moral ideals over economic and social considerations in marriage. By emphasizing parental affection for and obligations towards children, moreover, these movements complicated traditional ideals of unlimited parental authority and unquestioning filial submission. Finally, the portrayal of women as equally worthy, if by nature weaker, human beings whose greater capacity for love, moral virtue, and parental self-sacrifice deserved male respect challenged earlier images that depicted women as a source of sin and temptation who required stern male control.[71]

A similar influence was exerted by the ideas of several Western European social and political theorists and idealist philosophers who became popular in Imperial Russia after the mid-1830s. Following the French writer George Sand, for example, several Russian social critics in the 1840s stressed the importance of emotional and sexual fulfilment for self-realization and hence the need for both sexual equality and the freedom to form loving relationships.[72] The writings of British political economists fostered a belief in the superior productivity of free labour and consequently in the need to release the creative energy of individuals.[73] Perhaps most

[70] On these developments see the references cited above in Ch. 1 n. 2; on the nobility and on urban growth, see below, Chs. 6 and 8; on education, in addition to the references cited above in n. 66, see C. Johanson, *Women's Struggle for Higher Education in Russia, 1855–1900* (Kingston, Ont., 1987), and J. A. Ruckman, *The Moscow Business Elite: A Social and Cultural Portrait of Two Generations, 1840–1905* (DeKalb, Ill., 1984), 159–61.

[71] Ransel, *Mothers*, 7, 22–30, 59–60, 85–6, 100–5, 193–4, Tovrov, 'Action', 348–77, the essays by Tovrov and Wortman in Ransel, *The Family*, 15–43, 60–74, Engel, *Mothers and Daughters*, 16–42, Stites, *Women's Liberation Movement*, 13–25, Wortman, *Legal Consciousness*, 127–54, B. Heldt, *Terrible Perfection: Women and Russian Literature* (Bloomington, Ind., 1987), 12–37, M. Malia, *Alexander Herzen and the Birth of Russian Socialism* (Univ. Lib. edn., New York, 1965), I. Paperno, *Chernyshevskii and the Age of Realism: A Study in the Semiotics of Behavior* (Stanford, Calif., 1988), 60–8, L. Ia. Ginsburg, 'The "Human Document" and the Formation of Character', in A. D. and A. S. Nakhimovsky (eds.), *The Semiotics of Russian Cultural History* (Ithaca, NY, 1985), 188–224, and W. M. Todd, *Fiction and Society in the Age of Pushkin* (Cambridge, Mass., 1986).

[72] Stites, *Women's Liberation Movement*, 19–24, Engel, *Mothers and Daughters*, 35–41, 73, and Malia, *Herzen*, 257–77.

[73] A. A. Skerpan, 'The Russian National Economy and Emancipation', in A. D. Ferguson and A. Levin (eds.), *Essays in Russian History: A Collection Dedicated to George Vernadsky*

powerfully, Hegelian ideas led to an evolutionary view of history which emphasized the progressive liberation of the individual from the fetters of ignorance, instinct, and tradition.[74]

The statist jurist and professor of Russian legal history at Moscow University Konstantin Kavelin linked this latter idea to family structure in a seminal essay on Russian socio-juridical and political development in 1847.[75] Concerned primarily with refuting Slavophile arguments that stressed the distinctiveness of Russia from Western Europe and the need to return to native traditions, Kavelin sought to demonstrate that the historical development of Imperial Russia was internally consistent and was moving towards the same end as Western Europe. Hence, like Kranikhfeld and Nevolin, he credited Christianity with injecting critical values into the family and social life of both the early Russians and their Western European neighbours. But he concluded that therefore 'for all peoples of the new Christian world there is a single goal: the unconditional recognition of the worth of a human being, of an individual person, and his [*sic*] comprehensive development'.[76] Kavelin added that the resulting desire to realize this Christian ideal through conscious action distinguished the linear and thus progressive historical development of Russia and Western Europe from the cyclical and thus stagnant historical pattern of 'the East'.[77]

(Hamden, Conn., 1964), 161–229, Riasanovsky, *Parting*, 262, D. Offord, *Portraits of Early Russian Liberals: A Study of the Thought of T. N. Granovsky, V. P. Botkin, P. V. Annenkov, A. V. Druzhinin, and K. D. Kavelin* (Cambridge, 1985), 91, 123, 190–9, and P. K. Christoff, *An Introduction to Nineteenth-Century Russian Slavophilism: Iu. F. Samarin* (Boulder, Colo., 1991), 189, 308.

[74] D. I. Chizhevskii, *Gegel' v Rossii* (Paris, 1939), Malia, *Herzen*, 218–56, A. Walicki, *A History of Russian Thought from the Enlightenment to Marxism* (Stanford, Calif., 1979), 115–34, Offord, *Portraits*, 10–19, 48–50, 85–8, and Riasanovsky, *Parting*, 181–3, 207–11, 216–17, 221–4.

[75] 'Vzgliad na iuridicheskii byt drevnei Rossii', in *Sobranie sochinenii K. D. Kavelina* (Spb., 1900), i. 5–66. Born in 1818 and the son of a middling nobleman who was the first rector of St Petersburg University, Kavelin received his degree from the juridical faculty at Moscow University and eventually returned there to teach Russian legal history. Having resigned his position in 1848, in 1857 he was appointed professor in the same subject at St Petersburg University but again resigned in 1861. A 'Westerner' in the intellectual debates of the 1840s, Kavelin at this time advocated generally liberal reforms, including the abolition of serfdom. But he also stressed the progressive role of the state in Russian history and after the early 1860s his views grew more populist, nationalist, and monarchist. See D. Field, 'Kavelin and Russian Liberalism', *SR* 32 (1973), 59–78, N. Ia. Kuprits, *Iz istorii gosudarstvenno-pravovoi mysli dorevoliutsionnoi Rossii* (Mos., 1980), 73–4, 82–3, and Offord, *Portraits*, 175–213.

[76] Kavelin, *Sobranie sochinenii*, i. 16. [77] Ibid. i. 7–8.

Kavelin then outlined the dialectical process through which he claimed Imperial Russia was becoming a modern state capable of protecting the autonomous individual. According to him, Russian society originally had been composed of extended kin-groups that lived and utilized assets collectively under the leadership of several elders. The individual consequently had no identity or possibility for existence apart from such groups. The conflict engendered between these groups as they grew, divided, and multiplied, however, necessitated a more complex and consciously structured political organization. Kavelin contended that this organization caused kin-groups to adopt a patriarchal structure and to emphasize patrilineal relationships. Furthermore, conflict between the new political entities led to further political reorganization, resulting eventually in the appearance of a princely kin-group that reimposed order. This princely kin-group too ultimately fragmented into separate feuding branches, some of which restructured themselves on the basis of male seniority and descent within the narrower family group in order to avoid further fragmentation. Kavelin maintained that this restructuring enabled Muscovite princes to gain control over all other princely family groups, thereby converting Russia into their personal patrimony. The continued rationalization of what gradually became a state administration and the efforts of individual servitors to secure their position and property resulted in laws that further narrowed the family group as well as strengthened the rights of its individual members. Hence, Kavelin concluded, albeit by a path different from Western Europe, '[t]he principle of the individual personality has become legitimized in our life. Its turn has now come to act and to develop.'[78]

The historical process described by Kavelin was schematic and more conjectural than based on evidence. Yet it expressed the new sense of individuality and concern for self-realization emerging among the growing educated strata of tsarist society. Moreover, while affirming the view that the family and the political order were related directly to one another, it linked family structure and family law to an evolutionary process that implied the necessity—and indicated the direction—of further change.

[78] Kavelin, *Sobranie sochinenii*, i. 57. According to Kavelin, in Western Europe the task of Christian ideals and of history had been to tame the coarse, violent, and excessively egotistical nature of a primitive individualism that was most pronounced among the Germans. Interestingly, whereas Hegel explained this evolution from kin-group to family and individual in economic terms, Kavelin did so in political terms. See J. B. Landes, 'Hegel's Conception of the Family', in J. B. Elshtain (ed.), *The Family in Political Thought* (Amherst, Mass., 1982), 125–44.

Hence it is not surprising that in the 1840s at least a few members of educated society criticized both the autocratic political order and the patriarchal family for their stifling effects on the individual.[79]

Such criticism contributed to the emergence in the later 1850s of the 'woman question'. Emphasizing the equal creative potential of women, female and male critics of the traditional family and social order called for greater freedom of self-expression and opportunity for women, primarily through increased access to education and an expanded role outside the home. Radical critics went even further by challenging the institution of marriage itself and by suggesting that the subversion of the patriarchal family could help to undermine the authority of the autocratic state. Most critics, however, pursued the more moderate goal of improving the position of women within the family while enabling them to work outside it.[80]

By the late 1850s the social and intellectual bases for a critique of the patriarchal family and of the law that supported it had thus been created. As will be shown, over time this critique grew stronger and more widespread and increasingly became intertwined with questions of post-emancipation social and political reform in general, church–state relations, and reform within the Orthodox Church. It also coincided, however, with an increased resort to formal means of marital dissolution by a much broader spectrum of tsarist society.

As Table 2.1 indicates, the number of divorces granted by the Orthodox Church increased significantly in the mid-1860s and then again after 1900. In the decade prior to 1861, the church had granted about twenty-six divorces annually for causes other than penal exile, over which it had little control. In a typical year, about twenty divorces were granted on grounds of disappearance and three each on grounds of adultery and sexual incapacity. This number rose rapidly after the emancipation, averaging 657 throughout the 1870s. Even though the total number of divorces remained small, the number of divorces per 1,000 marriages also increased, suggesting either an increased demand for divorce, a change in

[79] Malia, *Herzen*, 259, 268, 274–5, Stites, *Women's Liberation Movement*, 21–4, Engel, *Mothers and Daughters*, 20–42, and Tovrov, 'Action', 385–94. In papers on Michael Bakunin and Alexander Herzen presented at the 23rd convention of the American Association for the Advancement of Slavic Studies in 1991, Marshal Shatz and Judith Zimmerman argued that criticisms of the family order provoked by personal experiences led to comparable criticisms of the social and political order.

[80] Engel, *Mothers and Daughters*, 45 ff., Stites, *Women's Liberation Movement*, 29–154, R. L. Glickman, *Russian Factory Women: Workplace and Society, 1880–1914* (Berkeley, Calif., 1984), 219–41, L. H. Edmondson, *Feminism in Russia 1900–1917* (Stanford, Calif., 1984), 8–22, and G. A. Tishkin, *Zhenskii vopros v Rossii v 50–60 gg. xix veka* (Lenin., 1983), *passim*.

church policy, or, perhaps, both.[81] At the same time, while the number of divorces granted on grounds of adultery increased, at first steadily and then rapidly after 1900, the number granted on grounds of disappearance initially rose sharply and then declined precipitously until becoming insignificant in the last years before the First World War.

Even though officially prohibited by statutory law, the incidence of formal marital separation also rose significantly over the same period. Prior to 1880 the Third Department of the Imperial Chancellery occasionally granted a wife a separate passport to live apart from her husband in cases of exceptional abuse or neglect. After 1881 the responsibility for such cases lay with the State Secretariat (after 1884 the Imperial Chancellery) for the Receipt of Petitions. Apparently increasing steadily since the early 1860s, the number of requests for separation reached over 1,500 per year by 1881 and rose rapidly in the 1890s.[82] From 1889 to 1896, for example, the number of petitions increased from 1,941 to 3,469 per year (Table 2.2). In over 40 per cent of cases where a passport was issued, moreover, it was against the will of the husband (Table 2.3). Throughout this period, in fact, the chancellery allowed marital separation at least as frequently as the Orthodox Church granted divorce.[83] Even after several Senate decisions in 1902 required the Ministry of Internal Affairs to issue separate passports to wives of peasants and members of unprivileged urban estates in cases of severe abuse or abandonment by their husbands, the number of requests for separation received by the Imperial Chancellery remained high, partly because local agencies of the ministry administered the new policy unevenly.[84] Complaining that ministry officials delayed the resolution of cases, for example, the philanthropic Society for the

[81] For the numbers of divorces in Western Europe and the United States at this time, see the references cited above in n. 22.

[82] TsGIA F. 797 op. 91–1898 d. 53 ll. 34–70, pp. 21–2; for examples, see F. 1405 op. 542 d. 124 ll. 67, 71–3, 75, 78–9, and F. 1412 op. 221 d. 183 and op. 223 d. 43 and 124 (I am grateful to Barbara Engel for the last reference). See also Maksimov, *Zakony*, 375–80, and I. V. Gessen, *Razdel'noe zhitel'stvo suprugov. Zakon 12 marta 1914 goda* (Spb., 1914), 4–7.

[83] Between 1890 and 1902 the Orthodox Church granted 12,870 divorces while the chancellery allowed 14,995 marital separations, although the totals are not strictly comparable because the chancellery figures include members of all religions. See the sources cited for Tables 2.1 and 2.3.

[84] TsGIA F. 797 op. 91–1898 d. 53 ll. 149–77, pp. 13–14, 18–20, *GU. Kn. 2-aia*, i. 227–32, and circulars of the Ministry of Internal Affairs dated from 1902 to 1912 contained in *Gosudarstvennyi Sovet. Sessiia VIII. Kommisiia*, Doklad no. 2 (Spb., 1913) (HLL). See also A. A. Oppengeim, *Ukazatel' voprosov prava razreshennykh Ministerstvom Iustitsii za vremia s kontsa 1885 po 1893 god* (Spb., 1895), 239–40, no. 92a (1888 no. 18), and S. Kozhukov, 'O praktike Pravitel'stvuiushchago Senata po voprosu o vydache krest'ianskim zhenam otdel'nyi vid na zhitel'stvo', *ZhMIu* (1901), 3: 158–68.

TABLE 2.2. *Petitions for marital separation/separate passports received by the Imperial Chancellery for the Receipt of Petitions, 1889–1896*

Year	Number
1889	1,941
1890 } 1891 } 1892 }	6,115
1893	2,161
1894	2,490
1895	2,736
1896	3,469
TOTAL	18,912

Source: TsGIA F. 797 op. 91–1898 d. 53 ll. 34–70, pp. 24–7.

Protection of Women reported that its local legal bureaux devoted most of their energy to helping women obtain separate passports, with each bureau handling several hundred cases annually.[85]

The change in the formal causes of successful divorce actions during the late Imperial period appears to have been due to a combination of church policy, shifting social attitudes, and cost. The procedure for cases of disappearance and adultery could be manipulated by spouses who wanted a divorce for other reasons, although the process remained lengthy and costly. Spouses therefore not infrequently employed fraudulent means to obtain a divorce, a practice that apparently was particularly common in cases of adultery, where an adulterous act would be staged with the help of paid witnesses.[86] Disappearance appears initially to have been a more

[85] *GSSO. 8-aia ses. (1912–1913)*, cols. 1130–1 (about 1,400 petitions were received each year between 1909 and 1911, and the number was again rising), circulars of the Ministry of Internal Affairs cited above in n. 84, M. B., 'Russkie otgoloski', *ZhD* (1899), 8: 77–8, G. S. N., 'K voprosu o razdel'nom zhitel'stve suprugov', *Pravo* (1900), 52, cols. 2484–7, *VE* (1891), 12: 804–7, and *Rossiiskoe obshchestvo zashchity zhenshchin v 1900 i 1901 g.* (Spb., 1902), 28, 36, *v 1902 g.* (Spb., 1903), 37, *v 1909 g.* (Spb., 1910), 8–9, 29, 40, 45, *v 1910 g.* (Spb., 1911), 20, 39, 45, *v 1912 g.* (Spb., 1913), 7, 55, *v 1913 g.* (Ptgd., 1914), 34, 57, 72–3, 81, *v 1914 g.* (Ptgd., 1915), 7, 51, 62, 71–2, 83.

[86] TsGIA F. 1405 op. 542 d. 665, Vysoch. utverzh. 1 marta 1877 zhur. soveshch. 25 noi. 1876 g. o merakh k presech. zloupotreb. po delam brakoraz., pp. 3–6, and Zapiska, soderzh.

TABLE 2.3. *Petitions from wives for marital separation/separate passports received, granted, and rejected by the Imperial Chancellery for the Receipt of Petitions, 1890–1902*

	Total no. of petitions		Granted, with husband's consent		Granted without consent		Total	Petitions rejected/terminated	% Granted	
	No.	%	No.	%	No.	%		No.	Group	All
SOCIAL ORIGIN										
Wives of nobles, officials, officers	3,106	10.3	997	59.3	683	40.7	1,680	1,426	54.1	11.2
Wives of honoured citizens, merchants, clergy	1,480	4.9	494	64.7	269	35.3	763	717	51.6	5.1
Wives of *meshchane*, *raznochintsy*	8,193	27.1	2,666	61.8	1,645	38.2	4,311	3,882	52.6	28.7
Wives of peasants[a]	17,461	57.7	4,572	55.5	3,669	44.5	8,241	9,220	47.2	55.0
TOTAL	30,240	100.0	8,729	58.2	6,266	41.8	14,995	15,245	49.6	100.0
PETITIONS										
Rejected	6,226	20.6								
Terminated due to reconciliation	6,277	20.8								
Terminated due to withdrawal of petition or failure to appear	2,742	9.1								
TOTAL	15,245	50.4								

[a] Includes factory workers.

Source: TsGIA F. 797 op. 91–1898 d. 53 ll. 149–77, pp. 18–20.

popular means of obtaining a divorce because it was the least costly, an important consideration especially among the peasantry and poorer urban classes, but the church could limit divorce on such grounds more easily than in the case of adultery simply by dragging out the search for the missing spouse. Disappearance declined rapidly as a formal cause of divorce after Konstantin Pobedonostsev became Chief Procurator of the Holy Synod in 1880 and virtually disappeared during the years that he sought actively to eliminate divorce fraud. It seems likely, then, that Pobedonostsev succeeded in limiting divorce on the grounds of disappearance by manipulating procedure but was unable to do so in the case of adultery, since the testimony of eyewitnesses to the latter act resulted in a fairly tight case, whatever church authorities might think about the matter.[87] (It may be, too, that by the late nineteenth century members of the poorer classes of society had simply given up trying to obtain the formal dissolution of marriages.) The dramatic rise in the number of divorces granted for adultery from the 1890s onward probably arose not from an increase in the incidence of marital infidelity, but rather from an increased determination of those members of society who possessed adequate means to obtain a divorce in a context where it had become socially more acceptable and church policy made adultery the most feasible method.

Certainly by the turn of the century the restrictive policy pursued by the church was producing frustration, resentment, and sometimes severe hardship. A young bride claimed, for example, that she had discovered on her wedding night that her new husband was syphilitic. Yet the church had refused to grant a divorce because her husband was still capable of having sexual relations, even though doing so endangered the health of his wife.[88] Similarly, in a petition to the Ministry of Justice in 1902, Don

v sebe krat. izlozh. zak. o sudoproiz. po delam brach., pp. 5–6, d. 666 ll. 74–144, pp. 21–8, d. 670 ll. 49–111, pp. 31–2, 80–9, d. 671 ll. 2–34, pp. 14–15, 47–8, and ll. 106–97, pp. 55–6, 95–6, F. 796 op. 445 d. 417 ll. 64–96, p. iv, and F. 797 op. 92–1901 d. 81[b] (t. ii) ll. 65–85, pp. 111–12, 116–17, 137–8. For various proposals made within the Holy Synod chancellery in 1901 to deal with these problems, see ibid. d. 81[a] (t. i) ll. 4–23. See also K. P. Pobedonostsev, *Pis′ma Pobedonostseva k Aleksandru III* (Mos., 1925, 1926), ii. 34–6, 358–64, Grigorovskii, *Prichiny*, 43–9, id., *O razvode. Prichiny i posledstviia razvoda i brakorazvodnoe sudoproizvodstvo. Istoriko-iuridicheskie ocherki* (Spb., 1911), 275–83 (Grigorovskii was director of the chancellery of the Holy Synod), Dvorzhitskii, 'Preliubodeianie', 46: 5–6, id., 'Iz kiny proektov (K voprosu o razvode)', *SG* (1903), 5: 2–4 (Dvorzhitskii served for many years as an examining magistrate), B——, 'Supruzheskoe pravo', 27: 2–4, and 'Delo brat′ev Skitskikh', in *Rechi izvestnykh russkikh iuristov* (Mos., 1985), 297–9.

[87] On Pobedonostsev's views, see below, Ch. 3.

[88] *Trudy pervago vserossiiskago zhenskago s″ezda pri Russkom Zhenskom (Vzaimno-Blagotvoritel′nom) Obshchestve v S.-Peterburge 10–16 dekabria 1908 goda* (Spb., 1909), 61–2.

cossack Iosif Petrunin complained that his wife had abandoned him three days after their wedding twenty-two years earlier. Again, however, the church had refused to grant a divorce because, so Petrunin contended, his wife had been located seventeen years later living in a neighbouring village with an Old Believer, by whom she had had three children. The situation, he asserted, had forced him to live out of wedlock because he needed a wife to help with the household economy and to satisfy his other needs.[89] Therein probably lies the reason for the decision of the church in this case. Even though abandoned by his adulterous wife, Petrunin himself was an adulterer and therefore equally guilty in the eyes of the church. However correct canonically, this position caused serious problems for people caught in such situations. As the writers of numerous letters to the Ministry of Justice and to the Holy Synod complained, their inability to obtain a divorce meant that their children suffered the indignities and legal disabilities of illegitimacy.[90]

If substantive and procedural rules, as well as cost, prevented people such as Petrunin from formally dissolving a marriage, they did not stop others from obtaining a divorce by staging an act of adultery with the help of professional witnesses. Such tactics did not always succeed, of course. At least one irate aspiring *divorcé* invited the consistory secretary and another priest to his next tryst after his petition had been denied, ostensibly because the witnesses belonged to different social estates.[91] And diocesan statistics for the period 1896–1900 reveal that, at least for those years, only slightly over half of the petitions for divorce on the grounds of adultery were approved.[92] Critics of the law charged, furthermore, that even in successful actions the stiff evidentiary rules established by the church often enabled the spouse who actually was guilty of adultery to compel an aggrieved spouse to accept the guilt as a desperate means of escaping an unhappy marriage. The law thus enabled anyone wealthy or brazen enough to obtain a divorce, such critics complained, while leaving

[89] TsGIA F. 1405 op. 542 d. 666 ll. 45–6.

[90] TsGIA F. 1405 op. 542 d. 666 ll. 149–58, 181–2, d. 668 ll. 457–9, and d. 671 ll. 249–52; ibid. d. 124 ll. 67, 71–3, 75, 78–9; and F. 797 op. 92 d. 51 ll. 1–7.

[91] M. M. Artsybashev, *Nash brakorazvodnyi protsess* (Spb., 1908), 11–12. See also 'Delo brat′ev Skitskikh' (n. 86 above), where a band of professional divorce 'expediters' may have murdered a recalcitrant priest in order to eliminate his opposition to a particular divorce.

[92] The totals of applications given by different sources vary somewhat, but the differences do not significantly alter the relative order of magnitude of successful and rejected petitions. Spouses were reconciled in about 5% of the cases, and about 40% of all petitions were rejected. TsGIA F. 1405 op. 542 d. 666 ll. 47–71 and ll. 74–144 (p. 88 n. 2), and d. 668 ll. 9–58 (p. 56 n. 1).

no exit for spouses who were genuinely offended or mistreated but unwilling to resort to, or unable to afford, such extreme measures.[93]

The increase in the number of both divorces and formal separations would appear to have more complex causes. These increases paralleled, although generally at a much lower level, trends in Western Europe and the United States from the mid-nineteenth century onward. In his comprehensive study of divorce in Western society, Roderick Phillips ascribes these trends principally to three causes. First, legal changes during this period increased access to divorce in most countries by expanding the allowable grounds and by reducing the cost of obtaining it. Secondly, as the laws regarding alimony and child custody became more favourable to women than previously, and as attitudes towards women and marriage changed, increasing the emphasis on affective relations between spouses and consequently raising expectations of marriage, women became more willing to initiate a divorce. Thirdly, and most importantly, as the household particularly among urban social groups changed from being primarily a unit of production to one of companionship and consumption, with production now taking place outside the home and income being generated apart from the family, the opportunities for women to support themselves outside marriage expanded. Hence not only did the number of divorces increase in Western Europe and North America before the First World War, but in most countries the majority of divorces were initiated by urban women.[94]

Similar influences appear to have underlain the rising number of divorces and marital separations in Imperial Russia after the early 1860s. Confronted by both increased public criticism and, apparently, an increasing tendency of Orthodox believers to resort to informal unions, in 1904 the Holy Synod relaxed its rules in cases of adultery. Thereafter even the guilty party in a divorce on these grounds could remarry, albeit only after a seven-year penance (often reduced in practice to only two years). By increasing the feasibility of divorce, this reduction in punishment quite probably contributed to the rapid increase in the number of divorces granted for adultery in the decade prior to the First World

[93] In addition to the references cited above in nn. 86 and 88–91, see A. L. Borovikovskii, 'Novyi zakonoproekt ob uluchshenii polozheniia nezakonnorozhdennykh detei', *ZhMIu* (1899), 8: 31–2, and 'Voprosy braka', *Nedelia* (1869), 22, cols. 681–9. See also Engel, *Between the Fields*, chs. 1, 2.

[94] Phillips, *Putting Asunder*, 260–3, 272, 316, 358–82, 394–478, 590–612, 638–40. See also M. Mitterauer and R. Sieder, *The European Family* (Oxford, 1982), 19–20, 39–44, 55–90, 120–39, and M. Anderson, *Approaches to the History of the Western Family 1500–1914* (London, 1980), 41–84 *passim*.

War.[95] Decisions by the Civil Cassation Department regarding child custody and payment of support to wives who lived apart from their husbands similarly made marital separation more feasible for women from the 1890s onward.[96]

As later chapters will demonstrate, after the late 1850s changed attitudes towards marriage and the family among members of the educated and upper strata of society made Imperial laws that previously seemed necessary, tolerable, and even enlightened now appear intolerably restrictive and oppressive. These new attitudes made behaviour such as wife-beating, adultery, or drunkenness among spouses appear more problematic than previously, even though there is no evidence that such behaviour increased precipitously after the emancipation, while also making divorce and separation more acceptable as solutions to marital problems. Of course attitudes on such issues varied, within as well as between social groups. But the fact that the overwhelming majority of petitions for formal marital separation submitted to the Imperial Chancellery came from the unprivileged and poorer groups of society suggests that the demand for greater flexibility in the law extended beyond the educated and upper strata (Tables 2.3–2.4).[97]

Post-emancipation economic development and urban growth also appear to have contributed to the increased incidence of divorce and formal separation, although more detailed information on family structures and individual cases is necessary before firm conclusions can be drawn. In the 1860s and 1870s, both commercial growth and the demands placed on the peasantry by the terms of emancipation resulted in considerable migration of peasants of both sexes into urban areas. During the same period, in some cases compelled by straitened family economic circumstances and in others motivated by the ideas that animated the 'woman question', a significant number of young noble and other educated women likewise

[95] Maksimov, *Zakony*, 80–4. In a report prepared apparently in 1916, the Petrograd diocesan consistory blamed the new law for the nearly 100% increase in the number of divorce petitions submitted to it after 1903. TsGIA F. 797 op. 96 d. 271 (no ll. assigned). See also *Mneniia i otzyvy po voprosu o prave lits, brak kotorykh rastorgnut po prichine narusheniia imi supruzheskoi vernosti, na vstuplenie v drugoi brak* (2nd edn., Spb., 1893). Remarriage was still to be prohibited in the case of second offenders. On the law, see Mazurenko, *Rastorzhenie braka*. Church officials also charged that the law of 17 April 1905 extending religious tolerance had likewise contributed to an increase in the number of divorces, especially in the Western Provinces, by legalizing conversion from Orthodoxy. TsGIA F. 1405 op. 542 d. 671 ll. 2–34, pp. 9–10, 17, and Grigorovskii, *O razvode*, 225–6, 241–4.

[96] See below, Ch. 5.

[97] Peasant women, too, sometimes sought similar protection through the reformed judicial process. See the references cited below in Ch. 3 n. 52, and Ch. 5 n. 24.

TABLE 2.4. *Social origin and sex of spouses petitioning the Imperial Chancellery for the Receipt of Petitions for marital separation/separate passports, 1893*

	No.	%
SEX		
Female	1,899	88
Male	262	12
TOTAL	2,161	100
SOCIAL ORIGIN OF WOMEN PETITIONERS		
Wives of nobility, officials, and officers	235	12
Wives of honoured citizens and merchants	73	4
Wives of *raznochintsy*	68	4
Wives of peasants (includes factory workers) and unprivileged urban estates	1,523	80
TOTAL	1,899	100

Source: TsGIA F. 797 op. 91–1898 d. 53 ll. 34–70, pp. 24–7.

moved to the cities, seeking self-fulfilment as well as some measure of independence and material security through employment. Although still limited and poorly paid, the occupations open to such women none the less expanded, to the point that in 1871 the tsarist government introduced regulations for women in state service.[98] While small, the total number of people involved in these movements was sufficient to account for the surge

[98] *2PSZ* xlvi (1871), pt. 1, no. 49137, pp. 36–7, which restricted women primarily to lower-level positions, particularly those perceived to be compatible with the nurturing role of women (e.g. teaching, midwifery, and paramedical work). For later rules, see *SZ* iii (1896), *Ust. o sluzh. po op. ot prav.*, arts. 156–7, and V. Mikhailova, *Russkie zakony o zhenshchine* (Mos., 1913), 6–11. Imperial law previously had not formally barred women from state service, but had simply assumed that they would not serve except in limited positions such as the educational and philanthropic institutions administered through the Administration of the Empress Mariia. See *SZ* (1833), i, pt. 2, *Uch. gos.*, bk. 7, *Stat. znak. otl. bez. sluzh.*, arts. 2738–50 (1857 edn., bk. 6, arts. 794–800). On the movement of women to cities and the expansion of employment for women during this period, see Ransel, *Mothers*, 161–75, Engel, *Mothers and Daughters*, 51, 71–2, 79, 156–61, id., *Between the Fields*, chs. 3, 5, 7, Stites, *Women's Liberation Movement*, 56–60, 80–7, 105–11, I. N. Kovaleva, 'Zhenskii vopros v Rossii v 50–60-kh godakh xix v.', in *Problemy istorii russkago obshchestvennogo dvizheniia i istoricheskoi nauki* (Mos., 1981), 126–7, J. H. Bater, *St. Petersburg: Industrialization and Change* (Montreal, 1976), 309, 313–15, 386, and C. Ruane, 'The Vestal Virgins of St. Petersburg: School Teachers and the 1897 Marriage Ban', *Russian Review*, 50 (1991), 163–82.

of divorces on grounds of disappearance and adultery which occurred during this period. After the mid-1880s, rapid industrial and urban growth greatly increased the number of urban working women and the incidence of seasonal migratory labour, thereby also increasing the number of spouses from the peasantry and poorer classes who lived apart for extended periods. Such developments strained traditional family relations and often compelled as well as enabled peasant and working-class women to live more independently, if usually still in poverty.[99]

Both the increased number and the sources of petitions for marital separation received after 1890 suggest that these developments increased the ability and willingness especially of wives to use separation as a means of escaping marital breakdown. Nearly 90 per cent of such petitions were submitted by women (Table 2.4), the vast majority of whom lived in St Petersburg (50+ per cent) or Moscow (17 per cent).[100] Predominantly from the poorest social classes, these women sought relief from what they alleged was misconduct and abusive treatment by their husband (Tables 2.3–2.5).[101] In most cases women petitioners also requested continued material support from their husband and custody of their children, questions left undecided by statutory law.[102] Similarly, the cases later handled by the legal bureaux of the Society for the Protection of Women overwhelmingly involved wives who sought to escape from what they described as the drunken brutality of their husbands.[103] Again, since there is no evidence that such behaviour by husbands had increased after emancipation, the growing number of urban women seeking a legal means to leave their husband suggests that employment outside the home and greater access to organizations that provided support were helping to break down the constraints that previously had induced or compelled women to remain within a discordant marriage.

99 On these phenomena, see Glickman, *Russian Factory Women*, esp. chs. 3, 4, R. Johnson, *Peasant and Proletarian: The Working Class of Moscow in the Late Nineteenth Century* (New Brunswick, NJ, 1979), esp. chs. 2–4, V. E. Bonnell, *Roots of Rebellion: Workers' Politics and Organizations in St. Petersburg and Moscow, 1900–1914* (Berkeley, Calif., 1983), 35–47, 52–60, 320, 361–5, 369–70, 442–3, and Engel, *Between the Fields*. See also Ransel, *Mothers*, 161–75.

100 TsGIA F. 797 op. 91–1898 d. 53 ll. 34–70 (pp. 21, 24–7), and ll. 149–77 (pp. 18–20). The number of petitions for separation increased more rapidly than the number of marriages in both St Petersburg and Moscow over the same period (see Table 2.6; see also Bater, *St. Petersburg*, 313–15, on the low number of marriages in St Petersburg).

101 TsGIA F. 797 op. 91–1898 d. 53 ll. 34–70 (pp. 21, 24–7), and ll. 149–77 (pp. 18–20).

102 Ibid., ll. 34–70, pp. 24–7. The sources do not state how frequently the chancellery awarded support to petitioners. But in 1893 it granted only 311 of 797 requests of women for custody of their children.

103 See the references to *Rossiiskoe obshchestvo zashchity zhenshchin* cited above in n. 85.

TABLE 2.5. *Reasons for granting wives marital separation/separate passports, Imperial Chancellery for the Receipt of Petitions, 1891*

Cause	No.	%
HUSBAND'S CONDUCT	(561)	(97.1)
Mistreatment, drunkenness, extortion, profligacy	226	39.1
Mistreatment and abuse	112	19.4
Failure to provide support	108	18.7
Depravity	51	8.8
Unfaithfulness	50	8.7
Unsettled lifestyle	14	2.4
ILLNESS	(17)	(2.9)
Mental illness	8	1.4
Venereal disease	5	0.8
Sexual incapacity	4	0.7
TOTALS	578	100

Source: TsGIA F. 797 op. 91–1898 d. 53 ll. 34–70, pp. 24–7.

This hypothesis also finds support in the rapid rise in the incidence of divorce in St Petersburg and Moscow from the 1890s onward, and in Kiev after 1902, although here the evidence is only suggestive. In all three dioceses, the rate of divorce exceeded that for the empire as a whole (Tables 2.1 and 2.6). A higher rate of divorce was not unusual for St Petersburg, where many well-connected and wealthy Russians came to pursue their cases directly through the Holy Synod. But the increasing frequency of divorce in each city coincided with the expansion of both the total population and the female work-force.[104]

Critics of Imperial family law claimed that this increase in the number of divorces and formal separations demonstrated the lack of correspondence between existing statutory law and social attitudes and needs. According to such critics, the result of this incongruence was not only marital disharmony and personal unhappiness, but also violence. Although women

[104] See the report of the Petrograd consistory for 1902–15, TsGIA F. 797 op. 96 d. 271 (no ll. assigned). On the growth of St Petersburg, Moscow, and Kiev during this period, see T. S. Fedor, *Patterns of Urban Growth in the Russian Empire during the Nineteenth Century* (Chicago, 1975), 188, 192, 198 (and 71 ff. on urban growth in general), M. F. Hamm (ed.), *The City in Late Imperial Russia* (Bloomington, Ind., 1986), 9–121, and Bater, *St. Petersburg*. On the growth of female employment, see the references to Glickman, Bonnell, Ransel, and Engel cited above in n. 99.

TABLE 2.6. *Divorces granted by the Orthodox Church and number of divorces per 1,000 Marriages, 1850–1914: St Petersburg, Moscow, and Kiev*

	St Petersburg			Kiev			Moscow		
Year	Total divorces	Total marriages	No. of divorces per 1,000 marriages	Total divorces	Total marriages	No. of divorces per 1,000 marriages	Total divorces	Total marriages	No. of divorces per 1,000 marriages
1850	0	n/a	—	1	n/a	—	0	n/a	—
1857	3	n/a	—	0	n/a	—	0	n/a	—
1865	0	n/a	—	1	n/a	—	0	n/a	—
1871	26	n/a	—	1	n/a	—	7	n/a	—
1880	29	6,956	4.17	7	20,615	0.34	4	13,113	0.31
1885	38	7,220	5.26	2	23,878	0.08	6	12,688	0.47
1890	56	8,036	6.97	4	20,868	0.19	13	13,632	0.95
1895	37	9,428	3.92	10	26,765	0.37	34	16,542	2.06
1900	61	11,226	5.43	21	26,656	0.79	29	18,807	1.54
1901	68	11,701	5.81	14	26,321	0.53	27	18,627	1.45
1902	106	12,804	8.28	37	29,716	1.25	36	18,279	1.97
1903	131	12,874	10.18	40	32,206	1.24	34	18,528	1.84
1904	149	12,466	11.95	86	25,794	3.33	57	15,016	3.80
1905	201	12,914	15.56	74	26,567	2.79	69	16,151	4.27
1906	199	16,942	11.75	93	36,960	2.52	69	22,468	3.07
1907	197	17,494	11.26	91	33,357	2.73	133	22,543	5.90
1908	253	14,879	17.00	139	28,728	4.84	179	19,331	9.26
1909	255	15,431	16.53	214	28,875	7.41	174	18,363	9.48
1911	229	15,542	14.73	120	33,008	3.64	133	22,062	6.03
1912	288	15,653	18.40	205	31,839	6.44	236	21,303	11.08
1914	197	17,828	11.05	212	25,540	8.30	201	21,370	9.41

Source: *VOOPSS* for 1850, 1857, 1865, 1871, 1880, 1885, 1890, 1895, 1900–9, 1911, 1912, 1914.

constituted a low proportion of convicted felons, they committed nearly half of all murders of one spouse by the other.[105] Hence, critics insisted, Imperial law urgently required revision to ensure the personal security, equality, and fulfilment of the moral obligations of each family member. Conversely, the same trends in divorce and formal separation strengthened conservative opposition to any change in the law which appeared likely to weaken the patriarchal family and thereby the social and political order. Conflict over the revision of family law therefore simultaneously reflected and contributed to the political and ideological divisions within the educated and upper strata of society, and within the tsarist government itself, during the late Imperial period. How the government managed this conflict provides a measure of its ability to deal with both social change in general and the changing attitudes and values among the educated élite.

[105] E. N. Tarnovskii, 'Voprosy sravnitel'noi prestupnosti polov', *RM* (1893), 12: 37, 47–9 (and 42–64 in general), N. V. Davydov, *Zhenshchina pered ugolovnym sudom* (Mos., 1906), 31–5, and *GU. Kn. 2-aia*, i. 213–14. Advocates of divorce law reform in France and the United States made similar arguments. Phillips, *Putting Asunder*, 310.

3

Jurists' Critique: Evolution of the Affective Family

AFTER the 1850s Russian jurists exerted strong pressure for the revision of Imperial family law. The changes demanded by jurists varied, however, depending on their view of the relationships that existed—and ideally should exist—between spouses and within the family generally. Like the tsarist government and the Orthodox ecclesiastical hierarchy, moreover, jurists believed that the family helped to shape fundamental social relationships, political attitudes, and moral values. Hence the revision of family law also represented for different groups of jurists an important medium for promoting their particular ideological ideals and objectives.

Two competing views of the family, each with different implications for the tsarist social and political order, emerged among jurists during the post-emancipation period. While the conservative, patriarchal, view of the family embodied the principles of unlimited personalized authority and unequal ascriptive status on which the autocratic order rested, the affective ideal, articulated by pro-reform jurists, contained conceptions of legality and individual rights which challenged this order and led frequently to demands for the secularization of both the law and its enforcement, thereby also challenging the authority and religious precepts of the Orthodox Church. Pro-reform jurists, moreover, generally drew on Western European precedents and identified existing Imperial Russian law with social and cultural backwardness. Underlying the disputes over the revision of family law, therefore, were deeper disagreements over the structure of post-emancipation society, the relationship between law, religion, and the state, and the relationship between Imperial Russia and Western Europe.

Moral and Utilitarian Critique of the Patriarchal Family

Both the educational developments, social changes, and intellectual trends discussed in the previous chapter and the increased familiarity of Russian jurists with Western European law and juridical literature provided important foundations for the post-emancipation debate among jurists over family law. But the conditions surrounding the Alexandrine reform era itself furnished the critical catalyst for this debate. Most broadly, the atmosphere of state reform encouraged jurists to believe that the systematization and revision of substantive law and its more efficient judicial administration could help to overcome the problems besetting both the government and society. Hence many jurists demanded that the judicial reform be followed by the codification of civil law, a process in which they expected to play a prominent role. In an address to the Moscow Juridical Society in 1868, for example, Nikolai Kalachov, an official in the Ministry of Justice who helped draft the judicial reform, declared that Russian jurists had a sacred duty to assist the government with the review and reformulation of Imperial civil law. He called on his peers to concentrate on critical analyses of existing law which the courts could use to perfect the law and to adjust it to current social needs. In preparation for the revision and codification of Imperial civil law, jurists also should compare it with Western European law to discover the universal values underlying them both.[1]

The relaxation of tsarist censorship in the late 1850s and the implementation of the judicial reform facilitated the reorientation of Russian jurists advocated by Kalachov. For the first time jurists could observe and comment critically on the administration of the law by the courts. As a result, they soon began to debate among themselves, in the new legal journals and juridical societies, both the inadequacies of existing law and different ways to overcome them.

Criticisms of both the law and particular judicial decisions in the general press also contributed to juristic debate. The emergence of the

[1] N. V. Kalachov, *Programma razrabotki nachal russkago grazhdanskago prava po svodu zakonov s ego istochnikami i po sudebnym resheniiam* (Mos., 1868); for similar arguments made at this time, see A. Dumashevskii, 'Nashe pravovedenie, chto ono i chem ono dolzhno byt'', *ZhMIu* (1867), 1: 3–32; 4: 3–34; and 11/12: 215–42, and Malyshev in G. F. Shershenevich, *Nauka grazhdanskago prava v Rossii* (Kazan, 1893), 84–5, 137–42. See also M. V. Shimanovskii, 'O proekte grazhdanskago ulozheniia i o tom uchastii, kotoroe mozhet okazat' Iuridicheskoe Obshchestvo v rabote sostavleniia proekta', *Protokol zasedaniia Iuridicheskago Obshchestva pri Novorossiiskom universitete No. 22, 24-go sentiabria 1882 goda* (Odessa, 1882), pril., pp. 171–4. Born in 1819 into a prosperous noble family, Kalachov graduated from the juridical faculty of Moscow University. While serving in the Ministry of Education, he also taught Russian legal history at Moscow University (1848–52). He then moved to the Second Department of the Imperial Chancellery, where he helped to edit a new edition of the *Digest of Laws* and assisted in the preparation of the judicial reform. See A. F. Bychkov, *Vospominaniia o d. chl. N. V. Kalachove* (Spb., 1886).

'woman question' in the late 1850s, for example, resulted in strong criticism of the treatment accorded women by Imperial law, which in turn persuaded some jurists that they had a special responsibility to use their expertise to alleviate this perceived injustice. In 1864, for example, the prominent jurist and future rector of St Petersburg University, Petr Redkin, asserted—paternalistically—that Russian women by themselves would never be able to attain their rightful social position. 'You, my young jurists', he exclaimed to the loud applause of his students, 'must extend a hand to Russian women and give them the possibility of occupying their appropriate place in society.'[2]

This combination of influences in the 1860s and 1870s led particularly younger jurists to formulate a moral and utilitarian critique of Imperial family law which characterized existing law as conflicting with the moral character ascribed to family relations and undermining the critical social role performed by the family.[3] While claiming to want only to adjust Imperial law to prevailing moral values and post-emancipation social conditions, however, juristic critics in fact sought also to shape these values and conditions through the redefinition of legal norms.

In essence, juristic critics formulated a new ideal of the family which rested on a conception of the relationship between authority, obligation, and individual rights which differed fundamentally from that of the past. The family was now depicted as a union of individuals in which mutual affection and the nature of the interrelations between members gave rise to a combination of individual rights and mutual obligations. Although these rights and obligations differed with respect to spouses and to parents and children, their purpose in both cases was to ensure the personal development and security of individual family members as well as the

[2] M. V. Shimanovskii, *Petr Grigor'evich Redkin (Biograficheskii ocherk)* (Odessa, 1890), 13. Born in 1808 and the son of a Ukrainian nobleman whose career had been primarily in the military, Redkin attended the Bezborodko Lycée in Nezhin before entering Moscow University in 1826. Among the students chosen by Speranskii to prepare for a career in law, he studied at Dorpat University and then in Berlin (1830–4), where he attended lectures by Savigny and Hegel. Initially a strong Hegelian, in 1835 Redkin became a member of the juridical faculty at Moscow University, where he lectured on jurisprudence, constitutional law, and various aspects of Western European law, including marriage law. Resigning his position in 1848, in 1863 he was appointed professor of jurisprudence at St Petersburg University. In addition to Shimanovskii, see *BSSU* ii. 155–68, and R. S. Wortman, *The Development of a Russian Legal Consciousness* (Chicago, 1976), 45, 223–30.

[3] Born in 1818, Konstantin Kavelin was the oldest of those jurists who undertook a detailed critique of Imperial family, property, and/or inheritance law during this period. A few such jurists were born in the mid or late 1820s; most were born in the 1830s or early 1840s. By contrast, jurists such as Nevolin, Kranikhfeld, Vasilev, and Kunitsyn, who had defended existing law or accepted it uncritically, were born prior to 1810.

welfare and happiness of the family as a whole. Hence individual rights and mutual obligations were now perceived to limit, and to a significant extent to take precedence over, marital and parental authority.

With respect to marriage, juristic critics stressed the voluntary and companionate nature of the relationship between spouses as the basis of their mutual obligations and nearly (although still not fully) equal rights. Indeed, in a critique of Imperial family law in 1861, the liberal jurist Mikhail Filippov came close to advancing a contractual understanding of marriage. Asserting that '[m]arriage is a private matter', he contended that '[t]he character of the relations between spouses must therefore be thus: in marriage the free will of the spouses must play the chief role'.[4] In contrast, in an article in 1874, the prolific and influential commentator on Imperial civil law Ilia Orshanskii rejected this contractual analogy and emphasized instead the unity between spouses. In this view, 'marriage produce[d] a communion of the personalities of both spouses', 'a communion of interests for the whole life of two people', and a 'moral bond'.[5] This difference proved to be more one of emphasis than of substance, however, since both Filippov and Orshanskii characterized spouses as simultaneously interdependent and independent personalities. This balance, in the opinion of Filippov, distinguished contemporary marriages both in the West and in Imperial Russia from those in Eastern cultures, where 'a woman unites with a man and loses her personality', and from those in the Russian past, when 'a woman was put in the position of a slave with respect to her husband'.[6] Hence, similarly to earlier juridical and Orthodox instructional writing, both jurists argued that the affective bond between spouses obligated them equally to respect and remain faithful to one another and to assist each other materially as well as

[4] M. Filippov, 'Vzgliad na russkie grazhdanskie zakony', *Sovremennik* (1861), 85: 562, and in general 526–63, and 86: 217–18. See also below, Ch. 7, for Filippov's critique of the inheritance rights of women, and G. A. Tishkin, *Zhenskii vopros v Rossii v 50–60 gg. xix veka* (Lenin., 1984), 46–57. Born in 1828 and educated first at the Richelieu Lycée in Odessa and then at the juridical faculty at St Petersburg University, Filippov gained prominence as a commentator on legal affairs for radical and liberal periodicals in the 1860s and 1870s.

[5] I. Orshanskii, 'Lichnyia i imushchestvennyia otnosheniia suprugov', in *Izsledovaniia po russkomu pravu semeinomu i nasledstvennomu* (Spb., 1877), 4, 17. Born in 1846 into a poor Jewish family in Ekaterinoslav, Orshanskii declined the offer to prepare for an academic career upon graduating from the juridical faculty at Novorossiia University because he would have had to abandon his faith. After briefly practising law, he turned to journalism and became a prominent spokesman for Jewish rights as well as an influential commentator on Imperial civil law. See his *Izsledovaniia*, intro., and P. A. Iampol'skii, *Vospominaniia ob I. G. Orshanskom* (Kiev, 1911).

[6] Filippov, 'Vzgliad', 86: 217, 218.

spiritually. Both spouses, too, should share equally in decisions regarding family matters, although as the natural head of the family the husband had the deciding voice in the event of disagreement.[7] Yet at the same time Filippov and Orshanskii insisted that both spouses retained a right to personal autonomy, which for a wife included not only control over her own property, but also the ability to engage in social and economic activities outside the home without the consent of her husband.[8]

The rights and obligations of parents and children, by contrast, were seen as necessarily asymmetrical and arising from the event of birth. 'Nature itself imposes on parents their sacred obligations,' Filippov asserted. 'Nature places in their hearts, as the instrument of a great act, the birth of a human being, a feeling of love and affection for their child. This moral phenomenon is a law of nature.'[9] This natural law resulted in the moral obligation of parents to protect, nurture, and educate their children, an obligation in fact already recognized by the *Digest of Laws*.[10] To fulfil their obligation, parents—both parents equally—had to possess some authority over their children, who consequently were obligated morally to obey and respect their parents.[11] But juristic critics again described the extent of authority as being limited, both by the requirements of the parents' obligations and by the right of individual children to sustenance and to personal security. The right of parents to direct the upbringing and education of their children therefore was, in Filippov's words, 'preferential' but not absolute.[12]

In this regard, juristic critics argued that the important social and political roles played by the family justified state intervention in its internal relationships. 'The family union constitutes the basis of the social and

[7] Ibid. 217–28, and 85: 526, 552–3, 561–2, and Orshanskii, 'Lichnyia i imushchestvennyia otnosheniia', 17–23, 39–49, 55, 72, 78–98, 129–30, 138, 192–8; see also A. Liubavskii, *Iuridicheskiia monografii i izsledovaniia* (Spb., 1875), iii. 434, 439–45.

[8] Filippov, 'Vzgliad', 85: 546–7, and 86: 220–3, 227–8, 240, Orshanskii, 'Lichnyia i imushchestvennyia otnosheniia', 116–29, 192–8, and A. Liubavskii, 'Ob uravnenii nasledstvennykh prav muzhchin i zhenshchin', *ZhMIu* (1864), 5: 399–400, 412–18.

[9] Filippov, 'Vzgliad', 86: 256.

[10] *SZ* (1857), x, pt. 1, arts. 172–5; Filippov, 'Vzgliad', 86: 256–65, A. F. Kistiakovskii, 'O nezakonnorozhdennykh', *Protokoly Kievskago Iuridicheskago Obshchestva za vtoruiu polovinu 1879 goda* (Kiev, 1880), 43, 46, 62–3, 75, S. I. Barshev, N. V. Kalachov, S. A. Muromtsev, and A. M. Fal'kovskii (eds.), *Pervyi s"ezd russkikh iuristov v moskve v 1875 godu* (Mos., 1882), 220–4, 232–7, and N. P. Liapidevskii, *O dopolnenii nashego deistvuiushchago zakonodatel'stva postanovleniiami ob uzakonenii i priznanii detei, rozhdennykh vne braka* (Mos., 1876), 1–2, 10–12.

[11] Filippov, 'Vzgliad', 86: 257–61. See also Orshanskii, 'Lichnyia i imushchestvennyia otnosheniia', 95–8, and Liubavskii, *Iuridicheskiia monografii*, iii. 439–45.

[12] Filippov, 'Vzgliad', 86: 257, and 256–64 in general.

the state union', asserted Filippov. 'From [this union] the state receives its members, and on its perfection depends the general good as well as social tranquility.'[13] But, Filippov argued, for the family to perform its role it had to enable the personal development of its members and to foster civic-spirited and patriotic citizens. These objectives could be achieved only if state law reinforced the rights and obligations that Filippov believed arose naturally from family relationships.[14]

Juristic critics charged, however, that by granting husbands and parents unlimited authority over their wives and children respectively, and by restricting the availability of divorce, Imperial family law, in fact, produced precisely the opposite results. In effect, the positive ideal of beneficent paternalism was transformed into a negative image of arbitrary power. According to juristic critics, such power led invariably to abuse and consequently also to oppression, the result of which was alienation, enmity, and even violent conflict between spouses and between parents and children. And not only the family suffered. '[W]hen in place of love, equality, and Christian fraternity, despotism, arbitrariness, and coercion reign in [the family]', Filippov argued,

> when wives are given over in slavery to their husbands and . . . children, especially daughters, are subject to the complete and unlimited power of their parents . . . in such a family union it is impossible to hope to draw healthy members [of society] and impossible to find either patriotic selflessness, or true Christian love, or hatred toward vice and despotism.[15]

The relationship between spouses was thought to suffer most severely from the pernicious effect of unlimited authority. In the view of juristic critics, Imperial statutory law erred doubly here, first by unreservedly subordinating a wife to her husband, and then by requiring that spouses live together regardless of the circumstances or their feelings towards one another. According to juristic critics, this combination of legal norms not only resulted in the mistreatment of wives by their husbands, but also compelled alienated spouses either to live together in hostility or to live apart illegally, situations that often led to illicit sexual activity. Hence existing statutory law weakened the institution of marriage, undermined respect for law, and fostered moral values, sexual behaviour, and attitudes

[13] Ibid. 265.

[14] Ibid. 85: 550–4, and 86: 222–3, 234, 237–42, 263, 265–6. See also Orshanskii, 'Lichnyia i imushchestvennyia otnosheniia', 48–9, 55, 68–71, 194–5, Liapidevskii, *O dopolnenii*, 14–15, and Barshev *et al.*, *Pervyi s''ezd*, 222–4.

[15] Filippov, 'Vzgliad', 86: 265, and in general 217–19, 223–7, 258–62, and 85: 527–30, 550–4; see also Orshanskii, 'Lichnyia i imushchestvennyia otnosheniia', 52–70, 184.

towards women that were regressive. 'I am convinced', Filippov asserted, 'that only an insane person, an obscurant, an ignoramus, a callous and complete egoist' would 'demand unlimited submission, or, in other words, slavery, from [his] wife', or would 'compulsorily, by means of the law, the court, and the police, force his wife to live with him.'[16] Concluding from a review of judicial practice that the legal obligation of spouses to live together in fact was difficult to enforce, Orshanskii asserted that none the less under existing law the courts lacked the means to protect wives from mistreatment by their husbands or to deal adequately with the marital problems constantly coming before them.[17]

Juristic critics similarly contended that the lack of rights accorded illegitimate children by Imperial law, and the limited possibility for their legitimization or adoption, unjustly deprived such children of the elementary right to care and support from their parents.[18] Nor did the state foundling homes provide an adequate alternative, the noted professor of criminal law at St Vladimir University Aleksandr Kistiakovskii argued in a critique of the law in 1879, as the high mortality rate in these homes demonstrated.[19] Again, society also suffered. The inferior legal status of illegitimate children bred an unhealthy resentment against society, Filippov claimed. Moreover, he added, 'laws that leave unpunished the debauchery through which base passions are indulged and that deflect the entire burden of this debauchery on to unfortunate and innocent illegitimate children' facilitated rather than discouraged illicit sexual activity, thereby weakening rather than protecting the institutions of marriage and the family.[20]

Breaking with pre-emancipation juridical writing, several jurists blamed the church for these deficiencies of Imperial law. '[R]unning throughout the entire history of the regulations on [marital relations] in Russian law', Orshanskii claimed, 'has been a struggle between two principles, the

[16] Filippov, 'Vzgliad', 86: 224, and in general 217–19, 223–7, and 85: 550–4.

[17] Orshanskii, 'Lichnyia i imushchestvennyia otnosheniia', 52–70, 184; see also Liubavskii, *Iuridicheskiia monografii*, iii. 429–38.

[18] Filippov, 'Vzgliad', 86: 229–42, Liapidevskii, *O dopolnenii*, 1–13, Barshev *et al.*, *Pervyi s"ezd*, 220–4, 232–7, and Kistiakovskii, 'O nezakonnorozhdennykh', 43, 46, 62–3, 75.

[19] Ibid. 73–5; see also Barshev *et al.*, *Pervyi s"ezd*, 234–7. Born in 1833, Kistiakovskii was the grandson of a freed serf and the son of a village priest. Upon completion of his studies at the Chernigov seminary, he entered the juridical faculty at St Vladimir University in Kiev. After serving briefly in several minor government posts, he returned to Kiev to teach at the university, where he became a distinguished professor of criminal law. See *BSUSV* 252–60, and *Kievskaia Starina* (1895), 1: 1–43, 64–102. On government attempts to deal with illegitimacy through state foundling homes, see D. L. Ransel, *Mothers of Misery: Child Abandonment in Russia* (Princeton, NJ, 1988).

[20] Filippov, 'Vzgliad', 86: 237; see also Liapidevskii, *O dopolnenii*, 14–15.

religious and the secular, a struggle in which the latter principle has increasingly gained superiority over the former.'[21] In fact exaggerating the effective—as opposed to the formal—power of the Orthodox Church in earlier periods, Orshanskii argued that the church had wrested control over marriage law from a weak Kievan state and then used its power to try to make popular practices and attitudes conform to its own doctrines. According to Orshanskii, this effort had distorted natural and customary marital relations, while at the same time the monopolistic control of the church over the law had prevented the state from regulating a critical area of social life. Welcoming the reassertion of state control over marriage law, which he believed had begun in the early eighteenth century, Orshanskii urged completion of the process of secularization.[22] At the First (and only) Congress of Russian Jurists, held in Moscow in 1875, the legal historian and renowned liberal defence attorney Vladimir Spasovich charged similarly that antiquated ecclesiastical law was strangling the development of Imperial family law.[23] And even Filippov contended that the early doctrines and practices of the Orthodox Church had resulted in the complete subordination of a wife to her husband, despite his profession that the church also had improved the status of wives in comparison with the pre-Christian Russian era. In his view, only the principles enunciated during the Reformation and the Enlightenment made possible the juridical recognition of the rights of women as individuals and therefore also their full liberation.[24]

To overcome its alleged shortcomings, juristic critics proposed several changes in Imperial family law. The authority of husbands and parents was to be limited through the reduction, and even elimination, of the

[21] Orshanskii, 'Lichnyia i imushchestvennyia otnosheniia', 27–8.

[22] Ibid., esp. 5–6, 28–30, 192–8, and id., 'Dukhovnyi sud i semeinoe pravo', *Zhurnal Grazhdanskago i Torgovago Prava* (1872), 3: 449, 455–6, and 4: 616–70; see also id., 'Reforma grazhdanskago suda i brachnago prava', *ZhGiUP* (1873), 6: 148–96, and id., 'Eshche po povodu dukhovno-sudebnoi reformy', *ZhGiUP* (1875), 2: 50–105. In fact, the Orthodox Church appears to have gained the ability to enforce its norms regarding marriage and divorce only slowly, in some instances not until the 18th c., and these norms themselves grew more restrictive after the 18th c. See the references cited above in Ch. 2 n. 23, and below in n. 45.

[23] Barshev *et al.*, *Pervyi s″ezd*, 222–4, 232–3. See also Liapidevskii, *O dopolnenii*, 11. Born in 1825 in the town of Rechitsa in Minsk prov. and the son of a doctor, Spasovich graduated from the juridical faculty at St Petersburg University. He served in the St Petersburg Criminal Chambers before teaching criminal law at St Petersburg University and the Imperial School of Jurisprudence. After the judicial reform Spasovich became an attorney and frequently acted for the defence in political cases. See A. F. Koni, *Ottsy i deti sudebnoi reformy. K piatidesiatiletiiu sudebnykh ustavov 1864–20 noiabria 1914* (Mos., 1914), 227–35, and M. M. Vinaver, *Nedavnee (vospominaniia i kharakteristiki)* (Ptgd., 1917), 1–58.

[24] Filippov, 'Vzgliad', 85: 526, 530–3, 546–56, 561–2, and 86: 218–19, 224–5, 265.

control of a husband over the economic activities of his wife and through the complete curtailment of parental authority after children reached the age of majority. In addition, the courts were to be given broad power to intervene in family affairs in order to protect the rights of wives and children.[25] Partly to protect wives from abuse, and partly to provide a way to avoid the problems perceived to result from marital breakdown in general, juristic critics also proposed that marital separation be permitted either by mutual consent of the spouses or by judicial action. In such cases, a wife was to retain the right to support from her husband unless she was found to be at fault for the separation. The same considerations led juristic critics to favour expansion of the grounds for divorce, in some cases to include mutual consent, and Orshanskii advocated the transfer of jurisdiction over divorce cases to the secular courts.[26]

Although favouring retention of the right of a wife to control her own property, in part as a protection against mistreatment by her husband, both Filippov and Orshanskii proposed that in the event of need she be obligated to contribute to family expenses or to help her husband. 'The idea of marriage', Orshanskii asserted, 'demands in this respect complete equality of the rights and obligations of both spouses.' Hence, 'just as spouses are obligated to render medical or in general personal assistance to one another, in the event of need they must also help one another with material means.'[27] For similar reasons, the existing statutory obligation of children to assist needy parents was also to be retained.[28]

Finally, juristic critics proposed to grant illegitimate children the same rights as legitimate children with respect to their mother and the right to support and an inheritance from their father. Legitimization of children was also to be facilitated and impediments to adoption eliminated. In addition, fathers were to be allowed to recognize their illegitimate children, thereby increasing the mutual rights and obligations between them.[29]

[25] Ibid. 226–8, 240, 260–2, and 85: 529–30, and Orshanskii, 'Lichnyia i imushchestvennyia otnosheniia', 48–55, 65–70, 98–9, 106–29, 188–96.

[26] Ibid. 39–70, 88–9, 187–94, and Filippov, 'Vzgliad', 85: 526, 549–62, and 86: 223–7, 249. See also the articles by Orshanskii cited above in n. 22 and Liubavskii, *Iuridicheskiia monografii*, iii. 429–38.

[27] Orshanskii, 'Lichnyia i imushchestvennyia otnosheniia', 22, and in general 22–3, 103, 194–8; see also Filippov, 'Vzgliad', 86: 227–8.

[28] Ibid. 264, and *SZ* (1857), x, pt. 1, art. 194.

[29] Kistiakovskii, 'O nezakonnorozhdennykh', 69–73, 97–101, Liapidevskii, *O dopolnenii*, 15–17, Barshev *et al.*, *Pervyi s"ezd*, 220–4, 232–7, 241, and Filippov, 'Vzgliad', 86: 228–55. See also K. D. Kavelin, *Sobranie sochinenii K. D. Kavelina* (Spb., 1900), iv. 622–3, and D. I. Meier, *Russkoe grazhdanskoe pravo, chteniia D. I. Meiera, izdannyia po zapiskam slushatelei pod redaktsieiu A. Vitsyna* (2nd edn., Spb., 1862), 538–9.

As juristic critics themselves sometimes acknowledged, these proposals went beyond mere adjustment of the law. 'During the last decade', Filippov argued,

> parental power has moderated significantly in our society. We have understood that children are not our subjects but our closest friends and collaborators. The backward and routine idea of severe and unlimited parental power remains only among coarse and ignorant people . . . But we are not speaking of these latter [people] . . . No, we speak of that leading element of society that has raised itself up to the understanding that even the peasant is a human being and our brother; it is this society that demands that our decrepit law of parental power be abolished.[30]

The conditions and attitudes to which the law was to be adjusted, in other words, were those of the 'leading element' of Imperial Russian society. For the majority of society, revision of the law meant assimilation of the values of this enlightened group.

For juristic critics such as Filippov, law thus represented an instrument as well as a measure of the progress of a society towards an ideal of civilization in which social relations were perceived to be inherently just and socially beneficial. Where traditional values and attitudes clashed with these natural norms of justice, the former had to give way. 'Law is an ideal', asserted Filippov.

> Morals must strive as their ideal towards the realization of law . . . [T]he development of man and his progress consist in his greater or lesser approach to perfection, and in its ultimate end perfection consists in justice and pure reason. Justice and truth, this is the path along which a developed person must walk undeviatingly, and this path can in no way be reconciled with morals that for the most part wear the worn clothes of an antiquated past, of ignorance, and of the original coarseness of society . . . such morals must be rooted out by the laws of a given country.[31]

Orshanskii, too, stated that his proposed changes in Imperial family law were intended to rationalize the law 'with the goal of placing our legal life on a level with other civilized peoples with respect to the protection of the legal rights and interests of spouses'.[32] And in his report to the First Congress of Russian Jurists advocating improvement of the rights of illegitimate children, the jurist Nikolai Liapidevskii contended that both the general trend of history and the 'postulates of civilization' reflected

[30] Filippov, 'Vzgliad', 86: 260, and see also 218, 224–6, 237, 251, 259–60, 265–6, and 85: 525.

[31] Ibid. 86: 225.

[32] Orshanskii, 'Lichnyia i imushchestvennyia otnosheniia', 192.

the movement to unite parents with their natural children and to facilitate the legitimization or parental recognition of children born out of wedlock.[33]

As it had earlier for jurists such as Kranikhfeld and Meier, civilization meant Western Europe, to which juristic critics contrasted the alleged backwardness and oppressiveness of Mongol, 'Eastern', and now also Byzantine and Orthodox legal norms and practices. Hence such critics felt justified in drawing heavily on Western European legal codes for models with which to purge from Imperial law—and from Imperial Russian society—legal norms and relationships that they considered to be both unjust and socially and culturally backward. Both Kistiakovskii and Liapidevskii, for example, based their proposals to improve the rights of illegitimate children on the most generous provisions existing at the time in Western European law.[34] And after reviewing several Western European civil codes, Orshanskii proposed to combine features of Austrian and Imperial Russian law in the way that he believed most equitably balanced the rights of individual spouses with the interest of society in stable marriages.[35]

Juristic critics obviously defined 'civilization' in broader terms than merely its juridical attributes. Like Kavelin and Meier had done earlier, for example, Filippov constantly contrasted the alleged ignorance and instinctual coarseness of early societies with the triumph of reason in civilized societies. And all juristic critics contrasted the unlimited patriarchal power, unequal status, and uncontrolled sexuality that allegedly characterized marriage in earlier times—and in Eastern cultures—with the limited authority, equality, and predominance of affective and spiritual ties over sexual passions that in their view distinguished marriage in a civilized society. Yet for such critics law played a crucial role in civilized society, precisely through its ability to limit authority and to guarantee the individual rights of all citizens. In sharp contrast to the emphasis in earlier juridical writing on moral self-restraint and legal minimalism, Orshanskii now asserted that the laws of all European countries 'represent the consistent development of the single idea of protecting the weaker member of the family from the arbitrary will of the stronger [member] through the

[33] Liapidevskii, *O dopolnenii*, 10. See also the comments of Spasovich and Plevako, in Barshev *et al.*, *Pervyi s″ezd*, 220–4, 232–7. Born in 1842 and apparently from the clerical estate, Liapidevskii studied at the Moscow Ecclesiastical Academy before entering the juridical faculty at Moscow University.

[34] Kistiakovskii, 'O nezakonnorozhdennykh', *passim*, and Liapidevskii, *O dopolnenii*, 3–10, 15–17.

[35] Orshanskii, 'Lichnyia i imushchestvennyia otnosheniia, 194–8.

courts, which is the sole motive that not only justifies, but insistently demands government intervention in the family life of its citizens'.[36] Similarly, Filippov declared that '[t]he strong know how to defend themselves, but law and society must defend the weak. This must be their sacred goal and the motto of each law.'[37] And linking the family to the overall structure of society, Kistiakovskii argued that 'an improvement in the fate of illegitimate children and a change in the general laws concerning them are urgently necessary . . . to introduce the principle of equality for all Russian subjects before the law and to eliminate the principle of separate social estates [*sosloviia*] from our civil laws'.[38] Through the revision of family law, in other words, the principles of legality and of equality before the law could be introduced into Imperial Russian society, thereby helping to establish a variant of the German ideal of a *Rechtsstaat*—a state in which the property and personal rights of all citizens would be secured by law.[39]

For juristic critics, the revision of Imperial family law thus served the same goal as other legal reforms being demanded at this time. Although the advocates of such reforms did not always agree over ultimate political objectives, their intention generally was to modify the autocratic system of government and to adapt tsarist institutions to their perception of changed socio-economic conditions and national needs.[40] In the final analysis, however, the principles of legality, individual rights, and legal equality embedded in most demands for legal reform conflicted fundamentally with the principles of unlimited personalized authority, beneficent paternalism, and unequal status on which the tsarist social and political order rested. Hence the constant tension between the desire of

[36] Ibid. 194. [37] Filippov, 'Vzgliad', 86: 262.

[38] Kistiakovskii, 'O nezakonnorozhdennykh', 97.

[39] On the German concept of a *Rechtsstaat*, see L. Krieger, *The German Idea of Freedom: History of a Political Tradition* (Chicago, 1972), 252–61, and M. John, *Politics and the Law in Late Nineteenth-Century Germany: The Origins of the Civil Code* (Oxford, 1989), 3–5, 42–3, 89–104. In 19th-c. Germany neither the liberal nor the conservative variant of the *Rechtsstaat* ideal contained the emphasis on the need to 'protect the weak' through law found among Russian jurists, a difference which suggests the influence of Russian cultural values on the formulation of this ideal by Russian jurists.

[40] It should be emphasized that juristic critics did not form a coherent group or even support identical political objectives, despite their common views regarding marriage, family, and the law. Jurists expressed their views independently, and their political positions ranged from the radical liberalism of Filippov to the moderate reformism of Aleksandr Liubavskii. Apparently from the hereditary nobility, Liubavskii graduated from the Imperial School of Jurisprudence in 1860 and served for a time both in the Ministry of Justice and on the committee that revised the Polish constitution. He wrote extensively on Imperial civil and criminal law. See G. Siuzor, *Ko dniu lxxv iubileia imperatorskago uchilishcha pravovedeniia 1835–1910 gg.* (Spb., 1910), 447; on Liubavskii's views regarding the revision of property and inheritance law, see Ch. 7 below.

juristic critics merely to adjust the law and their claims that reform was necessary to eliminate practices described as oppressive, unjust, and backward.

The implications of the legal changes demanded by Russian jurists during this period therefore differed significantly from those of similar demands being made at this time in Western Europe and the United States. To be sure, the arguments in favour of reform rested on similar ideals of the family, concepts of legal 'modernization', and concern for individual rights.[41] Yet however radical the demands for reform in Western Europe and the United States appeared to contemporaries, they could be accommodated within the existing political and legal cultures. For the tsarist socio-political order, by contrast, the principles underlying the demands for revision of the law were far more subversive.

But if through their arguments and proposals juristic critics challenged the fundamental principles on which the autocracy rested, they also unconsciously perpetuated paternalistic attitudes that derived from the interaction between tsarist tradition and Western European legal influences. Coming close to advocating a form of judicial tutelage, for example, Orshanskii argued that broad judicial discretion 'is indisputably the most satisfactory' method for settling family disputes because '[i]n the person of a dispassionate judge it guarantees identical justice for the personal interests of the spouses . . . and for the social interest in supporting the integrity of the family union'.[42] Similarly, a paternalistic conception of women as weaker by nature than men and therefore, like children, in need of special protection from the law often underlay jurists' demands for increased rights for married women and for divorce reform. Finally, the attempt of juristic critics to guide the development of post-emancipation Imperial Russian society by using the law to shape moral values and social relationships perpetuated both tsarist paternalism and an instrumentalist conception of law.

Unfortunately, it cannot be determined how widely held these views on the family were among Russian jurists during the 1860s and the 1870s. Few comprehensive studies of family law appeared during this period,

[41] e.g. see R. Phillips, *Putting Asunder: A History of Divorce in Western Society* (Cambridge, 1988), 310, 399–515, L. Holcombe, *Wives and Property: Reform of the Married Women's Property Law in Nineteenth-Century England* (Toronto, 1983), *passim*, N. Basch, *In the Eyes of the Law: Women, Marriage and Property in Nineteenth-Century New York* (Ithaca, NY, 1982), *passim*, C. Shammas, M. Salmon, and M. Dahlin, *Inheritance in America from Colonial Times to the Present* (New Brunswick, NJ, 1987), 83–101, and John, *Politics*, 202–40.

[42] Orshanskii, 'Lichnyia i imushchestvennyia otnosheniia', 49, and in general 48–52, 55, 65, 70, 78–94, 98–9, 116–17, 188–91, 194–8; see also Filippov, 'Vzgliad', 85: 527–30, 550.

and most juristic debate on this area of the law concerned the interpretation or judicial application of specific statutes. Participants in such debates sometimes expressed the same views of the family as those held by juristic critics. And these views were also reflected in several proposals for revision of the law put forward at this time by the Ministry of Justice.[43] Other jurists therefore shared the ideals articulated most fully by juristic critics. The percentage who did so, however, remains uncertain.

Evolution of the Affective Family

But whatever the extent of its initial popularity, the affective ideal of the family articulated by juristic critics during the Alexandrine reform era dominated juridical writing on Imperial law after the late 1870s. At the same time, this ideal—and consequently also the demands for changes in the law based on it—acquired an apparently objective foundation through the use of comparative historical methods by Russian jurists and the application of anthropological and sociological theories to the law. The evolutionary model constructed with these methods and theories, however, largely built on earlier arguments by Hegelian jurists such as Kavelin. Hence jurists depicted the development of family law, and of the law in general, as a progressive evolutionary process in which the legal institutions of a given society developed in correspondence with social, economic, and political conditions and in accordance with universal laws and patterns. Jurists believed that these laws and patterns could be discovered through the comparative historical study of the legal institutions of different societies and used to adjust Imperial law to post-emancipation conditions. As a result, Western European law again became the standard of measure for Imperial Russian law, since jurists considered it to have progressed further along the path of legal evolution.

The ideas of several Western social and legal theorists, including the British legal anthropologist Sir Henry Maine, the American ethnologist Lewis Henry Morgan, the French sociologists August Comte and Frédéric LePlay, and perhaps most influentially, the German jurist Rudolf von Ihering, inspired these trends in Russian jurisprudence. According to Ihering, legal rights originated in the struggles of individuals and social groups to defend their interests; every legal right, or law, therefore served some interest. Hence law changed as the interests, character, and interrelationships of social groups changed. Applying this idea to Imperial

[43] On these proposals, see below, Chs. 4 and 8.

Russia, progressivist jurists argued that the ends served by existing Imperial family law corresponded to the particular structure and conditions of pre-emancipation society but not to the needs and social relationships that had arisen after the abolition of serfdom. For his part, Ihering contended further that the assimilation of foreign ideas and the replacement of particular national legal conceptions by universal ones constituted the key determinants of legal and social progress. In his view, mature legal systems consequently were characterized by universality rather than by national particularity. In the political context of late Imperial Russia, this theory provided a powerful response to conservative claims that the unique national character allegedly embodied in existing family law should be preserved. Rejecting such claims, progressivist jurists argued instead that the task of jurists was to help identify universal institutions of civil law and adapt them to the needs of contemporary Imperial Russian society.[44]

[44] On the influence of Ihering's ideas in Imperial Russia, as well as on these ideas themselves and those of Maine, Morgan, *et al.*, see P. I. Novgorodtsev, *Istoricheskaia shkola iuristov, eia proiskhozhdenie i sud'ba* (Mos., 1896), esp. 115, 131–67, 218, *Politicheskie ucheniia: istoriia i sovremennost'. Marksizm i politicheskaia mysl' xix veka* (Mos., 1979), 192–212, D. R. Kelly, *The Human Measure: Social Thought in the Western Legal Tradition* (Cambridge, Mass., 1990), 229 ff., and P. Stein, *Legal Evolution: The Story of an Idea* (Cambridge, 1980), 65 ff. Most foreign references cited by Russian jurists during this period, however, were to continental European legal sources and to studies by mostly now little-known European, chiefly German, legal scholars. Although Russian intellectuals, and later jurists, had applied a comparative historical method to study of the law as early as the late 18th c., this method was employed more widely and rigorously after the 1860s, when it was reinforced by sociological and anthropological theories. The chief apostles of these methods and theories in Imperial Russia were Sergei Muromtsev (b. 1850) and Maksim Kovalevskii (b. 1851). Both noblemen, Muromtsev was the son of a Guards officer who owned a middling estate, while Kovalevskii came from a family of considerable landed wealth. Both men were members of the juridical faculty at Moscow University from the mid-1870s to the mid-1880s, when they were deprived of their positions for political reasons. For works by Muromtsev, see his *Iz lektsii po russkomu grazhdanskomu pravu (1898–1899)* (Spb., 1899) and *Stat'i i rechi* (Mos., 1910), i–v; for works by Kovalevskii, see his *Istoriko-sravnitel'nyi metod v iurisprudentsii i priemy izucheniia istorii prava* (Mos., 1880), *Modern Customs and Ancient Laws of Russia* (London, 1891), *Ocherk proiskhozhdeniia i razvitiia sem'i i sobstvennosti* (Spb., 1895), and *Rodovoi byt v nastoiashchem, nedavnem i otdalennom proshlom. Opyt v oblasti sravitel'noi etnografii i istorii prava* (Spb., 1905). On both men, and in general on the development of comparative historical and sociological methods in Imperial Russia after the mid-19th c., see A. Vucinich, *Social Thought in Tsarist Russia: The Quest for a General Science of Society, 1861–1917* (Chicago, 1976), esp. 125–72, Shershenevich, *Nauka*, 195–231, G. V. Shvekov, 'Sravnitel'nyi metod v russkoi istoriko-pravovoi nauke (istoricheskii obzor)', *Trudy vsesoiuznogo iuridicheskogo zaochnogo instituta*, xliii (Mos., 1977), *Problemy istorii gosudarstva i prava*, 188–223, and A. A. Tille and G. V. Shvekov, *Sravnitel'nyi metod v iuridicheskikh distsiplinakh* (Mos., 1978), 39–58. On Muromtsev, see also Vinaver, *Nedavnee*, 59–100, and *Sergei Andreevich Muromtsev* (Moscow, 1911); on Kovalevskii, see also N. Ia. Kuprits, *Kovalevskii* (Mos., 1978).

Drawing on these ideas, progressivist jurists depicted the socio-legal development of family relations as two parallel processes by which the conjugal family (*sem'ia*) gradually displaced the patrilineal kin-group (*rod*) and the autonomous individual emerged from subordination to the structure of patriarchal authority associated with the kin-group. These two processes were considered to be closely interrelated, with the conjugal family viewed as creating an environment that enabled the fullest development of each family member. Although clearly too universal, linear, and homogeneous, this account of family development served to legitimize the values and ideals of progressivist jurists by contrasting the negative qualities imputed to family relations in the past with the positive—civilized—qualities associated with such relations in the present.

Of course, progressivist jurists recognized that differences existed in the socio-legal arrangements and attitudes of particular social groups and regions, even within pre-Imperial and Imperial Russia. Indeed, their evolutionary paradigm often depended on the interaction of these differences to provide a dynamic for change. But progressivist jurists generally considered these differences to be less significant than the universal patterns and processes that they sought to uncover and described them largely as differences in the rate, rather than in the overall trajectory and the ultimate end, of development.

Hence progressivist jurists argued that in Russia, as elsewhere, society initially had been composed of patrilineal kin-groups that were organized on the basis of patriarchal authority, obedience, and unequal status. Because social identity and personal survival in this context depended on the kin-group, its individual members subordinated themselves completely to it. Women were seen to suffer particularly severely under these conditions. Daughters were accorded low status and considered expendable because they left their natal kin-group at marriage, while a wife was perceived by her husband's kin-group as an outsider. Moreover, because husbands acquired their wives initially by such means as abduction and then by purchase and parental arrangement, they considered them to be little more than chattel. Progressivist jurists therefore concluded that in patriarchal society marriage constituted primarily a means of furthering the interests of the kin-group and of satisfying instinctual desires and physiological needs. In such circumstances, the development of affective ties or ethical relationships within marriage or the family was believed to be extremely difficult.[45] A husband and wife 'were not two loving beings,

[45] For such arguments, see A. Smirnov, *Ocherki semeinykh otnoshenii po obychnomu pravu russkago naroda* (Mos., 1877), P. Iurenev, 'Semeistvennyia i grazhdanskiia prava zhenshchin

joined by mutual affection', declared Dmitrii Azarevich, professor of Roman law at the Demidov Juridical Lycée and then at Novorossiia University, in an article in 1880.

> [T]he most salient aspect of the relationship between spouses was the complete subordination of one side to the almost unlimited paternal power of the other. . . . [I]n the personal relations thus formed between spouses we cannot but see the logical outcome of the original organization of the family, that had as its necessary basis the complete subordination of all members of the community to a single person.[46]

Although agreeing that the patriarchal kinship structure gradually eroded under the impact of state, religious, and socio-economic forces, progressivist jurists disagreed over the relative importance and character of each of these forces. In an essay published in 1884, Konstantin Kavelin presented a modified version of his earlier Hegelian analysis in which he assigned principal importance to the state. As previously, Kavelin maintained that individual families, society as a whole, religious authorities, and the state were involved in a complex dialectical process in which state law both reflected and formed social relationships and moral values. State power played a central role in this process by gradually securing freedom

po russkim i pol'skim zakonam', *ZhGiUP* (1877), 4: 2, 4–29, D. I. Azarevich, 'Russkii brak', *ZhGiUP* (1880), 5: 82–132, and 6: 97–139, N. Lazovskii, *Lichnyia otnosheniia suprugov po russkomu obychnomu pravu* (Mos., 1883), esp. 1–12, 44–54, A. I. Zagorovskii, *O razvode po russkomu pravu* (Kharkov, 1884), 3–26, 264–300, 407–21, 487–90, id., *Kurs semeinnago prava* (2nd edn., Odessa, 1909), 1–7, 60–9, 127–43, 182–4, 256–60, id., 'Lichnyia i imushchestvennyia otnosheniia mezhdu suprugami', *RM* (1897), 1: 29–48, and 4: 45–68, A. F. Kazimir, *Ob otnosheniiakh suprugov po imushchestvu* (Spb., 1885), esp. 11–38, I. Tabashnikov, 'Zhelatel'noe otnoshenie budushchago grazhdanskago ulozheniia k nashemu obychnomu pravu', *ZhGiUP* (1885), 3, esp. pp. 83, 90–105, M. F. Vladimirskii-Budanov, *Obzor istorii russkago prava* (6th edn., Spb., Kiev, 1909), 409–506, G. F. Shershenevich, *Uchebnik russkago grazhdanskago prava* (10th edn., Mos., 1911), 674–5, 711–20, 729–30, 760, A. D. Sposobin, *O razvode v Rossii* (Mos., 1881), 13–17, 25–6, 50–2, and M. I. Kulisher, *Razvod i polozhenie zhenshchin* (Spb., 1895), esp. pp. v–vi, 1–2, 265–78. V. I. Sergeevich also followed this line of argument, although in his later work he allowed for a greater variety of patterns of development. Compare his *Lektsii i izsledovaniia po istorii russkago prava* (Spb., 1883), 927–40, with the later edn., *Lektsii i izsledovaniia po drevnei istorii russkago prava* (3rd edn., Spb., 1903), 445–507. A few jurists claimed that matriarchal and communal societies preceded this stage of social development. See e.g. the works by Kovalevskii cited above in n. 44 and A. N. Stoianov, *Zachatki semeinago prava u pervobytnykh narodov. Etiud po istorii zakonodatel'stv* (Kharkov, 1884).

[46] Azarevich, 'Russkii brak', 5: 102. Born in 1848 and the son of a law professor, Azarevich received his degree from the juridical faculty at St Petersburg University and then studied abroad. Upon his return to Imperial Russia, he taught Roman law at the Demidov Lycée before becoming professor of Roman law first at Novorossiia and then at Warsaw University. See *DINU* 483, 501–2.

for individual self-development while, Kavelin now added, at the same time curbing individual licence and ensuring the fulfilment of moral obligations towards other family members. Hence Kavelin concluded that the progressive regulation of family relations by the state constituted the chief means by which individuals in general, and women in particular, were liberated from patriarchal authority, the collectivist constraints of the kin-group, and restrictive ecclesiastical rules.[47]

Although similarly stressing the role of the state, Azarevich also repeated earlier arguments that Christian doctrine had contributed positively to these processes of change. Like Nevolin, Meier, and Filippov, he argued that Christianity had elevated the relationship between a husband and wife from its origins in merely the satisfaction of physiological needs and the pursuit of practical objectives by stressing the importance of mutual love between spouses and by emphasizing the equal worth of both spouses. But, Azarevich claimed, in Russia the efforts of the Orthodox Church to effect this transformation began to succeed only when, after the early eighteenth century, the state actively promoted Christian doctrine through secular law.[48]

Other progressivist jurists, in contrast, stressed the autonomous role of social and economic forces in these evolutionary processes, although such jurists disagreed over the significance of peasant custom. Jurists such as Nikolai Lazovskii and the eminent legal sociologist Maksim Kovalevskii contended that the peasant household constituted the strongest remaining bastion of the patriarchalism that had existed earlier among all social groups. While ascribing a positive effect to attempts by the state and the church to mitigate its harshness, Lazovskii and Kovalevskii argued that it was being transformed primarily by post-emancipation demographic and economic change. According to both jurists, the abolition of serfdom had led to a decrease in size of peasant households and a corresponding

[47] Kavelin, *Sobranie sochinenii*, iv. 1009–43, 1080–90, 1095–101 (and see also 1182–320, on inheritance law), and id., 'Russkoe grazhdanskoe ulozhenie', *ZhGiUP* (1882), 9: 1–24. For Kavelin's earlier argument and on Kavelin generally, see above, Ch. 2. For other jurists who assigned the state a central role in these processes, see the works by Shershenevich, Zagorovskii, Vladimirskii-Budanov, Lazovskii, and Kovalevskii cited above in n. 45.

[48] Azarevich acknowledged that during the pre-Petrine period the views of the church towards sexuality and towards women also had negative effects. See 'Russkii brak', 5: 84–5, 91–8, 123–32, and 6: 97–105, 135–8. For other authors ascribing a positive influence to the church, see Zagorovskii, *O razvode*, 264–81, 487–90, id., *Kurs*, esp. 3, 127–43, id., 'Lichnyia i imushchestvennyia otnosheniia', 1: 29–48, id., 'O proekte semeistvennago prava', *ZhMIu* (1903), 2: 58–9, Kazimir, *Ob otnosheniiakh*, esp. 17–20, 32–5, Sergeevich, *Lektsii* (1903), 459–60, 463–70, 492–4, and Vladimirskii-Budanov, *Obzor*, 409–66, 652–64. Kavelin, *Sobranie sochinenii*, iv. 1013–43, described religion as exerting first a positive and then a negative influence.

increase in the importance of a wife in the household economy, thereby enhancing her status and influence and undermining patriarchal authority.[49] Asserting that these changes represented 'the first step towards the emancipation of [peasant] women', Lazovskii urged, in a study of peasant custom published in 1883, that they be furthered through the revision of Imperial law, which could then 'serve as an escape from those outdated and patriarchal views of marriage which exist in customary law and, as an anachronism, even in our current positive law'.[50]

By contrast, jurists who subscribed to the populist variant of legal progressivism contended that peasant custom corresponded closely to the needs of post-emancipation society as a whole and therefore should provide the basis for the revision of Imperial family law. In fact, however, peasant custom often served as a means of justifying the introduction of Western European legal institutions into Imperial law without appearing to violate Russian cultural traditions. Hence populist jurists emphasized the alleged similarities between native custom and Western European law with regard to marital separation, the community nature of property within the family, adoption, and the treatment of illegitimate children. Such similarities, they asserted, stemmed from the same basic humanitarian principles.[51]

[49] Lazovskii, *Lichnyia otnosheniia*, esp. 23–5, 38–43, 57, and Kovalevsky, *Modern Customs*, esp. 24, 36–7, 65–8. For similar views, see Stoianov, *Zachatki*, Iurenev, 'Semeistvennyia i grazhdanskiia prava', (1877), 4: 12–16, 25–9, Kulisher, *Razvod*, esp. pp. v–viii, 265–8, 276–8, Tabashnikov, 'Zhelatel'noe otnoshenie', esp. 83, 90–106, Kazimir, *Ob otnosheniiakh*, esp. 3–38, Shershenevich, *Uchebnik*, 675, 711–16, and Vladimirskii-Budanov, *Obzor*, 409–66, 652–64. See also M. Ostrogorski, *The Rights of Women: A Comparative Study in History and Legislation* (London, 1893), esp. 190–200.

[50] Lazovskii, *Lichnyia otnosheniia*, 24, 52.

[51] See A. Savel'ev, *Iuridicheskiia otnosheniia mezhdu suprugami, po zakonam i obychaiam velikorusskago naroda* (Nizhny-Novgorod, 1881), esp. 3–7, 26, 88–91, I. M. Tiutriumov, 'Po povodu peresmotra i kodifikatsii grazhdanskikh zakonov', *RB* (1884), 3: 694–703, 4: 104–8, 112–19, and 5/6: 462–4, 472, id., in *ZNDGZ*, no. 1, A. M. Evreinova, 'Ob uravnenii prav zhenshchin pri nasledovanii (Protokoly grazhdanskago otdeleniia s.-p.-b. iuridicheskago obshchestva. XLI i XLII. Zasedaniia 1 i 15 maia)', *ZhGiUP* (1884), 3, pril., p. 133, [id.], 'Zasedanie komissii Ushinskago', *Pravo* (1905), 16, cols. 1324–5, and N. V. Reingardt, *O lichnykh i imushchestvennykh pravakh zhenshchin po russkomu zakonu* (Kazan, 1885), esp. 3, 19–20, 33, 38–40. On this group, see also Ch. 7 below, C. A. Frierson, 'Rural Justice in Public Opinion: The Volost' Court Debate 1861–1912', *SEER* 64 (1986), 529–36, and L. Engelstein, *The Keys to Happiness: Sex and the Search for Modernity in Fin-de-Siècle Russia* (Ithaca, NY, 1992), ch. 3. The idealization of peasant custom as the source of national law reflects the ideas of the Germanist branch of German legal historicism. On these ideas, see John, *Politics*, 23–5, 28–33, 39–41, 109–16, 244, and J. Q. Whitman, *The Legacy of Roman Law in the German Romantic Era: Historical Vision and Legal Change* (Princeton, NJ, 1990), 200–9. For critiques of populist arguments, see Tabashnikov, 'Zhelatel'noe otnoshenie', A. A. Kvachevskii, 'Semeistvennyia otnosheniia i budushchee grazhdanskoe ulozhenie', *IuV* (1887), 2: 325–35, L. I. Petrazhitskii, 'Obychnoe pravo i zhenskoi [*sic*] vopros', *Pravo* (1899), 18, cols. 901–12, and N. Brzheskii, *Ocherki iuridicheskogo byta krest'ianin* (Spb., 1902).

Where native custom diverged from these principles, for example in its treatment of women, populist jurists blamed the 'external' and regressive influence of Imperial law, which they claimed the tsarist state, the Orthodox Church, and the nobility had manipulated in pursuit of their own ends. Populist jurists therefore contended, not very persuasively, that state law and especially the church were obstructing the tendency of peasant communal organizations to improve the position of both illegitimate children and women.[52] Like Lazovskii, populist jurists consequently called for the assimilation into Imperial family law of Western European legal institutions that they hoped would accelerate trends in peasant custom considered to be desirable. '[W]e must not refrain from borrowing from foreign codes under the pretext that [what is borrowed] is foreign to us', argued Igor Tiutriumov, then chairman of the Kirillov congress of justices of the peace, in his comments to the commission formed to compose a new civil code.

In the interests of legal science, we must abandon this view and adopt as the principal criteria only usefulness and correspondence to the contemporary conditions of Russian life, without paying attention to whether a certain institution belongs to our law or is borrowed from the law of one or another people. A code that fully deserves its name must include principles characteristic to all humanity.[53]

[52] Tiutriumov, 'Po povodu', 3: 692–3, and 5/6: 455–8, 472, id., in *ZNDGZ*, nos. 1, 10, 14, 26, 86 (see also 109, 180, 293, 501, 573, 623, 642), Evreinova, 'Ob uravnenii', 3: 149–60, [id.], 'Zasedanie', cols. 1324–5, id., *O znachenii i predelakh obychnago prava pri razrabotke otdel'nykh institutov Grazhdanskago Ulozheniia* (Spb., 1883), 11–42, Reingardt, *O lichnykh*, 6, 18–19, 22–37, A. Efimenko, *Izsledovaniia narodnoi zhizni* (Mos., 1884), esp. 68–9, 73, 89, 91–2, 95, 99–100, 103, 106, 115, 122–3, and Savel'ev, *Iuridicheskiia otnosheniia*, 18, 27–9, 35–52, 57–64, 69–74, 84–91. The diversity of peasant legal customs and their unsettled character after the emancipation make generalizations about trends in such customs hazardous. During this period, however, in some instances peasant courts did grant a woman redress against actions by their husband or by his household. But the objective in such decisions appears to have been to enforce community standards or to ensure the material interests of the community as a whole, not to protect women against patriarchal authority *per se* or to challenge such authority. On this point, compare C. Worobec, *Peasant Russia: Family and Community in the Post-Emancipation Period* (Princeton, NJ, 1991), 64, 66, 69, 189–98, with B. Farnsworth, 'The Litigious Daughter-in-Law: Family Relations in Rural Russia in the Second Half of the Nineteenth Century', *SR* 45 (1986), 49–64.

[53] Tiutriumov, 'Po povodu' (1884), 4: 114. See also ibid. 3: 694–8, id., in *ZNDGZ*, nos. 1 (p. 3), 86 (pp. 62–5), Reingardt, *O lichnykh*, 36, and Evreinova, 'Ob urovnenii', 3: 133, 135, 160, and [id.], 'Zasedanie', cols. 1324–5. Born in 1855 and a hereditary nobleman and landowner from Novgorod prov., Tiutriumov received a gold medal upon graduation from the juridical faculty at St Petersburg University for his essay on the property relations of spouses under Imperial Russian, local non-Russian, and peasant customary law. In 1881 he was elected a district justice of the peace and chairman of the Kirillov (Novgorod) congress of justices of the peace. Tiutriumov then served as a judge in the regular courts until his appointment in 1901 as Assistant Chief Procurator of the Second Department of the Senate, which dealt with peasant cases (he became Chief Procurator in 1906). He also taught law at St Petersburg University and in the St Petersburg Higher Courses for Women. *PS* 160–1 (2nd pag.).

Despite the substantial differences in their arguments, and in the political implications of these arguments, progressivist and populist jurists therefore agreed on the direction of the changes in marital and family relations allegedly occurring in post-emancipation Imperial Russia. This agreement reflects the tendency of both groups to use the ends that they both imputed to the process of socio-legal evolution as a causal explanation of the process itself. 'The patriarchal house community will disappear in Russia, just as it has disappeared in France, Italy, and Spain, and as it is disappearing in our days in Servia [*sic*] and Croatia,' asserted Kovalevskii in a lecture in 1889. Everywhere, he continued, such social forms 'have been forced to yield to the requirements of individualism. I see no reason why the same thing should not happen in Russia.'[54] The result, progressivist and populist jurists alike agreed, would be the realization of the affective ideal of the family articulated earlier by juristic critics and the consequent liberation of the individual from the arbitrary rule of patriarchal authority.[55]

In the same way that the ideal of 'civilization' had done earlier for juristic critics, the progressive evolutionary conception of socio-legal development served progressivist and populist jurists as a mask for both the transformative character and the ideological and social basis of their proposals for the revision of Imperial family law. For however closely the limitation of patriarchal authority and the protection of the rights of individuals through law may have corresponded to the ideological beliefs, professional values, and social circumstances of predominantly urban progressivist and populist jurists, these goals conflicted with the principles that underlay the autocratic regime and the social norms and cultural values that still prevailed among substantial elements of tsarist society.[56] Paradoxically, the realization of these goals therefore could be achieved only through the intervention of the state, in the form of the law and the institutions that defined and administered it. As a result, the arguments made by progressivist and populist proponents of the revision of family law again revealed a tension between the professed objective of adjusting the law to changed conditions and the desire to use the law to shape social relations and attitudes.

[54] Kovalevsky, *Modern Customs*, 67, 68.

[55] In addition to the references cited above in nn. 45–54, see A. L. Borovikovskii, 'Sud i sem'ia', in *Otchet sud'i* (Spb., 1892), ii. 213–20, 238–40, 263–9, id., 'Konstitutsiia sem'i po proektu Grazhdanskago Ulozheniia', *ZhMIu* (1902), 9, esp. 32–7, K. N. Annenkov, *Sistema russkago grazhdanskago prava* (2nd edn., Spb., 1912), v. 2–8, 17–18, 23, and I. M. Tiutriumov, 'Razdel'noe zhitel'stvo suprugov', *Iurist* (1903), 11, cols. 364–9.

[56] See Ransel, *Mothers,* 96, 174–5, 192–4, 198–221, and the discussion of post-emancipation peasant society in Worobec, *Peasant Russia*.

The common allegiance of progressivist and populist jurists to the affective ideal of the family not surprisingly led them to propose essentially the same changes in family law, which repeated earlier demands of juristic critics. Hence, to protect children from parental abuse or neglect they advocated wide discretionary power for the courts to intervene in family affairs and complete termination of parental authority once children reached the age of majority. Arguing that children born out of wedlock should to some extent be considered part of the family of their natural parents, most progressivist and populist jurists also favoured extension to such children of the rights to receive support and an inheritance from their parents, particularly from their mother, and broad liberalization of the laws governing the legitimization, recognition, or adoption of one's own illegitimate children.[57]

Similarly, although most progressivist and even populist jurists continued to view the husband as the natural head of the family, they argued that the existing unlimited legal authority of a husband over his wife contradicted the voluntary and affective basis of the relationship between spouses. Such jurists therefore proposed sharply to reduce the authority of a husband, particularly with respect to the passport, employment, and further education of his wife. Henceforward his authority was to consist chiefly in the power to resolve disagreements over family matters, especially those that related to the upbringing and education of children.[58]

This continued priority for male authority, like the accompanying emphasis on the social role of the husband and the domestic role of the wife, of course reflected social attitudes and legal norms that were

[57] Kavelin, *Sobranie sochinenii*, iv. 1111–16, Borovikovskii, 'Sud i sem'ia', 298–307, id., 'Novyi zakonoproekt ob uluchshenii polozheniia nezakonnorozhdennykh detei', *ZhMIu* (1899), 8: 1–35, Shershenevich, *Uchebnik*, 755, Iurenev, 'Semeistvennyia i grazhdanskiia prava' (1877), 5: 21–4, and (1878), 1: 16–17, 131, A. I. Zagorovskii, 'O nezakonnykh detiakh', *VE* (1882), 3, esp. 379, 383–403, id., *O vnebrachnykh detiakh po novomu zakonu (3 iiunia 1902 g.) v sviazi s postanovleniiami o nikh zapadnoevropeiskikh grazhdanskikh kodeksov* (Odessa, 1903), intro., Annenkov, *Sistema*, v. 2–6, Tiutriumov, 'Po povodu' (1884), 4: 104–10, id., in *ZNDGZ*, nos. 1 (p. 3), 10 (p. 13), 128, 160, 180, id., 'Polozhenie detei ot nedeistvitel'nykh brakov', *Iurist* (1902), 1, cols. 14–17, id., 'Vnebrachnye deti', *Iurist* (1902), 2, cols. 41–5, id., 'Ogranichenie roditel'skoi vlasti', *Iurist* (1903), 13, cols. 437–42, id., 'Pravo roditelei nakazyvat' detei lisheniem svobody', *Iurist* (1903), 16, cols. 539–43, N. V. Davydov, *Zhenshchina pered ugolovnym sudom* (Mos., 1906), 41, and *ZNDGZ*, nos. 129–34, 136–43, 145–51, 154, 159–61, 164, 169–70, 174, 186–7.

[58] Zagorovskii, 'Lichnyia i imushchestvennyia otnosheniia', 1: 38–43, 47, id., *Kurs*, 201–2, 214, id., 'O proekte', 83–4, Iurenev, 'Semeistvennyia i grazhdanskiia prava' (1877), 4: 48–9, 54–63, 5: 7–12, 24–6, 6: 22–7, 54–5; and (1878), 1: 128–31, Reingardt, *O lichnykh*, 18–21, 36–40, Tiutriumov, in *ZNDGZ*, no. 86 (pp. 59, 66), Savel'ev, *Iuridicheskiia otnosheniia*, 69–74, and *ZNDGZ*, nos. 1025, 1040, 1059–61.

common throughout Europe and the United States during this period.[59] Only a few progressivist and populist jurists broke with these conventions by advocating complete legal equality in marriage and the consensual resolution of disputes. One of the few to do so was the appeals court judge and future senator in the Civil Cassation Department Aleksandr Borovikovskii, who contended in any essay in 1892 that parents should have no more difficulty achieving consensus than co-owners or partners in any other joint enterprise. '[T]he principle [of parental equality] is sacred', he asserted, 'and must lie at the basis of the human family.' Yet even Borovikovskii still considered the husband to be the head of the family and stressed the maternal role of the wife.[60] Rejecting even the former proposition, Kavelin and the populist legal ethnologist Anna Evreinova proposed to ensure full equality between spouses through the creation of family councils in which all adult family members would participate equally in the making of decisions.[61]

The question of the structure of property relations that ideally should exist in marriage provoked greater disagreement among both progressivist and populist jurists. Those populist and progressivist jurists who, like Orshanskii earlier, rejected the analogy between marriage and contract

[59] In addition to the references cited above in Ch. 2 n. 11, see M. Mitterauer and R. Sieder, *The European Family* (Oxford, 1982), Basch, *In the Eyes*, and Ostrogorski, *Rights*.

[60] Borovikovskii, 'Sud i sem′ia', 250–4; see also id., 'Brak i razvod po proektu Grazhdanskago Ulozheniia', *ZhMIu* (1902), 8: 8, id., 'Konstitutsiia', 3–10, 17–21, Annenkov, *Sistema*, v. 169–71, and Kazimir, *Ob otnosheniiakh*, 41–3, 50–1. Born in 1844 and a hereditary nobleman who owned a large estate in Ekaterinoslav prov., Borovikovskii graduated from the juridical faculty at Kharkov University and then entered the judicial service, eventually becoming Chief Procurator (1895) and then a senator (1898) in the Civil Cassation Department. While a member of the Odessa Court of Appeals he also taught civil law at Novorossiia University and served as a district justice of the peace. Borovikovskii practised what he preached, giving his wife and daughters separate passports. See TsGIA F. 1364 op. 15 d. 383, Koni, *Ottsy*, 250–4, A. A. Levenstim, *Ocherk deiatel′nosti sudebnykh uchrezhdenii Khar′kovskago okruga za istekshee tridtsatipiatiletie 1867–1902 gg.* (Kharkov, 1903), 114–16, and *DINU* 524–5.

[61] Kavelin also proposed to include a representative of the public, at least for issues relating to the use, disposition, and inheritance of property. See *Sobranie sochinenii*, iv. 1050–3, 1061–3, 1083, 1107–11, 1183–91, 1216–17, 1241–70, and 'Russkoe grazhdanskoe ulozhenie' (1882), 9: 1–24; and (1883), 1: 33–8, and 2: 85–91; see also Evreinova, 'Ob uravnenii', 3: 149–54, 159, and [id.], 'Zasedanie', cols. 1324–5. Because of the exclusion of women from most careers in the law, Evreinova was one of the few women to take part in the juristic debate over the law during this period. Born in 1844 and the daughter of the high-ranking commandant of Pavlovsk, she fled from her parents and went abroad to study law, first at Heidelberg and then at Leipzig University. The first Russian woman to receive a Doctorate of Law, she was unable to teach or practise law in Imperial Russia. In 1905 she helped found the All-Russian Union of Equal Rights for Women. See L. H. Edmondson, *Feminism in Russia 1900–1917* (Stanford, Calif., 1984), 36–7, and R. Stites, *The Women's Liberation Movement in Russia: Feminism, Nihilism and Bolshevism, 1860–1930* (Princeton, NJ, 1978), 106.

tended to argue that the existing system of separate property jeopardized the emotional and moral union created between spouses by marriage. 'At all times and in all places', Azarevich asserted in an article in 1883,

> marriage imposes an obligation to maintain the family, whether or not there are any children. In establishing the family, marriage gives birth to a special aggregate of interests which both spouses must serve. Marriage is incompatible with the dominance of egotistical personal interests. Upon entering a marriage, each person therefore knows that he [*sic*] is assuming an obligation to maintain the family and to serve its particular interests as distinct from his own personal [interests].[62]

Azarevich therefore proposed that both spouses be obligated to contribute to a special fund whose purpose would be to maintain the family as a whole. For similar reasons, Kavelin and populist jurists such as Tiutriumov proposed that the management of the property of both spouses be overseen by a family council in which the spouses would participate equally with other adult family members.[63] Still other jurists, such as Aleksandr Zagorovskii, professor of civil law at Kharkov and then at Novorossiia University, favoured the introduction of a form of community property patterned on Western European law. According to Zagorovskii, such a system would avoid the conflicts between spouses over property and the fraud with respect to third parties that allegedly often resulted from existing Imperial law while at the same time better securing the property of a wife through stricter judicial supervision over the actions of her husband.[64]

As even Zagorovskii's argument indicates, the objective of such proposals was not to increase the power of a husband over his wife, although in some cases this may have been the practical effect. On the contrary, the purpose was to limit the proprietary power of both spouses in order to ensure the welfare and rights of all members of the family. In this sense,

[62] Azarevich, 'Semeinyia imushchestvennyia otnosheniia po russkomu pravu', *ZhGiUP* (1883), 4: 105; but see his earlier statements in 'Russkii brak', 5: 102–7, and 6: 101–2.

[63] Kavelin, *Sobranie sochinenii*, iv. 1050–3, 1061–3, 1083, 1107–11, 1183–91, 1216–17, 1241–70, id., 'Russkoe grazhdanskoe ulozhenie' (1882), 9: 1–24; and (1883), 1: 33–8, and 2: 85–91, and Tiutriumov, 'Po povodu', 3: 698–703. Evreinova also may have favoured this form of arrangement, although she did not specifically connect her proposed family councils with the collective management of the property of both spouses.

[64] Zagorovskii, 'Lichnyia i imushchestvennyia otnosheniia', 4: 65–9, id., *Kurs*, 244–60, and id., 'O proekte', 92–9. See also Reingardt, *O lichnykh*, 6–8, 11–12, 22–6, 38–40, Ia. I. Gurliand, *Kakiia uzakoneniia mestnykh zakonov, a ravno iz innostrannykh kodeksov zhelatel'no vnesti v nashe budushchee grazhdanskoe ulozhenie?* (Odessa, 1884), 13–32, Savel'ev, *Iuridicheskiia otnosheniia*, 75–87, and A. M. Guliaev, *Edinstvo grazhdanskago prava i proekt grazhdanskago ulozheniia* (Kiev, 1903), 46–51. A graduate of the juridical faculty at St Vladimir University, Zagorovskii wrote extensively on family law. He adopted a somewhat more conservative position with respect to property and inheritance law (see below, Ch. 7).

these proposals reflected the same ambivalence towards individual ownership, and the same hostility to the notion of unfettered individualism, that emerged more forcefully in the parallel debate among jurists over property and inheritance law.[65]

In contrast, progressivist and populist jurists who stressed the contractual character of marriage generally also defended the existing right of a wife to control her own property. Such control, they argued, was both just and necessary to protect a wife against mistreatment by her husband. '[M]arriage by no means creates such a complete merging of two people of different sexes that the individuality of each of them disappears,' asserted the jurist A. F. Kazimir at a meeting of the St Petersburg Juridical Society in 1884. 'Each spouse is above all a person, with his or her individual characteristics, temperament, and inclinations, and only then a component part of that collective entity called the family.'[66] Since the right of a wife to separate property did not prevent co-operation between spouses, Kazimir continued, a system of community property normally was unnecessary. But, he contended, such systems were more vulnerable to abuse by a husband precisely when a wife most needed protection, that is, when marital relations had broken down or the husband had proved to be irresponsible.[67] None the less, Kazimir and other defenders of separate property also considered a wife to be obligated morally to contribute to common family expenses and therefore proposed that she be required legally to do so if she had separate means.[68]

If progressivist and populist jurists disagreed over the structure of property relations within marriage, they all agreed that the ability to dissolve a marriage should be increased to protect wives from mistreatment by their husbands and to reinforce the institution of marriage itself.[69]

[65] This point is made particularly forcefully in Iurenev, 'Semeistvennyia i grazhdanskiia prava' (1877), 6: 55–62, and (1878), 1: 129–30.

[66] Kazimir, *Ob otnosheniiakh*, 50–1, responding specifically to Azarevich.

[67] Ibid. 44–53.

[68] Ibid. 53–60, Annenkov, *Sistema*, v. 178–9, Iurenev, 'Semeistvennyia i grazhdanskiia prava' (1877), 4: 65–8, and 5: 58–62, Borovikovskii, 'Sud i sem'ia', 246–7 (and see also 236–8, 244–6), id., 'Konstitutsiia', 13–15 (and see also 32–7), and Shershenevich, *Uchebnik*, 717–20, 724–9; see also id., *Nauka*, 182–5. For arguments regarding the contractual aspects of marriage, see Annenkov, *Sistema*, v. 7–8, 17–18, Kazimir, *Ob otnosheniiakh*, 1–3, 43, 65–78, Savel'ev, *Iuridicheskiia otnosheniia*, 18, 27–9, 37–49, 64 (although he none the less advocated a system of matrimonial community property), *ZNDGZ*, no. 48, and the comments of Zmirlov in 'Zhurnal zasedaniia grazhdanskago otdeleniia Iuridicheskago Obshchestva 24 fev. 1896', *ZhIuOSU* (1896), no. 10, pril., pp. 10–11. See also Vladimirskii-Budanov, *Obzor*, 409, 414–15, and Kovalevsky, *Modern Customs*, 39–42.

[69] The lone exception was Azarevich, who favoured the indissolubility of marriage as an indication of its moral nature. 'Russkii brak', 5: 109–11.

To be sure, progressivist and populist jurists believed that spouses normally ought to live together, and where the husband wished, because of his greater role in providing materially for the family. But such jurists argued that because mutual affection and spiritual companionship constituted the basis for marriage, spouses should not be compelled to remain together once these qualities no longer existed in their relationship. The attempt to preserve a marriage intact in this instance, they contended, merely led to degenerate, immoral, or criminal behaviour, weakening the institutions of marriage and the family, and in turn threatening social stability and political order. In contrast, such jurists maintained, expansion of the grounds for divorce and the introduction of formal marital separation would not only avoid these problems, but also serve to inhibit abusive male behaviour, thereby reducing the likelihood of future marital breakdown.[70] Like the proponents of divorce law reform in Western Europe and the United States during this period, progressivist and populist jurists in Imperial Russia thus viewed divorce and marital separation as socially useful means for avoiding and dealing with marital breakdown rather than punishments to be imposed on spouses guilty of marital offences.[71]

This perspective brought progressivist and populist jurists into conflict with the Orthodox Church, whose sacramental view of marriage led church leaders to oppose efforts to liberalize divorce law during the post-emancipation period. Such opposition intensified the demand by jurists for secularization of both the law and its administration. But this demand also derived from a fundamental conflict over the relative roles of the church, the state, and the law in post-emancipation Imperial Russia. Although most progressivist and populist jurists considered marriage to be both a religious and a social institution, nearly all gave priority to its

[70] Kavelin, *Sobranie sochinenii*, iv. 1067–75, 1083, Borovikovskii, 'Sud i sem′ia', 213–20, 238–40, 263–9, id., 'Konstitutsiia', 23–6, 32–7, id., 'Brak i razvod', 34–5, 40–1, Shershenevich, *Uchebnik*, 699, 722–4 (who opposed separation as contrary to the nature of marriage but favoured wide access to divorce), Zagorovskii, *Kurs*, 187–208, id., 'Lichnyia i imushchestvennyia otnosheniia', 1: 33–7, 41–3, id., 'O proekte', 84–90, 99–101, id., *O razvode*, 392–3, 422–9, 455, 490, Annenkov, *Sistema*, v. 167–77, Tiutriumov, 'Po povodu', 3: 694–8, and no. 5/6: 475–6, id., in *ZNDGZ* nos. 26 (pp. 26–7), 86, id., 'Razdel′noe zhitel′stvo', Iurenev, 'Semeistvennyia i grazhdanskiia prava', (1877), 4: 49, 60–3, 5: 11–12; and (1878), 1: 129, Lazovskii, *Lichnyia otnosheniia*, 42–8, 57, Reingardt, *O lichnykh*, 14–20, Savel′ev, *Iuridicheskiia otnosheniia*, 30–52, 56–68, Sposobin, *O razvode*, 52, 86, 89, 92, 143, 156–76, 198–204, Kulisher, *Razvod*, 222–35, 265–78, and Davydov, *Zhenshchina*, 31–5.

[71] On this gradual shift in perception in Western Europe, colonial America, and the United States, see Phillips, *Putting Asunder*, 92, 168–72, 210–21, 422–32, 456–73, 481–8, 494–5, 526 ff.

social character and functions. Because '[b]oth for the individual person and for the whole state organism, marriage has such an important meaning, providing innumerable personal and social benefits,' Tiutriumov argued, 'the law [i.e. state law] must not refrain from establishing its norms and leave this to the discretion of the church'.[72] Secularization of the law therefore was necessary to enable the state to regulate an institution of vital interest to it and to society. Moreover, Tiutriumov continued, in a multi-religious state such as Imperial Russia, ecclesiastical jurisdiction produced a confusing hodgepodge of laws that impeded political integration through the introduction of uniform civil laws. 'The only escape from this labyrinth of contradictions', Tiutriumov asserted, 'can be for the law to take upon itself the normative definition of the juridical nature of marriage and to liberate it from those external political, estate, and religious restrictions that are foreign to its nature and that serve as unnecessary ballast in the laws.'[73] Tiutriumov's choice of words here is revealing. Marriage, he argued, should be subjected to the control of 'the law'. By thus emphasizing the law rather than the state in general, Tiutriumov expressed the ideal of legality that continued to underlie the proposals for the revision of family law made by pro-reform jurists. In so doing, he asserted the professional claims of progressivist and populist jurists, who perceived themselves as being the agents of the law.[74]

This aspiration to legality and to professional authority reflects the degree to which through their proposals for the revision of family law progressivist and populist jurists projected their own professional values, ideological ideals, and social attitudes onto the rest of tsarist society. Trained as jurists to think in terms of rights and obligations rather than authority and obedience, progressivist and populist jurists not surprisingly viewed family relations in these terms. Their assimilation of the Western ideal of legality, combined with the belief that the creative activity of individuals constituted the chief driving force of post-emancipation

[72] Tiutriumov, in *ZNDGZ*, no. 26 (p. 24), and in general nos. 26, 86; see also id., 'Po povodu', 3: 694–8, 701–2, and 5/6: 461–5, Kavelin, *Sobranie sochinenii*, iv. 1032–43, 1116–19, Borovikovskii, 'Brak i razvod', esp. 1–2, 10–13, 15–28, 59–62, Annenkov, *Sistema*, v. 7–8, 17–18, 23, Lazovskii, *Lichnyia otnosheniia*, 57, Sposobin, *O razvode*, 11–12, 53, 139–55, 177–94, Savel'ev, *Iuridicheskiia otnosheniia*, 35–7, 50–2, Davydov, *Zhenshchina*, 31–5, and Shershenevich, *Nauka*, 174–82.

[73] Tiutriumov, in *ZNDGZ*, no. 26 (p. 25). On the codification of civil law as an instrument for the political unification and integration of the empire, see especially Guliaev, *Edinstvo*, and id., *Proekt grazhdanskago ulozheniia* (Kiev, 1901).

[74] Not all progressivist jurists favoured the transfer of jurisdiction over divorce cases to secular courts. See Azarevich 'Russkii brak', Zagorovskii, 'O proekte', 58–60, and id., *Kurs*, 6–7; but cf. id., *O razvode*, 392–3, 424–5.

national and economic development, also led such jurists to emphasize the need to secure the rights of individual family members against interference by what they characterized as the arbitrary authority of husbands and fathers. When expressed within the context of a debate in which all participants attributed social and political influence to family relations, the demands of progressivist and populist jurists for the restructuring of the family on the basis of equality and legality implied an expansion of the civil rights of individuals in general, including the right of jurists to practise their profession without undue government interference. At the same time, although actual family relations among jurists undoubtedly varied, the image of such relations being propagated by progressivist and populist jurists at least expressed the ideal to which these relations were meant to aspire.

The mixture of traditional paternalism and radical reformism to which this projection of ideals led is illustrated by the critique of the position of women under Imperial law published by the liberal criminologist and instructor at Moscow University N. V. Davydov in 1906. Davydov depicted women as passive victims of men, of outdated Imperial laws, and of misogynist Orthodox doctrines. Echoing the sentiments expressed earlier by Redkin and by many juristic advocates of legal reform thereafter, Davydov contended that women therefore required the special protection of the law.[75] So, too, did the peasantry, especially peasant women. 'It is impossible to close one's eyes and accept on faith the proposition that hitherto our village population has remained moral and unspoiled,' Davydov asserted.[76] Education and law therefore should be used to inculcate among the peasantry values and attitudes that could protect them against corrupting influences. But among the legal protections advocated by Davydov were the 'equalization of the rights of wives and husbands', the 'elevation of the importance of the "wife" and the "mother" in the family', the 'abolition of any restrictions on the freedom of movement [of wives]', and the 'material . . . and spiritual responsibility . . . of the father [for] a child born out of wedlock',[77] changes in the law which challenged the patriarchal and inegalitarian structures and principles on which both the autocracy and the traditional social order rested.[78]

[75] Davydov, *Zhenshchina*, esp. 41–5. On similar views of women in both Imperial criminal law and debates over the law, see Engelstein, *Keys to Happiness*, chs. 2, 3.

[76] Davydov, *Zhenshchina*, 35. [77] Ibid. 35, 41.

[78] The critique of the law outlined above appeared frequently in legal periodicals after the early 1880s. See e.g. B——, 'Supruzheskoe pravo', *SG* (1895), 24: 2–4, 27: 2–4, 36: 2–4, and 40: 2–3, K. A. Dvorzhitskii, 'Preliubodeianie (grekh i prestuplenie)', *SG* (1895), 43: 8–9, 44: 6, 45: 6, 46: 5–6, and 47: 9, id., 'Vne braka', *SG* (1902), 29: 2–4, 'O detiakh

Authority and Order

This challenge to traditional structures and values did not go unanswered by conservative jurists, although such jurists defended existing family law—at least in print—less frequently than they did property and inheritance law and far less frequently than did other conservative writers. Particularly after the conservative resurgence following the assassination of Alexander II in 1881, the principal opposition to reform of Imperial family law came from political writers, state officials, and the Orthodox Church. Conservative jurists none the less contributed to this opposition by providing a juridical counter-argument to the proposals made by progressivist and populist reformers. Despite important variations, this counter-argument rested on the belief that the structure of patriarchal authority and unequal status reflected in current law existed naturally within the family and contributed to the maintenance of social and political order. By disrupting this natural family order, the assimilation of Western European legal institutions into Imperial law therefore would result in social and political instability. So, too, in the opinion of conservative jurists, would the secularization of either marriage law or divorce procedure, which would threaten the co-operation between the tsarist state and the Orthodox Church in protecting and strengthening the institutions of marriage and the family.[79]

uzakonennykh i usynovlennykh', *IuL* (1891), 6: 452–66, M. Levitskii, 'Po povodu 1016 st. ust. ugol. sud.', *ZhIuOSU* (1894), 2: 40–58, V. Volzhin, 'O protivozakonnom sozhitii', *IuV* (1890), 4: 646–63, id., 'Zamechaniia na semeistvennoe pravo po proektu Redaktsionnoi Komissii', *SG* (1902), 38: 4–6, 39: 3–5, 41: 3–4, 43: 3–4, and 44: 4–6, P. Lebedinskii, 'Neskol′ko slov o polozhenii russkoi zamuzhnoi zhenshchiny', *IuO* (1884), 171: 275–81, G. Petrov, 'Brak i sem′ia', *Iurist* (1903), 18, cols. 613–17, I. Nadezhdin, 'Vlast′ roditelei nad det′mi', *Iurist* (1902), 8, cols. 278–85, O. fon Kube, ' "Roditel′skaia vlast′ " i zhizn′ ', *Iurist* (1903), 19, cols. 648–53, I. M. Volkov, 'Pasporty zamuzhnikh zhenshchin', *IuV* (1888), 12: 649–53, B. G., 'Po povodu stat′i 19 polozheniia o vidakh na zhitel′stvo', *IuG* (1898), 30: 1–2, O. Portugalov, 'Kolliziia zakona s zhizn′iu', *IuG* (1902), 53: 2, I. V. Gessen, 'Budushchee grazhdanskoe ulozhenie. (Po povodu proekta semeistvennago prava)', *Pravo* (1902), 26, cols. 1251–9, id., 'Novyi zakon o vnebrachnykh detiakh', *Pravo* (1902), 28, cols. 1315–27, and 29, cols. 1352–63, id., 'Razdel′noe zhitel′stvo suprugov', *Pravo* (1911), 49, cols. 2755–67, and 50, cols. 2842–51, and A. I. Kaminka, 'Podsudnost′ i poriadok proizvodstva del o rastorzhenii brakov lits pravoslavnago ispovedeniia vsledstvie preliubodeianiia ili nesposobnosti k brachnomu sozhitiiu', *Pravo* (1908), 14, cols. 798–804. See also *ZNDGZ*, nos. 3, 27–31, 33, 35, 40, 48–9, 65, 68–77, 83, 85, 87–91, 93–4, 103, 132, 136, 159, 169, and the overwhelming majority of comments in *SZPGU. Kn. 2-oi.*

[79] In addition to the references cited below, see V. G. Demchenko, *Zapiski po grazhdanskomu pravu. Semeistvennoe pravo* (Kiev, 1894), L. A. Kasso, *Istochniki russkago grazhdanskago prava* (Mos., 1900), P. A. Matveev, *Krest′iane i Svod Zakonov (Po povodu sostavleniia novago Grazhdanskago Ulozheniia)* (Mos., 1883), V. R. Zavadskii in 'Kazanskoe iuridicheskoe obshchestvo', *Pravo* (1899), 15, cols. 797–9, L. N., 'Zakony o brakakh', *SG*

While agreeing that the family and the state orders reinforced one another, however, not all conservative jurists viewed this interaction identically. At a meeting of the Moscow Juridical Society in 1869, the professor of administrative law at Moscow University, Vasilii Leshkov, suggested that the state and the law should intrude only minimally into family matters. Reflecting the influence of Slavophile ideas, Leshkov argued that the family constituted an organic community. '[T]he rights of the people in this community follow from the idea of the family, or depend on the structure of the family,' Leshkov asserted, '[they do not follow] from the personality of the members themselves, or from these people viewed separately.'[80] If the rights of individual family members therefore were subordinated to the interests of the family as a whole, Leshkov contended that they also were inherently unequal, reflecting the hierarchy of authority that existed naturally within the family. Much like Nevolin and Meier, Leshkov concluded that family relations consequently did not fall within the scope of civil law, which, in his view, concerned only relations between equals. Hence, he argued, family matters should be the subject of a special field of 'social' law, and jurisdiction over such matters should lie primarily with religious and social bodies, whose decisions in turn should be based on inner conscience rather than on formal legal rules.[81]

Leshkov maintained that the existing legal authority of a husband over his wife and obligation of a wife to reside with her husband followed naturally from the character of the family community. According to Leshkov, the husband by nature was the head of this community and its chief actor, whereas the wife was primarily a helpmate to her husband and therefore naturally subordinate to him. This conception of the relationship between spouses also led Leshkov to conclude that the existing right of a wife to control her own property contradicted the nature of the family community. He therefore advocated the replacement of this right

(1896), 28: 2–3, I. Pobedonostsevich, *Opyt istolkovaniia 119 st. X t. Svoda Zakonov i 1033–1053 IX toma s tochki zreniia deistvuiushchago russkago, a ne innostrannago zakona* (Spb., 1906), and *ZNDGZ*, nos. 34, 41, 66.

[80] V. N. Leshkov, *Obshchiia zamechaniia na pervuiu knigu X t. 1 ch. sv. gr. zakonov, govoriashchuiu o pravakh i obiazannostiakh semeistvennykh* (Mos. 1870), 13. Born in 1810 and the son of a village deacon, Leshkov attended the Chernigov seminary before receiving a degree from the Main Pedagogical Institute in St Petersburg. He then studied law in Berlin, where he attended lectures by Savigny and Ranke. He was influenced strongly by both Savigny's historicism and Slavophile ideals. Leshkov also helped found the Moscow Juridical Society and edited the *Juridical Herald* [*IuV*] from 1871 to 1880.

[81] Ibid., esp. 10–13, 17–18.

by a system of community property under which the husband would manage the property of his wife. Leshkov insisted, however, that this relationship of unequal power and submission did not constrain the personal development of a wife, nor that of other members of the family, because the ultimate basis of the family was mutual love.[82] As they had earlier for jurists such as Nevolin and Meier, the affection and internal moral constraint of the husband and father thus transformed what pro-reform jurists characterized as the arbitrariness of patriarchal authority into beneficent paternalism. Any attempt to dismantle this paternalistic structure by reformulating family law on the basis of equality, Leshkov warned, would destroy the family, leaving only socialism or communism in its place.[83] Since Leshkov believed the family to be a microcosm of society, he presumably intended this Slavophile ideal of beneficent paternalism—and his warning regarding the likely result of its dismantlement—to apply to relations within tsarist society as a whole.

Slavophile idealism also led Leshkov, at the First Congress of Russian Jurists, to defend existing Imperial law with respect to illegitimate children and their legitimization or adoption. Imperial law justifiably treated such children more harshly than did Western European law, Leshkov asserted, because its provisions with respect to married women were more humane. Leshkov did not explain, however, why—even if true—this situation should influence laws that probably affected more unmarried than married women. Moreover, Leshkov continued, the cultural differences between Orthodox Russia and Protestant and Catholic Western Europe made any borrowing in this area of the law inappropriate.[84] Leshkov probably also shared the fear expressed by several speakers at the congress that any liberalization of the laws regarding illegitimacy would weaken the institution of marriage and threaten the honour and authority of fathers.[85] But in any case, the interests of the family as a whole, for him, again took precedence over the rights of individual illegitimate children, and the goal of the law was again to protect the legitimate family from intrusion.

By contrast, the arch-conservative jurist Konstantin Pobedonostsev gave a higher priority than Leshkov to state interests and therefore accepted a greater degree of state tutelage over marriage and the family. Moreover,

[82] Ibid., esp. 10–13.

[83] Ibid. 11–12. Leshkov probably also was reacting against the views of marriage and the family being expressed by radical and nihilist writers at this time. See Stites, *Women's Liberation Movement*, 45–6, 58–9, 89–114, 117–18.

[84] Barshev *et al.*, *Pervyi s"ezd*, 218–20.

[85] Ibid. 224–34, 238–41.

not only did he offer the most articulate defence of existing family law during the post-emancipation period, but his official positions enabled him to play a central role in the politics of family law reform in these years. A graduate of the Imperial School of Jurisprudence, Pobedonostsev was the author of a major study of Russian civil law.[86] He served as a senator in the Civil Cassation Department from 1868 to 1872, when he was appointed to the State Council. In 1880 he became Chief Procurator of the Holy Synod, a post that enabled him to influence the policies of both the state and the Orthodox Church.[87]

Drawing on the same comparative historical method and sociological and anthropological theories as progressivist jurists, Pobedonostsev claimed that family life was based on natural relationships of authority and submission, even though its specific form varied by culture and changed with historical circumstances.[88] These relationships were necessary for the maintenance of stability and order within the family, Pobedonostsev argued, because '[i]n any natural union that is connected with the intercourse of life and daily existence the balancing of personal relations is achieved through the unity of power'. And since 'the law by necessity confirms [this power] in the person to whom it belongs by nature', Imperial law rightly assigned superior authority in the family to the husband and father.[89] This structure of authority and obedience performed an important state role, Pobedonostsev continued, by fostering habits and

[86] K. P. Pobedonostsev, *Kurs grazhdanskago prava* (4th edn., Spb., 1896). The first edition of vols. i (property law) and ii (family and inheritance law) appeared in 1868 and 1871, respectively. On this work, see R. F. Byrnes, *Pobedonostsev: His Life and Thought* (Bloomington, Ind., 1968), 30, 36–7, 41–2, and Shershenevich, *Nauka*, 86–100.

[87] Born in 1827 and the son of an Orthodox priest who taught rhetoric and literature at Moscow University, Pobedonostsev was educated at home before entering the Imperial School of Jurisprudence. After graduating, he served first in the Senate and then as lecturer in Imperial civil law at Moscow University. Initially supporting the judicial reform of 1864, he helped to prepare the provisions regarding civil procedure and the courts of cassation. Pobedonostsev also tutored the sons of Alexander II, including the future Alexander III. For a full biography, see Byrnes, *Pobedonostsev*. Different aspects of his career and ideas are treated in P. A. Zaionchkovskii, *Rossiiskoe samoderzhavie v kontse xix stoletiia* (Mos., 1970), B. V. Vilenskii, *Sudebnaia reforma i kontrreforma v Rossii* (Saratov, 1969), F. B. Kaiser, *Die Russische Justizreform von 1864: Zur Geschichte der Russischen Justiz von Katharina II bis 1916* (Leiden, 1972), Wortman, *Legal Consciousness*, G. L. Freeze, *The Parish Clergy in Nineteenth-Century Russia: Crisis, Reform, Counter-Reform* (Princeton, NJ. 1983), I. Smolitsch, *Geschichte der Russischen Kirche 1700–1917* (Leiden, 1964), i, and G. Simon, *Konstantin Petrovič Pobedonoscev und die Kirchenpolitik des Heiligen Sinod, 1880–1905* (Göttingen, 1969).

[88] The following discussion is based on the 1896 edn. of *Kurs*, ii, which preserved Pobedonostsev's original argument but added passages intended to rebut his critics and to refute arguments in favour of progressivist reform of the law.

[89] Pobedonostsev, *Kurs*, ii. 112.

values that grew into social discipline and respect for state authority. Pobedonostsev concluded that because the patriarchal family thus contributed significantly to the preservation of social stability and political order, the state had a direct interest in supporting this natural family order.[90]

Similar considerations, as well as his own religious beliefs, led Pobedonostsev to defend the religious basis of Imperial marriage law. Pobedonostsev shared the belief of many Russian jurists that Christianity had elevated the meaning of marriage by transforming a predominantly physiological and instinctual relationship into a primarily moral and spiritual one. But more importantly, in Pobedonostsev's opinion, Christian doctrine had strengthened the institution of marriage by making it an indissoluble sacrament. According to Pobedonostsev, indissolubility, coupled with the submission to authority embedded in Orthodox teaching on marriage, reinforced the role of marriage as an instrument for inculcating individual and social discipline, not least because being bound together for life compelled spouses to learn to tolerate each other's faults. Religion thus combined with the naturally patriarchal family to preserve social stability and political order. Pobedonostsev maintained that this stabilizing role of religion and the family was particularly important in Imperial Russia, where the backwardness, ignorance, and unruliness of most of the population made survival and progress difficult without firm state guidance.[91]

Believing that they would weaken authority and discipline within the family, Pobedonostsev therefore opposed nearly every progressivist and populist proposal to revise Imperial family law made during the post-emancipation period. In his view, such proposals arose from the irresponsible infatuation of the Russian intelligentsia with abstract and alien ideas, particularly the doctrines of socialism and, even worse, individualism. '[T]he theory of radical individualism', he argued,

> rejects any authority in the state and in society. . . . This doctrine is distinguished by logic and consistency, for it insistently strives towards the complete destruction of any authority in all spheres of human life and, rejecting it in *religion*, in the *state*, and in *society*, just as decisively and with such passion banishes it from the *family*.[92]

[90] Ibid. 1–18, 44, 56–8, 79–84, 93–6, 110–13, 116–26, 166–8, 172, 176, 182–7; see also Byrnes, *Pobedonostsev*, 297–300, 310.

[91] Pobedonostsev, *Kurs*, ii. 1–18, 44, 56–8, 79–84, 93–6, 110–13, 116–26, 166–8, 172, 176, 182–7; see also Byrnes, *Pobedonostsev*, 297–300, 310.

[92] Pobedonostsev, *Kurs*, ii. 95, 96, emphasis original.

Holding the ideas of free marriage and individualism to be linked, Pobedonostsev especially opposed the introduction of marital separation or any broadening of the grounds for divorce. Both measures, he claimed, merely encouraged irresponsible and undisciplined behaviour and thereby sacrificed state interests to the whims of personal egotism. The state in fact should help the church to discourage divorce, Pobedonostsev asserted, because 'the state grows weaker the more the bonds of marriage are undone'.[93] Although admitting that 'the indissolubility of marriage entails great burdens for women because of their subordinate position', Pobedonostsev added consolingly that indissolubility also 'is bound with that high moral position that belongs to women' under the Christian ideal of marriage.[94] Regardless of the circumstances, a wife consequently was bound unconditionally to live with her husband. 'The husband and the wife are one body,' Pobedonostsev declared.

> The husband is the head of the wife. The wife is not distinguished from her husband. Those are the basic principles from which the provisions of our law proceed. . . . However severely a husband mistreats his wife, our law does not provide the wife with any direct means for requesting freedom from living with her husband or for refusing to return to him.[95]

Similar reasoning led Pobedonostsev to oppose the introduction of civil marriage or the transfer of jurisdiction over divorce cases to secular courts. According to him, the experience of Western Europe demonstrated that the introduction of civil marriage increased the incidence of divorce, thereby destabilizing the institutions of marriage and the family. Ideally, Pobedonostsev argued, the state and the church should co-operate to preserve the indissolubility of marriage and the stability of the family. Their failure to do so in Western Europe he blamed on the excessive political ambitions of the Catholic Church, which had driven the church into conflict with the state and ultimately compelled the state to take control of marriage law in order to protect its legitimate interests. Having deprived marriage law of its firmness in religious doctrine, however, the democratic states of Western Europe had pandered to the weaknesses of their citizens by facilitating divorce.[96]

While this argument greatly simplified, and distorted, the causes of the Reformation and the subsequent evolution of divorce law in both the

[93] Ibid. 95. [94] Ibid.

[95] Ibid. 116, 117, and in general 93–6, 114–26, 177–8, 210; see also K. P. Pobedonostsev, *Pis'ma Pobedonostseva k Aleksandru III* (Mos., 1925, 1926), ii. 34–6, 358–64.

[96] Pobedonostsev, *Kurs,* ii. 45–55, 69–72, 83–4, 99–101, 110–11.

Protestant and the Catholic states of Western Europe, it effectively called into question the applicability of Western European experience for Imperial Russia. In contrast particularly to progressivist jurists, Pobedonostsev maintained that the growth of secular control over marriage law did not represent a universal historical trend but, on the contrary, an abnormality produced by the peculiar historical conditions of Western Europe. The historical co-operation between the Orthodox Church and the tsarist state, he contended, had enabled the Russian empire to avoid this abnormality. But, Pobedonostsev argued, the elimination of the religious basis of marriage law would rupture this co-operation, at least in the area of family life, and thereby deprive the state of an important unifying as well as stabilizing force.[97]

Pobedonostsev never elucidated, however, how Orthodox doctrine on marriage helped to unify the multi-religious Russian empire. And although he did not exclude the possibility of the development between spouses and family members of the self-limiting relations of mutual love and affection idealized by Leshkov, as well as by progressivist and populist jurists, his expectations regarding human behaviour were more pessimistic. Hence while Pobedonostsev hoped that the family patriarch would act beneficently, he expected this authority figure above all to maintain order by restraining the egotistical, individualistic, and irresponsible impulses of family members. State law and the church were to assist in this endeavour by reinforcing the structure of patriarchal authority within the family, in part through the inculcation of a conservative Christian ideal of marriage. Pobedonostsev conceded that not all of the population accepted or fully shared this ideal. The peasantry in particular, he argued, treated marriage as a practical economic arrangement and consequently often resisted the efforts of the church to control it. State law and the church therefore had to civilize and educate the peasantry.[98] Despite his claims regarding the natural origin of the patriarchal family, Pobedonostsev thus viewed its existence as being dependent on state and ecclesiastical support.

Nearly all Russian jurists in the late Imperial period thus accepted the need for an active role for the law in shaping relations and attitudes within the family, and through this institution within society generally, even though their different ideological perspectives led them to disagree

[97] Ibid. 20, 32–3, 36–8, 41–55, 58, 61, 68–72, 79–84, 97–101, 110–11; see also Pobedonostsev, *Pis'ma*, ii. 34–6. On the evolution of the doctrines and legal norms governing divorce in both the Protestant and the Catholic areas of Western Europe, see Phillips, *Putting Asunder*.

[98] Pobedonostsev, *Kurs*, ii. 26–8, 61, 69–72, 79–82, 97–8, 110–11, 191–4.

sharply over the relations and attitudes to be fostered by the law. By defining ever more sharply alternative paths for the development of post-emancipation Imperial Russia in a context in which political debate and action were narrowly circumscribed, the emergence and intensification of these ideological differences after the late 1850s may in fact have contributed to the willingness of jurists to use the law in this way. Particularly prior to the introduction of the Duma system in 1906, the revision of law provided one of the few mediums through which social policy and political goals could be legally discussed and actively pursued. The increased use of family law for such purposes in Western Europe and the United States after the mid-nineteenth century may also have influenced Russian jurists and suggests the possibility of common sources, for example in the spread of the affective ideal of the family, positivist theories, and an ethos of professionalism and in processes of urban, educational, and industrial development.[99] Nor should one be surprised that professional jurists in Imperial Russia would use the law as a medium through which to respond to, interpret, and attempt to influence the various changes that they were experiencing. But in so doing, they also helped to perpetuate traditional tsarist paternalistic practices and conceptions of law.

Progressivist and populist jurists shared with conservative jurists not only an instrumentalist approach to law; the objectives and ideals of all three groups with respect to the family also exhibited important similarities. In contrast to more radical, especially socialist, critics of marriage and the family, progressivist, populist, and conservative jurists alike sought to preserve and to stabilize these institutions, even though their strategies for doing so differed fundamentally. Even those jurists who advocated the increased accessibility of divorce intended to relieve tensions within marriages, not to encourage their widespread dissolution. Hence the causes, as well as the process and legal consequences, of divorce and marital separation were to remain tightly controlled by the law and the courts. All three groups of jurists, too, emphasized the moral obligations and responsibilities of family members to one another, with even most progressivist jurists expressing ambivalence towards the concept of individualism. Moreover, if by the end of the nineteenth century conservative jurists had accepted the precedence of the conjugal family over the patrilineal kin-group even with respect to property and inheritance law, nearly all progressivist and populist jurists continued to view the

[99] See in particular Phillips, *Putting Asunder*, 403–515, M. Grossberg, *Governing the Hearth: Law and the Family in Nineteenth-Century America* (Chapel Hill, NC, 1985), esp. 10–15, 289–307, and Mitterauer and Sieder, *European Family*, 24–7.

husband and father as the natural head of this family and women as principally wives and mothers who needed special protection from the law. The proposals of these latter jurists to limit formal male authority within the family therefore simultaneously helped to perpetuate this authority, if in severely truncated form.[100] It is tempting to see in these similarities the persistence of traditional values and particularly of Orthodox ideals. Yet progressivist and populist jurists none the less broke fundamentally with both the past and the principles underlying the autocracy by espousing the need to limit authority through law and to recognize the rights and civil equality of all individuals. In so doing, they supplied a vocabulary of rights and supported a system of adjudication which could serve to limit patriarchal authority still further.

[100] On similar limitations in the ideas of Western European political philosophers, see S. M. Okin, *Women in Western Political Thought* (Princeton, NJ, 1979), 197–202, 226–30, and J. B. Elshtain (ed.), *The Family in Political Thought* (Amherst, Mass., 1982), 125–72. On property and inheritance law, and on the question of individualism, see below, Ch. 7.

4

The Limits of Legislative Revision

STATE officialdom and the educated strata of society were no less divided than jurists over the basis of the family and therefore also over the revision of Imperial family law during the post-emancipation period. As with jurists, this division grew more complex and politicized as the educated strata of society expanded and became more diverse, the process of professionalization broadened and intensified, and the ideological divisions within the government and educated society became delineated more sharply. While providing a unifying metaphor for its advocates, the affective ideal of the family in particular was expressed in ways that revealed important, and sometimes irreconcilable, differences in the professional interests and political objectives of ideological allies. Such division complicated attempts to provide legislative solutions even for commonly acknowledged legal problems, because different ideological and professional groups sought to solve these problems in ways that promoted their own ideals and interests.

But the tsarist legislative process itself made revision of the law difficult during this period. Both before and after the introduction of elected legislative bodies in 1906, major state agencies normally had to approve proposals that concerned their sphere of competence or affected their interests. The Holy Synod consequently reviewed proposed changes even in general Imperial family law and could obstruct proposals considered undesirable.[1] Any attempt by state officials or other members of lay

[1] Established in 1721 by Peter the Great, the Holy Synod constituted the supreme administrative body of the Russian Orthodox Church. The Synod itself consisted of twelve members of the higher clergy appointed by the tsar. A lay official, the Chief Procurator, also was appointed by the tsar to oversee the work of the Synod and to represent state interests generally. Composed of lay officials, often from a clerical background, the Synod Chancellery was subordinate to the Chief Procurator. Although the Synod was never subordinated to the state as completely as often is claimed, its relations with the Chief Procurator and the government fluctuated over time. On this relationship, see G. L. Freeze, 'Handmaiden of the State? The Church in Imperial Russia Reconsidered', *Journal of Ecclesiastical History*, 36 (1985), 82–102, id., *The Parish Clergy in Nineteenth-Century Russia: Crisis, Reform, Counter-Reform* (Princeton, NJ, 1983), I. Smolitsch, *Geschichte der Russischen Kirche 1700–1917*

society to change the law particularly with respect to marriage, moreover, unavoidably raised the question of the relative authority of church and state. While the resulting conflict resembled those over secularization of the law in Western Europe, in Imperial Russia few of the participants advocated, at least openly, the introduction of civil marriage. The majority of state officials apparently wished to preserve a Christian ideal in secular law as much as Orthodox Church leaders wanted the state to enforce church doctrines and policies.

State Reform and Legislative Impasse

Although during the first half of the nineteenth century church leaders and state officials had clashed occasionally over proposed changes in Imperial family law, sustained conflict emerged only during the 1860s. As part of the general attempt by state officials to overcome social, economic, and administrative problems through institutional and legal reform, both moderate reformist and conservative statist officials advocated the legalization of marital separation and the transfer of effective control over the resolution of divorce cases from ecclesiastical to secular courts. Although defeated by the combined opposition of conservative state officials and the Orthodox episcopate, these proposals generated institutional and ideological conflicts that persisted beyond the February Revolution of 1917.

But institutional conflict over family law had deeper sources in the growth of ministerial power and the professionalization of the Imperial bureaucracy. As both the desire and the ability of ministries to expand their control over social and economic life increased, the family inevitably received increased attention. In fact, the most significant proposals to change the law during the Alexandrine reform era were sponsored by conservative statesmen, the Minister of Internal Affairs, Petr Valuev, and the Chief Procurator of the Holy Synod, as well as Minister of Education, Count Dmitrii Tolstoi. Neither man wished to diminish the standing of the Orthodox Church or to weaken its role in preserving social order. But both men gave their primary loyalty to the state, and both believed that bureaucratically controlled legal and institutional reforms were necessary to stabilize the state and to further its development.[2] Differences in

(Leiden, 1964), and G. Simon, *Konstantin Petrovič Pobedonoscev und die Kirchenpolitik des Heiligen Sinod, 1880–1905* (Göttingen, 1969).

[2] On Valuev, Tolstoi, and their attitudes towards the church, see Freeze, *Parish Clergy*, 238–60, 298–34, 400–9; on Valuev, see D. T. Orlovsky, *The Limits of Reform: The Ministry*

priorities therefore brought even conservative state officials into conflict with Orthodox Church leaders over policy towards the family.

In addition, the training, the occupational concerns, and frequently also the professional orientation of state officials encouraged them to emphasize the social over the religious aspect of marriage. In the case of marital conflict, officials tended to be concerned more with containing the social effects of such conflict than with preserving the inviolability of a holy sacrament. From this perspective, marital dissolution appeared more as a solution to the problems caused by marital conflict than as a transgression against the sacrament of marriage. By the latter part of the nineteenth century this view predominated particularly among the jurists who staffed the Ministry of Justice and the reformed courts. The consensus over the relative roles in family life of state law and religious ethics, and hence of secular and ecclesiastical authority, reflected in pre-emancipation juridical and Orthodox writing, consequently broke down. The result was constant conflict especially between the Ministry of Justice and the Holy Synod.

There was therefore some foundation for the anxiety expressed in 1862 by Metropolitan Arsenii (Moskvin) of Kiev to the Archbishop of Kostroma that 'we are living in a time of cruel persecution of the sacred faith and the Church'.[3] Such anxiety stiffened the resistance of the Holy Synod to any changes in Imperial family law that contravened its interpretation of Orthodox doctrine. In practice, however, the Synod interpreted this doctrine to mean extensive ecclesiastical control over marriage and the preservation of the role of the episcopate in ecclesiastical justice. Defence of existing marriage law thus became bound up with the defence of the institutional interests of the church and the traditional prerogatives and authority of the higher clergy.

Ideological conflict over the revision of family law also had deeper roots in the politics of the Alexandrine reform era and in the conservative reaction provoked by the 'Great Reforms'. In the 1860s and 1870s it remained possible for moderate reformist officials who emphasized legality to ally with conservative statist officials such as Valuev and Tolstoi in

of Internal Affairs in Imperial Russia, 1802–1881 (Cambridge, Mass., 1981), 63–84 and *passim*, and the intro. by P. A. Zaionchkovskii to P. A. Valuev, *Dnevnik P. A. Valueva, Ministra vnutrennikh del, v dvukh tomakh* (Mos., 1961); on Tolstoi, see A. Sinel, *The Classroom and the Chancellory: State Educational Reform under Count Dmitry Tolstoi* (Cambridge, Mass., 1973), 34–54, and P. A. Zaionchkovskii, *Rossiiskoe samoderzhavie v kontse xix stoletiia* (Mos., 1970).

[3] 'Pis′ma mitropolita kievskago Arseniia k arkhiepiskopu kostromskomu Platonu', *RA* (1892), 1: 209; see also pp. 207, 211, and Freeze, *Parish Clergy*, 234–6, 246–7.

a mutual attempt to resolve what both groups considered to be important problems. But as the ideological divisions within the bureaucracy sharpened and hardened and different ideals of the family became identified more closely with particular ideological orientations, such co-operation became more difficult.

Both institutional and ideological considerations contributed to the failure of a proposal made by Valuev in 1864 to allow wives who were mistreated by their husbands to seek a formal separation through the courts. Contending that the existing means of handling such cases through administrative action or through criminal law were inadequate, Valuev argued that a civil remedy administered by the reformed courts could deal more effectively with what he claimed was a growing problem. His proposal therefore was intended to provide better protection for abused wives, not to challenge the doctrine or the authority of the Orthodox Church with respect to marriage. For similar reasons, the Director of the Third Department of the Imperial Chancellery, or gendarmerie, also supported the proposal.[4]

Despite such sponsorship, the proposal encountered strong opposition from the arch-conservative Director of the Second Department of the Imperial Chancellery, Count Viktor Panin. As Minister of Justice, Panin had opposed the judicial reform on the grounds that it threatened state administrative authority. He now sought to limit the influence of the new courts by preserving the authority of the church over marital affairs. But Panin also believed that ecclesiastical jurisdiction over marriage helped to maintain order and discipline in the family and thereby in society as a whole. Hence he proposed that local clergy should attempt to resolve cases of mistreatment through mediation and reconciliation. Where the mistreatment was severe, a wife might be allowed to live temporarily with her parents, a maiden aunt, or some elderly spinster until a reconciliation had been effected. For husbands convicted repeatedly by a criminal court of severely mistreating their wives, Panin advocated confinement in a

[4] TsGIA F. 797 op. 91–1898 d. 53 ll. 17–26, 34–70 (pp. 17–20), and 77–8. A similar proposal made in 1860 by the Director of the Third Department had been blocked by officials in the Second Department, who argued that such a measure could be introduced only if formulated in conjunction with the Orthodox Church. Ibid. ll. 34–70, pp. 14–17. Valuev did not mention the proposal in his diary, which suggests its relatively low priority for him. See also V. Ia. Maksimov, *Zakony o razvode pravoslavnago i nepravoslavnago ispovedenii i o razdel'nom zhitel'stve suprugov, s raz"iasneniiami Pravitel'stvuiushchago Senata i tsirkuliarnymi i separatnymi ukazami Sviateishago Synoda* (Mos., 1909), 375–7, I. V. Gessen, *Razdel'noe zhitel'stvo suprugov. Zakon 12 marta 1914 goda* (Spb., 1914), 4–7, and *GU. Kn. 2-aia*, i. 218–24.

monastery until the offenders learned to control themselves.[5] As other conservatives thereafter would do repeatedly, Panin attempted to use religion and the church as a defence against bureaucratic or judicial efforts to reform the patriarchal family.

But Orthodox Church leaders themselves opposed Valuev's proposal, on both doctrinal and institutional grounds. Metropolitan Filaret (Drozdov), for example, condemned the proposal as a covert attempt to establish civil marriage in Imperial Russia. According to Filaret, as a holy sacrament, marriage could be dissolved only by the church for reasons that the church condoned. He contended that, being unable to challenge this Scriptural doctrine directly, the state was trying to circumvent it through the introduction of what amounted to civil divorce. Hence Filaret concluded that the proposal violated both Orthodox doctrine establishing the indissolubility of marriage and ecclesiastical jurisdiction over divorce. If implemented, he added, it would induce spouses to obtain the illegal freedom to pursue illicit ends, thereby contributing to an already rapid degeneration of social morals.[6]

Making similar objections, the Holy Synod rejected the proposals of both Valuev and Panin when it reviewed them in September 1865, and again in March and April 1867. The Synod none the less left the door ajar for compromise, allowing the Third Department or the Ministry of Internal Affairs to take unspecified but 'appropriate action' once the efforts of local clergy to reconcile a husband and wife had failed. Since this position differed little from the existing situation, Valuev's effort to provide better protection for wives against abuse sputtered out.[7]

The same opponents also blocked efforts to eliminate the fraud, delays, and other problems alleged to result from existing divorce procedure by transferring effective control over such cases to secular courts.[8] Proposed initially as part of the judicial reform, such efforts sought both to apply

[5] TsGIA F. 797 op. 91–1898 d. 53 ll. 17–22, 34–70 (pp. 17–20); see also *Zhurnal soedinennykh departamentov zakonov i grazhdanskikh del Gosudarstvennago Soveta o preobrazovanii sudebnoi chasti v Rossii* (Spb., n.d.) (HLL), 114–15, 120, 147–9, 230–2, 276–7, 249–53, 283. On Panin, see R. S. Wortman, *The Development of a Russian Legal Consciousness* (Chicago, 1976), 167–96, and P. Maikov, *Vtoroe otdelenie sobstvennoi ego Imp. velichestva kantseliarii 1826–1882* (Spb., 1906), 466–98.

[6] TsGIA F. 797 op. 91–1898 d. 53 ll. 18–19, 77–8. On Filaret, see Freeze, *Parish Clergy*, 16–20, 23–4, and *passim*, and on his concern over civil marriage at this time, TsGIA F. 832 op. 1 d. 60 ll. 1–2, and d. 42 ll. 43–6.

[7] TsGIA F. 797 op. 91–1898 d. 53 ll. 17, 19–20, 24–6, 34–70 (pp. 17–20). See also S. P. Grigorovskii, *O razvode. Prichiny i posledstviia razvoda i brakorazvodnoe sudoproizvodstvo. Istoriko-iuridicheskie ocherki* (Spb., 1911), 307–15.

[8] On the procedure used in divorce cases, see above, Ch. 2.

the principles underlying the latter reform to divorce actions and to balance secular and ecclesiastical authority in an area of mutual concern. Hence the committee drafting the judicial reform proposed that divorce cases on grounds of adultery be submitted first to secular criminal courts to determine whether grounds for divorce existed. Ecclesiastical authorities would then grant or deny a divorce according to this finding. Proponents of the proposal argued that this procedure preserved ecclesiastical authority over the dissolution of a marriage while transferring the examination of evidence to secular courts, which allegedly were more suited to this task because of their procedural rules and the professional training of their personnel. But, echoing objections made by the Holy Synod, conservative critics in the State Council protested that this arrangement 'would substantially deprive the ecclesiastical court of its significance and would transform it into merely an executive body'.[9] Evidently persuaded by this argument, Alexander II rejected the proposal despite its acceptance by a substantial majority of the State Council in 1864.[10]

A more extensive version of the same proposal reappeared ten years later as part of a comprehensive plan for the reform of ecclesiastical courts sponsored by the Chief Procurator of the Holy Synod, Count Dmitrii Tolstoi, who ironically had opposed the earlier proposal. This similarity resulted partly from the strong representation of jurists on the committee established by Tolstoi in 1870 to prepare the reform. The committee also included several ecclesiastical scholars who employed similar analytical methods to those of jurists and evinced similar utilitarian and progressivist attitudes.[11] This composition had been dictated partly by the desire to reorganize ecclesiastical courts in accordance with the principles underlying the judicial reform. It also stemmed, however, from the growing conflict between Tolstoi and the majority of the Orthodox episcopate over the reform of the clerical estate and church organization

[9] TsGIA F. 1405 op. 542 d. 662 ll. 18–41, pril., p. 10.

[10] Ibid. 1–11, and d. 663 ll. 74–87, 114–23; see also d. 666 ll. 90–134, pp. 10–14, M. Levitskii, 'Po povodu 1016 st. ust. ugol. sud.', *ZhIuOSU* (1894), 2: 41–5, and I. S. Berdnikov, *K voprosu o reforme eparkhial'nago upravleniia i suda* (Kazan, 1906), 58–61, 71. When discussing the fundamental principles of the judicial reform, the State Council had implied that ecclesiastical jurisdiction should remain intact but had left the issue sufficiently vague to allow the jurists drafting the reform to justify their proposal. *Zhurnal soed. departamentov* (HLL), 114–15, 120, 147–9, 249–53, 283. On the similar failure of a comparable attempt made earlier by Count Speranskii, see the references cited above in Ch. 2 n. 26.

[11] TsGIA F. 797 op. 39 d. 295 ll. 1–7, 16–17; on the formation of the committee, see ll. 1–4 and *VOOPSS, za 1870*, 262–4; on the committee generally, see Freeze, *Parish Clergy*, 340–5, 401–4. Two earlier, similar proposals are contained in TsGIA F. 797 op. 87 d. 179 l. 1 and F. 796 op. 445 d. 409.

and administration in general. Through such reform Tolstoi hoped to create a more vigorous and competent parish clergy capable of fulfilling the pastoral, educative, and political functions expected of it by the state. But since the invigoration of the parish clergy threatened the power of the episcopate, Tolstoi's designs aroused episcopal opposition. As this opposition intensified, Tolstoi turned to the lower clergy, pro-reform faculty members at ecclesiastical academies, and other allies within the church for support. While the project drafted by the committee represented the outcome of this struggle, however, it also reflected the desire of jurists to resolve marital ills through legal regulation and judicial oversight.[12]

The committee majority supported its proposals with historical and utilitarian arguments.[13] According to the majority, advances in juridical science and the increased ability of the state to regulate civil relations necessitated the redefinition of the structure, the procedures, and, especially, the jurisdiction of ecclesiastical courts. The majority contended that such jurisdiction changed historically as society developed and as the state acquired the ability to perform functions that it earlier had ceded to the church only through to its own weakness. Applying this argument to marriage and divorce, the majority asserted that the growth of state power, which had enabled the state increasingly to assume responsibility for the definition of the laws that governed marriage and sanctions for marital transgressions, also required involvement of the secular courts in these cases.[14] Conceding a legitimate interest of the church in such cases,

[12] On Tolstoi's objectives and his relations with the Orthodox episcopate, see Freeze, *Parish Clergy*, 298–347, 400–9, esp. 298–301, 345–7. See also Freeze's essays in D. L. Ransel (ed.), *The Family in Imperial Russia: New Lines of Historical Research* (Urbana, Ill., 1978), 124–50, and R. L. Nichols and T. G. Stavrou (eds.), *Russian Orthodoxy under the Old Regime* (Minneapolis, 1978), 90–124.

[13] For the proposal, see TsGIA F. 1405 op. 542 d. 665, Ob. zap. k proektu osnov. polozh. preobraz. dukh.-sud. chasti. 1-aia i 4-aia ch., also published partly in 'O rabotakh po preobrazovaniiu dukhovno-sudebnoi chasti', *KhCh* (1873), 8: 618–91, and summarized in *VOOPSS, za 1873*, 229–42. An excellent description of the entire proposal and discussion of its fate can be found in Freeze, *Parish Clergy*, 342–5, 401–4; see also TsGIA F. 1405 op. 542 d. 666 ll. 74–144, pp. 14–15, Grigorovskii, *O razvode*, 276–80, and Berdnikov, *K voprosu*, 82–91.

[14] TsGIA F. 1405 op. 542 d. 665, Ob. zap. (n. 13 above), 1-aia ch., pp. 1–17, 20–5, and 4-aia ch., pp. 26–78, also published in 'O rabotakh', 649–51, 657–66 on divorce. See also the articles by Barsov and Sokolov cited below in n. 17, I. Orshanskii, 'Dukhovnyi sud i semeinoe pravo', *Zhurnal Grazhdanskago i Torgovago Prava* (1872), 3: 418–56, and 4: 616–70, id., 'Reforma grazhdanskago suda i brachnago prava', *ZhGiUP* (1873), 6: 148–96, id., 'Eshche po povodu dukhovno-sudebnoi reformy', *ZhGiUP* (1875), 2: 50–105 (for a hostile review of these articles, see N. V. Elagin [Lavrov], *Predpolagaemaia reforma tserkovnago suda* (Spb., 1873), esp. i. 146–76, ii. 92–142), *Mneniia dukhovnykh konsistorii otnositel'no proekta*

the committee majority none the less argued that dual jurisdiction was impracticable and concluded that in this situation secular courts should be preferred because they represented state interests and because jurists were more qualified than clergymen to evaluate competing claims and contradictory evidence in pursuit of a just verdict.[15] Whatever its merits, this justification of state priority was unlikely to persuade conservative and suspicious clergymen such as Arsenii, not least because it implied continued expansion of state authority and the right of the state to determine the relationship between secular and ecclesiastical courts.

Hoping none the less to forestall clerical opposition, the committee majority contended that its proposals regarding divorce did not deprive the church of its rightful control over the sacrament of marriage. According to the majority, this sacrament consisted only of the ceremonial celebration of marriage and excluded the subsequent life of the spouses together. The contrary proposition led inescapably to the Catholic position that Christian doctrine proscribed divorce entirely. The majority asserted, accurately but disingenuously, that in any case the proposals preserved ultimate ecclesiastical control over divorce because the final decision in each case still would be made by local bishops. Acknowledging that bishops in fact would be bound by the findings of the secular courts when making their decision, the majority argued that local bishops often delegated operational control over matters lying within their competence to other bodies and therefore could do so in this instance without threatening their authority.[16]

The support for these arguments among the jurists on the committee is not surprising. Their support by the majority of the clergy and ecclesiastical scholars on the committee is perhaps more surprising, and reflects the divisive impact of the processes of professionalization and ideological redefinition on the Orthodox Church itself. As part of these processes, clerics and especially ecclesiastical scholars subjected church doctrines and canons to the same types of critical analysis that jurists were applying to Imperial law. Comparing the development of the canons and ecclesiastical judicial practices on divorce in several Orthodox lands, for example, Timofei Barsov, a member of the committee and professor of canon law at the St Petersburg Ecclesiastical Academy, concluded that Orthodox

preobrazovaniia dukhovno-sudebnoi chasti (Spb., 1874), i. 23, 80–1, 482–3, and Berdnikov, *K voprosu*, 58–61, 71–91.

[15] TsGIA F. 1405 op. 542 d. 665, Ob. zap. (n. 13 above), 4-aia ch., pp. 28–53, 59–67, 74–8.

[16] Ibid. 64–6, 77–8.

canons constituted not immutable rules but general guide-lines whose interpretation and application varied culturally and changed historically. They therefore had to be reinterpreted and their practical meaning redefined as societies progressed.[17] 'Movement forward', Barsov asserted in an address in 1873,

> and development in all institutions constitute the fundamental law of existence for the church, whose assigned task is to educate not one, but all successive and consecutive generations in the spirit of the Evangels and of Christian commandments. Thus whatever forms and innovations the reform of Russian ecclesiastical courts has allowed into its plans, it must not fear any objections and criticisms as long as these forms and innovations, on the one hand, do not contradict the universal canons of the church and, on the other hand, are justified by the actual usefulness of their application and in addition promise to satisfy the demands of the time and the objectives of the ecclesiastical court in [our] fatherland.[18]

Post-emancipation conditions, in other words, necessitated an adjustment of the organization, practices, and canons of the church, a process in which ecclesiastical scholars such as Barsov could expect to play an important role.

The situation confronting the church appeared differently not only to the committee minority, but more importantly also to a majority of the Holy Synod as well as to much of the Orthodox episcopate and lower clergy. Denouncing the committee proposals as contrary to the laws of God, immutable church canons, and the fundamental principles of Orthodox theology, for example, Metropolitan Arsenii claimed that they would cause unrest by exciting evil passions.[19] And similarly, after presenting its own analysis of the church canons defining episcopal authority and ecclesiastical justice, the Riga diocesan consistory declared,

> let the Sokolovs and the Barsovs explain these rules as they will, of course they will find followers. But whoever has healthy eyes and a clear and direct view of

[17] T. Barsov, 'O dukhovnom sude', *KhCh* (1870), 9: 462–510, and 10: 587–626, and id., 'Rech′, chitannaia v torzhestvennom sobranii S.-Peterburgskoi Dukhovnoi Akademii ekstraordinarnym professorom T. V. Barsovym 17 fevralia 1873 goda', *KhCh* (1873), 3: 455–89. For similar arguments, see also the essays by the professor of canon law and church history at the Moscow Ecclesiastical Academy and Moscow University Nikolai Sokolov, 'O nachalakh i formakh dukhovnago suda v vidu sovremennykh potrebnostei', *PO* (1870), 5: 822–53, and 6: 973–1010, 'Tserkovnyi sud v pervye tri veka khristianstva', *PO* (1870), 9: 302–27, and 'Kanonicheskoe ustroistvo tserkovnago suda po nachalam vselenskago sobornago zakonodatel′stva', *PO* (1870), 11: 587–609, and 12: 752–68. For a polemical critique of both authors, see Elagin, *Predpolagaemaia reforma*, ii. 92–142. Like most faculty at ecclesiastical academies, Barsov and Sokolov were from the clerical estate.

[18] Barsov, 'Rech′', 489.

[19] TsGIA F. 797 op. 39 d. 295 l. 54.

the subject will never agree to call black, white, and white, black. . . . The Church of Christ is a Divine institution, and therefore both in its entirety and in its particular everyday practices it must strongly and unalterably maintain those fundamentals and principles that were established or decreed by Jesus Christ and the Apostles and confirmed and blessed by the centuries-old and uninterrupted practice of the Ecumenical Church. . . . The destabilization of Church doctrine on one point will destabilize others. It is impossible to remove one of the four corners of a building without destabilizing the whole building. And who can indicate the limit where human arbitrariness must stop?[20]

For conservative churchmen, doctrinal conservatism thus was reinforced by the belief that they were living through a period not of progressive change, but of secularizing and socially and morally degenerative attacks on the church. From this perspective, the proper response was not the adaptation of church organizations and canons but their determined defence.[21]

This defence included the preservation of ecclesiastical jurisdiction over divorce and therefore also of the influence of the Orthodox Church on Imperial family law. 'Marriage is a sacrament that is performed by the Church, and therefore the dissolution of marital bonds is . . . an exclusive right of the Church,' the Riga consistory asserted. The church 'therefore must not be a passive instrument of civil authority but an independent judge in the dissolution [of a marriage]'.[22] Agreeing with the committee that only one court could render the substantive judgement in a given case, the consistory concluded that ecclesiastical courts should be preferred to secular ones. Otherwise,

[g]uided by lay and purely carnal conceptions and views of marriage, secular authority can easily disregard those principles on the basis of which the Church with extreme circumspection and caution dissolves marital bonds. This would weaken marital unions, which in our time are already unstable and not firm, whereas the strength and holiness [of such unions] constitute the chief supports not only of family happiness, but also of social welfare and state prosperity.[23]

[20] *Mneniia dukhovnykh konsistorii*, i. 169, 167–8. On Sokolov, see n. 17 above.

[21] Orthodox doctrine almost invited conflict by treating marriage as a sacrament but then allowing divorce. See V. N. Myshtsyn, *K voprosu o printsipakh brakorazvodnago tserkovnago zakonodatel'stva* (Iaroslavl, 1911), esp. 5–13, 16–17, 48–9.

[22] *Mneniia dukhovnykh konsistorii*, i. 183. See also p. 264, TsGIA F. 1405 op. 542 d. 665, Ob. zap. (n. 13 above), 1-aia ch., pp. 17–20, and 4-aia ch., pp. 68–73, and Elagin, *Predpolagaemaia reforma*, i. 12, 88–9.

[23] *Mneniia dukhovnykh konsistorii*, i. 183. See also pp. 76–8, 167–9, 191, 233–43, 256–81, 356–8, 414–42, 459–60, 477–8, TsGIA F. 1405 op. 542 d. 665, Ob. zap. (n. 13 above), 1-aia ch., pp. 17–20, and 4-aia ch., pp. 35–8, 43–55, 59–73, and Elagin, *Predpolagaemaia reforma*, i. 5–6, 10–13, 18–19, 75–7, 82–5, and ii. 444–5 (for polemical reviews of the latter,

Clerical opponents also rejected the contention of the committee that members of the clergy were less qualified than jurists to assess the evidence in divorce cases. On the contrary, such opponents asserted, the pastoral activities of the clergy and their exposure in the confessional to the sins of daily life enabled them to discern the truth behind competing claims in a divorce action. Moreover, opponents argued, the concerns of the clergy for the spiritual and moral well-being of their flock made them more likely than secular judges to reconcile the spouses in such cases, thereby protecting them from the further sin of divorce. By contrast, 'not obligated to watch over the purity of morals, a secular court can view both marriages and the dissolution of marriages without the same strictness as members of the clergy, who bear the direct obligation to defend the purity of morals in a Christian society', the Vladimir diocesan consistory declared. 'Divorces therefore can occur more frequently, and respect for the sacrament of marriage will weaken, and [these results] can be accompanied by unfortunate consequences not only for individual families, but also for the state.'[24]

Hence, in the view of clerical opponents, the proposals of the committee threatened to undermine both society and the state by weakening the influence of the Orthodox Church on Russian family life. Indeed, many such opponents believed the proposals represented merely the first step in the introduction of the institution of civil marriage into Imperial law. '[I]t would be extremely regrettable', the Kostroma diocesan consistory complained, 'if the Russian Orthodox Church itself repudiated a right that gives it the possibility of supporting and strengthening good morals among its members. By denying itself this right, the Russian Church would itself lay the basis for the establishment of so-called civil marriages, after the introduction of which the corruption of morals and disorder in the family unavoidably would follow.'[25] '[T]o avoid this result', the Kishinev consistory warned, 'it is necessary to prevent the first step that unavoidably will lead to this result.'[26] Such attitudes left little room for compromise.

see Orshanskii, 'Reforma', and id., 'Eshche'). In general, see TsGIA F. 1405 op. 542 d. 662 ll. 1–45 (with pril., pp. 1–11), d. 663 ll. 82–7, 117–23, and d. 666 ll. 90–134 (pp. 10–15, 17–20, 87), Berdnikov, *K voprosu*, 58–61, 71–93, Grigorovskii, *O razvode*, 276–80, and Freeze, *Parish Clergy*, 401–4.

[24] *Mneniia dukhovnykh konsistorii*, i. 460. See also TsGIA F. 1405 op. 542 d. 666 ll. 74–144, p. 87, and Elagin, *Predpolagaemaia reforma*, i. 15–16, 77–8, 91, and ii. 346–51.

[25] *Mneniia dukhovnykh konsistorii*, i. 234.

[26] Ibid. 268. See also p. 235, TsGIA F. 1405 op. 542 d. 665, Ob. zap. (n. 13 above), 1-aia ch., pp. 17–20, and 4-aia ch., pp. 68–78, F. 797 op. 39 d. 295 ll. 54–8, and Elagin, *Predpolagaemaia reforma*, i, pp. i–iii, 1–4, 80, 90–9.

They also explain the hostile reception given by the Holy Synod both to the overall proposals of the committee and to those that related specifically to divorce when these proposals were discussed in mid-1873. The decision of the Synod to distribute the proposals to diocesan bishops and consistories for comment effectively doomed them, since most bishops and many consistories opposed them and the Chief Procurator lacked the power to implement such a reform on his own initiative. Conceding defeat, Tolstoi disbanded the committee even before most comments had been received.[27] But alarmed by the rising number of divorces obtained by allegedly fraudulent means, he tried to salvage the proposals regarding jurisdiction and procedure in divorce cases. In 1876 he received Imperial consent to form a special conference consisting of himself, the Minister of Justice, and the directors of the Second and Third Departments of the Imperial Chancellery to discuss means to eliminate the problem of fraud. Not surprisingly, the conference recommended that the proposals of the Tolstoi committee regarding divorce be implemented immediately and independently of the general reform of ecclesiastical courts. By making its recommendation contingent on the agreement of the Holy Synod, however, the conference demonstrated the reluctance of even high government ministers to challenge the authority of the Synod in this area directly. Consequently, the proposal was again blocked by the Synod majority, which twice rejected it, on one occasion quoting from Tolstoi's own argument against the earlier proposal of the committee on judicial reform.[28]

The Civil Code Commission

The replacement of Tolstoi as Chief Procurator of the Holy Synod by the arch-conservative Konstantin Pobedonostsev in April 1880, followed in March 1881 by the ascension of Alexander III to the Imperial throne after the assassination of his father Alexander II, soon led to an attempt to strengthen the autocracy through a combination of conservative reform,

[27] TsGIA F. 797 op. 39 d. 295 l. 49. The comments received from bishops and consistories are contained in F. 796 op. 445 d. 410–14, published as *Mneniia dukhovnykh konsistorii*, and F. 797 op. 39 d. 295 ll. 54–65. See also the references cited above in n. 13.

[28] TsGIA F. 1405 op. 542 d. 665, Vysoch. utverzh. 1 marta 1877 zhur. soveshch. 25 noi. 1876 g. o merakh k presech. zloupotreb. po delam brakoraz., and Zapiska, soderzh. v sebe krat. izlozh. zak. o sudoproiz. po delam brach., d. 662 ll. 1–41, 42b–45, and d. 666 ll. 74–144 (pp. 17–20). At Tolstoi's behest, the Ministry of Justice began examining the question in 1878, but it accomplished little apart from the preparation of a long memorandum, ibid., d. 662 ll. 82–260 (on adultery, ll. 86–8, 253–60). See also Berdnikov, *K voprosu*, 91–3, and Grigorovskii, *O razvode*, 280–5.

counter-reform, and the idealization of traditional values and institutions. The importance of both Orthodoxy and the patriarchal family for the maintenance of the tsarist social and political order received renewed emphasis, particularly under the influence of Pobedonostsev, and prospects for progressivist revision of Imperial family law appeared to diminish. And yet during this inauspicious period the most radical legislative proposal for the revision of the law to appear in the post-emancipation era was prepared by the editing commission of the special committee established to draft a new civil code.

The special committee was created in May 1882 on the initiative of the Minister of Justice, Dmitrii Nabokov.[29] At its only meeting, in June of that year, the committee formed an editing commission composed of seven of its members, which prepared the draft code. During the twenty-four years of its existence the commission also composed a number of legislative proposals concerning civil and commercial law, produced numerous treatises and articles on Imperial Russian and foreign civil law, and translated several foreign civil codes into Russian. The draft version of the code itself appeared between 1899 and 1903 and was circulated among government agencies, judicial personnel, commercial bodies, and public organizations for comments. Having slightly revised the code in view of these comments, the commission was disbanded in January 1906.[30] Although thereafter the Ministry of Justice established several special committees to revise the code further and to prepare it for submission to the State Duma, only small fragments of the code were enacted by the time of the February Revolution in 1917.[31] The principal reason for this

[29] *3PSZ* ii (1882), no. 872, pp. 206–7, *GU. Pribavlenie k proektu grazhdanskago ulozheniia* (Spb., 1906), 2–5, and *Ministerstvo iustitsii za sto let, 1802–1902. Istoricheskii ocherk* (Spb., 1902), 170–1, 270–4.

[30] Despite earnest efforts, the archivists of TsGIA (Leningrad) were unable to locate the archive of the editing commission. On its work, see *GU. Pribavlenie*, N. P. Druzhinin, *Obshchedostupnoe rukovodstvo k izucheniiu zakonov* (2nd edn., Spb., 1899), 32–59, A. Lykoshin, 'Pamiati A. A. Knirima (K istorii sostavleniia proekta grazhdanskago ulozheniia)', *ZhMIu* (1905), 10: 1–28, 'Redaktsionnaia kommisiia po sostavleniiu proekta grazhdanskago ulozheniia', *ZhGiUP* (1885), 8: 122–65, Z. [K. P. Zmirlov], 'Trudy kommisii po sostavleniiu novago grazhdanskago ulozheniia', *ZhGiUP* (1887), 2: 157–75, id., 'Trudy kommisii po sostavleniiu grazhdanskago ulozheniia', *ZhGiUP* (1890), 10: 109–19, 'Kommisiia po sostavleniiu grazhdanskago ulozheniia', *NV* (1894), 6737: 2, 'Neskol'ko zamechanii po povodu proekta grazhdanskago ulozheniia', *ZhIuOSU* (1895), 6: 85–104. For the draft code, see *GU* i–v.

[31] The first committee was established in 1906 but does not seem to have met, probably because the Holy Synod and several government ministries purposely delayed their responses. A second committee was formed in 1910. Admitting the political sensitivity of the proposals on family, property, and inheritance law, it spent two years revising those on contract, which were submitted to the Duma in 1913 but never enacted. Another committee was formed in May 1914, to discuss the remaining parts of the code, but never completed

outcome lay in the reformist character of the code, a character that had resulted both from the apparent objectives of Nabokov himself and from the composition of the commission.

It would appear that through the codification of Imperial civil law Nabokov sought not only to eliminate deficiencies in the law, but also to continue the programme of the reformist state officials who had drafted the judicial reform of 1864. A jurist with long judicial experience, Nabokov had been associated with reformist groups in the government since the 1850s, when he had helped Grand Duke Konstantin Nikolaevich to promote reform. As Minister of Justice, he defended the judicial reform against reactionary critics both within and outside the government until his dismissal in 1885.[32] Exploiting a brief resurgence of state reformism in the early 1880s, Nabokov gained approval for the project of codification by stressing the incongruence of existing civil law with post-emancipation social conditions and the obstacles to further economic growth created by the law. These circumstances, he accurately asserted, frequently compelled the courts to issue new legal norms, a point likely to provoke a reaction from an autocrat suspicious of the judiciary and jealous of his own authority. But even judicial action by itself could not adapt the law sufficiently to new conditions and needs, Nabokov continued, thereby making codification essential.[33]

Having obtained Imperial consent to proceed, Nabokov ensured a reformist orientation for the project by packing both the full committee and

its work. See *Obrazovannoe pri Ministerstve Iustitsii Osoboe Soveshchanie dlia obsuzhdeniia proekta grazhdanskago ulozheniia v sviazi s postupivshimi na onyi otzyvami vedomstv. Zhurnaly 1–23 (s 25 fevralia 1910 g. do 26 noiabria 1912 g.)* (Spb., n.d.) (HLL), i, ii, esp. i. 1–32, TsGIA F. 1405 op. 542 d. 670 l. 49, F. 1364 op. 15 d. 440 ll. 45, 86, 'Khronika', *Pravo* (1910), 22, col. 1415, and 45, col. 2723; (1912), 36, cols. 1939–40; (1913), 32, cols. 1880–2, and 33, col. 1933; (1914), 23, col. 1853, and 49, col. 3407; and (1915), 12, col. 905, and M. Ia. Pergament, 'Po povodu predstoiashchago vneseniia v gosudarstvennuiu dumu proekta grazhdanskago ulozheniia', *Pravo* (1913), 14, cols. 863–74.

[32] A nobleman and graduate of the élite Imperial School of Jurisprudence, Nabokov owned no land until given an estate in recognition of his long service. He was among the first senators in the Civil Cassation Department and became minister in 1878. See TsGIA F. 1364 op. 15 d. 728, A. F. Koni, *Ottsy i deti sudebnoi reformy. K piatidesiatiletiiu sudebnykh ustavov 1864–20 noiabria 1914* (Mos., 1914), 91–118, Zaionchkovskii, *Rossiiskoe samoderzhavie*, 84–7, 240–7, and H. Whelan, *Alexander III and the State Council: Bureaucracy and Counter-Reform in Late Imperial Russia* (New Brunswick, NJ, 1982), 159–67; on the 'konstantinovtsy', see W. B. Lincoln, *In the Vanguard of Reform: Russia's Enlightened Bureaucrats 1825–1861* (DeKalb, Ill., 1982), 141–8.

[33] See the references cited above in n. 29. Nabokov had used similar arguments a year earlier to gain permission to establish a commission to compose a new criminal code. See L. Engelstein, *The Keys to Happiness: Sex and the Search for Modernity in Fin-de-Siècle Russia* (Ithaca, NY, 1992).

TABLE 4.1. *Editing Commission of the Committee for the Compilation of a Civil Code, 1883–1906: Age*

	Members					
	Original[a]		Subsequent[b]		Total	
Year of Birth	No.	%	No.	%	No.	%
1820–5	2	29	0	0	2	10
1832–41	4	57	6	46	10	50
1847–51	0	0	4	31	4	20
1859–65	0	0	3	23	3	15
Unknown	1	14	0	0	1	5
TOTAL	7	100	13	100	20	100
Average Age at Appointment	48.3		47.7		47.9	

[a] Information for one member is unavailable.
[b] Does not include four members for whom information is unavailable, but who held juridical positions at the time of appointment.

Sources: TsGIA F. 1364 op. 15 d. 347, 400, 464, 471, 572, 588, 602, 670, 673, 722, 724, 767, 793, 848, 932, 1015; *GU. Pribavlenie k proektu grazhdanskago ulozheniia*, 57–61; *SChMIu, 1890*, ch. 1-aia, p. 58; *PS*.

the editing commission with jurists who had figured prominently in the preparation of the judicial reform of 1864. One of the original members of the editing commission had also served on the Tolstoi committee on ecclesiastical courts; all seven of the original members had received juridical training. Six had entered judicial service before 1864 and had spent their entire careers in judicial positions or in the Ministry of Justice; the seventh had taught civil law for thirty years before being appointed to the Civil Cassation Department. At the time of their appointment, four of the original members of the commission were serving as senators, and one as an assistant chief procurator, in the latter department. Another member was chairman of the Warsaw Court of Appeals, while the last had served as chairman of the Criminal Cassation Department before being appointed to the State Council. Although six of the original members of the commission belonged to the nobility, only one personally owned land. The seventh member was the son of a merchant (Tables 4.1–4.3).[34]

[34] *GU. Pribavlenie*, 2–5, 57–61, TsGIA F. 1364 op. 15 d. 471, 588, 602, 670, and 767, Lykoshin, 'Pamiati A. A. Knirima', M. M. Vinaver, *Nedavnee (vospominaniia i kharakteristiki)* (Ptgd., 1917), 165–91, and Koni, *Ottsy*, 91–118.

TABLE 4.2. *Editing Commission of the Committee for the Compilation of a Civil Code, 1883–1906: Social and religious background*

	Members					
	Original[a]		Subsequent[b]		Total	
	No.	%	No.	%	No.	%
SOCIAL ORIGIN						
Nobility	5	71	6	46	11	55
Official/officer's son	0	0	1	8	1	5
Merchant	1	14	3	23	4	20
Clergy	0	0	2	15	2	10
Unprivileged urban est. (*meshch.*)	0	0	1	8	1	5
Unknown	1	14	0	0	1	5
RELIGION						
Orthodox	3	43	8	62	11	55
Lutheran	1	14	3	23	4	20
Catholic	1	14	0	0	1	5
Unknown	2	29	2	15	4	20
TOTAL	7	100	13	100	20	100
Landowners	2[c]	29	2	15	4	20

[a] Information for one member is unavailable.
[b] Does not include four members for whom information is unavailable, but who held juridical positions at the time of appointment.
[c] Includes one member who personally owned no land but whose parents did.

Sources: TsGIA F. 1364 op. 15 d. 347, 400, 464, 471, 572, 588, 602, 670, 673, 722, 724, 767, 793, 848, 932, 1015; *GU. Pribavlenie k proektu grazhdanskago ulozheniia*, 57–61; *SChMIu, 1890*, ch. 1-aia, p. 58; *PS*.

The editing commission thus consisted originally of professional jurists who had helped to conceive and implement the judicial reform and who occupied positions at the apex of the system introduced by it.

The subsequent changes in the composition of the editing commission largely mirrored the development of the judiciary as a whole. The social background of members grew more diverse, the percentage of noble landowners declined, and graduates of university juridical faculties predominated increasingly over the graduates of such élite institutions as the Imperial School of Jurisprudence. Although both the age at the time of appointment and the length and character of prior service remained relatively constant,

TABLE 4.3. *Editing Commission of the Committee for the Compilation of a Civil Code, 1883–1906: Education and service*

	Members					
	Original		Subsequent[a]		Total	
	No.	%	No.	%	No.	%
EDUCATION						
Imperial School of Jurisprudence	3	43	2	15	5	25
Alexander Lycée	0	0	1	8	1	5
University Juridical Faculty	4	57	10	77	14	70
TOTAL	7	100	13	100	20	100
SERVICE						
Served in Civil Cassation Dept.:						
Prior to appointment[b]	4	57	9	69	13	65
After appointment	1	14	2	15	3	15
TOTAL[b]	5	71	11	84	16	80
Average years in juridical service prior to appointment	24.3[c]		21.8		22.6[c]	

[a] Does not include four members for whom information is unavailable, but who held juridical positions at the time of appointment.
[b] Most retained their position in the Civil Cassation Department while serving on the editing commission. Another member had served in the Criminal Cassation Department.
[c] Information for one member is unavailable.

Sources: TsGIA F. 1364 op. 15 d. 347, 400, 464, 471, 572, 588, 602, 670, 673, 722, 724, 767, 793, 848, 932, 1015; *GU. Pribavlenie k proektu grazhdanskago ulozheniia*, 57–61; *SChMIu, 1890*, ch. 1-aia, p. 58; *PS*.

the generational experiences of new members obviously also differed from those of the original members (Tables 4.1–4.3). Given this composition, it is not surprising that the proposals of the commission to a significant degree reflected the progressivist attitudes, values, and priorities that dominated Russian juridical writing after the early 1880s.

A more direct influence was exerted on the commission, however, by its three successive chairmen, Nikolai Stoianovskii, Aleksandr Knirim, and Iosif Karnitskii.[35] Stoianovskii and Knirim brought to the commission the reformist spirit that had animated the Alexandrine judicial reform. Both were noblemen who had graduated from the Imperial School of

[35] The original chairman, Staritskii, had resigned soon after the formation of the commission.

Jurisprudence and then served as judicial officials before playing a central role in the preparation and implementation of the latter reform. They had then been appointed, respectively, to the Criminal and the Civil Cassation Department of the Senate. More practitioner and politician than learned jurist, Stoianovskii frequently used his influential connections within the higher bureaucracy to shield the commission from criticism and dissolution until his death in 1900.[36] Knirim, by contrast, was the main operational and intellectual force behind the commission until he suffered a stroke in early 1901. Erudite, energetic, and dedicated to the law, he considered the code to be his crowning service to Imperial Russia. Also believing that Imperial Russian law was developing within a framework of universal legal principles, Knirim promoted the use of Western European models in the codification and revision of Imperial Russian law, both in the commission and through *The Journal of Civil and Criminal Law* (*Zhurnal Grazhdanskago i Ugolovnago Prava*), which he coedited.[37]

While often supporting the progressivist approach of Knirim, Karnitskii sometimes also provided the most conservative voice in the commission. A strong monarchist and Catholic from an eminent Polish noble landowning family, Karnitskii had served as a judge in Warsaw after completing his studies at the École de Droit in Paris. He had then been appointed an assistant chief procurator in the Civil Cassation Department, primarily to advise the high court on Polish law, which was based on the French civil code. This background led Karnitskii on the one hand to stress the protection of the rights of individuals and of religious and national minorities within the empire, and frequently also to advocate the adoption of Western European legal institutions, and on the other hand to defend the religious nature of marriage, ecclesiastical jurisdiction over divorce, and the pre-eminent authority of husbands and fathers. While his defence of ecclesiastical prerogatives undoubtedly derived from sincere religious convictions, it served also to protect Polish and Catholic interests against further encroachment by the predominantly Russian Orthodox Imperial state. Karnitskii had good reason to be sensitive to these issues, since his Polish nationality apparently blocked further advancement in his career.[38]

36 Stoianovskii owned a modest patrimonial estate. Koni, *Ottsy*, 91–118, Lykoshin, 'Pamiati A. A. Knirima', 6–9, and Wortman, *Legal Consciousness*, 217–18 and *passim*.

37 A Lutheran from the Baltic provinces, Knirim owned no land. He was a co-founder of the St Petersburg Juridical Society. Lykoshin, 'Pamiati A. A. Knirima', Vinaver, *Nedavnee*, 165–70, 172, and TsGIA F. 1364 op. 15 d. 602.

38 Karnitskii appears to have been the only Catholic member of the editing commission, although V. I. Golovinskii may also have been Catholic. Vinaver, *Nedavnee*, 171–91, TsGIA F. 1364 op. 15 d. 588, *ZhRKGU. Proekt knigi II (semeistvennoe pravo) (Zasedaniia Kommisii s 29 sentiabria 1899 g. po 19 ianvaria 1901 g.)* (Spb., 1903), *passim*, 'Zhurnal zasedaniia

Sensitivity to the social and political implications of codification also influenced the proposals and arguments of the commission. The public reaction to its formation had made these implications apparent to the commission from the outset. In meetings of juridical societies and in countless articles in legal journals progressivist and populist jurists had welcomed codification as an opportunity to overhaul the outdated character of existing Imperial civil law, particularly in the areas of family, property, and inheritance law.[39] Progressivist criticisms of existing law and demands for its reform had also been voiced by liberal publicists, who feared that a commission composed entirely of jurists would be too moderate and legalistic to introduce sufficiently far-reaching reforms and therefore demanded public participation in the process of codification.[40] Conversely, worried that the code would indeed be used in this manner,

grazhdanskago otdeleniia Iuridicheskago Obshchestva 24 fevralia 1896 g.', *ZhIuOSU* (1896), 10, pril., pp. 11–13, 'S.-Peterburgskoe iuridicheskoe obshchestvo', *Pravo* (1902), 22, cols. 1148–9, and 16, col. 1202, and *Gosudarstvennyi Sovet. Sessiia VIII. Kommisiia*, Doklad no. 2 (Spb., 1913) (HLL), special opinion by Karnitskii.

[39] In addition to the references cited above in Ch. 3 and below in Ch. 7, see Ia. I. Gurliand, *Kakiia uzakoneniia mestnykh zakonov, a ravno iz innostrannykh kodeksov zhelatel'no vnesti v nashe budushchee grazhdanskoe ulozhenie?* (Odessa, 1884), M. V. Shimanovskii, 'O proekte grazhdanskago ulozheniia i o tom uchastii, kotoroe mozhet okazat' Iuridicheskoe Obshchestvo v rabote sostavleniia proekta', *Protokol zasedaniia Iuridicheskago Obshchestva pri Novorossiiskom universitete No. 22, 24-go sentiabria 1882 goda, prilozhenie* (Odessa, 1882), 166–83, M. I. Malinin, *K voprosu ob osnovnykh printsipakh grazhdanskago prava i grazhdanskago ulozheniia* (Odessa, 1882), A. Filippov, 'O peresmotre Svoda nashikh grazhdanskikh zakonov', *IuV* (1882), 3/4: 570–83, K. D. Kavelin, 'Russkoe grazhdanskoe ulozhenie', *ZhGiUP* (1882), 8: 1–28, 9: 1–24; and (1883), 1: 33–66, and 2: 81–120, S. V. Pakhman, 'K voprosu o predmete i sisteme russkago grazhdanskago ulozheniia', *ZhGiUP* (1882), 8: 193–222, N. Zachinskii, 'Prakticheskiia zamechaniia na stat'i x t. ch. l zak. grazhd.', *IuV* (1883), 4: 640–64, K. K. Arsen'ev, 'Khronika—Razluchenie suprugov, kak neobkhodimyi institut brachnago prava', *VE* (1884), 3: 290–326, D. L., 'Proekt grazhdanskago ulozheniia', *Pravo* (1899), 38, cols. 1813–21, I. Tabashnikov, 'Zhelatel'noe otnoshenie budushchago grazhdanskago ulozheniia k nashemu obychnomu pravu', *ZhGiUP* (1885), 3: 67–107, K. P. Zmirlov, 'O nedostatkakh nashikh grazhdanskikh zakonov', *ZhGiUP* (1883), 3: 67–106, 9: 39–62, 10: 47–98; (1884), 1: 37–57, 5: 72–88, 6: 101–23; and (1885), 3: 31–51, A. M. Guliaev, *Proekt grazhdanskago ulozheniia* (Kiev, 1901), and id., *Edinstvo grazhdanskago prava i proekt grazhdanskago ulozheniia* (Kiev, 1903); this was the prevalent attitude among judicial officials and jurists responding to the commission's call for comments on the law, published in *ZNDGZ*.

[40] L. Z. Slonimskii, 'K voprosu o novom grazhdanskom kodekse', *VE* (1883), 8: 781–97, id., *O pozemel'noi sobstvennosti s tochki zreniia budushchago grazhdanskago ulozheniia* (Spb., 1885), *RM* (1883), 10: 77–80, *VE* (1882), 8: 726, and 9: 342–5; (1883), 3: 180–7; (1885), 12: 874–7; and (1887), 3: 369–73, A. A. Kvachevskii, 'Semeistvennyia otnosheniia i budushchee grazhdanskoe ulozhenie', *IuV* (1887), 2: 325–35, id., 'Chem zaderzhivaetsia delo grazhdanskago ulozheniia', *IuV* (1887), 1: 57–80, 'Po povodu proekta grazhdanskago ulozheniia', *RVed* (1895), 97: 3, and 104: 3, and 'Po brachnomu voprosu', *Nedelia* (1884), 22, cols. 731–3.

conservatives had argued that codification should only clarify existing legal relationships, not change them. Urging the commission to preserve traditional family, property, and inheritance laws, conservatives had cautioned also against borrowing what they considered to be inappropriate and socially disruptive foreign institutions.[41]

Attempting to deflect these latter criticisms in its final report in 1906, the editing commission tried to present its proposals in a conservative, utilitarian, and apolitical light. 'In general,' the commission asserted, 'the draft code does not depart from the principles of existing law without real necessity, and has as its goal only to correct, supplement, and renovate the law in correspondence with the demands of contemporary civil exchange.'[42] In reality, the proposals of the commission often broke radically with existing statutory law, precisely in such politically sensitive areas as property and inheritance law.[43] The commission contended further that the technical and substantive deficiencies of the Imperial *Digest of Laws* were so great in the field of civil law that some use of foreign models had been unavoidable. But it denied that such borrowing would disrupt existing social and economic relationships because 'the contemporary conditions of civil life in Russia and in other cultured countries, if not completely identical, in *many ways* closely approach one another'.[44] The deficiencies of Imperial Russian law in comparison with Western European law and the correspondence between Imperial Russian and Western European socio-economic life thus justified the use of Western European juridical norms and principles for the revision of Imperial Russian civil law.

This orientation led the editing commission to place the rights and inherent civil equality of individuals at the centre of the draft code. In sharp contrast to the inequality and the subordination to authority defined by the Imperial *Digest*, articles one and two of Book I of the code declared that

[41] A. Borzenko, 'Kommisiia dlia sostavleniia proekta russkago grazhdanskago ulozheniia', *MV* (1883), 238: 3, P. A. Matveev, *Krest'iane i Svod Zakonov (Po povodu sostavleniia novago Grazhdanskago Ulozheniia)* (Mos., 1883), A. A. Bashmakov, 'Institut rodovykh imushchestv pered sudom russkoi iurisprudentsii', *ZhMIu* (1897), 8, esp. 28–31, 52–3, id., *Ocherki prava rodovogo, nasledstvennago i obychnago* (Spb., 1911), 306–13, 352–3, 358–66, 421–3, L. A. Kasso, *Istochniki russkago grazhdanskago prava* (Mos., 1900), 13–15, and *ZNDGZ*, nos. 34, 41, 66, 320–3, 605, 607.

[42] *GU. Pribavlenie*, 45.

[43] On these areas of the draft code, see below, Ch. 8.

[44] *GU. Pribavlenie*, 47, emphasis original. In the introduction to its proposals on family law, however, the editing commission stated that this area of the law was least susceptible to such borrowing, in part because the gap between Imperial Russia and Western Europe was the greatest. *GU. Kn. 2-aia*, vol. i, pp. iv–v.

Each [individual] is recognized as being capable of having and acquiring civil rights, with respect both to the person and to property, from the day of birth until death.

Each person enjoys all civil rights without regard to sex, religious faith, origin, and status, except in those instances defined positively by law.[45]

These rights, moreover, were to enjoy greater legal security than heretofore. Article five of Book I asserted emphatically that '[n]o one can be deprived of [his or her civil] rights, or have [these] rights limited, except as the result of a criminal conviction by a court'.

Even sympathetic critics observed that these principles hardly corresponded to the conditions prevailing in an empire where society was still divided formally into legal estates.[46] They might have added that the attempt to secure the legal rights of individuals through the provision of clear statutory norms whose development was entrusted to an independent judiciary threatened the personalized authority and discretionary administrative power that constituted the essence of the autocratic system.[47] Indeed, at the very moment that the editing commission had issued its final report, special tribunals were sentencing thousands to prison, exile, and death under the emergency decrees of 1881, which permitted administrative suspension of all legal rights.

Hence the repeated assertion of the editing commission that the draft code sought merely to adjust the law to changed social and economic circumstances is questionable. To be fair, the members of the commission undoubtedly meant such claims sincerely, up to a point. After all, the commission members were not radical politicians but high civil officials who perceived themselves to be loyal state servants. Their faith in the objective character of juridical science, moreover, and their evolutionary conception of socio-legal development encouraged the belief that their

[45] *GU. Kn. 1-aia*, arts. 1–2 (with commentary); see also *Pribavlenie*, 50–1. By 'civil rights', the editing commission meant private rights in civil law, not political rights such as those of speech or assembly.

[46] e.g. see A. I. Vas'kovskii, 'Grazhdanskoe Ulozhenie', *SL* (1909), 4: 1–3, and 5: 7–8, Guliaev, *Edinstvo*, 126–33, and *SZPGU. Kn. 1-oi*, nos. 6, 9.

[47] The desire to preserve scope for the exercise of autocratic authority repeatedly complicated the process of codification in Imperial Russia, as did the tendency of codification to reconfigure authority. By adopting the abbreviated and generalized French, as opposed to the extended and detailed German, approach to codification (see *GU. Pribavlenie*, 50–1), the editing commission sought to expand the power of the judiciary at the expense of the state bureaucracy. It thereby differed from earlier efforts at codification in both Imperial Russia and Western Europe, where the reverse generally had been the case. On this question, see R. C. van Caenegem, *Judges, Legislators and Professors: Chapters in European Legal History* (Cambridge, 1987).

proposals constituted merely rational, socially and economically useful, and therefore necessary and impartial responses to the changing conditions and needs of the empire. But if these were not radical men, they were not unintelligent either. Their frequent criticisms of peasant practices and customs indicate their awareness of the gap between 'cultured' and peasant society. Members of the commission in fact hoped that the implementation of the draft code would help close this gap by assimilating the peasantry into the type of society that they believed was emerging in early twentieth-century Imperial Russia.[48] Similarly, their sensitivity to the need to address likely conservative criticisms demonstrates their awareness of the social and political implications of their proposals. In contrast to the recent German civil code, which had served as a model for the editing commission, the draft civil code therefore was not an institutionalization of the recent past, but an attempt to shape the future through the provision of a suitable legal framework.[49]

Members of the commission did not agree on every point, of course. While Karnitskii and Andrei Povorinskii, an assistant chief procurator of the Civil Cassation Department and a former appeals court judge, emphasized religious considerations, the former members of the high court Petr Iurenev and Sergei Lukianov stressed secular authority and the ideal of individual civil equality. In general, members of the commission drew on and revised Imperial Russian and foreign legal sources in accordance with the relative weight that each assigned to religion, national tradition, and allegedly universal socio-juridical norms and patterns in the process of Russian legal development. Despite their different conceptual approaches to the law, however, all members of the commission embraced both the affective ideal of the family and the ideal of a society regulated by rational and just laws.[50]

[48] See esp. *GU. Pribavlenie*, 38–41, and, in general, *GU* ii–iv.

[49] This is one of the main theses in M. John, *Politics and the Law in Late Nineteenth-Century Germany: The Origins of the Civil Code* (Oxford, 1989). The influence of the German civil code on its Imperial Russian counterpart is evident from the commentary accompanying the latter.

[50] *GU. Kn. 2-aia* (and earlier versions, *Proekt statei o soiuze brachnom s ob"iasneniiami (Pervaia redaktsiia)* (Spb., 1896) and *Proekt pravil ob uluchshenii polozheniia nezakonnorozhdennykh detei s ob"iasneniiami* (Spb., 1898) (both HLL)), TsGIA F. 797 op. 91–1898 d. 53 ll. 29–70, and *ZhRKGU. Proekt kn. II*. The first draft of the code on family law was completed by early 1896 and then discussed and revised in late 1899 and early 1901. At this time the commission consisted of eight members: Stoianovskii, Knirim, Karnitskii, Iurenev, Lukianov, Povorinskii, Kronid Malyshev, and Ernest Pirvits. Of this group, four were noblemen (two of whom owned land), two were sons of merchants, and two were from the clerical estate; four had graduated from university juridical faculties, three from the Imperial School of Jurisprudence, and one from the École de Droit in Paris; six had long judicial

Their proposals in the field of family law therefore proved to be highly controversial, even though these proposals were relatively moderate in comparison with other parts of the draft code. The editing commission attempted to redraw the boundary between the spiritual and the state domains by using the distinction between the external form and the internal relations of a marriage to expand secular authority over marriage and divorce. 'According to current law,' the commission asserted, ' "all matters relating to the verification of the conclusion of marriages, the recognition of their validity or invalidity, and divorce lie generally within the jurisdiction of ecclesiastical courts".' By contrast, '[t]he personal and property relations of spouses and children, which arise as the civil consequences of marriage, lie within the jurisdiction of the civil courts.'[51] Observance of the rules and procedures established by recognized ecclesiastical authorities thus was to remain necessary for both the conclusion and the dissolution of a marriage. Indeed, recognizing political reality, the commission asserted that 'the introduction in Russia of the general institution of civil marriage would be a rash and dangerous innovation'.[52] But once concluded, a marriage was to be primarily the concern of the state, which the commission contended had a duty to regulate the relations between spouses in accordance with the public good.[53]

Proceeding from this distinction, the draft code both defined the general laws that would govern the conclusion, annulment, and dissolution of all marriages and specified the particular rules applicable to members of each religious faith. Hence the code included both the Muslim acceptance of polygamy and the Catholic proscription of divorce. It also preserved existing limitations on inter-faith marriage.[54] Although religion therefore was still to exert a substantial influence over Imperial family law, Karnitskii,

careers that included periods in the Civil Cassation Department, one was an official in the Ministry of Justice, and one had taught civil law at St Petersburg University before becoming an official in the codification department of the State Council. TsGIA F. 1364 op. 15 d. 670, 793, and 1015, G. F. Shershenevich, *Nauka grazhdanskago prava v Rossii* (Kazan, 1893), 84–5, 137–42, *SChMIu, 1890*, ch. 1-aia, p. 58, and nn. 34, 36–8 above.

[51] *GU. Kn. 2-aia*, i. 239. On a similar intermingling of religious and secular norms in the draft criminal code, see Engelstein, *Keys to Happiness*, ch. 1.

[52] *GU. Kn. 2-aia*, i. 128. The commission referred explicitly to Pobedonostsev when making this statement. But recognizing that the institution of civil marriage had been introduced in practice in 1874 with respect to Old Believers, the commission preserved this arrangement and extended it to Baptists and other Protestant sects considered threatening by the Holy Synod and unacceptable by the government. Ibid., art. 85.

[53] *GU. Kn. 2-aia*, vol. i, pp. iv–v, and arts. 1–9, 12, 15–56, 59–88, 96–105, 216–23, 229, 260 (with commentary), and *ZhRKGU. Proekt kn. II*, nos. 1–2, 4–6.

[54] *GU. Kn. 2-aia*, arts. 12, 19–20, 45, 96–101, 157–9, 164, 232, and in general 1–107, 157–260.

in particular, sensed in the incorporation of all religious rules the seeds of future state encroachment. The ultimate result, Karnitskii feared, would be state control over the definition of canon law, since it was 'a mistake to assume that the transfer of individual rules from ecclesiastical to secular law will not influence their content'.[55]

Such fears were not groundless. Both under the guise of rationalization and clarification and in the name of the priority of state interest, the editing commission often changed the existing rules of individual religious faiths to accord with its own sense of justice, morality, and progress. The commission slightly modified Lutheran rules governing divorce, for example, because of 'the unclear formulation of individual articles in the Statute on Foreign Faiths and . . . the antiquated character of several of the rules contained in [this Statute]'.[56] Similarly, it abolished the right of a Jewish or Muslim husband to divorce his wife unilaterally because this right 'corresponds neither to the contemporary position of women nor to the equality of rights of both spouses with respect to divorce which is recognized by all jurisdictions'.[57] But perhaps most controversially, the commission revived earlier proposals to transfer control over the resolution of divorce cases to secular courts, arguing that

> [t]he transfer of such cases to secular courts in no way undermines the religious character of marriage as a sacrament and does not introduce civil marriage as an ordinary contract. . . . With such a transfer the ecclesiastical authority retains control over all that should belong to it in the present situation by right and by law, and from its jurisdiction is removed only that which by its essence is not related to the ecclesiastical domain and should be investigated on the general foundations of civil law.[58]

The legal relations within the family defined by the editing commission were no less controversial. The commission sought to realize both

[55] Ibid., i. 44, and in general 42–7, and *ZhRKGU. Proekt kn. II*, no. 27, pp. 248–53. The editing commission sought generally to promote the political, social, and economic integration of the empire through the promulgation of a uniform civil code. On this goal, see in particular *GU. Pribavlenie*, 41–7, *GU. Kn. 2-aia*, i. 42–52, and *ZhRKGU. Proekt kn. II*, no. 27.

[56] *GU. Kn. 2-aia*, i. 336, and 336–41 on the proposed changes themselves, contained in arts. 161, 186–9.

[57] Ibid., i. 272, and arts. 161, 190–6. Only Karnitskii resisted some of these proposals, probably in part because of their implications for Polish Catholics. But the editing commission also altered the rules governing the Orthodox population, e.g. by expanding the grounds for divorce, introducing formal marital separation, and eliminating the prohibition against remarriage in cases of divorce. Ibid., arts. 1–3, 141–56, 163, 172–3, 204, 207.

[58] Ibid., i. 316, and in general 272–4, 278–80, 289–90, 309–32, 341 (324–5 on the reasons for civil rather than criminal procedure) and arts. 160–2, 165–75, 181, 189, 217–18, 224, 233; see also *ZhRKGU. Proekt kn. II*, nos. 9, 27.

the ideal of legality and the affective ideal of the family promoted by progressivist and populist jurists. Hence the rights of individuals and the mutual obligations created by the natural and affective ties presumed to exist within the conjugal family were to replace unlimited obedience to superior authority within the patrilineal kin-group as the basis of Imperial family law. While acknowledging a need for authority within the family, the editing commission therefore sought to limit such authority narrowly to the amount necessary for the fulfilment of particular family functions and obligations. Conversely, those subordinate to authority were to enjoy the right to seek from the courts both protection from the abuse of authority and enforcement of the obligations owed them. Hence the exercise of authority within the family was to be constrained by legal norms and subjected to judicial oversight, with the courts having broad power to suspend or terminate the authority of a husband or parent if deemed necessary to secure the rights or welfare of individual family members. Since this conception of limited authority meant limited obedience, moreover, it further implied the right of individuals to act freely within a sphere of personal autonomy consisting of all matters not related directly to the family.

This approach resulted in the restriction of a husband's authority over his wife within the context of a reaffirmation of traditional gender roles. Hence, much like contemporary Orthodox writing and Western European and American law, the draft code declared that '[t]he deciding voice in family life belongs to the husband as the head of the family'.[59] And extending this principle to parental authority, the commission argued that '[i]n a union of two people, one of them must have dominance, and given the position in which women everywhere are placed, this dominance must belong to the father, in conformity with the fact that the deciding voice in questions of marital life belongs to the husband'.[60] But then contrasting this definition of a husband's authority with that contained in existing law, the commission asserted that 'the draft code speaks not of [unlimited] obedience or submission, but limits itself only to granting the husband the deciding voice in the event of disagreements with [his] wife on questions of family life'.[61] The commission therefore contended that its proposals constricted a husband's authority by confining it to the admittedly vague realm of family matters, a contention later challenged by progressivist critics.[62]

[59] *GU. Kn. 2-aia*, art. 109. [60] Ibid., i. 516, and art. 288. [61] Ibid., i. 162.

[62] On the relations between spouses, see esp. ibid., arts. 108–9, 197–9, 253–4, 288–9, 294, 302, 334 (and commentary, esp. pp. 490–2), and *Kn. 5-aia*, art. 423 and ii. 347–8; see also *ZhRKGU. Proekt kn. II*, nos. 1, 6, 16. For criticisms, see A. L. Borovikovskii, 'Brak i

The editing commission related the legal authority of a husband directly to his responsibility to provide materially for the family. 'The mutual position of spouses (parents) is not at all equal,' the commission asserted. On the contrary, 'the husband and father is the head of the household and primarily on him must lie the expenses for supporting the family'.[63] 'By nature and the general conditions of life,' the commission contended, 'a man has more possibilities than a woman to acquire the material means for the maintenance of the family.'[64] Having thus grounded male authority partly in unchanging nature and tied it to a consequent obligation to provide materially for the family, however, the commission tried to define the latter obligation in a way that facilitated its judicial enforcement.[65]

The rights and obligations of a wife conversely were to be based on her legal personality as an individual and her position as 'mistress of the household'.[66] Asserting that 'marriage does not affect the legal capacity of a wife in civil matters', the editing commission proposed to eliminate most of the controls of a husband over the activities of his wife, for example allowing a wife to engage in social and economic activities outside the home without the consent of her husband.[67] But then stating that '[t]he community of life established by marriage obligates spouses to [render each other] mutual assistance, which extends even to the labours necessary for the domestic economy and for obtaining the means of subsistence', the commission placed several conditional restrictions on a wife intended to ensure that her activities did not prevent her 'from fulfilling the obligations of a wife, mother, and mistress of the household'.[68] Hence the draft code obligated a wife to live with her husband except in the circumstances defined by law and to assist him in his economic activities when appropriate.[69] Similarly, a husband could

razvod po proektu Grazhdanskago Ulozheniia', *ZhMIu* (1902), 8: 8, id., 'Konstitutsiia sem′i po proektu Grazhdanskago Ulozheniia', *ZhMIu* (1902), 9: 3–10, 17–21, 39, [A. M. Evreinova], 'Zasedanie komissii Ushinskago', *Pravo* (1905), 16, col. 1325, *RM* (1902), 12: 428–30, Iurist, 'Lichnyia i imushchestvennyia otnosheniia suprugov', *RVed* (1902), 244: 2, and A. I. Zagorovskii, 'O proekte semeistvennago prava', *ZhMIu* (1903), 2: 83–4. See also A. Goikhbarg, 'Zamuzhniaia zhenshchina, kak neravnopravnaia lichnost′ v sovremennom grazhdanskom prave', *Pravo* (1914), 51, cols. 3545–8, and the speech by Tiutriumov reported in 'Khar′kovskoe iuridicheskoe obshchestvo', *Pravo* (1903), 3, cols. 177–9.

[63] *GU. Kn. 2-aia*, i. 506. [64] Ibid. 167.

[65] Ibid., arts, 110, 113–15, 121, 202, 257, 287–9, 305–6, 334 (with commentary).

[66] Ibid., art. 110. [67] *GU. Kn. 5-aia*, ii. 347.

[68] *GU. Kn. 2-aia*, i. 163 and *Kn. 5-aia*, art. 423.

[69] *GU. Kn. 2-aia*, art. 112. Although the draft code mutually obligated spouses to live together, it provided exceptions to this rule only for a wife and specifically obligated her to follow her husband. The obligation of wives to help with the household economy was directed specifically at the peasantry and poorer urban strata.

'demand the premature termination of a contract for personal employment concluded by [his] wife without his permission if this employment removes [his] wife from the home or diverts her from family obligations'.[70] In short, a wife was to be empowered to act as an autonomous individual, but subject to constraints imposed by family obligations conceived in terms that perpetuated traditional gender roles. The exceedingly unclear boundary between individual autonomy and collective obligation was to be determined in the first instance by agreement between a husband and wife, and in the event of their failure to agree, by the courts.

The property rights of married women defined by the draft code reflected the same tension between the wife's rights as an autonomous individual and her family obligations. Hence the editing commission retained the principle of separate property because

> [t]he separation of property and the independence of each spouse elevate the position of the wife and mother in the family, give her the possibility of herself exercising care for the material welfare of the family, and protect her property from the consequences of unwise or disordered dispositions by [her] husband which could be ruinous for the family.[71]

The right of a wife to control her own property thus remained bound up with the fulfilment of her family obligations. Hence the draft code obligated a wife who received unearned income to use an unspecified part of it for family expenses. It also included rules to protect the dowry of a wife against the actions of her husband while ensuring that, when so specified by the donors, the resources of the dowry were used to benefit the family.[72] The commission decided not to restrict a wife's use of her earned income, however, because a wife 'is not obligated to seek independent earnings to support [her] husband. If she has such earnings, then

[70] *GU. Kn. 5-aia*, art. 423, and ii. 347–8 for commentary. The editing commission intended a broad definition of what constituted permission from a husband, so that even previous behaviour by him could be construed as signifying such permission. Again, the rule was directed especially at the poorer urban strata.

[71] *GU. Kn. 2-aia*, i. 173.

[72] Ibid., arts. 110, 113–40, 197–9, 202, 257–8, 289 (with commentary, esp. pp. 167, 272–4, 278–9); see also *ZhRKGU. Proekt kn. II*, nos. 6–7. A woman also could be required to help support her former husband in limited circumstances after a divorce. Emphasis by the editing commission on the need to protect a wife and family from actions of the husband/father paralleled not only earlier arguments by such Russian jurists as Meier, but also those made by 19th-c. American and English advocates of separate property for women. See N. Basch, *In the Eyes of the Law: Women, Marriage and Property in Nineteenth-Century New York* (Ithaca, NY, 1982), 56–69, 115–20, 143–4, 152–3, 173–5, and L. Holcombe, *Wives and Property: Reform of the Married Women's Property Law in Nineteenth-Century England* (Toronto, 1983), 88–92, 148–9, 154–63.

these earnings justly remain freely at her disposal.'[73] The commission thus sought to provide material independence for a wife, but in a way that reinforced her traditional role.[74]

The same can be said of the editing commission's attempt to protect wives against abuse by a husband through an expansion of the grounds for divorce and the legalization of marital separation. Of course, neither change in the law applied solely to wives. But the arguments used by the commission and the grounds proposed for divorce and separation related largely to the behaviour of husbands. With respect to divorce, the draft code added severe cruelty or mistreatment as grounds for the dissolution of a marriage for all Imperial subjects except those belonging to the Catholic Church. Such behaviour, the commission argued, 'not only eliminates the possibility of [the spouses] living together, but also delivers a severe, deep, and indelible shock to the marital union'.[75] In part to ensure that in circumstances where divorce or separation was permitted a wife would be able to exercise her rights, the draft code obligated a (former) husband to continue to support his (former) wife, provided that she was found to be essentially an innocent victim.[76]

But anticipating opposition to further expansion of the grounds for divorce, the editing commission relied primarily on marital separation to protect wives from abuse or neglect by their husbands and to resolve marital discord in general. Asserting that '[t]he obligation of spouses to live together derives from the very essence of a marriage', the commission argued that none the less 'frequently there are instances when . . . living

[73] *GU. Kn. 2-aia*, i. 167. The latter rule was introduced in France in 1907. See T. Zeldin, *France 1848–1945: Ambition and Love* (Oxford, 1979), 356–7, and C. G. Moses, *French Feminism in the Nineteenth Century* (Albany, NY, 1984), 229–30.

[74] On this point, see esp. the discussion in *ZhRKGU. Proekt kn. II*, no. 6.

[75] *GU. Kn. 2-aia*, i. 297, and arts. 163, 172–3, 202 (with commentary, esp. pp. 296–8). Mistreatment and cruelty also constituted grounds for separation for Catholic subjects. Ibid., arts. 208–15.

[76] Ibid., arts. 147, 150, 176–7, 179, 197–9, 202 (with commentary, esp. pp. 287–9, 336–7, 387); see also arts. 157–9, *ZhRKGU. Proekt kn. II*, no. 27, and TsGIA F. 797 op. 91–1898 d. 53 ll. 34–70, pp. 33–7. For conflicting views by two members of the commission, Karnitskii and Pirvits, see 'Zhurnal zasedaniia grazhdanskago otdeleniia Iuridicheskago Obshchestva 24 fevralia 1896 g.', *ZhIuOSU* (1896), 10, pril., pp. 8–22. But either spouse could be denied support because of laziness or a depraved way of life, which gave a (former) husband limited control over the actions of his (former) wife, and in cases of separation the amount of support for a wife judged to be at fault was reduced. The concept of fault and the view of marital dissolution chiefly as a means to protect innocent women also underlay the rejection by the editing commission of mental illness, insanity, and mutual adultery as grounds for divorce and influenced its proposals regarding child custody in cases of divorce and separation.

together is unbearable'.[77] In such instances, 'separation can sometimes be preferable to divorce for an offended spouse because it can always be transformed through reconciliation into coresidence'. Hence, the commission contended, obviously in response to criticisms of earlier proposals, separation was 'not a threat to marriage, but a defence of its sanctity and a protection of its essence'. According to the commission, such considerations had led the government repeatedly since the 1860s to discuss the legalization of marital separation and both the courts and the state administration increasingly to allow such separation, despite its statutory proscription. 'At the present time', the commission concluded, 'it therefore is possible to speak properly only of the legalization of an existing fact.'[78] The commission proposed to allow formal separation for a number of reasons, including mistreatment, mental cruelty, perpetual drunkenness, abandonment, prodigality, and shameful or dissolute behaviour.[79] In the view of the commission, civil courts should have jurisdiction over such cases because they involved the internal relations of a marriage. The commission claimed, moreover, that all relevant questions of fact 'undoubtedly can be resolved most correctly only by a civil court, with the participation of the parties involved and through the use of adversarial procedure'.[80]

Citing the relationship between authority and obligation, the editing commission also limited parental authority, thereby increasing protection of the personal rights of children. '[I]t cannot be doubted', the commission asserted, 'that parental authority, whose goal is to give children the physical, mental, and moral development needed of a citizen, exists in the interests not of parents, but of children (and indirectly through them, of society).'[81] The draft code consequently linked the power of parents to control the actions of their children and to discipline them to the obligation of parents to support and educate their children and to prepare them for productive citizenship.[82] The actions of parents therefore could be

[77] *GU. Kn. 2-aia*, i. 207, 208.

[78] Ibid. 233, and in general, TsGIA F. 797 op. 91–1898 d. 53 ll. 34–70, pp. 1–32, 40–2, 56–9, 64–7.

[79] *GU. Kn. 2-aia*, arts. 112, 141–56 (with commentary) and, more completely, TsGIA F. 797 op. 91–1898 d. 53 ll. 29–70. See also *ZhRKGU. Proekt kn. II*, nos. 6, 11–13, and the views of Karnitskii in 'Zhurnal zasedaniia grazhdanskago otdeleniia'.

[80] *GU. Kn. 2-aia*, i. 240. [81] Ibid. 514.

[82] Ibid., arts. 3, 148–52, 197–9, 253–4, 284–302 (with commentary, esp. pp. 409–92), and *Kn. 5-aia*, arts. 396–7, 422; see also *ZhRKGU. Proekt kn. II*, nos. 15, 16, 17, 22. Hence parents exercised control over children with respect to residence, employment, the conclusion of contracts, and the use of their own property, and parents could still have a child confined, but only in an institution for juveniles, not for more than three months, and only with the approval of the local guardianship agency. *GU. Kn. 2-aia*, art. 297.

subjected to review and constraint, to the point where parents could be deprived of their authority and even of custody of their children. Empowering the courts to override both parental wishes and legally defined preferences when determining the custody of children in cases of divorce and separation, for example, the commission declared that 'the welfare of the children of course must be kept chiefly in view'.[83] And justifying the proposed power of local guardianship agencies to deprive abusive or neglectful parents of the custody of their children, the commission asserted that '[t]he state and society have a substantial interest in the fostering of good morals in the younger generation and in its health and morality not being subjected to danger'.[84] Moreover, arguing that '[w]ith respect to a person who has reached an age of maturity, parental influence can have the significance only of advice, the submission to which depends on the persuasiveness of the parents' arguments', the commission proposed to terminate parental authority altogether once children attained the age of majority (21) or, in the case of consent to marriage, 25.[85]

These arguments and proposals reflected the belief that parental care of children represented both a natural and a social obligation. This belief, coupled with its general concern for the rights of individuals, led the editing commission to propose the introduction of substantial rights for illegitimate children. Branding existing law as inadequate and incongruent 'with contemporary humanitarian views', the commission argued that 'the improvement of the legal position of extramarital children, and in particular the establishment of family rights between a child and a mother, is necessary not only in the interests of separate individuals, who bear no guilt for their origins, but also in the interests of society, on which a class of people deprived of family rights lays a heavy moral and economic burden'.[86] The commission emphasized the relationship of such children with their mother because '[f]rom a natural point of view, an extramarital child is as close to his *mother* as a legitimate child'. The rights of extramarital children had to be secured, however, 'without detriment to the sanctity of marriage and the significance of the legitimate family', by

[83] Ibid. i. 250, and in general 249–55, 381–3, 427–8 and arts. 148, 197–8, 253–4. As 'head of the family', a father had a preferential right to the custody of children in the event of disagreement between the spouses. But a court could award custody to the mother if it found the husband to be at fault or such custody to be in the best interests of the children.

[84] Ibid. 541, and in general 540–4 and arts. 305–6.

[85] Ibid. 10, and in general arts. 3, 284–5, 289, 293. The extension of parental authority beyond the age of majority in the event that a child continued to live with his or her parents at the latter's expense emphasizes the link between obligation and authority which underlay the proposals of the editing commission.

[86] Ibid. 560, 573.

which was meant chiefly the family of the father.[87] Hence the draft code granted extramarital children rights nearly identical to those possessed by legitimate children with respect to their mother. By contrast, they had a right only to support from their father, and only when their own resources combined with those of their mother were inadequate. Following French law, however, the code allowed a father voluntarily to expand his legal obligations and rights by formally recognizing his extramarital children.[88] The code also facilitated the adoption and the legalization of extramarital children, in the latter case in order to persuade 'the participants in an illicit union to transform it into a marital union' and thereby create for their children a family, which in turn would have 'beneficial meaning for both public morality and state interests'.[89]

The editing commission thus believed no less strongly than conservative officials or Orthodox Church leaders that the stability of the family was of critical importance for society and the state. Indeed, asserting that the present suffered from 'a weakening of family ties and a consequent increase in the number of instances in which children, the elderly, and other relatives unable to work are left without assistance', the commission argued that 'the development of begging and of a proletariat compel turning serious attention to measures to eliminate this evil, among the most important of which is to broaden the obligation of family members mutually to assist one another in [the event of] poverty and need'.[90] The draft code therefore obligated 'first of all . . . the spouse, and then in order of relationship . . . descendant [relatives], ascendant [relatives], brothers and sisters, and relatives-in-law of the first degree' to support a person in need.[91] While this legal reinforcement of the mutual obligations between family members clearly stemmed in part from a desire to counteract the negative effects of rapid economic and urban growth, it also

[87] Ibid. 573, emphasis original. The editing commission followed long-standing practice in assigning responsibility for illegitimate children primarily to their mothers. See D. L. Ransel, *Mothers of Misery: Child Abandonment in Russia* (Princeton, NJ, 1988), 39, 73, 79, 91, 97–103, 108–10, 129.

[88] *GU. Kn. 2-aia*, arts. 148–52, 311–36 (with commentary), and more completely, *Proekt pravil ob uluchshenii polozheniia nezakonnorozhdennykh detei* (HLL), ll. 1–15, 32–5, and arts. 1–33 (with commentary); see also *ZhRKGU. Proekt kn. II*, nos. 15, 18, 20.

[89] *Gu. Kn. 2-aia*, i. 630, and in general arts. 337–66 (with commentary); see also arts. 57, 229. These provisions extended a law enacted in 1891 which had allowed the legalization of extramarital children in limited circumstances. See *OGS*, *1891*, 502–58, *3PSZ* xi (1891), pt. 1, no. 7525, pp. 111–14, *SZ* x, pt. 1 (prod. 1891), arts. 132–3, 144^{1}, $145–156^{7}$, and Martynov, *Uzakonenie i usynovlenie*.

[90] *GU. Kn. 2-aia*, ii. 47.

[91] Ibid., art. 377, and in general arts. 137, 291, 377–91 (with commentary).

derived from the sense of the family as a moral community that bound its individual members as well as nurtured their individuality.[92] The draft civil code was meant not merely to recognize, but to enforce this ideal of the family.

The editing commission thus unavoidably perpetuated tsarist traditions of state paternalism and legal instrumentalism even while breaking sharply with the past. Although attempting to take account of social and cultural difference, the commission used the draft code to create a legal framework through which tsarist society could be reshaped in accordance with the values and ideals of moderate and progressivist Christian members of the educated and professional élite. The code, moreover, necessarily reflected the particular interests of jurists, whose authority and social standing would gain enormously from the shift of control over family matters to the courts. But herein also lay the radical character of the code, which through its emphasis on the rights of individuals and the limitation of authority proposed fundamentally to alter the existing relationship between the individual, established authority, and law. For this reason, proposals that in turn-of-the-century Western Europe or the United States would have appeared moderate or even conservative, in Imperial Russia had revolutionary implications.[93]

Legislative Compromise and Continued Impasse

Given these implications, it is not surprising that the proposed code on family law shared the fate of the draft code as a whole. None the less, a few sections of the code on family law did undergo legislative review. In

[92] See also the reformulation of inheritance law by the commission, discussed in Ch. 8 below. The provision also owed much technically to German law.

[93] For the reaction of jurists to the draft code, see I. V. Gessen, 'Budushchee grazhdanskoe ulozhenie. (Po povodu proekta semeistvennago prava)', *Pravo* (1902), 26, cols. 1251–9, Borovikovskii, 'Brak i razvod', id., 'Konstitutsiia', id., 'Novyi zakonoproekt ob uluchshenii polozheniia nezakonnorozhdennykh detei', *ZhMIu* (1899), 8: 1–35, V. Volzhin, 'Zamechaniia na semeistvennoe pravo po proektu Redaktsionnoi Komissii', *SG* (1902), 38: 4–6, 39: 3–5, 41: 3–4, 43: 3–4, and 44: 4–6, G. Petrov, 'Brak i sem'ia', *Iurist* (1903), 18, cols. 613–17, I. Nadezhdin, 'Vlast' roditelei nad det'mi', *Iurist* (1902), 8, cols. 278–85, I. M. Tiutriumov, 'Ogranichenie roditel'skoi vlasti', *Iurist* (1903), 13, cols. 437–42, id., 'Pravo roditelei nakazyvat' detei lisheniem svobody', *Iurist* (1903), 16, cols. 539–43, 'Proekt o razreshenii razdel'nago zhitel'stva suprugov', *SG* (1900), 3: 2–4, 4: 1–3, 5: 1–4, and 6: 1–3, 'Proekt ob uluchshenii polozheniia nezakonnorozhdennykh detei', *SG* (1900), 8: 1–3, 9: 1–3, 10: 1–3, 11: 1–3, and 12: 1–3, 'Proekt semeistvennago prava grazhdanskago ulozheniia', *SG* (1902), 28: 1–3, 29: 1–3, 30: 1–3, 31: 1–3, 32: 1–4, 33: 1–3, and 35: 1–2, 'Po povodu zakonoproekta o vnebrachnykh detei', *SG* (1901), 49: 1–3, 'Proekt pravil o razdel'nom zhitel'stve suprugov', *IuG* (1899), 89: 1–2, and *SZPGU. Kn. 2-oi*. For other reactions, see n. 122 below.

response to a request from the State Council, in 1898 the editing commission submitted its proposals regarding extramarital children and marital separation for consideration on the grounds that these areas of the law urgently required revision. And beginning in 1901, the Ministry of Justice responded to the repeated attempts of the Holy Synod to reform the rules governing divorce by proposing adoption of the relevant parts of the draft code.[94] While the conflicts provoked by these proposals reflect the way in which different groups used family law to promote competing visions of socio-political authority, their fate reflects the ability of conservatives and the church to control legislative development of the law, for the more directly a proposal appeared to conservative officials and the Holy Synod to threaten the existing basis of socio-political authority or the institutional authority of the church, the more difficult it was to enact.

Being the least threatening in this regard, the proposals to improve the rights of extramarital children were adopted relatively quickly. Progressivist and populist jurists and the liberal press endorsed the proposals, considering them to be both just and a step towards the full legal enshrinement of the affective ideal of the family.[95] In contrast to the past, Orthodox Church leaders did not oppose the proposals, perhaps hoping the new law would alleviate what they believed was a growing problem of child abandonment.[96] Nor did conservative officials object to the proposals in principle, perhaps because they assigned primary responsibility for extramarital children to the mother and in some cases actually reduced the obligations of the father.

Even without significant opposition, however, the proposals still underwent conservative revision in the State Council before being enacted

[94] The remaining proposals on family law were published in 1902. See *GU. Pribavlenie*, 51–2, Koni, *Ottsy*, 114–15, TsGIA F. 797 op. 91–1898 d. 53 ll. 34–70, *Proekt pravil ob uluchshenii polozheniia nezakonnorozhdennykh detei* (HLL), *GU. Kn. 2-aia*, arts. 311–36, and the references cited below in the discussion of divorce.

[95] In addition to the references cited below in n. 97, see 'Proekt ob uluchshenii polozheniia nezakonnorozhdennykh detei', 'Po povodu zakonoproekta', A. I. Zagorovskii, *O vnebrachnykh detiakh po novomu zakonu (3 iiunia 1902 g.) v sviazi s postanovleniiami o nikh zapadno-evropeiskikh grazhdanskikh kodeksov* (Odessa, 1903), and E. P. De-Turzhe Turzhanskaia, *Zhenskii vopros v sviazi s novym zakonom o 'nezakonnorozhdennykh'* (Smolensk, 1902).

[96] R. Stites, *The Women's Liberation Movement in Russia: Feminism, Nihilism and Bolshevism, 1860–1930* (Princeton, NJ, 1978), 165, 178–80. See also Borovikovskii, 'Novyi zakonoproekt', 31–5, V. Volzhin, 'O protivozakonnom sozhitii', *IuV* (1890), 4, esp. 649–50, *Trudy pervago vserossiiskago zhenskago s″ezda pri Russkom Zhenskom (Vzaimno-Blagotvoritel'nom) Obshchestve v S-Peterburge 10–16 dekabria 1908 goda* (Spb., 1909), 62, and Ransel, *Mothers*, who argues (p. 128) that, following the rate of illegitimacy, the incidence of abandonment in fact began to decline in the early 20th c.

in 1902. The State Council agreed with the editing commission both that existing law constituted an unjust remnant of a lower level of social and moral development and that extramarital children were linked to their parents, particularly their mother, by natural bonds and mutual obligations. But, influenced by Pobedonostsev, the State Council argued that reform of the law should be undertaken in conformity with national traditions in order to avoid social disruption. Threats to the reputation and authority of the father or to the stability of a legitimate family in particular had to be avoided. While accepting the basic proposals, the State Council therefore reduced the rights granted to extramarital children with respect to both parents. It also rejected the formal recognition of extramarital children by their father as an inappropriate foreign institution. To achieve comparable results in ways deemed more consistent with national legal traditions, the legitimization or unrestricted adoption of extramarital children by their parents was permitted instead.[97]

By contrast, the proposals to legalize marital separation and to facilitate and partially secularize divorce were more controversial and difficult to enact because they directly challenged the patriarchal conception of authority within the family and the institutional authority of the Orthodox Church. In this respect, the basic issues raised by the proposals had remained unchanged since the 1860s. But the different conceptions of social and political order implicit in the different ideals of the family articulated during the reform era had become more explicit by the late nineteenth century as the political implications of the Alexandrine reforms and the social effects of post-emancipation economic development

[97] *ODGS, 1901–1902*, 735–76, *3PSZ* xxii (1902), pt. 1, no. 21566, pp. 492–5, and I. V. Gessen, *Uzakonenie, usynovlenie i vnebrachnyia deti* (2nd edn., Spb., 1910), pp. vi–vii; see also A. G. Gasman, 'Vnebrachnyia deti na zapadnykh okrainakh i v imperii', *ZhMIu* (1914), 5: 1–66, 6: 1–84, and 8: 1–47, and, in general, Ransel, *Mothers*, 84–129. Unfortunately, the published account does not record any disagreements that occurred in the final discussion of the law in the State Council. While condemning the more conservative amendments to the law, progressivist and populist jurists and liberal writers none the less welcomed the improved rights for extramarital children that it introduced. See I. V. Gessen, 'Novyi zakon o vnebrachnykh detiakh', *Pravo* (1902), 28, cols. 1315–27, and 29, cols. 1352–63, I. M. Tiutriumov, 'Polozhenie detei ot nedeistvitel′nykh brakov', *Iurist* (1902), 1, cols. 14–17, id., 'Vnebrachnye deti', *Iurist* (1902), 2, cols. 41–5, K. A. Dvorzhitskii, 'Vne braka', *SG* (1902), 29: 2–4, I. Sobolev, 'O defektakh v zakone ot 3-go iiunia 1902 goda ob uluchshenii polozheniia nezakonnorozhdennykh detei', *SG* (1902), 51: 5–6, 'Novyi zakon ob uluchshenii polozheniia nezakonnorozhdennykh detei', *SG* (1902), 27: 1–2, 'Zakon 3 iiunia o vnebrachnykh detiakh i proekt sootvetstvuiushchei emu chasti grazhdanskago ulozheniia', *SG* (1902), 41: 1–3, Iurist, 'Vrednyi patriotizm', *Pravo* (1902), 32, cols. 1460–2, 'Kievskoe iuridicheskoe obshchestvo', *Pravo* (1902), 49, cols. 2425–7, *RM* (1902), 8: 200–1, and *Trudy 1-ago zhenskago s″ezda*, 62, 345–6, 348, 377–8, 825; see also A. Golubtsov, 'Po povodu zakona 3 iiunia 1902 g.', *ZhMIu* (1903), 2: 193–6.

became apparent. Moreover, the continued expansion and social and occupational diversification of the educated strata of society had resulted in a more complex ideal of the family, particularly among those who stressed the combination of affective relations, mutual obligations, and individual rights and security. Hence political conflict over revision of the law now encompassed a broader array of competing interests and goals than previously.

Women, especially from the educated strata of society, for example, demanded an expansion of the possibility of formal marital dissolution to enhance their personal security and legal status within the family and to increase their legal rights generally. While agreeing on the need to expunge all traces of patriarchy from existing family law, however, female critics of the law differed sharply over how the family should be restructured. Whereas a few such critics questioned the desirability of the family, most appear to have subscribed essentially to the same affective ideal as progressivist or populist jurists. Many female critics in fact used the protective attitude towards women and the idealization of maternity embedded in this ideal to justify increased access to marital dissolution.

In a pamphlet on marital ethics published in 1896, for example, one Serafima Argamakova drew on Western European medical and scientific literature, as well as on several Russian cases, to describe the physical, psychological, and moral dangers to which women and children were exposed by drunken and syphilitic husbands. 'Why', she exclaimed, 'has there still not been found an effective and simple means to protect a wife and family from such misfortune. That a woman must be given the freedom to choose whether to live with such a husband or to leave him has been proven by all that has been written recently on the influence of drunkenness on posterity.'[98] While justifying the facilitation of marital dissolution primarily in terms of protection from abuse and from physical or moral infection, however, Argamakova also viewed such legal change as a way to improve the position of women generally. 'I do not wish to impose on a woman the *petit-bourgeois* ideal by which a woman is consumed completely by marriage and the family,' she declared, 'but to assign her a prominent role in the task of social education.' And noting her grief at the death of her own daughter, Argamakova professed that she had 'found comfort only in knowing that fate had spared her [i.e. her

[98] S. Argamakova, *K voprosam etiki v sovremennom brake* (Polotsk, 1895), 9. Familiar with relevant Western European medical, scientific, and philosophic literature, Argamakova also appears to have had some clinical experience.

daughter], as a woman, from the multitude of degradations and sufferings that awaited her in society and in family life'.[99] Hence for Argamakova, the 'enslavement' of a wife to a drunken or syphilitic husband constituted merely an extreme example of the suffering that resulted generally from the inferior legal rights and subordinate status accorded women in the family and society. 'The church and school, of course, can to a significant extent help to ease the fate of slaves,' she asserted, 'but only positive law is capable of abolishing slavery.'[100]

The moderate feminist groups that became active in Imperial Russia after the late nineteenth century adopted a similar position. 'Our law deprives a woman even in the area specifically assigned to her, the family, of the most primitive human rights, the right to free movement and the right to labour, and completely subordinates her to the will of [her] husband,' declared Anna Shabanova, a co-founder and leader of the Russian Women's Mutual Philanthropic Society, at the First (and only) All-Russian Women's Congress held in St Petersburg in December 1908. 'Questions of marriage, the right to divorce, and the support of children fall in all their severity on a woman.'[101] Increased access to formal marital dissolution as part of a general reform of family law therefore constituted an important goal of the Society.

The same reformist approach to the family was followed even by women who advocated more extensive social and political change. Mariia Blandova, for example, a member of the radical Russian League of Equal Rights for Women, argued at the Women's Congress that 'if a wife is not personally free, if she does not have the right to dispose of her own person', then even her right to separate property could not protect her from an abusive husband and this right itself was 'no more than a fiction'. Blandova therefore maintained that 'the complete arbitrary authority of a husband must be limited by law for the sake both of humanity and justice and of the proper ordering and the mitigation of morals' and that to this end 'the facilitation of divorce . . . is an urgent need of society'. None the less, Blandova believed that divorce should not be undertaken lightly.

[99] Ibid. 53, 43. [100] Ibid. 37.

[101] *Trudy 1-ago zhenskago s″ezda*, 11, and 9–12 in general. Born in 1848 and a noblewoman, Shabanova had evinced radical views during the 1860s and had been imprisoned briefly for her participation in an illegal sewing co-operative. One of the first women medical students in Imperial Russia, she was a respected paediatrician as well as a feminist activist. See L. H. Edmondson, *Feminism in Russia 1900–1917* (Stanford, Calif., 1984), 9, 21, 28, 90, 147, 161–70, and Stites, *Women's Liberation Movement*, 194–7, 229–30, 281–3, 297–8, 307–8.

Regardless of the law, she asserted, 'spouses must first bear and suffer much before deciding to divorce'.[102] The predominance at the congress of views such as those expressed by Blandova and Shabanova led the delegates overwhelmingly to endorse the legalization of marital separation and the relaxation of divorce laws.[103]

The revisions of the law demanded by members of such feminist organizations as the Mutual Philanthropic Society and the League of Equal Rights therefore substantively were very similar, and often identical, to those being demanded by male critics of the law. This similarity stemmed partly from the similarity in social and occupational characteristics and the formal and informal relations between female and male advocates of legal reform. Like the feminist movement generally at this time, both the Mutual Philanthropic Society and the League of Equal Rights were composed predominantly of women from the well-to-do, educated, and professional strata of society. Frequently married to members of the professions or to state officials, these women themselves often were pursuing professional careers.[104] Members of feminist organizations therefore often shared with their male counterparts both comparable training and many of the same professional and personal frustrations caused by restrictive tsarist policies. Moreover, the philanthropic and civic activities of feminists often included co-operation with male activists, and after 1905 members of feminist organizations had ties with several of the newly founded and male-dominated political parties and Duma factions.[105] Despite important differences, particularly over the political

[102] *Trudy 1-ago zhenskago s"ezda*, 364, and 344, 359–67 in general. Blandova earlier had been active in the radical feminist Union of Equal Rights for Women. See Edmondson, *Feminism*, 134.

[103] See *Trudy 1-ago zhenskago s"ezda*, 11, 60–2, 344–8, 359–67, 374–86, 494–5, 512–19, 549–57, 589, 742, 754–60, 768, 825; on the Congress, see Edmondson, *Feminism*, 83–106, B. Glinskii, 'Pervyi zhenskii vserossiiskii s"ezd', *Istoricheskii Vestnik* (1909), 1: 384–407, and A. Ermanskii, 'Vserossiiskii zhenskii s"ezd', *Sovremennyi Mir* (1909), 1: 103–12. For other groups and opinions, see [Evreinova], 'Zasedanie', M. B., 'Russkie otgoloski', *ZhD* (1899), 8: 77–8, M. Ia. Pergament, 'K predpolagaemoi reforme brakorazvodnago protsessa', *Soiuz Zhenshchin* (1908), 5/6: 15–18, Stites, *Women's Liberation Movement*, 170–1, 180–1, 185–8, 202, 229–30, and Edmondson, *Feminism*, 38, 71–2, 95–8, 139–42.

[104] The majority of delegates to the 1908 Women's Congress, for example, conformed to this pattern. Even at its height, the membership of neither the Women's Mutual Philanthropic Society (est. 1895) nor the League of Equal Rights (successor to the Union of Equal Rights, est. 1905) ever exceeded about 2,000. On these organizations, and on Russian feminism in general at this time, see Edmondson, *Feminism*, Stites, *Women's Liberation Movement*, 191–232, R. L. Glickman, *Russian Factory Women: Workplace and Society, 1880–1914* (Berkeley, Calif., 1984), 229–32, 242–80, and *Trudy 1-ago zhenskago s"ezda*, 586–93.

[105] Edmondson, *Feminism*, chs. 3–7.

rights of women, the ideals and demands of feminist and progressivist, populist, and other critics of Imperial family law consequently overlapped and reinforced one another to a considerable extent.[106]

Other women, by contrast, rejected this reformist approach and challenged the very institutions of marriage and the family. Criticizing the position of women such as Shabanova and Blandova at the 1908 Women's Congress, for example, the radical feminist Anastasiia Chebotarevskaia argued that their proposals could not resolve the woman question because they 'in no way shake the basis of the bourgeois *state* or undermine its holy "foundations", *the bourgeois family and private property*'. '[I]n addition to the political and juridical equality of women, who find themselves in dual slavery, economic and sexual,' Chebotarevskaia therefore demanded '*the elimination of the institution of marriage* and the establishment of both the *social upbringing* of children and a *socialized economic system* (which includes the *domestic* economy)'. Only through such changes, Chebotarevskaia claimed, could 'women, particularly progressive thinking [women]', resolve the 'choice between a profession and motherhood' which she alleged economic growth compelled them increasingly to make.[107] Women were to be enabled to play a more active and self-fulfilling role in society, in other words, not through the restructuring of the family in accordance with the ideal of motherhood, but through the redefinition of the maternal role of women through the socialization of the family. Clearly, for women no less than for men, the revision of family law served as both a medium for ideological redefinition and a means for the pursuit of ideological ends during the late Imperial period.

A comparable process occurred within the medical profession, where the articulation of ideological ideals intersected with an attempt by physicians both to define the boundaries of their professional authority and to use such authority to establish a right to participate in the formulation of state policy. Influenced by discussions in Germany over the new Imperial civil code, physicians in Imperial Russia began to agitate for changes in divorce law in 1896, both at a congress of psychiatrists in Kiev and at the

[106] e.g. see Glinskii, 'Pervyi zhenskii s"ezd', 385–6, the reports by Petrazhitskii and Gessen in *Trudy 1-ago zhenskago s"ezda*, 13–17, 754–60, Stites, *Women's Liberation Movement*, 204–5, 209, and Edmondson, *Feminism*, 31–2, 40–6, 49–50, 54, 59–63.

[107] *Trudy 1-ago zhenskago s"ezda*, 550, 554, emphasis original, and 549–57 in general. A writer in her own right, Chebotarevskaia was the wife of the symbolist poet Fedor Sologub. Her views on the family were influenced strongly by the ideas of the German Marxist and social democratic leader August Bebel, hence their similarity to those of Russian social democratic women. On Chebotarevskaia, see Edmondson, *Feminism*, 95.

sixth congress of the national Pirogov Society of Russian Physicians.[108] Like other advocates of reform, physicians who demanded revision of the law subscribed to the affective ideal of marriage and emphasized the social role over the sacramental character of marriage. But they argued that the relations between spouses were physiological and psychological as well as juridical, spiritual, and moral. Hence when the former relations became impossible, neither the personal needs of spouses nor the social purposes of marriage could be satisfied. 'It is self-evident that in these conditions one cannot even speak of a spiritual communion between the spouses,' asserted the professor of psychiatry at Kazan University, Nikolai Popov, defending divorce in the event of incurable mental illness, at the seventh congress of the Pirogov Society in 1899. 'There is no longer a family,' he continued, 'factually it does not exist. . . . It is necessary to protect the family, [since] the whole social structure is based on it. I am for the family and that is precisely why I am for divorce!'[109] Similarly supporting divorce in the event of mental illness in an article published in the same year, the psychiatrist Pavel Rozenbakh added that divorce also should be permitted in cases of habitual drunkenness because of 'the danger for the family arising from this vice' and 'the impossibility of spouses living together due to the moral degradation of one of them'.[110]

Such views led an overwhelming majority of the physicians at both the sixth and the seventh congresses of the Pirogov Society, as well as at meetings of local medical and juridical societies, to support allowing divorce in cases of incurable mental illness.[111] At the same time the

[108] *Obshchestvo russkikh vrachei v pamiat′ N. I. Pirogova. Dnevnik shestogo s″ezda russkikh vrachei (byvshego v Kieve 21–28 aprelia 1896 goda)* (Kiev, 1896), no. 12, pril., pp. 66–9. Speakers frequently mentioned the new German civil code. On the Pirogov Society, see N. M. Frieden, *Russian Physicians in an Era of Reform and Revolution, 1856–1905* (Princeton, NJ, 1981).

[109] *Obshchestvo russkikh vrachei v pamiat′ N. I. Pirogova. Dnevnik sed′mogo s″ezda russkikh vrachei* (Kazan, 1899), no. 13, p. 285, and in general pp. 281–7 and no. 3, pp. 21–5. Born in 1854 and the son of a priest, Popov graduated from the St Petersburg Medical-Surgical Academy in 1877. After serving as a hospital staff physician, he was appointed professor of psychiatry first at Warsaw University and then at Kazan University.

[110] P. Ia. Rozenbakh, 'Rastorzhenie braka vsledstvie pomeshatel′stva', *ZhMIu* (1899), 3: 68. Born in 1858, Rozenbakh graduated from the St Petersburg Medical-Surgical Academy in 1881. After studying abroad, he became a staff physician and lecturer for nervous and mental disorders at the clinic associated with his Alma Mater.

[111] *Obshchestvo russkikh vrachei. Dnevnik 6-ogo s″ezda*, no. 12, p. 1, and pril., pp. 66–9, *Dnevnik 7-ogo s″ezda*, no. 3, pp. 21–5, and no. 13, pp. 281–7, *Desiatyi s″ezd russkikh vrachei v pamiat′ N. I. Pirogova. Moskva 25 Aprelia-2 Maia 1907 goda. Otchet* (Spb., 1907), 91–2, 'Zhurnal zasedaniia grazhdanskago otdeleniia', 'Kievskoe iuridicheskoe obshchestvo', *ZhMIu* (1899), 3: 237–8, and 'Kazanskoe iuridicheskoe obshchestvo', *Pravo* (1899), 15, cols. 797–9; see also L. Bertenson, *Fizicheskie povody k prekrashcheniiu brachnago soiuza. Nesposobnost′ k*

medical council of the Ministry of Internal Affairs, which examined applications for divorce based on sexual incapacity, tried to broaden these grounds, and somewhat later it advocated allowing divorce in cases of leprosy and syphilis.[112] Going even further, the physicians who served on a special committee established by the Holy Synod in 1907 to review the law added to this list physical or mental abuse, psychological incompatibility, and sexual incapacity due to psychological reasons.[113]

Again, however, the purpose of such expansion of the grounds for divorce was not to undermine but to strengthen the institution of marriage, both by ensuring that individual marriages were capable of performing their social role and by releasing spouses from oppressive conditions when a marriage had broken down irreparably. Advocating divorce in the event of incurable mental illness, in an article in 1898, for example, the physician B. I. Vorotynskii asked '[o]f what is the healthy spouse guilty in this situation? Why must she bear for life the full weight of the marital ties? Why must she be deprived of the joys of life and thereby subjected to material deprivations and moral suffering? This is both unjust and inhumane.'[114] Yet if the goal of divorce now was to avoid the harmful consequences of an unhealthy marriage for both society and the individual spouses, the authority to determine which situations were unhealthy was to be entrusted to those with appropriate professional expertise. Conspicuously omitting mention of the church, Vorotynskii asserted that divorce 'must be grounded firmly from both the juridical and the medical perspective, and this will serve as an adequate guarantee against a facility of divorce'.[115]

It was precisely over the question of authority that ecclesiastical advocates of divorce law reform parted company with their secular

brachnomu sozhitiiu. Bolezni. Durnoe ili zhestokoe obrashchenie (Ptgd., 1917), Grigorovskii, *O razvode*, 216–20, and Ransel, *The Family*, 248.

[112] See Bertenson, *Fizicheskie povody*, 33–89 (Bertenson was a member of the medical council at this time), TsGIA F. 1405 op. 542 d. 671 ll. 2–34 (pp. 37–41), 106–97 (pp. 163–5), 256, and Grigorovskii, *O razvode*, 216–20. See also Engelstein, *Keys to Happiness*, 48–51.

[113] TsGIA F. 1405 op. 542 d. 671 ll. 2–34 (pp. 21–45), 106–97 (pp. 163–5), F. 796 op. 445 d. 417 ll. 144–75, and Bertenson, *Fizicheskie povody*, 44–8, 68–85, 143–8 (Bertenson participated in the first committee).

[114] B. I. Vorotynskii, 'Dushevnaia bolezn′ odnogo iz suprugov, kak povod k rastorzheniiu braka', *Vrach* (1898), 45: 1308, and 1307–9 in general. Medical advocates of reform stated frequently that they sought to protect primarily wives, who they believed suffered more than husbands under existing law.

[115] Ibid. See also the references cited above in n. 111. For attempts by physicians to influence the reform of criminal law, see Engelstein, *Keys to Happiness*, chs. 1–3, 9.

counterparts. Like progressivist jurists with respect to civil law, reformist theologians and ecclesiastical scholars employed comparative historical methods and sociological theory to formulate an evolutionary conception of Orthodox canons according to which neither their content nor their subject was prescribed solely or clearly by Orthodox Christian doctrine. As had Barsov earlier, ecclesiastical advocates of reform concluded that the content and jurisdiction of church canons—both with respect to divorce and in general—therefore were not immutable but developed historically in response to changes in social conditions and needs and in the character of church–state relations.[116]

Also like secular proponents of reform, ecclesiastical reformers contended that changed conditions dictated an expansion of the grounds for divorce, in this instance to ensure achievement of what they claimed was the essential purpose of a Christian marriage. Asserting in a pamphlet published in 1906 that '[m]arriage with a mentally ill [person] is a crime against the idea of marriage', for example, the radical professor of canon law at the St Petersburg Ecclesiastical Academy, Archimandrite Mikhail, advocated allowing divorce in such cases because of the impossibility of any spiritual communion between spouses.[117] Agreeing with this argument, ecclesiastical members of the committees formed both by the Holy Synod and by two assemblies convened after 1906 to prepare for a general council of the Russian Orthodox Church employed similar reasoning to support proposals also to permit divorce in cases of physical or mental abuse, syphilis, abandonment, and the renunciation of Orthodoxy by

[116] In addition to the sources cited below in n. 118, see *Zhurnaly i protokoly Predsobornago Prisutstviia* (Spb., 1906–7), iv. 112–38 (3rd sect., *zhur.* no. 24), and 37–8, 43–9, 51, 55–7, 63–4 (combined meeting, 3rd, 6th, and 7th sects., *zhur.* nos. 1–4), *Protokoly kommissii po tserkovnomu pravu pri Moskovskom iuridicheskom obshchestve za 1911–1912 god* (Mos., 1913), 54–6, 59–60, *Mneniia i otzyvy po voprosu o prave lits, brak kotorykh rastorgnut po prichine narusheniia imi supruzheskoi vernosti, na vstuplenie v drugoi brak* (2nd edn., Spb., 1893), 87–168, N. S. Suvorov, *Uchebnik tserkovnago prava* (Mos., 1912), 1–9, 349–90, M. Gorchakov, *Tserkovnoe pravo. Kratkii kurs lektsii* (Spb., 1909), esp. 1–25, 238–86 (by the early 20th c. Gorchakov had shifted his position substantially from that expressed in *O taine supruzhestva* (Spb., 1880)), Grigorovskii, *O razvode*, id., *Prichiny i posledstviia razvoda i brakorazvodnyi protsess na sude dukhovnom* (Spb., 1898), A. Zav'ialov, *K voprosu o brake i brachnom razvode* (Spb., 1892), A. S. Pavlov, *Kurs tserkovnago prava* (Sviato-troitskaia Sergieva Lavra, 1902), esp. 17–34, 317–90 (and see also Shershenevich, *Nauka*, 185), N. Zaozerskii, *Zlonamerennoe ostavlenie odnim suprugom drugago kak osnovanie rastorzheniia braka* (Sviato-troitskaia Sergieva Lavra, 1904), and S. Bogoslovskii, *K voprosu o povodakh k brachnomu razvodu* (Kharkov, 1916).

[117] Arkhimandrit Mikhail, *Sumashestvie kak povod k razvodu* (Spb., 1906), 4. Born in 1874 and from the clerical estate, Arkh. Mikhail [Pavel Semenov] graduated from the Kazan Ecclesiastical Academy and eventually became professor of canon law at the St Petersburg Ecclesiastical Academy. Active in radical politics in 1905–7, he was dismissed from his academic position in 1906 and later became an Old Believer.

one's spouse.[118] To prohibit divorce in these instances, ecclesiastical reformers contended, was in fact counter-productive. So, too, was the imposition of harsh penalties for marital transgressions. '[S]ocial morals are never maintained by fear,' the professor of theology at the St Petersburg Ecclesiastical Academy, Nikolai Glubokovskii, argued in 1909 in one of the Synodal committees, 'but rather are prepared for a fatal crisis.'[119] And again, not only individual spouses suffered from the severity of the law. Describing existing laws as 'an eternal threat to the Church which hang over its head like an implacable Damoclean sword', an editorial in the *Church Herald* (*Tserkovnyi Vestnik*) in 1902 implied that the social influence of the church also was jeopardized.[120]

Herein lay the source of friction between ecclesiastical and secular proponents of reform. For through the revision of divorce law ecclesiastical reformers sought not only to release individual spouses from spiritually void and morally as well as physically harmful relationships, but also to reform the church in order to preserve its influence over society. Hence ecclesiastical reformers generally joined with conservatives to oppose any reduction in the authority of the church over such a central institution of social life as marriage. Although advocating considerable expansion of the grounds for divorce, for example, a committee of the Pre-council Conference held in 1912 echoed conservative arguments in declaring that

> [p]roceeding from the understanding of marriage as a sacrament performed by the Orthodox Church . . . only the ecclesiastical authority [has] the right to define

[118] On these committees, see *Zhurnaly i protokoly*, ii. 15–16 (4th sect.), 245, 320–3, and iv. 97–138 (3rd sect., *zhur*. no. 24), 1–88 (combined meeting 3rd, 6th, and 7th sects., *zhur*. nos. 1–4), TsGIA F. 1405 op. 542 d. 670 ll. 637, 639–41, d. 671 ll. 2–34, 106–97, and F. 796 op. 445 d. 417 ll. 1–13 (pp. 22–6), 64–96, 126–91, d. 420, 421, and Grigorovskii, *O razvode*, 199–266. On the Pre-council Assembly (1906) and Conference (1912), see also J. W. Cunningham, *A Vanquished Hope: The Movement for Church Renewal in Russia, 1905–1906* (Crestwood, NY, 1981), G. Simon, 'Church, State, and Society', in G. Katkov, E. Oberlander, N. Poppe, and G. von Rauch (eds.), *Russia Enters the Twentieth Century* (London, 1973), 205–12, and P. R. Valliere, 'The Idea of a Council in Russian Orthodoxy', in Nichols and Stavrou, *Russian Orthodoxy*, 183–201.

[119] TsGIA F. 1405 op. 542 d. 671 ll. 106–97, p. 61. A prominent theologian and church historian, Glubokovskii was born in 1863, graduated from the Moscow Ecclesiastical Academy, and eventually became professor of theology at the St Petersburg Ecclesiastical Academy.

[120] 'Mneniia i otzyvy (Po povodu peresmotra brakorazvodnykh zakonov)', *TsVest* (1902), 23, cols. 716–17. On the concern of church leaders with the waning social influence of the church in the early 20th c., see G. L. Freeze, '"Going to the Intelligentsia": The Church and Its Urban Mission in Post-Reform Russia', in E. W. Clowes, S. D. Kassow, and J. L. West (eds.), *Between Tsar and People: Educated Society and the Quest for Public Identity in Late Imperial Russia* (Princeton, NJ, 1991), 215–32.

whether a sacrament was performed legally or illegally and, equally, to judge in each case whether its beneficial action is subject to termination.[121]

Despite their disagreement over authority, feminist, medical, and ecclesiastical advocates of increased access to divorce none the less followed essentially the same general line of argument. So, too, did the moderate and liberal press, where criticisms of existing law had been appearing since the late 1860s. Again, emphasis was on redefining the law in order to foster mutually supportive marital relationships that could provide both for the personal fulfilment and security of each spouse and for the welfare and stability of the family as a whole. Where a marriage could not achieve these objectives, divorce was to be permitted in the interests of both the individuals involved and society generally. In this regard, the unlimited authority given a husband under existing law was perceived as being particularly prone to abuse and therefore a principal source of marital discord. By curbing this authority, the increased access to formal marital dissolution consequently would help to stabilize marriages.[122]

The similarity in reformist arguments indicates the emergence of a common ideological orientation among a substantial part of the educated, professional, and upper strata of tsarist society by the late Imperial period. Indeed, the campaign to revise divorce law not only reflected, but helped to create the ideals and aspirations that defined this ideological orientation. By emphasizing freedom of choice in marriage, the mutuality of rights and obligations between spouses, and the importance of personal self-fulfilment, it challenged the principles of ascriptive status and privilege on which the existing social system formally rested. In characterizing patriarchal authority as arbitrary and subject to frequent abuse, and by stressing the need to ensure personal security, it implied that social and state authority should be limited by legal, and perhaps also political, rights enjoyed by all. The evolutionary view of marriage as progressing

[121] TsGIA F. 796 op. 445 d. 417 ll. 64–96, p. i. See also ll. 126–91, d. 420, F. 797 op. 92–1901 d. 81[b] (t. ii) ll. 65–85 (pp. 106–19), op. 96 d. 271 (Proekty, pt. 7), and F. 1405 op. 542 d. 666 ll. 147–8, 161–6, d. 670 ll. 10–42, 49–111, 194–261, Berdnikov, *K voprosu*, M. M. Artsybashev, *Nash brakorazvodnyi protsess* (Spb., 1908), *Protokoly kommissii*, *Zhurnaly i protokoly*, iv. 97–109 (3rd sect., *zhur.* no. 24), *Strannik* (1915), 12: 1538, and Bogoslovskii, *K voprosu o povodakh*; but cf. 'Mneniia i otzyvy'.

[122] *BV* (1870), 270: 2, *Golos* (1871), 158: 1, and (1872), 46: 1–2, *SVed* (1872), 130: 1–3, 131: 1, *VE* (1877), 2: 828–30; (1891), 12: 804–7, and (1900), 2: 812–18, and 4: 801–3, 'Po brachnomu voprosu', *Nedelia* (1884), 22: 731–3, 'Popravki semeistvennago prava', *Nedelia* (1898), 5: 145–9, 'Razdel'nost' suprugov', *Nedelia* (1899), 48: 1584–7, *Nabliudatel'* (1889), 8: 39–43, 'Nashi vnutrenniia dela', *Nabliudatel'* (1899), 12: 35–9, and (1900), 1: 44–50, *Russkaia Zhizn'* (1891), 176: 1, *RVed* (1898), 299: 2, and (1899), 333: 2, and *RM* (1898), 2: 186–8; (1902), 12: 428–30, and (1903), 1: 38–40. See also the references cited below in nn. 147 and 152.

towards equality and freedom for the individual explained the changes occurring in late Imperial Russia in a way that offered considerable status, influence, and self-esteem to the educated and professional strata of society, whose understanding of this process and technical expertise enabled them to contribute to the development of Imperial Russia by adjusting the law to contemporary social needs. Opposition to such efforts could be dismissed as a self-interested attempt by outdated social groups to maintain their privileges.

Such implications, of course, merely strengthened the opposition of conservatives to the changes in the law being demanded by advocates of reform. Yet far from being simply members of allegedly outdated social groups clinging to anachronistic privileges, opponents of reform often shared the same social background, education, and careers as their adversaries. Not only did conservative jurists oppose changes in the law which might weaken traditional authority, for example, but a minority of physicians at the sixth and seventh congresses of the Pirogov Society in 1896 and 1899 also expressed similar opposition. Rejecting the proposal to allow divorce in cases of incurable mental illness, for example, the professor of psychiatry at Iurev University, Vladimir Chizh, feared that such a law would only 'be used by egoists, and the good-hearted will not wish to exercise their right, whereas the law should restrain egoism and encourage altruism'.[123] Indeed, Chizh denied that physicians had a right even to consider the law. The conditions governing divorce, he contended, 'are established by dogmatic law and therefore not only can we not influence existing law, but [we] cannot even discuss it'.[124] And as Chief Procurator of the Holy Synod between 1909 and 1911, the respected pathologist and professor of medicine, Sergei Lukianov, helped to block any relaxation of substantive divorce law or reduction in the authority of the church in this area.[125]

[123] *Obshchestvo russkikh vrachei. Dnevnik 7-ogo s″ezda*, no. 13, p. 284. Chizh also was concerned that only the wealthy would be able to take advantage of the law. Born in 1855 and educated at the Polotsk Cadet Corps, the St Petersburg Medical-Surgical Academy, and then abroad, Chizh served initially as a hospital staff physician in St Petersburg and later taught forensic psychopathology at St Petersburg University. He was appointed professor of psychiatry at Iurev University in 1891.

[124] *Obshchestvo russkikh vrachei. Dnevnik 6-ogo s″ezda*, no. 12, prib., p. 68.

[125] TsGIA F. 1405 op. 542 d. 671 ll. 106–97, pp. 131–4. See also D. P. Kosorotov, 'O nesposobnosti k brachnomu sozhitiiu', *ZhMIu* (1916), 5: 76–106 (Kosorotov was a member of the medical council of the Ministry of Internal Affairs). Born in 1855 and a graduate of the St Petersburg Medical-Surgical Academy, Lukianov served successively as professor of pathology at Warsaw University, director of the Imperial Institute of Experimental Medicine and a consulting member of the medical council of the Ministry of Internal Affairs, Assistant Minister of Education, and Chief Procurator of the Holy Synod. He also taught forensic medicine at the Imperial School of Jurisprudence.

Similar opposition was voiced by the conservative press. Rejecting the proposal of the draft civil code to shift effective jurisdiction in divorce cases from ecclesiastical to secular courts, for example, the ultra-conservative *Moscow Gazette* (*Moskovskiia Vedomosti*) contended in an editorial in 1902 that 'two substantial institutions that support the moral and the social order, the Church and the family, would be affected terribly' by such a transfer of authority. 'To transfer divorce cases to a secular court', the editorial continued, 'would mean to deprive the Church of a right that has belonged to it . . . from the very beginning of the Christian state.' The editorial feared, moreover, that 'a secular court will grant divorce more easily', thereby weakening the family and social stability.[126] The doctrine on marital separation developed by the Civil Cassation Department after the mid-1880s in fact provided some support for at least the former fear.[127] Condemning this doctrine as a usurpation of legislative power that threatened social stability, I. Kashkarov asserted in the same paper in 1900 that 'the laws that protect marriage as a holy sacrament, and the family as a fundamental state institution, must retain their force until abolished by the strength of new laws issued by the Supreme Power'.[128]

Ecclesiastical conservatives made the same argument. In their view, too, the restrictive approach to marital dissolution dictated by the sacramental nature of marriage helped to preserve social order by disciplining human weakness and restraining human egoism. 'A marital union is concluded not for a period, but for the whole life of the spouses,' the archpriest N. Favorov argued in an article opposing any expansion of the grounds for divorce in 1880. Hence

> [a]ny arbitrary separation of the spouses is a criminal violation of divine law. The inclination to seek the dissolution of a marital union for insufficient causes reveals in man a strong weakening of moral feeling and the dominance of sensual motives or sexual lust. And the facility of divorce in any civil society serves as an undoubted and dismal sign of the moral disintegration of [that] society.[129]

[126] 'Brak i sem′ia', *MV* (1902), 322: 1–2.

[127] See below, Ch. 5.

[128] I. Kashkarov, 'Senatskoe reshenie otmeniaiushchee zakon', *MV* (1900), 330: 2. See also id., 'Polurazvod i razvod', *MV* (1900), 61: 2, and 62: 2, and, on the practice of the high court, 'Mera sodeistvuiushchaia raspadeniiu krest′ianskoi sem′i', *MV* (1900), 295: 1–2. For examples of other statements by conservative journalists, see N. Znamenskii, 'Malenkiia zametki po povodu tolkov o razvode', *MV* (1900), 70: 2, and 71: 2, 'Razvod', *MV* (1902), 271: 1, N. N., 'Brak, otdel′noe zhitel′stvo i razvod', *Grazhdanin* (1901), 26: 7–9, and Provintsial, 'Zametka otnositel′no proekta o razdel′nom zhitel′stve suprugov', *Grazhdanin* (1900), 8: 8–9. For a response to some of these articles, see *VE* (1900), 4: 801–3, and 'Otzhivshie zakony', *SG* (1900), 28: 5–6.

[129] Protoierei N. A. Favorov, 'O khristianskoi nravstvennosti', *Trudy Kievskoi Dukhovnoi Akademii* (1880), 1: 102.

Reflecting the fear that such moral disintegration was accelerating in early twentieth-century Imperial Russia, Metropolitan Vladimir (Bogoiavlenskii) of Moscow not only rejected the proposals to expand the grounds for divorce made by a Synodal committee in 1908 but favoured further restriction of these grounds. 'The indissolubility of marriage is a necessary consequence of its unity, which is full and complete only when it excludes any substantial separation in the bodily and the spiritual union of spouses and any possibility of transferral to another person while the spouses are still alive.'[130] Linking demands for a relaxation of the law to lay criticism of the authority of the church, Vladimir exclaimed, '[n]eed we speak of how dangerous it would be to set off on the path of such concession especially in our time, when the materialistic world view has declared relentless war on Christianity, when we are threatened by the most dreadful revolution—the rising up of the spirit of this world against the spirit of God's [world]?'[131]

Similar concerns fuelled ecclesiastical opposition to both the legalization of marital separation and the involvement of secular courts in divorce cases. Both were perceived as an attempt to introduce the institution of civil marriage by indirect means.[132] 'If by "marital separation" is meant divorce, only disguised, then this would signify the introduction of a new institution into Russia—*civil divorce*,' contended an editorial in the *Church Gazette* (*Tserkovnye Vedomosti*) in 1911. Such an innovation would have dire consequences, the editorial warned, because '[t]he disintegration of the family is the most grievous phenomenon of our time. And the legalization of "marital separation", of course, would not be a barrier to such disintegration, but on the contrary would facilitate and reinforce it.' The end result of such disintegration would be 'the breakdown of society and the state', since the family constituted the foundation of both.[133] Arguing similarly that the transfer of jurisdiction over divorce cases to civil courts

[130] TsGIA F. 796 op. 445 d. 417 ll. 1–13, p. 19. [131] Ibid. 18.

[132] On ecclesiastical views of separation, see TsGIA F. 1405 op. 542 d. 671 ll. 106–97 (pp. 160–3, 173–82), F. 797 op. 92–1901 d. 81[b] (t. ii) ll. 65–85 (p. 108), and op. 92–1914 d. 185 ll. 1–3, 9–21, M. E. Krasnozhen, *Starye i novye zakony o razvode. Po povodu izdaniia proekta novago Grazhdanskago Ulozheniia* (Iurev, 1904), 37, and Grigorovskii, *O razvode*, 266, 299–341. Somewhat later the more liberal *TsVest* welcomed the reform ('Mneniia i otzyvy' (1911), 7, cols. 205–6, and 'Letopis′ tserkovnoi i obshchestvennoi zhizni v Rossii' (1911), 7, cols. 212–13, 18, cols. 551–2, and 48, cols. 1515–16), while the conservative *TsVed* opposed it (1911 no. 8, prib., p. 340). The only ecclesiastical scholar who strongly supported marital separation was Ilia Berdnikov, the conservative professor of canon law at Kazan University and the Kazan Ecclesiastical Academy, who believed that the measure would undermine liberal criticisms of the church and demands for reform of divorce law. TsGIA F. 797 op. 91–1898 d. 53 ll. 5–16; see also his comments in F. 796 op. 445 d. 417 ll. 14–32.

[133] *TsVed* (1911), no. 8, pril., p. 340.

likewise would represent the institution of 'civil divorce', one A. Volynets declared in the same paper in 1909 that '[c]ivil divorce would double the number of divorced spouses, that is of ruined families'. Moreover, Volynets continued, '[c]ivil divorce is the first step towards civil marriage'.[134] As during the Alexandrine reform period, ecclesiastical conservatives thus appealed to state interests as well as to what they described as universal and immutable church doctrines in defence of the institutional authority of the Orthodox Church—and within the church, of the episcopate—with respect to marriage and divorce.

Embedded in conservative arguments lay a view of marriage that expressed values, attitudes towards the individual and authority, and an understanding of historical and doctrinal development which were antithetical to those held by proponents of reform. Although conservatives and reformers alike wished to stabilize the social order by fostering stable and ethical relations within marriage, each group had fundamentally different conceptions both of the proper marital and social order and of the sources of stability and instability within marriage and society. Whereas advocates of reform defined marriage as a matrix of mutual rights and obligations that arose from affective relationships and fostered the individuality of both spouses, conservatives stressed the importance within marriage of patriarchal authority and of obedience to such authority as means of protecting the family and society against the inherently egoistic individual. Conservatives believed that this structure of authority was necessary for the preservation of order in the family and of stability in society, whereas reformers argued that by unduly constraining the individual it intensified discontent and thereby destabilized society. Similarly, while conservatives believed that marital indissolubility promoted marital and social stability by inculcating personal self-discipline and enforcing mutual responsibility, reformers contended that it contributed to instability and moral degeneration by compelling individuals to remain within relationships that no longer provided spiritual or personal fulfilment. The

[134] A. Volynets, 'Gosudarstvennaia Duma i dukhovenstvo', *TsVed* (1909), 43, prib., p. 2034. See also Arkhimandrit Sil′vestr, 'Est′-li kakiia-libo bezspornyia osnovaniia dlia peredachi brakorazvodnago protsessa iz vedeniia Tserkvi grazhdanskomu sudu, i vozmozhnyia sledstviia etoi peredachi', *Vera i Razum* (1903), 9: 541–52, Ieromonakh Mikhail, 'Dva slova o razvode brachnom', *TsVest* (1902), 48, cols. 1507–11, A. Bronzov, 'Khristos i "razvod"', *TsVest* (1917), 5/6, cols. 102–8, Berdnikov, *K voprosu*, Krasnozhen, *Starye i novye zakony*, TsGIA F. 796 op. 445 d. 417 ll. 1–13 (pp. 1–21), 64–96, 182–9 (views of Ostroumov and Archbishop Ioakim), and F. 1405 op. 542 d. 670 ll. 1–9 and d. 671 ll. 106–97 (the views of Ostroumov, Sokolov, Ispolatov, and Bishop Evlogii of Kholm), *Zhurnaly i protokoly*, iv. 106–9 (3rd sect., *zhur.* no. 24), 28–72 (combined meeting 3rd, 6th, & 7th sects., *zhur.* nos. 1–4), *Protokoly kommissii*, and Bogoslovskii, *K voprosu o povodakh*.

historical explanation and doctrinal definition of marriage offered by conservatives likewise suggested that order and stability derived from the continuity of tradition and from authority by a paternalistic élite. This élite could include members of the educated and professional strata of society, who saw themselves as defending national traditions and order against the self-interested and socially destabilizing pretensions of their reformist opponents. For both conservatives and reformers, then, marriage law represented a medium for ideological expression and an instrument for shaping the relations, attitudes, and values of society in accordance with their own ideals and interests.

Occupying the considerable space between conservatives and reformers were moderates and moderate conservatives who favoured a cautious approach to the revision of Imperial family law. Sharing the affective ideal of the family, they agreed that the law urgently required revision. But they also wished to ensure that such revision did not undermine marital and social stability or the religious side of marriage by giving too much rein to individuals. Moderate and moderate conservative writers therefore supported the legalization of marital separation, but only for narrowly defined reasons and only under close judicial supervision. Similarly, they advocated modest expansion of the grounds for divorce and welcomed the transfer of jurisdiction over divorce cases to civil courts as a way to combat fraud. But at the same time, they sought to preserve the religious character of marriage, both through sincere religious conviction and to help stabilize the family and society. They consequently sought to avoid conflict with the Orthodox Church by gaining its assent to revision of the law, an approach that contributed to the ability of the church to resist reform. In short, moderates and moderate conservatives agreed that the rights of individuals, particularly wives, had to be expanded and protected, for both moral and practical reasons, but they distrusted the ability of the individual to exercise these rights responsibly without state oversight.[135] This cautious approach to reform was reflected in the law of 1902 defining the legal position of extramarital children and it prevailed again in the case of marital separation.

But the key to the legalization of marital separation, as well as to the

[135] N. Rok, 'Iz Moskvy', *NiBG* (1899), 348: 2, and 356: 2, A. L., 'O razluchenii suprugov', *SVed* (1898), 169: 1, A. Pantserzhinskii, 'Po povodu stat′i "O razdel′nom zhitel′stve suprugov"', *SVed* (1899), 355: 3, N. A., 'Mimo zhizni', *SVed* (1902), 289: 1–2, 'Vodvorenie zhen', *NV* (1898), 7925: 2, 'Probel v zakonakh o sem′e', *NV* (1902), 9358: 3, A. Molchanov, 'Golos zhizni', *NV* (1902), 9358: 3, 'Nakanune brakorazvodnoi reformy', *NV* (1903), 9845: 1, and A. G., 'Razvod i raz″ezd', *RVest* (1900), 2: 749–56.

revision of divorce law and procedure, lay with the Holy Synod. Given both the tsarist legislative process and the deference shown by the government to the church in this area, Synod agreement was essential for legislative change. Such agreement was likely only if the Synod could be persuaded that a particular change in the law neither contravened Orthodox doctrine nor challenged the authority and prerogatives of either the Synod or the church as a whole.

In the case of marital separation, eleven years were required to find a formula that reassured the Synod on these points. The chief problem was whether to empower the civil courts to grant a marital separation or merely to determine the legal consequences of a separation that had occurred in fact. This distinction was not inconsequential, especially for women. As the evolving practice of the Civil Cassation Department made clear, empowerment of the courts to grant a separation enabled a wife to settle questions regarding the right to support and to the custody of children before separation, thereby reducing her risks in such an action. Moreover, such empowerment had important institutional and doctrinal implications, since recognizing the right of separation would draw the secular courts and state law more deeply into an area believed by church leaders to lie primarily within their own domain.

These latter concerns in particular aroused Synodal opposition to the project of the editing commission. In a report prepared in November 1898, Konstantin Dylevskii, the legal counsel to the Chief Procurator, rejected the distinction that the editing commission tried to draw between the external form and the internal relations of a marriage. '[I]n accordance with the doctrine of our church which holds marriage to be a sacrament,' Dylevskii argued,

> both the conclusion and the dissolution of a marriage, and equally also the discussion of the legality of the conditions of its existence, fall under the authority of the church. Not only did our entire marriage law arise and does it operate on the basis of this principle, but the family and social life of the Russian people also has been fostered [by it]. Whereas the project proposes to introduce among us an order under which the separation of spouses, for a fixed or a defined period, must be determined by the authority of secular courts, without the participation of the church. But this [order] unavoidably will undermine the meaning and holiness of marriage as a sacrament in the eyes of the people and will lead to a weakening of family bonds and of social morality.[136]

[136] TsGIA F. 797 op. 91–1898 d. 53 ll. 73–4 and in general 71–9. See also I. V. Gessen, 'Razdel'noe zhitel'stvo suprugov', *Pravo* (1911), 50, cols. 2842–5, and Grigorovskii, *O razvode*, 317–30.

The state's interest in family and social stability, in other words, was best served by preserving the authority of the church and religion over marriage and, by implication, by thereby limiting the authority of the secular courts and state law in this area.

Pobedonostsev, the Chief Procurator, incorporated these arguments in his own report, which was reviewed and approved by the Holy Synod only in October 1902 and submitted to the State Secretary only after repeated prodding. Also repeating the standard conservative objections to expansion of the grounds for divorce, Pobedonostsev added that marital separation was a foreign legal institution that had arisen in Western Europe due to the Catholic prohibition of divorce and the contractual nature of civil marriage. It therefore contravened Russian national traditions and popular religious beliefs. Pobedonostsev warned, moreover, that separation would be particularly ruinous to peasant households, which relied on the co-operative labour of both spouses for survival. Conceding that current conditions none the less necessitated some relaxation of existing statutory law, Pobedonostsev preferred administrative methods to judicial action. Hence he recommended that requests for marital separation continue to be dealt with through special petitions to the Imperial Chancellery and that a wife be permitted to obtain a separate passport without the consent of her husband. In that way, the courts would be limited to settling only questions such as support and child custody which might arise from the fact of separation.[137]

In contrast to the Holy Synod, other government departments had responded quickly and favourably to the project of the editing commission.[138] The opposition of the Synod therefore constituted the chief obstacle to approval of the project by the State Council. Attempting to overcome this opposition through mediation, a meeting in November 1903 of the combined departments of the State Council referred the project to a special conference that included the chief antagonists, Pobedonostsev and Iosif Karnitskii, who had replaced Knirim as chair of the editing commission.[139]

[137] TsGIA F. 797 op. 91–1898 d. 53 ll. 100–12. See also Grigorovskii, *O razvode*, 317–28.

[138] The comments of other government departments were reviewed by the editing commission in November 1899. See *ZhRKGU. Proekt kn. II*, nos. 12–13, pp. 105–14.

[139] For the Journal of the meeting of the Combined Departments, see TsGIA F. 797 op. 91–1898 d. 53 ll. 114–24. The journal of the special conference, which met in April and October 1904, is contained in *Gos. Sov. Ses. VIII. Kom.* (HLL), Doklad no. 2. See also Gessen, 'Razdel'noe zhitel'stvo', cols. 2842–5, and Grigorovskii, *O razvode*, 329–30. The special conference was composed of members of the State Council, including several who had served in the Civil Cassation Department.

Favourably disposed to the project, the moderate conservative officials who predominated in the special conference sought to find a formula that would enable the courts to regulate marital separation without appearing either to recognize the right of separation or to violate the sacramental conception of marriage. Hence, to reassure the Holy Synod, the conference declared the obligation of spouses to live together to be a basic principle of Orthodox doctrine which must remain the foundation of general state law. But the majority in the conference then asserted that this obligation represented a moral ideal that could not be enforced in practice. Reflecting the paternalism towards women and the social prejudices that pervaded much of the discussion of this area of the law, the majority argued that release from this formal obligation was necessary paticularly among the poorer classes of society, where the persistence of partriarchal attitudes allegedly resulted frequently in the cruel mistreatment of wives. Deferring to Pobedonostsev, however, the majority rejected the formal institution of marital separation as foreign to Russian national law and proposed instead to resolve cases of marital conflict by allowing a wife to obtain a separate passport without the consent of her husband. The majority then adopted the project of the editing commission virtually unchanged as a way to regulate the relations between spouses who had already separated. The discretionary power of the courts in determining the legitimacy of a separation and the right to the custody of children was greatly expanded indeed. Moreover, citing as justification the social and economic changes taking place in the empire, the majority proposed to eliminate the legal control of a husband over the employment and education of his wife.[140] Conversely, the special conference proposed to allow a husband to refuse to take back a wife whose conduct was deemed prejudicial to his reputation and to narrow the obligation of a husband to provide support by instituting a means test for the wife.[141]

The revolutionary events of 1905 intervened before either the State Council or the Holy Synod considered the proposals of the special conference. In 1907, when the Ministry of Justice submitted a revised version of the original project of the editing commission to the new Council of Ministers, the political landscape had changed considerably. The public had gained greater access to the legislative process through the creation of

[140] *Gos. Sov. Ses. VIII. Kom.* (HLL), Doklad no. 2, pp. 12–19, 22–8, 33–6, 43–6. Adopting the position of the editing commission on the draft civil code, and following the evolving practice of the Civil Cassation Department, the majority proposed that the courts be empowered to award custody of children based on the best interests of the latter.

[141] Ibid. 20–2.

the State Duma, admittedly elected in a manner that favoured the privileged strata of society, and the inclusion of elected members in the State Council.[142] The concession of limited civil rights and the legalization of political organization had broadened substantially the possibility of political debate and action. Although resulting in the legal organization of oppositional and reformist political movements, these developments also strengthened conservative resistance to reform, in part by intensifying apprehensions and provoking better organization on the political right. Moreover, the Holy Synod retained a powerful voice in legislative matters relating to the church. The agreement of the Synod therefore remained essential for any change in the law governing separation and divorce.

The continued importance of the Holy Synod became apparent when the Council of Ministers refused to approve the proposals of the Ministry of Justice after the new Chief Procurator of the Synod, Petr Izvolskii, objected that they would empower the civil courts to grant a marital separation.[143] There followed two years of mediation by the chairman of the Council of Ministers, revision by the Ministry of Justice, and negotiation between the ministry and Dylevskii, representing the Holy Synod, before the latter finally was persuaded that the revised version of the project did not legalize marital separation but merely allowed the courts to investigate the circumstances surrounding a factual separation in order to determine its legal consequences. In essence, the Ministry of Justice had adopted a slightly modified version of the project prepared earlier by the special conference of the former State Council.[144] The Holy Synod accepted the revised proposal in early April 1910, whereupon the Council of Ministers approved it. To eliminate any suggestion that the project established the right of spouses to separate, the phrase 'marital separation' was expunged from its title on the insistence of the Synod.[145]

Before this compromise could be submitted to the Duma, however, a large group of Duma deputies from the moderate Octobrist Party independently introduced a more radical bill to legalize marital separation on the urging of the Women's Mutual Philanthropic Society.[146] The proposal

[142] On the Duma and the reformed State Council, see above, Intro., esp. n. 24.

[143] TsGIA F. 797 op. 91–1898 d. 53 ll. 178–80. See also Grigorovskii, *O razvode*, 330–1.

[144] TsGIA F. 797 op. 91–1898 d. 53 ll. 125–9, 137–77, 181–207, and *Gos. Sov. Ses. VIII. Kom.* (HLL), Ob″iasnit. zap. k proektu Min. Ius. o rasshirenii lich. i imushch. prav zamuzh. zhen. (1911).

[145] TsGIA F. 797 op. 91–1898 d. 53 ll. 208–20, *Gos. Sov. Ses. VIII. Kom.* (HLL), letter dated 15 Apr. 1910 No. 3676, S. Luk′ianov (Chief Procurator of the Holy Synod) to P. Stolypin (Chairman of the Council of Ministers), and Grigorovskii, *O razvode*, 331–8.

[146] Gessen, 'Razdel′noe zhitel′stvo', col. 2851, Grigorovskii, *O razvode*, 340–1, and Edmondson, *Feminism*, 139–42.

elicited strong support from radicals, liberals, and moderate conservatives in the Duma and from the liberal, moderate, and feminist press, but the Synod opposed the proposal for the same reasons that it had rejected the original project of the editing commission.[147] Using this opposition as a lever, the Ministry of Justice persuaded the Duma committee on judicial reforms to substitute for the Octobrist proposal the project agreed to earlier by the ministry, the Synod, and the Council of Ministers.[148] Thereafter the moderate conservatives who held the balance in both the Duma and the State Council refused to deviate from the substance of this earlier agreement.[149]

The Duma discussed the proposed law three times between 1911 and 1914, passing the project in 1912 as drafted by the Ministry of Justice and in 1914 as amended by the State Council. Reviewing the project in 1913, the more conservative State Council adopted it after restoring the authority of a husband over the employment and education of his wife as long as she continued to live with him.[150] In all these instances the debate followed by now well-established lines of argument. From the left, the jurist David Grimm contended in the State Council that the existing statutory obligation of spouses to live together 'in practice encourages only arbitrariness and high-handedness on a legal basis. This [situation] is beneficial only for the worst elements, impedes the establishment of a more normal view of marital relations and of marriage in general as a moral union, and compels [state] authority either to decline to defend the defenceless or to violate the law.'[151] According to the liberal Progressivist

[147] I. G. [Gessen?], 'Davno pora', *Rech'* (1910), 297: 2, 'Tserkovnyia vesti', *NV* (1910), 12444: 5, *Zhenskii Vestnik* (1909), 7/8: 139, and TsGIA F. 797 op. 91–1898 d. 53 ll. 221–4. See also Grigorovskii, *O razvode*, 340–1, Gessen, 'Razdel'noe zhitel'stvo', V. Avseenko, 'Zaprosy zhizni', *Peterburgskaia Gazeta*, 1911 (1 May) (seen in TsGIA F. 1405 op. 542 d. 671 l. 255), 'V Gosudarstvennoi Dume', *SVed* (1911), 34: 4, 'Mneniia i otzyvy', *TsVest* (1911), 7, cols. 205–6, *ZhD* (1911), 5: 1, *Zhenskii Vestnik* (1914), 9: 199, and the views of the otherwise highly conservative Vasilii Rozanov, 'Zaputavsheesia delo', *NV* (1910), 12447: 3.

[148] *GDSO. 1911 g. 3-ii soz., ses. 4-aia*, ii. 1654, 2522, and *GDP. 3-ii soz., 5-aia ses. (1911–1912 gg.)*, i, no. 96, pp. 1–15. See also *GDP. 4-ii soz., 2-aia ses. (1913–1914 gg.)*, ii, no. 134, and I. G. [Gessen?], 'Davno pora'.

[149] *Gos. Sov. Ses. VIII. Kom.* (HLL), letter from the Assistant Minister of Justice to Baron Goiningen-Giune, 19 Feb. 1913, no. 1048, and the references cited below in nn. 161–3.

[150] *GDSO. 1911 g. 3-ii soz., ses. 4-aia*, ii. 1652–62, *1912 g. 3-ii soz., ses. 5-aia*, iii. 1876–83, 3075–7, *1914 g. 4-ii soz., ses. 2-aia*, ii. 362–427, *GDP. 3-ii soz., 5-aia ses. (1911–1912 gg.)*, i, no. 96, *4-ii soz., 2-aia ses. (1913–1914 gg.)*, ii, no. 134, *GSSO. 7-aia ses. (1911–1912)*, col. 3728, *8-aia ses. (1912–1913)*, cols. 1114–215, and *9-aia ses. (1913–1914)*, cols. 1451–2, 1501.

[151] *GSSO. 8-aia ses. (1912–1913)*, cols. 1126 and 1124–6 in general. Very weak in the State Council, the Left supported the position of the Centre, although its leader, Grimm,

Duma deputy from St Petersburg Mikhail Kalugin the 'defenceless' meant chiefly a wife, 'since under the action of the old laws precisely she . . . was always the side who suffered'. Condemning existing law as 'an instrument for the enslavement of a wife by her husband', Kalugin welcomed the current project but charged that, especially as amended by the State Council, it was still inadequate because '[i]t loses completely from view the fact that family life must not and cannot consist only in physical co-residence alone, but must also rest on moral foundations of mutual love and friendship, mutual understanding and respect. And as life grows constantly more complex this spiritual side begins to play an ever more important role in family relationships.'[152] To accommodate this alleged change in the nature of family relationships, liberal and socialist deputies in the Duma advocated even more radical reform of the law, including in some cases the introduction of civil marriage.[153]

From the right, conversely, the ultra-conservative state official Aleksandr Stishinskii asserted in the State Council that '[a]ccording to the teaching of our Church, the marital conjunction is a union indissoluble for life under the supremacy of the husband'. Despite the denials of its supporters, the project therefore violated Orthodox doctrine because, by defining the legal consequences of marital separation, it implicitly 'recognizes the legality of such abandonment of the family hearth by a wife'. Moreover, Stishinskii declared, 'in the form of a prize for the abandonment of co-residence, the project grants those [wives] who abandon their husbands rights that these married women did not enjoy when living with their husbands, that is the right independently, without the consent of a husband, to engage in employment and to enter educational institutions and service'.[154] The noble landowner and activist in the United Nobility Aleksei

clearly was dissatisfied with this moderation. See ibid., cols. 1124–8, 1164–7; see also cols. 1159–64. Born in 1864 and the son of the rector of the Imperial Academy of Fine Arts, Grimm held a series of academic positions after graduating from the juridical faculty at St Petersburg University and studying law abroad. For most of his career, he was professor of Roman law at St Petersburg University and instructor in that subject at the Imperial School of Jurisprudence and the Military-Juridical Academy. See *GS 1915*, 20–1 (2nd pag.).

152 *GDSO. 1914 g. 4-ii soz., ses. 2-aia*, ii. 366, 368. Founded in 1912 on the initiative particularly of several prominent Moscow merchant-industrialist magnates, the Progressive Party generally promoted a programme of constitutionalism and liberal reform. A landowner and an attorney in St Petersburg, Kalugin later joined the Kadet Party and in 1917 was elected to its central committee.

153 Ibid., cols. 366–82, 393–5, 399–404, 408, 410–13, 418–19, *1911 g. 3-ii soz., ses. 4-aia*, ii. 1654–8. Social Democratic deputies in particular advocated the introduction of civil marriage.

154 *GSSO. 8-aia ses. (1912–1913)*, cols. 1135–6. Born in 1857, a nobleman, and a graduate of the juridical faculty at Moscow University, Stishinskii held a number of promi-

Arsenev charged similarly in the same body that the proposed law would replace the concept of duty 'with the concept of personal good, of personal welfare', and would reward the illegal act of separation 'with a whole series of rights that are not granted except by a violation of the fundamental rule of our law regarding the co-residence of spouses'. Yet, Arsenev asserted, '[t]he imperative of duty is just as real as, if not stronger than, the imperative of right'.[155]

Rightists directed their sharpest criticism at the potential impact of the proposed law on the peasantry, however, whose traditions and values were portrayed as being under attack by the morally and socially degenerative values of the modern city. 'You, gentlemen of the intelligentsia, marry for the feeling of passion, love, and so on,' declared the reactionary noble landowner Nikolai Markov in the Duma in 1911, 'but the Russian peasant marries in order to have a worker and a helper for himself. If he did not have a wife, then it would be impossible for him to carry on an agricultural economy.' Hence, Markov accused his opponents, 'for the sake of your dissipated intelligentsia morals, you vainly want to ruin the life of the chaste Russian people (*narod*)'.[156] Repeating this argument in the State Council, Stishinskii contended that educated members of urban society would consider the law as tantamount to the establishment of civil divorce at the will of a wife, whereas 'among the peasantry marriage will become a pathetic semblance of a contract in which all the obligations are imposed on one side [the husband] and all the rights and privileges are granted to the other'. Stishinskii concluded that the proposed law would consequently 'have a corrupting influence on the strength of the marital union among the lower social strata, and from this perspective I find the bill to be an anti-state [measure]'.[157] Rightists in both the Duma and the State Council thus sought to limit the effects of the proposed law, as well as perhaps to derail it altogether by making it unacceptable to the Holy

nent positions in the state administration, chiefly in the Ministry of Internal Affairs, where he was assistant minister from 1899 to 1904. A strong proponent of reactionary counter-reform and of strengthening the landed nobility in order to buttress the autocratic regime, after 1905 he was active in the United Nobility and a leader of the Right in the State Council. On Stishinskii, see *GS 1915*, 88–9 (1st pag.), and on the United Nobility, Ch. 8 below.

155 *GSSO. 8-aia ses. (1912–1913)*, col. 1120. Arsenev had served as marshal of the nobility in Tula province.

156 *GDSO. 1911 g. 3-ii soz., ses. 4-aia*, ii. 1659–60. At least some of the peasant deputies in the Duma supported this argument. See the statements by Tarasov and Gorodilov in *1914 g. 4-ii soz., ses. 2-aia*, ii. 399, 404–5. Also a member of the United Nobility, Markov was a leader of the ultra-reactionary and anti-Semitic Union of the Russian People.

157 *GSSO. 8-aia ses. (1912–1913)*, cols. 1139, 1140.

Synod, by attempting—ironically as well as unsuccessfully—to amend it to allow separation only after judicial review in each case.[158]

Rejecting the proposed amendments, as well as the arguments, of the right, the socialist Duma deputy and future premier of the ill-fated Provisional Government Aleksandr Kerenskii declared by contrast that '[i]t is necessary to make the peasant woman a free person. It is necessary to make a woman a completely equal member of society and of state life. And as one of the stages towards this complete emancipation of a woman, towards the recognition of a woman as a free person and as our comrade in social and state work, as one of the stages towards this goal, we recognize this bill.'[159] Likewise proclaiming the project to be a step towards the equalization of the rights of women and men, the Progressivist Kalugin asserted that 'this equality of rights is not only a demand of the most elementary justice, but it is called forth by the demand of the times, by the need for the normal development of culture and for progress'.[160] Both left and right thus agreed that the proposed law challenged traditional structures of authority and socio-cultural practices, in part by promoting formal sexual and social equality. They disagreed profoundly, however, over the desirability of such effects.

Attempting to mediate between the socio-cultural and ideological vision of left and right, the moderate conservatives who controlled the outcome in both legislative chambers sought, through the bill, to adapt Imperial law to their perception of prevailing social conditions without risking social disorder or promoting fundamental social change. Supporting the bill in the State Council, the Civil Cassation Department Senator Baron Emilii fon Goiningen-Giune therefore maintained that statutory law should continue to proclaim the obligation of spouses to live together. But, he continued, '[i]n an abnormal marriage, life sometimes becomes unbearable for one spouse due to the guilt of the other. In such a situation a wife often leaves her husband, lives separately, and cannot be compelled forcibly to live with her husband by either a court or the police.' Although legal regulation of such abnormal situations was necessary, 'the institution of marital separation contradicts the canonical rules of the Orthodox Church regarding the sacramental character of marriage'. In the view

[158] On these efforts and the arguments of the Right in general, see ibid., cols. 1120–4, 1133–47, 1173–9, 1188–92, 1197–1200, *GDSO. 1911 g. 3-ii soz., ses. 4-aia*, ii. 1658–60, *1914 g. 4-ii soz., ses. 2-aia*, ii. 383–5, 395–9, 404–5, 408–10, 414–17, 419–20, and *Gos. Sov. Ses. VIII. Kom.* (HLL), Doklad no. 2. The chief spokesmen for the Right were Markov in the Duma and Stishinskii, Arsenev, A. A. Khvostov, and P. N. Durnovo in the State Council.

[159] *GDSO. 1914 g. 4-ii soz., ses. 2-aia*, ii. 411.

[160] Ibid., col. 367.

of fon Goiningen-Giune, as well as of the moderate conservative Centre faction in the State Council, the current bill represented an acceptable alternative to the formal institution of separation because it offered protection to women in discordant marriages through revision of the passport regulations while enabling the courts to regulate such cases through resolution of the legal questions that arose from the fact of separation.[161] The moderate conservative zemstvo activist and former state official Vladimir Gurko added in the same body that the bill was necessary not only to relieve the misery and suffering caused by irreparable marital breakdown, but also to ensure social stability. 'We favour planned evolution,' Gurko declared, 'and it is self-evident that were we to oppose [such evolution], we would come to only one thing—to disorderly revolution.'[162] Further reflecting their cautious approach to legal reform, moderate conservatives in the State Council deleted from the proposed law the provision that would have allowed a wife who was living with her husband to undertake employment or pursue formal education without his consent, a change that even Octobrists in the Duma criticized strongly but accepted in order to ensure passage of the bill.[163]

[161] *GSSO. 8-aia ses. (1912–1913)*, cols. 1114–15, 1118. Born in 1842 and a landless Baltic nobleman, fon Goiningen-Giune held a series of positions in the Senate after graduating from the Imperial School of Jurisprudence and studying law abroad. Appointed a senator in the Civil Cassation Department in 1889, he also was a high official in the Evangelical Lutheran Church. Appointed to the State Council in 1908, he joined the moderate conservative Centre group. See TsGIA F. 1364 op. 15 d. 468 and *GS 1915*, 29 (1st pag.).

[162] *GSSO. 8-aia ses. (1912–1913)*, col. 1157. Born in 1863 and a member of a distinguished noble landowning and servitor family, Gurko graduated from Moscow University and then entered state service, where he spent most of his career dealing with peasant and agrarian affairs in the Kingdom of Poland, the State Chancellery, and the Ministry of Internal Affairs. Forced to resign his position in 1906, in 1912 he was elected as a zemstvo representative to the State Council, where he joined a small 'non-party' group that favoured moderate reform. See V. I. Gurko, *Features and Figures of the Past: Government and Opinion in the Reign of Nicholas II* (Stanford, Calif., 1939). For the arguments of moderate conservatives, see *GDSO. 1911 g. 3-ii soz., ses. 4-aia*, ii. 1652–4, 1660–2, *1912 g. 3-ii soz., ses. 5-aia*, iii. 1876–83, *1914 g. 4-ii soz., ses. 2-aia*, ii. 362–6, 385–93, 405–8, 421–6, *GSSO. 8-aia ses. (1912–1913)*, cols. 1114–19, 1128–33, 1167–8, 1179–87, 1191–5, 1200–2, *Gos. Sov. Ses. VIII. Kom.* (HLL), Doklad no. 2, and TsGIA F. 797 op. 96 d. 219 ll. 1–4.

[163] *GDSO. 1914 g. 4-ii soz., ses. 2-aia*, ii. 365, 390–2, 405–8, 411–13, 418, 421, and *GSSO. 9-aia ses. (1913–1914)*, cols. 1451–2, 1501. Representatives of the Centre, the Ministry of Internal Affairs, and the Holy Synod apparently reached an agreement on this point in committee. Defending the original proposal in the Duma in 1912, Liudvig Liuts, the chief spokesman for the Octobrists on the bill and an assistant procurator in the Odessa District Court, had declared that 'in those circles where material circumstances compel a married woman, equally with [her] husband, to seek a supplementary wage, the prohibition against engaging in such work without the consent of the husband does not correspond at all with our social conditions'. *GDSO. 1912 g. 3-ii soz., ses. 5-aia*, iii. 1878. On the Synod's espousal of strong authority for the husband, see TsGIA F. 797 op. 92–1906 d. 68 l. 33.

On 12 March 1914 marital separation thus finally received statutory sanction in Imperial law, fifty-four years after first being proposed and more than thirty years after being legitimized in judicial practice by the Civil Cassation Department.[164] Although still obligated legally to live with her husband, a wife now could obtain a separate passport without his consent. As several speakers in the legislative debate over the law had pointed out, as long as a wife had not left the locale of her husband's residence, in practice even previously she had been able to live apart from him and work without his consent.[165] Now, however, in cases of separation a wife could move and act freely. Albeit cautiously, the law thus recognized the individual rights of married women. Equally importantly, the courts had acquired statutory sanction for their practice of awarding a wife support from her husband and custody of her children when deemed appropriate, considerations that in Western Europe and the United States strongly influenced the willingness of women to resort to separation.[166]

Passage of the law on marital separation in the end had been possible because a version of the law acceptable to the Holy Synod had been found, thereby undercutting secular conservative opposition. Such compromise proved unattainable in the case of divorce, however, in part because the proposed reforms of the law challenged ecclesiastical or episcopal authority and the established interpretation of Orthodox doctrine even more directly than did marital separation. But divisions within the church also limited the possibility of compromise.

As in the 1870s, the demand within the Orthodox Church for the reform of divorce law intersected with internal conflicts over church governance and structure and over the interpretation of Orthodox doctrine. Simmering since the 1870s, these conflicts had re-emerged in the turmoil of 1905. They now received added impetus, however, from the perception of ecclesiastical reformers and conservatives alike that the social influence of the church was declining. In response, both reformers and conservatives demanded greater independence for the church from

[164] *SUzak*, 1914 no. 76, item 902 (12 March), 1369–72. The text of the law, together with extensive commentary, can also be found in Gessen, *Razdel'noe zhitel'stvo*, and P. S. Tsypkin, *Zakon 12 marta 1914 goda o nekotorykh izmeneniiakh i dopolneniiakh deistvuiushchikh uzakonenii o lichnykh i imushchestvennykh pravakh zamuzhnikh zhenshchin i ob otnosheniiakh suprugov mezhdu soboiu i k detiam* (Spb., 1914). See also E. Fleishits, 'Novella semeistvennago prava', *Pravo* (1914), 14, cols. 1113–29.

[165] *GSSO. 8-aia ses. (1912–1913)*, cols. 1149–50.

[166] R. Phillips, *Putting Asunder: A History of Divorce in Western Society* (Cambridge, 1988), 398, 599–603, 611–12.

the state, despite their disagreement over the internal reforms necessary to revitalize the church.[167] Ecclesiastical proposals to relax substantive divorce law and to reform ecclesiastical courts arose in this context.

Indeed, the basic ecclesiastical programme for reform of the law was formulated initially at the Pre-council Assembly, a meeting composed predominantly of prominent members of the higher clergy and the faculty of ecclesiastical academies which was convened in St Petersburg in 1906 to lay the groundwork for a general church council.[168] Under the chairmanship of the relatively liberal Archbishop Iakov of Iaroslavl, and consisting chiefly of ecclesiastical scholars and lay officials of the Holy Synod, the third section of the Assembly reviewed ecclesiastical courts and the regulations governing marriage among Orthodox believers. Concluding that restrictive and outdated substantive laws more than antiquated procedural rules caused the fraud and other problems alleged to plague divorce cases, this group advocated the inclusion of mutual adultery, severe mistreatment of a spouse, incurable mental illness, venereal disease, and abandonment among the grounds for divorce. At the same time, all but one of the members of the third section believed that divorce cases should remain under the jurisdiction of ecclesiastical courts, whose deficiencies they proposed to eliminate through restructuring on the basis of the 1864 judicial reform.[169]

In February 1907 Chief Procurator Izvolskii persuaded the Holy Synod to form a committee to review the proposals of the Pre-council Assembly regarding substantive divorce law, particularly as a way to stem the tide of conversions from Orthodoxy taking place in the wake of a recent law extending religious tolerance. Chaired by the moderate Bishop Innokentii (Beliaev) of Tambov, the committee otherwise was composed of lay officials in the Synod and advised by several physicians. Not only did the committee accept the recommendations of the Pre-council Assembly, but it proposed to expand the grounds for divorce still further to include mental cruelty, the abandonment of Orthodoxy by one's spouse, and sexual incapacity arising even after marriage or for psychological

[167] In addition to the references cited above in n. 118, see Freeze, *Parish Clergy*, 449–74, id., '"Going to the Intelligentsia"', Simon, *Konstantin Petrovič Pobedonoscev*, 249–64, Smolitsch, *Geschichte*, 306–30, J. S. Curtiss, *Church and State in Russia: The Last Years of the Empire: 1900–1917* (New York, 1940), and the essays by Treadgold and Meyendorff in Nichols and Stavrou, *Russian Orthodoxy*, 21–43, 170–82.

[168] On this assembly, see the references cited above in n. 118.

[169] *Zhurnaly i protokoly*, iv. 97–138 (3rd sect., *zhur.* no. 24); see also ii. 15–16 (4th sect.), 245, 320–3, and Grigorovskii, *O razvode*, 199–222.

reasons.[170] After the Synod had rejected these proposals in November 1908, the committee was augmented by several theologians and Synodal officials and by the conservative Bishop Evlogii (Georgievskii) of Kholm.[171] Despite a more conservative complexion, greater disagreement, and more frequent reference to canon law, however, the committee in the end excluded from the proposed grounds for divorce only abandonment, mental cruelty, and post-marital or psychologically caused sexual incapacity.[172] After a delay of four years, the Synod also rejected this proposal in May 1913.[173] Finally, in 1916 a third committee, associated with the Pre-council Conference of 1912, drafted a project that included as proposed grounds for divorce the original proposals of 1907, excluding only that regarding sexual incapacity and adding leprosy.[174]

Although all three committees drew heavily on the arguments of ecclesiastical and medical advocates of reform to justify their proposals, they appear to have reflected a fairly broad spectrum of opinion within the church. While continuing to stress the traditional interpretation of church doctrine on marriage, for example, Bishop Innokentii considered the proposals of the two committees he chaired to be a necessary response both to the needs of the time and to human fallibility.[175] Dylevskii, who as legal counsel of the Chief Procurator served on the same committees as Innokentii, similarly supported most of their proposals, even though he generally adopted a conservative position on other issues. The unifying thread among proponents of reform appears to have been a common belief that in the changing social and economic conditions of early twentieth-century Imperial Russia the relaxation of divorce law was necessary both to provide a legitimate solution for cases of irreparable marital breakdown and, especially, to maintain the influence of the church. The latter goal found further reflection in the defence of ecclesiastical jurisdiction made by all three committees and in the proposals for the reform of the procedure used by ecclesiastical courts in divorce actions formulated

[170] TsGIA F. 1405 op. 542 d. 671 ll. 2–34 and Grigorovskii, *O razvode*, 225–66. Grigorovskii played an influential role in the committee, and even the more conservative Dylevskii supported modest reform of the law.

[171] TsGIA F. 796 op. 445 d. 417 ll. 1–13 and F. 1405 op. 542 d. 671 ll. 106–97.

[172] Ibid. The committee also narrowed the definition of some of the other grounds for divorce.

[173] TsGIA F. 1405 op. 542 d. 670 ll. 1–9 and Grigorovskii, *O razvode*, 229.

[174] TsGIA F. 796 op. 445 d. 417 ll. 1–13 (pp. 22–6), 64–96, 126–91, d. 420, and d. 421, and F. 1405 op. 542 d. 670 ll. 637, 639–41.

[175] See also the comments of Archbishops Aleksei of Tver and Gurii (Okhotin) of Novgorod in TsGIA F. 796 op. 445 d. 417 ll. 1–13, pp. 22–6.

by the last committee. The structure and procedure of these courts were to be revised not only to facilitate the adjudication of cases, but also to provide more effective pastoral counselling of spouses.[176] Changes in substantive and procedural law therefore represented an integrated programme of reform designed to perpetuate an active role for the church in marital affairs.

Despite this objective, the proposals encountered strong opposition in the Holy Synod, especially from the influential Metropolitans Vladimir of Moscow and Antonii (Vadkovskii) of St Petersburg. Accepted as necessary by all factions, the reform of ecclesiastical courts none the less remained unattainable largely because of its implications for the distribution of authority within the church. And as for substantive law, the reactionary Chief Procurator of the Synod Vladimir Sabler informed the Minister of Justice in 1913 that 'proceeding from the lofty goal of preserving a Christian marital union from collapse through the facilitation of its dissolution', the Holy Synod had rejected the proposal of its own committees to allow divorce in cases of mutual adultery, since in such instances neither spouse could be considered an innocent victim of the sinful actions of the other. The Synod similarly had found the proposals of the first of these committees regarding sexual incapacity to be 'completely unacceptable from the point of view of the understanding of a Christian marriage, which has in view the spiritual union and perfection of spouses rather than their sexual pleasure'. Likewise, Sabler continued, the Synod considered allowing divorce in cases of incurable mental illness, venereal disease, and abandonment to be

> incompatible with the fundamental goals and characteristics of a truly Christian marriage, in which spouses must see not a means for the satisfaction of base physical needs but a method for limiting them. [Marriage] must be fulfilled through Christian self-denying care of the other spouse and with Christian forgiveness and tolerance of his [*sic*] weaknesses and the misfortunes that befall him.[177]

In the view of the Synod, Sabler stated, only the extreme mistreatment of a spouse, mental cruelty, and the abandonment of Orthodoxy by one's spouse were acceptable as additional grounds for divorce.[178] Clearly, the majority of the Synod believed the inculcation of greater personal discipline through the re-emphasis of a strict interpretation of church doctrine,

[176] The latter are contained in ibid., ll. 64–96; see also d. 420, 421.

[177] TsGIA F. 1405 op. 542 d. 670 ll. 1–9 (quotes on ll. 1, 3–4, 8). See also F. 796 op. 445 d. 417 ll. 1–13, pp. 1–21.

[178] TsGIA F. 1405 op. 542 d. 670 ll. 5–7.

rather than concessions to public demands for reform, to be the appropriate response to changing social conditions.

Sabler's letter also contained the response of the Holy Synod both to the relatively modest proposals of the draft civil code with respect to divorce and to the highly favourable review by the Ministry of Justice of the more radical proposals of the first two Synodal committees.[179] Having received this response, in 1914 the Ministry of Justice established a special committee to revise the relevant section of the draft code in preparation for its submission to the Duma. Deferring to the Synod, the special committee included in the revised version of the code only those grounds for divorce which had been accepted by the Holy Synod. The spirit of conservatism affected even the rhetoric accompanying the revised code. In place of references to progressive evolutionary change, the explanatory memorandum now declared that

> [m]arriage is one of the most stable religious–legal institutions of a Christian society, and the juridical norms that define it are subject in general only to very insignificant changes over the course of even thousands of years. This capacity to hold its basic traits inviolable, at the same time that other institutions of life are being transformed and are disappearing in the historical flow of time and events, is inherent in marriage not only as a result of its religious nature, which in essence is unchanging, but also in view of its state and social significance as the original basis of the entire structure of our fundamental relationships.[180]

Despite such rhetoric, however, the special committee adopted, virtually unchanged, the original provisions regarding alimony, the custody of children, and the other consequences of divorce contained in the draft civil code.[181] In April 1916 this new version of the draft code was resubmitted to the Holy Synod for review, at roughly the same time that the third Synodal committee also completed its project.

The nearly simultaneous submission of these two projects brought to a head the conflict over jurisdictional control in which the Ministry of Justice and the Holy Synod had been engaged since 1901. In November of that year Pobedonostsev had proposed to the Minister of Justice that a special committee be formed to prepare legislation regarding the

[179] In 1910 the ministry strongly endorsed several proposals for considerably expanding the grounds for divorce made by ecclesiastical reformers, and its representatives supported similar proposals in a special committee created by the Chief Procurator of the Synod in 1916. TsGIA F. 1405 op. 542 d. 671 ll. 199–248 and F. 796 op. 445 d. 417 ll. 126–91.

[180] TsGIA F. 1405 op. 542 d. 671 ll. 49–111, p. 8.

[181] Ibid., d. 670, ll. 1–42, 49–111, 194–261, and F. 1364 op. 15 d. 440 ll. 45, 86. The committee was chaired by the Assistant Minister of Justice, Ilia Iliashenko, who earlier had been a member of the editing commission.

involvement of secular courts in divorce cases.[182] Through such involvement Pobedonostsev did not intend the church to relinquish its control over divorce. On the contrary, he sought to use the secular courts to help the church perform its pastoral mission of preserving marriages intact by curbing the fraud and corruption that he believed explained the rise in the number of divorces granted for adultery at the turn of the century.[183] Unable to address this problem through the reform of ecclesiastical courts, Pobedonostsev had adopted the approach favoured by a number of Synodal officials and, apparently, by many consistorial clergy, who felt overburdened by the increasing number of divorce cases. According to this approach, the secular courts would determine the facts of a case, with ecclesiastical courts then seeking to reconcile the spouses and deciding whether to grant a divorce.[184]

The jurists who dominated the committee established by the Ministry of Justice in early 1902 clearly intended, however, to assert secular judicial control over the process of divorce.[185] In doing so they were motivated not only by the desire to eliminate fraud, but also by the belief that by attempting a reconciliation, the clergy both prolonged the suffering of spouses and obstructed their right to a divorce under the law. Drawing on the proposals contained in the draft civil code as well as the arguments advanced by the various committees of the 1860s and 1870s, the jurists on the committee therefore argued that only trained jurists in secular courts could reduce corruption in divorce cases and reconcile the legitimate interests of the church, the state, and individual litigants. The committee majority consequently proposed that effective jurisdiction over divorce cases for adultery and for sexual incapacity be transferred to secular civil courts. To safeguard the rights of litigants, ecclesiastical courts would be bound by the decisions of their secular counterparts, their efforts to reconcile spouses would be limited to three months, and attorneys would

[182] TsGIA F. 1405 op. 542 d. 666 ll. 3–4, 6–7, 10–11, 13–18, 20, 28–9, 36, and K. P. Pobedonostsev, *Kurs grazhdanskago prava* (4th edn., Spb., 1896), ii. 110–11.

[183] K. P. Pobedonostsev, *Pis'ma Pobedonostseva k Aleksandru III* (Mos., 1925, 1926), ii. 34–6, 358–64, and *TsVest* (1901), 30, cols. 950–1. On the rise in the number of divorces, see above, Ch. 2 and Table 2.1.

[184] TsGIA F. 797 op. 92–1901 d. 81[a] (t. i) l. 4–9, 14–23, Grigorovskii, *Prichiny*, 5–7, 41–3, and id., *O razvode*, 204–5. On the problem of overburdened ecclesiastical courts, see TsGIA F. 797 op. 96 d. 371, first item, and 'Po povodu peresmotra brakorazvodnykh zakonov', *TsVest* (1902), 23, cols. 716–17.

[185] The committee was chaired by Assistant Minister of Justice Sergei Manukhin and composed of five jurists from the Ministry of Justice and the Civil Cassation Department (including the chief advocate of secular jurisdiction on the editing commission, Andrei Povorinskii), two officials from the Holy Synod (Dylevskii and Grigorovskii), and another state official. TsGIA F. 1405 op. 542 d. 666 ll. 3–4, 6–7, 10–11, 13–18, 20, 28–9, 36.

be permitted to represent litigants in these courts. While barring divorce in the event of collusion between spouses, the committee also proposed to allow divorce in cases of mutual adultery on the grounds that in such instances the moral basis for a marriage no longer existed.[186]

Although accepted by all relevant government departments, the project was rejected by nearly every faction in the Orthodox Church as an unacceptable limitation of ecclesiastical independence and an improper extension of state control into spiritual affairs. Ecclesiastical conservatives and reformers alike contended that jurisdiction over divorce lay rightfully with the church and that ecclesiastical courts would provide a more appropriate forum for the resolution of cases of marital discord than would the narrowly legalistic and adversarial arena of the secular courts.[187] Even the Synodal representatives on the committee thought that the project too narrowly constricted the activities of ecclesiastical courts and the ability of the church to perform its pastoral mission. In a report prepared in early 1905, nearly two years after submission of the project to the Holy Synod, Dylevskii therefore recommended that the project be accepted only if the independence of ecclesiastical courts was ensured and the time limit imposed on pastoral efforts to reconcile the spouses eliminated.[188] The Synod essentially followed this recommendation when it considered the issue over a year later, in June 1906.[189]

The project thus brought jurists and the Ministry of Justice into direct conflict with Orthodox clergy, ecclesiastical scholars, and officials in the Holy Synod over control of the enforcement and interpretation of divorce law. To satisfy their different institutional and professional priorities, each side sought to control the decision to grant a divorce. Moreover,

[186] Ibid., ll. 13–18, 22–6, 72–144, and d. 667. For the reactions of jurists to the proposal, universally favourable, see 'Kavkazskoe iuridicheskoe obshchestvo', *ZhMIu* (1902), 5: 257, 'Kievskoe iuridicheskoe obshchestvo', *Pravo* (1902), 20, cols. 1045–8, M. A. Levitskii, 'Ne poiavilos′ li v dannom sluchae pod formoi grazhdanskago protsessa rastorzhenie braka i pravo na otdel′noe zhitel′stvo suprugov?', *SG* (1902), 15: 7–8, A. I. Kaminka, 'Podsudnost′ i poriadok proizvodstva del o rastorzhenii brakov lits pravoslavnago ispovedaniia vsledstvie preliubodeianiia ili nesposobnosti k brachnomu sozhitiiu', *Pravo* (1908), 14, cols. 798–804, and Pergament, 'K predpolagaemoi reforme'; but cf. TsGIA F. 797 op. 92 d. 51 ll. 3–4.

[187] Ibid., op. 92–1901 d. 81[b] (t. ii) ll. 65–85 (pp. 106–19), op. 96 d. 271 (item 2), and F. 1405 op. 542 d. 666 ll. 147–8, 161–6, Berdnikov, *K voprosu*, Artsybashev, *Nash brakorazvodnyi protsess*, 16–20, Volynets, 'Gosudarstvennaia Duma', Arkhim. Sil′vestr, 'Est-li kakiia-libo bezspornyia osnovaniia', Ierom. Mikhail, 'Dva slova o razvode', *Protokoly kommissii*, 54–6, 59–60, 67–8, 71–2, and *Strannik* (1915), 12: 1538.

[188] TsGIA F. 797 op. 92–1901 d. 81[a] (t. i) ll. 45–61; see also Grigorovskii, *O razvode*, 285–98.

[189] TsGIA F. 1405 op. 542 d. 666 ll. 146–80; for similar objections by Lutheran and Moslem representatives, see ibid., d. 672 l. 14 and *ZhRKGU. Proekt kn. II*, no. 27, pp. 260–2.

given their different perspectives, each side perceived the position of the other as a threat to the well-being of society as well as to its own self-defined social and professional role. Both sides consequently refused to budge on the central issue of the relative autonomy of ecclesiastical courts. Ignoring the objections of the Synod, the Ministry of Justice in 1907 and 1909 forwarded the project essentially unchanged to the Council of Ministers for submission to the Duma, only to be obliged by the Council on each occasion to withdraw the project when the Synod protested. For its part, the Synod insisted that ecclesiastical courts be able to act independently and without time limits and contended that the Duma had no right to consider the issue because it involved affairs of the church, which after 1906 had been assigned by the Fundamental Laws to the exclusive purview of the Emperor.[190] Since the government as a whole refused to accept the project until approved by the Synod, the opposition of the latter proved sufficient to block the project indefinitely, even though the Ministry of Justice continued to promote it.[191]

Indeed, the project was incorporated into the proposals on substantive divorce law sent by the Ministry of Justice to the Holy Synod in April 1916. Now in receipt of competing secular and ecclesiastical projects for the reform of both substantive and procedural law, the Chief Procurator received Imperial permission to form an inter-departmental committee within the Synod to reconcile the conflicting proposals.[192] When the committee met in late 1916 and early 1917, it broke down along predictable lines. Juristic and ecclesiastical advocates of reform agreed to adopt the considerably expanded grounds for divorce proposed by the third Synodal committee, provoking the conservative Chief Procurator of the Judicial Department of the Senate, S. Ia. Utin, to utter in despair: 'why make the possibility of divorce still easier and easier for spouses and in that way weaken the already by no means firm foundations of the family and the marital union?'[193] Juristic and ecclesiastical reformers likewise agreed to adopt the proposals of the Ministry of Justice regarding alimony, the custody of children, and the other consequences of divorce. But these allies parted company over the question of jurisdiction, with the February Revolution intervening before they could resolve their

190 TsGIA F. 1405 op. 542 d. 668 ll. 2–58, 90, 92, 186, 279–81, 283, 291–6, 303–4, 307–10, 345–52, 356, 361–5, 367, 457–9, F. 796 op. 445 d. 417 ll. 92–108, and F. 797 op. 92-1901 d. 81[b] (t. ii), letter 21 Nov. 1912 from V. Sabler (Chief Procurator of the Holy Synod) to I. Shcheglovitov (Minister of Justice).

191 TsGIA F. 1405 op. 542 d. 670 ll. 10–42.

192 Ibid., ll. 313, 317–423, 637–41.

193 TsGIA F. 796 op. 445 d. 417 ll. 183–4.

differences. It seems unlikely that the Holy Synod would have accepted their overall recommendations in any case.[194]

Taken together, these conflicts over the revision of Imperial family law during the last decades of the old regime reveal sharp divisions within educated society, state officialdom, and the Orthodox Church over fundamental social ideals and cultural values. On one level, of course, such conflict constituted merely a struggle over relative authority provoked by the expansion of state institutions, emergence of professional groups, and changes within the Orthodox Church which had occurred especially after the first third of the nineteenth century. But on a deeper level, conflict over the law reflected both the ideological divisions produced within the educated and upper strata of society by the changes taking place in late Imperial Russia and the competing strategies proposed for dealing with such changes. In a context where all factions believed that the family constituted the foundation of the social and political order and that processes such as industrialization and rapid urban growth were causing social instability, it is not surprising that different ideological factions used the revision of family law as a means to restore social stability. Where some sought stability through the direction of social change via a legal framework derived from Western Europe, others believed that social change could be contained and order restored only through the re-emphasis and adaptation of traditional values and relationships. Legislative revision of the law consequently became extremely difficult because the measures for resolving marital discord proposed even by moderate advocates of reform appeared to conservatives as likely only to undermine authority in the family and to accelerate what they considered to be an already alarming rise in the instance of marital dissolution.

Legislative revision of the law was made still more difficult by an institutional structure that enabled conservative members of the Orthodox episcopate to establish the boundaries of marital law reform. In every instance, the conservative majority in the Holy Synod proved able to block or force the revision of proposals for legal reform which it deemed undesirable, regardless of their origin. This ability rested on the willingness of the government to defer to the church on these issues, a willingness that in turn reflects the complex relationship between the Orthodox Church and the tsarist state during the post-Petrine period. Although the state attempted to use the church for its own purposes, the Orthodox Church in turn used Imperial law as a means to pursue its own interests, in this

[194] Ibid., ll. 126–91.

case to reinforce its jurisdiction and doctrines with respect to marriage and the family. On many issues, of course, church and state leaders agreed. But the conflicts between the Holy Synod and the Ministry of Justice over the revision of family law illustrate the friction that resulted when the agenda and priorities of the church leadership and the state administration differed. By the early twentieth century this friction had grown to the point where nearly every faction in the church desired institutional independence from the state. Had such independence been achieved, however, one of its costs might have been the loss of ecclesiastical jurisdiction over divorce and of the ability of the Holy Synod to block 'undesirable' changes in family law.[195]

In the mean time, the cost of the Synod's success in obstructing legal reform was to embitter lay advocates of reform. Blaming the Holy Synod for the delay in the reform of both substantive and procedural divorce law, an author in the *Petersburg Gazette* (*Peterburgskaia Gazeta*) complained in 1911 that '[t]he ecclesiastical authority has insisted on the immutability of canons that appeared a millennium and a half ago under social circumstances that have nothing in common with either the contemporary state or the conditions of contemporary civil life'. In the view of the author, 'consistorial *batiushki*, constrained by decrepit canons', therefore should be deprived of their role in divorce actions, with jurisdiction being transferred to secular judges, who better understood the conditions and needs of real life.[196] More tactfully, the Octobrist Duma deputy Ivan Godnev declared similarly in 1914 that

> [t]he current bill [on marital separation] is nothing other than the result of the unsatisfactory state of our current divorce laws, which at the present time provide no outlet for those people who get caught in such a distressing state of family life in marriage that their further life [together] becomes impossible. . . . Historically it is indisputable that the canon law of the early church was much broader and more humane, and viewed the question of marriage and divorce much more correctly, than our current law and our current practice.[197]

Godnev's implicit criticism of the current leadership of the church reflects the conservatism often underlying the demands for revision of the law. While some advocates of reform favoured complete severance of

[195] The experience of the Catholic Church in Western Europe and of the Church of England after the late 18th c. is instructive. See Phillips, *Putting Asunder*, esp. 191–226.

[196] *Peterburgskoe Gazeta* (1 May 1911), found in TsGIA F. 1405 op. 542 d. 671 l. 255. A colloquial expression for a priest, *batiushka* here is used condescendingly.

[197] *GDSO. 1914 g. 4-ii soz., ses. 2-aia*, ii. 385, 388. The Duma voted overwhelmingly for a relaxation of divorce law. Ibid., cols. 421–7.

the link between the religious and the secular aspects of marriage through the introduction of civil marriage,[198] Godnev—like most other advocates of reform—preferred to preserve this link, in this instance by grounding proposals for reform in earlier church traditions and practices. In the same way, most reformers sought to provide individual family members, especially wives and children, with greater freedom and security, but without eliminating either the superior authority of the husband and father or the moral obligations of individuals to the family as a whole. This attempt to adjust the legal expression of the traditional patriarchal and collectivist structure of the family to changes in social and economic relationships and in cultural ideals parallels the experience of Western Europe and the United States at this time.[199] But in the context of Imperial Russia, the principles and values embedded in the proposals for revision of the law had radical implications for the autocratic order. This combination of conservatism and reformism also characterized the practice of the Civil Cassation Department.

[198] For example, see P. Liakub, 'Nechto o sushchestve grazhdanskago braka na Zapade', *SG* (1890), 43: 4–6, 'S.-Peterburgskoe iuridicheskoe obshchestvo', *Pravo* (1903), 16, col. 1201, *RM* (1903), 1: 38–40, *'Kak smotrit' obshchestvo na tserkovnyi ili grazhdanskii brak?' Otvety na anketu, postavlennuiu knigoizdatel'stvom, so stat'eiu I. Tertichnago 'ot chego ne prochny nashi braki?'* (Kiev, 1908), 9–12, 14–16, *Protokoly kommissii*, 71–2, and G. Grigorovskii, *Grazhdanskii brak* (Ptgd., 1917). See also Borovikovskii, 'Brak i razvod', 1–2, 15–28, 59–62.

[199] See Phillips, *Putting Asunder*, esp. 494–5, 505–6, 513–15, Basch, *In the Eyes*, esp. 38–41, 110–12, 224–32, and M. Grossberg, *Governing the Hearth: Law and the Family in Nineteenth-Century America* (Chapel Hill, NC, 1985), esp. 10–11, 289–307. See also S. M. Okin, *Women in Western Political Thought* (Princeton, NJ, 1979), 197–202, 226–30, and for comparable arguments regarding attempts to reform Imperial criminal law, Engelstein, *Keys to Happiness*, chs. 2, 3, and 9.

5

The Possibilities of Judicial Revision

THE limited success of legislative attempts to revise Imperial family law during the post-reform period increased the role of the courts in adapting the law to changing social conditions and attitudes. Confronted by actual cases of marital conflict and the effects of legal discrimination against illegitimate children, judges responded by redefining the law in the process of enforcing it. At the highest level, the practice of the Civil Cassation Department came to reflect the affective ideal of the family that underlay most legal writing on the law from the 1870s onward. The decisions of the high court gradually crystallized into a policy that protected the welfare and rights of individual family members while seeking to ensure their fulfilment of what the court considered to be their moral obligations to one another. The ability of judges to pursue these objectives through judicial action was constrained, however, both by the language of statutory law and by ethical limitations on judicial law-making. Three countervailing influences thus shaped judicial development of family law in late Imperial Russia: the conservative limitations of statutory law, the reformist implications inherent in the view of the family that predominated among jurists, and the tendency of judicial ethics to limit reformist impulses by adherence to statutory law.

The way in which the Civil Cassation Department treated the property and personal rights of wives both demonstrates the ability of the high court to amend family law and reveals the principles that guided the court's development of the law. By strictly enforcing the statutory right of a wife to separate property while deviating from statutory law to create the right for her to leave her husband, the high court pursued the same objective: security of the welfare and rights of wives as individuals, albeit within the limits imposed by the family union. In the view of the Civil Cassation Department, this union constrained particularly the wife. The court upheld repeatedly, for example, the statutory power of the husband in his capacity as head of the family to limit the employment of his wife and to determine their place of mutual residence. But from the 1870s onward, the decisions of the high court began to emphasize the affective ties between spouses, the voluntary nature of their union, the mutuality of their moral obligations, and their equality, particularly with regard to their parental role.[1] Indeed, after the 1870s the Civil Cassation Department described the family in terms of relations of power and submission to authority only in a single decision made during the conservative reaction following the revolution of 1905. Yet even in this decision the high court gave equal weight to the moral bonds alleged to unite the family and to the need to protect individual family members from abuses of power by the husband or father.[2] Nor did the court alter significantly its position on substantive issues. Despite occasional inconsistencies in its rulings, then, after the 1870s the Civil Cassation Department protected and even expanded the legal rights of a wife, interpreting statutory law strictly or loosely to achieve this objective.

Protecting Women's Property Rights

From its inception, the Civil Cassation Department opposed all efforts by husbands, in-laws, or the creditors of husbands to erode the control of a wife over her own property. In so doing, the high court sought to secure the independent property rights of wives and to strengthen the general principle of individual ownership.[3] Rejecting the argument that marriage gave a husband the right to manage the property of his wife while they lived together, for example, the Civil Cassation Department declared in *Murashkovskaia* v. *Murashkovskii* in 1870 that

> [n]ot only does the property of a wife not become the property of her husband, but he does not even acquire through marriage the right to use or manage it. . . . the dowry of a wife, just as any property acquired by her during marriage through purchase, gift, inheritance or any other legal means, therefore is considered her separate property, and spouses have an equal right to dispose of their own property independently of one another . . .[4]

[1] *SRGKD* 1867 no. 70, 1869 no. 292, 1871 no. 761, and *RGKD* 1913 no. 92 (on the nature of marriage); *SRGKD* 1870 no. 1130, 1871 no. 504, 1880 no. 38, and 1898 no. 16 (on the husband's powers; but cf. *ZNDGZ*, no . 1059), 1883 no. 20, 1890 no. 18, and 1908 nos. 48 and 56 (on the spouses' relations). On the character of cassation department decisions, see above, Ch. 1, n. 51.

[2] *SRGKD* 1908 no. 95; but see 1908 no. 48 and *RGKD* 1913 no. 92 for different views.

[3] On property, see below, Ch. 9.

[4] *SRGKD* 1870 no. 59; see also 1868 no. 466, 1869 no. 16, 1871 no. 991, 1872 no. 334, 1875 no. 63, and 1901 no. 124.

In *Zhuravlev* v. *The Estate of Zhuravleva* in 1901 the high court extended this principle beyond the grave, holding that a surviving husband was not obligated to pay for the funeral and wake of his deceased wife if she had left sufficient property of her own.[5] Statutory law considered only the household effects found in a common residence to be community property. Yet even here the court held that a wife could protect such property from her husband or his creditors by proving sole ownership of it.[6]

Wives needed the protection of the courts especially to retain control of their dowries and to avoid responsibility for the debts of their husbands. Juridical literature and the frequency of judicial actions on the former issue suggest that the practice of giving the dowry of a wife to her husband to use for common family needs continued to be widespread in prerevolutionary Russia. Unregulated by statutory law, this custom created problems for the courts in determining the liability of a husband to his wife for the use of her dowry.[7] In this situation, the Civil Cassation Department consistently recognized the exclusive ownership of a dowry by the wife, upheld her right to demand control over her dowry at any time, and held the husband responsible for maintaining its value.[8] Moreover, in *Kollezhinskaia* v. *Kollezhinskii* in 1868 the high court ruled that a husband must surrender the dowry to his wife even though doing so would enable her to leave him. According to the court, a wife's control over her dowry constituted a property right that was independent of her obligations to her husband.[9] Hence even where local law expressly gave the husband the right to possess and use the dowry of his wife for family expenses, as in Bessarabia, the high court ruled that he must return it intact to her once they had separated for any reason.[10]

The high court likewise defended the interests of a wife against claims made by the creditors of her husband. In this instance, however, the

[5] *SRGKD* 1901 no. 124.

[6] *SRGKD* 1873 no. 57, 1880 no. 122, and 1899 no. 14; but in 1909 no. 21, the court ruled that spouses voluntarily could establish some form of community property.

[7] K. Zaborovskii, 'O vzaimnykh otnosheniiakh suprugov po imushchestvu', *Zhurnal Ministerstva Narodnago Prosveshcheniia* (1849), 63: 192–3, A. M. Khotkevich, 'Neskol′ko slov ob otnosheniiakh suprugov po imushchestvu', *Moskovskiia Universitetskiia Izvestiia* (1869), 7: 375–84, A. Savel′ev, *Iuridicheskiia otnosheniia mezhdu suprugami, po zakonam i obychaiam velikorusskago naroda* (Nizhny-Novgorod, 1881), 81–4, A. F. Kazimir, *Ob otnosheniiakh suprugov po imushchestvu* (Spb., 1885), 56–7, 68–72, A. I. Zagorovskii, *Kurs semeinago prava* (2nd edn., Odessa, 1909), 254–5, and *GU. Kn. 2-aia*, i. 184–5; see also A. L. Borovikovskii, 'Sud i sem′ia', in *Otchet sud′i* (Spb., 1892), ii. 246–7.

[8] *SRGKD* 1867 nos. 279, 314, 1870 nos. 1329, 1524, 1872 no. 908, and 1881 no. 14; see also I. G. Danilov, *Ukazatel′ voprosov grazhdanskago prava razreshavshikhsia na konsul′tatsii pri Ministerstve Iustitsii uchrezhdennoi 1867–1871* (Spb., 1873), 56–7, no. 61.

[9] *SRGKD* 1868 no. 466. [10] *SRGKD* 1871 no. 991 and 1908 no. 21.

court balanced its concern for the wife with the need to protect the creditors against fraud. For example, a heavily indebted husband might execute a fictitious bill of sale, mortgage, or loan agreement with his wife, thereby sheltering property in her name or giving her the rights of a preferred creditor.[11] Although statutory law tried to eliminate this problem by extending debt liability to gifts between spouses and by requiring proof that the wife had at least possessed sufficient means to make the purchase or loan, the potential for fraud remained high.[12] None the less, the Civil Cassation Department rigorously protected the separate property of the wife and generally placed the burden of proof of fraud on the creditors.[13]

In *Zinoveva* v. *The Bankruptcy Administration over Zinovev*, for example, the plaintiff Praskovia Zinoveva sought ownership of a building in St Petersburg that her husband had mortgaged to her for 10,000 roubles two months before being declared insolvent. The bankruptcy administrators of her husband contested her claim on the grounds that the mortgage was fictitious. Even though Zinoveva proved that she possessed sufficient capital at the time of the transaction, both the St Petersburg District Court and the Court of Appeals denied her suit because she had not also proved that she had actually given the money to her husband. Setting the decision aside, the Civil Cassation Department ruled that Zinoveva had to demonstrate only her ability to make the loan to her husband from her own resources, whereas the bankruptcy administration had to show that she had not actually made it.[14]

The Civil Cassation Department also broadly defined the power of a wife to dispose of her own property. As the court ruled in *Ivanova* v. *Parfenovskaia* in 1870, wives and children had an unlimited right to dispose of their own property without the consent of their husbands or parents. Hence in this case the court held that the husband of the respondent had no right to challenge the issuance by his wife of a loan note to their daughter solely on the grounds that he had not agreed to it.[15] By

[11] Zaborovskii, 'O vzaimnykh otnosheniiakh', 194–5, Khotkevich, 'Neskol'ko slov', 375–6, I. Orshanskii, 'Lichnyia i imushchestvennyia otnosheniia suprugov', in *Izsledovaniia po russkomu pravu semeinomu i nasledstvennomu* (Spb., 1877), 130–42, Kazimir, *Ob otnosheniiakh*, 36–40, Zagorovskii, *Kurs*, 254–5, *ZNDGZ*, nos. 120–2, and *GU. Kn. 2–aia*, i. 176–8.

[12] *SZ* (1857), x, pt. 2, *Zak. sud. grazh.*, arts. 2270–4, and xi, pt. 2, *Ust. torg.*, arts. 1932–7 (1893 edn., *Ust. sudoproiz. torg.*, arts. 554–8, 624).

[13] The burden of proof was reversed in the case of the household effects in a common residence. See *SRGKD* 1867 nos. 53, 279, 1870 no. 1645, 1871 no. 459, 1872 nos. 334, 908, 1873 no. 57, 1874 nos. 377, 889, 1875 nos. 63, 101, 724, 1876 no. 589, 1877 nos. 285, 355, 1879 no. 122, 1895 no. 67, 1898 no. 67, and 1899 no. 14.

[14] *SRGKD* 1876 no. 589.

[15] *SRGKD* 1870 no. 1130; see also 1870 no. 59.

contrast, the court did enforce the few specific limitations imposed by statutory law on the powers of disposition enjoyed by a wife, which concerned chiefly bills of exchange. Even here, however, the Civil Cassation Department did not invalidate such dispositions, but merely deprived them of the special guarantees extended to bills of exchange by law.[16]

From its inception, then, the Civil Cassation Department rigorously defended the interests of a wife as an independent property owner. While grounded in statutory law, this practice also reflected the prevailing view of women in legal literature as both individuals with equal rights and inherently weaker members of society in special need of protection by the law. The beliefs of jurists thus reinforced the provisions of statutory law, with the result that the property rights of married women received considerable protection in the courts.

Marital Separation

Protecting mistreated wives and resolving marital conflict posed a more difficult and controversial problem for the Civil Cassation Department because the only remedies considered feasible conflicted rather than coincided with statutory law. While statutory law proscribed marital separation except when granted by the Catholic or the Evangelical Lutheran Church, divorce lay outside the purview of the civil courts. Hence judges faced an agonizing dilemma. On the one hand, conscientious exercise of their role as guardians of the law produced results that many judges considered unjust, socially harmful, and contrary both to their own social values and to their professional self-image of protectors of the weaker members of society. On the other hand, the provision of equitable or effective relief for marital strife appeared to require contravention of the law that judges had sworn to uphold.

The Civil Cassation Department at first responded to this dilemma by preserving the integrity of the law. Hence in its decision in *Vagner* v. *Vagner* in 1868 it excluded any form of marital separation. In this case, St Petersburg resident Feodosiia Vagner had sought a monthly allowance of 40 roubles from her husband, Lieutenant-Colonel Pavel Vagner, who she claimed had agreed to pay her this amount after being transferred to Kronstadt. Because her husband had ceased to make these payments, Vagner asserted, she and her two children had fallen into destitution. Contesting the suit, Colonel Vagner argued that he had no obligation to

[16] *SRGKD* 1880 no. 38 and 1898 no. 16.

provide for his wife since she had abandoned him and now led a disreputable life. Although the St Petersburg District Court denied the suit on the grounds that Vagner had not proved the existence of an agreement with her husband, the St Petersburg Court of Appeals reversed this decision. The court held that the law obligated a husband to maintain his wife regardless of whether they lived together. The court added that although the respondent had not proved his charges against his wife, she had demonstrated that he had left her and had initially paid her 40 roubles per month.[17]

Setting this decision aside, the Civil Cassation Department adopted a strict interpretation of the law that denied the possibility of marital separation. The high court argued that the law required spouses to live together and predicated their legal rights and obligations on such co-residence. Hence, the court continued, the law not only did not, but could not define any rights or obligations for spouses living apart owing to marital discord. Indeed, to do so would violate the very foundation of the law. In short, a wife separated from her husband had no rights. The court asserted, moreover, that recognition of the right to support for a wife who was separated from her husband would violate the property rights of the husband by establishing a claim on his property. Yet Imperial law granted spouses completely independent property rights, with each spouse retaining the freedom to dispose of his or her own property without reference to the other. The high court concluded that the only legal remedy available to a wife in this situation was restoration of co-residence.[18] In subsequently confirming its position, the Civil Cassation Department also stressed the sacramental nature of marriage and held any agreement or judicial decision that resulted in the separation of spouses to be invalid because it contributed to an illegal objective, the wilful dissolution of a marriage.[19]

The position of the Civil Cassation Department attracted sharp criticism from both legal commentators and the general press. In his essays in the early 1870s, for example, the jurist Ilia Orshanskii branded the rulings of the high court as unjust, socially harmful, and contrary to the moral union of spouses that lay at the basis of marriage. He advocated a more flexible interpretation of the law that would allow the courts to grant marital separation and to obligate a husband to support his wife in appropriate circumstances.[20] Advancing a similar critique of high court

[17] *SRGKD* 1868 no. 461. [18] Ibid.

[19] *SRGKD* 1868 no. 526, 1870 nos. 799, 1145, 1873 no. 1385, and 1875 no. 291; see also *SRPS* i, pt. 2, no. 662, and Danilov, *Ukazatel' voprosov*, 3–4, 1868 no. 93.

[20] On Orshanskii, see above, Ch. 3; for a more moderate position, see A. Liubavskii, *Iuridicheskiia monografii i izsledovaniia* (Spb., 1867, 1875, 1878), iii. 429–38.

decisions in 1871 and 1872, the liberal newspaper *Voice* (*Golos*) blamed the inflexibility of the court and severity of the law on the religious basis of family law. It called on both the court and government legislators to distinguish between the unattainable religious ideal of marriage and its social and juridical aspects. Otherwise, the paper argued, lower courts would be unable to render just decisions, protect abused wives, or adjust the law to the changing needs of society.[21] Even the moderate *St Petersburg Gazette* (*Sankt-Peterburgskie Vedomosti*) accused the high court of undermining rather than supporting the sanctity and moral basis of marriage. In the view of the editors, the obligation of a wife to love and live with her husband did not require her to share in his degeneracy or suffer his abuse. Hence the courts needed the power to allow a wife to leave her husband when her welfare demanded it. By stripping lower courts of this power, the editors complained, the Civil Cassation Department had left wives helpless before the tyranny of their husbands.[22]

The actions of lower courts seemed to corroborate these charges. Apparently believing that they needed greater flexibility to deal with the realities of marital life, lower courts resisted the doctrine on marital separation established originally by the Civil Cassation Department.[23] Many justices of the peace in particular asserted that they frequently encountered marital disputes that could be resolved only by allowing the spouses to separate. More concerned with alleviating what they considered to be a serious social problem than with reinforcing a religious sacrament, they argued that allowing a wife to leave her husband while retaining the right to support from him often provided the only effective means of avoiding brutal mistreatment or severe neglect. The peasant who hitched his wife to a cart and whipped her all the way back from her parents' to his own village to teach her the proper respect for his authority represented only an extreme example of the kind of behaviour that justices sought to curtail.[24] Lower court judges added that in any case the

[21] *Golos* (1871), 158: 1 and (1872), 46: 1–2. The paper clearly also was attacking the views of Pobedonostsev and Leshkov (see above, Ch. 3).

[22] *SVed* (1872), 130: 1–2, and 131: 1; see also 'Voprosy braka', *Nedelia* (1869), 22, cols. 681–9, and *BV* (1870), 270: 2.

[23] See the decisions of one or both lower courts in *SRGKD* 1868 no. 526, 1870 nos. 799, 1145, 1871 no. 970, 1872 no. 407, 1873 nos. 1385, 1666, 1874 no. 689, 1875 no. 291, and 1876 no. 41; Borovikovskii, 'Sud i sem′ia', 227–33, Orshanskii, 'Lichnyia i imushchestvennyia otnosheniia', 19–22, 28–30, 39–47, 52–65, 88–9, 184, 188–91, *VE* (1877), 2: 828–30, Savel′ev, *Iuridicheskiia otnosheniia*, 62–5, 69–74, and *GU. Kn. 2-aia*, i. 213–15.

[24] This and other cases are described in M. I. Kulisher, *Razvod i polozhenie zhenshchin* (Spb., 1896), 148–53, 183. See also V. Nazar′ev, 'Sovremennaia glush′. Iz vospominanii mirovogo sud′i', *VE* (1872), 2: 609–22 (but cf. (1876), 5: 126, 145–7), Ia. Ludmer, 'Bab′i

interpretation of the law adopted by the Civil Cassation Department could not be enforced. Court bailiffs could return a wife to her husband against the wishes of one or the other, but they could not prevent either spouse from leaving moments later. Trying to enforce the law under these circumstances, judges claimed, merely undermined respect for law in general without either strengthening the institution of marriage or resolving marital disputes.[25]

Underlying the complaints about the difficulty of enforcing the law lay a belief in its basic injustice. Influenced by the moral and utilitarian critique of the law advanced by their peers, many judges concluded that the law conflicted with the affective nature of the contemporary family. It also appeared incompatible with their concept of legality and their desire to resolve social problems and to protect the weaker members of society through law. As a result, members of the judiciary both advocated legislative reform of the law and revised the law through their decisions. As an assistant chief procurator in the Civil Cassation Department in the late 1870s, for example, the noted liberal journalist, attorney, and zemstvo activist Konstantin Arsenev proved instrumental in modifying the position of the high court on marital separation. In an address in 1883 to the St Petersburg Juridical Society he advocated still further relaxation of the law in order to bring it into conformity with changing social needs and attitudes.[26] Similar sentiments were later expressed by Aleksandr Borovikovskii, an appeals court judge, instructor at Novorossiia University, and eventually senator in the Civil Cassation Department, whose skilful analysis of the law helped justify the doctrine ultimately adopted

ston′i', *IuV* (1884), 11: 446–67, and 12: 658–79, A. A. Vereshchagin, 'O bab′ikh stonakh', *IuV* (1885), 4: 750–61, I. M. Tiutriumov, 'Po povodu peresmotra i kodifikatsii grazhdanskikh zakonov', *RB* (1884), 3: 694–8, and in *ZNDGZ*, pp. 59–66, ibid., nos. 31, 39, 49, 71, 90, 95, 97–100, 104, I. N. Zakharin, 'Mirovoi sud v Podolii', *RS* (1897), 3: 565–6, and 4: 138–41, *GU. Kn. 2-aia*, i. 210–15, TsGIA F. 797 op. 91–1898 d. 53 ll. 34–70, pp. 4–8, B. Farnsworth, 'The Litigious Daughter-in-law: Family Relations in Rural Russia in the Second Half of the Nineteenth Century', *SR* 45 (1986), 49–64, and B. Engel, *Between the Fields and the City: Women, Work, and Family in Russia, 1861–1914* (Cambridge, forthcoming), ch. 3.

[25] Borovikovskii, 'Sud i sem′ia', 215–21, 234, 269, A. F. Koni, *Sobranie sochinenii* (Mos., 1966–9), i. 244–8, *ZNDGZ*, nos. 27–30, 67, 83, 88–9, 94, 'Isk zheny o sovmestnom zhitel′stve s muzhem', *IuG* (1896), 5: 2–3, *SRGKD* 1872 no. 407, M. I. Pen′kovskii, *Kassatsionnaia praktika. Ne voshedshiia v ofitsial′nyi sbornik resheniia Grazhdanskago Kassatsionnago Departamenta Pravitel′stvuiushchago Senata s 1897 g. po 1914 g., s postateinym i predmetnym ukazateliami* (Ptgd., 1915), no. 181, and TsGIA F. 797 op. 91–1898 d. 53 ll. 34–70, pp. 9–13.

[26] K. K. Arsen′ev, 'Khronika—Razluchenie suprugov, kak neobkhodimyi institut brachnago prava', *VE* (1884), 3: 290–326. Arsenev helped write the decision in *SRGKD* 1879 no. 309.

by the high court. In his view, not only was the position articulated initially by the court unenforceable, but it also undermined the moral basis of marriage by relieving the husband of having to earn the love of his wife and by encouraging his abuse of authority.[27]

Confronted by this criticism and by the contrary decisions of lower courts, the Civil Cassation Department modified its position and thus also the practical meaning of the law. The high court proved to be responsive to this pressure, however, at least partly because of changes in its composition which occurred during the 1870s. Of the sixteen senators who served in the Civil Cassation Department between its establishment in 1866 and 1870, eight had been born prior to 1813, five between 1816 and 1821, and three between 1824 and 1827. As a result, only six members of the high court had received a juridical education, and all members of the court had matured professionally during a period when there had been little critical discussion of Imperial civil law. Nor had the majority of senators had to view the formal requirements of statutory law through the prism of marital conflict conducted by the spouses in an open courtroom. Although most members of the high court had served extensively in the Ministry of Justice and the judicial departments of the Senate prior to their appointment to the Civil Cassation Department, only six had even brief experience in the lower courts, where in any case pre-reform civil procedure had shielded the judiciary from the people and drama involved in a case. Considerably younger than the majority of senators, the four members of the procuratorial staff similarly lacked experience in the lower courts, although three had received a juridical education. Hence little in the education or experience of most members of the high court inclined them to depart from the letter of the law on the question of marital separation.[28]

During the 1870s, however, the composition of the Civil Cassation

[27] Borovikovskii, 'Sud i sem′ia', 213–50, 263–9. See also his articles 'Brak i razvod po proektu Grazhdanskago Ulozheniia', *ZhMIu* (1902), 8: 1–62, and 'Konstitutsiia sem′i po proektu Grazhdanskago Ulozheniia', *ZhMIu* (1902), 9: 1–38.

[28] *SChMIu, 1866*, 57–8, *1870*, 33–4, *Lichnyi sostav kassatsionnykh departamentov Pravitel′stvuiushchago Senata za 1866–1891 gody* (Spb., 1891), and TsGIA F. 1364 op. 15 d. 356, 366, 396, 425, 447, 479, 496, 505, 511, 523, 675, 694, 728, 738, 781, 786, 793, 857, 927, and 949. The presentation of reports in the relevant high-court decisions suggests that Senators A. D. Bashutskii (1792), A. I. Voitsekhovich (1806), A. E. Matiunin (1810), and N. E. Tornau (1810), and the procurators D. G. fon Derviz (1829) and I. N. Nikolaev (1827), formed a conservative core on this issue. The four senators were among the oldest men in the court. Only fon Derviz possessed a juridical education, and only Tornau had served briefly in a lower court. Voitsekhovich had spent most of his career in the chancellery of the Holy Synod and in the Main Administration for Foreign Faiths.

Department began to change, in terms of both specific personnel and their background. By the middle of the decade, few members of the court of 1870 remained. Although the new members of the high court often resembled in age, education, and service experience those whom they replaced, men like Arsenev, Aleksandr Knirim, and Pavel Korobin also joined the court. All three had graduated from the Imperial School of Jurisprudence and shared extensive experience in the lower courts prior to their appointment to the Civil Cassation Department. Arsenev had practised for eight years as an attorney in St Petersburg, Knirim had served for six years as assistant chairman of the St Petersburg District Court and chairman of the St Petersburg Commercial Court, and Korobin had served for eight years as chairman of the Riazan District Court and a department chairman of the St Petersburg Court of Appeals. Considerably younger than their predecessors on the high court, Arsenev and Knirim began their careers in the idealistic and critical atmosphere that accompanied preparation of the judicial reform, and in their writings both used European law to expose what they considered to be the defects of Imperial civil law.[29] A core of jurists with experience of the difficulties resulting from a strict interpretation of the law and with knowledge of alternative means of resolving cases of marital conflict thus had appeared in the Civil Cassation Department. Not surprisingly, Knirim, Arsenev, and Korobin delivered the reports that formed the basis for the decisions in the 1870s which most significantly modified the position of the high court on marital separation.[30]

By the early 1880s, the backgrounds of most members of the Civil Cassation Department resembled those of Knirim, Arsenev, and Korobin. Of the twenty-five senators in the high court in 1884, for example, only four had been born prior to 1821. In contrast, twelve had been born after 1834 and therefore had received their education and begun their careers in the same atmosphere that influenced Knirim and Arsenev. Twenty

[29] TsGIA F. 1364 op. 15 d. 337, 602, and 624. Arsenev and Knirim were born in 1837, and Korobin in 1826. All three belonged to the nobility. While Knirim owned no land, both Arsenev and Korobin owned substantial estates, although it is not clear when Korobin acquired his property. Entering state service in the Senate in 1846, Korobin became chairman of the Riazan District Court on its foundation in 1866. On Knirim, see above, Ch. 4.

[30] Knirim, Arsenev, and Korobin prepared the reports for the decisions in *SRGKD* 1872 no. 407, 1879 no. 309, and 1882 no. 152. Although all members of the high court discussed the decisions that were to be published for the guidance of lower courts, the chief responsibility for drafting a decision rested with the senator and procurator who prepared reports on the case. For a description of the procedure followed by the court, see K. P. Zmirlov, 'Zhelatel'naia reforma v nashem kassatsionnom proizvodstve i sudoustroistve', *ZhMIu* (1896), 5: 38–82.

senators had received a juridical education, and eighteen had served in the lower courts prior to their appointment to the Civil Cassation Department. Similarly, of the ten members of the procuratorial staff, nine had been born after 1833, five had received a juridical education, and eight had served in the lower courts.[31] These trends in the background of members of the high court continued to strengthen, so that by 1900 twenty-two of the twenty-six senators had received a juridical education and twenty-one had served in the lower courts prior to their appointment. At least eight of the eleven members of the procuratorial staff also had been educated in the law, and all had experience in the lower courts.[32] Although education and experience by themselves, of course, did not determine the attitude towards the law of a particular member of the high court, the background of most senators and procurators at least familiarized them with the juridical arguments in favour of marital separation and with the human dimension of the cases coming before them, when personal experience did not. Whether for idealistic or other reasons, eight of the twenty-eight members of the high court in 1900 whose records indicate they were married gave their wives or daughters separate passports after the introduction of new regulations in 1895, while one senator had remarried shortly after receiving a divorce.[33]

The staged retreat by the Civil Cassation Department from its initial interpretation of the law reflects this evolution in the composition of the high court. In a series of decisions in the 1870s the court acknowledged the impracticality and inequity, particularly for wives, of a strict interpretation of the law. Groping for a workable doctrine that would preserve the fiction of observing statutory law, the court gradually formulated the rule that a wife was not obligated to live with her husband, yet retained the right to support from him, if for reasons beyond her control co-residence with him proved impossible. Wary of loosening marital ties too far or of overstepping its authority by altering the law too drastically, the

[31] *SChMIu, 1884*, 45–8, *Lichnyi sostav*, and TsGIA F. 1364 op. 15 d. 347, 352–3, 406, 439, 465, 471, 484, 513, 556, 571, 602, 604, 624, 666, 670, 714, 735, 738, 746, 759, 808, 810, 849, 854, 857–8, 916, 919–20, 947, 997, 1009, 1015, and 1019.

[32] *SChMIu, 1900*, 35–8, *Lichnyi sostav*, and TsGIA F. 1364 op. 15 d. 340, 347, 352–3, 383, 394, 410–11, 451, 468, 479, 484, 490, 536, 547, 556, 603, 665, 688, 712–13, 762, 793, 810, 813, 849, 854, 904, 919, 929, 943, 950, 988, 990, 1005, and 1009. See also above, Ch. 1, Tables 1.7–1.10.

[33] TsGIA F. 1364 op. 15 d. 383, 394, 411, 479, 484, 547, 665, 813, and 849. Their writings on the law would suggest that at least A. L. Borovikovskii, N. V. Grave, and K. P. Zmirlov were motivated partly by their ideological beliefs. Four of the eight—Grave, Zmirlov, Ia. V. Saburov, and D. A. Viktorov—prepared reports for relevant decisions of the high court: *SRGKD* 1886 no. 29, 1892 no. 111, 1895 no. 44, and 1902 no. 48.

high court initially construed these circumstances narrowly. Hence it accepted the lack of a fixed residence for the husband, his refusal to live with his wife, or his mental incapacity as valid reasons for separation but resisted lower court efforts to include marital discord in general or the immoral or abusive conduct of a husband, provided the husband still wished to live with his wife.[34] At the end of the decade, however, in a landmark decision shaped partially by Arsenev and Korobin, the high court held that the spouses could agree to separate as long as the lower courts found the reasons for separation to be valid and the intention of the agreement not to be the permanent dissolution of the marriage.[35]

To justify its evolving doctrine, the Civil Cassation Department abandoned or revised many of its previous arguments against marital separation. To be sure, the court still believed that spouses were obligated to live together, but it now considered this obligation conditional, especially on the actions and circumstances of the husband, rather than absolute. Moreover, the court now argued that obligating the husband to support his wife when their separation was his fault provided the only effective means of securing the legal rights and personal welfare of the wife. Not only did such arrangements protect the wife, the court reasoned in *Kokoraki* v. *Kokoraki* in 1872, but they helped to preserve the marriage because they remained binding only as long as the circumstances causing the separation continued.[36] For this reason, the court now held, these arrangements did not violate the property rights of the husband because they constituted a personal obligation that depended on his willingness and ability to live with his wife rather than an unlimited right of the wife to the property of her husband.[37] In sum, the Civil Cassation Department no longer viewed marital separation as an unlawful act but instead considered it to be a useful device for protecting wives while preserving their marriages.

At the end of the 1870s the Civil Cassation Department still hesitated to apply its new doctrine on marital separation widely. From the mid-1880s onward, however, as criticisms of the law by jurists intensified and the composition of the Civil Cassation Department continued to change,

[34] For instances where separation was recognized, see *SRGKD* 1871 no. 970 (which was a rehearing of 1870 no. 1145), 1872 no. 407, 1873 no. 1666, and 1882 no. 152; for instances where the right was recognized in principle but denied in the particular case, see 1874 no. 1689 and 1876 no. 41; the court reiterated its earlier position in 1875 no. 291.

[35] *SRGKD* 1879 no. 309; the court partially revoked this principle in *RGKD* 1913 no. 95.

[36] *SRGKD* 1872 no. 407; see also 1871 no. 970, 1873 no. 1666, 1879 no. 309, and 1882 no. 152.

[37] *SRGKD* 1873 no. 1666 and 1882 no. 152.

the high court broadened the application of its doctrine. In particular, in two decisions in 1886 and 1889 it upheld the right of a lower court to award a separated wife support despite the profession by her husband that he wished to live with her, provided the court found that the conduct of the husband did not support his statement. The lower courts therefore could consider the behaviour of the husband as legitimate grounds for granting his wife a separation against his will, which significantly increased their ability to protect a wife from abuse or neglect by her husband.[38]

The high court expressed its doctrine on marital separation most fully, however, in its decision in M——a v. M. in 1906.[39] The decision also increased still further both the ability of wives to seek protection from the courts and the flexibility enjoyed by the courts in resolving such cases. The plaintiff, Sofiia M——a, had brought suit against her husband for support, even though she still lived with him. M——a claimed that because of his infatuation with another woman, her husband refused to speak to her, gave her no money and only meagre portions of tea and sugar, and had even taken the curtains from her room in order to drive her from his house. Lacking other means of support and therefore unable to leave her husband, M——a sought 83 roubles per month from him. Her husband, Colonel Ivan M., referred to previous decisions of the high court in countering that a wife had no right to sue her husband for support unless they had actually separated. The St Petersburg District Court rejected this argument and granted M——a's suit.

In upholding this decision, the St Petersburg Court of Appeals held that the obligation of a wife to live with her husband and her right to support from him depended on the moral relations between them. According to the court, '[o]nly when the husband fulfils [his] moral obligations towards his wife can the latter be considered obligated to live together with her husband in accordance with the [law]'.[40] The court concluded that a wife was not required to live with her husband when he failed to fulfil his obligations towards her. Attempting to refute the argument presented by Colonel M. while accepting implicitly its main premiss, the court argued that he had treated his wife so abysmally that in essence they had separated; M——a therefore had a right to demand support from her husband even though they resided in the same house. The court added

[38] *SRGKD* 1886 no. 29 and 1890 no. 18; see also 1906 no. 8 and *RGKD* 1913 no. 95, and, where the principle was confirmed but the suit denied, *SRGKD* 1892 no. 111, 1893 no. 106, and 1908 no. 48.

[39] *SRGKD* 1906 no. 8. [40] Ibid.

that the law could not be understood so narrowly as to allow the wife a right to support only after she had been thrown out on the street. Such an interpretation, it argued, would compel a wife either to continue living with her husband under abusive conditions or to become homeless in order to acquire the right to sue him for support. The court concluded that such a situation 'would not only be an injustice, but a barbarity'.[41]

Upholding the main points of this decision, the Civil Cassation Department confirmed the right of a wife to leave her husband and for the first time recognized her right to sue him for appropriate support while still living with him. Using its previous decisions to justify the former right, the court sought to base the latter on statutory law. Clearly, however, the same notion of the reciprocal rights and obligations between spouses that had guided the court of appeals also influenced the high court. The court asserted that statutory law assumed that the spouses lived together and therefore failed to define their rights and obligations when they lived apart. Hence the statutory obligation of a husband to support his wife arose from the obligation of the spouses to live together and referred only to the period when they actually did so. The high court acknowledged that it had recognized as an exception the obligation of a husband to support a wife from whom he was separated, but only in cases where he had caused the separation. Concluding that a husband was obligated generally to support his wife, the court rejected the argument of Colonel M. that a wife could claim support only after a separation. On the contrary, the court declared, a wife could seek defence of her marital rights from the moment her husband had violated them, regardless of whether they still lived together, and in certain circumstances also could petition a court to recognize that married life with her husband was impossible. But in either case, the high court concluded, she possessed the right to an appropriate level of support from her husband.[42]

The decision of the Civil Cassation Department in *M——a* v. *M.* represented the culmination of a process through which the high court significantly modified statutory law while claiming formally to uphold it. In essence, through its practice the court created the right for a wife to leave her husband while retaining the right to support from him. In so doing, the high court reflected the progressivist view of the relationship between spouses which dominated contemporary juristic writing. In the practice of the court, the authority of the husband as head of the family

[41] Ibid.

[42] Ibid. For the fullest statement on the procedure for determining the level of support, see *SRGKD* 1882 no. 152.

had become limited by the rights of his wife, whose obligations towards her husband now were considered conditional on the fulfilment of his obligations towards her.[43] Hence the wife emerged as an individual commanding equal respect, if not authority, with her husband within the family. The high court also apparently believed that the inferior legal position as well as the presumed natural weakness of a wife entitled her to special protection, since it formulated its doctrine on marital separation exclusively with respect to wives and made separation contingent on the behaviour of the husband. The court established no corresponding right for the husband, although in 1908 it did rule that a wife operating a successful business could not evict her drunken and indolent husband from her apartment, thereby demonstrating that moral obligations worked both ways.[44] Indeed, to further protect the wife, the Civil Cassation Department held in *Rykhlis et al.* v. *Rykhlis* in 1895 that a separated wife who had been awarded support from her husband could have him declared insolvent or have his property distrained in order to force him to pay her.[45]

Similar objectives led the court gradually to grant illegitimate children the right to bring civil actions against their father for support.[46] The court asserted that even though no statutory obligation existed, 'a natural bond exists between illegitimate children and their parents, and . . . from this bond arises the obligation of the father to assist the mother in supporting their illegitimate child in an amount commensurate with his means'.[47] Hence for both illegitimate children and wives, the moral obligations believed to arise from natural family ties became the source of enforceable legal rights in post-reform judicial practice.[48]

Aware that their actions were controversial, judges justified them by depicting their development of the law as a necessary response to objective

[43] Similarly, the high court held that the main considerations in assigning custody of children should be their welfare and security, even though the position of the father as head of the family gave him preference. *SRGKD* 1890 no. 18; see also the lower court decisions in 1883 no. 20, 1908 no. 56, and Pen′kovskii, *Kassatsionnaia praktika*, no. 181.

[44] *SRGKD* 1908 no. 95. For a contrary decision by a district congress, see N. Sh——ov, 'Isk o vodvorenii muzha k zhene', *IuG* (1896), 90: 2.

[45] *SRGKD* 1896 no. 104; see also 1882 no. 152, 1890 no. 18, 1895 no. 44, 1906 no. 8, and *RGKD* 1913 no. 95.

[46] *ROSPKD* 1868 no. 657; *SRGKD* 1873 no. 1383, 1888 no. 17, and 1893 no. 105; see also *ROSPKD* 1899 no. 21, which reversed 1893 no. 23.

[47] *SRGKD* 1893 no. 105.

[48] For other decisions emphasizing the affective ties and moral obligations between family members, see *SRGKD* 1871 no. 995, 1883 no. 20, 1893 no. 106, 1898 no. 32, 1899 no. 2, 1902 no. 48, 1908 no. 56, and *RGKD* 1913 no. 92.

circumstances. Echoing an argument made frequently by their peers, for example, the authors—mostly members of the high court—of the draft civil code asserted in 1898 that

> all efforts to insist on the strict application of the unconditional law obligating spouses to live together have proved unsuccessful, and . . . under the pressure of the just demands of life itself, [the courts] have allowed so many unavoidable deviations from the law, which seem almost to be new legislative statutes, that in practice [the law] has acquired a meaning incompatible with its literal content.[49]

Yet as use of the word 'just' (*spravedlivye*) suggests, the values and attitudes of judges influenced their assessment of contemporary social needs and thus shaped their perception of the problems created by statutory law.

Judges attempted to mitigate the problems believed to be caused by formal statutes by introducing greater flexibility into the law, thereby compensating partially for the limited ability of the government to revise the law through legislation. In this way they rendered the law more responsive to changing conditions and attitudes, at least as these changes were understood by the educated and largely urban professional strata of society from which the judiciary sprang. In the final analysis, the image of the family that emerged from the treatment by the Civil Cassation Department of the personal and property rights of wives and illegitimate children corresponded closely to that contained in the draft civil code and portrayed in contemporary legal literature.

Although sometimes lagging behind lower courts, the Civil Cassation Department played a crucial role in the process of judicial transformation of the law because it legitimized and generalized the actions of these courts. In addition, the practice of the high court influenced other government bodies concerned with administration of the law. At a parallel level with the Civil Cassation Department, for example, the First General Meeting and the Second Department of the Senate from the later 1880s onward used the interpretation of the law made by the high court to justify their own decisions instructing police officials, land captains, and other state officials with administrative authority over the peasantry to allow wives of peasants to leave their husbands in cases of abusive or neglectful treatment. This ruling later was extended to the unprivileged strata of the urban population.[50] While these instructions concerned only

[49] TsGIA F. 797 op. 91–1898 d. 53 ll. 34–70, p. 13.

[50] A. A. Oppengeim, *Ukazatel' voprosov prava razreshennykh Ministerstvom Iustitsii za vremia s kontsa 1885 po 1893 god* (Spb., 1895), 239–40, no. 92a (1888 no. 18); circulars

the issuance of separate passports and did not address the question of support from the husband, they none the less recognized the right of a wife to personal security and offered her greater protection than she had enjoyed previously under the law.

But the Civil Cassation Department did not possess unlimited power to alter the law. In particular, divorce lay completely outside its purview. Even where it enjoyed some latitude, the high court acted hesitantly when its preferred remedies appeared to contravene statutory law or to be politically controversial. Hence it defended the property rights of wives more readily and completely than their personal rights. As a result, its doctrine on marital separation remained tenuous and incomplete. Moreover, determination of the impossibility of joint married life and of the fault for this situation was highly subjective, resulting in frequent disagreements between lower courts and the Civil Cassation Department.[51] Many, and probably most, forms of marital conflict remained unaffected by the rulings of the high court, and lower court judges with cautious or conservative inclinations undoubtedly were reluctant to apply these rulings even when possible. In the event that a court did reject the suit of an abused, neglected, or simply discontented wife, prior to passage of the law of 1914 she had no legal recourse apart from a petition to the Imperial Chancellery. The position of women under the law therefore remained harsh, and tragedies like Sharapova's leap from the Kaluga courthouse window continued to occur. In the final analysis, then, the courts provided only a partial solution to the problems attributed by critics to Imperial family law.

Frustration with this situation helps explain the ambiguous response of liberal and progressivist jurists to the development of the law by the Civil Cassation Department. Although welcoming the effects of the later decisions by the high court, several progressivist jurists also criticized the court for violating statutory law to achieve them. Their criticism rested in part on a professional rivalry with the Civil Cassation Department over

of the Ministry of Internal Affairs dated from 1902 to 1912 contained in *Gosudarstvennyi Sovet. Sessiia VIII. Kommisiia*, Doklad no. 2 (HLL), S. Kozhukhov, 'O praktike Pravitel'stvuiushchago Senata po voprosu o vydache krest'ianskim zhenam otdel'nyi vid na zhitel'stvo', *ZhMIu* (1901), 3: 158–68, M. B., 'Russkie otgoloski', *ZhD* (1899), 8: 77–8, and G. S. N., 'K voprosu o razdel'nom zhitel'stva suprugov', *Pravo* (1900), 52, cols. 2484–7.

[51] e.g. see *SRGKD* 1892 no. 111 and 1893 no. 106, Pen'kovskii, *Kassatsionnaia praktika*, nos. 84, 181, 'Isk zheny o sovmestnom zhitel'stve s muzhem', *IuG* (1896), 5: 2–3, S. B. Gomolitskii, 'Iz tekushchei praktiki Grazhdanskago Kassatsionnago Departamenta', *VP* (1902), 4/5: 178–86, and V. V. Bykhovskii, *Brak, razdel'noe zhitel'stvo i razvod* (Mos., 1912), 45–6. See also TsGIA F. 797 op. 91–1898 d. 53 ll. 34–70, pp. 4–13.

their relative roles in defining the law and in part on their concern that the high court itself might undermine the principle of legality by combining legislative with judicial powers.[52] But equally importantly, progressivist critics feared that judicial action would reduce the pressure for legislative revision of the law, especially through the medium of a civil code, which for liberals and progressivists represented one of the chief hopes for the progressive transformation of the legal basis of society and thus for the peaceful reform of society itself.

Conservative reaction to the development of the law by the courts split for similar reasons. Most conservatives condemned the actions of the courts and considered their development of Imperial family law to be further proof of the subversive nature of the new judicial system.[53] By the turn of the century, however, several conservative jurists had come to view judicial action as a way of adjusting civil law to the needs of contemporary life while confining its development within the boundaries set by existing statutory law. In this way, introduction of the draft civil code, considered by conservatives to be a Trojan Horse bearing subversive reforms, could be avoided.[54] It is ironic that as the limitations on the power of the courts became apparent, liberals became more critical of them and despaired of their ability to resolve social problems, whereas conservative jurists shed some of their fear of the courts and began to view judicial action as a less threatening means than codification to effect change.

[52] M. Levitskii, 'Nash kassatsionnyi Senat i obshchee sobranie pervago i kassatsionnago departamentov Senata', *SG* (1902), 32: 4–5, and 33: 3–6, I. V. Gessen, 'Razdel'noe zhitel'stvo suprugov', *Pravo* (1911), 49, cols. 2755–67, and 50, cols. 2842–51, A. Kondiurev, 'K state o vysylke zhen v postoiannoe mestozhitel'stvo ikh muzhei i o primenenii pasportnago ustava', *IuG* (1901), 73: 2, and N., 'K voprosu'.

[53] e.g. see 'Mera sodeistvuiushchaia raspadeniiu krest'ianskoi sem'i', *MV* (1900), 295: 1–2, I. Kashkarov, 'Senatskoe reshenie otmeniaiushchee zakon', *MV* (1900), 330: 2, and TsGIA F. 797 op. 92 d. 51 ll. 1–4.

[54] L. A. Kasso, *Istochniki russkago grazhdanskago prava* (Mos., 1900), 7–15, and TsGIA F. 1226 op. 1 d. 1 ll. 34–50 (pp. 25–7), 209.

PART II

Restructuring Property and Inheritance Law

6

Traditional Law: Patrimonial Property and Pressures for Change

WEARIED by incessant disputes over land with fractious relatives, in the early 1760s the grandfather of Sergei Aksakov abandoned his patrimonial estate in Simbirsk province and moved his family, serfs, and other belongings eastward to the uncrowded steppes of Orenburg. There he at last found peace from the endless quarrels and vexatious constraints on his proprietary power produced by Imperial Russian inheritance law.

> No petitions, no complaints, no disputes, no disturbance! No tiresome relations, no divided ownership! No thieves to fell his trees, no trespassers to trample down his corn and meadows! He was undisputed master at last in his own house, and beyond it: he might feed sheep, or mow grass, or cut firewood where he pleased without a word from any one.[1]

The difficulties experienced by Asksakov's grandfather reflect some of the common effects of tsarist property and inheritance law. The constant division and dispersal of property caused by the law not only resulted in conflict among relatives and neighbours, but also sometimes frustrated the efforts of those apparently few landowners who wished to organize their property in a more productive manner. Among the nobility, moreover, the fragmentation of landholdings also affected the relative standing of individual families as well as the relationship between the autocracy and the nobility as a whole. Concern over these problems already had been voiced by some state servitors from the landed nobility in the early eighteenth century. Demands for revision of the law intensified after the abolition of serfdom in 1861, when noble landowners simultaneously became more reliant on the commercial exploitation of their land and confronted a more competitive market for the land itself.

[1] S. Aksakov, *Memoirs of the Aksakov Family: A Russian Gentleman* (reprint edn., Westport, Conn., 1977), 13. This is the first part of a trilogy that recounts the family history of the noble landowner, state official, and author Sergei Aksakov (1791–1859).

The Limitations of Patrimonial Property

The problems experienced by landowners like the elder Aksakov derived primarily from the patrimonial principle that underlay Imperial property and inheritance law. Under this principle, certain property became identified with the kin-group (*rod*), with the result that the owner's power to dispose of it was limited, especially at death.[2] In essence, any immovable property inherited by a member of the patrilineal kin-group of the deceased owner or bequeathed by an owner to his or her direct legal heirs became classified as 'patrimonial'. Thenceforward such property could not be transferred to anyone other than the direct legal heirs except by sale. The direct heirs therefore enjoyed a secure right to inherit their share of patrimonial property in kind which the owner could not overcome, at least by any legal means, either in life or at death. Heirs could not be compelled to accept other property or the payment of a cash equivalent in place of the patrimonial property due them by law. Moreover, if sold to non-kin, patrimonial property could be redeemed by any member of the kin-group, with some limitations, within three years and on generally favourable terms.[3]

All remaining immovable property and all movable property, including money and stocks as well as tangible objects, was considered 'acquired property', over which the owner enjoyed unlimited powers of disposition during his life and at death.[4] But the inheritance of acquired immovable property by the legal heirs converted it into patrimonial property. The property remained so classified until acquired by non-kin, for whom it again became 'acquired property'. An owner therefore could transform patrimonial into acquired property by selling it to, and then repurchasing it from, non-kin. Although sometimes used to gain greater control over property, this device was expensive as well as risky. Even if the sale itself involved no actual exchange of cash, both the sale and the repurchase were liable to taxation. Moreover, the property was temporarily vulnerable

[2] *SZ* (1857), x, pt. 1, art. 420, defined full ownership as the right to possess, use, and dispose of property.

[3] *SZ* (1857), x, pt. 1, arts. 399–400, 967, 970, 996–8, 1001, 1003, 1068, 1086, 1100, 1110 pt. 1, 1111–18, 1120, 1138, 1140, 1346–72, 1506 (and also *Prod.* 1876, art. 116 prim.), and ix, arts. 222, 550 pt. 2; Imperial property and inheritance law in general was contained primarily in *SZ* x, pt. 1, arts. 383–1537. A detailed analysis of prerevolutionary literature on property and inheritance law is provided below in Ch. 7.

[4] *SZ* (1857), x, pt. 1, arts. 396–8, 401–3, 967, 970, 996, 1011, 1086, 1347; xi, pt. 2, *Ust. kred.*, arts. 293, 1199; and ix, arts. 222, 550.

to redemption by a relative or to the treacherous act of an untrustworthy accomplice. And if a relative redeemed such property, it once again became patrimonial.[5]

The patrimonial principle also resulted in male preference in inheritance. Males perpetuated the kin-group, formally possessed predominant authority within it, and constituted its chief public actors. In contrast, the ties of women with their paternal kin-group diminished substantially on marriage. As the elder Aksakov declared, 'daughters . . . what's the good of them? They look out of the house, not in; if their name is Bagroff today, it may be anything on earth tomorrow; my hopes rest entirely on my boy, Alexei.'[6] In fact, in descendant lines each woman received only one eighth of the movable and one fourteenth of the immovable property of the deceased, while her brothers shared the remaining estate equally. Only when the number of sisters was such that the share of each would exceed the amount of movable or immovable property received by each brother was each type of property divided equally among male and female heirs. In the absence of descendant heirs, an inheritance passed to the nearest collateral lines, with males or their descendants completely excluding females of equivalent relationship and again sharing the estate equally. In both descendant and collateral lines, women of equivalent relationship divided an estate equally in the absence of male heirs or their descendants. In collateral lines, patrimonial property followed appropriate kinship lines while acquired property passed only to the paternal relatives of an owner. Following this principle, paternal half-brothers displaced full sisters in the inheritance of patrimonial and, apparently, acquired property. Not being related by kinship to a deceased spouse, the surviving spouse—referred to generally in statutory law as a widow—had no right of inheritance but instead could claim only one seventh of the immovable and one quarter of the movable property of the deceased as provision for support. But however meagre the share of patrimonial

[5] Because it constituted an involuntary transfer that relied on the still-existing property interest of the clan, redemption of patrimonial property by a member of the kin-group produced different legal results than repurchase of the property by its former owner. See *SZ* (1857), x, pt. 1, arts. 1346–73, A. E. Nol'de, 'O prave rodstvennikov zhenskago pola na vykup rodovago imeniia', *ZhMIu* (1911), 8; 139–56, and the works cited below in Ch. 7. Writing in the late 1860s and early 1870s, the jurist Aleksandr Liubavskii claimed that collusive acts to transform patrimonial into acquired property occurred infrequently. *Iuridicheskiia monografii i izsledovaniia* (Spb., 1867, 1875, 1878), iii. 11–12. Until the mid-18th c., the period allowed for redemption was forty years. M. F. Vladimirskii-Budanov, *Obzor istorii russkago prava* (6th edn., Spb., Kiev, 1909), 579.

[6] Aksakov, *Memoirs*, 4. In the story, Aksakov renamed his family 'Bagroff' ('Bagrov').

property due a surviving spouse or female heirs, they had the right to receive this property in kind.[7]

These restrictions significantly limited the flexibility of owners in arranging a settlement of their property. An owner who wished to avoid the difficulties produced by the division of patrimonial property in particular had few options. He or she might induce his or her spouse to accept possession of a larger amount of property for life rather than absolute title to the share due by law. Similarly, a daughter might be persuaded to accept a large dowry of movable property in return for renouncing her right to the future inheritance.[8] Division of the property among the sons usually was unavoidable, however, and could be controlled only partially through a will or the allotment of shares during the lifetime of the owner. But even these strategies had limitations. The legal status of testamentary directions regarding the division of patrimonial property remained uncertain. And since statutory law generally excluded ascendant relatives from an inheritance, property allotted to sons would pass to the collateral lines if they predeceased their parents and died without issue, thereby leaving the parents without support.[9]

An owner enjoyed much greater legal power to control the devolution of his acquired property. But even here the vagueness and frequent silences of statutory law limited his options and often rendered his arrangements insecure. Statutory law in fact said little about the substantive

[7] *SZ* (1857), x, pt. 1, arts. 1068, 1104–221, 1234, 1241–8, and, on the rights of adopted children, 145–6, 149–51, 155–6, 161; ix, arts. 227, 259, 267, 305–6, 356–7, 1372–4, 1525; xi, pt. 1, *Ust. in. isp.*, art. 116; and xiv, *Ust. ssyl.*, arts. 785–6, 789–94.

[8] On the substitution of possession for life for an absolute title to the share of patrimonial property due a spouse by law, see *SZ* (1857), x, pt. 1, art. 116 prim. (1887, 1900 edns., arts. 116, 1070, 1148). Prior to 1862, Imperial consent was required in each case; thereafter, such estates could be established generally via certain types of wills. *2PSZ* xxxvii (1862), pt. 1, no. 38005, pp. 153–5, and I. Orshanskii, 'Lichnyia i imushchestvennyia otnosheniia suprugov', in *Izsledovaniia po russkomu pravu semeinomu i nasledstvennomu* (Spb., 1877), 3–4. On renunciation of the right to a future inheritance by a daughter who received a dowry, see below, Ch. 9.

[9] Heirs enjoyed considerably more freedom to divide a patrimonial estate than did the deceased owner, provided they could agree among themselves. On this issue, as well as on the inheritance rights of ascendant relatives and on gift, allotment, and dowry, see below, Ch. 9. On the difficulties created by the law for parents, at least in the second half of the eighteenth century, see *SIRIO* iv (1869), 252, 371, 418, 471; viii (1871), 444, 482, 514, 524–5; xiv (1875), 287, 447; xxxvi (1882), 138–9; xliii (1885), 26, 174–5, 176–9; lxviii (1889), 6, 31–2, 115, 330, 411, 459, 489, 493, 516, 551–2; xciii (1894), 170, 430; and cvii (1900), 128. For contrasting views on the power of an owner in his will to divide his patrimonial property among his legal heirs, see N. N. Novosil'tsev, 'Mnenie senatora Novosil'tseva, poddanoe v Sovet Kommissii sostavleniia zakonov 1809 goda, o nasledovanii imushchestvom vo Rossii', *ChOIDR*, ii (1859), 125–33, and K. P. Pobedonostsev, *Kurs grazhdanskago prava* (4th edn., Spb., 1896), ii. 569.

content of testamentary power. Although it defined a will as the distribution of property by the owner in the event of his death, it did not state clearly whether a will was revocable, when it took effect, or whether it could include property acquired after its composition. The law did permit an owner to bequeath his acquired property in full ownership or with only limited rights of use and possession, the latter either for the life of the recipient or for a defined term. Bequests of cash also were allowed, although the heirs of patrimonial property were not obligated to pay them. But statutory law said nothing about the conditions or obligations under which bequests of any type could be made. Moreover, no testamentary arrangement could extend beyond the lives of the heirs, whether by law or under the will. Hence a will that attempted to assign immovable property to one or two children while providing for the others with legacies or annuities from the income would be very insecure, not least because the obligation to make these payments would lapse with the death of the person paying rather than receiving them. Nor was it clear whether an owner could make a series of conditional bequests in order to provide for various contingencies.[10] Under Imperial law, then, the security of all but the simplest testamentary arrangements remained uncertain.

By protecting the property interests of the patrilineal kin-group and giving priority to males in inheritance, Imperial property and inheritance law reinforced the patriarchal family structure embodied in family law. This linkage between family structure, proprietary power, and inheritance rights reflected in part the historical experience of the upper strata of Muscovite society, especially the service nobility. In Muscovy, both princes and servitor families had an interest in ensuring that the adult male members of a kin-group commanded sufficient resources to fulfil their service obligations. These resources also enabled male servitors both to secure the fate of their immediate family and to further the interests of the kin-group, with whose fortunes their own fate generally was bound. For this reason, Muscovite law gave preference to male members first of the family, and then of the patrilineal kin-group, in the succession to both service tenements and hereditary lands of all types. In the absence of male

[10] On the substantive content of testamentary power, see especially *SZ* (1857), x, pt. 1, arts. 229–30, 295, 1010–11, 1067–8, and 1086, and Ch. 9 below; for testamentary law in general, see arts. 984–5, 991, 1010–89, 1110 pts. 2 and 3, 1222; ix (1857), arts. 222, 259, 267, 298, 304, 309, 550 pt. 2, 1536, and *Osob. pril.* (1876), I. *Obshch. pol.*, art. 91 *prim.* 1, XIX. *Pol. zakav.*, art. 84 *prim.* 3; xi, pt. 1 (1857), *Ust. in. ispov.*, arts. 115, 609, and pt. 2 (1857), *Ust. kred.*, arts. 293, 1199, 1204–9; see also *2PSZ* xli (1866), pt. 1, no. 43186, pp. 346–62, and xliv (1869), pt. 1, no. 46935, pp. 297–9. Prerevolutionary legal literature is discussed below in Chs. 7 and 9.

descendants, female descendants did have the right to inherit certain forms of hereditary land. But in most instances daughters, other female relatives, and widows were excluded from the inheritance of land and had the right to receive only a limited amount of such property as a dowry or as provision for support until (re)marriage, death, or entry into a convent, at which time the property normally reverted to sons or to other male representatives of the kin-group. And while the rights of kin did not limit the power of landholders to manage their property, nor, at least by the late Muscovite period, to sell or exchange it, members of the kin-group possessed the right to redeem most forms of hereditary land within forty years after its transfer to non-kin. Embodied ultimately in the Law Code of 1649, these practices in turn provided many of the concepts and institutions that underlay Imperial law until the collapse of the tsarist regime in 1917.[11]

None the less, similarities between peasant custom during the Imperial period and both Muscovite and Imperial law suggest that the roots of the patrimonial system of property and inheritance lay deeper than merely the relationship between political organization, service, and land tenure in medieval Muscovy. Despite wide regional variations among the peasantry, property generally was held by the predominantly kin-based household, although in most areas the commune also exercised control over the land. The head of a household possessed limited power to dispose of its property, most property was divided equally among adult males when the household split, women were severely discriminated against with respect to both the acquisition and the management of property, and yet certain property remained under the exclusive control of individual household members, including women.[12] Like positive law, peasant custom thus

[11] The power of women to manage and dispose of land acquired in inheritance, as a dowry, or by other means varied over time as well as regionally, socially, and by marital status. On these variations, as well as on the complex structure of rights in land and succession to such rights during the pre-Petrine period, see A. G. Man'kov, *Ulozhenie 1649 goda. Kodeks feodal'nago prava Rossii* (Lenin., 1980), esp. 58–93, 216, Iu. G. Alekseev, *Pskovskaia Sudebnaia gramota i ee vremia* (Lenin., 1980), 92–110, N. L. Pushkareva, *Zhenshchiny drevnei Rusi* (Mos., 1989), 113–39, 198–209, A. M. Kleimola, '"In Accordance with the Canons of the Holy Apostles": Muscovite Dowries and Women's Property Rights', *Russian Review*, 51 (1992), 204–29, and the prerevolutionary works cited below in Ch. 7.

[12] There is a substantial body of literature on peasant inheritance customs. For works representing different perspectives, see V. F. Mukhin, *Obychnyi poriadok nasledovaniia krest'ian. K voprosu ob otnoshenii narodnykh iuridicheskikh obychaev k budushchemu grazhdanskomu ulozheniiu* (Spb., 1888), A. Efimenko, *Izsledovaniia narodnoi zhizni* (Mos., 1884), N. Brzheskii, *Ocherki iuridicheskogo byta krest'ianin* (Spb., 1902), P. Czap, 'Peasant-Class Courts and Peasant Customary Justice in Russia, 1861–1912', *Journal of Social History*, 1 (1967/8), 149–78, W. T. Shinn, 'The Law of the Russian Peasant Household',

reinforced the patriarchal family structure and sought to reproduce it in succeeding generations. This similarity suggests common sources in the structure and functioning of the patriarchal family and the patrilineal kin-group, in the perceived need to conserve landed property within these groups, and in the cultural and religious matrices in which they operated, despite otherwise substantial differences between peasant and non-peasant society and between Imperial law and peasant custom.

Pressures for Change

Despite the close relationship between family, property, and inheritance law, pressure to revise the latter two areas of the law emerged earlier than did the pressure to change family law. Moreover, early efforts to change the law related chiefly to the landed nobility. Other social groups were either less affected by the restrictiveness of statutory law or less able publicly to voice their views and to influence government policy. Prior to the abolition of serfdom in 1861, both state peasants and, albeit subject to seigneurial power, serfs generally followed their own customs.[13] Local custom or law also prevailed among many of the non-Russian groups in the empire as well as among various unprivileged social groups.[14] And while governed by general Imperial law after 1785, merchants and other townsmen also were subject to special rules that mitigated the potentially negative effects of statutory law. Moreover, the restrictions contained in the law affected the property commonly held by merchants and manufacturers less negatively. Shops, factories, mines, and similar establishments were legally as well as physically indivisible. As 'acquired property', capital, trade goods, and similar wares could be disposed of freely by their owners. Although merchants, small traders, and manufacturers had to contend with the restrictiveness of patrimonial property and the system of partible

SR, 20 (1961), 601–21, C. D. Worobec, *Peasant Russia: Family and Community in the Post-Emancipation Period* (Princeton, NJ, 1991), 42–75, and V. A. Aleksandrov, *Obychnoe pravo krepostnoi derevni Rossii XVII-XIX v.* (Mos., 1984).

[13] *SZ* (1857), x, pt. 1, art. 1184; ix, arts. 672, 827; and xii, pt. 2, *Ust. o blag. v kaz. sel.*, arts. 114–15, 117–18.

[14] *SZ* (1857), x, pt. 1, arts. 1184, 1238, and xii, pt. 2, *Svod uch. i ust. o kol. ino.*, arts. 169–79. See also N. Korevo, *Ob izdaniiakh zakonov Rossiiskoi Imperii. 1830–1899. Sbornik svedenii ob izdaniiakh Svoda zakonov i Prodolzhenii k nemu, Polnago Sobraniia Zakonov, Svodov Voennykh i Morskikh Postanovelenii, a takzhe ob izdaniiakh mestnykh zakonov* (Spb., 1900), 83–104, Pobedonostsev, *Kurs*, ii. 356–8, A. E. Nol'de, 'Kolliziia raznomestnykh zakonov o nasledovanii v dvizhimostiakh po russkomu pravu', *VP* (1900), 7: 1–42, and id., *Ocherki po istorii kodifikatsii mestnykh grazhdanskikh zakonov pri grafe Speranskom, Vypusk 2, Kodifikatsiia mestnago prava pribaltiiskikh gubernii* (Spb., 1914).

inheritance, they therefore could avoid the difficulties created by the law more easily than could landowners.[15]

For noble landowners, in contrast, the assimilation of service into hereditary landholdings and shifts in state regulations governing the use of various resources during the eighteenth century necessitated clarification and reformulation of the law. At the same time, at least a few noble landowners and officials began to press for changes in the law to alleviate problems perceived to stem from the limited power to dispose of patrimonial property within a system of partible inheritance.[16] This combination resulted in the constant division of landed property, the effects of which were exacerbated by the practice of dividing even single estates into smaller and often vaguely defined parcels. Law and custom together thus produced a pattern of landholding in which the property of an owner frequently lay scattered among several districts or provinces and, within a district, was fragmented into numerous holdings that were intermingled with those of other owners. The continued operation of the

[15] None the less, the law also tended to cause the dispersal of commercial capital. See *SIRIO* xciii (1894), 100, 308, 432, E. Karnovich, *Zamechatel'nyia bogatstva chastnykh lits v Rossii. Ekonomichesko-istoricheskoe izsledovanie* (Spb., 1874), 174 ff., 203–6, and A. von Haxthausen, *Studies on the Interior of Russia*, ed. S. F. Starr, trans. E. L. M. Schmidt (Chicago, 1972), 214. For statutory law, see *SZ* (1857), vii, *Ust. gorn.*, arts. 476–8, 562, 2439 (1893 edn., arts. 221, 227–9; 1912 edn., arts. 263, 272–4); xi, pt. 2 (1857), *Ust. torg.*, arts. 154–77, 758–61 (1887, 1900 edns., x, pt. 1, art. 1238 prim., pril.: 1–20; 1887 edn., xi, pt. 2, *Ust. torg.*, arts. 73–5; 1903 edn., arts. 64–6); and xi, pt. 2 (1857), *Ust. prom. fab. i zav.*, art. 72 (1887 edn., art. 87; 1893 edn., art. 82); see also I. V. Vasil'ev, *Noveishee rukovodstvo k poznaniiu rossiiskikh zakonov, izdannoe dlia vospitannikov Moskovskago kommercheskago uchilishcha* (Mos., 1826, 1827), ii. 87–9. Although the merchants who submitted instructions to the Legislative Commission assembled by Catherine II in 1767 rarely mentioned inheritance law, occasional comments suggest that inheritance among the urban estates was governed by a combination of custom and Imperial law. Complaining of the disorder that resulted from this system, the merchants of St Petersburg and Moscow requested that either new legislation be formulated specifically for their estate or general Imperial law be applied to them. *SIRIO* xciii (1894), 129; cvii (1900), 219. Even though Imperial law was extended to the urban estates in 1785, a traveller to Imperial Russia in the first half of the nineteenth century noted that customary law still applied in many towns. *1PSZ* xxii (1785), no. 16188, arts. 4, 88, pp. 359, 367, and Haxthausen, *Studies*, 233.

[16] It is difficult to determine the percentage of land in late Imperial Russia that was classified as patrimonial property and therefore subject to the effects of the law. In 1877, 85% of all privately owned land (70% by 1914) in the 49 provinces of European Russia was held by individuals and therefore could have been affected by the law. G. T. Robinson, *Rural Russia under the Old Regime: A History of the Landlord-Peasant World and a Prologue to the Peasant Revolution of 1917* (New York, 1932), 268–70. The service records that I and other scholars have examined suggest that, at least among noble servitors, the percentage may have been on the order of 68–75%, with this percentage declining after emancipation. P. A. Zaionchkovskii, *Rossiiskoe samoderzhavie v kontse xix stoletiia* (Mos., 1970), 113–15, and R. S. Wortman, *The Development of a Russian Legal Consciousness* (Chicago, 1976), 56, note to table 3.2. See also L. P. Minarik, *Ekonomicheskaia kharakteristika krupneishikh zemel'nykh sobstvennikov Rossii kontsa xix-nachala xx v.* (Mos., 1971), 75–7 (43–75 in general).

law led to progressively smaller and more fragmented landholdings with each generation. Adroit marriages or purchases of land could mitigate the impact of the law, as did the Muscovite system of service tenure and the grants of land made by rulers to noble servitors. But the long-term effects of the law were difficult to avoid. Sir Donald Mackenzie Wallace, an astute British traveller to Imperial Russia, observed in the 1870s that

> we can find in the neighbourhood a number of poor, uneducated nobles, who live in small, squalid houses, and are not easily to be distinguished from peasants. In other parts of the country we might find men in this condition bearing the title of prince! This is the natural result of the Russian law of inheritance.[17]

In the latter part of the eighteenth century and the early nineteenth century, however, noble landowners appear to have been concerned less with the impact of the law on the overall size of their domain than with its effects on the security of their property, particularly in a context of increased land sales. In their instructions to the Legislative Commission convened by Catherine II in 1767 to codify Imperial law, for example, noble landowners complained of the same problems that had led the elder Aksakov to flee to the Orenburg frontier. Most complaints dealt with quarrels over boundaries and the use of common lands, encroachment by aggressive neighbours who had purchased a scrap of the family patrimony, and the lengthy and costly legal disputes that ensued from such situations.[18] A few nobles also claimed that the law prevented them from organizing and managing their lands more efficiently and profitably.[19]

[17] Sir D. M. Wallace, *Russia on the Eve of War and Revolution*, ed. C. E. Black (Vintage edn., New York, 1961), 159. See also J. Blum, *Lord and Peasant in Russia from the Ninth to the Nineteenth Century* (Princeton, NJ, 1961), 376–9, R. O. Crummey, *Aristocrats and Servitors: The Boyar Elite in Russia, 1613–1689* (Princeton, NJ, 1983), 112–23, B. Meehan-Waters, *Autocracy and Aristocracy: The Russian Service Elite of 1730* (New Brunswick, NJ, 1982), 77–8, M. Confino, *Systèmes Agraires et Progrès Agricole: L'Assolement Triennal en Russie aux xviii–xix Siècles* (Paris, 1969), 104–6, Haxthausen, *Studies*, 250–7, Karnovich, *Zamechatel'nyia bogatstva*, 34–5, 52–3, A. Ia. Antonovich, 'Chrezpolosnoe zemlevladenie, ego proiskhozhdenie i khoziaistvennoe znachenie', *SKhiL* 127 (1878), 301–19, and id., 'Ekonomiko-iuridicheskiia osnovaniia razverstaniia cherezpolosnykh zemel'', *SKhiL* 128 (1878), 55–75; but cf. Minarik, *Ekonomicheskaia kharakteristika*, 9–24, 43–77.

[18] *SIRIO* iv (1869), 325, 342, 345, 364, 368–9, 378, 388, 430–1; viii (1871), 462, 481, 526–7, 539, 547–51; xiv (1875), 390–1, 428–9, 448; and lxviii (1889), 106–7, 347–8, 381–2, 401–2, 405–6, 458–9, 623. In all, 80 of 124 instructions from the nobility mentioned problems relating to inheritance law. These are summarized in W. R. Augustine, 'Notes Toward a Portrait of the Eighteenth-Century Russian Nobility', *Canadian Slavic Studies*, 4 (1970), 395–408.

[19] *SIRIO* iv (1869), 275, 423–4, 451; viii (1871), 455, 462, 481, 497–8, 501; xiv (1875), 244, 286, 390–1, 448, 459–60, 464–5 475–6; lxviii (1889), 3, 401–2, 405–6, 440–1, 443, 458–9, 488–9, 496–7, 623. See also iv (1869), 240, 315–16, 448–9, 470; xiv (1875), 405, 419, 437; and lxviii (1889), 21–2, 25–6, 381–2, 414–15, 529, 554, 585–6, 606–7.

That this latter complaint was echoed later in the eighteenth century by the noted diarist and noble landowner Andrei Bolotov and by noble landowners during the first half of the nineteenth century testifies to the persistence of the problems attributed to the law.[20]

Yet nobles seldom advocated abolition of the institution of patrimonial property as a way to overcome these problems. On the contrary, even those noble landowners who complained most bitterly of the effects of the law none the less generally favoured the retention of this institution. The instructions from the nobility to the Legislative Commission, for example, strongly supported the preservation of patrimonial property. To eliminate the effects of the law, noble landowners most frequently proposed reducing the number of shares in the inheritance of such property by granting daughters and widows the right only to a monetary payment or to the use and possession of patrimonial property for life.[21] Some nobles requested unlimited testamentary power over their patrimonial property or at least the right to distribute it freely among their legal heirs.[22] A few proposed that separate villages and fields remain indivisible in inheritance,[23] while even fewer, most notably the nobility of Moscow district, supported the conversion of some noble lands into permanently indivisible and inalienable—i.e. entailed—hereditary estates.[24] Although dissatisfied with the effects of the law, noble landowners therefore simultaneously wished generally to preserve its underlying principles and disagreed markedly over how to eliminate its negative effects.

[20] A. T. Bolotov, *Zhizn′ i prikliucheniia Andreia Bolotova, opisannye samim im dlia svoikh potomkov* (reprint edn., Cambridge, 1973), ii. 321–7 (410–73, 504–25 generally on the difficulty of disentangling intermingled holdings), Zhitel′ Saratovskikh stepei, *O cherezpolosnykh vladeniiakh. Pis′mo k Al. St. Khomiakovu* (2nd edn., Mos., 1836), 39, A. A. Khomiakov, 'O cherezpolosnom vladenii', *Moskovskii Nablidudatel′* (1835), ch. 1, pp. 792–802, and D. N. Strukov, 'Otvet na otkrytyi vopros: pochemu ne visakoe blagopriobretennoe imenie mozhet byt′ obrashcheno v maiorat i ne vedet li takoe zapreshchenie k razdrobleniiu imenii po bol′shei chasti vrednomu i v otnoshenii razvitiia sel′skago khoziaistva i dlia samikh naslednikov?', *Gazeta dlia Selskikh Khoziaev* (1861), 7, cols. 102–5. See also M. M. Speranskii, 'O rodovykh imeniiakh', *Arkhiv Istoricheskikh i Prakticheskikh Svedenii, otnosiashchikhsia do Rossii* (1859), 5: 62–70, and the statistics on civil actions in the Senate departments and the provincial chambers given in the tables in *OMIu* for 1835, 1840, 1845, 1850, 1855, and 1859.

[21] *SIRIO* iv (1869), 252, 368–71, 393, 424; viii (1871), 481–2; xiv (1875), 398–9, 448, 494; xxxvi (1882), 98, 138–9; xliii (1885), 176–9; and lxviii (1889), 7–8, 25–6, 115, 331, 344, 368–9, 441, 488–9, 492, 532, 622–4.

[22] Ibid., iv (1869), 242, 369, 403, 462; viii (1871), 444, 455, 482, 488, 496–7, 508; xiv (1875), 288, 397–8, 446–7, 459–60, 481; and lviii (1889), 6.

[23] Ibid., iv (1869), 228, 275–6, 423–4; viii (1871), 455, 481; xiv (1875), 244, 460; lxviii (1889), 496–7, 624; and xxxvi (1882), 98.

[24] Ibid., iv (1869), 228; lxviii (1889), 624; see also iv (1869), 275–6; xiv (1875), 244; and Karnovich, *Zamechatel′nyia bogatstva*, 260.

Beginning in the early eighteenth century, prominent noble landowners and state officials also sometimes expressed the fear that the constant division of noble landholdings could cause political and social instability. In typically grandiose fashion, in 1714 Peter the Great had tried to avoid this problem by declaring all lands of the nobility henceforward to be indivisible, inalienable, and heritable by a single, preferentially male, heir. But the unpopularity of the measure among its intended beneficiaries compelled Empress Anna to repeal it in 1731 and to restore a system of partible inheritance and patrimonial property which retained many of the basic principles of Muscovite law.[25]

Despite this initial failure, the proposal to allow entail of noble land resurfaced periodically as a means for avoiding the threat thought to be posed by the law both to social and political stability and to individual noble families.[26] To help the wealthiest of these families, beginning in the late eighteenth century the government permitted a few prominent noblemen to carve entailed estates from their vast holdings, provided their other heirs also were secured. A statute enacted in 1845 regularized this practice but established criteria for size that limited eligibility to only about 1 per cent of all noble estates.[27] Moreover, the requirement that substantial provision be made for the other legal heirs indicates that attitudes towards entail remained ambiguous. Catherine II herself had expressed the source of this ambiguity in her own instructions to the Legislative Commission. Although concerned over the harmful effects allegedly produced by the constant division of property, she argued that a system of partible inheritance none the less served state interests more effectively by ensuring adequate material means for more people, including

[25] *1PSZ* v (1714), no. 2789, pp. 91–4, Vladimirskii-Budanov, *Obzor*, 503–6, *GU. Kn. 3-ia*, iii. 1–2, Karnovich, *Zamechatel'nyia bogatstva*, 260, and Meehan-Waters, *Autocracy*, 118–22. As a result of these measures, the real property formerly due women and widows only as a dowry or as provision for support until death or remarriage was now given to them in absolute ownership and the size of the share was expanded modestly.

[26] In addition to the references cited above in n. 24, see A. Romanovich-Slavatinskii, *Dvorianstvo v Rossii ot nachala xviii veka do otmeny krepostnago prava* (Spb., 1870), 255, and D. Field, *The End of Serfdom: Nobility and Bureaucracy in Russia, 1855–1861* (Cambridge, Mass., 1976), 41, 224.

[27] *2PSZ* xx (1845), pt. 1, no. 19202, pp. 528–38, and TsGIA F. 1151 op. xii d. 1–1896 g. ll. 325–32; for the statutory regulations, see *SZ* (1857), x, pt. 1, arts. 391, 395, 432 pt. 3, 467–93, 564, 969, 1069, 1184 pt. 7, 1192–213, 1641, and x, pt. 2, *Zak. sud. grazh.*, arts. 2252–6 (1876 edn., arts. 1467–71). See also *GU. Kn. 3–ia*, iii. 2–3, Blum, *Lord*, 368–9, Field, *End of Serfdom*, 224, Karnovich, *Zamechatel'nyia bogatstva*, 38–43, 165–7, and Iu. B. Solov'ev, *Samoderzhavie i dvorianstvo v kontse xix veka* (Lenin., 1973), 205. The entailed estates formed under these provisions are listed in A. M. Anfimov, 'Maioratnoe zemlevladenie v tsarskoi Rossii', *Istoriia SSSR* (1962), 5: 151–9.

widows and daughters.[28] Most noble landowners apparently shared this view, albeit as regarded from the perspective of the family and the kin-group rather than from that of the state.

In the early nineteenth century criticism of the treatment of women under the law also began to appear. To be sure, such criticism does not seem to have been widespread, at least among men. The instructions sent from all social estates to the Legislative Commission, for example, generally had expressed acceptance of the existing inheritance rights of women. While a few nobles had suggested modest improvements in these rights,[29] most had advocated their further limitation in order to reduce the negative effects of the law. Count Speranskii, too, had advanced similar proposals in the late 1820s as an alternative to the entail of noble land.[30] But in a memorandum submitted to the commission on the compilation of laws, formed by Alexander I in another vain attempt to codify Imperial law, one of the commission's officials, Nikolai Ilinskii, proposed that the inheritance rights of men and women be made equal. According to Ilinskii, the provision of regular salaries and pensions to males for state service now obviated their need for a larger share of an inheritance than that received by their sisters, who in fact often had greater financial need because of their inability to earn their own living. Although the commission apparently did not find this argument persuasive, it none the less did propose to increase the inheritance rights of women.[31]

By the early nineteenth century, then, Imperial statutory law had attracted considerable criticism. It none the less remained basically unchanged

[28] *Catherine the Great's Instruction (Nakaz) to the Legislative Commission, 1767*, trans. and ed. P. Dukes (Newtonville, Mass., 1977), arts. 416–27, and A. K. Rikhter, *O neobkhodimom nasledovanii* (Spb., 1893), 196–201. See also Speranskii, 'O rodovykh imeniiakh', and TsGIA F. 1151 op. XII d. 1–1896 g. ll. 325–32. On debates over entail in Western Europe at this time, see the essays by Thirsk and Cooper in J. Goody, J. Thirsk, and E. P. Thompson (eds.), *Family and Inheritance: Rural Society in Western Europe, 1200–1800* (Cambridge, 1976), 177–305.

[29] *SIRIO* viii (1871), 508–9, 519; xiv (1875), 446–8, 459–60, 487–8; lxviii (1889), 488–9; see also xliii (1885), 177. For instructions that explicitly accepted existing rights for women, see iv (1869), 283, 326, 369; viii (1871), 456; xiv (1875), 397–8; and lxviii (1889), 342, 345. In the 19th c., only three provincial assemblies of the nobility appear to have proposed that the inheritance rights of women be made equal with those of men: Smolensk (1864), Kursk (1890), and Kostroma (1899). *GU. Kn. 4-aia*, intro., p. 27.

[30] See the references cited above in nn. 21–4 and Speranskii, 'O rodovykh imeniiakh'.

[31] 'Iz zapisok N. S. Il'inskago', *RA* (1879), 12: 431–2. Influenced strongly by the French civil code, the commission did propose to abolish the institution of patrimonial property, introduce a system of obligatory shares in inheritance, and increase the share of an inheritance due daughters. See *Trudy kommisii sostavleniia zakonov* (2nd edn., Spb., 1822), ii. 108–57, and S. V. Pakhman, *Istoriia kodifikatsii grazhdanskago prava* (Spb., 1876), i. 447–59, 467.

prior to the emancipation. Indeed, one observer noted the reluctance of high state officials to alter the system of inheritance in any way, however insignificant, during the early nineteenth century.[32] While this reluctance undoubtedly stemmed partly from the ethos of nationalist conservatism that dominated the reign of Nicholas I, it also appears to have derived from an acceptance of the legitimacy of the basic principles underlying the law.

Equally importantly, prior to emancipation the harm caused by the law apparently did not outweigh its benefits for many nobles. Especially given the limited availability of careers outside government service, land settled by serfs represented a crucial source of income and security for noblemen, quite apart from any status or psychological satisfaction that ownership of such property may have provided.[33] And in prevailing conditions, gaining control over the labour power, potential income, and mortgage value of individual serf households was more important than receiving a consolidated plot of land. Capital was scarce, agriculture was relatively unprofitable, market relations and institutions were poorly developed, and the infrastructural problems hindering development of an agricultural market were formidable. Hence there were few economic incentives for noble landowners to reorganize their estates on a more productive basis, a task for which their background as a service élite in any case had ill prepared them. In these conditions, noble landowners seldom departed from the traditional system of cultivation based on individual peasant households working small plots of land. In many cases, landowners simply expropriated a share of the income produced by the agricultural, trading, and other activities of their serfs. The result, in either case, was that households rather than land represented the critical object of division among heirs.[34]

These economic conditions made difficult the payment of monetary or other forms of compensation to some of the co-heirs in order to avoid the

[32] A. E. Nol'de, 'O poriadke nasledovaniia rodstvennikov bokovykh linii nasledodatelia v ego blagopriobretennom imushchestve (Arkhivnaia spravka)', *ZhMIu* (1907), 10: 83–91.

[33] Both Field, *End of Serfdom*, 134–41, 359, and S. Becker, *Nobility and Privilege in Late Imperial Russia* (DeKalb, Ill., 1985), 29–31, argue that by the mid-19th c. the paternalistic ethos described so brilliantly by Aksakov in *Russian Gentleman* had disappeared among noble landowners, who now regarded their estates essentially as a source of income.

[34] See Confino, *Sytèmes*, Field, *End of Serfdom*, 8–35 and *passim*, Blum, *Lord*, 375–6, 379–85, 390, Robinson, *Rural Russia*, 52–63, O. Crisp, *Studies in the Russian Economy before 1914* (London, 1976), 96–7, 114–15, and R. Manning, *The Crisis of the Old Order in Russia: Gentry and Government* (Princeton, NJ, 1982), 4–8. See also Haxthausen, *Studies*, 37–40, 78, 81–2, 86, 215, 248–58, Karnovich, *Zamechatel'nyia bogatstva*, 4–5, 11–12, 15–22, 33–5, 48–50, 67–8, 70–4, 80–1, 125–41, 213–31, and A. V. Iakovlev, 'Zemledelie, zemlevladenie i kredit', *TVEO* (1886), 1: 1–29.

physical division of settled land in inheritance. Equally importantly, the deficiencies of both tsarist statutory law and the pre-reform courts left such arrangements legally insecure, particularly if attempted by an owner through his will. In a context where inheritance provided one of the chief means of acquiring serf households, few nobles apparently wished to jeopardize receipt of a future inheritance by changing the law, even though they might complain about the practical problems resulting from it.

Finally, government action was stymied by a dilemma in which reforms that might solve one problem appeared only to create or compound others. Entailing estates or expanding the testamentary power of owners to eliminate the fragmentation of property appeared likely to lead only to the potentially equal or worse problems caused by the widespread disinheritance of children. Equalizing the inheritance rights of women and men appeared only to increase the problem of fragmentation. This dilemma in fact frustrated the only significant attempt to reform the law undertaken in the last decades before the abolition of serfdom.

In 1848, as part of a general review of selected aspects of Imperial civil law, the Second Department of the Imperial Chancellery proposed several changes in inheritance law. The proposals were heavily influenced by the director of the department, Count Dmitrii Bludov, a well-educated and extremely wealthy noble landowner with strong ties to St Petersburg literary society. Bludov believed firmly in the need for both autocratic authority and the preservation of historical continuity to maintain political order and to avoid social chaos. Yet he was also influenced by the values of sentimentalist literature, particularly its emphasis on love, affective relations, and moral idealism.[35]

The proposals made by the Second Department reflected both Bludov's personal values and the tangle that resulted from trying to resolve the various problems attributed to existing statutory law. The Second Department began by asserting that inheritance law must both satisfy the demands of justice and serve state interests. Defining justice as the moral obligation of an owner to provide adequately for his family, the Second Department advocated restricting the power to dispose of acquired property in order to safeguard the spouse, children, and parents of an owner from irresponsible or capricious acts by him. For similar reasons, it was

[35] On Bludov, see Wortman, *Legal Consciousness*, 142–66, and on the Second Department under his direction, see P. Maikov, *Vtoroe otdelenie sobstvennoi ego Imp. velichestva kantseliarii 1826–1882* (Spb., 1906), 276–401 (330–4, 345–73 on activities in the field of civil law).

proposed that the inheritance rights of women and men be made equal. After forty years, the sentiments expressed by Ilinksii thus apparently had gained official sanction. But, the Second Department continued, 'for the good of the state economy and especially of agriculture, for which large, extensive material means concentrated in a single owner are still essential, it seems necessary to allow inequality in division at least with respect to immovable, particularly settled, estates'. Daughters therefore were granted the right only to one half the share of such property due their brothers in inheritance.[36] The principle of male and female equality in inheritance thus was to be sacrificed to the economic interests of the state and of noble landowners.

Justice, as understood by the Second Department, likewise gave way to the interest of both the state and parents in maintaining order through strong patriarchal authority within the family and the kin-group. In a revised version of its project, the Second Department claimed that the state

> must be concerned constantly with the greatest possible observance and confirmation of the sacred ties of kinship and the patriarchal submission to the elders in the kin-group, even outside the circle of the immediate family, that is based on them—a submission that is among the most important guarantees of order in civil societies, the first link . . . in the great chain that unites them.[37]

To strengthen this submission to patriarchal authority, the institution of patrimonial property was to be preserved and parents granted the right to disinherit children. The proposals of the Second Department therefore simultaneously expanded and constricted the testamentary power of owners and increased the inheritance rights of women while making them less secure in order to satisfy the conflicting social, political, and economic demands placed on the law.[38]

The dilemma created for government legislators by these conflicting demands emerges clearly from the fate of the Second Department's proposals. Accepting them in principle, Nicholas I none the less directed that the proposed restrictions on the power to dispose of acquired property apply only when an owner left no patrimonial property. Otherwise, Nicholas believed, an owner should retain unlimited control over his

[36] A. G. Goikhbarg, *Zakon o rasshirenii prav nasledovaniia po zakonu lits zhenskago pola i prava zaveshchaniia rodovykh imenii* (3rd edn., Spb., 1914), 8.

[37] Rikhter, *O neobkhodimom nasledovanii*, 210.

[38] On these proposals, see ibid. 206–13, *GU. Kn. 4–aia*, intro., pp. 7–19, Goikhbarg, *Zakon*, 6–8, A. Kaminka, 'Proekt nasledstvennago prava', *Pravo* (1903), 47, cols. 2640–2, and TsGIA F. 797 op. 92–1910 d. 53 ll. 6–18, pp. 5–7.

acquired property. Nicholas also stipulated that disinheritance must be approved in each case by appropriate state authorities.[39] Hence while more reluctant than the Second Department to tamper with the right of owners to dispose freely of their acquired property, Nicholas placed no greater trust in them to exercise their testamentary powers responsibly. The state therefore would intervene where necessary to prevent injustice or avoid social harm. Nicholas also requested that the Second Department 'examine the possibility of reconciling, at least to some degree, the demands and feelings of justice with the necessity of trying to preserve inherited property in noble kin-groups as far as possible without division by establishing a system whereby patrimonial immovable, particularly settled, estates would pass indivisibly to the eldest heir in his own right or by representation, and all acquired and movable property would be divided equally among the remaining co-heirs of each sex'.[40] Like the Second Department, Nicholas thus seemed to accept in principle that women and men should have equal inheritance rights while simultaneously advocating continued inequality for political and economic reasons. Nor was it clear how the need to provide for the remaining heirs of an owner from his acquired property could be reconciled with preservation of his power to dispose freely of this property. Unable to square these circles, Bludov abandoned the attempt to improve the inheritance rights of women. After encountering opposition in the State Council, his proposal to reform testamentary law died at the hands of his successor as head of the Second Department, the arch-conservative Count Viktor Panin.[41]

Government inability to reconcile competing objectives thus combined with an official ethos of conservatism and an apparent lack of urgency to prevent any substantial revision of property and inheritance law prior to emancipation. The conditions produced by the abolition of serfdom in 1861 made revision of the law seem more urgent, however, although again not equally to all social groups. As before, the subordination of the peasantry to local custom largely excluded them from the purview of statutory law, although the Civil Cassation Department gradually applied Imperial law to property acquired by peasants outside the commune.[42]

[39] Rikhter, *O neobkhodimom nasledovanii*, 207. [40] Goikhbarg, *Zakon*, 8.

[41] Rikhter, *O neobkhodimom nasledovanii*, 213–30, and *GU. Kn. 4-aia*, intro., pp. 7–19; see also the references cited above in n. 38.

[42] *SZ* x, pt. 1 (*Prod.* 1876, and 1887, 1900 edns.), art. 1184; and ix (*Prod.* 1863), *Osob. pril.*, *Ob. pol.*, art. 38 (1902 edn., art. 13), (*Prod.* 1876), *Osob. pril.*, IV, art. 110, V, art. 93, XV, art. 19, XX, art. 2 prim. 2, pril.: 42, 81 (1902 edn., IV: i, art. 15, ii, art. 66, vi, arts. 296, 587, v, art. 41); see also *2PSZ* xlvi (1871), pt. 1, no. 49705, *pravila*, art. 19, p. 819. For judicial practice, see *SRGKD* 1873 no. 1507, 1875 no. 839, 1878 no. 225, 1880 no. 174, 1882 no.

And the classification by the Civil Cassation Department of corporate assets, shares, financial instruments, and the other forms of property that appeared or became more widespread after the 1860s as 'acquired property' enabled merchants, industrialists, and other entrepreneurs to avoid the restrictions contained in statutory law. Hence newspapers directed at commercial and industrial interests treated the debate over the revision of inheritance law that took place in the latter part of the nineteenth century as if it concerned only the nobility and the question of agricultural development.[43]

In contrast, as a result of emancipation the nobility lost a considerable portion of its land to its former serfs and the rest was thrown open to ownership by people of any social estate. Mortgage credit, restructured on market principles, was now largely in private hands. Like all private landowners after emancipation, noble landowners thus had to adapt their estates to new market conditions in order to survive. At the same time, extensive railroad construction, industrial development, and European economic growth expanded considerably the domestic and foreign markets for Russian agricultural goods, providing both commercial opportunities and financial pitfalls for noble landowners. In addition, participation in the zemstva, the new institutions of local and provincial self-government introduced in 1864, was based on a land qualification for each district. As the importance of these bodies grew, maintenance of sufficient land to ensure a role in them became highly desirable. In these changing circumstances, problems of management, impediments to reorganization,

225, 1884 nos. 22, 105, 1885 nos. 3, 74, 1890 no. 110, 1891 no. 86, 1893 nos. 66, 77, 1898 no. 71, 1901 no. 69, and 1902 no. 37, *ROSPKD* 1892 nos. 33, 41, 42, 1894 no. 11, 1898 no. 2 (*SRGKD* 1898 no. 71), 1909 no. 19, and 1910 no. 1, and Pobedonostsev, *Kurs*, ii. 356–62. For contrary arguments regarding the basis and economic effects of government policy towards the peasantry, see O. Crisp, 'Peasant Land Tenure and Civil Rights Implications before 1906', in O. Crisp and L. Edmondson (eds.), *Civil Rights in Imperial Russia* (Oxford, 1989), 33–64, and A. Gerschenkron, 'Russia: Agrarian Policies and Industrialization, 1861–1914', in *Continuity in History and Other Essays* (Cambridge, Mass., 1968), 140–248.

[43] On the use of high-court decisions by merchants and industrialists, see below, Ch. 9. For journalistic comments on the law, see *NiBG* (1892), 58: 2 ('Russkaia pechat′'), 73: 2 ('Otkliki'), 74: 2 ('Russkaia pechat′'), and 77: 1–2, V. Bystrenin, 'Zemledel′cheskii "krizis"', *NiBG* (1898), 330: 1, *BV* (1892), 65: 2 ('Nasha pechat′'), 92: 2 ('Nasha pechat′'), and 95: 1, and (1893), 173: 1–2 ('Novosti i otkliki'). In their discussions of the legal questions that concerned merchants and industrialists from the 1850s onward, neither Thomas Owen nor L. E. Shepelev mentions inheritance law or patrimonial property. T. C. Owen, *The Corporation under Russian Law, 1800–1917: A Study in Tsarist Economic Policy* (Cambridge, 1991), and L. E. Shepelev, *Tsarizm i burzhuaziia vo vtoroi polovine XIX veka. Problemy torgovo-promyshlennoi politiki* (Lenin., 1981), 34–44, 93–8, 108–13, 207, 229–36. See also *ZNDGZ*, no. 154.

TABLE 6.1. *Decline in noble landownership, 1862–1914*

Acreage at End of Year			Average Annual Decrease		
Year	No. of des. (m.)	% of 1862 Acreage	Period	No. of des. (000s)	Average % Decline
1862	87.2	100.0	—	—	—
1867	83.9	96.3	1863–7	638	0.73
1872	80.7	92.6	1868–72	652	0.78
1877	77.0	88.4	1873–7	736	0.91
1882	71.2	81.7	1878–82	1,146	1.49
1887	66.8	76.7	1883–7	880	1.24
1892	62.9	72.2	1888–92	781	1.17
1897	58.4	67.1	1893–7	896	1.42
1902	53.2	61.0	1898–1902	1,061	1.82
1905	51.3	58.8	1903–5	630	1.18
1909	45.6	52.3	1906–9	1,418	2.76
1913	41.5	47.6	1910–13	1,036	2.27
1914	41.1	47.1	1914	400	0.96

Source: S. Becker, *Nobility and Privilege in Late Imperial Russia* (DeKalb, Ill., 1985), 32.

and questions of fragmentation assumed much greater importance than previously.

Adjusting to these new conditions often proved difficult for noble landowners, who were accustomed to thinking of their estates as sources of status and income rather than as economic enterprises. Consequently, whether forced by circumstances or lured by other opportunities, nobles increasingly parted with their land after emancipation. By 1877 they had lost nearly 12 per cent of their land to non-nobles, and between 1877 and 1905 their holdings declined a further 33 per cent. Moreover, the rate of decrease accelerated in the 1880s and 1890s as a depression gripped world grain markets and affected private landowners in Imperial Russia particularly severely (Table 6.1). Although higher grain prices helped to stabilize noble landownership in the early twentieth century, the massive agrarian unrest of 1905–6 again increased noble flight from the land, so that by 1914 the nobility owned less than one half the amount that it had held in 1862 (Table 6.1).

This general pattern of decline, of course, was marked by significant variations. The wealthiest magnates, possessing tens or even hundreds of thousands of desiatin, commanded sufficient resources to reorganize their estates, diversify their economic activities, and undertake industrial enterprises on their land. In many instances, large parts of their vast holdings were protected by entail in any case.[44] Petty owners, receiving too little compensation for their land and serfs to make up for their lack of livestock, agricultural implements, and other inventory, often sold their land or leased it back to their former serfs. Differences in such variables as soil quality, population density, relative labour costs, the accessibility of markets, the relative profitability of agriculture or ability to maintain traditional methods of cultivation, and the degree of previous commercial experience produced significant regional variations in both the extent and the rate of declining noble landownership. But regardless of these variations, this decline occurred everywhere after emancipation.[45]

Unfortunately, available information does not allow measurement of the degree to which restrictive inheritance laws contributed to this phenomenon. The pattern of change in noble landholding portrayed in Table 6.2 suggests that the influence of the law was significant. The proportion of smaller to larger estates increased steadily throughout this period and the number of noble estates did not decrease as rapidly as did the amount of land owned by nobles, both phenomena consistent with the division of estates in inheritance. In fact, between 1877 and 1895 the number of estates actually increased slightly, despite the substantial loss of noble land by this time.[46] But these changes also could have been produced by the sale of land for reasons unrelated to inheritance. Indeed, a comparison of the amount of rural land sold with that transferred by all means without consideration (i.e. without receiving an equivalent value in exchange) in the early twentieth century indicates that the former was primarily responsible for changes in noble landholding, although the amount of land passing by the latter still was substantial (Tables 6.3–6.4).

[44] e.g. compare the names of the largest noble landowners listed in Minarik, *Ekonomicheskaia kharakteristika*, 13–19, with the owners of the entailed estates listed in Anfimov, 'Maioratnoe zemlevladenie'.

[45] N. A. Proskuriakova, 'Razmeshchenie i struktura dvorianskogo zemlevladeniia evropeiskoi Rossii v kontse xix–nachale xx veka', *Istoriia SSSR* (1973), 1: 55–75, A. P. Korelin, *Dvorianstvo v poreformennoi Rossii 1861–1904 gg. Sostav, chislennost', korporativnaia organizatsiia* (Mos., 1979), 52–76, G. M. Hamburg, *Politics of the Russian Nobility 1881–1905* (New Brunswick, NJ, 1984), 31–8, 84–101, Manning, *Crisis*, 3–24, 37–44, and Becker, *Nobility*, 28–54. For good prerevolutionary studies, see V. V. Sviatlovskii, *Mobilizatsiia zemel'noi sobstvennosti v Rossii (1861–1908 g.)* (2nd edn., Spb., 1911), V. V. [Sviatlovskii?], 'Dvorianskoe zemlevladenie posle reformy', *RM* (1898), 10: 69–98, and P. I. Liashchenko, 'Mobilizatsiia zemlevladeniia v Rossii', *RM* (1904), 1: 39–60, and 2: 1–26.

[46] V. V. [Sviatlovskii?], 'Dvorianskoe zemlevladenie', 73–4.

TABLE 6.2. *Decline in noble landownership, 1877–1905*

Stratum	No. of Owners					Land Owned: (1,000 des.)					Average Size of Estate:	
	1877	%	1905	%	% Change	1877	%	1905	%	% Change	1877	1905
Petty (1–100 des.)	56,551	49.3	60,910	56.8	7.7	1,924.4	2.6	1,662.6	3.1	–13.6	34.0	27.3
Medium (101–1,000 des.)	44,827	39.1	37,003	34.5	–17.5	16,264.7	22.2	13,218.8	24.9	–18.7	362.8	357.2
Large (1001+ des.)	13,388	11.7	9,324	8.7	–30.4	54,976.4	75.1	38,290.0	72.0	–30.4	4,106.4	4,106.6
TOTAL	114,766	100.0	107,237	100.0	–6.6	73,165.5[a]	100.0	53,171.4[a]	100.0	–27.3	637.5	495.8

[a] Although these totals differ slightly from those given by Becker (Table 6.1), the amount is not significant for the purposes of my argument.

Source: N. A. Proskuriakova, 'Razmeshchenie i struktura dvorianskogo zemlevladeniia evropeiskoi Rossii v kontse xix–nachale xx veka', *Istoriia SSSR* (1973), 1: 68.

TABLE 6.3. *Transfers of rural land by sale and without consideration, 1900–1902*[a]

Year	No. of transactions			No. of des. (1,000)			Value (m. roubles)		
	1 Sale	2 Without consideration	2 as % of 1	3 Sold	4 Without consideration	4 as % of 3	5 Sold	6 Without consideration	6 as % of 5
1900	38,470	8,424	21.9	3,905	1,748	44.8	265.5	93.9	35.4
1901	39,054	8,382	21.5	3,333	1,809	54.3	260.7	102.5	39.3
1902	39,877	6,970	17.5	3,599	1,459	40.5	265.9	104.1	39.2
TOTAL	117,401	23,776	20.3	10,837	5,016	46.3	792.1	300.5	37.9

[a] 47 provinces of European Russia.

Source: V. V. Sviatlovskii, *Mobilizatsiia zemel′noi sobstvennosti v Rossii (1861–1908 g.)* (2nd edn., Spb., 1911), 59–61.

TABLE 6.4. *Transfers of title without consideration, 1897–1902*[a]

Year	No. of Transfers	Land (m. des.)	Value (1,000 roubles)
1897	9,566	2.1	90,684
1898	9,061	1.4	90,199
1899	8,689	1.4	99,801
1900	8,424	1.7	93,902
1901	8,382	1.8	102,523
1902	6,970	1.4	104,062
TOTAL	51,092	9.8	581,171

[a] 47 provinces of European Russia.

Source: V. V. Sviatlovskii, *Mobilizatsiia zemel'noi sobstvennosti v Rossii (1861–1908 g.)* (2nd edn., Spb., 1911), 59–61.

Since the amount of rural land transferred as a gift was relatively small, inheritance probably accounted for most land transferred without consideration. In any case, landowners often used gifts, dowries, and similar devices to settle part of their inheritance, especially after the Civil Cassation Department facilitated such practices.[47] Moreover, throughout this period heirs submitted a sizeable number of claims for confirmation of inheritance rights to district courts, even though the number of divisions of an estate recorded by senior notaries or imposed by district courts was not great, which suggests that most inheritances were divided informally to avoid state fees and taxes (Tables 6.5–6.6).[48] While secondary to sales, the transfer of land in inheritance thus accounted for a significant portion of the changing pattern of noble landowning after the emancipation. The constantly rising number of sales in relation to transfers of rural land without consideration, however, suggests that this influence was diminishing as commercial relationships spread throughout the countryside (Tables 6.3–6.5).[49]

But the impact of the law on noble landownership cannot be assessed solely by measuring the amount of land that passed in inheritance, whether directly or by surrogate means. Both conservative and reformist critics of the law claimed that its restrictions also compelled owners or heirs to sell their land. According to these critics, owners sometimes sold their

[47] See Ch. 9 below and the references to *SIRIO* cited above in n. 9.

[48] On the rules governing division of an estate, see below, Ch. 9.

[49] See also Sviatlovskii, *Mobilizatsiia*, 99.

patrimonial estates in order to gain greater testamentary control over their property, while heirs often sold entire estates and divided the proceeds because of disagreements over division of the land or the small size of each share. Being less profitable, the smaller estates remaining to heirs who retained the land became more vulnerable to future sale. Conversely, critics asserted, heirs who purchased either the portion of their co-heirs' or surrounding land in order to obtain a more viable holding frequently burdened themselves with substantial debt, thereby reducing the profitability and security of their new estates.[50]

The large amount of land purchased by the nobility during the post-emancipation period provides limited support for this latter claim.[51] Nor is it unlikely that at least some of the rapidly growing mortgage debt of the nobility arose from efforts to deal with the effects of restrictive inheritance laws, although most of this debt clearly resulted from the attempts of owners to hold on to or improve their land or to use its rising capital value for other ventures.[52] Given the impossibility of measuring the different situations that led nobles to sell, buy, or mortgage land, perhaps the best that can be said is that the law made a difficult situation worse and often may have provided the final impetus for abandoning an estate.

The law threatened particularly those middle-sized owners whose estates provided an adequate living and who dominated the zemstva, noble associations, and provincial politics.[53] Its restrictions threatened to undermine the social status, political power, and economic security of the heirs of these owners by reducing their holdings below the amount needed for economic viability and for the right of direct participation in provincial political life. The discomforting spectre of diminished family status

[50] This debate is discussed below in Ch. 8.

[51] Korelin, *Dvorianstvo*, 55–6, Solov'ev, *Samoderzhavie*, 199–200, Becker, *Nobility*, 31–6, Liashchenko, 'Mobilizatsiia', 52–4, and Sviatlovskii, *Mobilizatsiia*, 93–4, 107–20, who questions the interpretation of Liashchenko.

[52] In contrast to other historians, Becker argues that most noble landowners used mortgage loans rationally to make productive investments both in agriculture and in other areas. The case of Baltic noblemen, who were the most indebted but also among the most successful noble landowners, provides support for this claim. But the extremely high percentage of noble landowners whose mortgage payments were in arrears, especially in the 1880s and 1890s, suggests that Becker takes his argument too far. Becker, *Nobility*, 47–54, 77–85, *Statistika dolgosrochnago kredita v Rossii. 1894 g. Vypusk III. Dolgi po dolgosrochnym zaimam v gosudarstvennykh i chastnykh kreditnykh uchrezhdeniiakh k 1894 g.* (Spb., 1895), *1900 g. Vypusk IX.* (Spb., 1900), *1907 g. Vypusk XIII.* (Spb., 1907), E. I. Zhigachev, 'Zadolzhennost' chastnago zemlevladeniia v Rossii', *RM* (1892), 11: 41–69, Solov'ev, *Samoderzhavie*, 231, 235–6, and Hamburg, *Politics*, 88–100.

[53] On this group, see Manning, *Crisis*, 11–12, 17–23, 30, 38–43, Hamburg, *Politics*, 15–19, 25–7, Becker, *Nobility*, 53–4, 136–52, and Korelin, *Dvorianstvo*, 60–70, 127.

TABLE 6.5. *Deeds of purchase, divisions of inheritance, and gifts of immovable property confirmed by senior notaries, 1884–1914*[a]

Purchase Deeds			Divisions				Gifts			
RURAL PROPERTY										
Year	No.	Value (m. roubles)	No.	Value (m. roubles)	As % of Purchases		No.	Value (m. roubles)	As % of Purchases	
					No.	Value			No.	Value
1884	21,436	101.2	510	33.4	2.4	33.0	730	5.8	3.4	5.7
1889	19,978	97.4	558	37.9	2.8	38.9	964	5.9	4.8	6.1
1894	23,197	114.0	729	36.7	3.1	32.2	1,138	6.1	4.9	5.4
1899	36,474	271.5	1,013	65.5	2.8	24.1	1,820	10.5	5.0	3.9
1903	38,480	269.1	1,137	82.8	3.0	30.8	2,685	16.2	7.0	6.0
1906	31,189	310.1	887	33.6	2.8	10.8	2,196	15.6	7.0	5.0
1908	80,255	369.5	1,062	46.7	1.3	12.6	3,038	10.3	3.8	2.8
1910	191,019	464.2	1,550	60.6	0.8	13.1	3,777	12.9	2.0	2.8
1913	322,192	602.8	1,414	108.6	0.4	18.0	7,728	18.2	2.4	3.0
1914	308,032	452.5	1,258	63.1	0.4	13.9	7,892	16.9	2.6	3.7

URBAN PROPERTY

1884	11,752	52.9	303	17.4	2.6	32.9	444	5.8	3.8	11.0
1889	13,301	64.9	366	13.4	2.8	20.6	612	3.7	4.6	5.7
1894	15,000	74.9	452	15.8	3.0	21.1	681	3.4	4.5	4.5
1899	22,846	199.0	646	19.2	2.8	9.6	1,013	6.6	4.4	3.3
1903	20,506	127.9	626	22.4	3.1	17.5	1,270	7.0	6.2	5.5
1906	20,246	106.6	649	21.8	3.2	20.5	1,192	7.5	5.9	7.0
1908	23,785	147.2	731	35.2	3.1	23.9	1,470	11.8	6.2	8.0
1910	29,965	205.5	878	36.0	2.9	17.5	1,458	5.8	4.9	2.8
1913	34,355	278.8	995	41.2	2.9	14.8	1,710	12.2	5.0	4.4
1914	30,385	232.1	816	29.8	2.7	12.8	1,674	13.2	5.5	5.7

[a] Judicial districts of European Russia, excluding Warsaw and, for the period 1884–1908, Tiflis.

Source: *SSSMIu. chast' 1* for 1884, 1889, 1894, 1899, 1903, 1906, 1908, 1910, 1913, 1914.

TABLE 6.6. *Requests for confirmation of inheritance and judicial divisions of inheritance executed, District Courts of European Russia, 1885–1908*

Year	No. of cases submitted	Requests for confirmation of inheritance	%	No. of judicial divisions executed
1885	122,118	11,644	9.5	511
1889	117,089	12,167	10.4	411
1893	138,636	14,398	10.4	472
1897	140,088	16,265	11.6	528
1901	174,459	17,509	10.0	632
1905	186,958	18,789	10.0	575
1908	238,805	22,082	9.2	711

Source: *SSSMIu* for 1885, 1889, 1893, 1897, 1901, 1905, 1908.

helped persuade many mid-level nobles to agitate for revision of the law in the late nineteenth and early twentieth century.[54]

At the same time that pressure for revision of property and inheritance law was building among noble landowners and others concerned with the political and economic role of the landed nobility, an extensive critique of the law also developed within the growing professional strata of society, especially among jurists. Based on the same values and ideological ideals that animated criticisms of family law, this critique rested on conceptions of property, the family, and individuality that differed fundamentally from those underlying statutory law. The jurists and other writers who formulated this critique, of course, included many noblemen who had severed their ties with the land and come to rely primarily on their professional expertise for their status and income.[55]

By the late nineteenth century, then, a broad consensus existed within the government, educated society, and the landowning nobility that inheritance law needed substantial revision. These groups disagreed strongly, however, over the objectives that such revision should pursue and the form that it should take. Where some stressed the political effects of fragmenting noble landholdings, others gave priority to the needs of economic development. Still others sought to adjust the law to the social

[54] See below, Ch. 8.

[55] This critique is discussed below in Ch. 7. On the migration of noble landowners to cities and towns after emancipation, see Becker, *Nobility*, 28–31, 53–4, and Korelin, *Dvorianstvo*, 122–31.

circumstances, values, and ideals of the growing professional and largely urban strata of society. Moreover, while the practical problems attributed to the inflexibility of the law provided a major impetus for its revision, further pressure arose from the attempt of competing groups to use the law as a means of resolving political and ideological conflicts. In this situation, the actions of the tsarist regime again provide a measure of its ability to resolve the social and economic problems confronting it and to respond to changing attitudes among its educated élite.

7

Jurists' Critique: The Ascendancy of Individual Ownership

LIKE other groups in the educated and upper strata of tsarist society, jurists in the post-reform period agreed on the need to revise Imperial property and inheritance law but disagreed sharply over how to do so. To be sure, by the late 1870s most Russian jurists appear to have believed that in post-emancipation economic conditions owners required greater power to dispose of patrimonial property, particularly by will. And influenced by the changing views on the family discussed above, most jurists favoured some improvement in the inheritance rights of women. But jurists viewed these common goals from profoundly different ideological perspectives that entailed contrasting conceptions of authority, individuality, the appropriate ordering of the family and of society, and the relationship between Imperial Russia and Western Europe.

Emergence of the Individual

This ideological cleavage began to open, at least publicly, in the late 1850s and the early 1860s. Prior to then tsarist censorship had combined with the influence of German legal historicism on Russian jurists to mute criticism of existing property and inheritance law. While presenting existing law as the natural outcome of national historical development, however, early studies of the law also assigned it a positive role in maintaining the tsarist order. Hence, in his doctoral dissertation, published in 1839, the historicist professor of philosophy and civil law at St Petersburg University, Nikolai Rozhdestvenskii, argued that the institution of patrimonial property ensured both the participation of the patrilineal kin-group in social affairs and the supply of male servitors to the state. Believing that the law could support the autocratic order still further, Rozhdestvenskii proposed to strengthen parental authority—on which he believed the power and welfare of the state ultimately rested—by permitting parents to disinherit their children. Conversely, reflecting the same sentimentalism that later motivated Bludov, Rozhdestvenskii added that the equal love of parents for daughters and sons necessitated an equal right to the inheritance of property other than land.[1] Rejecting this last proposition, Aleksei Kunitsyn, professor of civil law at Kharkov and then at Novorossiia University, asserted in 1844 that 'a woman always and everywhere by the nature of her sex needs to be defended by a man and, sharing his work, she is no more than his helper'. By contrast, he contended, a man bears the principal obligations of society 'as statesman, soldier, citizen, and father of a family'. Kunitsyn concluded that men therefore required more material means than women in order to fulfil their social obligations, and thus they also needed a greater share of an inheritance.[2]

In his study of Imperial civil law published in 1843, Aleksandr Kranikhfeld, the professor of law at St Petersburg University, offered a moral as well as a historical defence of existing property and inheritance law. Kranikhfeld asserted that ties of kinship and resulting patrimonial forms of property characterized all early human societies and arose from the nature of man. Reflecting the influence of Hegelian ideas, he stated that historically these ties and property forms tended to weaken as the state intruded into affairs that previously had concerned only the kin-group and as individual private property and the conjugal family consequently grew in social importance. Kranikhfeld contended that kin ties none the less continued to retain vitality and therefore the principles underlying the institution of patrimonial property also retained their legitimacy. Hence the kin-group preserved an interest in the inherited property of an individual owner even while the power of the latter over this property increased. Kranikhfeld concluded that the need to protect the property interest of the kin-group from violations by the owner, and thereby ensure fulfilment by an owner of his obligations to his kin-group

[1] N. F. Rozhdestvenskii, *Istoricheskoe izlozhenie russkago zakonodatel'stva o nasledstve* (Spb., 1839), esp. 37–9, 45–53, 74–90. Born in 1800 and apparently from the hereditary nobility, Rozhdestvenskii graduated from the philosophical-juridical faculty at St Petersburg University in 1823, where he subsequently taught philosophy and, from the 1830s to 1853, civil law.

[2] Cited in G. F. Shershenevich, *Nauka grazhdanskago prava v Rossii* (Kazan, 1893), 40–1. See also A. Kunitsyn, 'O prave plemianits na ukaznyia chasti iz nasledstva (otvet g. Motovilovu)', *ZhMIu* (1866), 4: 33–46, and G. A. Tishkin, *Zhenskii vopros v Rossii v 50–60 gg. xix veka* (Lenin., 1984), 32–4. Born in 1807 into the clerical estate, Kunitsyn studied at the St Petersburg Ecclesiastical Academy after graduating from the Tver seminary. Among the students chosen by Speranskii to study law, he studied under Savigny in Berlin. See *DINU* 498–9, 509–13.

as well as to his family, justified both the restrictions imposed on the disposition of patrimonial property and male preference in intestate succession.[3]

Challenges to these arguments began to emerge in juridical literature only after the late 1850s. In his published lectures on Imperial civil law, Kazan University law professor Dmitrii Meier denied both the historical legitimacy and the socio-economic utility of existing property and inheritance law. In contrast to Kranikhfeld, Meier argued that the constant expansion of the rights and powers of the individual since the Petrine period had so eroded ties of kinship that the law had been deprived of its social basis. The institution of patrimonial property therefore constituted an outdated relic that conflicted with current social and state needs by unduly restricting individual property owners.[4] In his address to the Moscow Juridical Society in 1868 advocating the formulation of a civil code, the prolific legal commentator Nikolai Kalachov likewise characterized Imperial property and inheritance law as anachronistic, incongruent with current social needs, and the area of civil law most in need of reform.[5] But apart from an expansion of the proprietary power of owners, neither Kalachov nor Meier proposed specific changes in the law.

Juristic criticism of Imperial property and inheritance law grew more focused and detailed during the reform era, partly as a result of the same socio-economic, educational, intellectual, and institutional trends that produced a parallel critique of family law. The common foundation of all three areas of the law and their complementary roles in supporting the kin-group and patriarchal authority made this interconnection unavoidable. Hence juristic criticisms of family law and of property and inheritance law frequently complemented one another and often were made by the same people.

[3] A. I. Kranikhfel'd, *Nachertanie rossiiskago grazhdanskago prava v istoricheskom ego razvitii* (Spb., 1843), 38–40, 51–5, 62–8, 91–7, 141–8, 173–4, 188–9, 212–13. For a similar approach, see K. A. Nevolin, *Polnoe sobranie sochinenii K. A. Nevolina* (Spb., 1857, 1858), iv. 26–36, v. 94–111. On both Kranikhfeld and Nevolin, see above, Ch. 2 n. 48. See also N. Varadinov, *Izsledovaniia ob imushchestvennykh ili veshchestvennykh pravakh po zakonam russkim* (Spb., 1855), 58–92, 100–4, V. N. Leshkov, *O chastnom pozemel'nom prave, po svodu zakonov, ili neskol'ko zamechanii na II-iu knigu t. X, ch. I Svoda Grazhdanskikh Zakonov ob imushchestvakh, pravakh na imushchestva i sposobakh ikh priobreteniia* (Mos., 1871), K. P. Pobedonostsev, 'Imenie rodovoe i blagopriobretennoe', *ZhMIu* 8 (1861), pt. 2, ch. neof., pp. 3–74, and Shershenevich, *Nauka*, 43–8.

[4] D. I. Meier, *Russkoe grazhdanskoe pravo, chteniia D. I. Meiera, izdannyia po zapiskam slushatelei pod redaktsieiu A. Vitsyna* (5th edn., Mos., 1873), 110–12, 634, 659–60. On Meier, see above, Ch. 2 n. 52.

[5] N. V. Kalachov, *Programma razrabotki nachal russkago grazhdanskago prava po svodu zakonov s ego istochnikami i posudebnym resheniiam* (Mos., 1868), 1–2. On Kalachov, see above, Ch. 3 n. 1.

Also as in the case of family law, the atmosphere of the Alexandrine reform period encouraged jurists to examine existing property and inheritance law in light of the general goal of state and social development. More specifically, the abolition of serfdom focused attention on these areas of the law because it forced the reorganization of the economies of both master and serf. The officials who drafted the emancipation decrees apparently intended the long-term guiding principle for this reorganization to be individual private ownership within the context of an expanded agricultural market. Hence after the redemption of their land even peasant households were expected eventually to sever their ties with the commune and to hold their land individually. The emancipation thus encouraged jurists not only to examine the economic implications of existing property and inheritance law, but to do so from a perspective favourable to individual ownership.[6] This orientation in turn found reinforcement in Western European juridical writing on individual ownership during the first half of the nineteenth century, a source with which Russian jurists were familiar.

This combination of influences led several Russian jurists particularly of a younger generation in the 1860s and early 1870s to formulate a moral and utilitarian critique of existing property and inheritance law which paralleled their critique of family law.[7] In its desire to increase the legal security of family members and to make the law more equitable, this critique reflected sentiments similar to those that had motivated Bludov's earlier proposals to change the law. In both instances, too, there was a wish to use the law to promote the productive use of resources. While Bludov never questioned the legitimacy of the institution of patrimonial property and had sought to strengthen patriarchal authority, however, juristic critics of the law now condemned both. In their view, the law should seek to maximize both the power of individual property owners and the security of their family members, in the latter instance without sexual discrimination.

Juristic critics contended that the creative activity of individuals and

[6] On the provisions regarding the peasantry, see O. Crisp and L. Edmondson (eds.), *Civil Rights in Imperial Russia* (Oxford, 1989), 21, 38–42; but cf. A. Gerschenkron, 'Russia: Agrarian Policies and Industrialization, 1861–1914', in *Continuity in History and Other Essays* (Cambridge, Mass., 1968), 140–248. On the economic ideas current at the time of the emancipation, see the references cited above in Ch. 2 n. 73, R. S. Wortman, *The Development of a Russian Legal Consciousness* (Chicago, 1976), 255–7, and M. G. Korotkikh, 'Sudebnaia reforma v Rossii', *Voprosy Istorii* (1987), 12: 32. See also n. 23 below.

[7] In addition to the references cited below, see Tishkin, *Zhenskii vopros*, 39–45, and N. L. Pushkareva, *Zhenshchiny drevnei Rusi* (Mos., 1989), 178–87. On the generational difference between juristic critics and earlier juristic defenders of the law, see above, Ch. 3 n. 3.

the free mobility of resources constituted the basis for post-emancipation economic development. Existing law restricted both, they charged, and thereby depressed national wealth and overall social welfare. The main culprit was the institution of patrimonial property. Critics argued that by constraining the power of individual owners and by limiting the transfer of resources, legal rules intended to preserve property within the kin-group obstructed individual initiative, discouraged investment, and impeded trade.[8] Critics also condemned the right to redeem patrimonial property, claiming that it was used primarily to extort payments from purchasers and thereby discouraged improvement by the property's new owners.[9] Summarizing these arguments at the First Congress of Russian Jurists in 1875, the legal historian and renowned liberal defence attorney Vladimir Spasovich concluded that the very concept of patrimonial property constituted 'a restriction of free will'. Spasovich asserted that inheritance law therefore should be reformulated on the basis of 'the principles of personal right and complete freedom, [and] the principle of the sovereignty of the person over the thing and of capital over land', in order to bring the law into conformity with what he and other pro-reform jurists perceived to be current social attitudes and economic needs.[10]

The sexual inequality established by existing inheritance law also was condemned as outdated and unjust, on the basis of the same affective ideal of the family and conception of the status of women within both the family and society which underlay contemporaneous juristic criticisms of family law.[11] In a detailed critique of inheritance law published in 1864, for

[8] M. Filippov, 'Vzgliad na russkie grazhdanskie zakony', *Sovremennik* (1862), 92: 24–8, 453–9, 473–8, A. Liubavskii, 'Ob uravnenii nasledstvennykh prav muzhchin i zhenshchin', *ZhMIu* (1864), 5: 414, id., *Iuridicheskiia monografii i izsledovaniia* (Spb., 1867, 1875, 1878), iii. 34–5, 415–19, and V. D. Spasovich, 'Sledovalo by razreshit′ svobodnoe rasporiazhenie po dukhovnym zaveshchaniiam rodovymi imushchestvami', in *Pervyi s″ezd russkikh iuristov v moskve v 1875 godu*, eds. S. I. Barshev, N. V. Kalachov, S. A. Muromtsev, and A. M. Fal′kovskii (Mos., 1882), 151–64. For similar arguments by critics of Imperial corporate law, see T. C. Owen, *The Corporation under Russian Law, 1800–1917: A Study in Tsarist Economic Policy* (Cambridge, 1991), 72–8.

[9] Liubavskii, *Iuridicheskiia monografii*, iii. 34–5, 415–19, and M. Daragan, 'O vykupe rodovykh imushchestv', *Sovremennaia Letopis′* (1862), 41: 1–4; but see Filippov, 'Vzgliad', 459–73.

[10] Spasovich, 'Sledovalo by', 151, 153. On Spasovich, see above, Ch. 3 n. 23, and Tishkin, *Zhenskii vopros*, p. 39.

[11] Filippov, 'Vzgliad', 24–8, 453–9, 473–8, K. D. Kavelin, *Sobranie sochinenii K. D. Kavelina* (Spb., 1900), iv. 585–90, 620–6, and 536–626 in general, Liubavskii, 'Ob uravnenii', 399–424, id., *Iuridicheskiia monografii*, iii. 9–38, I. Orshanskii, 'Nasledstvennyia prava russkoi zhenshchiny', *ZhGiUP* (1876), 2: 1–38, and 3: 1–31, Spasovich, 'Sledovalo by', 154–7, 161–3, 'Obozrenie spetsial′nykh zhurnalov', *Otechestvenniia Zapiski* (1865), 1: 204–8, and Fal′kovskii and Markonet in 'Protokol ocherednago zasedaniia moskovskago iuridicheskago

example, Aleksandr Liubavskii charged that the law 'was based on Eastern-patriarchal and kinship principles that were outlived long ago'.[12] According to Liubavskii, these principles excluded women from inheritance because they were considered simultaneously to have left their natal kin-group but not to be a member of their husbands' kin-group. Asserting that the kin-group's survival in Muscovy was due largely to the interrelated system of state service and land tenure, Liubavskii argued that the elimination of this system during the eighteenth century and the consequent extension of full rights of property ownership to women and to social estates other than the nobility had accelerated the natural process by which the conjugal family displaced the kin-group. The perpetuation of sexual inequality in inheritance rights therefore now 'contradicts . . . the demands of human nature and of justice', he concluded, because in the context of the conjugal family parents loved their children equally and consequently had a moral obligation to provide equally for each child without regard to sex.[13]

Juristic critics argued that the failure of existing law to conform with this moral obligation of parents was not only unjust, but also harmful. Reflecting the socio-economic circumstances particularly of the educated and upper strata of society, critics asserted that the exclusion of women from most means of earning a living forced them to rely primarily on inheritance and marriage to acquire adequate sources of support. The right to only a meagre portion of an inheritance consequently often compelled women to marry solely for convenience, which increased the dependence of wives on their husbands and thereby also their vulnerability

obshchestva aprelia 26 dnia 1871 goda', *IuV* (1871), 4: 3–15. See also P. Tsitovich, *Iskhodnye momenty v istorii russkago prava nasledovaniia* (Kharkov, 1870), 168–9, although he was more conservative than the other authors on social issues (see n. 13 below).

[12] Liubavskii, 'Ob uravnenii', 400. On Liubavskii, see above, Ch. 3 n. 40.

[13] Ibid. 400. The most sophisticated statement of this argument was made by Kavelin, *Sobranie sochinenii*, iv. 536–626. Although he arrived at similar conclusions, Tsitovich argued that property and inheritance rights in ancient Rus had been based originally on the family, on whose rights the kin-group gradually encroached. Despite discrimination against them, women at that time consequently had enjoyed much more independence than they did later. Tsitovich attributed this deterioration in their rights both to the strengthening of the kin-group and to the Mongol occupation. *Iskhodnye momenty*, 87–144, 153–67. The son of a village priest, Tsitovich graduated from the juridical faculty at Kharkov University and then taught civil law both there and, later, at Novorossiia University. After 1880 he combined a career in government service, chiefly in the Senate and in the Ministry of Finance, with teaching commercial law, first at St Vladimir University and then at St Petersburg University. A strident critic of radical and nihilist positions on marriage in the 1870s, he has been characterized by some as reactionary, although he appears to have held moderately conservative views. See *DINU* 513–16, and R. Stites, *The Women's Liberation Movement in Russia: Feminism, Nihilism and Bolshevism, 1860–1930* (Princeton, NJ, 1978), 97, 269.

to abusive treatment by a husband.[14] Critics also charged that the frequent attempts allegedly made by owners to circumvent the law in order to provide equitably for daughters as well as sons bred disrespect for the law in general. Conversely, they added, the inability of owners who observed the law to arrange their inheritances in accordance with the needs and merits of each heir sowed discord within the family. Warning that such discord threatened social stability, the liberal jurist Mikhail Filippov concluded that 'since . . . [the institution of patrimonial property] is only a cause of endless suits and hatred among relatives, this institution must be abolished in the sense in which it presently exists'.[15]

In response to arguments in defence of existing law, Filippov and other juristic critics claimed that the law no longer served any political purpose. In fact, drawing to some extent on the arguments of their opponents, juristic critics contended that existing property and inheritance law had been shaped largely by the need of Muscovite princes for servitors. They then argued that the changes introduced into the autocratic political system since the time of Peter the Great had deprived the institution of patrimonial property and male preference in inheritance of their political function. Applying his Hegelian explanation of the evolution of tsarist socio-juridical institutions to the development of Imperial property and inheritance law in an address at St Petersburg University in 1860, for example, the statist jurist Konstantin Kavelin maintained that during the eighteenth century rights to land had finally become disassociated from state service and converted into the private rights of individuals. This conversion in turn furthered the changes occurring during this period in the socio-economic role of the individual and in the nature of the family.[16] Hence Kavelin and other critics concluded, with surprisingly little empirical support, that existing law no longer corresponded to either the political, the economic, or the social needs of Imperial Russia.

[14] Liubavskii, 'Ob uravnenii', 399–400, 412–18, id., *Iuridicheskiia monografii*, iii. 28–31, 35, and Orshanskii, 'Nasledstvennyia prava', esp. 2: 3–5, 11–14, and 3: 17–19, 27–30.

[15] Filippov, 'Vzgliad', 459, and in general 24–8, 453–9, 473–8, Liubavskii, 'Ob uravnenii', 418–19, and id., *Iuridicheskiia monografii*, iii. 27, 29, 34–5. See also L. F. Snegirev, 'O prave nasledovaniia v bokovykh liniiakh edinokrovnykh i edinoutrobnykh brate′ev i sester', *IuV* (1871), 9: 18–22. On Filippov, see above, Ch. 3 n. 4.

[16] Kavelin, *Sobranie sochinenii*, iv. 537–69, 585–90, 620–6; for his earlier argument, see above, Ch. 2. See also Liubavskii, 'Ob uravnenii', 419–23, id., *Iuridicheskiia monografii*, iii. 31–6, Filippov, 'Vzgliad', 24–8, 453–9, 473–8, 493–502, and Spasovich, 'Sledovalo by', 151–64. Liubavskii did not oppose use of the law to support noble landownership, but argued that only entail could achieve this objective. Filippov opposed entail on the grounds that it encouraged absenteeism and economic inefficiency. In his view, the smaller holdings that resulted from the division of an estate were economically more efficient than the larger estate and also produced a more equitable distribution of property.

To reinforce their conclusions, and to undercut historicist arguments in defence of national particularity, juristic critics placed Imperial Russia in the context of what they claimed was a universal process of historical development, depicting history as the movement by individual nations towards a universal ideal of 'civilization' that was defined by Western European jurisprudence and juridical norms. Hence Kavelin felt justified in using contemporary French and Prussian law as a basis both for criticizing and for predicting the future development of Imperial Russian law. Likewise, adopting the property and inheritance rights of women as a measure, Liubavskii concluded that although Imperial Russia had progressed beyond the backward patriarchies of Asia, 'of all the jurisdictions of civilized peoples there is not one in which women are in a more disadvantageous position relative to men with respect to intestate succession than in our fatherland'.[17]

This use of Western European juridical norms suggests the underlying objectives and motives of juristic critics of the law during this period. Although, from their perspective, they were merely developing and extending to property and inheritance law the principles that they believed underlay the Alexandrine reforms in general, in effect they sought to replace those institutions which they associated with serfdom, unlimited patriarchal authority, and the backwardness of Imperial Russia. Hence they advocated sexual equality in inheritance rights in part as a means to promote the general ideal of civil equality.[18] Both this proposal, by providing women with independent resources, and that to guarantee all family members an appropriate share of an inheritance were intended in part as means to limit the exercise of patriarchal authority.[19] Conversely, elimination of the restrictions imposed on individual ownership by the institution of patrimonial property and by other tsarist legislation was seen as a way to create the legal basis for civil liberty. Proposing not only sexual equality in inheritance rights, for example, but also civil equality for Jews, Filippov asserted that 'there, where there are no free institutions,

[17] Liubavskii, 'Ob uravnenii', 412, and in general 399–400, 407–11, 414–15, 423, and id., *Iuridicheskiia monografii*, iii. 10, 13–14, 16, 18, 20, 35–7; Kavelin, *Sobranie sochinenii*, iv. 590–626. See also Filippov, 'Vzgliad', 10–16, 24–8, 453–9, 473–8, 484–5, and Orshanskii, 'Nasledstvennyia prava', 2: 6–11, 15–23, and 3: 6–10, 27–30.

[18] Ibid. 2: 3–5, 11–14, and 3: 17–19, 27–30, Filippov, 'Vzgliad', 24–8, 453–9, 473–8, Liubavskii, 'Ob uravnenii', 399–400, 412–18, id., *Iuridicheskiia monografii*, iii. 28–31, 35, Spasovich, 'Sledovalo by', 153–7, 161–7, Kavelin, *Sobranie sochinenii*, iv. 585–6, 620–6, and Tsitovich, *Iskhodnye momenty*, 168–9.

[19] Liubavskii, 'Ob uravnenii', 423, and id., *Iuridicheskiia monografii*, iii. 21, 23–34. See also iii. 429–45, Orshanskii, 'Nasledstvennyia prava', and Tsitovich, *Iskhodnye momenty*, 74, 167–8.

where a person's personality and property are not secure, there look not for enlightenment and humane principles'.[20] However much these ideals and goals may have suited the circumstances of jurists such as Filippov, Spasovich, and Liubavskii, who for the most part lived in cities and towns and derived their livelihood and status from the exercise of their professional expertise, they obviously were incompatible with—and unacceptable to—the autocratic regime.

To effect their desired transformation of the social and legal order, juristic critics proposed several changes in property and inheritance law. All critics favoured the introduction of sexual equality in intestate succession and either the elimination of all restrictions on the power of owners to dispose of patrimonial property or the abolition of this form of property altogether. All, too, advocated giving priority in inheritance to a surviving spouse and other members of the conjugal family rather than to more distant members of the kin-group. Exposing an important tension between their goals of freedom and security, however, critics disagreed over the degree to which the liberation of individual property owners from existing restraints on their power should in turn be limited by the right of the individual members of their families to security. A few jurists, such as Filippov, rejected any constraint on proprietary power, both because this position followed logically from their arguments regarding the benefits of individual ownership and because they believed that owners would use their power to distribute their property in accordance with the specific needs and merits of each family member. But most juristic critics supported the introduction of a system of obligatory shares patterned on French law, which reserved a substantial portion of an owner's property for his heirs. Critics contended that such systems most fairly balanced the competing interests of owners, heirs, and the state economy because they left an owner with unrestricted control over a large part of his property while still ensuring the fulfilment of what critics considered to be his moral obligations to his family.[21]

[20] Filippov, 'Vzgliad', 484–5, and 483–90 in general. See also the comments of Spasovich, 'Sledovalo by', 151, 153, who was Polish and identified strongly with Polish culture.

[21] Filippov, 'Vzgliad', 24–8, 453–9, 473–8, 493–502, Kavelin, *Sobranie sochinenii*, iv. 585–6, 620–6, Liubavskii, 'Ob uravnenii', 399–400, 412–18, 423, id., *Iuridicheskiia monografii*, iii. 21–34 (and see also ii. 192–202), Spasovich, 'Sledovalo by', 151–64, and Orshanskii, 'Nasledstvennyia prava'. During the Revolution, French law established sexual equality in inheritance and severely limited the power of owners to dispose of property. Under the civil code enacted in 1804, an owner could dispose freely of only one half to one quarter of his property, depending on the number of his children. The rights of a wife varied depending on the type of property arrangement agreed upon at the time of marriage. In most cases, however, she recovered her personal property and one half of the property considered to be

The willingness of most juristic critics to limit proprietary power in favour of the members of an owner's family suggests that their objections to existing property and inheritance law lay less with its restrictiveness *per se* than with the specific character of the restrictions and the purposes served by them. Existing law appeared to such critics to protect an outdated structure of authority and social unit, the kin-group, whereas it did not effectively secure the rights and welfare of individual members of the more important conjugal family. Moreover, in its terminology, its association of property with the kin-group, and its treatment of women the law connoted to pro-reform jurists the backwardness of Imperial Russia relative to Western Europe. Conversely, adoption of the civilian system of obligatory shares would both ensure fulfilment by the owner of his obligations to his family and reduce the distance perceived by jurists to exist between Imperial Russia and Western Europe. Hence most pro-reform jurists were prepared to limit the property rights of individual owners in the pursuit of socially desirable ends, provided that these ends conformed with their own ideological beliefs and objectives. Even such a staunch advocate of the property rights of individuals as Filippov argued that these rights could be violated by the state in order to ensure the equitable distribution of property throughout society, a power he considered to have been exercised appropriately in the case of the emancipation.[22]

Despite their emphasis on the need to liberate individual property owners from legal restrictions deemed to be anachronistic, juristic critics thus exhibited an ambivalence towards the concept of individual private ownership, resulting from the interaction between native and Western European attitudes. Although long influenced by aspects of Roman law, especially through the medium of the Orthodox Church, Muscovy none the less had not experienced any counterpart to the extensive reception and systematic reworking of Roman law which had occurred in Western

the community property of both spouses. Variants of these provisions were adopted widely throughout continental Europe after 1804. The codes adopted in German areas not affected by French law placed fewer restrictions on the disposition of property by an owner and secured the interests of family members through their right to the value of a specified share of the deceased's property. See M. Ostrogorski, *The Rights of Women: A Comparative Study in History and Legislation* (London, 1893), 208–31, J. F. Traer, *Marriage and the Family in Eighteenth-Century France* (Ithaca, NY, 1980), 137–91, T. Zeldin, *France 1848–1945: Ambition and Love* (Oxford, 1979), 143–8, 287–91, 343–4, 356–7, and K. Zweigert and H. Kötz, *An Introduction to Comparative Law*, trans. T. Weir (Amsterdam, 1977), i. 74–80, 86, 90–101, 137–8, 157–65, 288, 291–2. For an early attempt to introduce a system patterned on French law into Imperial Russia, see the references cited above in Ch. 6 n. 31.

[22] Filippov, 'Vzgliad', 10–16, 479–80, 484–5, 493–502.

Europe after the twelfth century. Hence the very concept of unlimited individual ownership as it came to be defined in Western European civilian jurisprudence was relatively novel in the Russian cultural and legal contexts. Only in the latter part of the eighteenth century did this concept percolate into Imperial Russia and begin to affect both legal terminology and, especially, the complex structure of coincident interests in real property through which the rights and powers of the state and other collective entities limited those of individuals.[23] And even then, Imperial Russia did not possess a juridical establishment capable of propagating such a concept as effectively as those in Western Europe.

If the juridical forces that helped to break down feudal concepts and structures of property in early modern Europe were weak in Imperial Russia, the message being sent from Western Europe was itself ambiguous. Since the Enlightenment, Western European jurisprudential and other theories of property had promoted both the absolute character and inviolability of individual private property and the legitimacy of state intervention in property rights for the general good, a dichotomy that found reflection in the legal codes enacted in many continental European countries after the late eighteenth century. These codes included restrictions on testamentary power, for political purposes or to protect an owner's heirs.[24] Hegel, whose ideas several Russian professors of law had

[23] See V. I. Gsovski, 'Roman Private Law in Russia', *Bulletino dell'Instituto di Diritto Romano*, 46 (1939), 363–75, D. P. Hammer, 'Russia and the Roman Law', *American Slavonic and East European Review*, 16 (1957), 1–13, K. P. Pobedonostsev, *Kurs grazhdanskago prava* (4th edn., Spb., 1896), i. 131–9, ii. 291–302, and M. F. Vladimirskii-Budanov, *Obzor istorii russkago prava* (6th edn., Spb., Kiev, 1909), 584–5. On Roman and Western European civil law concepts of absolute ownership, see below, Ch. 9 n. 56. The attempt of noble landowners to resist the abolition of serfdom by referring to the inviolability of their property rights indicates the degree to which at least this élite group had assimilated new concepts of ownership after the late 18th c. (See D. Field, *The End of Serfdom: Nobility and Bureaucracy in Russia, 1855–1861* (Cambridge, Mass., 1976).) But since this conflict concerned the security of their property rights against the state, it sheds little light on the attitude of noble landowners towards the type of family interests in property represented by patrimonial property.

[24] A. Ryan, *Property and Political Theory* (Oxford, 1984), 82–3, 91–5, 106–7, 129, 158–9, J. Q. Whitman, *The Legacy of Roman Law in the German Romantic Era: Historical Vision and Legal Change* (Princeton, NJ, 1990), 165–89, M. John, *Politics and the Law in Late Nineteenth-Century Germany: The Origins of the Civil Code* (Oxford, 1989), 3–5, 15–18, D. R. Kelly, *Historians and the Law in Postrevolutionary France* (Princeton, NJ, 1984), 49, 129–30, Zeldin, *France*, 142–3, and the references cited above, n. 21, and below, Ch. 9 n. 56. The authors of the draft civil code of 1809/14 tried to incorporate the dichotomy of absolute ownership and legitimate state intervention into Imperial law, and their successors did so in *SZ* (1857), x, pt. 1, arts. 420, 424–6, 575–608. See *Trudy kommisii sostavleniia zakonov* (2nd edn., Spb., 1822), ii. 94–5, and S. V. Pakhman, *Istoriia kodifikatsii grazhdanskago prava* (Spb., 1876), i. 440–1.

encountered while studying in Germany, had defended such restrictions on the grounds that the freedom to distribute property by will meant the freedom to act not arbitrarily, but responsibly in the fulfilment of one's obligations.[25] Other Russian jurists were familiar with these Western European ideas and legal institutions, either directly or through the teaching and publications of Russian jurists themselves.[26] The filtering of Western European ideas through traditional Russian values and legal concepts thus appears to have made Russian jurists particularly sensitive to the inherent potential of individual private property to serve not only as a means for the attainment of personal self-realization and security, but also as an inducement to place self-centred interests before moral obligations and the needs of the community.

The desire of pro-reform jurists to eliminate all vestiges of the serf order and to limit the exercise of patriarchal authority by legal norms also contributed to the tension in their demands regarding proprietary power. On the one hand, by promoting the equal right of all members of society to acquire and use property, the principle of individual ownership provided a powerful weapon for subverting the formal hierarchies of status and privilege which jurists associated with serfdom. On the other hand, as Rozhdestvenskii, Bludov, and later conservative writers made clear, an increase in testamentary power could reinforce patriarchal authority.[27] The European civilian institution of obligatory shares offered a way to avoid this result and to compel a father to fulfil what pro-reform jurists considered to be his moral obligations to his family without losing the social and economic benefits of individual ownership.[28] But in thus using the law to shape behaviour and moral values, pro-reform jurists unconsciously perpetuated tsarist paternalistic attitudes and practices; and by accepting the right of the state to intervene in the property rights of individuals in order to achieve social and moral goals, they may have weakened the security of the personal rights of individuals which they sought to strengthen, not least because they implicitly legitimized the violation of the individual's rights by the state.[29]

[25] Ryan, *Property*, 129 (118–41 in general). See also J. B. Landes, 'Hegel's Conception of the Family', in J. B. Elshtain (ed.), *The Family in Political Thought* (Amherst, Mass., 1982), 125–44.

[26] See above, Ch. 2 n. 64. [27] See below, Ch. 8.

[28] Russian jurists generally conducted their discussions of testamentary power within the paradigm of the relations between a husband and father and his wife and children.

[29] On this point, see R. S. Wortman, 'Property Rights, Populism, and Russian Political Culture', in Crisp and Edmondson, *Civil Rights*, 13–32, L. Schapiro, 'The Pre-Revolutionary Intelligentsia and the Legal Order', in R. Pipes (ed.), *The Russian Intelligentsia* (New York, 1961), 19–31, and A. Walicki, *Legal Philosophies of Russian Liberalism* (Oxford, 1987).

Freedom, Obligation, Security, and Utility

Although the expanded use of comparative historical methods and the application of anthropological and sociological theories after the late 1870s increased the sophistication and the detail of their arguments, pro-reform jurists never managed to resolve these tensions. Indeed, the tensions only intensified in the economic conditions and the reactionary political atmosphere that prevailed after the assassination of Alexander II in 1881. Conservative concern over the rapid loss of land by the nobility fuelled a debate over revision of the law in which the demand for greater freedom for property owners conflicted directly with the demands for greater security for family members and for sexual equality in inheritance. In the course of this debate, unlimited testamentary power became associated not only with increased economic productivity and with the expansion of individual freedom, but also with the preservation of existing social relations and structures of authority. The conflict between the values underlying the tsarist socio-political order and the demands for sexual equality in inheritance and for the introduction of a system of obligatory shares consequently emerged more clearly.[30] Similarly, the defence of the traditional order mounted by reactionaries after 1881, and the criticism of the use of foreign models for key Alexandrine reforms, made more apparent the transformative character of the changes in the law sought by pro-reform jurists.

Partly in response to such criticism, pro-reform jurists formulated a progressive evolutionary explanation of the development of property and inheritance law which complemented their arguments on family law. As in the latter case, this explanation appeared to provide objective support for the practical proposals of pro-reform jurists. By functionally linking existing law to pre-emancipation social conditions and political institutions, it supported the conclusion that the law served no useful purpose in post-emancipation conditions. Conversely, by demonstrating the similarity between existing Imperial Russian law and earlier Western European legal institutions, and between the direction of Russian and Western European social development, it legitimized the use of Western European juridical norms and concepts for the evaluation and revision of Imperial Russian law.

Progressivist jurists portrayed the development of family, property, and inheritance law as a single, interrelated evolutionary process. Hence such jurists argued that in early Rus, as elsewhere, rights to an inheritance

[30] On this debate, see below, Ch. 8.

and to private property—as opposed to state, ecclesiastical, or community property—had emerged from the initial organization of society into family groups. Both movable and, later, immovable property had belonged originally to such groups and had been managed by the head of the group in the interests of all its members. While some progressivist jurists contended that in medieval Russia the Orthodox Church and the state gradually expanded the circle of relatives who held a right in the property of the family group and therefore also a right to share in the inheritance of such property, most simply accepted the primordial existence of the extended kin-group. All agreed, however, that under the system of family property the power of disposition had been restricted severely, even for the head of a family group. Moreover, apart from gifts to the church, the inheritance of such property had been limited to members of the kin-group. Women had enjoyed even more limited rights to manage or inherit property than men, progressivist jurists claimed, because of their subordinate position and the perception that they left their natal kin-group on marriage. Males therefore had excluded females from an inheritance because they perpetuated the kin-group and acted publicly for it while women only carried its resources away.[31]

According to progressivist jurists, state, socio-economic, and/or ecclesiastical pressures had begun to break down the system of family property

[31] Kavelin, *Sobranie sochinenii*, iv. 1217, 1251–7 (which somewhat modified his earlier argument in ibid., cols. 536–626), id., 'Russkoe grazhdanskoe ulozhenie', *ZhGiUP* (1882), 9: 13–19, D. I. Azarevich, 'Semeinyia imushchestvennyia otnosheniia po russkomu pravu', *ZhGiUP* (1883), 4: 101–36, id., 'Svoboda i ogranichenie dukhovnykh zaveshchanii', *ZhGiUP* (1889), 8: 64–115, N. M. Reinke, 'Dvizhenie zakonodatel'stv ob imushchestvennykh pravakh zamuzhnei zhenshchiny', *ZhGiUP* (1884), 3: 39–72, K. P. Zmirlov, 'Znachenie instituta rodovykh imushchestv dlia budushchago grazhdanskago ulozheniia', *ZhGiUP* (1889), 3: 51–98, id., 'Otmena ili preobrazovanie nashikh zakonov o rodovykh imushchestvakh?', *ZhMIu* (1898), 4: 75–124, I. E. Il'iashenko, 'Institut rodovogo imushchestva s tochki zreniia budushchago grazhdanskago ulozheniia', *ZhMIu* (1900), 2: 96–130, 3: 110–42, and 4: 110–36, id., 'O prave nasledovaniia suprugov s tochki zreniia budushchago grazhdanskago ulozheniia', *VP* (1902), 4/5: 70–90, A. K. Mitiukov, *Obshchnost' imushchestva v sem'e, kak istoricheskaia osnova nasledovaniia* (Kiev, 1900), V. I. Kurdinovskii, 'Vymorochnyia imushchestva', *ZhMIu* (1902), 8: 134–47, P. N. Gussakovskii, 'Nasledstvennoe pravo po proektu Grazhdanskago Ulozheniia', *ZhMIu* (1903), 9: 1–52, A. N. Gedda, 'Obiazatel'naia dolia v nasledstve po proektu novago grazhdanskago ulozheniia', *ZhMIu* (1904), 2: 56–84, M. Ia. Pergament, ' "Predely nasledovaniia" v grazhdanskom prave', *VP* (1906), 3: 293–312, Vladimirskii-Budanov, *Obzor*, 470–588, esp. 548–56, and *ZNDGZ*, nos. 294, 305–6, 309–10, 314, 317–18, 486. See also V. G. Demchenko, *Sushchestvo nasledstva i priznanie k nasledovaniiu po russkomu pravu* (Kiev, 1877), although Demchenko also expressed conservative views on the family. For a contrary argument that the principle of individual private ownership was firmly established in Rus by at least the 11th c. and subsequently was only limited by Muscovite rulers, see V. I. Sergeevich, *Lektsii i izsledovaniia po drevnei istorii russkago prava* (3rd edn., Spb., 1903), 514–31, 561–2.

in Muscovy in the late fifteenth century. As in their discussion of family law, however, jurists tended to confuse the ends imputed to this process with its causes. Employing this teleological technique, they traced the legislative path by which the power of individuals to dispose of property gradually expanded and the interests of kin correspondingly contracted, eventually to include only the rights to share in an inheritance and to redeem alienated ancestral land. In the view of progressivist jurists, the institution of patrimonial property therefore had emerged from the disintegration of the system of family property. This institution in turn had disintegrated steadily after the late seventeenth century, as state political and economic development provided the individual with a social identity and the ability to survive apart from the kin-group. Hence, during the eighteenth century, the right to redeem patrimonial property had contracted and the individual had acquired full rights of ownership over all but patrimonial property. At the same time affective ties within the conjugal family had begun to gain precedence over blood-ties within the kin-group, with the result that the property and inheritance rights of women also had expanded. Pointing to the further changes in social relations and the tsarist political structure introduced by the emancipation and the other Alexandrine reforms, progressivist jurists concluded that the institution of patrimonial property and sexual inequality in intestate succession now constituted merely the remnants of earlier systems of family and patrimonial property which no longer corresponded to prevailing social attitudes or served state needs.[32]

To reinforce this conclusion, some progressivist jurists contended that the institution of patrimonial property had been created by the Muscovite state to secure the services of the male members of noble kin-groups and extended inappropriately to other social groups only in the eighteenth century as the right to own land expanded.[33] Most jurists, however, subscribed to the position presented most comprehensively by Ilia Iliashenko, an assistant to the civil code commission, who later became a

[32] See the references cited above in n. 31.

[33] Zmirlov, 'Znachenie', 51, 54–65, 83–4, 98, id., 'Otmena', 75–81, 117–19, Ia. I. Gurliand, 'O neravenstve prav zhenshchin s pravami mushchin [*sic*] pri nasledovanii po zakonu', *IuO* (1885), 209: 392–4, and 210: 417–18, G. F. Shershenevich, *Uchebnik russkago grazhdanskago prava* (6th edn., Spb., 1907), 131–3, 'O nasledovanii zhenshchin po zakonu', *SG* (1891), 8: 1–3, 'K voprosu ob uravnenii nasledstvennykh prav muzhchin i zhenshchin', *SG* (1893), 14: 1–4, and *ZNDGZ*, nos. 294, 305, 308, 311–12, 574. Sergeevich similarly argued that a statutory right of redemption was created by the Muscovite state, in 1550, but in response to dissatisfied heirs rather than in pursuit of state political interests. *Lektsii* (1903), 524–31 [1st edn., *Lektsii i izsledovaniia po istorii russkago prava* (Spb., 1883), 945–8].

senator in the Civil Cassation Department and, ultimately, Assistant Minister of Justice. Iliashenko argued that although '[t]he institution [of patrimonial property] developed organically in history through the gradual constriction of the rights of the kin-group in favour of the private person, under the influence of the development of the economic and civil life of the people', it none the less had been identified closely with the nobility because of the virtual monopoly of private landownership in Muscovy by the higher service estates. While the legal rules defining the institution of patrimonial property therefore had not arisen exclusively for political reasons, these rules had been influenced strongly by the system of service tenure. Consequently, Iliashenko concluded, when after the late seventeenth century other social groups began to acquire the right to own land, the rules developed for the nobility had been extended to them without considering whether these rules fitted the customs, circumstances, and needs of the groups involved.[34] Whatever their view of the role of the state and the nobility in the historical evolution of the institution of patrimonial property, progressivist jurists thus came to the same conclusion: existing law did not reflect unique Russian legal conceptions but instead derived from an historically common institution that in Russia had developed primarily in association with a single social group and been applied only recently (and inappropriately) to other social groups.

This evolutionary argument reinforced the assertion of progressivist jurists that in post-emancipation economic conditions the aim of property and inheritance law should be to provide the maximum mobility of resources as well as secure rights and maximum powers for property owners. '[T]here can be no doubt', declared Iliashenko, 'that the freedom to dispose of landed property is extremely important for the proper development of the economic life of the state, since this property constitutes the foremost and chief source of popular wealth.'[35] Yet Iliashenko and other

[34] Il'iashenko, 'Institut', 3: 131–2, and in general 3: 113 ff., and 4: 111 ff. From the hereditary nobility, Iliashenko graduated from the juridical faculty at St Petersburg University. He personally owned no land until, near the end of his life, he inherited a small patrimonial estate from his parents. He drafted the final version of the intro. to *GU. Kn. 4-aia*, on inheritance, and as Assistant Minister of Justice was charged with overseeing revision of the code and securing its passage through the Duma and the State Council. TsGIA F. 1364 op. 15 d. 572 and *PS*, p. 40. For similar arguments, see Vladimirskii-Budanov, *Obzor*, 548–61, V. I. Kurdinovskii, *Ob ogranicheniiakh prava sobstvennosti na nedvizhimyia imushchestva po zakonu. (po russkomu pravu)* (Odessa, 1904), 316–17, *ZNDGZ*, no. 318, and the earlier essay by Kavelin, *Sobranie sochinenii*, iv. 537–90.

[35] Il'iashenko, 'Institut', 4: 126. See also Azarevich, 'Svoboda', 80–2, 90–7, Pergament, '"Predely"', 298–9, Zmirlov, 'Otmena', 75–6, 98–101, 120–1, 124, and *ZNDGZ*, nos. 292, 294, 305, 307–13, 316–18, 324, 507.

progressivist jurists believed that existing law impeded rather than promoted economic development. Echoing the complaints of noble landowners themselves, and in contrast to their predecessors in the 1860s and the 1870s, progressivist jurists stressed the harm allegedly caused to well-organized agricultural operations by their unavoidable division in inheritance into parcels that eventually became unprofitable and even incapable of supporting the families of their owners. Avoiding the division of an estate through the payment of compensation to the co-heirs offered no solution to these problems because the heir who retained possession of the estate often was so crippled by debt that he lacked the resources needed for the introduction of necessary improvements. Indeed, they contended, merely the knowledge that the future division of an estate was unavoidable discouraged investment in or reorganization of an estate.[36]

Progressivist jurists also repeated earlier claims that the right to redeem patrimonial property likewise created disincentives to acquire and develop land.[37] To this argument Iliashenko added that redemption 'can destroy the agricultural or industrial significance of a property, devalue the parts remaining to the owner, and even leave him only such land which, without the redeemed section, is completely useless to him'.[38] For this reason, he continued, since the early eighteenth century the state had progressively restricted the right of redemption, preferring 'real and substantial economic interests requiring security in land transactions . . . to the doubtful interests of the kin-group'.[39]

The evolutionary framework formulated by progressivist jurists also reinforced earlier arguments that existing law unjustly treated certain family members, particularly women, spouses, and parents. According to progressivist jurists, even though family relationships now were based on the mutual affection and obligations that bound members of the conjugal family, statutory law continued to give priority in inheritance to blood relationships in the patrilineal kin-group. Hence the bulk of an inheritance frequently passed to distant relatives who meant little to an owner, while family members closer to the deceased, such as parents or a surviving spouse, were deprived of security. Indeed, arguing that the courts had

[36] Il'iashenko, 'Institut', 4: 113–17, 131–3, Shershenevich, *Uchebnik*, 137, Gussakovskii, 'Nasledstvennoe pravo', 3–8, and *ZNDGZ*, nos. 294, 306–7, 309–10, 312–13, 507, 720–5.

[37] Ibid., nos. 309, 720–25, Il'iashenko, 'Institut', 4: 123–31, K. P. Zmirlov, 'O nedostatkakh nashikh grazhdanskikh zakonov', *ZhGiUP* (1885), 3: 51, and Gussakovskii, 'Nasledstvennoe pravo', 3–4. For examples of such cases, see the letters from L. and G. in *NV* (1900), 8879: 2, and (1901), 9039: 4, and *SRGKD* 1891 no. 40.

[38] Il'iashenko, 'Institut', 4: 124. [39] Ibid. 3: 137.

misunderstood the historical evolution of tsarist legislation and consequently had interpreted existing law too restrictively, the former appellate court judge Nikolai Tovstoles asserted in 1914 that 'owing to [the spiritual and moral bond that exists in marriage] the spouse stands as close to the deceased as even children'. 'The inheritance right of spouses', he added, 'without doubt has as its basis the presumption that property acquired during the marriage was obtained by mutual effort, and if it was acquired prior to marriage, then it was preserved, and perhaps even improved, by mutual effort.'[40]

But progressivist jurists most harshly criticized the unequal treatment of women under the law. In essence, they repeated earlier arguments that the equal love of parents for all their children and the equal moral obligation of parents to children of both sexes required the introduction of sexual equality in inheritance, and that women needed a large share of an inheritance because both law and convention restricted their ability to support themselves through work.[41] They also charged that the frequent

[40] N. N. Tovstoles, 'Ukaznaia chast′ supruga v imushchestve svekra (testia)', *ZhMIu* (1914), 5: 154–5. Born in 1872 into the clerical estate, Tovstoles entered the judicial service in 1896 after graduating from the juridical faculty at St Vladimir University. He spent most of his career in courts in the Western Provinces, attaining the position of judge in the Vilnius Court of Appeals before leaving service sometime after 1911. He generally argued that the property and inheritance rights of women had deteriorated during the Muscovite period, begun to improve in the 18th c., but, because of incorrect judicial rulings, again narrowed somewhat during the 19th c. See also id., 'Nasledovanie suprugov po russkomu pravu, v sviazi s proektom grazhdanskago ulozheniia', *ZhMIu* (1911), 5: 48–58, Azarevich, 'Semeinyia imushchestvennyia otnosheniia', 122 ff., Kavelin, *Sobranie sochinenii*, iv. 1256–7, 1266, id., 'Russkoe grazhdanskoe ulozhenie' (1882), 9: 2–9, 13–23, Zmirlov, 'O nedostatkakh' (1884), 5: 72–4, id., 'Znachenie', 67–8, 94–5, Iurist-Praktik, 'Zhelatel′nyia izmeneniia v russkom nasledstvennom prave', *SG* (1892), 7: 4–5, Il′iashenko, 'O prave', 70–5, 81–8, Gussakovskii, 'Nasledstvennoe pravo', 1–3, 10–24, 28–36, Kurdinovskii, 'Vymorochnyia imushchestva', 8: 133–47, A. Goikhbarg, 'K reforme nasledovaniia po zakonu', *Pravo* (1909), 38, cols. 2023–6, and 39, cols. 2081, 2084–7, and *ZNDGZ*, nos. 3, 309, 574–9, 609, 618–20, 624–34.

[41] Kavelin, *Sobranie sochinenii*, iv. 1251–4, id., 'Russkoe grazhdanskoe ulozhenie', 15–17, Zmirlov, 'O nedostatkakh' (1884), 5: 72–4, id., 'Otmena', 93, Gurliand, 'O neravenstve', esp. nos. 203, 208, L. I. Petrazhitskii, 'Obychnoe pravo i zhenskoi [*sic*] vopros', *Pravo* (1899), 18, cols. 901–3, 910–11, Il′iashenko, 'Institut', 4: 120, A. K. Mitiukov, *Obshchnost′ imushchestva v sem′e, kak istoricheskaia osnova nasledovaniia* (Kiev, 1900), 12–13, Gussakovskii, 'Nasledstvennoe pravo', 20–7, I. V. Gessen, 'Vliianie zakonodatel′stva na polozhenie zhenshchin', *Pravo* (1908), 51, cols. 2834–7, N. N. Tovstoles, 'Iuridicheskoe polozhenie zhenshchiny pri otkrytii nasledstva po russkomu zakonodatel′stvu', *ZhMIu* (1910), 1: 56, 77–81, *ZNDGZ*, nos. 305, 309, 320 574–9, 586–604, 609–12, and the articles in *SG* cited above in n. 33. See also A. E. Nol′de, 'O poriadke nasledovaniia rodstvennikov bokovykh linii nasledodatelia v ego blagopriobretennom imushchestve (Arkhivnaia spravka)', *ZhMIu* (1907), 9: 85–6.

resort of parents, spouses, and other property owners to illegal and fictitious acts to avoid the inequities and other problems resulting from the law undermined respect for law in general.[42]

As in the case of family law, the progressivist evolutionary conceptual framework formulated after the late 1870s thus provided powerful support for the changes in property and inheritance law demanded by earlier pro-reform jurists. History itself seemed to decree these changes. Again, if in retrospect the universality, linearity, and homogeneity of this view of history appear unfounded and its characterization of the Russian past at times seems too harsh, the very harshness of the past depicted by progressivist jurists served to highlight the superiority imputed to their own values, ideals, and attitudes.[43] Moreover, by making legal development integral to the historical development of a given society, this ideology of progress assigned to progressivist jurists an important social role. Through their command of juridical science and their understanding of the dynamics of socio-legal development, they could best explain the sources of the practical problems attributed to existing property and inheritance law and discover the most effective solutions to these problems. It is not surprising, therefore, that during the 1880s progressivist views and proposals came to dominate juridical writing on these areas of the law.[44]

Despite consensus on the direction of legal reform, however, progressivist jurists continued to disagree over the extent of testamentary power to be allowed a property owner. Advocates of unlimited testamentary power continued to base their arguments on both the juridical concept and the assumed economic utility of absolute individual ownership. At a

[42] Kavelin, *Sobranie sochinenii*, iv. 1217, Zmirlov, 'Otmena', 92–3, N. A. Poletaev, 'Darenie', *VP* (1899), 5: 87 ff., Il′iashenko, 'Institut', 4: 116–17, 120–1, and *ZNDGZ*, nos. 3, 292, 294, 305–6, 308–17, 324, 486, 565, 574, 576, 586–604, 624–34, 724. See also Ia. K. Gorodyskii, 'Nashi sudy i sudebnye poriadki po dannym revizii 1895 g.', *ZhMIu* (1901), 5: 116–18, and 6: 112–13. For similar sentiments in the general press, see *VE* (1880), 2: 823–30, and (1903), 11: 360–7, *RM* (1890), 3: 231–2, and (1899), 10: 222–3, 'Prava zhenshchin po nasledovaniiu', *SVed* (1893), 73: 1 *RVed* (1903), 97: 2, and, by the highly conservative V. Rozanov, 'Synov′ia i docheri pri nasledovanii', *NV* (1903), 9752: 3.

[43] Since the 10th c., e.g., the rights of women to inherit and otherwise acquire land appear to have fluctuated significantly both over time, regionally, and with respect to social group. On the period from the 10th to the late 17th c., see the references to Pushkareva, Alekseev, Man′kov, and Kleimola cited above in Ch. 6 n. 11. While noting the influence of ideological beliefs and nationalist sentiments, Pushkareva attributes the harshness of the picture drawn by prerevolutionary authors primarily to the deficiencies in their methods and sources. *Zhenshchiny*, 177–87.

[44] Much of the juridical commentary on existing law also was devoted to the elimination of the technical confusion and the inconsistencies found in the law, although even here criticisms often were made from a progressivist perspective. For broad critiques of all aspects of the law, see *ZNDGZ* and Zmirlov, 'O nedostatkakh'.

meeting of the Kiev Juridical Society in 1902, for example, the Kiev District Court judge Aleksandr Gedda opposed the introduction of a system of obligatory shares in inheritance on the grounds that

> [b]y its nature this institution is indisputably a limitation of testamentary freedom, of the freedom to dispose of one's property in the event of death, and, being a restriction of the freedom to dispose of one's property in general, this limitation constitutes a violation of the right of ownership.[45]

Moreover, Gedda argued, because among all social groups except the peasantry the family now consisted of equal and independent members, no member of the family had a claim to the property of any other member. Family members therefore could not be deprived of their rights to property through the arbitrary exercise of an owner's will because they possessed no such rights. Nor, Gedda contended, did unlimited testamentary freedom encourage an owner to violate his moral obligations to his family. According to Gedda, where love truly existed within the family, an owner voluntarily would fulfil these obligations; where love was absent, no such obligations existed. Hence unlimited testamentary power ensured that heirs received what they deserved. Echoing conservative arguments, Gedda claimed that, in contrast, guaranteed rights to an inheritance bred laziness and disrespect for parents. He therefore conceded a right to statutory provision from an inheritance only to minor children because only they had not yet attained independence. Adding that a system of obligatory shares also would merely perpetuate the disastrous economic effects allegedly produced by existing law, Gedda concluded that only unlimited testamentary freedom could ensure the most equitable and economically efficient distribution of property in inheritance.[46]

The overwhelming majority of progressivist jurists, however, rejected such arguments. In their view, the affective ties and interdependent relations that existed ideally between family members gave rise to moral

[45] Gedda, 'Obiazatel'naia dolia', 58. A majority at the meeting rejected Gedda's arguments and supported the introduction of a system of obligatory shares. *Pravo* (1903), 46, cols. 2617–19. Born in 1861 and a Lutheran nobleman, Gedda entered the judicial service in 1887 after graduating from the juridical faculty at St Petersburg University. He held a number of judicial positions in the Ukraine before becoming a department chairman of the Moscow Court of Appeals in 1915. On the civilian concept of absolute ownership, see below, Ch. 9 n. 56.

[46] Gedda, 'Obiazatel'naia dolia'. See also *ZNDGZ*, nos. 305, 309–10, 313, 317, 324, 507 (and possibly also 308, 316), 'O nasledovanii zhenshchin po zakonu', *SG* (1891), 8: 1–3, and the comments of Karnitskii in A. M. Evreinova, 'Ob uravnenii prav zhenshchin pri nasledovanii (Protokoly grazhdanskago otdeleniia s.-p.-b. iuridicheskago obshchestva. XLI i XLII. Zasedaniia 1 i 15 maia)', *ZhGiUP* (1884), 7, pril., pp. 160–6.

obligations that should be legally enforceable. Allowing an owner to violate these obligations through the arbitrary exercise of his will would not only be unjust, such progressivist jurists argued, but would also contravene state and social interests by threatening the stability and welfare of the family. Hence most progressivist jurists favoured the introduction of some system of restrictions on proprietary power which would balance the rights of individual owners with their obligations and with the right of the members of their families to security. Since in most instances these restrictions would have limited property owners even more than did existing law, in the final analysis the majority of progressivist jurists clearly gave a higher priority to the enforcement of moral obligations and to the provision of security to family members than they did to the extension of the rights of individual owners.[47]

Most progressivist jurists believed that the competing claims of freedom, obligation, and security could be balanced most effectively through the adoption of a system of obligatory shares patterned on French or Italian law.[48] Hence such progressivist jurists proposed to exclude a substantial portion of an estate (usually at least half) from the testamentary control of an owner. This property would be reserved for the legal heirs, who would now be defined as principally the surviving spouse, the descendants, and the parents of an owner. The owner would enjoy unlimited testamentary power over his remaining property. Contending that this degree of testamentary control would provide sufficient flexibility for economic needs, the proponents of such arrangements argued that they consequently would serve the public interest in both the welfare of families and increased productivity better than did existing law. In fact, proponents claimed, the level of security enjoyed by the members of an owner's family actually would increase under this system because its restrictions would apply to all property rather than only to that immovable property that the owner himself had inherited. For the same reason, they asserted, these restrictions would be less easy to circumvent than those currently in force.[49]

[47] See the references cited below in nn. 49–53.

[48] On these systems, see above, n. 21.

[49] Kavelin, *Sobranie sochinenii*, iv. 1190–2, 1241–5, 1260–70, id., 'Russkoe grazhdanskoe ulozhenie' (1882), 9: 1–24, (1883), 1: 33–8, and 2: 85–91, Azarevich, 'Svoboda', 80–2, 90–7, G. Dormidontov, *K voprosu o vliianii zakonov o nasledstve na raspredelenie nedvizhimoi sobstvennosti* (Kazan, 1885), 27–8, 36–9, 61–4, 73–7, Zmirlov, 'Znachenie', 69–80, id., 'O nedostatkakh' (1883), 9: 49, 53, and 10: 59, 70, and (1884), 5: 83, id., 'Otmena', 93–4, 108–9, Gurliand, 'O neravenstve', 210: 419–20, Poletaev, 'Darenie', 90–101, Il'iashenko, 'Institut', 4: 116–17, 120–1, 133–6, P. I. Beliaev, 'Istoricheskiia osnovy i iuridicheskaia priroda

The arguments used in support of these proposals demonstrate the persistence of the ambivalent attitude towards individual private property exhibited by earlier pro-reform jurists. Branding *laissez-faire* liberalism as outworn, for example, the Kiev appellate court judge and future Civil Cassation Department senator, Konstantin Zmirlov, argued in 1889 that the fulfilment of the moral obligations of an owner to his family took precedence over all other considerations. Characterizing the family as the foundation of the state and of society, Zmirlov concluded that the law must limit the testamentary power of an owner in order to protect his family, regardless of the economic consequences. In another article on the same theme he declared that such limitations would not unjustly constrain the freedom of owners because absolute freedom was never possible to attain. In all societies, Zmirlov asserted, the rights of others and the interests of society inevitably constrained the freedom of the individual.[50] Yet as a doctrinaire adherent of the progressive evolutionary view of Imperial Russian socio-legal development, Zmirlov also strongly criticized the social and economic disutility of the restrictions imposed by existing law on the proprietary power of individual owners.[51] Similarly, also in 1889 the former Novorossiia and then Warsaw University law professor, Dmitrii Azarevich, contended that state interests dictated that priority should be given to moral considerations in the formulation of inheritance law. Even more forcefully than Zmirlov, however, Azarevich also defended the institution of individual private property on the grounds that it provided a necessary incentive for productive labour. Hence, believing unlimited testamentary power to foster self-centred materialism and a system of obligatory shares to be too restrictive, Azarevich proposed in place of either arrangement to allow the courts in each case to divide an inheritance

sovremennago russkago zaveshchaniia', *ZhMIu* (1903), 6: 69, Gussakovskii, 'Nasledstvennoe pravo', 14–18, 23–7, 'S.-Peterburgskoe iuridicheskoe obshchestvo', *Pravo* (1903), 43, cols. 2439–40, 44, cols. 2506–7, and 45, cols. 2557–8, and *ZNDGZ*, nos. 123, 125, 292, 313–14, 318, 486, 502, 504–5, 562–3. See also Demchenko, *Sushchestvo*, 29–30, 74–8.

[50] Zmirlov, 'Znachenie', 51–98, esp. 69–80, and A. K. Rikhter, *O neobkhodimom nasledovanii* (Spb., 1893), 268–70, 323–37, 368–70, 390–1, 404–5; see also Zmirlov, 'O nedostatkakh' (1883), 3: 105–6, 9: 49, and 10: 59, 70, and (1884), 5: 83, and id., 'Otmena'. Born in 1847 and originally from the *meshchanstvo*, Zmirlov served in a number of judicial positions after graduating from the mathematics faculty at Kharkov University. An aid to the civil code editing commission, he eventually became a senator in the Civil Cassation Department. See TsGIA F. 1364 op. 15 d. 547, and B. Levin-Stankevich, 'Cassation, Judicial Interpretation and the Development of Civil and Criminal Law in Russia, 1864–1917: The Institutional Consequences of the 1864 Court Reform in Russia' (Ph.D. diss. SUNY, Buffalo, 1984), 279–80.

[51] Zmirlov, 'Otmena', esp. 98–101, 120–4.

in the manner deemed to be most equitable and economically efficient.[52] Even more radical was the somewhat earlier proposal of the statist jurist Konstantin Kavelin, who favoured the formation of a council composed of the adult members of the conjugal family, close relatives and in-laws, and a representative of the public interest to oversee the disposition by an owner of most of his property both during his lifetime and at death. According to Kavelin, the disposition of property and the fate of the family were too vital to the present and future welfare of society to be left entirely to the arbitrary will of any individual.[53]

The debate among progressivist jurists over revision of the law thus concerned chiefly the resolution of the conflict perceived to exist between the freedom of individual owners and the economic needs of the state on the one hand and the obligations of owners to their families and the right of individual family members to security on the other. Especially after 1889, however, this juristic debate intersected with a political debate over possible means to alleviate the alleged impact of existing property and inheritance law on noble landholdings. In the course of this latter debate, conservatives demanded first the extension of the right of entail and then virtually unlimited testamentary power over patrimonial property in order to prevent the further loss of land by the nobility. Conversely, they opposed the introduction of both sexual equality in inheritance and a system of obligatory shares, in part because they feared such measures would increase the fragmentation of estates via inheritance and thereby add to the instability of noble landholdings.[54]

In the context of this latter debate, the arguments and proposals made by progressivist jurists clearly had subversive implications for the tsarist socio-political order. In particular, the assertion by most progressivist jurists that moral considerations had a higher priority than economic needs served to justify proposals for changes in the law which not only conservatives believed would weaken one of the chief props of the old

[52] Azarevich, 'Svoboda', esp. 80–2, 90–7, 113–14. On Azarevich, see above, Ch. 3 n. 46.

[53] Kavelin, *Sobranie sochinenii*, iv. 1183–91, 1216–17, 1241–70, and 'Russkoe grazhdanskoe ulozhenie' (1882), 9: 1–24, and (1883), 1: 33–8, and 2: 85–91. On Kavelin, see above, Ch. 2 n. 75. Kavelin remained consistently concerned with the development of moral and ethical values even as his views on the individual evolved from a belief in the need to liberate the individual to an ideal that sought to balance individual and collective interests, rights, and obligations. For a favourable review of his proposal, see A. I. Zagorovskii, 'K voprosu o budushchem zakonodatel'stve o nasledstve', *IuV* (1886), 4: 730–43. Born in 1818, Kavelin belonged to an older generation than Zmirlov and Azarevich, who were born in 1847 and 1848 respectively. For similar critiques, see Dormidontov, *K voprosu*, esp. 61–4, and Reinke, 'Dvizhenie', 39–40.

[54] On these arguments, see below, Ch. 8.

regime, the landed nobility. Seeking to counter conservative opposition to the introduction of sexual equality in inheritance, for example, the Civil Cassation Department senator Petr Gussakovskii declared in a positive review of the draft civil code in 1903 that

> [t]he thought . . . that in formulating the extent of the inheritance rights of women legislation must retreat from the demands of justice in order to achieve general economic or social advantages is fundamentally untrue. Legislation establishing the norms of private property relations must not defer from the demands of justice in the interests of the general good, because the very concept of the general good embraces the interests of the whole population and therefore excludes the possibility of allowing any sort of injustice with respect to particular groups . . . the greater fragmentation of properties to which the equalization of the inheritance rights of women unavoidably will lead is not such a harmful phenomenon in the economic life of the state that for its prevention the institution of legislative measures recognized to be unjust in principle would be necessary. On the contrary, the concentration in a few hands of large sums of capital in general exerts a disadvantageous influence on the development of the general welfare of the state, and therefore inheritance laws that enable the fragmentation of this capital and its more even distribution among a larger number of people can only be recognized as desirable.[55]

Hence for progressivist jurists such as Gussakovskii the introduction of sexual equality in inheritance was not only an intrinsically just goal, but also a means through which the socio-legal order identified with patrimonial property could be transformed into one based on civil equality and a more equitable distribution of wealth.[56]

The populist variant of juristic progressivism pursued essentially the same goal, albeit in a different way. While progressivist jurists relied primarily on their evolutionary construct to refute conservative claims that existing property and inheritance law reflected deeply rooted conceptions of national law, populist jurists employed native peasant customs for the same purpose. Such customs also served to legitimize the positive proposals for revision of the law made by populist jurists. Despite these

[55] Gussakovskii, 'Nasledstvennoe pravo', 23, 25. Born in 1847 and a Catholic nobleman, Gussakovskii graduated from the juridical faculty at St Vladimir University in 1868 and served in a number of posts in the courts and the Ministry of Justice before becoming a senator in 1901. Although he personally owned no land, his wife owned a patrimonial estate of 1,600 des. See TsGIA F. 1364 op. 15 d. 494.

[56] Although I have not been able to determine the political sympathies of all the progressivist jurists referred to, most fell along the spectrum between the Octobrists and the Left Kadets. One, Alexander Goikhbarg, was a Menshevik who later joined the Bolshevik Party and helped to draft the first Soviet civil code.

differences, however, populist jurists also declared civil equality, the security of individual family members, and the development of the individual personality to be the primary goals of the law.[57] Like progressivist jurists, they therefore advocated the abolition of patrimonial property, the introduction of sexual equality in inheritance, and the reassignment of inheritance rights on the basis of the affective ideal of the family. And populist jurists, too, maintained that 'in the interests of family and social welfare it is necessary to introduce into the civil code certain limitations on the arbitrary disposition of property of a kind that in fact, and not fictitiously, would secure the material condition of the members of the family'.[58] Among the limitations proposed by populist jurists was the introduction of a system of obligatory shares patterned on Western European law.

Populist jurists claimed that their proposals represented merely the further development and extension to Imperial law of the principles of equality and interdependent labour which allegedly determined property relations in the peasant household. According to populist jurists, the mutual efforts of all family members to provide for their common welfare and security bound the household together into a co-operative social unit. Each person who contributed to the welfare of the household consequently shared equally in its assets. Populist jurists contended that property and inheritance rights among the peasantry therefore arose from real interpersonal relations rather than from formal ties of kinship. Hence, they asserted, not entirely accurately, both blood relatives who under Imperial law lacked legal status, such as illegitimate children, and non-relatives who participated in the common labour of a household were entitled to use the property of the household and to share in the division of its assets, whereas any relative who had left the household enjoyed no such rights. Populist jurists concluded that peasant custom therefore was more equitable, just, humane, and progressive than Imperial law because it provided greater security to the family and more effectively ensured the fulfilment of interfamilial moral obligations. Declaring that '[e]ven at the present time . . . our peasant customary law . . . with regard to the inner strength of its principles in many respects can be placed higher than the extremely decrepit principles of the *Digest of Laws*', the populist jurist and chairman of the Kirillov congress of justices of the peace, Igor

[57] Evreinova, 'Ob uravnenii', 133, 160, and Tiutriumov in *ZNDGZ*, nos. 1, 14. See also the references cited below in n. 59.

[58] Tiutriumov, in *ZNDGZ*, no. 109.

Tiutriumov, thus urged the civil code commission to adopt peasant custom as the basis for the revision of Imperial statutory law.[59]

Despite their idealization of native peasant custom, however, populist jurists also judged it according to a standard of progress derived partly from Western European jurisprudence and juridical norms. Hence, in terms similar to those used by progressivist jurists with respect to Imperial statutory law, they condemned the limited rights of peasant women to succeed to household property as being 'legalized theft'.[60] Yet the limited rights of peasant women also seemed to contradict the populist ideal of peasant egalitarian co-operativism. To avoid this threat to their ideal, populist jurists located the source of these limited rights not in the patriarchal structure of the household but in such external influences as German and Polish law, the political policies of the Muscovite state, or the authoritarianism of state officials. This explanation enabled populist jurists to conclude that sexual inequality in inheritance constituted an anomaly rather than a fundamental principle of Russian national law.[61] It therefore ought to be abandoned, populist jurists contended, and Imperial Russian law revised to reflect the progressive principles alleged to underlie both Russian peasant custom, at least in most instances, and the Western European civilian norms governing inheritance. For populist jurists, the alleged similarity between Russian peasant custom and Western European juridical norms and institutions thus provided a justification for using the latter as a means to transform both peasant custom and Imperial statutory law.

By the mid-1880s, then, both progressivist and populist jurists had formulated a systematic critique of property and inheritance law and an extensive programme for the revision of the law which complemented their criticisms of family law. Taken together, the proposals to revise all three areas of the law comprised a comprehensive critique of traditional Russian society as well as a plan for its fundamental transformation. The

[59] Ibid.; on Tiutriumov, see above, Ch. 3 n. 53. See also Tiutriumov in *ZNDGZ*, nos. 1, 10, 14, 180, 293, 501, 573, 623, 642, id., 'Po povodu peresmotra i kodifikatsii grazhdanskikh zakonov', *RB* (1884), 4: 122–31, and 5/6: 465–71, 478–81, Evreinova, 'Ob uravnenii', 3: 133, 149–60, and 7: 161–3, id., *O znachenii i predelakh obychnago prava pri razrabotke otdel'nykh institutov Grazhdanskago Ulozheniia* (Spb., 1883), 1, 26–37, 41–2, A. Savel'ev, *Iuridicheskiia otnosheniia mezhdu suprugami, po zakonam i obychaiam velikorusskago naroda* (Nizhny-Novgorod, 1881), 18–23, 43–7, 69–91, N. Zachinskii, 'Prakticheskiia zamechaniia na stat'i x-ago t. ch. 1 zak. grazhd.', *IuV* (1890), 7/8: 643–53, and N. V. Reingardt, *O lichnykh i imushchestvennykh pravakh zhenshchin po russkomu pravu* (Kazan, 1885), 31–40, although he had more conservative views on women than did the other authors.

[60] Evreinova, 'Ob uravnenii', 3: 133–5, and 7: 161–3.

[61] See the references cited above in n. 59.

values and ideals of both groups of jurists were remarkably similar, moreover, despite the important difference in the professed orientation of each group. Both groups placed the principles of equality, legality, and security for the rights of individuals at the centre of their critique of Imperial law and their proposals for its revision. Both therefore threatened to undermine the foundations of autocratic power as well as the traditional bases of social and familial authority. Both, too, sought to use the law to enforce what they considered to be morally responsible behaviour and thereby ensure that personal freedom did not become individualistic licence. In this sense, both groups were bourgeois and anti-feudal rather than individualist and pro-capitalist,[62] even though populist jurists considered themselves also to be anti-bourgeois.

Herein, perhaps, lies another source of the tension between individual freedom and paternalistic state intervention which characterized the arguments and proposals of progressivist and populist jurists. Few practising or academic jurists themselves appear to have been engaged in entrepreneurial economic activities. Most lived in urban areas and relied primarily on their professional expertise for their livelihood; few appear to have owned much real property, most normally rented their accommodation.[63] Acting in conjunction with the doctrines of civilian jurisprudence, this combination of circumstances appears to have predisposed most jurists to regard property in terms more of partible and transferable rights than of tangible objects, especially objects whose identification with a particular kin-group limited their transferability. As Spasovich had proclaimed at the First Congress of Russian Jurists, property and inheritance law in the post-emancipation period must now be based 'on the sovereignty

[62] Ryan, *Property*, 129, applies this characterization to Hegel. See also L. Krieger, *The German Idea of Freedom: History of a Political Tradition* (Chicago, 1972), 129–38. Laura Engelstein notes a similar ambiguity towards individualism in debates over criminal law in *The Keys to Happiness: Sex and the Search for Modernity in Fin-de-Siècle Russia* (Ithaca, NY, 1992), ch. 3.

[63] All regular courts and juridical faculties were located in cities, although sometimes relatively undynamic provincial ones. According to the annual *SSSMIu* and to Gorodyskii, 'Nashy sudy', 2: 42, 5: 128, and 6: 124, the overwhelming majority of sworn attorneys also lived in cities (for example, 1,937 out of 2,120 in 1895). Justices of the peace constituted the main exception with respect to judicial personnel, at least until 1889, when they were replaced by land captains. On property and income, see Tables 1.6 and 1.8 (and the sources cited there), Gorodyskii, 'Nashy sudy', 2: 9–10, 22, 39, 41, and *Soveshchaniia starshikh predsedatelei i prokurorov sudebnykh palat po nekotorym voprosam sudebnoi praktiki v sviazi s peresmotrom zakonopolozhenii po sudebnoi chasti* (Spb., 1895) (HLL), 89–103, 244–89. On the prevalence of renting rather than owning property among urban professionals and officials, see D. Brower, 'Urban Russia on the Eve of World War One: A Social Profile', *Journal of Social History*, 13 (1979–80), esp. tables I and II, pp. 429, 432.

of the person over the thing and of capital over land'.[64] This view of property enabled equity in inheritance, defined in terms of both sexual equality and security for family members against abuses of authority by the owner (implicitly, the husband–father), to take precedence over avoidance of the economic disadvantages attributed to the fragmentation especially of landed estates. Indeed, both Filippov and Gussakovskii had stated explicitly that such fragmentation actually was desirable because the resulting diffusion of property more broadly throughout society provided more individuals with security and the means for personal development.

Although justified most frequently in terms of its economic utility, this demand for increased freedom and security for the activities of the individual also corresponded with the professional and personal interests of progressivist and populist jurists. The formation of a self-conscious legal profession had created associations, an identity, and criteria for determining status and for guiding behaviour which cut across those which had existed previously and which in many cases continued to exist. In particular, members of the new legal profession had to establish their personal and collective status and authority in a context in which social deference still was paid chiefly to formal rank and in which administrative suspicion of jurists often resulted in limitations on their activities. In these conditions, legal security for the rights and activities of individuals included the freedom for progressivist and populist jurists to pursue without undue state interference professional activities that they considered to be socially important.[65] Yet despite their apparent influence on the arguments and proposals of progressivist and populist jurists, the professional circumstances and social background of Russian jurists, as well as their common exposure to Western European jurisprudence, did not result uniformly in reformist ideologies, as the arguments and proposals of conservative jurists make clear.

[64] Spasovich, 'Sledovalo by', 153. See also Mrts. [S. A. Muromtsev], 'Kassatsionnoe reshenie po voprosu o rodovykh imushchestvakh', *IuV* (1880), 3: 560–8, Liubavskii, 'Ob uravnenii', 413, and Gurliand, 'O neravenstve', no. 210.

[65] In 'The Politics of Punishment: A History of Russia's Main Prison Administration and Related Topics from 1863 to 1917' (unpublished manuscript), 326–43, Bruce Adams argues that by the end of the 19th c. increased government restrictions on the activities of jurists had politicized juridical societies and made them more active advocates for the professional prerogatives of their members. Even members of the judiciary complained of pressure by state officials to sacrifice their professionalism to state political interests in particular cases. For example, see V. Volzhin, 'Iz memuarov V. A. Volzhina', *Istoricheskii Vestnik* (1912), 7: 50, and 8: 451–3, 457–60, 462, 466, 472–3, *Zapiski sud'i* (3rd edn., Spb., 1912), 25–7, 35–6, 43–58, and A. F. Koni, *Sobranie sochinenii* (Mos., 1966–9), ii. 72–4, 85–8.

Order and Tradition

Although expressing what appears by at least the late 1870s to have become a minority view, conservative jurists continued to argue that existing property and inheritance law was not only historically legitimate, but also more just and of greater utility than were the alternatives being proposed by pro-reform jurists. While their arguments overlapped considerably, however, conservative defenders of Imperial law themselves tended to divide into two groups. Influenced strongly by historicist and sometimes by Slavophile ideas, some conservative jurists emphasized the belief that existing legal institutions embodied ancient and unique national traditions that reflected deeply rooted Russian legal values. The abandonment of these institutions, especially in deference to Western European juridical influences, therefore would result in the disruption of the natural course of Russian development. Other conservative jurists, in contrast, gave a higher priority to the ability of the law to meet vital state needs than they did to its historical pedigree. Cautiously accepting change, such statist conservatives none the less sought to avoid what they feared would be the destabilizing effects of radical reform by preserving and only modifying existing legal institutions in response to new social and economic conditions.

The Pan-Slav and later extreme right politician Aleksandr Bashmakov provided the most detailed nationalist conservative defence of existing law in a series of articles published in 1897, when he was an assistant to the civil code commission. Using the same legislative and other historical evidence cited by progressivist jurists, Bashmakov attempted to demonstrate that the concept of patrimonial property constituted an integral part of the body of national legal conceptions that allegedly had developed in Russia from earliest times. Hence existing law represented merely the current expression of a fundamental principle of national law whose survival and evolution over several centuries reflected its vitality rather than its decay.[66]

[66] A. A. Bashmakov, 'Institut rodovykh imushchestv pered sudom russkoi iurisprudentsii', *ZhMIu* (1897), 7: 1–34, and 8: 1–62, id., 'Institut rodovykh imushchestv nakanune ego otmeny ili preobrazovaniia', *ZhIuOSU* (1897), 9: 98–130, and id., 'Opyt kriticheskoi otsenki instituta obiazatel'noi doli', *ZhIuOSU* (1897), 7: 36–69; see also id., *Ocherki prava rodovogo, nasledstvennago i obychnago* (Spb., 1911). For a critical review of Bashmakov's arguments, see Zmirlov, 'Otmena'. A graduate of the juridical faculty at Novorossiia University, Bashmakov served as a justice of the peace in the Western Provinces and briefly assisted the civil code editing commission before joining the Ministry of Foreign Affairs in 1898. He later moved to the Ministry of Internal Affairs. On Bashmakov, see V. I. Gurko, *Features*

Like progressivist jurists, Bashmakov located the origin of patrimonial property in the social and property relations believed to have obtained within the kin-group. He then asserted that this type of property had existed in some form in Russia since before the *Sudebnik* of 1550 and therefore had not been created by the Muscovite state for political purposes. Bashmakov conceded that the state had used the institution of patrimonial property for its own ends and thereby had distorted the natural evolution of this institution. And he also acknowledged that because the state at that time had been concerned chiefly with its servitors, Muscovite legislation regarding patrimonial property had related primarily to the nobility. Bashmakov none the less contended that prior to the sixteenth century the basic principle embodied in the institution of patrimonial property had affected all real property regardless of who owned it and that even afterwards this principle had continued to apply in the customary law that governed most civil relations between non-servitors. Hence, Bashmakov argued, as Muscovite restrictions on the right of non-servitors to own real property were eliminated and as the state abandoned its use of patrimonial property to support the service élite, the institution of patrimonial property had reacquired its purely private character and after the early eighteenth century had properly been recognized as applying to the inherited property of all social estates. Even though over this same period the growth of individual property rights had weakened the institution of patrimonial property and had transformed it into an aspect of individual ownership, Bashmakov added, the principle underlying this institution had remained unimpaired.[67]

According to nationalist and statist conservative jurists alike, the fundamental principle of both national law and justice which underlay the institution of patrimonial property arose from the distinction between inherited and self-acquired property. 'It is entirely rational', argued the statist conservative jurist A. F. Brandt in 1888 in his oft-cited defence of the institution of patrimonial property,

and Figures of the Past: Government and Opinion in the Reign of Nicholas II (Stanford, Calif., 1939), 150–2, 161, 384, 634 n. 26.

[67] Bashmakov, 'Institut rodovykh imushchestv pered sudom', 7: 13–18, and 8: 1, 17–27, 30–2, 52–3, and id., 'Institut rodovykh imushchestv nakanune', 98–101, 111–12, 123–30. See also Pobedonostsev, *Kurs*, i. 53–4, 64–5, ii. 293–302, 441–3, 487–8, id., 'Imenie', 3–5, V. N. Nikol'skii, *Ob osnovnykh momentakh nasledovaniia* (Mos., 1871), 73–80, 127–54, and Saburov in *GU. Kn. 4-aia*, intro., pp. 112–15. See also A. I. Zagorovskii, 'K voprosu o zakonnoi nasledstvennoi dole', *ZhMIu* (1896), 5: 118–20, and 6: 34–5, although his views generally tended to be more moderate, particularly with respect to the family. Like populist jurists, nationalist conservatives appear to have been influenced by the ideas of the Germanist branch of German legal historicism.

to allow a person who has acquired property with his own labour and capital or who has inherited it not solely due to the fact of kinship, but as a result of special personal qualities, broader rights of ownership than a person who received property exclusively because he is the nearest relative of the previous owner.[68]

In the latter case, Brandt and other conservative jurists contended, property passed from one generation to the next with the objective of securing the future of the descendants of the person who originally had acquired it. Each succeeding generation developed the property and added to its value. Conservative jurists therefore considered restrictions on the transfer of such property, particularly to persons outside the kin-group and by means that did not involve equivalent compensation, to be just and rational. Otherwise, they asserted, the efforts of previous generations would be wasted and the security of both current and future heirs would be jeopardized. Conceding that it would be neither practical nor consistent with present state economic needs to restrict the power of the current owner to dispose of inherited property for equivalent compensation, conservative jurists claimed that in any case the value received in exchange for such property adequately safeguarded the interests of both the immediate heirs and the future descendants of the seller. Hence existing law was both just and practical, they concluded, because its restrictions on the disposition of patrimonial property protected the family and the posterity of an owner while the unlimited power to dispose of acquired property and the right to sell patrimonial property provided owners with sufficient flexibility for economic purposes.[69]

As this argument demonstrates, conservative jurists were no less concerned than progressivist and populist jurists with finding the proper balance between proprietary freedom, family security, and economic utility. Statist conservative jurists such as Brandt in fact tended to give much greater weight to these considerations than to the preservation of romanticized national legal institutions *per se*. Hence, in defending patrimonial property, Brandt stressed its utility. In his view, it provided a better

[68] A. F. Brandt, 'O rodovykh imushchestvakh', *ZhGiUP* (1888), 6: 1–44, and 7: 1–55; quote from 7: 36. For a critical review of this article, see Zmirlov, 'Znachenie'.

[69] Nikol'skii, *Ob osnovnykh momentakh*, 74–80, Leshkov, *O chastnom pozemel'nom prave*, 15–17, Spasovich, 'Sledovalo by', 158–9, 163–4, Pobedonostsev, *Kurs*, i. 64–5, ii. 487–8, Brandt, 'O rodovykh imushchestvakh', 6: 10–12, and 7: 31–45, Rikhter, *O neobkhodimom nasledstve*, pp. i–vii, 375–84, Zagorovskii, 'K voprosu o zakonnoi', 5: 118–20, and 6: 33–40, Bashmakov, 'Institut rodovykh imushchestv nakanune', 112, 121–3, 128–30, id., 'Institut rodovykh imushchestv pered sudom', 7: 13–15, 18, and 8: 1, 10–14, 36–7, 47–51, id., 'Opyt', 36–69, Malyshev and Saburov in *GU. Kn. 4-aia*, intro., pp. 104–8, 112–36, Demchenko in *Pravo* (1903), 46, cols. 2617–19, L. A. Kasso, *Russkoe pozemel'noe pravo* (Mos., 1906), 19, 149 and *ZNDGZ*, nos. 320–3, 607.

balance of flexibility for property owners and security for their families than did either unlimited testamentary power or a system of obligatory shares. According to Brandt, the former risked widespread and unjust disinheritance, whereas the latter would merely increase the economically harmful division of estates. By contrast, Brandt contended, existing law ensured an adequate mobility of economic resources by allowing the disposition of all property for equivalent value and by prohibiting only those methods of disposing of patrimonial property which had no commercial significance. Moreover, he added, by enabling the adjustment of an inheritance to suit the needs, capabilities, and merits of each heir, the unlimited testamentary control over acquired property accorded an owner under Imperial law both strengthened parental authority and discouraged sloth among family members. Somewhat inconsistently, Brandt then also claimed that existing law protected family members from the arbitrary authority of fathers by restricting testamentary control over patrimonial property.[70]

This latter inconsistency reveals the difficulty posed for conservative jurists, as opposed to conservatives in general, by the desire to reconcile the affective ideal of the family with the social assumptions underlying the institution of patrimonial property. Initially adhering to traditional assumptions, conservative jurists continued to assign social significance to the patrilineal kin-group. As a result, they also defended the inferior rights of women in inheritance. The historicist professor of law at the Demidov Juridical Lycée and then at Moscow University, Vladimir Nikolskii, for example, argued in 1871 that patrimonial property belonged to the entire kin-group. According to Nikolskii, such property was intended to serve the interests of the kin-group as a whole and therefore was only entrusted to the current tenant for this purpose. And since 'not all members of the family have an identical position and significance in the kin-group or in society', he continued, '[they] consequently have different inheritance rights'.[71] Repeating the earlier arguments of Rozhdestvenskii and Kunitsyn, Nikolskii claimed that the role of men in perpetuating the kin-group, in maintaining society, and in defending the fatherland justified their greater share of an inheritance, whereas the potential of women leaving the kin-group on marriage required their exclusion from the inheritance of patrimonial property. Advancing a similar argument in an article in 1861, Pobedonostsev asserted that

[70] Brandt, 'O rodovykh imushchestvakh', esp. 6: 8–12, 21, and 7: 31–51.

[71] Nikol'skii, *Ob osnovnykh momentakh*, 127; on Nikol'skii, see Shershenevich, *Nauka*, 43–8, 188–91.

> [t]he fate of males is to serve the state with their property and person, and therefore the property fund of the kin-group passes to males. The fate of females is to build a new family and a new home, and to add to the fund of their husband. . . . But in order to enter a different family, a woman must be separated from her kin-group.[72]

Hence both Pobedonostsev and Nikolskii concluded that the female relatives and the surviving spouse—by which they meant primarily the widow—of a deceased owner did not share in the inheritance proper but received only a dowry or a statutory provision for support.[73]

As the nineteenth century wore on, however, this view of the kin-group weakened even among conservative jurists. In contrast to Nikolskii, Bashmakov asserted that patrimonial property represented 'a form of personal ownership which is limited with respect to the right of disposition in order to safeguard the interests of the kin-group'.[74] Distinguishing carefully between the conjugal family and the kin-group, Bashmakov contended that the moral obligations of an owner to the former created a right to security from his property for all family members, including women. By contrast, he continued, more distant members of the kin-group had only the right to ensure that patrimonial property remained within this group.[75] Brandt declared that the interest of family members in security in fact took precedence over the interests of the kin-group and therefore had to be protected against the latter.[76] And in defending the retention of patrimonial property in the civil code commission, the State Councillor and former senator in the Civil Cassation Department Andrei Saburov argued that the kin-group no longer had any social relevance but the concept none the less should be maintained as a legal fiction to support provisions of the law that in essence were just and practical.[77]

[72] Pobedonostsev, 'Imenie', 10.

[73] Ibid. 9–12, 52–6, id., *Kurs*, i. 54–7, ii. 297–301, 309–13, 316–18, 337, and Nikol'skii, *Ob osnovnykh momentakh*, 73–8, 127–56. See also Liubimtsev and Leshkov in 'Protokol', Malyshev and Saburov in *GU. Kn. 4-aia*, intro., pp. 103–8, 112–41, and *ZNDGZ*, nos. 322–3, 583, 605, 607.

[74] Bashmakov, 'Institut rodovykh imushchestv pered sudom', 8: 9.

[75] Ibid. 7–14 and id., 'Institut rodovykh imushchestv nakanune', 60–4. See also Pobedonostsev, *Kurs*, i. 64–5, ii. 487–8, *ZNDGZ*, no. 320, and Demchenko in *Pravo* (1903), 46, cols. 2617–19.

[76] Brandt, 'O rodovykh imushchestvakh', 7: 31–2, 338. See also Rikhter, *O neobkhodimom nasledstve*, pp. i–vii, 375–84, and Zagorovskii, 'K voprosu o zakonnoi', 6: 33–44, who advocated equal rights for women and recognition of extensive rights for illegitimate children.

[77] Saburov in *GU. Kn. 4-aia*, intro., pp. 111–44. Born in 1837, a nobleman, and the owner of an hereditary estate of 1,300 des., Saburov graduated from the élite Alexander Lycée in 1857 and served in a number of judicial and Senate positions thereafter. He was

As Saburov's argument suggests, both statist and nationalist conservative jurists considered the mere preservation of the institution of patrimonial property to be useful, however the substantive content of the law might be revised. From their perspective, the abolition of such a long-standing legal institution would threaten social stability by undermining belief in traditional institutions in general. After providing a historical analysis of the law which essentially supported the position of his opponents, for example, the arch-conservative Pobedonostsev declared that

> [i]t is impossible not to wish that the criticism of our old laws concerning immovable property, a criticism that has been growing especially strong recently, would proceed more carefully to the evaluation of the historical phenomena of our life. It is frightful to condemn and destroy that which is not fully understood.[78]

Bashmakov charged even more stridently that the arguments and demands made by progressivist critics of Imperial law stemmed from an obsessive desire to conform with Western European patterns and ideas rather than from the deficiencies of the law itself. Such jurists rarely considered whether their abstract notions were applicable to Russian conditions, he claimed, whereas a glance at peasant custom demonstrated that the principles underlying existing law were rooted firmly in the legal consciousness of the people.[79] And according to Brandt, the proposals of progressivist jurists not only contravened the rights of owners and threatened to exacerbate the economic harm already caused by current law, but also transgressed basic popular and national legal norms. In his view, necessary revision of the law should remain consistent with existing legal concepts.[80]

Yet the proposals of conservative jurists themselves demonstrated that in post-emancipation conditions such consistency was difficult to achieve. In the final analysis, conservative jurists proved to be no more successful in reconciling their desire to preserve the institution of patrimonial property

also curator of the Dorpat educational district from 1875 to 1880 and acting Minister of Education in 1880–1. See TsGIA F. 1364 op. 15 d. 848, and *PS*, p. 8.

[78] Pobedonostsev, *Kurs*, i. 65; for Pobedonostsev's analysis of the law, see i. 53–104, 131–50, ii. 291–645, esp. 293–302, 309, 337–43, 401–3, 441–5, 487–8. For similar sentiments, see Leshkov in 'Protokol', Brandt, 'O rodovykh imushchestvakh', 7: 35–9, 45, and Bashmakov, 'Institut rodovykh imushchestv pered sudom', 8: 8, 28–31.

[79] Bashmakov, 'Institut rodovykh imushchestv nakanune', 112, 123–6. For similar views, see Nikol'skii, *Ob osnovnykh momentakh*, 74–5, 132–3, and Rikhter, *O neobkhodimom nasledstve*, 270–5.

[80] Brandt, 'O rodovykh imushchestvakh', 7: 35–50. See also Pobedonostsev, *Kurs*, ii. 487–8, Malyshev and Saburov in *GU. Kn. 4-aia*, intro., pp. 96–8, 104–8, 121–34, and *ZNDGZ*, no. 605.

with their desire to increase the power of property owners and to provide greater security for family members than were pro-reform and progressivist jurists in reconciling their own demands regarding freedom, obligation, and security. Hence, for the same reasons as the latter, and in sharp contrast to other conservatives, nearly all conservative jurists advocated the elimination of the right of relatives to redeem patrimonial property, which constituted the sole remaining interest of kin in such property apart from the right of inheritance itself.[81] To avoid the economic problems believed to result from the excessive division of estates, conservative jurists also regularly proposed that an owner be allowed to distribute his patrimonial property freely among his legal heirs, with the latter retaining a secure right at best to only a much reduced share of an estate. To this proposed power Brandt added the right to substitute other property for the statutory share of patrimonial property due a surviving spouse.[82] Conversely, to protect the immediate family of an owner, Bashmakov favoured not only the retention of existing restrictions on the disposition of patrimonial property, but also the application of a system of obligatory shares patterned on French law to acquired property. At the same time, he proposed to adapt the concept of patrimonial property to altered family patterns by classifying as patrimonial only that property that had descended through two generations and by restricting to only the descendants of the original purchaser the property rights associated with ties of kinship. The consent of these latter relatives would then be required, however, before an owner could sell or mortgage more than half of his patrimonial property.[83]

The sharp divergence in these approaches to the revision of the law reveals not only the tensions inherent in the position of conservative jurists generally, but also the substantial difference in the priorities of nationalist and statist conservatives. On the one hand, the romanticization

[81] Brandt, 'O rodovykh imushchestvakh', 7: 48–9, Pobedonostsev, *Kurs*, ii. 443, Bashmakov, 'Institut rodovykh imushchestv pered sudom', 8: 55–8, id., 'Institut rodovykh imushchestv nakanune', 98–101, 123, 127, Kasso, *Russkoe pozemel'noe pravo*, 148–9, *ZNDGZ*, no. 727, and Malyshev in *GU. Kn. 4-aia*, intro., pp. 103–4. Saburov also agreed, but believed that the right should be retained for the descendants of the original owner. Ibid. 130–1. On the contrary demand of other conservatives, see below, Ch. 8.

[82] Brandt, 'O rodovykh imushchestvakh', 7: 13, 36–45, 49–52. For similar proposals, see Spasovich, 'Sledovalo by', 151–4, 163–4, *ZNDGZ*, nos. 320, 564–5, 590, and Pobedonostsev, Malyshev, and Saburov in *GU. Kn. 4-aia*, intro., pp. 86–7, 104–8, 112–41. See also Pobedonostsev, *Kurs*, i. 64–5, ii. 487–8, Kasso, *Russkoe pozemel'noe pravo*, 19, 218, and *ZNDGZ*, nos. 596, 605.

[83] Bashmakov, 'Institut rodovykh imushchestv pered sudom', 8: 10–14, 44–58, id., 'Institut rodovykh imushchestv nakanune', 98–101, 120–3, 127–8, and id., 'Opyt'. Zagorovskii made a similar proposal in 'K voprosu o zakonnoi', 6: 36–44.

of the institution of patrimonial property led nationalist conservative jurists such as Bashmakov to propose an expansion of the rights to such property possessed by members of the kin-group not in order to facilitate or support any function actually being performed by this group, but in order to provide a significant role for the institution of patrimonial property itself. Yet this attempted resuscitation of the kin-group was accompanied by recognition of the priority of the conjugal family and by the imposition of new restrictions on proprietary power which conservative jurists themselves acknowledged to be economically debilitating.[84] On the other hand, the concentration of statist conservative jurists such as Brandt and Saburov on the social, economic, and political utility of the law led them to favour a reduction or even elimination of the restrictions on proprietary power which were essential to the institution of patrimonial property. Indeed, by the time of the publication of the draft civil code in 1902 the social basis of patrimonial property had become for Saburov no more than a useful fiction. Following this utilitarian line of reasoning to its logical conclusion, at a meeting of the St Petersburg Juridical Society in 1903 Brandt repudiated his former position and endorsed the proposal of the civil code commission to replace the institution of patrimonial property with a system that combined expanded testamentary power with a flexible form of obligatory shares. He now believed that such a system would satisfy state economic interests and protect the family of a property owner more effectively than did existing law.[85]

The endorsement by Brandt of the draft civil code only underscores the parallels in the substance of the proposals made by progressivist, populist, and conservative jurists during the post-emancipation period, despite the sharp ideological differences between these jurists. Whatever their ideological orientation, all Russian jurists appear to have been concerned with working out the legal consequences not only of the emancipation and the resulting growth of commercial activities, but also of a heightened sense of individuality and the spread of the ideal of the affective family among the educated and upper strata of tsarist society.[86] In ways

[84] Ibid., Spasovich, 'Sledovalo by', 151–4, 163–4, Brandt, 'O rodovykh imushchestvakh', 6: 21, and 7: 13, 38–45, 49–50, Bashmakov, 'Institut rodovykh imushchestv pered sudom', 8: 44–7, 55–8, id., 'institut rodovykh imushchestv nakanune', 127–8, Pobedonostsev, Malyshev, and Saburov in *GU. Kn. 4-aia*, intro., pp. 86–7, 104–8, 112–41, Kasso, *Russkoe pozemel'noe pravo*, 19, Pobedonostsev, *Kurs*, i. 64–5, ii. 487–8, and *ZNDGZ*, nos. 320, 564–5, 590.

[85] *Pravo* (1903), 43, cols. 2439–40. On the draft code, see below, Ch. 8.

[86] For a particularly striking example of an attempt by a Russian jurist to accommodate a heightened sense of the self within a traditional matrix of values that connected the individual with, and obligated him or her to, the community, see M. I. Malinin, *K voprosu ob osnovnykh printsipakh grazhdanskago prava i grazhdanskago ulozheniia* (Odessa, 1882). See

reminiscent of the movement for the reform of civil law in Western Europe and the United States from the late eighteenth century onward, these concerns led in late Imperial Russia to pressure for the expansion of the power of individual owners.[87] Although progressivist jurists viewed such increased power in terms of the extension of individual freedom, and conservative jurists in terms of the reinforcement of parental authority, all considered it to be necessary for economic reasons. At the same time, few Russian jurists embraced Western notions of unfettered individualism and unlimited proprietary power. Nearly all Russian jurists expressed a belief that family relationships gave rise to moral obligations that legitimately limited the power of owners to dispose of their property, particularly in the event of death. Within this consensus, jurists disagreed sharply over the definition of the family itself, the extent to which the right of family members to security should limit the exercise of parental authority and be shaped by both conventional gender roles and state economic considerations, and the degree to which the kin-group—viewed now more historically than contemporaneously—retained significance.

The positions taken by jurists on these issues both reflected and defined their different ideological orientations. In this sense, these orientations were shaped as much by the disputes among jurists themselves as they were by the social, economic, and other changes being experienced by jurists. For jurists, ideology became the medium through which change was understood and a new identity expressed. Where conservative jurists saw continuity and adaptive potential, progressivist and populist jurists saw obsolescence and decay. Where progressivists saw evolutionary progress, and populists saw the progressive potential of peasant customs, conservatives saw threats to national tradition and to social stability. Where progressivist and even populist jurists looked to Western Europe for 'modern' solutions to the practical problems attributed to existing property and inheritance law, conservative jurists looked to the Russian

also the jurists discussed by Walicki in *Legal Philosophies*. For an attempt to justify greater autonomy for the individual by demonstrating, not very persuasively, that this principle was rooted deeply in ancient Russian civil law, see A. S. Muliukin, *Ob individualizme drevniago russkago grazhdanskago prava* (Odessa, 1911).

[87] On the reworking of property law in Western Europe under the influence of Enlightenment notions of individualism, see the references cited above in n. 24. On the way in which changing conceptions of motherhood and the family contributed to the movements in Britain, France, and the United States for increased property rights for married women, see L. Holcombe, *Wives and Property: Reform of the Married Women's Property Law in Nineteenth-Century England* (Toronto, 1983), C. G. Moses, *French Feminism in the Nineteenth Century* (Albany, NY, 1984), and esp. N. Basch, *In the Eyes of the Law: Women, Marriage and Property in Nineteenth-Century New York* (Ithaca, NY, 1982).

past, at least rhetorically, to preserve the integrity of basic social relations and cultural values while adjusting them to meet new conditions. The motives of each ideological faction in revising the law differed fundamentally, and consequently their mutual suspicions of each other were well founded. But if the common professional training and experiences of Russian jurists in the end produced ideological diversity and conflict rather than uniformity and concord, they also appear to have resulted in a shared belief in the importance of the role played by civil law in managing social change and by jurists in defining the law.

8

The Limits of Legislative Revision

As in the case of family law, the disputes among jurists over property and inheritance law took place within a wider context of conflict over revision of the law. Again, legislative attempts to adjust the law to post-emancipation conditions became intertwined with the pursuit of broader social, political, ideological, and institutional goals, with the result that effective action was blocked until 1912. On the most immediate level, conflict over the law revolved around the interrelated issues of the extent of an owner's testamentary power, the degree of security to be accorded his family, and the relative inheritance rights of women and men. But underlying these issues lay more fundamental disagreements over the appropriate structure of society and basis of social relations, the relationship between authority and law, and the proper governmental response to socio-economic change.

The redefinition of property and inheritance law thus served in post-emancipation Imperial Russia as a medium for the articulation of competing ideological beliefs and the redefinition of social identity. As noble landowners adjusted differentially to the expansion of market relations, large numbers of noblemen abandoned the land and turned to new occupations, and members of other social estates also crowded into these occupations as well as into the state bureaucracy, the character and identity of the nobility grew even more amorphous than previously.[1] At the same time, formal categories of social status declined in practical significance within the urban commercial economy, the civic, professional, and municipal

[1] The nobility in Imperial Russia never constituted a homogeneous and cohesive social estate but was in fact divided by regional, religious, and ethnic differences as well as by differences in wealth and formal rank. For discussions of the changes occurring in the nobility after the emancipation, see G. M. Hamburg, *Politics of the Russian Nobility 1881–1905* (New Brunswick, NJ, 1984), 9–84, S. Becker, *Nobility and Privilege in Late Imperial Russia* (DeKalb, Ill., 1985), 28–54, 110–15, 125–8, 143–9, R. T. Manning, *The Crisis of the Old Order in Russia: Gentry and Government* (Princeton, NJ, 1982), 25–44, and A. P. Korelin, *Dvorianstvo v poreformennoi Rossii 1861–1904 gg. Sostav, chislennost', korporativnaia organizatsiia* (Mos., 1979), 122–31.

organizations, and the new occupational groups that developed rapidly after the 1860s.[2] In this context, different groups demanded changes in the law that not only suited their socio-economic interests and circumstances, but also reflected their self-image. Hence, for example, even though by the turn of the century a broad consensus on the desirability of expanding proprietary power for economic reasons had emerged, this demand was expressed in ways that either idealized traditional legal institutions and social relationships or measured them critically against a standard drawn from Western European experience. Ideological conceptions of the law therefore did not correspond neatly with particular social or occupational groups, even though the principal proposals for revision of the law emerged from among noble landowners, professional jurists, and moderate feminists respectively.

A minor skirmish in the mid-1860s between reformist jurists in the Ministry of Justice and the arch-conservative director of the Second Department of the Imperial Chancellery, Count Viktor Panin, demonstrates how from the reform era onwards ideological conflict affected even relatively modest proposals to revise property and inheritance law. In 1862 the Second Department resubmitted to the State Council a revised version of the project on wills that had been prepared initially under the direction of Count Bludov.[3] In addition to improving the procedure for composing and verifying wills, the project sought to increase the security of the immediate family of an owner by limiting his right to dispose of acquired property in the event that he left no patrimonial property. To ensure that this restriction of proprietary power would not undermine parental authority, the Second Department proposed to allow an owner to disinherit any heir, albeit only with Senate approval and for statutorily defined causes that had been verified judicially. Finally, the Second Department also proposed to permit an owner of patrimonial property to assign binding legacies on the heirs of such property for a total amount not exceeding a fixed proportion of its annual income. Without reviewing the project, however, the State Council returned it to the Second Department for co-ordination with the impending judicial reform.[4]

In the course of this revision, jurists in the Ministry of Justice proposed

[2] For an attempt to synthesize recent research on the effects of urban growth on social identity among the upper strata of society, see D. R. Brower, *The Russian City between Tradition and Modernity, 1850–1900* (Berkeley, Calif., 1990), 54–6, 104–24.

[3] See above, Ch. 6.

[4] *GU. Kn. 4-aia*, intro., pp. 13–15, A. K. Rikhter, *O neobkhodimom nasledovanii* (Spb., 1893), 218–19, and *Proekt polozheniia o dukhovnykh zaveshchaniiakh* (Spb., 1862), esp. arts. 13–29.

to the Second Department that testamentary power be expanded even further and that the inheritance rights of women and men be made equal. Reflecting the view of the family and of the purpose of inheritance which was forming among jurists, the memorandum submitted by the ministry asserted that inheritance law should be based on the assumption that an owner wished to provide for the security of his nearest relatives. According to the memorandum, this assumption led to the conclusion that sexual inequality in inheritance was no longer justified. 'At the present time,' the memorandum continued,

> when property laws and social and private civil life have changed completely, when the distinction between service tenure and hereditary right has disappeared, the existence of this inequality has become incompatible with juridical concepts and directly contradicts both the principle now lying at the basis of our inheritance law and the position afforded women by current legislation.[5]

Arguing that parents loved their sons and daughters equally and that married women were no longer slaves of their husbands but fully equal individuals with the right to dispose of their own property, the memorandum concluded that the law should establish the principle of sexual equality in inheritance and then allow an owner to adjust the share of each heir in accordance with individual needs and deserts.[6]

Reflecting Panin's conservatism, however, the revised project resubmitted to the State Council in 1867 not only ignored the recommendations of the Ministry of Justice, but abandoned the attempt to revise substantive law altogether. '[I]n the formulation of separate projects on civil law', declared the memorandum accompanying the project, 'the basic principles of existing national law must be preserved.'[7] Any restriction of existing testamentary power over acquired property therefore was impermissible because it would constitute 'an unjust constriction of a right that has long existed in Russia and that rests on the natural and universal conviction that every person has the full right to dispose of property acquired by his own labour at his discretion'.[8] Stating further that the inherited character of patrimonial property justified the limitations

[5] TsGIA F. 797 op. 92–1910 d. 53 ll. 6–18, p. 8.

[6] Ibid., ll. 6–18, pp. 8–12, *GDP. 3-ii soz., 4-aia ses. (1910–1911)*, iii., no. 212, pp. 5–6, and A. Liubavskii, *Iuridicheskiia monografii i izsledovaniia* (Spb., 1867, 1875, 1878), iii. 22–3.

[7] Rikhter, *O neobkhodimom nasledovanii*, 223. On Panin's historicism, see P. Maikov, *Vtoroe otdelenie sobstvennoi ego Imp. velichestva kantseriarii 1826–1882* (Spb., 1906), 474–5, and 466–85.

[8] Rikhter, *O neobkhodimom nasledovanii*, 220.

placed on its disposition, the memorandum implied that these limitations adequately ensured fulfilment of the moral obligations of an owner to his family. The Second Department also rejected its previous proposals to allow the imposition of binding legacies on the heirs of patrimonial property and the disinheritance of heirs, fearing now that the former might overburden estates with debt while the latter might be abused and thereby engender family disharmony.[9] The revised project consequently contained only those procedural changes necessitated by the reforms of the judicial and notarial systems.

Although prodded by the State Council, two separate joint commissions failed to reconcile either the practical or the conceptual differences between the Second Department and the Ministry of Justice. Consequently, only the proposed changes in procedural law were enacted, in 1869.[10] Fundamental disagreement within the bureaucracy over the approach to legal reform, and indirectly over the general direction of state policy, thus had blocked any revision of substantive inheritance law. But the abstract character of the arguments used by advocates of reform may also have contributed to this outcome. In the end, reformist officials adduced little evidence in support of their claim that the law urgently required revision. This situation altered dramatically, however, after the mid-1880s.

From Entail to Testamentary Freedom

In 1887 the Poltava provincial assembly of the nobility petitioned the government for the right to create entailed estates, thereby provoking a public and governmental debate over property and inheritance law which lasted until the eve of the First World War. Over the next five years sixteen more provincial assemblies submitted similar petitions.[11] On one

[9] Ibid. 219–30.

[10] *GU. Kn. 4-aia*, intro., pp. 16–19, 'Zakonodatel'nyia raboty po izmenenii zakonov o dukhovnykh zaveshchaniiakh,' *MV* (1870), 224: 3, and *SVest* (1870), 273: 1.

[11] The petitions can be found in TsGIA F. 1151 op. xii d. 1 ll. 120–94, the contents of which are reproduced in *Dvorianskoe zemlevladenie, material 1893* (Spb., n.d.) (HLL), with the petitions contained in 'Khodataistva dvorianstva o merakh k podderzhaniiu dvorianskago zemlevladeniia'. See also Iu. B. Solov'ev, *Samoderzhavie i dvorianstvo v kontse xix veka* (Lenin., 1973), 201–16, 316–26, Hamburg, *Politics*, 118–31, and Becker, *Nobility*, 66–75. Formed at the district and provincial levels in the provinces of European Russian, assemblies of the nobility normally met every three years, chiefly to elect the local marshal of the nobility and to deal with a variety of mostly minor matters. Often serving primarily as a social occasion, they generally were less well attended than zemstvo assemblies and had a more conservative complexion. See Korelin, *Dvorianstvo*, 137–54, Becker, *Nobility*, 136–44, and Manning, *Crisis*, 83–5.

level, these demands formed part of a broad campaign by noble landowners for state relief from the severe depression that gripped European and American grain markets in the late nineteenth century. Indeed, nearly identical demands were advanced in Germany at this time. And the American Homestead Exemption laws cited frequently by both Russian and German advocates of entail had a similar purpose.[12] Significantly, most noble assemblies in the agriculturally rich black-earth and southern provinces supported the demand for a right of entail, whereas none in the central industrial region did so, perhaps reflecting differences in the attractiveness of agriculture and the incidence of mortgage debt in these areas.[13]

But the petitions and the responses they elicited from other noble landowners also reflected the anxieties, evolving self-images, and growing political assertiveness especially of the owners of middle-sized estates who dominated provincial noble and zemstva assemblies. Members of this group used traditional values and an idealization of their past to justify diametrically opposed demands for revision of the law as they simultaneously reacted against and adjusted to the commercialization of agriculture and to state efforts to extend bureaucratic control deeper into the countryside. In the end, the most appealing strategy for balancing even conservative socio-political values and ends with the economic conditions of the market-place proved to be increased, rather than diminished, proprietary power.

In part responding to the reactionary rhetoric of the government under Alexander III, the noble landowners who composed the petitions on entail portrayed themselves as performing an important state service by '[s]tanding guard over conservative values and guiding and directing to the good the masses of our ignorant peasantry'. Hence, concluded Nizhegorod nobleman Vladimir Khvoshchinskii, 'the landed nobility are

12 On Germany, see M. John, *Politics and the Law in Late Nineteenth-Century Germany: The Origins of the Civil Code* (Oxford, 1989), 127–43. On US homestead exemption laws, see C. Warren, *Bankruptcy in United States History* (Cambridge, Mass., 1935), 9, 13, 81–92, 100–12, 122–3, 146–50, and J. H. Thomas, 'Homestead and Exemption Laws of the Southern States', *The American Law Register*, xix (1871), 1–17, 137–50.

13 A partial exception was Kaluga prov., which straddled the two regions. Seventeen out of thirty-seven noble assemblies in European Russia submitted petitions, including eight out of thirteen back-earth provinces (Tula, Riazan, Kursk, Penza, Kazan, Simbirsk, Poltava, Kharkov), four out of five southern provinces (Ufa, Ekaterinoslav, Kherson, Tauride), and five others (St Petersburg, Pskov, Smolensk, Kaluga, and Nizhegorod). According to *Statistika dolgosrochnago kredita v Rossii. Dolgi po dolgosrochnym zaimam v gosudarstvennykh i chastnykh kreditnykh uchrezhdeniiakh* (Spb., annual) for 1894 and 1898, the nobility in these provinces were among the most heavily in debt.

necessary to our state as the link that unites tsar and people'.[14] Capturing the contradictions in petitioners' arguments, a district marshal from Kursk province, S. Zhekulin, asserted similarly that

> hitherto within the general structure of the state the hereditary nobility has remained a repository of the continuous traditions of unshakeable loyalty to the tsar and conscientious service to the people. . . . It has been predominantly the middle landed nobility that heretofore has been the sole propagator of efficient agricultural methods in the country. If this task has not yet yielded brilliant or very weighty results, the cause lies in the necessity of dividing estates among the heirs. . . . With few exceptions, each noble estate constitutes a vital, more or less cultured agricultural centre.[15]

Why, then, did noble estates need special protection from the state?

Because, according to noble petitioners, traditional values and relationships were being undermined by the actions both of propertyless and therefore venal government officials and of unscrupulous capitalist and peasant exploiters. To the ideal of selfless paternalism allegedly cultivated among the landed nobility by its tradition of service to tsar and people, petitioners counterposed the selfish egoism and lack of moral scruples imputed to state bureaucrats and non-noble landowners. Thus, argued Prince Aleksandr Meshcherskii, whose memorandum to the Poltava nobility had initiated the campaign for entail, unless restrained by economically independent noble landowners, 'the unlimited power of tsarist officials becomes an unlimited evil, because the further it goes the worse it gets'.[16] And as for the new capitalist landowners, Meshcherskii characterized them as

> Rippers and Strippers because they generally pursue a policy of squeezing to the last drop the juice from the peasant and the land, a policy of getting the quickest possible commercial return on the money and interest spent on buying an estate. Of course, the new person sees no harm in this because the exhausted peasant is transformed into a slave, a slave on the basis of the unwritten laws of the exploitation of neighbours, and the exhausted land can always be sold.[17]

Peasant institutions similarly were now dominated by 'the peasant exploiter, a drunken brawler, or the tavern-keeper with the help of the village scribe', claimed Khvoshchinskii. 'With such leaders,' he continued,

[14] 'Khodataistva dvorianstva', 25. This self-image of the noble landowner in fact preserved substantial continuity with the immediate pre-emancipation period. See D. Field, *The End of Serfdom: Nobility and Bureaucracy in Russia, 1855–1861* (Cambridge, Mass., 1976), 15.

[15] 'Khodataistva dvorianstva', 48–9, 51. [16] Ibid. 18. [17] Ibid. 10.

the people are developing more and more disrespect for property rights, for family rights, and even for governmental authority, assuming that any decision or directive of legally constituted authority can be overturned if one hires a clever lawyer. All authority is ceasing to exist.[18]

In the view of noble petitioners, the perpetuation of the values that sustained the tsarist socio-political order thus depended on the preservation of their property.

But having depicted themselves as both a source of agricultural progress and a guarantor of social and political stability, noble petitioners then argued somewhat inconsistently that a combination of current economic conditions, misguided state policies, and the unavoidable effects of inflexible inheritance laws was weakening their ability to play these roles. Reflecting the problems caused generally for Russian agriculture by the scarcity and resulting high cost of capital relative to low and fluctuating income, petitioners complained that the replacement of cheap state credit after the emancipation with more expensive and rigidly enforced private credit had put noble landowners at the mercy of heartless capitalists and the vagaries of market prices. Lured into debt by the need to adjust to new conditions or to obtain operating capital, they had become ensnared in ruthless capitalistic tentacles that squeezed them off their land once falling grain prices in the early 1880s had depressed their income. Catastrophe was unavoidable under these conditions, asserted Meshcherskii, and 'the most capable, the apparently most intelligent people suffered more than most and, though blameless, were condemned completely'.[19]

While exonerating themselves, however, noble petitioners found the state partly culpable for their problems. Since the emancipation, argued Iu. D. Rodionov, a district marshal from Simbirsk province, state economic policies 'have sacrificed noble landowning to capital, especially foreign [capital]'.[20] And in the view of Tula noblemen R. I. Zmeev and A. N. Parenyi, the Alexandrine reforms in general

were directed towards the elimination of the privileged position of the noble estate . . . The undermining of material welfare, the licentiousness of the peasantry, the enthronement of the tavern, the final collapse of the prestige of the nobility, the dragging in the mud of its ancient traditions of valour, honour, and nobility—

[18] Ibid. 25. [19] Ibid. 10.

[20] Ibid. 64. For Rodionov's views, see also P. [A. D. Pazukhin?], 'Zapovednyia imeniia', *MV* (1889), 26: 2.

all this taken together has forced the nobility to bow its head and has rendered life on its estates hateful for it.[21]

Petitioners urged the state to reverse its policies and to arrest the declining fortunes of noble landowners by insulating them from the pitfalls of the market before the autocratic order itself was undermined. After all, Meshcherskii lamented, '[w]hat state, local, or governmental goals could be served by an assembly of completely impoverished nobles, the last remnants of a great past, the useless children of pitiable fathers—because the future will brand us pitiable for the legacy we have prepared and left to it'.[22]

According to the petitioners, the survival of the landed nobility depended in particular on the revision of existing inheritance law. In contrast to their eighteenth-century ancestors, noble petitioners now complained that the law threatened their economic well-being and undermined patriarchal authority within the family. Echoing arguments made by progressivist jurists, as well as by French critics of obligatory partible inheritance, petitioners like Khvoshchinskii claimed that the law frequently compelled landowners or heirs to sell an estate, and '[t]hose lands which are not sold are divided obligatorily among the children and the portions grow increasingly smaller, thereby transforming their owners into impoverished noblemen who are little capable of bearing the social obligations which the government wishes to impose on the nobility'.[23] Forced to borrow heavily to maintain themselves, these impoverished heirs often eventually sold their land to non-nobles. Nor did the law affect only landholdings. According to Rodionov, guaranteeing a share of the inheritance gave 'children proprietary independence from the head [of the family], thereby reducing his authority and undermining the family'.[24]

To eliminate these problems, noble petitioners demanded the right to entail all or part of their estates. Reflecting the political concerns of the middle landed nobility who had drafted them, eleven of the seventeen petitions tied the minimum size for entailed estates to the amount of land needed for direct participation in noble assemblies or for election as a justice of the peace, thereby ensuring the right to take part in provincial affairs.[25] Only three noble assemblies proposed to extend the law to their

[21] 'Mneniia o nedelimykh dvorianskikh uchastkakh chlenov kommisii po voprosu o zapovednykh imeniiakh, P. I. Zmeeva, A. N. Parenago i Iu. V. Arsen′eva', 7–8, in *Dvorianskoe zemlevladenie* (HLL).

[22] 'Khodataistva dvorianstva', 11. [23] Ibid. 27. [24] Ibid. 59.

[25] This amount varied from 200 to 600 desiatin in the provinces concerned.

lesser brethren, while the nobility of Tauride province failed to agree on this issue.[26] And to forestall the possibility of foreclosure, nearly all petitions favoured allowing entailment of estates that already were mortgaged to the State Noble Land Bank, which had been established in 1885 in response to earlier requests from the nobility for easier credit. A few assemblies also proposed that noble estates be declared indivisible below a certain size or that owners of estates above a minimum size be allowed to declare their estates indivisible in inheritance.[27] Finally, echoing several earlier petitions, the Penza nobility requested elimination of the restrictions that the Civil Cassation Department had imposed on the right to redeem patrimonial property.[28]

Emphasizing the political aspect of these proposals, several individual nobles demanded that entailment of estates be compulsory and accompanied by new service obligations that would have extended the role of the middle landed nobility in provincial administration. Referring to the past and expected future service of the landed nobility to justify these concessions, Khvoshchinskii declared that 'estate privileges cannot be harmful if they correspond to the benefit which the state expects from one or another social estate'.[29] Moreover, argued Rodionov, concessions like entail guaranteed the state

> a strong, settled agricultural population, secured the family from need, established a link between the family and the land, transformed the domestic hearth into an unassailable fortress, and ensured the state's best people eternal freedom from enserfment to capital—the worst of all slaveries.[30]

Similar political motives led ultra-conservative and reactionary writers to adopt the proposal for compulsory entail as a means of protecting the autocratic socio-political order from the allegedly corrosive effects of the Western principle of civil equality. In the view of such authors, the misguided propagation of this principle through the reforms of Alexander II had destabilized the empire by fostering the class antagonisms, selfish individualism, and chaotic conflict characteristic of democratic capitalist societies. The slide towards national disintegration, disorder,

[26] See the petitions from Ufa, Kursk, Simbirsk, and Tauride, ibid.; the issue was not mentioned in the petitions from the Kazan and Tula assemblies.

[27] See the petitions from Kursk and Smolensk, ibid.

[28] Ibid. 1–7, 106, 109–12; see also Korelin, *Dvorianstvo*, 258–9, 261–2, 265. On the practice of the Civil Cassation Department, see below, Ch. 9.

[29] 'Khodataistva dvorianstva', 33; see also the memoranda of Zhekulin and of Zmeev and Parenyi in *Dvorianskoe zemlevladenie* (HLL).

[30] 'Khodataistva dvorianstva', 63; see also the reference to P. cited above in n. 20.

and moral degeneracy could be arrested, warned ultra-conservative pamphleteers and writers in such papers as the *Moscow Gazette* and *Citizen* (*Grazhdanin*), only through the preservation of strong autocratic authority, national traditions, and a corporate social structure. Such authors concluded that the landed nobility, with its alleged tradition of selfless service and loyalty to the autocracy, therefore had to be reinforced to provide a shield against the pretensions of landless bureaucrats and intellectuals, whose selfish and socially disruptive actions sacrificed national interests to their own.[31]

Like Khvoshchinskii and Rodionov, ultra-conservative writers hoped that the compulsory entail of all noble estates would arrest the decline in both the overall extent of noble landholdings and the number of noble landowners resident in the provinces.[32] To further consolidate the political role of noble landowners, ultra-conservatives also proposed that they be granted control over key provincial administrative institutions, exclusive right to certain central governmental posts, and free and preferential access to secondary and higher education. Rejecting criticisms of these proposals, ultra-conservatives argued that disinherited sons could be supported from the income of entailed estates and educated to perform other valuable social functions, thereby presumably enlarging the number of landless professionals, officials, and entrepreneurs who conservatives believed were disrupting the traditional order. Although they also claimed that entail would enable owners to use their land more efficiently, ultra-conservatives asserted that economic considerations should be subordinated to the political need for a strong landed nobility. This emphasis on

[31] For such views, see Navrotskii, 'Po povodu khodataistv o podderzhanii dvorianskago zemlevladeniia', *Grazhdanin* (1892), 63: 1, and 64: 1, A. A. Planson, *O dvorianstve v Rossii. (Sovremennoe polozhenie voprosa)* (Spb., 1893), id., *Sosloviia v drevnei i sovremennoi Rossii. Ikh polozhenie i nuzhdy (o tsentre)* (Spb., 1899), D. Bodisko, 'Dvorianskii vopros—vopros gosudarstvennyi', *Grazhdanin* (1897), 37: 4–7, and 39: 3–5, id., '"Novoe Vremia" i G. Evreinov o dvorianskom voprose', *MV* (1898), 60: 2, id., 'Pravda i krivda o dvorianskom voprose', *MV* (1898), 70: 2, 72: 2, 78: 2–3, 84: 3, 116: 2, 118: 2, and 119: 1–2, Prince D. N. Tsertelev, 'K voprosu o dvorianskom zemlevladenii', *RVest* (1897), 2: 411–23, 3: 397–402, and 4: 426–44, id., 'Dvorianstvo i intelligentsiia', *SVed* (1897), 207: 1, Prince P. N. Tsertelev, 'Podderzhanie dvorianskago zemlevladeniia i zapovednost′ imenii', *MV* (1897), 110: 2, 111: 2, and 112: 2, id., 'Gosudarstvennoe znachenie dvorianstva', *SVed* (1897), 200: 1, and (1898), 137: 1, P. N. Semenov, 'Krest′ianskoe i dvorianskoe zemlevladenie v Rossii', *Grazhdanin* (1898), 97: 2–8, and 98: 2–9, Byvshii Predvoditel′ Dvorianstva, 'Kak uprochit′ pomestnoe dvorianstvo?', *MV* (1898), 32: 2–3, id., 'Dopolnenie k moei programme', *MV* (1898), 49: 2, Dvorianin, 'Po povodu myslei G. Romera o "Budushchem dvorianstva"', *Grazhdanin* (1900), 12: 7–10, and 13: 5–9, and 'Dvorianskii vopros', *MV* (1897), 38: 1, 79: 1–2, 80: 2, 83: 1–2, 85: 1–2, 89: 2, 103: 2, 104: 1–2, 111: 1–2, 112: 2, and (1898), 157: 2.

[32] Throughout this period the number of noble landowners eligible to participate directly in noble and zemstvo assemblies was declining significantly. See Becker, *Nobility*, 136–8.

political and ideological objectives brought the proponents of reactionary reform into conflict with even the majority of noble petitioners, who in demanding a right of voluntary entail had sought primarily to solve their pressing economic and personal problems, albeit in a way that promoted conservative values. For most ultra-conservatives, then, while the landed nobility as a group represented an essential instrument for the pursuit of their political agenda, the desires of individual noble landowners were irrelevant. Indeed, those nobles who expressed ideologically unacceptable views were to be deprived of their status.[33]

Conversely, progressivist and liberal writers opposed entail on the grounds that it violated the principles of civil equality and social status based on individual merit. For them, entail represented an anachronistic device intended solely to serve the political purpose of preserving an historically outdated aristocracy and a social structure based on legal inequality. The liberal *Russian Gazette* (*Russkie Vedomosti*) asserted, for example, that

> entailed landholding was never in any place free from political motives, which frequently outweigh economic considerations. In general, the reform of inheritance law has been resorted to historically more than once with purely political objectives, and in such instances the principle of entail always played a prominent role, attracting hostility or enjoying support depending on what political, and not economic, tasks the government was pursuing.[34]

Confirming the fears of their opponents, progressivists and liberals concluded that the political task of the moment consisted in completion of the transition to civil equality and legality begun by the reforms of Alexander II, in part by extending the underlying principles of the latter to substantive civil law.

Progressivist and liberal writers also raised several practical objections to the measures proposed by the provincial assemblies. They contended that the disinheritance and impoverishment of an owner's children would not only be unjust, but also result in family disharmony and possibly even

[33] In addition to the references cited above in n. 31, see 'Dnevnik', *Grazhdanin* (1892), 56: 3–4, 58: 3, and 92: 3, 'Dvorianskii vopros', *Grazhdanin* (1893), 18: 1, V. G. K., 'Dvorianstvo i dvorianskiia zapovednyia imeniia', *MV* (1893), 193: 2 (letter), *MV* (1893), 311: 2, 313: 2, 349: 2, and 351: 3; (1894), 18: 2, 27: 1–2, 39: 2, 44: 2, and 47: 2–3, 'Zapovedniia dvorianskiia imeniia', *MV* (1895), 343: 5, 'Neotchuzhdaemost′ dvorianskago zemlevladeniia', *MV* (1898), 37: 2, and 200: 1, 'Vremenno-zapovednyia imeniia', *MV* (1899), 192: 2, 'Nedelimyia imeniia', *MV* (1901), 36: 1–2, *RVest* (1893), 8: 364–7, and (1899), 9: 371–4, and V. K. Lilienfel′d, *Kak predupredit′ dvorianskoe zemlevladenie ot neminuemoi gibeli? Malenkoe izsledovanie pomeshchika Penzenskoi gubernii* (Spb., 1894).

[34] *RVed* (1892), 353: 2.

social unrest, particularly given an alleged inadequacy of alternative sources of income. Pointing to the experience of Western Europe, they also charged that entailment of noble estates would restrict the availability of credit and discourage innovation, thereby retarding agricultural development.[35] Many progressivist and liberal critics of entail went even further and claimed that agricultural progress necessitated the demise of the landed nobility. Characterizing the nobility as historically a service estate that had been uninterested and incompetent in agricultural affairs, these critics asserted that most noble landowners simply could not compete successfully when deprived of free labour. The operation of the market therefore should be allowed to replace this historically as well as financially bankrupt group with dynamic new men who could use national resources more effectively. 'At the present time,' declared the liberal economist E. I. Zhigachev,

> the personal activity of people, their energy and enterprise, is the factor deciding the economic position achieved by people. As a consequence, noble landowners, as unzealous owners, have not delayed in falling to one of the lowest economic levels . . . In such conditions . . . the ring of the auctioneer's hammer is merely the triumphant victorious note of that new economic motif which has begun to resound in the province of landownership as the logical consequence of the new post-reform bases of social life.[36]

The political significance of the refusal of progressivist and liberal writers to extend this line of reasoning to peasant landholdings was not lost on their conservative opponents.[37]

[35] For such views, see *RVed* (1890), 32: 2, and 237: 1; (1892), 71: 1, 119: 1, and 353: 2; and (1899), 192: 1, *RM* (1888), 3: 183–93; and (1892), 4: 229–32, and 5: 196–9, *VE* (1887), 12: 810–18; (1892), 4: 839–55; (1894), 4: 823–33; (1898), 3: 366–71; and (1899), 9: 344–51, and *NiBG* (1892), 58: 2 ('Russkaia pechat''), 73: 2 ('Otkliki'), and 77: 1–2 ('K voprosu maioratov').

[36] E. I. Zhigachev, 'Zadolzhennost' chastnago zemlevladeniia v Rossii', *RM* (1892), 11: 67. For other progressivist criticisms, see A. Radtsig, 'Ekonomicheskii krizis vo Frantsii i u nas', *Ekonomicheskii Zhurnal* (1888), 4: 90–5, D. K. Grishenko, 'Gde osnovy sel'skokhoziaistvennago krizisa?', *TVEO* (1893), 6: 183–200; and (1894), 1: 19–23 (*zhur.*), L. V. Khodskii, 'K voprosu o sel'skokhoziaistvennom krizise', *TVEO* (1895), 2: 1–30, 171–94, *RVed* (1893), 66: 1–2, and 286: 4; (1895), 138: 1; (1899), 86: 4; and (1912), 38: 1, *VE* (1896), 10: 800–8. G. A. Evreinov, *Proshloe i nastoiashchee znachenie russkago dvorianstva* (Spb., 1898), V. V. [Sviatlovskii?], 'Dvorianskoe zemlevladenie posle reformy', *RM* (1898), 10: 69–98, I. F. Tsyzyrev, 'O russkom dvorianstve', *Pravo* (1903), 19, cols. 1345–60, B. Landau, 'Otzhivshii institut', *Pravo* (1908), 23, cols. 1367–77, and A. A. Chuprov, 'Dvorianskoe zemlevladenie posle reformy', *RVed* (1911), 40: 5.

[37] e.g. compare the argument in 'Podderzhka dvorianskago vladeniia', *Nedelia* (1891), 52, cols. 1681–3, with that in 'Okhrana melkago zemlevladeniia', *Nedelia* (1891), 3, cols. 68–70, or the arguments in the articles in *RVed* cited above in nn. 34–6 with those in 'Mery k

Concerns over the practical effects of entail also led noble landowners themselves to reject it as a solution to the problems attributed to property and inheritance law, even when they shared the anti-capitalist, anti-bureaucratic, and anti-Western sentiments of the petitioners. For example, as the rightist Kursk landowner Count V. F. Dorrer complained, 'to deprive those of us who conduct the difficult and thankless task of agriculture without resorting to any credit, troubling no one and asking nothing, of the right to dispose freely of our land, simply because we are noblemen, seems to me somewhat . . . high-handed'.[38] Hence only seventeen of thirty-seven provincial assemblies ultimately supported the campaign for a right of entail. And even in assemblies that adopted the measure, strong opposition sometimes was encountered.[39] A special conference of twenty-two provincial marshals of the nobility assembled in 1897 to review draft legislation on entail similarly split over the issue. Although all the participants agreed on the urgent need to revise existing inheritance law, a minority none the less rejected entail as both unjust and impractical in prevailing economic conditions. In contrast to this continued disagreement over entail, however, all the marshals endorsed a plan to expand testamentary power over patrimonial property.[40]

For moderate conservatives and conservative liberals, the expansion of testamentary power in fact represented a preferable strategy for adapting

preduprezhdeniiu perekhoda nadel'nykh krest'ianskikh zemel' v postoronniia ruki', *RVed* (1893), 142: 3, 145: 3, and 147: 3. On this point, see also R. S. Wortman, 'Property Rights, Populism, and Russian Political Culture', in O. Crisp and L. Edmondson (eds.), *Civil Rights in Imperial Russia* (Oxford, 1989), 13–32, and L. Schapiro, 'The Pre-Revolutionary Intelligentsia and the Legal Order', in R. Pipes (ed.), *The Russian Intelligentsia* (New York, 1961), 19–31.

[38] Graf V. Dorrer, 'Neobkhodimaia popravka', *MV* (1898), 60: 2 (letter); see also *NV* (1892), 5754: 1 ('Dvorianin' and 'Golos iz provintsii'), and 5808: 1, and A. Lykoshin, 'Rodovyia imushchestva i dvorianskoe zemlevladenie', *SVed* (1900), 213: 1–2.

[39] 'Khodataistva dvorianstva', 89, 102–3, 109–12. For example, the Penza nobility initially adopted its petition by a vote of only 118 to 82. See also Hamburg, *Politics*, 125–7, Becker, *Nobility*, 141–2, and Korelin, *Dvorianstvo*, 263–4.

[40] 'Zhurnal Vysochaishe uchrezhdennoi Osoboi Kommisii dlia obsuzhdeniia vozbuzhdennago dvorianskimi sobraniiami voprosa o merakh k podderzhaniiu dvorianskago zemlevladeniia [for 29 Nov. 1893]', *Dvorianskoe zemlevladenie* (HLL), TsGIA F. 1151 op. XII d. 1–1896 g. ll. 345–7, and F. 1284 op. 223 d. 45–1896 g. ll. 4–6, 16–17, 28–9, 47–50; see also Solov'ev, *Samoderzhavie*, 222–7, on a similar conference held in 1896, where entail also was discussed. For other moderate conservative and conservative liberal criticisms of entail, see N. Shatilov, 'Eshche po povodu proekta o zapovednykh imeniiakh', *NV* (1892), 5791: 2, 'Nedelimye dvorianskie uchastki', *NV* (1888), 4269: 1, and 4271: 1, 'Beznadezhnyi vopros', *NV* (1888), 4378: 1, 4285: 1, *SVed* (1888), 11: 1, 'Tendentsiia maioratov', *SVed* (1892), 58: 1, 'Zapovednyia imeniia', *SVed* (1893), 185: 1, and S. P. Petrovskii, 'Plody zapovednosti', *Grazhdanin* (1892), 91: 2.

traditional values and institutions to changed economic circumstances. Like proponents of entail, they considered the landed nobility to be the only group that could promote economic progress and cultural enlightenment in the countryside while simultaneously ensuring social stability. '[T]he country cannot get on without a class of people that can conscientiously, intelligently, and honourably conduct local administration either by election or government appointment,' contended the conservative noble landowner and journalist Konstantin Golovin.[41] But moderate conservatives also recognized that the landed nobility needed to adopt new attitudes and habits in order both to play this leadership role and simply to survive in post-emancipation conditions. Moreover, echoing the emphasis of progressivists on individual merit, they argued that noble leadership should be exercised through such all-class institutions as the zemstva and be based on superior ability and economic competence, not on privileges justified by the past services of ancestors. Opposing any concessions to his social estate, for example, the moderate noble landowner V. Chicherin argued that

> [t]here is no question that the entire question of the preservation of noble landownership arises solely from the sale and indebtedness of a significant number of estates belonging to those noblemen who are coming to ruin either because they do not know how to conduct agriculture or, primarily, because they do not live within their means, and no measures can save such noblemen from ruin. . . . The salvation of such noblemen depends entirely on themselves.[42]

To help noble landowners save themselves, moderate conservatives favoured changes in the law that they believed would facilitate the development of agriculture in general. Increasing the power of owners to dispose of patrimonial property appeared to provide a particularly propitious means to this end.[43]

[41] K. Golovin, 'Dvorianskii vopros', *NV* (1898), 7937: 2–3; this article was continued in 7938: 2, and 7939: 2. On the ideological divisions within the landed nobility, see Manning, *Crisis*, 49–64.

[42] V. Chicherin, 'Po povodu stat′i byvshago predvoditel′ia dvorianstva o pomestnom dvorianstve', *SVed* (1898), 104: 2–3; see also id., 'Po povodu statei "pravda i krivda o dvorianskom voprose" g. Bodisko', *SVed* (1898), 130: 2.

[43] The boundaries of this broad and admittedly amorphous group were defined by Golovin, who was active in rightist circles that supported the nobility *qua* nobility, and by Boris Chicherin, a classic Hegelian liberal who saw the nobility as playing primarily a transitional role. See Golovin, 'Dvorianskii vopros', id., 'Neizbezhna li likvidatsiia zemlevladeniia?', *MV* (1895), 349: 2–3, id., 'K voprosu o zapovednykh imeniiakh', *SVed* (1896), 17: 1, and 18: 1–2, id., 'Kak pomoch′ zemlevladeniiu?', *MV* (1896), 75: 2, id., 'V chem prichina khronicheskikh nedoimok?', *NV* (1898), 7896: 2, and B. N. Chicherin, 'O sovremennom polozhenii russkago dvorianstva', *SVed* (1897), 28: 1; see also G. Romer, 'K

The most extensive proposal with this objective was formulated by Prince Petr Trubetskoi, marshal of the nobility in Moscow province and an opponent of entail at the conference of provincial marshals in 1897. An innovative agriculturalist long active in provincial politics, Trubetskoi well understood the difficulties of adjusting to post-emancipation economic conditions. Also a moderate Slavophile, he sought to perpetuate Russian national traditions by adapting them to prevailing circumstances and needs. Hence his proposals for the revision of inheritance law attempted to eliminate the practical problems attributed to existing law while preserving intact both the institution of patrimonial property and the paternalistic values underlying it. The proposals were drafted after the 1897 conference and subsequently submitted for consideration both to the Moscow nobility and to special conferences convened by the government to review the needs of agriculture and the nobility.[44]

Declaring that 'there is not a single area of the law that exerts so decisive and serious an influence on family and social relations as the norms of inheritance law',[45] Trubetskoi sought to restructure these norms in a way that would strengthen both the landed nobility and paternalistic authority within the family and society. In his view, both objectives would be served by eliminating the restrictions imposed by the law on the owners of patrimonial property. According to Trubetskoi, these restrictions constituted inappropriate alien additions to Russian law that had been introduced only recently. Yet their effect on the nobility had been devastating. '[A]s long as the obligatory division of an inheritance into equal parts still exists,' he asserted,

> as long as the will of the testator is powerless to protect the interests of the kin-group and of individual members of his family from mechanical application of the absolute proscription against distributing patrimonial property in the event of death, any attempt firmly and radically to improve noble landholding will inevitably

dvorianskomu voprosu', *SVed* (1898), 3: 1–2, id., 'Obosoblennost′ dvorianstva', *NV* (1898), 7987: 2–3, id., 'Budushchee dvorianstva', *NV* (1900), 8571: 2–3, and 8616: 2–3, E. Markov, 'Sol′ zemli', *NV* (1900), 8869: 2–3, and 8870: 3, S. T., 'O pravitel′stvennoi podderzhke dvorianskago sosloviia', *SVed* (1897), 176: 1 (letter), L. Bukh, 'O pasynkakh zakona', *SVed* (1902), 290: 2, Sh., 'Dvorianstvo v Rossii', *VE* (1887), 3: 239–84, 4: 531–71, 5: 186–210, and 6: 421–52, F. G. Terner, 'Dvorianstvo i zemlevladenie', *VE* (1903), 3: 5–55, F. K. Glinka, *K voprosu ob uluchshenii polozheniia zemel′nago dvorianstva* (Mogilev-on-Dnieper, 1899), *NV* (1897), 7617: 2; (1898), 7286: 1; and (1903), 9736: 2–3, and I. Ivaniushenkov, 'K dvorianskomu voprosu. Pis′mo nedvorianina', *MV* (1898), 157: 2–3.

[44] [P. N. Trubetskoi], *Zapiska o zhelatel′nykh izmeneniiakh v sushchestvuiushchem poriadke nasledovaniia po zakonu i po dukhovnym zaveshchaniiam* (Mos., 1900), TsGIA F. 1283 op. 1–1897 g. d. 18 ll. 2–16, 20–7, and F. 1233 op. 1 d. 99 ll. 1–2, 13–20.

[45] [Trubetskoi], *Zapiska*, 3.

clash with and be paralysed by the action of existing laws, which ineluctably and systematically lead to the parcelling of landed property and thereby, in the final analysis, threaten to diminish seriously the role of the nobility in Russian landowning.[46]

Trubetskoi concluded that the power of owners to dispose of patrimonial property therefore had to be increased rather than restricted still further by the adoption of yet another alien institution such as entail.

Trubetskoi claimed that the expansion of testamentary power over patrimonial property would be more consistent with Russian legal tradition than existing law because it would reinforce the principle of beneficent paternalism that lay at the basis of Russian family and social relations. Approvingly citing an earlier petition by the Chernigov nobility, he argued that

[u]nder our laws the family, the embryo of society, has received the proper organization, and it has been subordinated to almost unlimited parental power. Parents manage this small society at their discretion, educating their children without any outside interference and providing them with sustenance during their life. Their power ends only with their life.[47]

Restrictions on testamentary power therefore interfered unjustifiably in family matters, Trubetskoi contended, because they prevented parents from making adequate arrangements for their children after their own death. For similar reasons, Trubetskoi denied that equality of inheritance rights even among males constituted a fundamental principle of Russian law. In his view, real equity among the heirs based on their individual needs and deserts could be ensured only by the firm exercise of parental authority in a will, not by the specious, mechanical equality established by statutory law. Expansion of testamentary power thus would strengthen traditional socio-political authority and values as well as eliminate the practical problems attributed to existing law.[48]

Trubetskoi none the less acknowledged the need for some restrictions on testamentary power in order to protect the legitimate interests of both the heirs and the kin-group of an owner. Hence he proposed that an owner be given unlimited testamentary power over one half of his acquired property, free disposition within the family of one half of his acquired and patrimonial property, and the right to bequeath his remaining patrimonial property to any heir, provided that the remaining heirs received

[46] Ibid. 6. [47] Ibid. 8.

[48] Ibid. For a later version, which emphasizes the role of the landed nobility even more strongly, see TsGIA F. 1283 op. 1–1897 g. d. 18 ll. 2–16.

compensation for this latter property equivalent to one half of the share due each by law. In addition, an owner could disinherit any heir for just cause and impose a variety of conditions and limitations on the use and disposition of property bequeathed in a will. Finally, Trubetskoi also urged adoption of a government proposal to allow an owner to bequeath intact, or any heir to retain, an integrated, economically well-ordered estate, with partial compensation being paid to the remaining heirs.[49] Trubetskoi concluded,

> while enabling attainment of the . . . basic goal—the support of noble landowning—all these proposals also correspond to the demands of justice and comprise the further consistent development of the principles of parental authority and the strength of family bonds that lie at the basis of our family law.[50]

In contrast to their failure to support entail, the Moscow provincial nobility endorsed the proposals of Trubetskoi in special meetings in 1900 and 1903.[51] Indeed, going even further, they demanded unlimited testamentary control over their patrimonial property, with only a bare majority conceding to descendant heirs the right to receive one half the value of the share of such property due each by law. Moreover, to limit the tendency of heirs to divide an inherited estate, the Moscow nobles also proposed to alter the rules of intestate succession so that the eldest son would receive one half of all immovable property, with the other heirs dividing the remaining property under the guidance of provincial and district marshals of the nobility. Admitting that these proposals broke with traditional legal principles, the Moscow nobles argued that

> even though completely founded, [r]eferences to the injustice of division created in this way, [an injustice] foreign to the spirit of Russian law, none the less must be relegated to the background in view of the great importance [of strengthening both the landed nobility and parental authority].[52]

Similar reasoning led the Moscow nobles to reject the introduction of sexual equality in inheritance and to demand the right to declare their estates indivisible, although not inalienable, for two generations.[53]

[49] [Trubetskoi], *Zapiska*, 9–13, 16–21. Given existing law, under Trubetskoi's proposals sons would be guaranteed a right to only the value of a quarter of an owner's patrimonial property, daughters a right to the value of only one twenty-eighth of such property, and a spouse a right to the value of only one fourteenth of such property.

[50] Ibid. 12.

[51] Ibid. 24, TsGIA F. 1283 op. 1–1897 g. d. 18 ll. 2–16 and F. 1233 op. 1 d. 99 ll. 13–20; see also 'Volg.', *Pravo* (1903), 22, cols. 1554–5, *RVed* (1903), 36: 1, 42: 1, and 103: 2, and *GU. Kn. 4-aia*, intro., pp. 86–92.

[52] [Trubetskoi], *Zapiska*, 24.

[53] TsGIA F. 1283 op. 1–1897 g. d. 18 ll. 2–16, pp. 1–2, 9.

The contrasting approaches to the revision of property and inheritance law embodied in noble demands for a right of entail and for expanded testamentary power reflect a landed noble élite in transition. Supporters of both approaches emphasized the preservation of tradition, idealized the past service ethos of noble landowners while stressing their current public role in ensuring social stability and economic progress, and asserted the need to reinforce inegalitarian social structures based on paternalistic authority. Their common goal was to preserve a corporatist state in which order would be maintained by the interdependent and mutually reinforcing authority of the emperor, the landed nobility, and the beneficent family patriarch. But proponents of entail sought to achieve this goal by insulating noble landowners against the competitive pressures of the market-place, whereas advocates of testamentary freedom sought a way to do so that would enable landowners to compete more effectively. A similar debate also took place during this period among noble landowners in Imperial Germany, where most favoured a synthesis between traditionalism and greater legal flexibility in the disposition of property.[54] Even though this synthesis may not have been durable in the long run, either in Imperial Russia or in Germany, it demonstrates both the persistence of traditional values and attitudes even among noble landowners who had adjusted successfully to changed economic conditions and the adaptability of these values and attitudes themselves.[55]

The treatment accorded both the petitions for entail and Trubetskoi's proposals reflect the ambiguous relationship that developed between the tsarist government and the landed nobility after the emancipation, even during the period of intense reaction that followed the assassination of Alexander II in 1881. On the one hand, as part of a general effort to reinforce the autocratic order, the government itself encouraged the idealization of the landed nobility and supported it through a variety of means. Hence in 1891 the government responded to noble demands for entail by forming a special commission to review the matter under the chairmanship of the moderate former governor of Riazan province, Nikolai Abaza. On the other hand, even though several provincial marshals of the

[54] John, *Politics*, 90–3, 96, 111–16, 127–39, 176–7, 184–7, 197–8, 201–3. See also D. Blackbourn and G. Eley, *The Peculiarities of German History: Bourgeois Society and Politics in Nineteenth-Century Germany* (Oxford, 1984), 181–2, 230–3, 271–4, and R. S. Neale, 'The Bourgeoisie, Historically, Has Played a Most Revolutionary Part', in *Writing Marxist History: British Society, Economy and Culture Since 1700* (Oxford, 1985), 67–85.

[55] For contrary arguments regarding the degree to which noble landowners retained or had shed traditional values, and thus by the late Imperial period had come to constitute a politically reactionary privileged estate or the core of a new and broader class of landowners, see especially Manning, *Crisis*, and Becker, *Nobility*.

nobility participated in some of its sessions, the commission itself was composed exclusively of state officials, primarily from the Ministries of Finance, Justice, Internal Affairs, and State Domains.[56] Moreover, the majority of officials on the commission did not consider state interests to require indiscriminate support for the nobility, even when they themselves were prominent noble landowners.

Indeed, despite pressure to do so, a majority of members on the commission refused to sacrifice economic utility, the security of family members, and equity to the narrowly political objectives of ultra-conservative advocates of entail. The same considerations that had complicated previous efforts to revise property and inheritance law thus also influenced the work of the commission, even though each manifested itself differently in the particular circumstances of the late nineteenth century. Attempting to balance these competing considerations, the commission linked the stabilization of noble landownership for political purposes with the economic viability of individual landholdings. '[Its] goal', declared the commission, 'consists precisely in protecting from fragmentation the middle-sized estates that comprise a single organized economic operation and which yield an income sufficient for the modest existence of a single noble family.' And 'since the existing regulations for intestate inheritance of patrimonial property provide[d] the chief cause of the fragmentation of such estates,'[57] the commission sought to furnish noble landowners with the means for circumventing these regulations, but not at the cost of impoverishing their heirs or shielding economic incompetence. This objective led the commission to formulate two projects, each of which reflected one of the two contrary approaches to revision of the law emerging among noble landowners themselves.

Given its charge, conservative composition, and the interest of Alexander III in the issue, it is hardly surprising that a majority on the commission favoured the introduction of some form of entail. Contending that 'entail protects a middle-sized noble estate from fragmentation into small pieces, which inevitably disrupts its economy, devalues the land, and frequently leads to its sale outside the family',[58] the commission

[56] The noble landowner and economist Konstantin Golovin also participated in some sessions of the commission, which met throughout 1892 and briefly in 1893. Its journals and related material are contained in TsGIA F. 1151 op. XII d. 1–1896 and in *Dvorianskoe zemlevladenie* (HLL); see also Solov'ev, *Samoderzhavie*, 201–16, 316–26, Hamburg, *Politics*, 127–30, Becker, *Nobility*, 66–75, K. Golovin, *Moi vospominaniia* (Spb., 1910), ii. 229–42, and 'Dnevnik', *Grazhdanin* (1892), 56: 3–4.

[57] 'Zhurnal Vysochaishe uchrezhdennoi Osoboi Kommisii [for 1892]', 70.

[58] Ibid. 17. The strongest opponents of entail in the commission were Prince Aleksandr Obolenskii and Prince Viazemskii, the director of the Appanage Administration; ibid. 12–15.

proposed to establish a provisional form of entail for estates that consisted of between two and ten times the amount of land required locally for participation in zemstva assemblies. For larger estates, the more stringent regulations for the permanent entailment of latifundia would be applied. To expand the eligibility of estates for provisional entail, entailment of estates that were mortgaged for no more than 60 per cent of their value would be permitted, although to protect creditors such estates would remain liable to sale in the event of default. Hence provisional entailment was not to serve as a refuge for heavily indebted noble landowners. Reinforcing this point, the commission limited provisional entail to estates that constituted an integrated economic operation and included the owner's residence. And to ensure access to adequate credit for future economic improvements, it recommended that owners be allowed to mortgage an entailed estate to the State Noble Land Bank for up to a third of its value. Again, such estates would be liable to trusteeship and sale in the event of default. Finally, the commission restricted the period of provisional entail to only two generations in order to avoid any problems that might result from the long-term immobilization of land.[59]

The commission similarly sought to limit the impact of entail on individual family members. Unless otherwise specified by the original owner, succession to a provisionally entailed estate would be based on male primogeniture. But to secure the welfare of a surviving spouse and of descendant heirs not succeeding to the estate, the commission proposed to establish a right to partial monetary compensation for the share of the estate that each normally would have inherited, with these payments being guaranteed by the estate itself. Attempting to forestall criticism, the commission argued that this arrangement actually would increase the security of most heirs. 'There can be no doubt', it asserted optimistically,

> that in amicable families, where the children have been raised with feelings of love for parents and for one another, this result will be much more beneficial for each family member than would the loss of the family hearth and the receipt in its stead of an insignificant sum that could not secure even the modest existence of a nobleman.[60]

The commission none the less expected most noblemen to rely primarily on income derived from the expertise acquired through education to ensure their welfare.[61]

[59] Ibid., esp. 9–27, 33–41, 62–7; for the existing law on entail, see above, Ch. 6.

[60] 'Zhurnal Vysochaishe uchrezhdennoi Osoboi Kommisii [for 1892]', 69–70.

[61] Ibid. 17–18, 55–90. On changing career patterns among the nobility, see Becker, *Nobility*, 28, 51–3, 110–14, 125–8, Korelin, *Dvorianstvo*, 122–31, and Brower, *Russian City*, 55–6.

The commission also advocated the expansion of testamentary power over patrimonial property as a way to avoid the problems attributed to existing law. Acknowledging that the law resulted in the disruption of estates of all sizes, the commission asserted that the entailment of small landholdings none the less was neither economically wise nor politically necessary. Yet it still wished to enable smallholders to avoid the harmful effects of the law. 'So that well-organized smallholdings do not collapse after the death of the owner,' the commission argued,

> it is necessary to introduce into the civil laws regarding the inheritance of agricultural estates certain isolated corrections without violating the basic principles [of these laws] . . . the first of these corrections must be a modest expansion of the testamentary freedom of the owners of well-organized patrimonial estates who have several descendant heirs. These people must be given the right to bequeath their patrimonial property intact to a single heir of their choice, with this *chief* heir being obligated to satisfy his co-heirs with money.[62]

Attempting to balance economic considerations with the right of family members to security, the commission proposed to allow an owner to reduce by up to one half the amount of compensation due any of the remaining heirs in order to avoid overburdening the 'chief heir' with debt. Conversely, in the event of intestate succession, any heir (with preference based on male seniority) would be permitted to retain an estate intact, although in this case with the obligation to compensate the remaining heirs in full. Again hoping to avert criticism, the commission concluded that '[t]he direct purpose [of these proposals] was by no means the enrichment of the chief heir at the expense of the property rights of the other members of the family, but solely the protection of the integrity of well-ordered estates and their preservation within the kin-group'.[63]

Recognizing the general usefulness of these proposals, the commission recommended that they be applied to all small landholdings, regardless of the social estate to which their owners belonged. Several members of the commission also sought to extend them to middle-sized estates in order to provide an alternative to entail. Fearing that most noble landowners would eschew entail if granted greater testamentary power, however, the commission majority restricted application of its proposals to estates smaller than the minimum size stipulated for provisional entail.[64]

The proposals of the commission demonstrate that by the 1890s the unreconstructed traditionalism and resistance to reform exhibited earlier

[62] 'Zhurnal Vysochaishe uchrezhdennoi Osoboi Kommisii [for 1893/1894]', 14.
[63] Ibid. 34, and 15–17, 24–6, 28–37 in general.
[64] Ibid. 17–23.

by Panin had become untenable. The commission now sought to preserve traditional social structures, legal institutions, and their underlying values by consciously adapting them to changed circumstances. Hence, while idealizing the social and political role of noble landowners in traditional terms, the commission linked their survival to success in a commercial world where credit, mortgages, and similar financial arrangements were commonplace. Although recognizing the pernicious economic effects of legal institutions designed to protect the family patrimony, the commission preserved and only modified these institutions. Indeed, as a further concession to noble petitioners, the commission proposed to eliminate the restrictions imposed by the Civil Cassation Department on the right to redeem patrimonial property.[65] Finally, the commission attempted to make legal rules concerned with the preservation and distribution of land within the kin-group serviceable in a context where the integrity of agricultural operations was becoming important and the security of heirs increasingly was expected to be provided by capital, dividends, and occupational income.[66]

The responses within the government to the proposals of the commission demonstrate the difficulty of this endeavour. Although cautious in challenging a measure supported by the emperor, several prominent officials none the less questioned the economic soundness of the provisions regarding entail and expressed concern over their potential impact on an owner's heirs.[67] Arguing that '[t]he chief goal in formulating the present project was not to establish the boundary of privileges that could be extended to debtors who have mortgaged their estates to the [State] Noble [Land] Bank', for example, the Minister of Justice, Nikolai Manasein, favoured severe restrictions on the entail of mortgaged

[65] 'Zhurnal Vysochaishe uchrezhdennoi Osoboi Kommisii [for 12 Nov. 1892]'.

[66] This shift in the form of wealth was only beginning to take place in Imperial Russia and was still limited to only a small percentage of the population. In C. Shammas, M. Salmon, and M. Dahlin, *Inheritance in America from Colonial Times to the Present* (New Brunswick, NJ, 1987), the authors trace the significant changes in both formal inheritance law and testamentary practices produced by a comparable, although much more extensive, shift in the form of wealth in the United States during the 19th c. See also L. Holcombe, *Wives and Property: Reform of the Married Women's Property Law in Nineteenth-Century England* (Toronto, 1983), 34. On the demand of landowners for greater flexibility in response to commercial development, see also T. Zeldin, *France 1848–1945: Ambition and Love* (Oxford, 1979), 143–8, 287–91, John, *Politics*, 90–3, 96, 111–16, 127–31, 137–9, A. W. B. Simpson, *An Introduction to the History of the Land Law* (Oxford, 1961), chs. 8, 9, and Neale, 'The Bourgeoisie'.

[67] The comments of all ministries are contained in *Dvorianskoe zemlevladenie* (HLL) and in TsGIA F. 1151 op. XII d. 1–1896 ll. 214–42, 533–42. The Ministries of Internal Affairs, Finance, and State Domains submitted generally uncritical reviews.

estates.[68] And opposing any reduction in the minimum size required for hereditary entailed estates, the director of the codification department of the State Council, Eduard Frish, asserted that

> [i]t can scarcely be disputed that the establishment of a large number of hereditary entailed estates is justified from neither a juridical . . . nor especially an economic point of view, since such estates, having been withdrawn from general civil circulation, cannot be alienated . . . mortgaged, or burdened with debts or obligations . . . [and] at the present time, as even the commission recognizes, mortgage credit comprises one of the most substantial conditions for the proper and successful conduct of the economy of an estate.[69]

Such concerns led a majority of members of the State Council first to delay consideration of the measure and then to impose tighter restrictions on the indebtedness allowed for provisionally entailed estates and to establish more generous guarantees for the surviving spouse and heirs of an owner. The majority likewise rejected an attempt by ultra-conservative members to increase the number of estates eligible for hereditary entail by lowering the minimum size required for such estates to 5,000 desiatin. Thus having been largely stripped of its political and economic significance, provisional entail was introduced in May 1899.[70]

The predictions by both advocates and opponents of entail that the new law would have little effect proved accurate.[71] By 1914 only thirty-five

[68] 'Ministerstvo iustitsii, 21 Maia 1893 goda. No. 13554', 6, in *Dvorianskoe zemlevladenie* (HLL); for similar views, see ibid., 'Osoboe mnenie chlena Kommisii Senatora Shidlovskago'.

[69] 'Glavnoupravliaiushchii Kodifikatsionnym otdelom pri Gosudarstvennom Sovete. 30 Ianvaria 1893 goda. No. 73', 4, in *Dvorianskoe zemlevladenie* (HLL); for similar remarks by Obolenskii, see 'Zhurnal Vysochaishe uchrezhdennoi Osoboi Kommisii [for 29 Nov. 1893]', 5–6. In 'Peasant Land Tenure and Civil Rights Implications before 1906', in Crisp and Edmondson, *Civil Rights*, 33–64, Olga Crisp noted a similar conflict at this time between government officials who advocated private ownership and mobility of peasant allotment land for economic reasons and those who favoured restrictions on mobility for social and political reasons.

[70] Nicholas II accepted the minority proposal to lower the minimum size for a hereditary entailed estate to 5,000 des. Prior to consideration by the State Council, special conferences of provincial marshals of the nobility, and on the needs of the nobility, also reviewed the proposals, with majorities in both instances recommending only minor modifications. *OGS, 1899*, 216–69, *3PSZ* xix (1899), no. 16949, pp. 527–36, and *SZ* (1900), x, pt. 1, arts. 395, 493^{1-46}, 1069^{1}, 1070^{1}, 1213^{1-9}, 1222^{1}; for a detailed description of the law, see W. G. Wagner, 'Legislative Reform of Inheritance in Russia, 1861–1914', in W. E. Butler (ed.), *Russian Law: Historical and Political Perspectives* (Leiden, 1977), 161–6. See also *GU. Kn. 3-ia*, iii. 3–4, 8–52, Hamburg, *Politics*, 130–1, Solov′ev, *Samoderzhavie*, 316–26, and Becker, *Nobility*, 71–7.

[71] For opponents, see D. L., 'Zakon o vremenno-zapovednykh imeniiakh', *VP* (1899), 8: 138–49, *RVed* (1899), 192: 1, *NiBG* (1899), 187: 2 ('Otkliki'), and *VE* (1899), 9: 344–51; for advocates, see V. N. Semenkovich, 'O zapovednykh imeniiakh', *MV* (1899), 214: 2, 215: 2,

provisionally entailed estates had been created, mostly by members of prominent aristocratic families.[72] Although the stringent requirements established for provisional entailment undoubtedly helped to account for this result, the inflexibility of the law and the timing of its passage appear to have been more important. Entail constrained both those nobles who wished to realize the rapidly rising capital value of their land by selling or mortgaging it and those who wanted to rationalize or expand their holdings in order to increase profitability. Being not only the largest sellers of rural land, but until the early twentieth century also the largest buyers, most noble landowners apparently had little interest in restricting the mobility of their chief asset.[73] If the agricultural depression of the late nineteenth century had led many anxious noble landowners to support the call for entail by more politically motivated peers as a possible escape from foreclosure, the depression had ended and the threat of foreclosure had receded by the time the law was enacted. Noble proprietors consequently had little incentive to resort to such a restrictive institution. Hence, after 1899, even the formation of hereditary entailed estates, which had been unusually high during the depression, declined dramatically.[74]

Concern over its allegedly harmful economic effects also provoked harsh criticism of the proposal made by the Abaza commission to restore the right of noble landowners to redeem patrimonial property.[75] In this instance, these concerns led the majority in the State Council to reject the proposal, arguing that '[w]ith the development of industry and trade, the inconveniences [caused by redemption] are growing constantly'.[76] At least

241: 1, 243: 1–2, and 245: 2, 'Vremenno-zapovednyia imeniia', *MV* (1899), 192: 2, 'Nedelimyia imeniia', *MV* (1901), 36: 1–2, *RVest* (1899), 9: 371–4, 'Nedelimyia imeniia i krest′ianskie dvory', *NV* (1903), 9674: 3, and TsGIA F. 1233 op. 1 d. 99 ll. 13–26 and F. 1283 op. 1 d. 26 l. 211. See also Hamburg, *Politics*, 130.

72 Provisionally entailed estates are listed in the annual volumes of *SSSMIu* for 1900–14. Since such estates could be established by will, landowners who were still alive in 1914 may also have taken advantage of the law.

73 Becker, *Nobility*, 31–6, and Solov′ev, *Samoderzhavie*, 199–200.

74 See the lists of such estates in A. M. Anfimov, 'Maioratnoe zemlevladenie v tsarskoi Rossii', *Istoriia SSSR* (1962), 5: 151–9, and in *Obshchii obzor deiatel′nosti Ministerstva iustitsii i Pravitel′stvuiushchago Senata za tsarstvovanie Imperatora Aleksandra III* (Spb., 1901), 65. In fact, after the turn of the century owners tried to gain greater power over such estates, generally for economic reasons. See the letters by Iu. Kartsov and R. Kutsynskii in *NV* (1901), 9252: 3, and 9268: 5, Landau, 'Otzhivshii institut', and *GSSO. 8-aia ses. (1912–13)*, cols. 740–57, 2622–3, 2744.

75 e.g. see 'Glavnoupravliaiushchii Kodifikatsionnym otdelom', 22–7, and 'Ministerstvo iustitsii', 15; see also 'Ministerstvo gosudarstvennykh imushchestv. 28 Fevralia 1893 goda. No. 292', 2–4, in *Dvorianskoe zemlevladenie* (HLL).

76 *OGS, 1899*, 255–6.

for the majority of officials in the State Council, the needs of economic development thus again outweighed both the demands of noble petitioners and any desire to preserve a long-standing legal institution.

Although greeted more sympathetically, the commission's proposal to expand testamentary power over patrimonial property also fared poorly. Some officials who favoured an extension of testamentary power, like the Minister of Agriculture and State Domains, Aleksei Ermolov, and the new Minister of Justice, Nikolai Muravev, none the less questioned the equity and efficacy of allowing an owner to reduce the value of the share due an heir.[77] Seeking to retain the initiative for revision of the law within his own ministry, Muravev later succeeded in having all such proposals referred to the civil code editing commission, which was in the process of revising its own project on inheritance law.[78] Other officials preferred a measure that was oriented less narrowly towards the political objective of supporting the landed nobility. For this reason, both Ermolov and the Chief Procurator of the Holy Synod, Konstantin Pobedonostsev, also opposed Trubetskoi's proposals, even though they believed that an expansion of testamentary power was necessary.[79] While substantial agreement on the desirability of increasing the testamentary power of property owners thus existed by the early twentieth century, considerable disagreement remained over how to achieve this end.

The Civil Code Commission

In late 1902 the civil code editing commission thrust its own proposal into this already complex situation. The commission had discussed the question of inheritance law during the same years that conservative noble landowners and publicists had been conducting their campaign for entail. Having reviewed the initial draft of its project in late 1889 and early 1890, the commission completed work on the final draft in mid-1901.[80] It could

[77] TsGIA F. 1151 op. XII d. 1–1896 ll. 533–4, 536–41. Ermolov had been a member of the commission prior to his appointment as minister. For reactions to the proposal, see ibid., ll. 533–42, and *Dvorianskoe zemlevladenie* (HLL).

[78] TsGIA F. 1283 op. 1–1897 g. d. 18 ll. 20–2, 24–7 and op. 1 d. 187ᵃ–1897 g., F. 1233 op. 1 d. 99 ll. 1–2, 13–20, 30–31 (marginal notation to point 9), 75, 78–9, 81–4, and, for a similar proposal, ll. 62–74.

[79] *SKhiL*, 202 (1901), 294–310, TsGIA F. 1233 op. 1 d. 99 ll. 97–128, F. 1283 op. 1–1897 g. d. 18 ll. 18–19; for Pobedonostsev's views on entail in general, see *Kurs grazhdanskago prava* (4th edn., Spb., 1896), i. 479–86, and ii. 354–5, 441–52, 466, 570–1. On the scepticism of the powerful Minister of Finance, Sergei Witte, see Gurko, *Features*, 57–68, 201–2, Hamburg, *Politics*, 130–1, and Solov′ev, *Samoderzhavie*, 316–17.

[80] *GU. Kn. 4-aia*, intro., pp. 147–8, and *ZhRKGU. Proekt o nasledovanii.*

not have been unaware of either the problems attributed to existing law by noble landowners or the politically controversial nature of its own solutions to them. It none the less proposed to transform Imperial inheritance law radically by replacing the system of patrimonial property based on male preference in the kin-group with a system of obligatory shares based on sexual equality within the conjugal family.[81]

There were, of course, differences in motives and disagreements over specific proposals within the editing commission. But, as in the case of family law, these divisions generally reflected professional and ideological disputes that transcended differences in social background. Not surprisingly, the fate of patrimonial property provoked the sharpest controversy. The initial draft of the project, prepared primarily by the moderate conservative A. K. Rikhter, in fact had retained the distinction between patrimonial and acquired property while reassigning inheritance rights on the basis of the affective ties and moral obligations imputed to the conjugal family.[82] Conceding in a later treatise that the institution of patrimonial property created serious practical problems, Rikhter argued that a modified form of this institution none the less would be more just, flexible, and therefore appropriate for the social and economic needs of Imperial Russia than would the European system of obligatory shares.[83] Supporting Rikhter, the historicist jurist Kronid Malyshev likewise claimed that the abolition of patrimonial property would constitute an inexpedient abandonment of national legal traditions.[84] The balance within the editing commission tilted in the opposite direction, however, with the death of Rikhter in 1893 and the addition of jurists from a younger generation. While the commission gained an effective advocate of progressivist transformation of the law in the person of Ilia Iliashenko,[85] another addition, the conservative nobleman Aleksandr Lykoshin, viewed the abolition of patrimonial property as necessary to protect the landed nobility and the traditional socio-political order.[86] In the final deliberations on the issue,

[81] *GU. Kn. 4-aia* (with commentary).

[82] *ZhRKGU. Proekt o nasledovanii*, 10, 41, 128, 212, 214, and *GU. Kn. 4-aia*, intro., p. 147.

[83] Rikhter, *O neobkhodimom nasledovanii*, esp. the intro. and pp. 375–84.

[84] *GU. Kn. 4-aia*, intro., pp. 103–8. On Malyshev, see above, Ch. 4.

[85] *GU. Kn. 4-aia*, intro., pp. 147–8; on Iliashenko's views and background, see above, Ch. 4.

[86] On Lykoshin's views, see 'Rodovyia imushchestva'. A graduate of the Imperial School of Jurisprudence, Lykoshin served first in the Ministry of Justice and then as an assistant chief procurator in the Civil Cassation Department before becoming Assistant Minister of Internal Affairs in 1907. He joined the rightist group when appointed to the State Council in 1914. Although Lykoshin himself owned no land, his wife had a sizeable patrimonial

all members of the editing commission from the nobility favoured the abolition of patrimonial property.[87]

Anticipating strong conservative opposition, the editing commission prefaced its proposals with a lengthy introduction intended to demonstrate that they represented the natural development of Imperial law and also corresponded with prevailing social attitudes and socio-economic needs. Like progressivist jurists, the editing commission placed Imperial law within a context that stressed the evolution of universal juridical institutions and concepts. According to the commission, the institution of patrimonial property, the limited rights of spouses, and the inferior inheritance rights of women represented merely the remnants of a Russian variant of the system of family property commonly found during the early stages of a society's development. The need of Muscovite princes for servitors and the desire of noble kin-groups to secure their status had shaped and preserved this system, the editing commission contended, even as the patriarchal kin structure that had produced it was being undermined by influences that emphasized affective ties within the conjugal family and the primacy of the individual. The intensification of these influences after the early eighteenth century had resulted in constant efforts by the state to alter the law and in frequent demands for its revision by different social groups, particularly the landed nobility. Citing the recent petitions of the provincial nobility as evidence, the editing commission asserted that the inflexibility inherent in the institution of patrimonial property now threatened both noble landholding and state security by obstructing productive economic activity. 'There can be no doubt', the commission argued,

> that the freedom to dispose of landed property, which constitutes the first and most important source of popular wealth, is extremely important for the proper development of the economic life of the state. Only with such freedom can land pass into the control of people capable of using it with the greatest benefit to themselves and the state. From this point of view, restricting the transfer of landed property is generally an impediment to the natural development of the productive forces of the country.[88]

estate. See TsGIA F. 1364 op. 15 d. 673, *GS 1915*, 131 (1st pag.), and Gurko, *Features*, 150–1, 462, 634.

[87] The members from the nobility included Knirim, Karnitskii, Iliashenko, Iurenev, and Lykoshin. For the backgrounds of Knirim, Karnitskii, and Iurenev, see above, Ch. 4. A former member of the editing commission from the landowning nobility, Andrei Saburov, opposed the abolition of patrimonial property, although he admitted that the family had displaced the kin-group. *GU. Kn. 4-aia*, intro., pp. 111–41.

[88] *GU. Kn. 4-aia*, intro., p. 77.

The problems created by existing statutory law therefore could not be eliminated simply by modifying the specific characteristics of the institution of patrimonial property along the lines proposed by conservative jurists or by Trubetskoi, the editing commission claimed, because the proprietary power of owners would still be restricted and certain family members, especially women, would still be discriminated against unjustly. Hence the commission concluded that it was necessary '*to abolish the laws of patrimonial property as unnecessary and even harmful remnants of the past*'.[89]

The adoption of this evolutionary conceptual framework effectively established contemporary Western European law as the standard against which Imperial Russian law was to be measured. Adoption of this standard implied in turn that one purpose of the new civil code was to move Imperial Russia further towards the realization of its own form of the European ideal of a *Rechtsstaat*, in which the restriction of authority by uniformly applied legal norms would assure civil equality, establish spheres of autonomous personal and civic action, and guarantee the security and rights of individuals, particularly with respect to property. The linkage between European and Imperial Russian legal development served also to justify the use of German, French, Austrian, Swiss, and Italian (and even Californian) codes as sources for the redefinition of Imperial law in a way that promoted the ideals of legality and civil equality and overcame the practical problems attributed to existing law by its many critics.

Like the Abaza commission, the editing commission therefore attempted to balance the economic needs of property owners, including noble landowners, with the right of their family members to security. And like Trubetskoi, the commission concluded that this balance could be achieved most effectively through the expansion of testamentary power.[90] But influenced by both the principle of individual ownership and the practice of the Civil Cassation Department, the editing commission went much further in this direction than had Trubetskoi. Defining a will as merely the distribution of property by an owner in the event of his death, the commission declared that 'the general guiding principle indicating the point of view of the law [is] . . . that the testator can make any type of

[89] Ibid. 95, emphasis original; for the editing commission's argument in general, see pp. 1–95, 109–10, 141–4, and commentary, esp. 30–49, 72–95, 238–43, 276–8; for the response to the Moscow nobility, see intro., pp. 84–92. See also *ZhRKGU. Proekt o nasledovanii*, nos. 3–6, 12, 13.

[90] *GU. Kn. 4-aia*, arts. 39–120 (with commentary, esp. pp. 114–270, 282–3, 293–4, 443–5); see also *ZhRKGU. Proekt o nasledovanii*, nos. 3, 4, 7, 11–16, 18.

disposition with respect to property. Freedom of disposition thus constitutes a general principle which is set aside only as far as there is a law that limits this freedom.'[91]

In fact, the editing commission proposed few such laws and granted the courts wide discretion in applying them, thereby ensuring broad scope for judicial law-making. For example, the editing commission permitted the courts to disallow bequests deemed contrary to good morals or the social order, by which it meant any restraint on a beneficiary's freedom of action which the courts considered unjustifiable. Nor, chiefly for economic reasons, did the commission allow the use and disposition of property to be limited for long periods of time.[92] Otherwise, any bequest of full or limited rights of use, possession, or disposition and any condition, restriction of powers, or charge to the heir in principle was permitted. Moreover, testamentary conditions could stipulate the substitution of one beneficiary for another, provided that ownership of the property involved had not yet been vested in the former. Even in the latter case an exception was allowed for bequests to a surviving spouse, which could be terminated in favour of the children of the deceased if the spouse remarried, a limitation on the actions of the latter which the commission did not consider unjustifiable.[93] The editing commission thus enabled an owner to provide for multiple contingencies and to control the devolution of his property for at least two, and possibly three, generations. More importantly, the commission recognized the power of an owner to separate the management of property from the enjoyment of its income and to assign each to different parties, thereby greatly increasing the ability of an owner to pursue a variety of economic, familial, and socio-political objectives.[94]

But the editing commission also recognized a need to limit the testamentary power of an owner in order to protect the members of his family. 'Elimination from the future code of all limitations on the freedom of testamentary disposition', it declared,

> and the granting to the testator of the right to dispose of his property in favour of third parties in the presence of descendants, a spouse, or parents would not

[91] *GU. Kn. 4-aia*, commentary, p. 190; see also 282–3 and arts. 39, 66.

[92] Ibid., arts. 66, 68, 70–4 (with commentary); see also *ZhRKGU. Proekt o nasledovanii*, 10–14, 19–20, 78–83, 89–103, 116–23, 131–9.

[93] A will was also to be revocable and ambulatory. *GU. Kn. 4-aia*, arts. 66–88 (with commentary); see also *ZhRKGU. Proekt o nasledovanii*, 10–14, 19–20, 78–102, 107–23.

[94] *GU. Kn. 4-aia*, art. 70 (with commentary). The disputes over testamentary power that arose within the editing commission generally involved the inevitable conflict between the testator's and the heir's rights of ownership, although the desire to preserve tradition also motivated some members. see *ZhRKGU. Proekt o nasledovanii*, nos. 3, 4, 7, 11–16, 18.

correspond to the natural close bond that exists between family members and that is expressed in law by their mutual right to sustenance.[95]

To secure this right against violation by an owner, a majority in the editing commission favoured the introduction of a system of obligatory shares. Hence the commission proposed to reserve a portion of the property left by a deceased for his or her 'necessary heirs', i.e. the deceased's surviving spouse, descendant heirs, and, in the absence of the latter, parents. Moreover, testamentary bequests made prior to marriage or to the birth of a child would be considered invalid to the extent that they deprived the spouse or child of the share of an inheritance due by law.[96]

The editing commission realized, however, that a system of obligatory shares could be as restrictive for a property owner and therefore as debilitating economically as the existing institution of patrimonial property. Hence it drew heavily on German law to devise an arrangement that would maximize the power of an owner to dispose of his property while still effectively protecting his immediate family. To achieve this balance, the editing commission proposed to grant an owner unlimited testamentary power over his property. But in the event that he did not leave to any of his 'necessary heirs' at least one half of the value of the property due by law, such an heir would have the right to obtain up to this amount from the beneficiaries of the deceased's will.[97] The majority argued:

> Limiting the claim of the necessary heirs to only the right to demand *one half of the value* of that part of the inheritance due them under the order of intestate succession . . . not only eliminates the mandatory physical division of an estate, but also significantly extends the limits of the testator's discretion. At his discretion he can bequeath a separate immovable property to each of his necessary heirs or he can grant all his immovable property to one of these heirs, satisfying the others with legacies; in general he is completely free to dispose of his property as long as the value of the property received by each necessary heir is not less than the amount established by law.[98]

The majority contended that this arrangement would also avoid overburdening landed estates or other economic units with debt in order to

[95] *GU. Kn. 4-aia*, intro., p. 95.

[96] Ibid. 95–103, 141–4, and arts. 93, 121–43 (with commentary, esp. pp. 271–84). Within the editing commission, conservative opposition came from Malyshev and the former member Andrei Saburov, who argued that the proposal broke too strongly with national legal tradition and limited too severely the owner's rights over self-acquired property. See ibid., intro., pp. 96–8, 103–10, 121–3.

[97] Ibid. 101–3, and arts. 121–43 (with commentary, esp. 282–3).

[98] Ibid. 283, emphasis original; see also intro., pp. 102–3.

compensate co-heirs because the total amount due all necessary heirs could never exceed half the net value of an estate and often would be less. Finally, to increase the flexibility enjoyed by an owner still further, the majority allowed an owner to disinherit a necessary heir for statutorily defined causes, ranging from a serious criminal act against the owner to marital infidelity or a substantial insult to a parent.[99]

As the editing commission claimed, its proposed system of obligatory shares would have gone far towards eliminating the economic disabilities of existing law, even for noble landowners. Yet the system rested on the conception of a deceased's estate as an undifferentiated fund and of property as an infinitely partible value rather than tangible objects. However well these conceptions corresponded to the circumstances and training of urban jurists, they ignored both the allegiance of conservatives to traditional institutions and the special meaning of land in a still predominantly agrarian society. Moreover, while the editing commission had increased the power of an owner to dispose of property that was classified as patrimonial, it had simultaneously constrained his previously unlimited power over property that was considered acquired. The more wealth was composed of capital, corporate shares, and other forms of intangible property, the greater would be the restrictive impact of the proposed system on an owner. Hence the proposals of the editing commission were not unproblematic from either an ideological or a practical perspective.

Finally, the editing commission also reassigned inheritance rights on the basis of the affective ideal of the family. The bonds of affection and the mutual obligations presumed to unite the conjugal family therefore replaced blood-relationship in the patrilineal kin-group as the criteria for determining relative rights to an inheritance. Moreover, the purpose of the law no longer was to protect the interests of the kin-group as a whole by preserving property within it, but now was to ensure the welfare of individual family members through the fulfilment of their obligations towards one another. Attempting to justify such radical changes in the basis and function of the law, the editing commission claimed that it was merely formalizing existing legislative trends and judicial practices. '[B]y giving *unconditional* force to the prohibition against the testamentary disposition of patrimonial property only to protect *the inheritance rights of the owner's children, his descendants generally, and his spouse*,' the editing

[99] Ibid., arts. 137–41 (with commentary). In most cases, the courts would have the power to review such provisions.

commission argued, '[c]urrent law thus gives preference to the family principle before that of the kin-group.'[100] The commission contended that because its proposals pursued this principle more systematically than did existing statutory law, they would more effectively achieve the fundamental objectives already motivating the law, thereby eliminating the cause of many fraudulent practices currently encountered in the courts.[101]

The draft code therefore made the surviving spouse, descendants, and parents of a property owner the principal heirs. In the event of intestacy, a surviving spouse would inherit one quarter of the property left by the deceased in the presence of descendant heirs, one half in the presence of only parents, grandparents, or their descendants, and the entire estate in all other circumstances. Otherwise, an estate passed equally to the children of the deceased or to their descendants, then equally to the parents of the deceased or to their descendants, then to the grandparents and so on up to the fifth degree of ascendant relationship. Beyond this point property would pass to the state or to various social organizations because, the editing commission argued, family ties no longer had significant meaning. At every level, women enjoyed the same rights to an inheritance as men.[102] Moreover, the editing commission also established mutual inheritance rights between a mother and her illegitimate children. But reflecting the practice of several European countries and American states, and also wary of ecclesiastical reaction, the commission refrained from extending these rights to the relatives or legitimate children of the mother. Nor would illegitimate children inherit property from their father unless he formally recognized them.[103]

Few in the editing commission dissented from these basic proposals. Karnitskii and Malyshev favoured granting a surviving spouse only a life interest in immovable property in order to prevent such property from passing away from the family of an owner.[104] Fearing increased fragmentation of landed estates and disruption of economic enterprises, a

[100] *GU. Kn. 4-aia*, intro., p. 66, emphasis original.

[101] Ibid., intro., pp. 40–74, 93, 141–4 and commentary, pp. 30–45, 72–95, 238–43, 276–8; see also *ZhRKGU. Proekt o nasledovanii*, nos. 3–6, 12, 13.

[102] *GU. Kn. 4-aia*, arts. 14–21, 28–38 (with commentary, esp. pp. 30–45, 72–95, 238–43, 276–8); See also *ZhRKGU. Proekt o nasledovanii*, nos. 3–6, 12, 13.

[103] Adopted children likewise enjoyed only limited inheritance rights. *GU. Kn. 4-aia*, arts. 22–7 (with commentary); see also *ZhRKGU. Proekt o nasledovanii*, 16–18, 20–4, and above, Ch. 4.

[104] *GU. Kn. 4-aia*, intro., pp. 105–6, 108–9, and commentary, pp. 72–88, 276–8; see also *ZhRKGU. Proekt o nasledovanii*, nos. 5, 6, 12, 13.

former member of the editing commission, Andrei Saburov, opposed the introduction of sexual equality in inheritance.[105] But the remaining members of the commission contended that the continued discrimination against women and spouses in inheritance would be unjust once the original social and political basis of this treatment had disappeared. Although offering other arguments, the majority clearly was motivated most strongly by the belief that the current position of women in both the family and society demanded recognition of their right to security and to legal equality.[106]

Indeed, the editing commission applied these ideals of legal equality and security even more rigorously in its proposals regarding inheritance law than it did in the case of family law, where it continued to define the husband as the head of the family. As under existing law, the property of spouses would remain separate and they would possess an identical power to dispose of their own property. They would also continue to enjoy the same rights of inheritance with respect to one another. But their share of the property left by a deceased spouse was increased considerably and made more secure, which on balance probably benefited wives more than husbands. There can be little doubt that the equalization of the inheritance rights of women and men represented a substantial gain for daughters and for other female relatives of a deceased property owner. Only in the case of illegitimate children was any inequality on the basis of sex preserved. Hence, at least when measured according to the criteria accepted by late nineteenth-century European jurisprudence, the draft code compared favourably with the rules governing inheritance elsewhere in Europe and in the United States.[107]

This congruity between the draft code and the most recent European and American legislation on inheritance emphasizes the radical character of the changes being proposed by the editing commission. Imperial Russia, after all, was not Western Europe. However closely the provisions of the draft code may have corresponded to changing conditions, relations, and attitudes among the educated and upper strata of Imperial Russian society, these social strata constituted only a small percentage of the total population. And by no means all members of even these social strata

[105] *GU. Kn. 4-aia*, intro., pp. 131–6; see also *ZhRKGU. Proekt o nasledovanii*, 25; on Saburov, see above, nn. 87 and 96 and Ch. 4.

[106] *GU. Kn. 4-aia*, commentary, pp. 30–40, 72–95, 276–8.

[107] On continental European, English, and American law, see the references cited above in Ch. 7 n. 21, and J. Goody, J. Thirsk, and E. P. Thompson (eds.), *Family and Inheritance: Rural Society in Western Europe, 1200–1800* (Cambridge, 1976), 202–33.

subscribed to the ideals of legality, civil equality, and individuality that underlay the draft code. Hence while the editing commission claimed sincerely that its proposals were meant only to adjust inheritance law to social, economic, and cultural changes that already had taken place, the draft code in fact represented an attempt to provide a suitable legal framework for directing further change along a path defined by the experience of Western Europe. In this sense, the editing commission unconsciously perpetuated the tsarist paternalistic tradition even as it promoted values and relationships that challenged the very foundation of the autocratic regime.

The political and ideological implications of the draft code help to explain its mixed reception. The progressive press, juridical societies, and most jurists writing in legal periodicals warmly greeted the proposals and frequently urged the editing commission to go even further in uprooting allegedly outworn remnants of the past, particularly with respect to illegitimate children. As a reviewer in *The Herald of Law* (*Vestnik Prava*) declared, 'the heart of every healthy-minded Russian jurist, who sees in the law the means for the social and ethical upbringing of the people, must be overjoyed when reading' the proposals of the editing commission.[108] Moderates, too, generally commended the commission for its work. Ermolov, for example, hailed the basic propositions of the code for providing a framework that would effectively adjust the law to current economic conditions and needs.[109]

In contrast, conservatives generally condemned the proposals as the abstract and useless creation of cloistered juridical bureaucrats who were

[108] A. I. Bugaevskii, *VP* (1904), 5, cited in *SZPGU. Kn. 4-oi*, 121. For other positive reviews, see ibid., 'Zhurnal obrazovannoi pri grazhdanskom otdelenii iuridicheskago obshchestva kommisii dlia razsmotreniia proektov knig I i IV grazhdanskago ulozheniia' and nos. 8, 13, 27, 28, 32, 37, 124, 127, 129, 134–8, A. I. Kaminka, 'Proekt nasledstvennago prava', *Pravo* (1903), 37, cols., 2638–48, 'S.-peterburgskoe iuridicheskoe obshchestvo', *Pravo* (1903), 43, cols. 2439–40, 44, cols. 2506–7, and 45, cols. 2557–8, A. Goikhbarg, 'K reforme nasledovaniia po zakonu', *Pravo* (1909), 38, cols. 2023–30, and 39, cols. 2080–7, P. N. Gussakovskii, 'Nasledstvennoe pravo po proektu Grazhdanskago Ulozheniia', *ZhMIu* (1903), 9: 1–51, N. N. Tovstoles, 'Iuridicheskoe polozhenie zhenshchiny pri otkrytii nasledstva po russkomu zakonodatel'stvu', *ZhMIu* (1910), 1: 56–83, id., 'Nasledovanie suprugov po russkomu pravu, v sviazi s proektom grazhdanskago ulozheniia', *ZhMIu* (1911), 5: 1–63, *RVed* (1903), 97: 2, and 103: 2, *VE* (1903), 11: 360–7, V. A., 'Vopros o reforme nasledstvennago prava pered Gosudarstvennoi Dumy', *SVed* (1911), 40: 1, id., 'Sud'ba rodovykh imushchestv', *SVed* (1911), 46: 1, and A. N. Gedda, 'Obiazatel'naia dolia v nasledstve po proektu novago grazhdanskago ulozheniia', *ZhMIu* (1904), 2: 56–84 (discussed in *Pravo* (1903), 46, cols. 2617–19), who generally welcomed the proposals but opposed any system of obligatory shares as a violation of the individual's property rights.

[109] *SZPGU. Kn. 4-oi*, nos. 2, 35.

out of touch with real social conditions and attitudes. Although grudgingly accepting the abolition of patrimonial property because of its harmful effects on the landed nobility, for example, the reactionary *Moscow Gazette* somewhat inconsistently called for preservation of the right to redeem such property and renewed its campaign for the permanent entailment of noble estates.[110] Most conservative critics, however, opposed even the abolition of patrimonial property.[111]

The harshest condemnation of the draft code came from noble landowners, many of whom found the proposals contrary to their practical interests as well as to their traditionalist beliefs and values. Leading the way, in late 1903 the assembly of the nobility in Moscow province unfavourably compared the draft code with its own earlier proposals.[112] 'If at first glance', declared the report of the assembly, 'it seems that the draft project of the new Code in many respects satisfies the proposals of the Nobility, on closer examination this turns out to be only a purely fortuitous coincidence within the complete dissimilarity of basic principles.'[113] The Moscow nobility had sought to preserve the institution of patrimonial property through an expansion of testamentary power, the report continued, whereas the editing commission proposed to abolish this institution and to limit testamentary power in order to protect the family. In the view at least of the noble landowners gathered at the meeting of the Moscow assembly, both proposals of the editing commission threatened their vital interests. Again romanticizing rural landownership, they linked the preservation of patrimonial property with the perpetuation of traditional values and relationships, including their own privileged status. They also rejected as unjust and inexpedient any restriction of their power to dispose of acquired property. Despite a common desire to increase the flexibility of property owners for economic reasons, the Moscow nobility and the editing commission thus remained deeply divided politically and ideologically over how to achieve this objective.

Similar concerns led the director of the recently created chancellery for the affairs of the nobility in the Ministry of Internal Affairs, Nikolai Mordvinov, to attempt to enlist other provincial assemblies in a campaign to defeat the draft code. Assisted by Trubetskoi and by several other provincial marshals, Mordvinov circulated to provincial assemblies both the proposals made originally by the Moscow provincial nobility and

110 *MV* (1902), 190: 1.
111 e.g. see *SZPGU. Kn. 4-oi*, nos. 4, 5, 9, 12, 25, 36, 70, 98.
112 TsGIA F. 1233 op. 1 d. 99 ll. 21–8, contained also in *SZPGU. Kn. 4-oi*, no. 4.
113 TsGIA F. 1233 op. 1 d. 99 ll. 21–6, p. 2.

their critique of the draft code. His terse rejection of a proposal made by the Smolensk nobility to study the issue further at the local level suggests that Mordvinov's primary concern was to block a measure considered to be politically repugnant, not to respond to the actual needs of the landed nobility.[114] Despite a disappointing response from the provinces, Mordvinov therefore submitted to his superiors a somewhat misleading report that urged the ministry to oppose the draft code on the grounds that the landed nobility had unanimously rejected it.[115]

In fact, although generally critical, the responses of provincial assemblies to the draft code were more complex than Mordvinov had reported. As in the late eighteenth century, the nobility were uniformly dissatisfied with existing statutory law but divided over what to do about it. Responses therefore depended on the relative importance placed on political and economic considerations. Swayed by the arguments of their arch-conservative provincial marshal, V. A. Drashusov, for example, the Riazan nobility rejected the proposals of the editing commission and supported those of the Moscow nobility. 'In whomever's hands land [remains],' Drashusov had declared to his fellow noblemen, 'in those hands also [resides] predominant influence. Thus to preserve this influence for the nobility, it is necessary also to preserve the land of the nobility.'[116] In contrast, emphasizing the need for greater flexibility for economic reasons, the Smolensk nobility accepted the basic premisses of the draft code and demanded even greater testamentary power over their property.[117] In the end, while most provincial assemblies favoured the retention of patrimonial property in some form, all sought greater control over their property. They tended to combine elements from both the draft code and the proposals of the Moscow nobility in a way that maximized their proprietary power while minimizing the challenge to traditional values.[118]

By the early twentieth century two competing projects for the revision of property and inheritance law thus had emerged. Although, partly for common economic reasons, both made the expansion of testamentary power a central demand, each rested on a different ideological premiss and envisioned a different future for Imperial Russia. For conservatives, the expansion of testamentary power also represented a means of preserving

[114] TsGIA F. 1283 op. 1 d. 26 ll. 183–93, 196–7.

[115] Ibid., ll. 3–11, 64–8, 72–3, 100–1, 107–8, 137, 166, 169, 225–38, 283–5.

[116] Ibid., l. 155, and 153–6 in general.

[117] Ibid., ll. 181–93; see also the response of the Tambov nobility, ll. 103–4.

[118] Sixteen provincial assemblies responded to Mordvinov's circular. Ibid., ll. 103–4, 110, 135–6, 153–6, 160–5, 171–94, 199–207, 210–23, 245–80.

hierarchical relationships and patriarchal authority, both in the family and in society generally. From this perspective, property—especially landed property—constituted not only a resource for development and welfare, but primarily an instrument of social and familial power and the medium through which the landed nobility fulfilled its redefined public roles. For progessivists, in contrast, the expansion of testamentary power also represented a means of disencumbering the individual property owner in order to allow both personal and national development. From this perspective, property—tangible or intangible—provided a resource for productive activity, the basis of personal independence and security, and a medium for the fulfilment of family obligations.

In an important sense, the two positions were not incompatible. The bestowal of unlimited testamentary power on a property owner in accordance with the principle of individual ownership could easily serve to strengthen patriarchal authority within the family. In part to prevent the abuse of this authority, progressivist reformers sought to place limitations on the testamentary power of individuals even while proposing to expand it. The same conflict over the nature of authority which complicated efforts to revise family law thus also shaped the competing projects for the revision of inheritance law. Before being fully joined, however, the struggle between these projects was pushed far into the background by the revolutionary events of 1905. By the time it re-emerged, the editing commission had been disbanded and the draft civil code buried by bureaucratic infighting,[119] Trubetskoi had been displaced within noble institutions by far more conservative men, and the political process had been broadened by the introduction of national representative bodies.

Legislative Compromise

The last substantial attempt to revise tsarist inheritance law began with the efforts of feminists, particularly those in the moderate Women's Mutual Philanthropic Society, to gain legal equality with men.[120] Like Russian feminists generally, the largely well-to-do women who dominated the Society expected revision of the law to yield important practical as well as symbolic gains. Most importantly, they believed that sexual

[119] See above, Ch. 4.

[120] R. Stites, *The Women's Liberation Movement in Russia: Feminism, Nihilism and Bolshevism, 1860–1930* (Princeton, NJ. 1978), 224, L. H. Edmondson, *Feminism in Russia 1900–1917* (Stanford, Calif., 1984), 139; on the Women's Mutual Philanthropic Society and other feminist organizations, see above, Ch. 4.

equality in inheritance would not only advance their goal of civil equality for women, but also better enable women to attain the economic independence thought necessary to achieve personal security and liberation. Hence several speakers at the Women's Congress in 1908 had demanded the elimination of all discrimination against women in inheritance law, and the Congress had included this demand among its final resolutions.[121] Pressed by members of the Mutual Philanthropic Society, in early 1909 a group of Octobrist deputies introduced into the Duma a bill with this objective.[122] Sympathetic with the proposal, and seeing in it a means to challenge the autocratic regime by eroding its underlying values, progressivist writers, Duma deputies, and jurists also warmly endorsed the bill.[123]

This agreement between moderate conservatives and progressivists on the need to revise the law ensured a relatively smooth passage of the bill through the Duma. The competing demands of equity, security, and flexibility, as well as the desire to use revision of the law for the pursuit of political and institutional objectives, none the less continued to provoke conflict over the specific content of the bill. Instructed to compose appropriate legislation, for example, the Ministry of Justice tried to use the opportunity to lay the groundwork for acceptance of the draft civil code and to eliminate the alleged inflexibility of existing statutory law. Its proposal not only established complete sexual equality in the event of intestate succession, but also allowed an owner to dispose freely of his patrimonial property among descendant heirs. As proposed in the draft code, moreover, any heir deprived of the share of patrimonial property due by law as a result of the will of the owner would have the right to receive as compensation one half of the value of this share.[124] Seeking to undermine the institution of patrimonial property and its underlying values still further, progressivists in the Duma commission on judicial

[121] *Trudy pervago vserossiiskago zhenskago s″ezda pri Russkom Zhenskom (Vzaimno-Blagotvoritel′nom) Obshchestve v S-Peterburge 10–16 dekabria 1908 goda* (Spb., 1909), 9–12, 344, 359–67, 495, 589, 754–60, 825; see also B. Glinskii, 'Pervyi zhenskii s″ezd', *Istoricheskii Vestnik* (1909), 1: 386, and, on the congress in general, Edmondson, *Feminism*, 83–106.

[122] *GDP. 3-ii soz., 4-aia ses. (1910–1911 gg.)*, iii., no. 212, p. 1, and 'Gos. Duma', *NV* (1909), 11819: 3.

[123] e.g. see 'Gos, Duma', *Rech′* (1909), 45: 3, I. G. [Gessen], 'Reforma nasledstvennago prava', *Rech′* (1911), 48: 2, Goikhbarg, 'K reforme', id., 'Kolliziia novykh i starykh zakonov v sviazi s predstoiashchei reformoi nasledovaniia zhenshchin', *Pravo* (1910), 11, cols. 647–56, and 12, cols. 734–43, V. A., 'Vopros o reforme', id., 'Sud′ba rodovykh imushchestv', and A. E. Nol′de, 'O prave rodstvennikov zhenskago pola na vykup rodovogo imeniia', *ZhMIu*, (1911), 8: 139–56.

[124] TsGIA F. 797 op. 92–1910 d. 53 ll. 2–36, *GDP. 3-ii soz., 4-aia ses. (1910–1911 gg.)*, iii., no. 212, and Goikhbarg, 'K reforme', no. 38, id., 'Kolliziia', no. 11, and id., *Zakon o rasshirenii prav nasledovaniia po zakonu lits zhenskago pola i prava zaveshchaniia rodovykh imenii* (3rd edn., Spb., 1914), 12–15.

reforms managed to eliminate all restrictions on testamentary power in its version of the bill.[125] Reluctant to threaten the security of heirs and wary of inciting conservative opposition in the State Council, however, the moderate Octobrists who dominated the Duma rejected any change in testamentary power. Hence in March 1911 the Duma sent to the State Council a bill intended solely to establish sexual equality in inheritance.[126]

The caution of the Duma Octobrists proved to be well founded but futile. As in the case of marital separation, the decisive struggle over revision of the law took place in the State Council and pitted moderate conservatives against the reactionary right. Before a gallery packed with women, the chamber ultimately debated the equity and efficacy of an expansion of their inheritance rights almost entirely in terms of its effect on noble landholding.[127] Although the revision of inheritance law provided the formal issue at hand, the real issue clearly was whether tsarist society should be structured on the basis of legality, civil equality, and status derived from personal achievement or on the traditional foundation of a hierarchy of authority and privilege dominated by the landed nobility. The results of the debate proved to be ambiguous.

Rightist opposition to the bill in the State Council reflected essentially the same sentiments and concerns as those expressed earlier by ultra-conservative advocates of entail and by supporters of Trubetskoi's proposals. Hoping to block passage of the bill altogether, rightists in the commission on legislative proposals thus argued that it would undermine the socio-political order by subverting the male role in society, harm agriculture by increasing the fragmentation of noble estates, and provoke social instability by challenging traditional values among the peasantry and other groups. When this effort failed, they then tried unsuccessfully to minimize the impact of the bill on the landed nobility, chiefly by amending it to preserve a larger share for males in the inheritance of rural property.[128]

Backed by the United Nobility, a loose association formed by conservative noble landowners to safeguard their interests in the wake of the events of 1905, the Right pursued the same tactics on the floor of the State Council. Apparently hoping to enlist more support from moderate conservatives, rightists now stressed the potential impact of the bill on

[125] *GDP. 3-ii soz., 4-aia ses. (1910–1911 gg.)*, iii., no. 212, pp. 7–12.

[126] *GDSO. 1911 g. 3-ii soz., ses. 4-aia*, ii. 2238–45, iii. 1142–66, 3772, 3803–6.

[127] 'V Gos. Sovete', *NV* (1912), 12899: 2.

[128] *Gosudarstvennyi Sovet. Sessiia VII. Kommisiia Zakonodatel'nykh Predpolozhenii, no. 7.*, Doklad po zakonoproektu ob uravnenii lits zhenskago pola v pravakh nasledovaniia po zakonu s litsami muzheskago pola. Zasedaniia 24 Noiabria, 1 i 8 Dekabria 1911 goda (HLL), and *GSSO. 7-aia ses. (1911–1912)*, cols. 1499–1507.

noble landowners.[129] Alluding to allegedly comparable methods used to break up noble estates during the French Revolution, for example, the conservative jurist and former Civil Cassation Department senator Petr Kobylinskii claimed that the law would increase the fragmentation of noble landholdings and thereby destroy their economic viability.[130] Aleksandr Stishinskii added,

> the current needs of the state, society, and social estates . . . consist in the preservation of agricultural estates from fragmentation . . . [through which] is lost not only the agricultural significance of such estates, but also their political significance, for they cease to provide the land qualification which in local districts ensures the proper composition of participants in all organs of local self-administration.[131]

In the view of rightists, these political and economic considerations should take precedence over any moral claims arising from parental affection in the formulation of inheritance law. In any case, contended Ananii Strukov, former marshal of the Ekaterinoslav provincial nobility and a reactionary leader of the United Nobility, men required a greater share of an inheritance than did women because they performed more demanding social roles and contributed more to the productivity of property.[132] Indeed, concluded Count Dmitrii Olsufev, a former district marshal and chairman of the provincial zemstvo administrative board from Saratov, the proposed law seemed more appropriate to bourgeois capitalist societies than to still largely agrarian Imperial Russia. Hence, he observed caustically but accurately, the strongest supporters of the bill came from the free professions, whose members he accused of incautiously advocating the inappropriate adoption of foreign laws.[133]

[129] *Trudy VIII s″ezda upolnomochennykh dvorianskikh obshchestv 37 gubernii* (Spb., 1912), 144–50, *GSSO. 7-aia ses. (1911–1912)*, cols. 1512–22, 1536–54, 1566–83, 1591–6, 1643–5, 1649–55, 1667–9, 1676–7, 1681–2, 1695–1700, 1705–7, 1712–15, 1721–7, 1735–6, 1740. For contrasting views of the United Nobility, see Becker, *Nobility*, 161–9, and G. A. Hosking and R. T. Manning, 'What Was the United Nobility?', in L. H. Haimson (ed.), *The Politics of Rural Russia, 1905–1914* (Bloomington, Ind., 1979), 142–83 (and 164–9 on the relationship between the United Nobility and the State Council).

[130] *GSSO. 7-aia ses. (1911–1912)*, cols. 1512–22. A hereditary but landless nobleman, Kobylinskii served in various judicial and central administrative positions and as a sworn attorney in Saratov after graduating from the Imperial School of Jurisprudence in 1868. TsGIA F. 1364 op. 15 d. 603, *GS 1915*, 51 (1st pag.).

[131] *GSSO. 7-aia ses. (1911–1912)*, col. 1722; on Stishinskii, see above, Ch. 4.

[132] *GSSO. 7-aia ses. (1911–1912)*, cols. 1536–47; on Strukov, see *GS 1915*, 90 (1st pag.).

[133] *GSSO. 7-aia ses. (1911–1912)*, cols. 1547–54. From the prominent aristocracy, Olsufev served in the élite Guards horse artillery and the Ministry of State Domains after graduating from Moscow University in 1885. He helped found the Octobrist party in 1905 but joined the Right in the State Council, where he represented the Saratov zemstvo. See *GS 1915*, 61 (2nd pag.).

In contrast, the position taken by representatives of moderate conservative factions in the State Council demonstrates the degree to which changed attitudes towards women and the family had penetrated the upper strata of society. Supporting the bill, the moderate conservative majority in the commission on legislative proposals asserted that

[a]t the present time, when the position of women in both family and social life has changed substantially, when their activity is no longer confined within the narrow framework of the family hearth, when women have attained access not only to occupations in the free professions, in the fields of education, science, and the arts, but also to positions of responsibility in state and private service, it is scarcely possible to maintain that sufficient grounds still exist to preserve the limited rights of women in inheritance which formed under the influences of the already outdated customs of patriarchal family life and the structure of the kin-group and the anachronistic view of women as people possessing neither independence nor full rights.[134]

And in the debate in the State Council itself the right Centrist and former judge Vladimir Deitrikh attempted to counter rightist contentions by arguing that the obligatory division of estates among the male heirs would continue to threaten their economic viability regardless of the size of the share due to women in inheritance. He therefore concluded that there was no reason to deny women the equality due to them in inheritance as a result of equal parental love and obligation. Considerations of justice based partly on a changed view of family relations thus led Deitrikh and his moderate conservative colleagues to support equal inheritance rights for women and men.[135]

But concerned with the problem alluded to by Deitrikh, moderate conservatives turned to a familiar solution. Ostensibly to avoid any harmful effects on noble landholdings which might result from the expansion of the inheritance rights of women, the majority in the commission on legislative proposals amended the bill to allow free testamentary disposition of patrimonial property among descendant heirs. In contrast to the draft code and to the comparable proposal made by the Ministry of Justice, moreover, the majority did not established a right to compensation

[134] *Gos. Sov. Ses. VII. Kom. Zak. Pred. no. 7.* (HLL), Doklad, p. 14.

[135] *GSSO. 7-aia ses. (1911–1912)*, cols. 1583–92, 1679–80, 1727–30. A landless hereditary nobleman, Deitrikh occupied a series of judicial posts after graduating from the juridical faculty at St Petersburg University in 1873. Holding strong Russian nationalist views, he became an assistant to the Governor-General of Finland in 1902. See *GS 1915*, 34 (1st pag.), and *SChMIu, 1890*, ch. 2-aia (Spb. Court of Appeals). See also the speeches by fon Goiningen-Giune, Ermolov, Gasman, and Manukhin, *GSSO. 7-aia ses. (1911–1912)*, cols. 1501–7, 1596–609, 1630–42, 1663–5, 1676, 1700–5, 1715–21, 1731–3, 1738–40.

for an heir who was deprived by the will of an owner of the share of such property due by law.[136] While meeting the demand of feminists and progressivists for equality, the commission thus also satisfied the long-standing demand of noble landowners for greater testamentary power. The amendment therefore not surprisingly met with overwhelming approval in the State Council, and not only among its moderate conservative members.

The small band of progressivists in the State Council, chiefly academics and jurists, also supported the bill, albeit for different reasons. While professing their desire to adjust the law to changed socio-economic conditions and to recognize the gains already made by women, they believed that the proposed law would help create the social foundation necessary for a more far-reaching transformation of the tsarist political system. In particular, they hoped that by undermining the institution of patrimonial property and by proclaiming the principles of civil equality, legality, and testamentary freedom, the law would foster the values and relationships that undergirded constitutional democratic government. As the eminent legal sociologist Maksim Kovalevskii put it, political freedom and equal political rights had to be based on civil freedom and equal civil rights.[137] By thus linking the transformation of the political order with the revision of civil law, Kovalevskii made clear that for many the objective of legal reform had grown well beyond merely the creation of a *Rechtsstaat*.

Perhaps for this reason, the moderate conservatives who composed the Centre group refused to embrace fully the principle of equality for women, particularly where it affected the interests of noble landowners.[138] Although willing to grant women an equal right to the inheritance of most forms of property, a majority in the State Council gave greater priority to enabling landowners to preserve their estates intact, whether for economic or political reasons. Consequently, while sizeable majorities voted to grant women equality with respect to movable property and not to reject the bill entirely, a slim majority (74–64) adopted a proposal made by the Right to limit the share of female heirs to one seventh of the immovable property of a deceased owner when there where male heirs. Manœuvring

[136] *Gos. Sov. Ses. VII. Kom. Zak. Pred. no. 7.* (HLL), Doklad, and *GSSO. 7-aia ses. (1911–1912)*, cols. 1499–507.

[137] Ibid., cols. 1611–20; see also 1522–30 and the speeches by Koni and Bagalei, 1507–12, 1555–65, 1620–8. On Kovalevskii, see above, Chs. 3 and 7.

[138] 'V Gos. Sovete', *Rech'* (1912), 41: 4–5, and Goikhbarg, *Zakon*, 15–22, 58–9. It should be noted, however, that in 1905 a few provincial assemblies of the nobility had accepted the proposal of the civil code editing commission to establish complete sexual equality in inheritance. TsGIA F. 1283 op. 1 d. 26 ll. 103–4, 199–205, 210–19, 245–59.

by Centre leaders managed to restrict this limitation to only rural immovable property, although acquired as well as patrimonial property was included on the urging of Stishinskii. And while the State Council also defeated (74–58) a proposal by the Right to allow male heirs to redeem any immovable property inherited by women, it adopted a motion by the Right (66–52) that instructed the Ministry of Justice to draft legislation granting sons a right of preferential purchase in the event that daughters or a surviving spouse sold such property.[139] Being supported by all factions, the proposal to expand testamentary power over patrimonial property carried easily.[140]

Approved by the Duma, the amended bill became law in June 1912, far too late to have much practical impact.[141] In terms of resolving the long-standing conflicts over the revision of inheritance law, the new law went far towards meeting the desire of property owners for greater flexibility, recognizing the principle of civil equality, and acknowledging changed attitudes towards women and the family, at least within the educated and upper strata of society. But the desire of most jurists and progressivist reformers to limit the power of a property owner in order to protect the welfare and rights of his family had been sacrificed almost completely to the interests of noble landowners and to the goal of state economic development. In fact, the new law had the effect of reducing considerably the level of security enjoyed both by descendant heirs and by a surviving spouse. As Trubetskoi, several noble assemblies, and conservative jurists had proposed, the institution of patrimonial property remained, with the owner receiving the right to bequeath such property freely among his descendant heirs. An owner was not obligated to compensate an heir deprived of the share of such property due by law, although he could elect to do so and for this purpose was given greater power with respect to the assignment of legacies. When combined with his existing testamentary power over acquired property and over patrimonial property in the absence of descendants, an owner therefore now enjoyed considerable flexibility in arranging his inheritance and commanded substantial means to influence the future actions of his heirs.[142] In its passage through the State Council, the Octobrist proposal to establish sexual equality in

[139] *GSSO. 7-aia ses. (1911–1912)*, cols. 1642–3, 1675, 1684–90, 1712–42.

[140] Ibid., cols. 1708–10.

[141] *GDSO. 1912 g. 3-ii soz., ses. 5-aia*, iv. 2078, 2598, and *SUzak*, 1912 (3 June) no. 107, item 914; Goikhbarg, *Zakon*, provides an extensive analysis of the law.

[142] *SZ* (1900, *Prod.* 1912), x, pt. 1, arts. 1068, 1068^{1}, 1126–8, 1130, 1132, 1135, 1148. In the absence of descendant heirs, an owner could bequeath all or part of his patrimonial property to a single member of the relevant kin-group, regardless of the degree of relationship.

inheritance had thus been transformed into a law that vastly increased the power of property owners at the expense of their heirs.

But if the law of 1912 eliminated many of the practical problems attributed to inheritance law, it failed to resolve the ideological conflict that repeatedly had plagued efforts to revise the law. Frustrated and disappointed, the progressivist and liberal press bitterly denounced the amendments made to the bill in the State Council as the handiwork of a backward-looking clique of noble landowners and bureaucrats who had selfishly sacrificed justice, civilized values, and state interests to their own narrow interests. While perpetuating a grave injustice, the liberal *Russian Gazette* intoned, the new law none the less would be unable to stem the historical forces that were sweeping away noble landholdings and, by implication, the old regime.[143] Even the moderate *New Times* (*Novoe Vremia*) condemned the Right in the upper chamber for needlessly sacrificing the legitimate rights of women and the forward movement of state legislation in a vain attempt to arrest the division of noble estates. 'The division of land in inheritance is a natural process of life itself . . .', declared the editor, and 'this process will continue, of course, independently of whether or not women participate equally with men in the division of immovable property'.[144]

In contrast, the reactionary paper *Citizen* complained that the law had come too late to save the landed nobility, which had now deteriorated too far to rise up in defence of 'old Russia' and the autocracy. An alliance of intelligentsia and bureaucrats, lamented the editor, had destroyed the landed nobility and produced in the Duma merely the parody of a parliament.[145] The intensity of these feelings, on both sides of the issue, suggests that the ideological conflict dividing the educated and upper strata of society in Imperial Russia on the eve of revolution was irresolvable. That both sides numbered state bureaucrats among their enemies indicates, moreover, the extent to which this conflict also split the tsarist government even while it alienated society from the government as a whole.

If in this regard the struggle to revise property and inheritance law paralleled the attempt to change family law, it also differed from this

[143] *RVed* (1912), 38: 1; see also A. S. Izgoev, 'Politicheskaia zhizn′ v Rossii', *RM* (1912), 3: 7–8, *VE* (1912), 3: 412–14, *Rech′* (1912), 41: 2, 'Za nedeliu', *Rech′* (1912), 42: 2, Goikhbarg, *Zakon*, 15–22, and *GDSO. 1912 g. 3-ii soz., ses. 5-aia*, iv. 2077–8.

[144] 'Zhenskaia opasnot″', *NV* (1912), 12902: 4, and see also 'V Gos. Sovete', *NV* (1912), 12904: 3.

[145] 'Dnevniki', *Grazhdanin* (1912), 8: 12–13.

latter effort in an important respect. In contrast to the latter struggle, attempts to revise inheritance law originated more from society than from the government. Reflecting the widened political process in late Imperial Russia, first conservative noble landowners and then moderate political actors and activist women managed to place reform on the legislative agenda, thereby forcing the government to respond. To be sure, until 1906 the government retained exclusive control over the legislative process and generally shaped any changes in the law to suit its own interests, or at least those of competing factions within it. But the law of 1912 resulted entirely from social initiative and corresponded to the demands of a variety of social and political groups.

Conservative noble landowners in particular exerted a strong influence on the legislative development of the law, although their success generally depended on the ability to find factions within the state bureaucracy with parallel interests, either in supporting noble landowners for political reasons or in assisting them to become more efficient agricultural producers. In this regard, the law of 1912 represented not only a compromise between competing social and political groups, but also a synthesis between old and new values among noble landowners themselves. While recognizing the apparent need of noble landowners for greater power to dispose of their property in response to the demands of the market-place, the law also introduced a new legal distinction between rural and urban property that reflected their traditionalist ideal of landownership. And while conceding that changes in the position of women required an expansion of their inheritance rights, many members of the State Council from the conservative nobility had also supported this change in the law because of a paternalistic belief that the natural weakness of women relative to men justified additional legal protection. Moreover, this improvement in the inheritance rights of women was accompanied by an expansion of testamentary power that, in the absence of safeguards for heirs of either sex, reinforced patriarchal authority within the family as a whole. While revealing important changes in the attitudes of members of the educated and upper strata of Imperial Russian society, then, the law of 1912 also demonstrated the persistence of traditional values and the political predominance of conservative forces on the eve of the First World War.

9

The Possibilities of Judicial Revision

As with family law, limited legislative revision of property and inheritance law increased the role played by the courts in adapting the law to post-emancipation conditions. Judges, and especially senators in the Civil Cassation Department, again responded to this opportunity by redefining the law in accordance with their perception of current social and economic needs, a perception influenced strongly by the criticisms of the law made by progressivist jurists. Guided particularly by the principle of individual ownership, the high court effectively changed property and inheritance law even more extensively than it proved willing to do in the field of family law. But again the Civil Cassation Department did not reform the law as substantially as progressivist jurists had desired. Both judicial ethics and the language of statutory law placed limits on the reformist impulses of judges. In addition, however, the same tension between freedom, equity, and security which characterized juristic writing on property and inheritance law also limited the willingness of the high court to revise the law.

Limiting Patrimonial Property

From the outset, the Civil Cassation Department exhibited an ambiguous attitude towards the institution of patrimonial property. On the one hand, especially in its earliest decisions, the high court stressed the goal of preserving patrimonial property within the kin-group and even asserted that members of the kin-group possessed an independent right to such property. Hence the court routinely protected members of the kin-group against the claims of non-kin in disputes over the inheritance or ownership of patrimonial property.[1] On the other hand, the high court tended

[1] e.g. see *SRGKD* 1872 nos. 474, 1288, 1874 no. 804, 1875 no. 302, 1876 no. 214, 1880 no. 1, 1881 no. 30, 1883 no. 32, 1890 no. 41, 1891 nos. 40, 61, 1897 no. 72, 1899 no. 11, 1901 no. 41, 1902 no. 98, 1906 no. 38, 1908 no. 13, and, on the independent property right of kinsmen, 1896 no. 93 and 1900 no. 8. On the published decisions of the high court, see above, Ch. 1 n. 51.

to increase the power of owners to dispose of patrimonial property and to reduce the incidence of such property, thereby reflecting the antipathy to this institution found in juridical literature after the mid-1860s. This antipathy in turn was counterbalanced by recognition that under Imperial law the institution of patrimonial property provided the sole means for protecting family members from an abuse of power or actions of an owner considered by the courts to be capricious. These conflicting considerations led the Civil Cassation Department to weaken the legal restrictions on owners of patrimonial property except where they appeared to protect the material welfare of the nearest heirs of an owner. And even in these instances, the high court sought to ensure that the heirs received an appropriate value, not necessarily a share of the family patrimony.

As with marital separation, the Civil Cassation Department shifted its position and began to redefine the purpose of patrimonial property in the 1880s. For example, in 1884, in two separate decisions, in the case of *Cherepovy* v. *Pishchevich* the high court clearly was concerned primarily with securing the material welfare of the heirs, even though it referred to the interests of the kin-group as a whole to justify its position.[2] In these decisions, the legal heirs of Andrei Cherepov had contested his bequest of the livestock, farm inventory, and crops from his patrimonial estates to his niece. The plaintiffs argued that such objects were inseparable from the land and therefore in this instance could not be disposed of by will because the land itself was patrimonial.

In finding for the plaintiffs, the Civil Cassation Department stressed the importance of maintaining the viability of economic enterprises such as landed estates, a goal that it believed served the interests of both the heirs and the state. The high court therefore used the institution of patrimonial property to establish the general rule that the inventory of a landed estate was inseparable from the land itself. 'The owner of patrimonial property', the high court argued,

> . . . by no means can be considered its unlimited owner, since in the interests of his kin-group he is limited in the disposition of this property, particularly in the event of death. From this it follows that in this event he has no right to separate and bequeath to a person not being a member of the kin-group or having a right of inheritance those movables that constitute the necessary appurtenances of a patrimonial estate and to leave the legal heirs bare earth in place of an economically organized estate.[3]

[2] *SRGKD* 1884 nos. 75 and 108.

[3] *SRGKD* 1884 no. 75. Appurtenances are objects or incorporeal interests that are not naturally and originally appendant to an object but have been attached to it by law,

The Civil Cassation Department concluded that the owner of any landed estate or economic enterprise classified as patrimonial therefore could not separate from it by will the inventory essential for its operation. Revealing its primary concerns in this case, the high court then extended its ruling to include acquired property. The court declared that even in this instance the inventory of an estate or an economic enterprise could not be separated from it by such general bequests as a grant of 'all movable property' to another person, although here the court recognized that a specific bequest to this effect would be legal.[4]

Although after 1884 the Civil Cassation Department asserted repeatedly that the main purpose of patrimonial property was to protect the material welfare of the heirs, it expressed this view most forcefully in its decision in *Shanshieva* v. *Lapteva* in 1910.[5] Petr Laptev had bequeathed all his property, including several thousand desiatin of patrimonial land, to his wife Aleksandra. Their son Dmitrii had failed to contest the provisions of the will concerning his father's patrimonial property, even though they were clearly illegal. Several years after the death of Dmitrii, his remarried widow, now Anna Shanshieva, contested the bequest and requested ownership of the property for her children and herself. The Riazan District Court denied the suit. On appeal, however, the Moscow Court of Appeals reversed this decision, holding that an owner could not circumvent the prohibition against the testamentary disposition of patrimonial property simply by using such general phrases as Laptev had employed in his will. Contending further that when interpreting a will the courts must assume that the testator intended his bequest to be legal, the court of appeals concluded that in this case Laptev must not have meant his bequest to include his patrimonial property.

In setting this decision aside, the Civil Cassation Department asserted that the courts could not assume that an owner who expressed a bequest in the proper form intended its content to be legal, especially when it involved patrimonial property. 'The law does not deny the testator's right of ownership of patrimonial property,' the court continued,

> it only limits his right to dispose of [such property] in the event of his death in violation of the rights of the legal heirs. Any private right lies in the complete

prescription, or a specific act. Imperial statutory law did not provide any general rule on appurtenances but only defined the appurtenances of a few specific objects, such as houses, factories, and shops. *SZ* (1857), x, pt. 1, arts. 386–92.

[4] See also *RGKD* 1912 no. 71, where the court again stressed the necessity of an economic link.

[5] *SRGKD* 1910 no. 51; see also 1890 no. 42 and 1899 no. 49.

disposition of its owner, who is free to use it or not to use it, and if the person, in this instance the heir by law, in whose favour the will [*volia*] of the testator concerning property is limited wishes not to use his right or to lose it by non-exercise within the period established by law, then obviously the limitation collapses and the freedom of the testator to dispose of his property is restored in full measure. . . . Thus the law itself allows the possibility of testamentary dispositions which are illegal in content but are expressed in legal form, and which, not having been contested within the designated period, acquire legal force. In particular, such are wills concerning patrimonial properties.[6]

Under the ruling of the high court, an illegal bequest of patrimonial property therefore became valid if not contested by the legal heirs within two years. If they failed to do so, the high court appeared unconcerned that patrimonial property would pass from the kin-group as a result.

The decision of the Civil Cassation Department in *Shanshieva* v. *Lapteva* demonstrates one way in which the court expanded the power of owners to dispose of patrimonial property. Although the high court never challenged the prohibition against testamentary disposition of patrimonial property,[7] it facilitated circumvention of the law by limiting both the right to dispute an illegal bequest of such property and the period allowed for doing so. Hence the court ruled that an illegal bequest of patrimonial property could be disallowed only if contested by the legal heir. The courts by themselves could not disallow such a bequest even if they knew it to be illegal, nor could any other member of the kin-group or third party challenge it.[8] In cases involving illegal bequests, moreover, the high court adhered rigidly to the two-year period set by law for contesting wills in general, even though it had recognized in *Cherepovy* v. *Pishchevich* and elsewhere that members of the kin-group possessed an independent right to patrimonial property. By contrast, the high court normally extended to ten years the time allowed the holder of an independent property right to challenge other types of illegal bequest, most notably those attempting to control property for long periods of time.[9]

[6] *SRGKD* 1910 no. 51.

[7] e.g. see *SRGKD* 1878 no. 235.

[8] *SRGKD* 1876 no. 302, 1878 no. 60, 1880 no. 243, 1881 no. 30, 1900 no. 73, 1901 no. 105, 1906 no. 15, 1910 no. 51, and *RGKD* 1911 no. 14; but cf. *SRGKD* 1910 no. 15, where the court allowed a more distant relative who was not the direct heir to contest a will. In 1875 nos. 27 and 695 the high court even allowed illegal bequests of patrimonial property to stand when contested by the legal heirs on other grounds. See also *SZ* (1857), x, pt. 1, art. 1102 (*Prod.* 1876, art. 1012 pril.: 22; 1887, 1900 edns., art. 1066^{3}), and A. Liubavskii, 'O vneshnei forme zaveshchanii', in *Iuridicheskiia monografii i izsledovaniia* (Spb., 1867, 1875, 1878), ii. 104–8, 189–92.

[9] On the two-year period for contesting a bequest, see *SZ* (1857), x, pt. 1, art. 1098 (*Prod.* 1876, art. 1012 pril.: 35; 1887, 1900 edns., art. 1066^{12}), and *SRGKD* 1900 no. 73 and 1910

This discrepancy in the practice of the high court rested on its assessment of the different state and social interests involved in each type of case. As the court declared most forcefully in its decision in *Berkolova et al.* v. *Zakorkova* in 1913, arrangements that limited the power of an owner and the mobility of resources for long periods of time contravened state economic interests. The court therefore allowed heirs the maximum opportunity to contest such arrangements.[10] The Civil Cassation Department considered the institution of patrimonial property similarly to limit the owner, but with the legitimate objective of protecting his heirs against capricious acts. The court therefore declined to enforce the restrictions on the power of owners to dispose of such property when the person being protected failed to contest the actions of the owner. Clearly, the high court believed that two years provided sufficient time for the heir to defend his interests. After then the will of the owner should prevail.

In a similar way, the Civil Cassation Department expanded the power of owners of patrimonial property to obligate their heirs to pay legacies to third parties, giving them greater flexibility in settling their estates. The high court argued that the statutory rules restricting the testamentary power of owners of patrimonial property did not prohibit the imposition of legacies on the heirs of such property but only released the heirs from the obligation to pay a legacy that would result in the loss of this property. Hence such bequests to third parties as the right to reside in a patrimonial home or to receive periodic payments from the income of an estate were permissible because they would not result in loss of the property.[11] In its decision in *Podgornaia* v. *Serdiukov* in 1880, moreover, the high court ruled that an heir who inherited both patrimonial and acquired property had to pay all the legacies stipulated by the owner even if their total amount exceeded the value of all acquired property received.

no. 51. On the ten-year period and its application to other types of bequest, see *SZ* (1857), x, pt. 1, arts. 692, 694 prim., pril., and *SRGKD* 1891 no. 112, 1906 no. 11, and *RGKD* 1913 no. 62; see also *SRGKD* 1872 no. 1233, 1875 no. 695, 1876 no. 246, 1886 no. 20, 1900 no. 85, and 1907 no. 11, where the court extended the two-year period in cases involving other types of bequest, and 1876 no. 302, 1878 nos. 60, 138, and 1883 no. 16, where the court ruled that a person could not be deprived of an independent property right by the testamentary bequest of a person not entitled to dispose of the right.

[10] *RGKD* 1913 no. 62; for similar cases, see the references cited above in n. 9.

[11] *SRGKD* 1880 no. 1, 1899 no. 11, and 1907 no. 11. See also K. Annenkov, 'Otkazy po dukhovnym zaveshchaniiam', *ZhGiUP* (1892), 1: 58–9, K. P. Pobedonostsev, *Kurs grazhdanskago prava* (4th edn., Spb., 1896), i. 86–7, ii. 567–8, and G. F. Shershenevich, *Uchebnik russkago grazhdanskago prava* (6th edn., Spb., 1907), 775; but cf. *Pravo* (1915), 40, cols. 2510–11.

Since most heirs inherited both forms of property, this decision greatly weakened the restrictions on the disposition of patrimonial property because an heir most probably would have to use some of this property to pay the legacies bequeathed by the owner.[12] Finally, the court also held that heirs were obligated to pay promissory notes given by an owner to third parties even though he had received nothing in return and payment of the notes would result in the loss of patrimonial property.[13]

Although the decisions of the Civil Cassation Department weakened the statutory restrictions on the testamentary disposition of patrimonial property, these restrictions remained substantial. As a result, the owner of such property could more easily avoid these restrictions and arrange the devolution of his property to his heirs by transferring all or part of it to the heirs during his lifetime.[14] But this strategy involved considerable risk, since the owner lost control of the property. Moreover, if the recipients were childless and predeceased him, the property would pass to collateral heirs, thereby leaving the former owner without support. By reducing these risks, the Civil Cassation Department increased the attractiveness of using such acts as a gift, allotment, or dowry to arrange the generational transfer of patrimonial property. The high court achieved this effect by allowing an owner to impose appropriate conditions on the use and disposition of the property transferred by these means, particularly gifts, and by strengthening the right of parents to the return of property given by them to their children.[15]

[12] *SRGKD* 1878 no. 54 and 1880 no. 78.

[13] *SRGKD* 1872 no. 474. See also N. A. Poletaev, 'Darenie', *VP* (1899), 5: 99–101, and *Pravo* (1914), 5, cols. 370–1.

[14] On these means of transferring property, see *SZ* (1857), x, pt. 1, arts. 967–1009; ix, arts. 222, 550 pt. 2; and xi, pt. 2, *Ust. torg.*, arts. 1932–7. See also K. N. Annenkov, *Sistema russkago grazhdanskago prava* (2nd edn., Spb., 1912), iv. 101–20, Pobedonostsev, *Kurs*, i. 66–70, 74–7, 88–95, 371–83, and ii. 430–41, Shershenevich, *Uchebnik*, 487–94, 652–6, Poletaev, 'Darenie', K. P. Zmirlov, 'O nedostatkakh nashikh grazhdanskikh zakonov', *ZhGiUP* (1883), 9: 39–62, and 10: 47–52, N. N. Tovstoles, 'Darenie po deistvuiushchemu pravu v sviazi s proektom grazhdanskago ulozheniia', *ZhMIu* (1906), 8: 1–34, and B. Popov, 'Dogovor ob otrechenii ot nasledovaniia po russkomu pravu', *Pravo* (1912), 26, cols. 1409–15.

[15] *SRGKD* 1872 no. 872, 1873 no. 865, 1874 no. 889, 1878 no. 221, 1879 no. 178, 1886 no. 14, 1893 no. 12, 1899 no. 30, 1900 no. 8, 1901 no. 97 (on gifts); 1867 nos. 279, 314, 1869 no. 16, 1872 nos. 16, 872, 1880 no. 183, 1881 no. 3, 1893 no. 12, 1903 no. 133 (on parents' rights); and the cases reported in *SG* (1892), 28: 2–3, *Pravo* (1913), 12, cols. 754–8, and 35, cols. 2037–40, and A. E——v, 'Baryshnikovskoe nasledstvo', *MV* (1899), 326: 2, 328: 2, 330: 2, and 333: 2. See also Pobedonostsev, *Kurs*, i. 92–5, 371–2, 375, and ii. 432–3, Annenkov, *Sistema*, iv. 108, 113–14, Shershenevich, *Uchebnik*, 487–94, 652–6, Poletaev, 'Darenie', 103, Tovstoles, 'Darenie', 26, and V. L. Isachenko, 'Nasledovanie v voskhodiashchikh stepeniakh po deistvuiushchemu pravu', in *Pamiati Aleksandra Vladimirovicha Zavadskago. Sbornik statei po grazhdanskomu i torgovomu pravu i grazhdanskomu protsessu* (Kazan, 1917), 1–32.

The Civil Cassation Department also used a statutory provision regarding the renunciation of future inheritance rights to weaken the rule that limited transfer of patrimonial property via gift, allotment, or dowry to the amount due under the rules of intestate succession. Again, the high court considered the purpose of this limitation to be the protection of the interests of the heir. By renouncing the right to the inheritance, the court argued, the recipient of a gift, allotment, or dowry signified that his or her interests had been satisfied. Such a renunciation deprived both the heir and his or her own heirs of the right to contest any future disposition of patrimonial property by the owner, regardless of its legality or illegality.[16] As a result of this ruling, it became possible for an owner to control or even prevent the division of his patrimonial property by substituting capital or other acquired property for shares of a landed estate, provided that at least some of the heirs agreed to this arrangement.

The case of *Sipiagin* v. *Sipiagin* in 1899 illustrates the increased flexibility enjoyed by owners of patrimonial property as a result of the decisions of the Civil Cassation Department.[17] The decision in this case also reflects the desire of the high court to balance the freedom of an owner to dispose of his property with the right of his heirs to security. In this case, an owner had transferred his entire patrimonial estate to one son as a gift and compensated his second son with other property. The latter son in turn had formally renounced his right to any future inheritance from his father, declaring it to have been satisfied fully by this arrangement. After becoming insolvent, however, he contested the gift to his brother on the grounds that it exceeded the amount of patrimonial property due the latter by law. The Moscow Court of Appeals denied his suit.

In upholding this decision, the Civil Cassation Department restated its view that the primary purpose of the law was to protect the welfare of the heirs. The high court did acknowledge that legal heirs normally could receive a gift or allotment of patrimonial property only in an amount not exceeding that due them by law. 'However,' it continued,

[16] *SZ* (1857), x, pt. 1, arts. 998, 1002, *SRGKD* 1888 nos. 74, 91 (on the transfer of patrimonial versus acquired property); 1876 no. 280, 1879 no. 178, 1886 no. 60, 1890 no. 40, 1891 no. 82, 1894 no. 95, 1899 no. 49, 1906 no. 15, and *RGKD* 1912 no. 46, 1913 no. 72 (on renunciation); see also *SRGKD* 1888 no. 91, 1890 no. 41, and 1900 no. 8. See also I. Kharlampovich, 'Otrechenie ottsa ot nasledstva vlechet′ li za soboiu lishenie syna prava na to zhe nasledstvo?', *ZhMIu* (1900), 5: 198–215, id., 'Primenenie 1002 st. t. X ch. 1 v sviazi s poniatiem "otrechenie" ', *ZhMIu* (1901), 2: 185–91, and Shershenevich, *Uchebnik*, 653; but cf. Popov, 'Dogovor', no. 26, cols. 1410–11.

[17] *SRGKD* 1899 no. 49.

in thus limiting the freedom of an owner to dispose of patrimonial property with respect to both allotment and gift, the law pursues the same objective in both instances, which consists exclusively in protecting the private interest of the nearest heirs from the disadvantageous consequences for them of being deprived of their lawful share of patrimonial property by a one-sided, arbitrary act of the owner. Therefore, although an allotment or gift of patrimonial property made by the father in favour of one of his sons in violation of the rules cited above undoubtedly can in general be contested by the other son with respect to that part due him as his share as nearest heir, he cannot be recognized as having this right if he himself voluntarily accepted this transaction and in it renounced his right to receive patrimonial property in return for the receipt of his share from other property.[18]

In other words, the Civil Cassation Department saw no reason to enforce the statutory restrictions on the disposition of patrimonial property once the interests and welfare of the legal heirs had been secured.[19]

The Civil Cassation Department also limited the incidence of patrimonial property, thereby leaving more property under the full control of the owner, by defining certain forms of property as movable property. This classification permanently excluded a wide range of objects and property relationships from the legal restrictions imposed on patrimonial property. Owners consequently retained maximum control over the forms of property that appeared after emancipation or that grew in importance as the economy developed.[20] For example, the treatment by the high court of stocks, shares, and corporate assets in such decisions as *Ananev* v. *The St Petersburg Curtain-Lace Co.* in 1878 and *Bashkirovy* v. *Bashkirovy and Piatovaia* in 1907 enabled an owner to gain unrestricted powers of disposition over his property through incorporation or formation of a partnership. The court ruled that in such cases an owner enjoyed unlimited power to dispose of his shares in a corporation or partnership because they constituted movable property. But as manager of the partnership or corporation he also

[18] Ibid.

[19] The data in Table 6.5 provide indirect evidence that after the mid-1880s landowners especially took advantage of the opportunities created by the rulings of the high court.

[20] *SRGKD* 1869 nos. 14, 16, 816, 865, 1873 nos. 334, 1179, 1874 no. 126, 1878 nos. 81, 164, 256, 1879 nos. 178, 364, 1880 nos. 217, 302, 1881 nos. 3, 45, 1886 no. 67, 1887 no. 42, 1890 no. 19, 1893 no. 92, 1896 no. 28, 1897 no. 11, 1898 nos. 31, 99, 1899 no. 56, 1903 no. 133, and 1907 no. 61. See also *SZ* (1857), x, pt. 1, arts. 401–3, 417 (and also in 1900 edn., arts. 415, 698 pt. 10, 1238 prim. 1 and pril.); xi, pt. 2 (1903), *Ust. torg.*, arts. 59–70, and *Ust. sud. torg.*, art. 58; xvi, pt. 2, *Ust. grazh. sud.*, arts. 35, 220–2; and K. P. Zmirlov, 'Mozhet li byt′ priznana rodovym imushchestvom chast′ imushchestva torgovago doma polnago tovarishchestva, pereshedshaia posle smerti polnago tovarishcha k ego zakonnomu nasledniku, esli do smerti oznachennago tovarishcha eta chast′ ne sostavliala sobstvennosti umershago?', *ZhMIu* (1907), 7: 129–39.

possessed unrestricted power to dispose of its assets. These assets could not become patrimonial property because they were owned by a juridical person that could never be part of any kin-group. Nor did the shares become patrimonial property when transmitted by inheritance because they constituted movable, and hence always acquired, property.[21] By transferring his patrimonial property to a corporate entity, then, an owner could gain complete control over it. Not only did he enjoy greater power over his property during his lifetime, but he could also prevent its physical division in inheritance while still providing for his relatives by distributing the managerial powers and the rights of enjoyment inherent in his shares as he deemed appropriate.

By the late nineteenth century large landowners in the south-western Ukraine had begun to use incorporation to avoid the division of their agricultural and food-processing operations through inheritance.[22] Many prominent merchant and industrialist families, particularly in older industries such as textiles and food processing, also used the rulings of the high court to maintain maximum control over property while retaining it within the family group. Family members held shares in the family operations, which they could distribute to their heirs as, and on whatever terms, they chose. Although the family tried to prevent these shares from passing from its control through such devices as a right of preferential purchase, the decision of the Civil Cassation Department in *Koniukov* v. *The Iaroslavl Grand Manufacturing Co.* in 1898 shows that these efforts did not always succeed. In this decision, the high court held that the personal identity of shareholders was of no interest to a company since they possessed only a limited interest in its total assets rather than a direct interest in a specific object. Hence the court found no legal basis for limiting the disposition of shares by their owner.[23]

[21] *SRGKD* 1873 no. 1179, 1878 no. 81, 1887 no. 42, 1898 no. 31, 1899 no. 56, and 1907 no. 61. See also Zmirlov, 'Mozhet li byt'', and the references to the *SZ* cited above in n. 20.

[22] *SKhiL*, 202 (1901), 301–2, V. Ia. Laverychev, 'K voprosu ob osobennostiakh imperializma v Rossii', *Istoriia SSSR* (1971), 1: 84, and T. C. Owen, 'Entrepreneurship and the Structure of Enterprise in Russia, 1800–1880', in G. Guroff and F. V. Carstensen (eds.), *Entrepreneurship in Imperial Russia and the Soviet Union* (Princeton, NJ, 1983), 72–3. See also L. P. Minarik, *Ekonomicheskaia kharakteristika krupneishikh zemel'nykh sobstvennikov Rossii kontsa xix–nachala xx v.* (Mos., 1971), 30–6.

[23] *SRGKD* 1898 no. 31; the court distinguished a shareholder from a co-owner, who did have a direct personal interest in an object. See also the case described in P. A. Buryshkin, *Moskva kupecheskaia* (New York, 1954), 58–9, where implementation of a similar decision by the lower courts required over ten years. On use of the strategy of incorporation by merchants and industrialists, see J. A. Ruckman, *The Moscow Business Elite: A Social and Cultural Portrait of Two Generations, 1840–1905* (DeKalb, Ill., 1984), 53–4, T. C. Owen, *The Corporation under Russian Law, 1800–1917: A Study in Tsarist Economic Policy* (Cambridge,

The Civil Cassation Department further reduced the incidence of patrimonial property by narrowly defining the acts which transformed acquired into patrimonial property while broadly defining those which converted patrimonial into acquired property. For example, although patrimonial property normally retained its classification when transferred between kin, the high court used a literal reading of statutory law to rule that such property became acquired when bought by kin at public auction or inherited by a surviving spouse who happened to be kin of the deceased.[24] More importantly, the high court treated leniently attempts by owners to convert their patrimonial into acquired property through such acts of collusion with non-kin as a fictitious sale and repurchase or mortgage, foreclosure, and repurchase of their property. In such cases, the property became acquired on passing to the fictitious buyer or mortgagee, and it remained so classified when formally reacquired by the original owner.[25] By contrast, the Civil Cassation Department again used a literal interpretation of statutory law to rule that acquired property became patrimonial only when received in inheritance by the direct heir. Acquired property therefore retained its classification when bequeathed to a relative who was not the direct heir or when transferred to the direct heir by means other than inheritance. The high court even went so far as to hold that the acquired property bequeathed to the direct heir in excess of the amount due by law remained acquired.[26]

While generally applauding the restriction of patrimonial property by the Civil Cassation Department, most jurists disagreed with its ruling that property remained acquired when transferred by the owner to his

1991), 50–3, L. E. Shepelev, 'Aktsionernoe uchreditel'stvo v Rossii (istoriko-statisticheskii ocherk)', in *Iz istorii imperializma v Rossii. Akademiia Nauk SSSR. Trudy Leningradskago otdeleniia instituta istorii*, ed. M. P. Viatkin, vyp. 1 (Mos., Lenin., 1959), 135 n. 6, and I. F. Gindin, 'Russkaia burzhuaziia v period kapitalizma, ee razvitie i osobennosti', *Istoriia SSSR* (1963), 2: 63.

[24] *SRGKD* 1892 no. 80, 1905 no. 96; see also 1871 no. 1256, 1901 no. 97 (but cf. 1876 no. 246), 1905 no. 82, and 1908 no. 13.

[25] *SRGKD* 1872 no. 474, 1889 no. 83, 1896 no. 93, 1902 no. 120, 1908 no. 13; 1881 no. 187, 1890 no. 41, 1892 no. 80, 1905 no. 82 (probably fictitious acts); and 1876 no. 246 and 1906 no. 38, where the court disallowed an agreement to alter the legal classification of property. See also E——v, 'Baryshnikovskoe nasledstvo', Ia. K. Gorodyskii, 'Nashi sudy i sudebnye poriadki po dannym revisii 1895 g.', *ZhMIu* (1901), 5: 116–18, and 6: 112, and Mrts. [S. A. Muromtsev], 'Simulirovannyia sdelki kassatel'no nedvizhimykh imenii', *IuV* (1880), 5: 158–9.

[26] *SRGKD* 1867 no. 144, 1876 no. 214, 1877 nos. 168, 286, 1879 nos. 3, 58, 1880 nos. 1, 150, 183, 1892 no. 80, 1897 no. 68, 1899 no. 30, 1901 no. 97, 1902 no. 98, 1907 no. 90, and 1909 no. 20. See also Pobedonostsev, *Kurs*, i. 71–4, and Mrts. [S. A. Muromtsev], 'Kassatsionnoe reshenie po voprosu o rodovykh imushchestvakh', *IuV* (1880), 3: 560–8.

children as an allotment or dowry. The high court argued in this instance that no change took place in the character of the property because neither of these acts constituted a form of inheritance. In contrast, most jurists and often the lower courts asserted that both allotment and dowry represented an anticipated inheritance and therefore acquired property transferred in this manner became patrimonial by analogy with inheritance.[27] Although the juridical point at issue in this dispute concerned the nature of allotment and dowry, lurking behind it lay the conflict between the desire of jurists to remove allegedly outdated restrictions on proprietary power and their desire to provide adequate security for children of an owner. Denial of the tie between inheritance and allotment or dowry enabled the high court to limit the incidence of patrimonial property, whereas recognition of this tie would have strengthened the sole legal rules providing for some equity between the children of a deceased owner.

Again the Civil Cassation Department maintained its initial position until the 1880s, whereupon it reversed its decision.[28] In two decisions in 1888 the high court now argued that since property received as an allotment or dowry counted towards the share of the recipient in the future inheritance of the donor, 'an allotment of acquired property, just as an allotment of patrimonial property, acquires the significance of an anticipated inheritance, and consequently the character of property received in this manner must be determined on the same basis as if it had been received by right of legal inheritance'.[29] The court limited its new rule solely to instances of allotment and dowry, however, and in later decisions reaffirmed its earlier practice with respect to all other forms of conveyance, including gifts and testamentary bequests.[30] Depending on their objectives, parents consequently could transfer their acquired immovable property to their children with or without it becoming patrimonial.[31]

[27] The lower courts advanced the contrary argument in *SRGKD* 1879 nos. 3, 58, and 1880 no. 183; see also *ZNDGZ*, nos. 320–2. For the debate among jurists, see Annenkov, *Sistema*, iv. 109–11, Pobedonostsev, *Kurs*, i. 66–70, Shershenevich, *Uchebnik*, 134–5, 625, Liubavskii, *Iuridicheskiia monografii*, iv. 28–32. D. Dovnar-Zapol'skii, 'Prevrashchaetsia-li posredstvom vydela blagopriobretennoe imenie v rodovoe?', *ZhGiUP* (1880), 3: 106, and A. F. Brandt, 'O rodovykh imushchestvakh', *ZhGiUP* (1888), 6: 9–11.

[28] *SRGKD* 1888 nos. 74, 91; see also 1906 no. 15. Since none of the members of the court who had prepared reports for the decisions in earlier cases took part in these decisions, a change in the composition of the court may also help to explain this reversal of position.

[29] *SRGKD* 1888 no. 74.

[30] *SRGKD* 1897 no. 68, 1899 no. 30, and 1901 no. 97. For a favourable reaction of jurists to this new position, see *ZhMIu* (1900), 10: 168–9.

[31] The court explicitly recognized this ability in *SRGKD* 1874 no. 889 and 1901 no. 97. See also Pobedonostsev, *Kurs*, i. 67–8, 77.

The antipathy of the Civil Cassation Department towards the institution of patrimonial property emerged most strongly, however, in its curtailment of the right of relatives to redeem such property sold by the owner to non-kin. The high court apparently shared the view expressed by both conservative and reformist jurists that relatives used their right more for extortion and fraud than for the preservation of family property. Nor did the right appear to protect the material welfare of the heirs, which the court came to regard as the principal objective of the law. Hence the Civil Cassation Department consistently limited exercise of the right of redemption, for example by narrowly interpreting the time period within which redemption could be requested and by broadly defining the actions of a relative that signified agreement to a sale and thereby barred redemption. The high court also treated leniently the various fictitious acts through which purchasers of patrimonial property might protect their investment.[32] But the court limited exercise of the right of redemption most extensively, and controversially, by defining 'settled' and 'unsettled' land so that all rural land in post-emancipation Imperial Russia eventually became classified legally as 'unsettled', which by law could not be redeemed if sold to a member of a different social estate than the seller.[33]

The Civil Cassation Department first formulated its doctrine on unsettled land and redemption in 1869 and adhered strictly to its position thereafter. The doctrine attracted a storm of criticism from conservative political writers and noble landowners, especially in the reactionary years after 1881. Its most serious legal challenge, however, occurred in the Nazimov case in 1900.[34] The petitioner, Guards Lieutenant P. I. Nazimov, sought to redeem 274 desiatin of patrimonial land in Tver province, which his brother had sold to a *meshchanin* named Chukhlin. Following the

[32] *SRGKD* 1882 no. 48, 1905 no. 82, and *RGKD* 1913 no. 31 (limitations of right); *SRGKD* 1891 no. 40, 1903 no. 52, 1904 no. 12, 1906 no. 17, and 1907 no. 90 (fictitious acts). See also *ZNDGZ*, nos. 720–5, Shershenevich, *Uchebnik*, 343, 351, 353 ff., and Mrts. [Muromtsev], 'Simulirovannyia sdelki'.

[33] *SZ* (1857), x, pt. 1, art. 1350. When deciding cases of redemption, the high court also defined social estates in the way that minimized exercise of the right. *SRGKD* 1903 nos. 52, 62, 75, and *RGKD* 1911 no. 40.

[34] On the Nazimov case, see *NV* (1899), 8361: 4, (1900), 8600: 5, 8624: 2, 8630: 2, and (1901), 9194: 2, and *MV* (1899), 129: 5, (1900), 117: 2, 131: 2, and 340: 2; on the practice of the high court, see *SRGKD* 1869 no. 138, 1870 no. 772, 1895 no. 59, 1900 no. 11, and 1904 no. 88. For conservative criticism of this practice, see the references cited above on the Nazimov case and *Grazhdanin* (1900), 18: 8, and 20: 13, P. N. Tsertelev, 'Podderzhanie dvorianskago zemlevladeniia i zapovednost′ imenii', *MV* (1897), 110: 2, 111: 2, and 112: 2, P. [A. D. Pazukhin?], 'Zapovednyia imeniia', *MV* (1889), 26: 2, and 31: 2, and TsGIA F. 1233 op. 1 d. 99 ll. 13–19 (p. 13), 20, 21–6 (pp. 5–6), F. 1664 op. 1 d. 126 ll. 213–14, and F. 1283 op. 1 d. 26 ll. 156, 171–3, 199–205 (pp. 2–3).

previous decisions of the high court, Nazimov argued that the presence first of serfs, and then of temporarily obligated peasants, had distinguished settled from unsettled land. The emancipation, and then in 1881 the mandatory termination of the temporarily obligated status of former serfs, therefore had eliminated the category of settled land. But then extending the reasoning of the Civil Cassation Department, Nazimov asserted that the category of unsettled land also had become meaningless at this point and therefore land was no longer legally either settled or unsettled. Nazimov referred to a number of government proclamations after 1861 that appeared to support his contention. He then argued, accurately, that the restriction of the right to redeem unsettled land had been introduced in the early nineteenth century to enable non-nobles to acquire land from the nobility.[35] The rule made sense prior to emancipation because restrictions on the ownership of settled land still protected noble patrimonies. But it had lost its historical justification after emancipation and therefore should lapse. Otherwise, Nazimov concluded, noble landowners would be left with no means for protecting their hereditary estates.

Although the Civil Cassation Department did not include the Nazimov case in its published decisions, it responded to his arguments in its decision in the Shcherbacheva case in the same year.[36] The high court agreed that the category of settled land had disappeared because the object of the category, land inhabited by serfs, had ceased to exist. But the court then asserted that the category of unsettled land had not been abolished by any legislative act nor had the rule restricting redemption of such property been repealed. The court therefore had to decide whether land remaining at the complete disposition of owners after the termination of all dependent relations with former serfs was subject to the rule restricting the right of redemption. Answering this question, the Civil Cassation Department declared that

> the unsettled lands not subject to redemption in the event of their sale to a person of another social estate are lands on which no peasants who have dependent relations with the owner are settled. The lands referred to in the [statute], that is estates which have lost the characteristic of settled [estates] as a consequence of

[35] Nazimov referred to *SZ* (1899), ix, art. 88 prim., pril., and x, pt. 1 (1887, 1900), art. 385 prim., which were based primarily on *2PSZ* xxxvi (1861), pt. 1, no. 36674, pp. 399–402, and xxxvii (1862), pt. 1, no. 38214, pp. 372–3, and to *3PSZ* xix (1899), pt. 1, no. 16949, sect. iv, p. 528. For the original legislation, see *1PSZ* xxvi (1801), no. 20075, pp. 862–3, and M. F. Vladimirskii-Budanov, *Obzor istorii russkago prava* (6th edn., Spb., Kiev), 586–7.

[36] *SRGKD* 1900 no. 11.

the collapse of the above-mentioned substantive and sole characteristic of the so-called 'state of being settled', that is the settling on them of peasants who are dependent on the owner, seem now to be indistinguishable from the 'unsettled' lands referred to in article 1350, and as a result in all respects must be considered as having entered this category, without any necessity of their being so reclassified by a special act of law. Hence this article, which previously related to a particular part of all lands in general, has now acquired the significance of a general rule for all lands.[37]

The court added consolingly that its decision did not eliminate the right of redemption, but merely limited its exercise.

Given the thrust of its practice on this issue, the decision of the Civil Cassation Department in the Schmidt case in 1881 is difficult to explain.[38] The nobleman Baron Vasilii Schmidt had petitioned the court to redeem a house in the city of St Petersburg which the guardians of his niece had sold to a peasant named Aleksei Kornilov. Despite Kornilov's references to previous decisions of the high court, both the St Petersburg District Court and the Court of Appeals granted the petition on the grounds that the categories of settled and unsettled land applied only to rural property. Hence the restriction on the redemption of unsettled land did not apply to urban property. The Civil Cassation Department upheld this decision, arguing that although the right of redemption applied to patrimonial property owned by people of any social estate, the rule restricting this right had been introduced to allow non-nobles to acquire rural realty. The restriction therefore did not apply to urban realty, which consequently could be redeemed even when the seller and buyer belonged to different social estates. Taken in conjunction with its other decisions, the ruling of the high court meant that while the landed nobility had been largely deprived of the right to redeem patrimonial estates, urban property owners could exercise this right without restriction. This turn of events understandably incensed conservative writers, who accused the courts of purposely undermining noble landownership.[39]

37 Ibid.

38 *SRGKD* 1881 no. 136; see also 1900 no. 11 and *RGKD* 1911 no. 40.

39 See the references cited above in n. 34. Although after emancipation a substantial amount of rural land changed hands within the nobility, most transactions appear to have been between persons belonging to different social estates, and most of the land sold was to buyers who belonged to a different estate than the seller. V. V. Sviatlovskii, *Mobilizatsiia zemel'noi sobstvennosti v Rossii (1861–1908 g.)* (2nd edn., Spb., 1911), 93–5, 107–8, 115–16, and P. I. Liashchenko, 'Mobilizatsiia zemlevladeniia v Rossii', *RM* (1904), 1: 54, and table IV, p. 52.

Expanding Testamentary Power

In the case of patrimonial property, the Civil Cassation Department limited and redefined a long-standing legal institution that was treated extensively in statutory law. The high court faced a different problem with respect to testamentary power: the need to develop a body of law where the statutes were relatively silent. Statutory law provided detailed rules for the composition of wills in order to ensure their authenticity. It likewise extensively restricted testamentary power in order to preserve patrimonial property within the kin-group and to limit the transfer of resources to the church. On the content of testamentary power, however, statutory law said little save that, with a few exceptions, acquired property could be disposed of by will and property could be bequeathed in ownership or in possession and use. Precisely what rights and powers could be granted, to whom, under what conditions, with what obligations, and for what period of time remained unspecified.[40]

This lack of definition led to many, often sharp disputes among Russian jurists over the extent of testamentary power under Imperial law. In these disputes, the strong influence of categories and concepts derived from Roman law and from European civilian jurisprudence was evident. Jurisprudential orientation, personal concepts of equity and of the general spirit of Imperial law, and ideological perspective also shaped the position of each author. But in the end, the Civil Cassation Department determined the effective extent of testamentary power. In doing so, it again tended to maximize the power and flexibility enjoyed by owners, not infrequently despite the predominance of contrary views in juridical literature.

The Civil Cassation Department began from the proposition that a will constituted merely the distribution of property by an owner in the event of his death. Hence, in the case of the heir by will, the high court appeared to reject the Roman law and civilian concept of universal succession, according to which the heirs took the place of the deceased and succeeded to the totality of his property rights and obligations. In practice, this understanding of succession tended to limit the testamentary power of an

[40] For references to statutory law and to prerevolutionary secondary literature, see above, Ch. 6 n. 10. For surveys of the law written prior to the judicial reform, see P. V. Polezhaev, 'O zaveshchaniiakh', *Arkhiv istoricheskikh i prakticheskikh svedenii, otnosiashchikhsia do Rossii* (1859), 1: 21–104, N. Sbitnev, 'O dukhovnykh zaveshchaniiakh po russkomu pravu', *ZhMIu*, 8 (1861), 181–244, A. Lukanin, *Svod vsekh neobkhodimykh uzakonenii o dukhovnykh zaveshchaniiakh* (Kiev, 1865), and the relevant sections of the works by Kranikhfeld, Nevolin, and Meier discussed above in Ch. 7.

owner by the ownership rights of his successors, regardless of whether the latter were determined by law or appointed by will.[41] In contrast, the Civil Cassation Department held that since '[a] will is nothing other than a grant to the heir to enjoy the inheritance left by the testator not on the basis of the law, but on the basis of the special dispositions made by the testator', the beneficiary of a will acquired only the rights and powers assigned specifically by the owner.[42] This approach led the high court to allow nearly any testamentary provision, under whatever terms or conditions, that was not prohibited specifically by statutory law. As it declared in its decision in *Kikiny* v. *Shirov* in 1875, 'instances in which the freedom of action of the testator is limited are an exception from the general rule granting discretion to the owners of the property bequeathed when making testamentary dispositions and are defined positively by law'.[43] Since statutory law contained few such limitations, the illegality in principle of most types of testamentary bequests became difficult to prove.

The apparent unwillingness of the Civil Cassation Department to admit the principle of universal succession into Imperial law, as many Russian jurists advocated, was stated most forcefully in its decision in *Sergeev* v. *The Executors of the Will of Z. Shibalkin* in 1870.[44] In his will, Shibalkin had directed his executors to use most of his property for charitable works. But he had failed to mention all his property in his will, including several bank certificates worth a considerable sum. Shibalkin's legal heir, A. Shibalkina, on her death had bequeathed her right to the inheritance to a peasant named Vasilii Sergeev. He in turn had brought suit against the executors of Shibalkin's will for ownership of the bank

[41] On the concept of universal succession in Roman law, see B. Nicholas, *An Introduction to Roman Law* (Oxford, 1962), 235–43, 258–64. Although influenced strongly by this concept, the law in European civilian jurisdictions varied substantially as a result of different historical conditions and cultural traditions. In all cases, however, it was more complex and defined more extensively than Imperial Russian statutory law.

[42] *SRGKD* 1881 no. 16.

[43] *SRGKD* 1875 no. 429; see also 1868 no. 110, 1869 nos. 816, 1334, 1870 no. 917, 1871 no. 274, 1874 no. 583, 1875 nos. 91, 429, 1876 nos. 302, 460, 1878 nos. 60, 138, 274, 1880 no. 56, 1881 nos. 16, 131, 1888 no. 63, 1901 no. 111, 1902 nos. 104, 112, 1903 no. 28, 1904 no. 85, and 1906 no. 88.

[44] *SRGKD* 1870 no. 917. For arguments by jurists in favour of universal succession, see Zmirlov, 'O nedostatkakh' (1883), 10: 52–3, 78–80, P. I. Beliaev, 'Istoricheskiia osnovy i iuridicheskaia priroda sovremennago russkago zaveshchaniia', *ZhMIu* (1903), 5: 103 ff., and 6: 60–5, N. N. Tovstoles, 'Svoboda zaveshchatel'noi voli po russkomu pravu v razlichnye periody ego razvitiia', *ZhMIu* (1902), 8: 108–9, V. G. Demchenko, *Sushchestvo nasledstva i priznanie k nasledovaniiu po russkomu pravu* (Kiev, 1877), 1–25, and L. Rudnev, *O dukhovnykh zaveshchaniiakh po russkomu grazhdanskomu pravu v istoricheskom razvitii* (Kiev, 1894), 181–2.

certificates and the other property not mentioned in the will. Sergeev argued that any acquired property of an owner not specifically disposed of in his will remained outside the will and therefore passed to the heirs by law.

Although the St Petersburg District Court had found for Sergeev, the Court of Appeals reversed this decision. Reflecting the influence of the concept of universal succession, the court argued that the very act of making a will signified that the owner intended to dispose of all of his acquired property by these means. It concluded that, unless an owner specifically excluded property from his will, all of his acquired property passed to the executors of his will for disposition in accordance with his directions, and therefore no property remained to be inherited by the legal heir.

Setting this decision aside, the Civil Cassation Department asserted that under Imperial law a will concerned solely the distribution of property and not the appointment of an heir. The high court then stated that although an owner could distribute all of his acquired property by will, he need not do so. The courts therefore could not assume that by itself the act of composing a will implied the intention of an owner to dispose of all of his acquired property. The Civil Cassation Department concluded that only the property mentioned specifically in a will came under its provisions, while any property not mentioned passed to the heirs by law.[45] Developing this line of reasoning still further in its decision in *Gladilina* v. *Gladilin* in 1903, the high court ruled that an owner could not formally disinherit a legal heir.[46] Hence only the law, not an owner, could create or eliminate the right of inheritance. The court added, however, that an owner could prevent his legal heirs from inheriting any of his acquired property by bequeathing all of it to other people.

But the position of the Civil Cassation Department was more complicated than appears at first glance. Although the high court ruled consistently that an owner could not create an heir through his will, it still had to define the status of the beneficiary of a bequest. Again, Imperial statutory law said nothing on this subject. In particular, the responsibility of the beneficiary for the debts and other obligations of the deceased remained unclear. The only rule of relevance concerned the heirs by law, who upon accepting an inheritance became liable for the debts and obligations of the deceased regardless of whether they exceeded the total

[45] *SRGKD* 1870 no. 917; see also 1874 no. 583, 1902 no. 104, and 1903 no. 28.

[46] *SRGKD* 1903 no. 28; see also 1868 no. 25, 1874 no. 583, 1881 no. 16, and 1902 no. 104.

value of the estate.[47] Interpreted literally, and in conjunction with the finding of the high court that the beneficiary of a will was not an heir, this rule would cause the legal heirs to bear a disproportionate responsibility for the debts of the deceased. If treated like the recipient of a gift, the beneficiaries of a will would have no liability for these debts; otherwise, their liability would be limited to the value of the bequest. In the former instance, the property bequeathed also might elude the creditors of the deceased, thereby opening the door to fraud. To avoid these results, in cases involving responsibility for the debts of the deceased the Civil Cassation Department deviated from its general position and defined the beneficiary of a will as an heir. Hence in its decision in *Saltykova* v. *The Executor of the Will of Hereditary Honoured Citizen Butorin* in 1868 the court declared that

> [a] person receiving property by testamentary disposition enters into possession of this property in the capacity of the heir of the testator. With the realization of the right of inheritance the heir, having become the owner of the property included in the inheritance, simultaneously accepts responsibility for the obligations incumbent on it in proportion to the share of the inheritance received, and in the event of its insufficiency, is responsible even with his own property.[48]

From its inception, then, the Civil Cassation Department adopted a contradictory but workable definition of the beneficiary of a will. When determining the testamentary power of an owner, the high court compared the beneficiary of a will with the recipient of a gift. Hence a beneficiary held the property bequeathed only under the conditions stipulated by the deceased and failure to fulfil these conditions caused the loss of the right to this property. When determining liability for the debts and obligations of the deceased, however, the court considered the beneficiary to be one of the heirs and therefore proportionately liable for these debts even

[47] *SZ* (1857), x, pt. 1, art. 1259; see also arts. 112, 566, 1000 prim., 1009 prim., 1104, 1255, 1257–8, 1262, 1268, 1298, 1329–30, 1543–4; x, pt. 2, *Zak. sud. grazh.*, arts. 214, 2268–76; xi, pt. 2, *Ust. kred.*, arts. 90, 149, 286–7, 292, 357–8, 659, 760, 1199, 1271, and *Ust. torg.*, arts. 154, 159–63, 166, 1932–7, 1950; xv, *Ulozh. nak.*, art. 61; *Ustav grazh. sud.* (1866), arts. 457–8; and *Ustav ugol. sud.* (1866), art. 18. This extended liability resembled the position of the heirs in the Roman and civilian system of universal succession and may in fact have entered Imperial law only as a result of borrowing from French law by the editors of the *Digest of Laws*. See N. N. Tovstoles, 'Otvetstvennost′ naslednika pered kreditorami voobshche i pered legatariem v chastnosti', *ZhMIu* (1915), 7: 77–81, 89, Beliaev, 'Istoricheskiia osnovy', 6: 25 ff., and Rudnev, *O dukhovnykh zaveshchniiakh*, 171–81. Unlike Roman or civilian law (Nicholas, *Roman Law*, 239–41), Imperial law provided no formal mechanism to enable an heir to assess the net value of an estate before accepting it, except in the case of merchants. But the Civil Cassation Department allowed such an assessment to be made in practice. *SRGKD* 1890 no. 22.

[48] *SRGKD* 1868 no. 777.

beyond the value of the bequest.[49] Although criticized by jurists for being theoretically inconsistent, this position safeguarded the interests of all parties involved in an inheritance while maximizing the testamentary power of owners.

The Civil Cassation Department similarly increased the testamentary power of owners in several other ways. Clarifying previously uncertain points, for example, the high court held that an owner could revoke a will and could include in it any property acquired after its composition.[50] Equally importantly, the court ruled that an owner could bequeath numerous combinations of rights and powers, each hedged with limitations and conditions. Hence it became possible to assign various rights and powers over the same property to different people in order to achieve a variety of objectives and to provide for multiple contingencies. In this way, more easily and securely than before, an owner could reconcile considerations of economic need, family continuance, and social status with the desire to secure the welfare of individual family members by separating the management of a property from the enjoyment of its income and assigning each to different parties.[51]

The decisions of the Civil Cassation Department in *Chernov* v. *Chernov* in 1879 and *Novitskaia* v. *Filimonov* in 1881 illustrate the kind of flexibility now enjoyed by an owner.[52] In the first case, the merchant D. Chernov

[49] *SRGKD* 1868 no. 25, 1869 no. 816, 1870 no. 1856, 1871 nos. 863, 945, 1872 nos. 643, 863, 1873 no. 1074, 1874 no. 583, 1875 nos. 302, 322, 1073, 1876 no. 460, 1879 no. 27, 1880 no. 70, 1881 nos. 16, 62, 131, 1882 nos. 63, 83, 1886 no. 23, 1904 no. 85, 1907 no. 26, 1908 no. 77 (on testamentary conditions); 1868 nos. 610, 777, 1871 nos. 392, 675, 781, 1872 no. 624, 1875 no. 91, 1877 no. 373, 1878 no. 274, 1879 no. 294, 1907 no. 11, and 1909 no. 40 (on liability for debt). For criticisms by jurists, see Beliaev, 'Istoricheskiia osnovy', 5: 103 ff., and 6: 25 ff., 60–5, Tovstoles, 'Svoboda', 108–9, Rudnev, *O dukhovnykh zaveshchaniiakh*, 179–82, and Zmirlov, 'O nedostatkakh' (1883), 10: 68–70.

[50] *SRGKD* 1899 no. 66, 1904 no. 85 (revocability); 1870 no. 917, 1872 no. 624, 1875 nos. 27, 429, 1876 no. 302, 1877 nos. 191, 289, 291, 1878 nos. 169, 274 (ambulatory nature of wills); see also 1869 no. 72, 1875 nos. 199, 854, 1882 no. 83, 1883 no. 16, 1888 no. 63, and 1899 no. 66. See also Beliaev, 'Istoricheskiia osnovy', 5: 74–5, 79–81, 85–102, and Zmirlov, 'O nedostatkakh' (1883), 10: 54–5, 79–80.

[51] *SRGKD* 1869 nos. 816, 1334, 1870 no. 1856, 1871 no. 643, 1874 nos. 155, 583, 709, 1879 no. 205, and 1881 no. 116. The high court granted owners similarly broad power with respect to gifts and, to a lesser extent, allotment and dowry. See *SZ* (1857), x, pt. 1, arts. 975–7, *SRGKD* 1871 no. 333, 1872 no. 765, 1873 no. 865, 1874 no. 179, 1876 nos. 134, 299, 1878 no. 221, 1879 no. 178, 1886 no. 14, 1894 no. 95, 1899 nos. 30, 49, and 1904 no. 7, and *Pravo* (1912), 11, cols. 633–6, and (1914), 5, cols. 571–3; see also Pobedonostsev, *Kurs*, i. 92–5, 371–2, 375, ii. 432–3, Annenkov, *Sistema*, iv. 108, 113–14, Shershenevich, *Uchebnik*, 487–94, 652–6, Poletaev, 'Darenie', 103, and Tovstoles, 'Darenie', 26; for contrary views, see Liubavskii, *Iuridicheskiia monografii*, iii. 398–400, iv. 28–32, *ZNDGZ*, nos. 483, 491, and 'Po povodu odnogo sudebnago resheniia', *SG* (1892), 28: 2–3.

[52] *SRGKD* 1879 no. 205 and 1881 no. 116.

had bequeathed his trading and manufacturing enterprises to his ten grandsons equally in ownership. But to ensure the growth and tranquil operation of these enterprises, he had granted the eldest grandson sole rights of management and disposition with respect to commercial matters. In upholding the legality of this arrangement, the high court argued that the eldest grandson managed the property as a co-owner who enjoyed greater rights of disposition than the other co-owners but who none the less remained accountable to them for his actions.

In the second case, the merchant Maksim Vinogradov had bequeathed most of his property, including a factory, to the minor children of his deceased son Nikolai. Vinogradov had also directed his executor, Feodor Filimonov, to manage all commercial and manufacturing operations during the minority of the grandchildren and to use the resulting income to provide for their support and education and for the maintenance of their mother. She had brought suit for control of the estate, even though its value had doubled in six years under Filimonov's management, on the grounds that the rights of management and disposition could not be separated from that of ownership. Nor, she contended, could an executor be given such broad and undefined powers of management as those assigned to Filimonov. Both the Ekaterinburg District Court and the Kazan Court of Appeals had denied the suit.[53]

In upholding these decisions, the Civil Cassation Department articulated a doctrine of management that gave owners broad power to settle their property in an equitable yet economically efficient manner by separating the power to manage property from the right to enjoy its income. According to the high court, ownership consisted of the rights to use, possess, and dispose of property. The power of management by itself therefore was not a constituent part of ownership but was only realized through the exercise of these other rights. Hence, the court argued, the assignment of powers of management in a will constituted only an allocation of narrowly defined powers by the owner for the achievement of particular objectives and not the grant of a separate property right. Not having an independent property right, the recipient of managerial powers was bound by the will of the deceased and therefore could take only those actions necessary for its fulfilment. Moreover, the court continued,

> if on the one hand the testator has the right to express his will on the form of use and management of the property bequeathed for the course of a specified period, and on the other hand the testator can lay the execution of his will as expressed

[53] *SRGKD* 1881 no. 116.

> in his testament not on the heir but on an executor, then it is impossible not to recognize the right of the testator to entrust the temporary management of property to the executor, despite the grant in the will of ownership to the heir designated. Managing the property, the executor remains only the executor of the will of the testator . . . until the factual transfer of property to the heir in agreement with the testamentary disposition.[54]

Since elsewhere the Civil Cassation Department had ruled that the rights of an heir could be limited for his entire life, its decision in this case enabled an owner to establish a trust in favour of his heirs or other beneficiaries for at least one generation and possibly even longer.[55]

The doctrine of management formulated in the above decision underlay the treatment by the Civil Cassation Department of the contentious issues of conditional ownership and the validity of bequests to persons yet unborn. Imperial statutory law ignored both subjects. In the absence of any statutory guidance, most Russian jurists employed a concept of absolute and unlimited ownership derived from civilian jurisprudence to deny the legality of either conditional ownership or a bequest to a person who was not alive when a will took effect.[56] In a particularly controversial and well-publicized case in 1870, the lower courts also had followed this line of reasoning in disallowing testamentary provisions granting Count Zubov the right to use and possess a large amount of property for his lifetime. At his death ownership of the property was to lie either with any offspring born to the still childless count or, in their absence, with the already living children of a certain Sazonov. Both the lower courts and juristic commentators considered these arrangements to be invalid because unconditional ownership had to vest immediately in some living person. It therefore was impossible to await either the death of Zubov or the possible birth of his children to determine ownership. Some jurists then argued that the illegality of the bequest to Zubov's still unborn children invalidated the bequest to the Sazonov children and therefore

[54] Ibid.

[55] *SRGKD* 1868 no. 25, 1875 no. 322, 1890 no. 42, 1892 no. 76; on management, see also 1875 nos. 27, 322, and 1902 no. 104. For the rules regulating life tenancies in the absence of more specific instructions from the testator, see *SZ* (1857), x, pt. 1, arts. 533^{1}–533^{13}, 1692^{1}, which the high court extended to all life tenancies in *SRGKD* 1878 no. 7 and 1879 no. 248 (these decisions reversed 1867 no. 275); see also 1892 no. 11.

[56] Under Roman and civilian law, the rights, powers, and immunities composing ownership tend to be much less divisible or separable than in Anglo-American law. See Nicholas, *Roman Law*, 129–30, 153–7, 242–3, the intro. by O. Kahn-Freund to K. Renner, *The Institutions of Private Property and their Social Functions* (London, 1949), 17–24, and C. R. Noyes, *The Institution of Property: A Study of the Development, Substance and Arrangement of the System of Property in Modern Anglo-American Law* (New York, 1936), esp. 517–21.

unlimited ownership of the property should pass immediately to Zubov. In contrast, other jurists contended that the Sazonov children should receive immediate and unlimited ownership because the bequest to Zubov's unborn children was illegal and the count himself had received only the limited right of use.[57]

The St Petersburg Court of Appeals avoided ruling on the legal issues raised by this case by holding that Countess Zubova had bequeathed the property to her son in ownership rather than in use. Any further arrangements concerning the property therefore were invalid. But statements by the court in this case and in an earlier decision suggest that it had interpreted the contents of the will in this way in order to achieve what it considered to be the most equitable result. Had Zubov received only the right of use, the court argued, ownership of the property would have vested immediately and unconditionally in the Sazonov children, thereby frustrating the intentions of the countess and unjustly depriving any future grandchildren of their rights.[58]

Because the court of appeals had framed its decision as an interpretation of the substantive content of the will, the Civil Cassation Department could not rule on the main points of law raised by the Zubov case. But in its decision in *Bek and Bek* v. *Bloss, Schitz and Muirstedt* in 1875, the high court defied dominant legal opinion and introduced the principle of conditional ownership into Imperial law.[59] In her will, G. Bek had instructed that all her property be held in trust for her two daughters until both attained the age of majority, with the income of the property in the

[57] *SRGKD* 1870 no. 1856. That the bequest to a conditional beneficiary as yet unborn particularly troubled the court of appeals is suggested by its decisions in 1868 no. 25 and 1875 no. 1073, where this issue did not arise and the court appeared open to a more liberal interpretation of the other points of law raised by the case. For discussions of the Zubov case see *MV* (1869), 90: 1, 115: 1–2, and 273: 3, N. Sokolovskii, 'Iuridicheskiia zametki', *SVed* (1869), 159: 1–2, A. N. Unkovskii [plaintiff's attorney], 'Eshche neskol'ko zamechanii po povodu dukhovnago zaveshchaniia grafini Zubovoi', *Sovremennaia Letopis'* (1869), 23: 14–16, P. Vel'iashev [guardian of Sazonov children], 'Pis'mo k izdateliam', *MV* (1869), 99: 3, A. Ostriakov [Zubov's attorney], 'Vozrazhenie na stat'iu v No. 90-m Moskovskikh vedomostei po povodu dela o dukhovnom zaveshchanii grafini Zubovoi', *MV* (1869), 115: 3, Pobedonostsev, *Kurs*, ii. 584–8, 658–60, N. Moiseenko, 'O substitutsii v zaveshchanii po russkomu polozhitel'nomu pravu', *Izvestiia i uchenyia zapiski Imp. Kazanskago Universiteta* (1874), 5: 787–8, and Liubavskii, 'O vneshnei forme', 192–202.

[58] In *SRGKD* 1870 no. 1856 the court of appeals required a specific statement in the will granting limited rights for life, whereas in 1868 no. 25 it had argued that such a bequest could be inferred from the general content of the will.

[59] *SRGKD* 1875 no. 1073. On this question in general, in addition to the references cited above in n. 57 see V. N. Nikol'skii, *Ob osnovnykh momentakh nasledovaniia* (Mos., 1871), 183–95, 203–4, Shershenevich, *Uchebnik*, 707–9, and P. N. Gussakovskii, 'Nasledstvennoe pravo po proektu Grazhdanskago Ulozheniia', *ZhMIu* (1903), 9: 40–4.

interim being used for the support and education of the girls. Bek also had stipulated that if both daughters died before their twenty-first birthday, the bulk of her estate was to pass to her sister B. Bloss, with smaller bequests going to her mother, B. Schitz, her brother-in-law, Nikolai Bek, and the manager of her commercial operations, F. Muirstedt. After the death of both daughters prior to the age of 21, Bek's two brothers-in-law, Nikolai and Andrei Bek, contested the provisions of the will that concerned this eventuality. Following the reasoning of the St Petersburg Court of Appeals in the Zubov case, the Beks argued that the daughters had acquired unconditional, albeit temporarily limited, ownership of the property bequeathed by their mother at the moment her will had taken effect. Any further disposition of the property under the will therefore was invalid and the property should pass to the plaintiffs as the legal heirs of Bek's daughters. No doubt much to the surprise of the Beks, the St Petersburg Court of Appeals now reversed its position on the question of conditional ownership and denied their suit.

In upholding this decision, the Civil Cassation Department ruled that statutory law allowed an owner to bequeath his acquired property unconditionally or conditionally either in ownership or in limited possession and use. Hence the law did not preclude a bequest of ownership that was conditional on some future event. The identity of the unconditional owner of the property need not be known immediately, the high court argued, as long as the property was not left unmanaged (*bezkhoziainoe*). Although the court had yet to define precisely what it meant by 'management', it implied that a manager was someone who possessed sufficient power over the property to look after it and to ensure its legal defence until the requisite event had determined unconditional ownership and the owner himself could perform these actions. The Civil Cassation Department concluded that in this case the rights of possession and use held by the daughters provided sufficient management of the estate to support the bequest of conditional ownership.[60]

The Civil Cassation Department likewise defied dominant legal opinion by allowing bequests to beneficiaries not yet born at the time a will took effect. Although the high court first established this principle in its decision in *Shilovy* v. *Rusanova* in 1873, it formulated its position most clearly in its decision in *Shulman and Meniaevy* v. *Kolontarov* in 1888.[61]

[60] *SRGKD* 1875 no. 1073; see also 1882 no. 63, 1888 no. 63, 1901 nos. 52, 111, and 1908 no. 77.

[61] *SRGKD* 1873 no. 1530, 1888 no. 63; see also 1875 no. 1073, 1882 no. 63, 1901 no. 52, and 1908 no. 77. For the views of jurists, in addition to the references cited above in nn. 57

In this case, commercial councillor and honoured citizen Petr Meniaev had bequeathed the use, possession, and income from his commercial operations in St Petersburg to his youngest son Nikolai for life, with ownership passing to the surviving children of Nikolai at his own death. After the death of Nikolai, the creditor of one of his children, his surviving children, and the heirs of his deceased children each put forward competing claims for the property. The creditor sought to exclude most of the children by arguing that an heir had to be alive at the time a will took effect, and therefore only those children who had both been born prior to the death of Petr Meniaev and survived their father Nikolai had a right to the inheritance. The surviving children each claimed an equal share of the estate on the grounds that under the terms of the will all of the grandchildren of Petr Meniaev who had survived their father possessed an equal right to the inheritance regardless of when they had been born. The heirs of the deceased children argued that only those children who were alive at the time Petr Meniaev had died had a right to his estate, irrespective of which of them survived their father Nikolai. Both the St Petersburg District Court and Court of Appeals agreed with this last position and ruled accordingly.

In setting this decision aside, the Civil Cassation Department ruled that the conditional beneficiary of a will need not be alive at the time the will took effect. The high court therefore found the court of appeals to have erred in excluding some of the grandchildren of Petr Meniaev from his inheritance solely on the grounds that they had not been born prior to his death. The court then added that

> [w]hereas . . . it is clear that the will of the testator concerning acquired property is not subject to any limitations in so far as it does not contravene the law, the owner of acquired property can dispose of it freely and without constraint . . . the designation by the testator of his heir under a suspensive condition [a condition that delays vesting of a right until the occurrence of a future event], dependent upon a time or obligations indicated in the will, is neither prohibited by nor contravenes any law; consequently, even a person not yet born, but living by the occurrence of a particular time or event, can be designated as heir . . . having granted his property in possession for life, the testator therefore is not deprived of the right to make the determination of his heir dependent on the death of the life tenant and to bequeath his property in ownership to the surviving children of

and 59 see Sbitnev, 'O dukhovnykh zaveshchaniiakh', 193–4, Demchenko, *Sushchestvo*, 82–5, V. L. Isachenko, 'Zaveshchatel'nyia rasporiazheniia uslovnyia. Podnaznachenie', *Pravo* (1911), 1, cols. 15–16, and A. A. Bashmakov, *Ocherki prava rodovogo, nasledstvennago i obychnago* (Spb., 1911), 123–35.

the latter, even though they were not born by the death of the testator. Such a will does not contravene [the law], for the persons to whom the estate is bequeathed are designated exactly, the life tenant is indicated, and the owners are defined in the person of his children at the moment the life tenancy terminates; the estate itself does not remain unmanaged from the death of the testator, [as] it is in the possession and use of the life tenant, and the right of ownership belongs from the very death of the testator to precisely designated persons, however only under a suspensive condition, with the occurrence of which the identity of the designated owners must be revealed.[62]

This ruling increased substantially the testamentary power of owners by enabling them to control the devolution and use of their property for several generations through bequests of life estates, with conditional ownership passing to heirs still to be born. The rights of use and possession enjoyed by the conditional owners then could be restricted for their entire lifetime.

Throughout its existence, the Civil Cassation Department thus constantly expanded the testamentary power of owners. This policy reflected both the principle of individual ownership that underlay most juridical writing on property law and the belief common among jurists that extensive testamentary power best served state, social, and family interests by enabling owners to settle their property in the most equitable and economically efficient manner. Indeed, the only significant limitation imposed on testamentary power by the high court arose from both its concern with state economic interests and its conception of ownership.

Believing the immobility of property for long periods of time both to be contrary to state economic interests and to violate the ownership rights of the heir, the Civil Cassation Department built from an extremely vague statutory reference a strict rule of law that might be called the 'Russian rule against perpetuities'.[63] Under this rule, no testamentary bequest, limitation, or other provision could extend beyond the combined lives of any life tenants and the original heirs in ownership, i.e. normally

[62] *SRGKD* 1888 no. 63. Roman and European civilian law allowed both conditional bequests and bequests of limited rights and established detailed rules to govern testamentary provisions of either type. See Nicholas, *Roman Law*, 242–3, 258–70, and Kahn-Freund, intro. to Renner, *Institutions*, 17–24.

[63] *SZ* (1857), x, pt. 1, art. 1011 prim. To prevent the permanent or excessively long immobility of property, the 'rule against perpetuities' in English law forbids any disposition that postpones the absolute vesting of property beyond the life or lives of any number of persons alive at the time of the disposition and a further period of twenty-one years. See A. W. B. Simpson, *An Introduction to the History of the Land Law* (Oxford, 1961), 195–8, 204–17, 239–40. On the efforts of Roman law to avoid this problem, see Nicholas, *Roman Law*, 268–9.

no more than three generations. Nor was any form of perpetual or hereditary right of use to be allowed. The rule applied to any form of property and consequently excluded perpetual trusts. The high court permitted an exception only in the case of charitable bequests. But even here the motives of the court were consonant with its otherwise strict enforcement of the rule. Charitable trusts, requiring perpetual rights of use, benefited society and therefore were permissible; perpetual personal trusts or effectively entailed property harmed society by immobilizing resources and therefore were prohibited.[64]

Finally, the Civil Cassation Department also expanded the power to make legacies, i.e. testamentary gifts of money or property. Roman and civilian law distinguished carefully between heirs and legatees. Not being considered the successors of the deceased, legatees bore no responsibility for his debts and other obligations, at least not beyond the value of the legacy itself. But their rights also generally were less secure than those of an heir. In most instances a legacy was treated as a personal obligation of the heir and therefore depended on the latter. None the less, because they could serve so many purposes, legacies greatly increased the power of owners to arrange a settlement of their property. They proved especially useful in enabling owners to avoid the physical division of their property while still providing for the members of their family.[65] Imperial statutory law, however, said virtually nothing on this subject and made no distinction between the beneficiaries of a will.

In this situation, Russian jurists essentially debated how much of the civilian institution of legacy to assimilate into Imperial law. In addition to differing over the question of assimilation itself, jurists disagreed over the identity of a legatee in Imperial law, the extent of his responsibility for

[64] *SRGKD* 1868 no. 25, 1869 no. 1334, 1870 no. 1856, 1873 no. 201, 1874 no. 299 (with 1875 no. 695), 1879 nos. 21, 27, 78, 1882 nos. 83, 130, 1886 no. 20, 1887 no. 11, 1892 no. 76, and *RGKD* 1912 no. 75 (in general); *SRGKD* 1871 no. 643 , 1875 nos. 27, 322, 1883 no. 86, 1891 no. 112, 1902 no. 104, 1903 no. 60, 1906 no. 85, 1909 no. 75 (charitable uses); 1891 no. 112 and *RGKD* 1913 no. 62 (ten-year period). Although a perpetual succession of life estates may have been possible, the high court apparently never confronted this question in practice. On this possibility, see *OGS, 1870*, 188–9, Moiseenko, 'O substitutsii', 787–8, Pobedonostsev, *Kurs*, ii. 574–5, 577–80, and Isachenko, 'Zaveshchatel'nyia rasporiazheniia', cols. 14–16. Jurists overwhelmingly supported the position of the high court on this issue. See ibid., cols. 10–18, Rudnev, *O dukhovnykh zaveshchaniiakh*, 167–9, Moiseenko, 'O substitutsii', 767–8, 773–9, Pobedonostsev, *Kurs*, ii. 571–9, 593, 601–4, Zmirlov, 'O nedostatkakh' (1883), 10: 81–4, Shershenevich, *Uchebnik*, 713–15, Bashmakov, *Ocherki*, 126–9, and A. Grinevich, 'O substitute ili o podnaznachenii naslednika po russkomu pravu', *IuV* (1867/8), 4: 12, 16–19; for a dissenting view, see A. I. Zagorovskii, 'O podstave naslednika (substitutsii)', *RM* (1906), 11: 13 ff.

[65] On legacies under Roman law, see Nicholas, *Roman Law*, 264–70.

the debts of the deceased, and the relative security of his rights against both the heir and the creditors of the heir. Jurists who favoured borrowing extensively from civilian law argued that all but the principal beneficiaries of a will were legatees, who therefore had no responsibility for the debts of the deceased but also no greater right to the inheritance than creditors of the heir.[66] At the other extreme, a handful of jurists denied that legacies existed at all in Imperial law and therefore contended that all beneficiaries of a will were equal heirs who enjoyed a direct right to the inheritance but also an equal liability for the debts of the deceased.[67] Most jurists tried to find an intermediate position that admitted the existence of legatees but defined them more narrowly than did those jurists who advocated broad assimilation. These jurists agreed with the latter, however, on the limited nature of the rights and liabilities of legatees.[68]

Although formally denying it, the Civil Cassation Department effectively adopted the intermediate position and emphasized practicality and equity over theoretical consistency in defining the law. The high court initially denied that legacies existed under Imperial law and argued instead that all beneficiaries of a will were equal co-heirs. This policy protected the creditors of the deceased by ensuring that none of his property escaped responsibility for his debts while it also secured legatees against both the legal heirs and their creditors by giving legatees a direct right to the inheritance.[69] But the high court found its position difficult to maintain in instances where the owner had directed an heir to pay a sum to, or to perform a service for, another party. In such cases the court in practice

[66] Writing in the 1860s–1870s, Sbitnev, 'O dukhovnykh zaveshchaniiakh', 195–6, 198–202, Demchenko, *Sushchestvo*, 1–25, and Nikol'skii, *Ob osnovnykh momentakh*, 11–14, 169–71, simply assumed the applicability of civilian norms. Later authors were more conscious of the controversial nature of the issue. See Shershenevich, *Uchebnik*, 772–6, Tiutriumov in *ZNDGZ*, nos. 501–2, Zmirlov, 'O nedostatkakh' (1883), 10: 55–9, A. A. Bashmakov, 'Byt' ili ne byt' poniatiiu zaveshchatel'nago otkaza v russkom zakonodatel'stve', *ZhMIu* (1901), 7: 71–101, and S. A. Beliatskin, 'Naslednik i legatarii', *Pravo* (1909), 43, cols. 2297–307, 44, cols. 2360–5, and 46, cols. 2518–22.

[67] Rudnev, *O dukhovnykh zaveshchaniiakh*, 171–81, N. A. Poletaev, 'O zaveshchatel'nykh otkazakh v nashikh deistvuiushchikh i budushchikh zakonakh', *ZhMIu* (1902), 6: 175–98, I. A. Ostrikov, 'Kassatsionnyi Senat i zakon o pravakh otkazoprinimatelei (legatariev)', *ZhMIu* (1903), 4: 151–72, and *Pravo* (1909), 46, cols. 2518–22.

[68] Annenkov, 'Otkazy', Beliaev, 'Istoricheskiia osnovy', 6: 45–56, 72, Tovstoles, 'Otvetstvennost'', nos. 9 and 10, N. G. Vavin, 'Poniatie zaveshchatel'nago otkaza po deistvuiushchemu russkomu pravu', *ZhMIu* (1913), 10: 118–41, id., 'O nekotorykh vazhneishchikh momentakh legatarnago prava', *ZhMIu* (1914), 3: 52–97, and Pobedonostsev, *Kurs*, ii. 566, 609–10, 635–43, 666, who vacillated between this and the more assimilationist position.

[69] *SRGKD* 1868 no. 777, 1874 no. 596, 1879 nos. 294, 340, 1886 no. 60, 1904 no. 99, 1907 no. 11, 1908 no. 77; see also 1874 no. 284 and 1876 no. 66.

adopted much of the civilian doctrine on legacy by defining the beneficiary as a creditor of the heir, albeit with a greater claim than other creditors on the resources of an inheritance and with a proportional responsibility for the debts of the deceased.[70] The decision of the Civil Cassation Department in *Shcheglov and Smolentseva* v. *Vasileva* in 1909 essentially formalized this position by declaring these beneficiaries to be true legatees.[71]

While increasing the attractiveness of legacies by providing them with greater legal security, however, the Civil Cassation Department could not eliminate their chief disadvantage under Imperial law. The obligation to pay a legacy still died with the heir rather than with the legatee, and therefore the imposition on an heir of the obligation to make periodic payments to another person remained a risky means for securing the welfare of the latter.[72] But the high court eventually provided a way around even this restriction by enabling the owner to create a secure right to periodic payments for the life of the recipient through the medium of a gift.[73]

Intestacy, Equity, and Women

In contrast to its redefinition of patrimonial property and extensive development of testamentary power, the Civil Cassation Department proved either unable or unwilling to expand the inheritance rights of women or spouses. The atypical clarity of the statutory rules governing these subjects offered the high court few opportunities to revise the law. But the court also declined to exploit some of the opportunities open to it and in one case even reduced the rights of spouses to an inheritance. The chief

[70] *SRGKD* 1868 no. 610, 1870 no. 79, 1871 nos. 643, 675, 1872 no. 1223, 1873 no. 620, 1874 no. 284, 1875 no. 288, 1880 no. 78 (continuation of 1878 no. 54), 1886 no. 60, 1891 no. 112, 1903 no. 122; see also 1874 no. 284. A comparison of the decisions in 1879 no. 340 and 1900 no. 104 demonstrates the concern of the court primarily with practicality and equity rather than with theoretical consistency. A change in the rules governing inheritance taxation led the court to reverse its position with respect to legatees in order to ensure that the burden of taxation continued to be distributed fairly. *SZ* (1857), v, *Ust. o posh.*, arts. 372, 396–7, and (1893 edn., *Prod.* 1895), arts. 153, 163.

[71] *SRGKD* 1909 no. 40, reconfirmed in the decisions reported in *Pravo* (1915), 46, cols. 2959–60, and 47, cols. 3020–2; preliminary traces of the new position can be found in *SRGKD* 1900 no. 104, 1903 no. 122, and 1908 no. 83. See also K. G. Ginkul, *O legatakh* (Tiraspol, 1912), N. Rabinovich, 'Otvetstvennost′ naslednika pered legatariem', *Pravo* (1915), 51, cols. 3311–15, Beliatskin, 'Naslednik', Vavin, 'Poniatie', and id., 'O nekotorykh'.

[72] *SRGKD* 1871 no. 643, 1880 no. 78, 1886 no. 60, and 1891 no. 112; see also I. G. Danilov, *Ukazatel′ voprosov grazhdanskago prava razreshavshikhsia na konsul′tatsii pri Ministerstve Iustitsii uchrezhdennoi 1867–1871* (Spb., 1873), p. 92, no. 89 (will of Koniaev).

[73] *Pravo* (1912), 11, cols. 633–6, and (1914), 5, cols. 571–3.

cause of this action, or inaction, on the part of the high court lay in the intersection between the inheritance rights of women and spouses on the one hand and the goals of strengthening the power of individual owners and providing adequate security for their heirs on the other. Expanding the inheritance rights of women or spouses generally required the limitation of the testamentary power of owners or the reduction of the share of descendant heirs in an inheritance. In the few instances where an improvement in the rights of women or spouses could be achieved while avoiding these effects, the Civil Cassation Department tended to revise the law in their favour.[74]

The conflict between the goals of freedom for the owner and security for his family emerges clearly in two cases in the late 1860s in which, in each instance, the widow of the owner sought to secure her share of the acquired property of her husband by limiting his testamentary power over it.[75] In each case, the husband had distributed all of his acquired property by will, leaving nothing for his wife to inherit. The widow argued that the legal obligation of a husband to love and provide for his wife, as well as his Christian duty towards her, precluded him from depriving his wife of her statutory share of his acquired property in this way. According to the widows, the law granted a husband testamentary control over his acquired property not so that he could deprive his wife of her share of it, but so that he could increase this share. Unmoved by this argument, the lower courts in both cases denied the widows' suits.

In upholding these decisions, the Civil Cassation Department ruled that an owner enjoyed unlimited power to dispose of his or her acquired property by will. A surviving spouse therefore had a right only to the relevant portion of such property that remained unbequeathed by the owner. The high court added that the duty of a husband to provide for

[74] These opportunities lay primarily in determining relative rights to an inheritance within collateral lines; e.g. in *SRGKD* 1877 no. 132, 1879 no. 264, 1880 no. 210, 1881 no. 52, 1888 no. 74, 1894 no. 72, and *RGKD* 1913 no. 41 the high court accepted the interpretation of the law which favoured female over male relatives. In contrast, in *SRGKD* 1868 no. 25, 1872 nos. 88, 505, 1874 no. 123, 1875 nos. 199, 854, 1880 no. 210, 1888 no. 74, 1905 no. 24, and *RGKD* 1912 no. 46 and 1913 no. 62 the high court adopted a traditional interpretation of the law, sometimes against the more reformist impulses of the lower courts.

[75] *SRGKD* 1870 no. 1599 and N. S., 'Po povodu st. 1148 i 106 Zakonov Grazhdanskikh,' *IuV* (1869), 12: 74–7; see also *SRGKD* 1873 no. 1074, 1884 no. 23, 1890 no. 42, 1897 no. 68, and *SRPS* i, no. 356. In contrast, the court also held that local laws in Chernigov and Poltava provs. and for Moslems in Transcaucasia did limit the testamentary power of husbands. *SRGKD* 1884 no. 8 and 1911 no. 14. For statutory law, see *SZ* (1857), x, pt. 1, arts. 1068, 1105, 1120, 1123, 1148–55, and (*Prod.* 1876), art. 116 prim., pril.: 3 (1887 edn., art. 1148 prim.).

his wife constituted a personal obligation that died with him. For the same reason, the court later held that the right of parents to the reversion of property given to a child who later predeceased them and died without issue did not prevent the child from bequeathing this property to whomever he or she chose.[76] Underlying these decisions presumably lay the belief that had the affective ties assumed to create moral obligations within the family actually existed, the spouse or child would have recognized them in his or her will. In the absence of these ties, the high court saw no reason to limit the rights of the owner.

A similar regard for the rights of owners led the high court narrowly to restrict the right of a surviving spouse to property that would have come to the deceased spouse had he or she survived his or her father. Russian jurists universally condemned this right as having no basis in either a kinship or a moral relationship between the owner and his daughter- or son-in-law. Several critics also charged that the right unjustifiably gave the spouses of the children of an owner a greater claim to his property than that enjoyed by his own children because in some instances it could be realized even during the lifetime of the owner.[77]

Evidently agreeing with these criticisms, the Civil Cassation Department gradually limited the rights of surviving spouses in such instances. The high court argued that because children could not demand any portion of their father's property while he lived, the surviving spouse of one of these children could claim only that property that necessarily would have come to the deceased spouse had he or she survived his or her father. The court concluded that during the lifetime of the father-in-law the surviving spouse of any of his children who predeceased him therefore had a right only to his patrimonial property because only this property passed unavoidably to his own children. In the case of acquired property, however, a surviving spouse had a right only to share in any such property that remained undistributed by the will of his or her father-in-law because the latter enjoyed an unlimited right to dispose of his acquired property

[76] *Pravo* (1913), 12, cols. 754–8, and 35, cols. 2037–40. For statutory law, see *SZ* (1857), x, pt. 1, arts. 1121, 1141–7.

[77] *SZ* (1857), x, pt. 1, arts. 1149, 1151, 1153–4; see also *ZhMIu*, 7 (1861), 118–25. For criticisms by jurists, see A. Liubavskii, 'Ukaznaia chast′ iz nedvizhimago imushchestva testia ili svekra', *ZhMIu* (1864), 8: 209–18, K. D. Kavelin, *Sobranie sochinenii K. D. Kavelina* (Spb., 1900), iv. 1256–7, Zmirlov, 'O nedostatkakh' (1884), 6: 113–15, I. M. Tiutriumov, 'Po povodu peresmotra i kodifikatsii grazhdanskikh zakonov', *RB* (1884), 5/6: 465–70, Pobedonostsev, *Kurs*, ii. 338–41, 'K voprosu o poriadke nasledovaniia suprugov', *SG* (1891), 44: 2–3, I. E. Il′iashenko, 'O prave nasledovaniia suprugov s tochki zreniia budushchago grazhdanskago ulozheniia', *VP* (1902), 4/5: 89–90, and *GU. Kn. 4-aia*, intro., pp. 19–20, and commentary, pp. 88–95.

during his lifetime or at his death.[78] Although the Civil Cassation Department referred extensively to the historical sources of statutory law to reinforce its argument, its position appeared, even to sympathetic jurists, to deviate substantially from the clear meaning of the relevant statutes. As in the case of marital separation, they consequently criticized the action of the high court for being arbitrary and unfounded even while they welcomed its effects.[79]

The ultimate resolution by the Civil Cassation Department of the conflict between the inheritance rights of full sisters and paternal half-brothers demonstrates, however, that the high court was willing to improve the inheritance rights of women when doing so did not limit the rights of owners. Statutory law compelled the courts either to exclude full sisters in favour of paternal half-brothers or vice versa when the inheritance of acquired property passed to the collateral lines. Since the ambiguity of the statutes themselves and their historical sources allowed either interpretation, the courts effectively had to choose between supporting the traditional system of male preference based on the kin-group or adopting the principle of mutual obligation based on the affective ideal of the family as the basis of the law.[80]

Two decisions by the pre-reform Senate favouring full sisters over their paternal half-brothers sparked the debate among jurists over this issue.[81] Critics of these decisions argued that since the patrilineal kin-group formed the basis of Imperial inheritance law, paternal half-brothers excluded full sisters from an inheritance in collateral lines. The fact that the children of a common father issued from unions with different wives did not alter the blood relationship between the father and his children and therefore did not affect membership within the patrilineal kin-group. Hence, critics concluded, full and paternal half-brothers stood in an identical relationship to their common father and enjoyed equal rights to

[78] *SRGKD* 1868 no. 869, 1884 no. 23, 1897 no. 68; see also *SRPS* i, no. 356.

[79] Kavelin, *Sobranie sochinenii*, iv. 1256–7, Zmirlov, 'O nedostatkakh', (1884), 6: 113–15, Tiutriumov, 'Po povodu peresmotra', 5/6: 469–71, Pobedonostsev, *Kurs*, ii. 338–41, Shershenevich, *Uchebnik*, 745–7, and N. N. Tovstoles, 'Ukaznaia chast′ supruga v imushchestve svekra (testia)', *ZhMIu* (1914), 5: 152–5.

[80] *SZ* (1857), x, pt. 1, arts. 1135, 1138, 1140. No dispute arose with respect to patrimonial property because both full and half-siblings were equal members of the patrilineal kin-group of their common parent. Hence a half-brother excluded a full sister when an inheritance passed to the collateral lines. *SRGKD* 1874 no. 804, 1876 no. 214, 1881 no. 30, and 1908 no. 13. For the legislative sources, see *1PSZ* xxxiv (1817), no. 26867, pp. 313–14; and xxxv (1818), no. 27579, p. 620, and A. A. Vereshchagin, 'O nasledovanii nepolnorodnykh vo bokovykh liniiakh po deistvuiushchemu russkomu pravu', *ZhMIu* (1898), 10: 48–100.

[81] *ZhMIu* 3 (1860), sud. prak., pp. 116–17, and 7 (1861), 613–16.

his inheritance. Under the general rules of intestate succession, both full and paternal half-brothers therefore excluded full sisters from the inheritance of acquired property in collateral lines. Jurists who advocated this position concluded that the statute in dispute consequently admitted maternal half-siblings to an inheritance on an equal basis with paternal half-siblings solely as an exception when no full siblings had survived.[82]

In contrast, jurists who supported the Senate decisions argued that the familial bonds of the deceased with a full sister were closer than those with a half-brother and took precedence over formal kin relationships. A full sister therefore should exclude from an inheritance any half-sibling, whether paternal or maternal. Likewise, these jurists continued, half-siblings through either parent stood equally close to the deceased and were closer to their deceased half-sibling than were more distant collateral relatives. Maternal and paternal half-siblings therefore should inherit equally and should exclude more distant collateral relatives from an inheritance. The jurists who defended this position claimed that the original legislation in fact had been intended to achieve precisely these results, thereby providing legal recognition to family as well as to kin ties.[83]

In resolving this conflict, the Civil Cassation Department initially favoured the patrilineal kin-group. Indeed, the high court explicitly rejected the contrary argument in its decision in *Gerakova* v. *Demidova and Stoikovich* in 1872.[84] Setting aside the ruling of the Moscow Court of

[82] 'G.' in N. V. Kalachov, 'Otvet g. G. na vopros: "ne dolzhny li edinokrovnye brat′ia vladel′tsa, umershago bezdetnym i bez zaveshchaniia, nasledovat′ emu v imushchestve blagopriobretennom vmeste s rodnymi ego brat′iami i iskliuchat′ brat′ev ego edinoutrobnykh?" ', *IuV* 2 (1860–1), 56–7, ——n, 'Vozrazhenie Redaktoru na otvet ego g. G. po stat′e 1140 t. X Zak. Grazhd.', *IuV* 4 (1860–1861), 38–40, 'Oproverzheniia i zashchita mneniia Redaktora po stat′e 1140 Zakonov Grazhdanskikh', *IuV* 9 (1860–1), 15–30, F. Zhukov, 'Iuridicheskiia zametki, pri chteniia statei, pod zaglaviem: "Oproverzheniia i zashchita mneniia Redaktora po stat′e 1140-i Zakonov Grazhdanskikh", v 9-m vypuske "Iuridicheskago Vestnika" 1860–1861 g.', *IuV* 18 (1860–1), 2–10, 15–18, 23, and A. Liubavskii, 'Spornye voprosy grazhdanskago prava. I. Nasledovanie edinoutrobnykh i edinokrovnykh brat′ev i sester', *ZhMIu* (1865), 11: 238–42. See also Vereshchagin, 'O nasledovanii', 76–100.

[83] Kalachov, 'Otvet g. G.', 55–62, id., 'Eshche zametka po stat′iam 1138-i i 1140-i Zak. Grazhd.', *IuV* 14 (1860–1), 29–31, 'Oproverzheniia', 34–7, A. Truvorov, 'Zakliuchitel′noe slovo o stat′e 1140-i zakonov grazhdanskikh', *IuV* 18 (1860–1861), 27–65, Kavelin, *Sobranie sochinenii*, iv. 587–8, P. Kititsyn, 'Zametka o tolkovanii 1140 st. 1 ch. X t. sv. zak.', *ZhMIu* (1865), 9: 399–404, and L. P. Snegirev, 'O prave nasledovaniia vo bokovykh liniiakh edinokrovnykh i edinoutrobnykh brat′ev i sester', *IuV* (1871), 9: 17–39; see also Pobedonostsev, *Kurs*, ii. 324–30, and S. F. Deliusto, 'O poriadke nasledovaniia v bokovoi linii mezhdu polnorodnymi i nepolnorodnymi brat′iami i sestrami v blagopriobretennom imushchestve, po st. 1140 t. X ch. I Sv. Grazhd. Zak.', *Protokoly Kievskago Iuridicheskago Obshchestva za vtoruiu polovinu 1879 goda* (Kiev, 1880).

[84] *SRGKD* 1872 no. 1188; see also 1868 no. 25, 1874 no. 738, and 1876 nos. 102, 515.

Appeals in favour of the full sisters of the deceased, the high court declared that the law

in no way concerns the relative inheritance rights of full brothers and sisters with respect to the rights of paternal and maternal half-brothers and sisters; on the contrary, it has in view the instance when there are no full brothers and sisters, and only paternal and maternal half-brothers and sisters are surviving, and in this instance alone defines the preference of these latter to all other collateral relatives of more distant lines.

The general rules of intestate succession governed all other situations, the court continued, and these rules were based on the patrilineal kin-group. 'Both full brothers and paternal half-brothers are included within the definition of the kinship or blood-kin group,' the court continued,

and as they belong to one and the same kin-group, both must have an identical right of inheritance in all those instances when the inheritance passes to that kin-group to which they belong . . . it is impossible not to conclude that in the order of succession in collateral lines, children of paternal half-blood must enjoy rights identical with those of full blood, that the law makes no distinction between one and the other, and that with respect to the order of inheritance they all are recognized as full members of the kin-group.[85]

Clearly, at this point the Civil Cassation Department had chosen the kin-group over the family.

Fifteen years later, however, the pressure of juristic opinion and the lower courts again combined with changes in the composition of the Civil Cassation Department to produce a shift in policy. In its decision in *Zinovev* v. *Shchulepnikovy and Novitskii* in 1887 the high court now declared that the bonds uniting the conjugal family took precedence over the blood ties of the kin-group. Although formally basing its decision on an historical analysis of statutory law, the high court also asserted that

the interpretation of [the law] now established by [the court] corresponds more closely to those moral ties which usually exist between children of one or of different marriages. There is no doubt that brothers and sisters originating from a common father and mother stand incomparably nearer to one another than children from different marriages; the law of inheritance in general must correspond to the moral bond between those seeking the inheritance and the deceased.[86]

While resulting in a modest expansion in practice of the inheritance rights of women, this reasoning also implied that in principle women

[85] *SRGKD* 1872 no. 1188. [86] *SRGKD* 1887 no. 106.

should enjoy rights equal with men in inheritance since the strength of moral bonds within the family was not perceived to vary on the basis of sex.[87]

By the mid-1880s, then, the Civil Cassation Department had come to view the affective ties and mutual obligations arising from relations within the conjugal family as the principal justification of inheritance law. As a result, where possible it effectively revised the law to reflect this view. For example, it broadly interpreted the rights of parents to the property of their children who predeceased them and were childless, declaring in its decision in *The Chernigov Provincial Nobility* v. *Ilenko* in 1893 that

> the law grants [parents] this property not on the strength of any general principle of civil law, but, on the contrary, in the form of an exception to these general principles in view of the fact that in the absence of the deceased's own children or brothers or sisters, his parents must be considered the persons nearest to him.[88]

Similarly, in its decision in 1913 regarding the petition of Elena Petrashevskaia to become guardian of her mentally ill husband, the high court abandoned its long-standing position that spouses were not true heirs of one another and now defined the wife as a relative of her husband in order to enable Petrashevskaia to protect the interests of her husband against his more distant blood relatives. 'The purpose of the law', the court declared,

> is to entrust the guardianship of a mentally ill person to the person nearest to him, with the goal of ensuring sufficiently considerate care for him, and, with the exception of rare anomalies, no one can be nearer to the afflicted person and can relate with him more considerately than his spouse. This is especially true when the nearest members of his kin-group are those relatives and heirs who, being distantly related to him, perhaps do not even know him and can be considered his relatives only because they descend from the same ancestor as he.[89]

[87] Despite occasional prodding by lower courts and jurists, the high court did not apply this reasoning to patrimonial property. *SRGKD* 1908 no. 13 and V. Katsnel'son, 'O nasledovanii edinokrovnykh brat'ev pri polnorodnykh sestrakh', *Pravo* (1903), 8, cols. 531–4; see also Pobedonostsev, *Kurs*, ii. 324–5, 330–4.

[88] *SRGKD* 1893 no. 12; see also the references cited above in n. 15.

[89] *RGKD* 1913 no. 92. For the argument by the high court that a surviving spouse was not an heir, but only the recipient of a provision for maintenance, see *SRGKD* 1868 no. 563, 1871 no. 1224, 1879 no. 2, 1888 nos. 71, 95, 1905 no. 96, and *RGKD* 1913 no. 41; a spouse therefore had to request his or her statutory share to establish a right to it (*SRGKD* 1867 no. 279, 1869 no. 16, 1877 no. 373, 1882 no. 101, 1888 nos. 71, 95, 1904 no. 23), but also had only a limited liability for the debts of the deceased spouse (1868 no. 563, 1877 no. 373, 1888 no. 71). For contrasting views of jurists see Graf Vol'tke, 'Ob ukaznoi dole ovdoveishago supruga', *ZhIuOSU* (1896), 4: 42–56, Nikol'skii, *Ob osnovnykh momentakh*, 127–52, and Pobedonostsev, *Kurs*, i. 56–9, and ii. 297–300, 309, 337, 341–3, all of whom emphasized

The conflict between the principles underlying the decision of the Civil Cassation Department and existing statutory law could hardly have been greater. In the view of the high court, the mutual obligations arising from familial affection had displaced kin ties as the primary basis of the law. As they had with family law, these obligations became a source of enforceable legal rights for family members, provided of course that they did not interfere with the proprietary rights of owners.

Flexible Division

The power of the heirs themselves to dispose of inherited property also affected the legal means available for avoiding the fragmentation of estates and the other problems attributed to statutory law. In defining this power, the Civil Cassation Department scrupulously protected the rights of each heir while granting the heirs as a group the same broad power and flexibility as that enjoyed by individual owners. Hence the high court defined the role of the courts in cases involving the division of an inheritance to be only the determination and protection of the relative rights of the heirs to the total inheritance and not the distribution of specific objects among them. Unless the heirs failed to agree on the disposition of an inheritance, the courts could not intervene in the allocation of the assets of an estate.[90] The heirs therefore could either divide an estate or remain in co-possession of it. In the latter case, the high court defined the heirs as co-owners and rigorously protected the property rights of each heir, including the right to dispose freely of his or her share.[91] In this way the heirs could retain an estate intact and simply divide its income if they so wished.

It is not clear, however, how often heirs adopted this latter strategy. On the one hand, the frequency of cases involving co-ownership suggests that the practice was common, especially among merchants. A Soviet study of the largest noble estates in the early twentieth century also

kinship as the basis of inheritance rights, and Tovstoles, 'Ukaznaia chast′', 152–5, and 'Nasledovanie suprugov po russkomu pravu, v sviazi s proektom grazhdanskago ulozheniia', *ZhMIu* (1911), 5: 33–41, who stressed affective ties.

[90] *SRGKD* 1893 no. 4 and 1905 no. 7; for statutory law, see *SZ* (1857), x, pt. 1, arts. 1315–45. See also A. N. Butovskii, 'O razdel′nykh aktakh', *ZhMIu* (1905), 3: 29–83, Shershenevich, *Uchebnik*, 766–8, Pobedonostsev, *Kurs*, i. 97–9, and ii. 421–30, and L. A. Kasso, *Russkoe pozemel′noe pravo* (Mos., 1906), 172–8. The data in Table 6.5 suggest that the courts only infrequently became involved in the division of an inheritance.

[91] *SRGKD* 1871 no. 931, 1875 no. 178, 1876 no. 559, 1885 no. 103, 1900 no. 55, and 1904 no. 88. For statutory law on co-ownership, see *SZ* (1857), x, pt. 1, arts. 545–56.

suggests that a significant number of these estates were held in co-possession. In addition, a participant at a meeting of the agricultural council of the Ministry of Agriculture and State Domains in 1901 stated that co-ownership by the heirs especially of large commercially oriented estates occurred frequently in the south-western provinces.[92] On the other hand, a majority of the landowners at this meeting rejected co-possession as impractical, awkward, and risky, and in its comments to the civil code editing commission in the late 1880s the Alatyr congress of justices of the peace stated that the practice was declining among landowners because families no longer stayed together.[93]

In any case, it seems clear that in most instances the heirs divided an inheritance. Since the courts would not intervene in this process except in the event of disagreement, the heirs collectively enjoyed unlimited power to dispose of an estate. But the courts ultimately had to recognize the legality of any action taken by the heirs for it to be secure against third parties, such as creditors of the deceased or of one of the heirs, or against any of the heirs themselves in the future. The willingness of the Civil Cassation Department to sanction the legality of the arrangements made by the heirs therefore defined the legal boundaries for these arrangements. In practice, the high court defined these boundaries extremely broadly.

The development of the law by the high court rested on its conception of an inheritance as a fund or total value in which each heir had a specified but general interest. Each heir therefore had a right to a specific value or share in the total property fund rather than the right to particular objects. Hence the Civil Cassation Department sought to ensure that each heir received the value due to him or her in an inheritance and normally was not concerned with the form that this value assumed. This approach gave the heirs considerable flexibility in disposing of an inheritance because they could divide its assets in any manner they chose, under whatever conditions, as long as each heir was satisfied that he or she had received the appropriate value. Since this value could take the form of compensatory payments or the right to an annuity, heirs easily could avoid any

[92] Minarik, *Ekonomicheskaia kharakteristika*, 43–74, and *SKhiL*, 202 (1901), 301–2; see also Sviatlovskii, *Mobilizatsiia*, 43–4, who shows that between 1877 and 1905 the share of privately owned land held by partnerships, companies, corporations, and similar entities had increased from 2.6% to 15.5%. For examples of legal cases, see *SRGKD* 1868 no. 891, 1869 no. 199, 1871 nos. 432, 931, 1872 nos. 277, 456, 1873 no. 713, 1875 no. 209, 1880 no. 150, 1885 no. 124, 1901 no. 41, and 1910 no. 93.

[93] *SKhiL*, 202 (1901), 301–2, and *ZNDGZ*, no. 521.

disruptive physical division of an estate.[94] To protect such arrangements, in debt and bankruptcy actions the Civil Cassation Department assigned a higher priority to heirs who had accepted compensatory payments or annuities than to creditors of the heir who had retained the estate. To protect the heirs against each other, the high court also treated the voluntary division of an estate as an irrevocable contract, even if some heirs had accepted a share lower in value than that due them by law. Seeing its duty as the defence of the rights of an heir against the illegal or unjust claims of others, the court obviously felt no obligation to protect a property owner against his own voluntary actions.[95]

The case of Iakov-Tadeush Loskevich in 1889 illustrates the way in which the Civil Cassation Department increased the ability of the heirs to secure their own interests as well as what the court considered to be the economic interests of the state.[96] On the death of Dionisii Loskevich, his three sons agreed that one of them, Iakov-Tadeush, would retain sole ownership of the landed estate of their father in Kiev province and would pay each of his brothers 5,550 roubles as compensation. Both the Kiev District Court and Court of Appeals, however, denied Loskevich's petition for ownership of the full estate on the grounds that the law prohibited people of Polish origin from acquiring non-urban land in the nine Western Provinces by any means other than intestate succession. According to the lower courts, Loskevich was entitled to inherit only one third of the estate of his father. His acquisition of the remaining two-thirds of the estate from his brothers therefore represented a new, and hence illegal, acquisition of land.

In setting this decision aside, the Civil Cassation Department defended both the general right of ownership and the power of heirs to divide an inheritance as they deemed appropriate. The high court first established the right of Loskevich to acquire the entire estate by interpreting narrowly the law restricting the acquisition of land by people of Polish origin in the Western Provinces. The court argued that the law 'had in view halting the further inflow of people of Polish origin, while preserving as inviolable,

[94] *SRGKD* 1867 no. 518, 1868 no. 891, 1869 no. 199, 1871 nos. 432, 443, 1872 nos. 456, 1049, 1875 no. 209, 1876 no. 302, 1877 no. 142, 1878 no. 274, 1879 nos. 2, 344, 1880 no. 150, 1883 no. 32, 1885 no. 124, 1889 nos. 33, 54, 55, 1893 no. 4, 1905 no. 7, 1907 no. 90, and 1909 no. 90. See also Butovskii, 'O razdel′nykh aktakh', 40–1, 47–55, 74–6.

[95] *SRGKD* 1868 no. 891, 1875 no. 209, and 1905 no. 7; see also 1872 no. 1049 and K. P. Zmirlov, 'Iz praktiki grazhdanskago kassatsionnago departamenta Pravitel′stvuiushchago Senata', *ZhMIu* (1902), 5: 206–18.

[96] *SRGKD* 1889 no. 54.

however, the property rights of current owners and the rights of their legal heirs'.[97] Since the law preserved the right of Polish people to inherit land in this area, the high court asserted, it also protected all rights that followed from the general right of inheritance. In the view of the Civil Cassation Department, these rights included the power to divide an inheritance in a way that enabled each heir to realize his particular rights in the general inheritance.

Turning to the right of heirs to divide an inheritance, the Civil Cassation Department argued that while the law required the share of each heir to be equal in quality and benefit, this requirement could not 'be interpreted in the sense of an obligation to compose the lots exclusively from the material parts of the property being divided'. The rule referred only to the means of ensuring the just division of an estate, the court contended, as did the rule allowing payment of monetary compensation to some heirs if physical division of the estate proved to be inconvenient. In the view of the high court, such a payment represented 'only an auxiliary means for the equalization of lots . . . and it preserved this meaning even if this payment constitutes the entire lot of the co-heir because of the inconvenience of allotting any physical part of the property to one or another co-owner'.[98] The high court therefore considered valid an act of division in which some of the heirs received monetary payments in place of their share of an estate while the heir obligated to make the payments received physical assets that exceeded the value of the share of the inheritance to which he was entitled. In the opinion of the court, this arrangement provided for the security of the heirs as well as, or better than, an equal division of the landed estate itself.

As it had with family law, then, the Civil Cassation Department constituted an important means for adjusting property and inheritance law to post-emancipation social and economic conditions, thereby at least partially resolving the problems attributed to the law by its critics. Indeed, the effective changes introduced into these areas of the law by the high court proved to be much more substantial than in the case of family law, perhaps because both reformers and conservatives agreed that statutory law allowed owners too little flexibility. By limiting patrimonial property, expanding the proprietary power of owners and heirs, and recognizing the principle that the mutual obligations arising from family relationships provided the proper basis of inheritance law, the Civil Cassation Department also did much to realize the proposals for reform of the law advanced

[97] Ibid. [98] Ibid.

by progressivist jurists. But the ability of the courts to alter the effective content of the law still was limited. By themselves they could not abolish completely the institution of patrimonial property and reformulate the law on the basis of individual ownership, civil equality, and security for family members. Nor could they introduce equal inheritance rights for women, assuming they even wished to do so. Such reform required legislative action. Yet legislative action proved difficult to achieve because of the political connotations surrounding revision of property and inheritance law. In the end, significant revision of the law therefore awaited resolution of a political conflict over fundamental values and ideals that far transcended the simple resolution of practical legal problems.

Yet the courts, and especially the Civil Cassation Department, did provide solutions to many of the problems attributed to the inflexibility of statutory law. The Baryshnikov case at the turn of the century perhaps best illustrates the way in which owners could use the legal means provided by the high court to gain greater control over their property, for whatever ends.[99] The courts finally resolved this case in 1899, moreover, when the political battle over the status of the nobility and its loss of land was at its height. On his death in 1878, noble landowner Andrei Baryshnikov had left 50,000 roubles in cash, bank certificates, and similar assets and an unmortgaged estate of 23,576 desiatin in Smolensk province which included extensive forests and several profitable mills. To preserve the estate intact for her only son, Baryshnikov's widow had persuaded her three daughters to renounce their right to the inheritance in exchange for 35,000 roubles each. Confirmed as co-heirs, the widow Baryshnikova and her son then had divided the estate, with the son taking only 500 desiatin. Baryshnikova herself had received 23,076 desiatin despite being entitled to only one seventh of the landed estate. On acquisition by Baryshnikova, all this property became classified legally as 'acquired' rather than 'patrimonial' because Baryshnikova was not a member of her husband's kin-group. Over the next four years Baryshnikova then transferred over 19,000 desiatin to her son, for whom the property remained acquired because he ostensibly had received it as a gift. Clearly, both the act of division and the subsequent gifts had been intended to transform the legal classification of the property in order to increase the control of the son over it, and in fact he apparently had never relinquished management of the property. Baryshnikova and her son then had composed wills naming each other as principal beneficiary.

99 E——v, 'Baryshnikovskoe nasledstvo'.

In 1890 Baryshnikova had inherited the entire estate after the unexpected death of her son. Since the estate had not passed to the legal heir, it remained classified as acquired property. This turn of events understandably upset at least one of the two surviving daughters of Baryshnikova, E. A. Ostrikova, because had the property remained patrimonial she would have inherited half the estate on the death of her childless brother. Ostrikova challenged the legality of the original act of division and hence the validity of all subsequent acts disposing of the property. Her suit was denied by the lower courts, however, which based their decisions on the practice of the Civil Cassation Department with respect to gifts, the division of inheritances, and the transformation of patrimonial into acquired property. Not surprisingly, the high court upheld their decisions. In the mean time, Baryshnikova had become so incensed at the insubordination of her daughter that she composed a new will directing that on her death the entire estate be sold and the proceeds used for charity. Although Ostrikova also contested this will, the courts ruled that it, too, was valid, given the definition of testamentary power by the high court. Enraged that such a large estate had passed from the hands of the nobility, the conservative press branded the outcome of the case as a lamentable but unavoidable consequence of the reformist activities of the new courts.[100]

The ability of Baryshnikova and her son to gain complete control over a large patrimonial estate through manipulation of the law as developed by the courts raises an important question. Given the opportunities created by the Civil Cassation Department, many of the effects attributed to the law by its critics from the 1880s onward were due at least as much to the action or inaction of owners and heirs as to the restrictions of the law itself. Of course many of these critics were pursuing political objectives and consequently exaggerated the severity of existing problems in order to strengthen their case for changes in the law which supported either reformist or reactionary ends. Also, many of the means provided by the high court for avoiding the problems attributed to the law were technically complicated and costly, the latter especially being an important consideration in impoverished rural Russia. Unlimited powers of disposition, particularly of testamentary disposition, provided a simpler, less expensive solution to these problems. None the less, the persistence of the complaints about the restrictiveness of the law, despite the flexibility introduced into it by the courts, suggests that the roots of the extreme fragmentation of estates, the unequal treatment of women in inheritance,

[100] Ibid.; see also the references cited above in n. 34.

and the other problems attributed to statutory law in fact lay much deeper than the law. The sources of these phenomena can be found, in varying degrees, in the weight of tradition, the difference of priorities between generations, the poverty and difficulties of agriculture and the scarcity and high cost of capital in prerevolutionary Imperial Russia, apathy, ignorance of the law, and the persistence of the patriarchal mentality and of discriminatory attitudes towards women. Given these conditions, one may well question how effective the changes in the law demanded by its critics would have been in either resolving the problems attributed to it or changing society in accordance with the progressivist or conservative ideals of these critics. In the final analysis, the ability of the courts and of jurists to reform the law therefore proved to be much greater than their ability to change society.

Conclusion

Ends and Beginnings

THE impact of the judicial reform, at least in the areas of family, property, and inheritance law, was mixed. On the one hand, the reform had created a judicial system capable not only of defining general legal norms and applying them reasonably uniformly to particular cases, but also of adapting the law creatively to changing conditions and attitudes. Such judicial law-making was constrained both by the content of statutory law and by prevailing ethical standards. Equally importantly, it was shaped, and hence also constrained, by the European juridical concepts assimilated by Russian jurists through their training and professional activities and by the ideological perceptions and values that predominated within the legal profession.[1] But at least with respect to marriage, the family, property, and the individual, these latter perceptions and values were shared more widely, particularly among members of the growing educated and professional strata of society. Moreover, the changes introduced into the law by the courts responded to the demands of an even broader circle of the population. The desire of property owners for increased flexibility and of spouses—especially wives—for access to formal separation, for example, each received some satisfaction. Indeed, the recognition by the Civil Cassation Department of a right of marital separation, some thirty years before it was established legislatively, demonstrates how far the process of judicial law-making could be taken. By adapting the law to social, economic, and cultural change, the new courts acted as a stabilizing force in the late Imperial period.

On the other hand, neither the Civil Cassation Department nor the new courts in general could resolve the ideological, political, and institutional conflicts over the law which took place during this period, not least because they were principal actors rather than neutral brokers in

[1] In this sense the pattern of judicial law-making in late Imperial Russia supports the argument of Alan Watson in *The Evolution of Law* (Baltimore, 1985) that legal development generally is shaped and constrained by the culture of lawyers.

these conflicts. By granting the new courts both independence and the ability effectively to make law, the judicial reform invested the judiciary—composed now overwhelmingly of members of the new juridical profession—with substantial power. The mere exercise of this power challenged traditional centres of authority, in particular the state administration and, with respect to marriage, the higher clergy of the Orthodox Church. But by using its power to develop civil law in the direction advocated generally by moderate conservative and progressivist jurists, the judiciary also challenged the principles of arbitrary and personalized authority and unequal ascriptive status on which the autocratic order rested. Both institutionally and ideologically, the new courts therefore also acted as a destabilizing and even revolutionary force in the last years of the autocracy.

This ambiguous outcome resulted largely from the self-contained character of the judicial system established by the 1864 reform. To be sure, the state administration retained superior authority within the tsarist governmental system and was able to redefine the jurisdiction of the courts in ways that preserved substantial discretionary power for itself. But the institutional structure of the judicial system, the technical nature of the law and the judicial process, and a strong base of political support within the state administration preserved the autonomy of the courts and thereby also their power to shape Imperial civil law. This structural autonomy was reinforced by the presence of a professional peer group that on the whole was committed to the principle of legality and that played a central role in fostering the ideals and values promoted by judges through their decisions in individual cases. The self-contained structure of the courts, however, also limited their impact to those areas of life over which they exercised control.[2] The different legal orders represented by the courts and by the state administration thus remained in conflict, with the boundary between them constantly being contested. This struggle between competing legal orders recalls that which in Western Europe had led to the arrangements, practices, and theories comprehended ultimately by the concept of legality. But it differed crucially in that it took place within a single governmental system in which one side possessed predominant power and both sides acknowledged the supreme authority of the tsar and within a political culture that stressed the personalized

[2] On the self-contained nature of the reformed judicial system, see B. Levin-Stankevich, 'Cassation, Judicial Interpretation and the Development of Civil and Criminal Law in Russia, 1864–1917: The Institutional Consequences of the 1864 Court Reform in Russia', (Ph.D. diss., SUNY, Buffalo, 1984), esp. 285–99.

nature of authority, the pursuit of particular interests by working through such authority, and the priority of results over process or rules.[3]

By challenging the fundamental principles of this political culture, the proposals for the revision of family, property, and inheritance law made by progressivist and populist jurists, feminists, and other proponents of reform threatened the autocratic order. Conservatives responded by reasserting traditional values and by attempting to adapt traditional legal institutions to changed conditions. Efforts to address what often were generally perceived as being significant practical legal problems consequently became intertwined with the attempt by different ideological factions within and outside the state administration to use the law to promote their respective ideals. The family in particular served as a medium for such attempts, with all factions believing that as the foundation for the social order as a whole it should and could be structured through legal norms to foster the values, attitudes, and relationships necessary to support their competing ideal orders. Although this belief over-simplified the relationship between the family and general social and political structures, and exaggerated the power of law, it found firm support in Russian Imperial and Orthodox ideology and reinforcement in ideas assimilated from Western Europe after the late eighteenth century. Indeed, the conflict over competing family ideals in late Imperial Russia resembles those which preceded and formed an important part of earlier revolutionary upheavals in Western Europe and colonial America, suggesting the revolutionary implications of reformist proposals for legal change, however moderate they appear from a late—or even an early—twentieth-century Western perspective.[4]

The chief cause of conflict over the law, however, remained the growing incongruity between statutory civil law and the changing social and economic conditions of post-emancipation Imperial Russia. The further change proceeded, the more intense, complex, and diffuse conflict over the law became. Even where some sort of consensus eventually emerged, for example as with the belief that owners needed increased power over the devolution of their property, the particular circumstances and interests

[3] Without stretching the analogy too far, the struggle over legality in Imperial Russia thus may resemble that within the Catholic Church over papal authority more closely than those between the church and other sources of power. See esp. H. J. Berman, *Law and Revolution: The Formation of the Western Legal Tradition* (Cambridge, Mass., 1983), B. Tierney, *Religion, Law, and the Growth of Constitutional Thought 1150–1650* (Cambridge, 1982) and K. Pennington, *The Prince and the Law, 1200–1600: Sovereignty and Rights in the Western Legal Tradition* (Berkeley, Calif., 1993).

[4] See the references cited above in the Intro., n. 8.

of different social groups prevented agreement on how to change the law. Such conflicts over competing interests, of course, neither are unusual nor were new in tsarist Russia, where the political élite had ruled as much through concession and mediation as through coercion. What was new was the tendency to envelope such conflict in divergent ideological perspectives, thereby greatly complicating—and perhaps precluding—any mediation between competing interests.[5]

The conflicts over the revision of family, property, and inheritance law therefore formed an integral part of the social, economic, and cultural changes taking place in post-emancipation Imperial Russia. In the context of such change, these areas of the law served as a medium through which different ideological, occupational, social, and other groups not only pursued their particular interests, but also articulated their values, ideals, and self-image. This use of the law reveals sources of both unity and disunity within the educated and professional strata of tsarist society on the eve of the First World War. Clearly, proponents of all approaches to revision of the law valued specialized expertise and used it to support their own proposals as well as to refute the arguments of their opponents. All likewise believed that the law shaped as well as reflected social relations and values and therefore sought to use the law to fashion society in accordance with their own attitudes, beliefs, and interests. This common ability to use specialized education, willingness to engage in public debate over socio-political issues, and paternalistic desire to shape social development in correspondence with ideological beliefs demonstrates the emergence in late Imperial Russia of both a national dialogue over public issues and a civic-minded public capable of participating in political life. Like its Western European counterparts, however, this public remained divided by competing occupational, economic, and other interests and by divergent ideological perspectives, which in this case supported as well as challenged the autocratic order. The resulting conflict fostered political division within the educated and professional strata of society while simultaneously helping to undermine the autocracy by eroding faith in its underlying values and irreconcilably dividing the élites on which it relied.

Although less broad in range, similar divisions split state officialdom,

[5] On the non-ideological character of politics in Russia prior to the 19th c., see esp. N. Shields Kollman, *Kinship and Politics: The Making of the Muscovite Political System, 1345–1547* (Stanford, Calif., 1987), R. O. Crummey, *Aristocrats and Servitors: The Boyar Elite in Russia 1613–1689* (Princeton, NJ, 1983), B. Meehan-Waters, *Autocracy and Aristocracy: The Russian Service Elite of 1730* (New Brunswick, NJ, 1982), and D. L. Ransel, *The Politics of Catherinian Russia: The Panin Party* (New Haven, Conn., 1975).

suggesting that the distance between it and at least the educated and professional strata of society was narrower than normally claimed. The conflict produced by this intra-governmental division caused attempts to change the law legislatively to follow a pattern seen frequently during the late Imperial period.[6] Despite agreement on the need for legislative action, ideological differences and institutional and similar rivalries made consensus on any specific proposal difficult to obtain, with the result that extended discussion yielded only the belated introduction of modest, albeit important, changes in the law. Although incorporating new perceptions of the family, society, and individuality, these changes also demonstrated the persistence of traditional values and the ability of conservatives within both the pre- and the post-1906 legislative process to set the boundaries of legal change. One effect of such limited legislative change was to increase the importance of the courts as a medium for adapting civil law to changing conditions. But more ominously, it also embittered both the proponents and, their relative success notwithstanding, the opponents of progressivist and similar changes in the law towards the state bureaucracy. While the former blamed the bureaucracy for the inadequacy or lack of legal reform, the latter accused it of undermining the existing socio-political order by carrying reform too far.

This outcome suggests that the structure and methods of the tsarist governmental and political order were incapable of accommodating the ideological diversity that had emerged within both state officialdom and society during the late Imperial period, in part as a result of state policy itself. The resulting ideological conflict, however, helped to perpetuate tsarist traditions of legal paternalism and instrumentalism, even among those who challenged the tsarist order in the name of legality, civil equality, and the rights and security of individuals. In the final analysis, these latter principles constituted ideological ideals whose realization—like that of alternatives on both the left and the right—entailed the use of law as a means to shape the relations, values, and attitudes of the majority of the population.[7]

Hence the conflicts over civil law in late Imperial Russia in part constituted a struggle over the power to use law to shape society. The unfolding of events eventually gave this power to the Bolsheviks. With respect to the legal order, they used it ultimately to preserve the external forms of legality while subverting this principle in essence through the

[6] See the references cited above in the Intro., n. 21.

[7] On legality as an ideology, see J. Shklar, *Legalism: Law, Morals, and Political Trials* (Cambridge, Mass., 1964).

resubordination of the courts to political authority, thereby restoring the unity of the judicial system, the state administration, and political leadership which conservatives such as Pobedonostsev had desired. Conversely, despite significant twists and turns, Soviet family and inheritance law implemented essentially a radical version of the progressivist programme: monogamous marriage and the family remained but were recast on the basis of formal sexual equality, civil marriage was introduced and marital dissolution facilitated, inheritance rights—albeit initially restricted severely—were reassigned on the basis of sexual equality and the conjugal family, and the rights of children born out of wedlock were expanded. Patrimonial property disappeared, of course, with the socialization of land and other forms of immovable property. Yet the Soviet experience, too, demonstrates that although the law affects behaviour, it is far easier to change the law than to use it effectively to inculcate specific values, control behaviour, or shape social relations in conformity with ideals. As the people of the successor states to the Soviet Union embark upon the legal redefinition of their fundamental social and economic institutions and the reconstitution of their respective legal orders, they—and we—would do well to remember this limitation of the law and to recall the origin and basis of legality in the West in the struggle for power.

Select Bibliography

The bibliography lists only archival sources, legal materials, and the records and reports of legislative and governmental bodies. Rare materials located at the Harvard Law Library, Cambridge, Massachusetts, are marked 'HLL'.

Archival Sources

Tsentral'nyi Gosudarstvennyi Istoricheskii Arkhiv, Leningrad (now Rossiiskii Gosudarstvennyi Istoricheskii Arkhiv, St Petersburg):

Fond 796, Kantseliariia Sinoda.

Fond 797, Kantseliariia ober-prokurora Sviateishago Sinoda.

Fond 832, Bumagi Mitropolita Moskovskago i Kolomenskago Filareta.

Fond 1151, Gosudarstvennyi Sovet.

Fond 1226, Delo Vysochaishe uchrezhdennago Osobago Soveshchaniia ob izmenenii v sostave i poriadke deistvii Kassatsionnykh Departamentov Pravitel'stvuiushchago Senata.

Fond 1233, Osoboe Soveshchanie o nuzhdakh sel'sko-khoziaistvennoi promyshlennosti.

Fond 1278, Gosudarstvennaia Duma.

Fond 1283, Ministerstvo Vnutrennykh Del: Osoboe Soveshchanie po delam dvorianskago sosloviia; Kantseliariia Ministerstva Vnutrennykh Del po delam dvorianstva.

Fond 1284, Departament obshchikh del Ministerstva Vnutrennykh Del.

Fond 1364, Pravitel'stvuiushchii Senat. Kantseliariia Ober-Prokurora grazhdanskago kassatsionnago departamenta.

Fond 1405, Ministerstvo Iustitsii.

Fond 1587, Gosudarstvennyi Sovet, otdelenie del gosudarstvennago sekretaria po osobomu soveshchaniiu.

Fond 1664, Pechatnyia zapiski. Krest'ianskoe i dvorianskoe zemlevladenie.

Law Codes, Collections of Laws, Statutes, and Judicial Decisions, and Records of Legislative and Governmental Bodies

Danilov, I. G., *Ukazatel' voprosov grazhdanskago prava razreshavshikhsia na konsul'tatsii pri Ministerstve Iustitsii uchrezhdennoi 1867–1871* (St Petersburg, 1873).

Dvorianskoe zemlevladenie, material 1893 (St Petersburg, n.d.) (HLL).

Gessen, I. V., *Uzakonenie, usynovlenie i vnebrachnyia deti* (2nd edn., St Petersburg, 1910).

—— *Razdel'noe zhitel'stvo suprugov. Zakon 12 marta 1914 goda* (St Petersburg, 1914).

Goikhbarg, A. G., *Zakon o rasshirenii prav nasledovaniia po zakonu lits zhenskago pola i prava zaveshchaniia rodovykh imenii* (3rd edn., St Petersburg, 1914).

Gosudarstvennaia Duma. Prilozheniia k stenograficheskim otchetam. Tretii sozyv, chetvertaia sessiia (1910–1911 gg.) (St Petersburg, 1911).

—— *Tretii sozyv, piataia sessiia (1911–1912 gg.)* (St Petersburg, 1911), i.

——*Chertvertyi sozyv, vtoraia sessiia (1913–1914 gg.)* (St Petersburg, 1914), ii.

Gosudarstvennaia Duma. Stenograficheskii otchet. 1911 g. Tretii sozyv, sessiia chetvertaia (St Petersburg, 1911), i–iii.

——*1912 g. Tretii sozyv, sessiia piataia* (St Petersburg, 1912), i–v.

——*1914 g. Chetvertyi sozyv, sessiia vtoraia* (St Petersburg, 1914).

Gosudarstvennyi Sovet 1915 (Petrograd, 1915).

Gosudarstvennyi Sovet. Sessiia VII. Kommisiia Zakonodatel'nykh Predpolozhenii, no. 7, Doklad po zakonoproektu ob uravnenii lits zhenskago pola v pravakh nasledovaniia po zakonu s litsami muzheskago pola. Zasedaniia 24 Noiabria, 1 i 8 Dekabria 1911 goda (HLL).

——Dopolnitel'nyi doklad po zakonoproektu 'ob uravnenii lits zhenskago pola v pravakh nasledovaniia po zakonu s litsami muzheskago pola'. Zasedanie 12 Marta 1912 goda (HLL).

Gosudarstvennyi Sovet. Sessiia VIII. Kommisiia, Doklad no. 2 (St Petersburg, 1913) (HLL).

Gosudarstvennyi Sovet. Stenograficheskii otchet. Sed'maia sessiia (1911–1912) (St Petersburg, 1912).

——*vos'maia sessiia (1912–1913)* (St Petersburg, 1913).

——*deviataia sessiia (1913–1914)* (St Petersburg, 1914).

Grazhdanskoe Ulozhenie. Pribavlenie k proektu grazhdanskago ulozheniia (St Petersburg, 1906).

Grazhdanskoe Ulozhenie. Proekt Vysochaishe uchrezhdennoi Redaktsionnoi Kommisii po sostavleniiu Grazhdanskago Ulozheniia, Kniga pervaia. Polozheniia obshchiia (St Petersburg, 1903).

——*s ob''iasneniiami* (St Petersburg, 1903).

——*Kniga vtoraia. Semeistvennoe pravo* (St Petersburg, 1902).

——*s ob''iasneniiami* (St Petersburg, 1902), 2 vols.

——*Kniga tret'ia. Votchinnoe pravo* (St Petersburg, 1902).

——*s ob''iasneniiami* (St Petersburg, 1902), 3 vols.

——*Kniga chetvertaia, Nasledstvennoe pravo* (St Petersburg, 1902).

——*s ob''iasneniiami* (St Petersburg, 1903).

——*Kniga piataia. Obiazatel'stva* (St Petersburg, 1899).

——*s ob''iasneniiami* (St Petersburg, 1899), 5 vols.

Istoriia Pravitel'stvuiushchago Senata za dvesti let, 1711–1911 gg. (St Petersburg, 1911), 5 vols.

Kalashnikov, S. V., *Sbornik dukhovnykh i grazhdanskikh zakonov po delam brachnym i o zakonnosti rozhdeniia* (Kharkov, 1891).

Maksimov, V. Ia., *Zakony o razvode pravoslavnago i nepravoslavnago ispovedanii i o razdel'nom zhitel'stve suprugov, s raz"iasneniiami Pravitel'stvuiushchago Senata i tsirkuliarnymi i separatnymi ukazami Sviateishago Synoda* (Moscow, 1909).

Martynov, N. K., *Uzakonenie i usynovlenie detei (zakon 12 marta 1891 goda), s zakonodatel'nymi motivami, raz"iasneniiami Senata i obraztsami bumag* (4th edn., St Petersburg, 1902).

Mazurenko, N. N., *Rastorzhenie braka i zakon 28 maia* (St Petersburg, 1905).

Obrazovannoe pri Ministerstve Iustitsii Osoboe Soveshchanie dlia obsuzhdeniia proekta grazhdanskago ulozheniia v sviazi s postupivshimi na onyi otzyvami vedomstv. Zhurnaly 1–23 (s 25 fevralia 1910 g. do 26 noiabria 1912 g.) (St Petersburg, n.d.), 2 vols. (HLL).

Mikhailova, V., *Russkie zakony o zhenshchine* (Moscow, 1913).

Ministerstvo iustitsii za sto let, 1802–1902. Istoricheskii ocherk (St Petersburg, 1902).

Mneniia dukhovnykh konsistorii otnositel'no proekta preobrazovaniia dukhovno-sudebnoi chasti (St Petersburg, 1874, 1876), 2 vols.

Oppengeim, A. A., *Ukazatel' voprosov prava razreshennykh Ministerstvom Iustitsii za vremia s kontsa 1885 po 1893 god* (St Petersburg, 1895).

Otchet Ministerstva Iustitsii (St Petersburg, 1835, 1840, 1845, 1852, 1857, 1861).

Otchet po deloproizvodstvu Gosudarstvennago Soveta (St Petersburg, 1894–1907).

Otchet po Gosudarstvennomu Sovetu (St Petersburg, 1870–92).

Pen'kovskii, M. I. (ed.), *Kassatsionnaia praktika. Ne voshedshiia v ofitsial'nyi sbornik resheniia Grazhdanskago Kassatsionnago Departamenta Pravitel'stvuiushchago Senata s 1897 g. po 1914 g., s postateinym i predmetnym ukazateliami* (Petrograd, 1915).

Polnoe sobranie postanovlenii i rasporiazhenii po vedomstvu pravoslavnago ispovedaniia Rossiskoi Imperii. Tsarstvovanie Gosudaria Imperatora Pavla Pervago, 6 noiabria 1796 g. – 11 marta 1801 g. (Petrograd, 1915).

——*Tsarstvovanie Gosudaria Imperatora Nikolaia I* (Petrograd, 1915), 2 vols.

Polnoe Sobranie Zakonov Rossiiskoi Imperii (St Petersburg, 1830–1917), lst ser., enactments 1649–Dec. 11, 1825; 2nd ser., Dec. 12, 1825–Feb. 28, 1881; 3rd ser., Mar. 1, 1881–1913.

Polnyi Svod Reshenii Grazhdanskago Kassatsionnago Departamenta Pravitel'stvuiushchago Senata, 1866–1910 (Ekaterinoslav, 1910), vols. by year.

Pravitel'stvuiushchii Senat (St Petersburg, 1912).

Prilozhenie k svodu zamechanii na proekt knigi chetvertoi grazhdanskago ulozhenia o nasledstvennom prave. Zhurnaly zasedanii Kommisii, obrazovannoi pri S.-Peterburgskom iuridicheskom obshchestve dlia obsuzhdeniia proekta knigi IV grazhdanskago ulozheniia (St Petersburg, 1904).

Proekt polozheniia o dukhovnykh zaveshchaniiakh (St Petersburg, 1862).

Proekt pravil ob uluchshenii polozheniia nezakonnorozhdennykh detei s ob"iasneniiami (St Petersburg, 1898) (HLL).

Proekt statei o soiuze brachnom s ob"iasneniiami (Pervaia redaktsiia) (St Petersburg, 1896) (HLL).

Resheniia Grazhdanskago Kassatsionnago Departamenta pravitel'stvuiushchago Senata (St Petersburg, 1867–1915).

Rotenberg, L. M. (ed.), *Polnyi svod reshenii obshchago sobraniia pervago i kassatsionnykh departamentov i kassatsionnykh departamentov Pravitel'stvuiushchago Senata* (Ekaterinoslav, 1909, 1910), 2 vols.

Sbornik reshenii Pravitel'stvuiushchago Senata (St Petersburg, 1864, 1865), 2 vols.

Sbornik statisticheskikh svedenii ministerstva iustitsii. chast' 1. Svedeniia o lichnom sostave i o deiatel'nosti sudebnykh ustanovlenii Evropeiskoi Rossii (St Petersburg, 1884–1916).

Sistematicheskii svod sushchestvuiushchikh zakonov Rossiiskoi Imperii, s osnovaniiami prava iz onykh izvlechennymi. Izdavaemyi Kommisieiu sostavleniia Zakonov. Pravo grazhdanskoe. (St Petersburg, 1818–22).

Sobranie Uzakonenii i Rasporiazhenii Pravitel'stva, izdavaemoe pri Pravitel'stvuiushchem Senate (St Petersburg, Petrograd, 1863–1917).

Soveshchaniia starshikh predsedatelei i prokurorov sudebnykh palat po nekotorym voprosam sudebnoi praktiki v sviazi s peresmotrom zakonopolozhenii po sudebnoi chasti (St Petersburg, 1895) (HLL).

Spisok chinam Pravitel'stvuiushchago Senata i Ministerstva iustitsii. 1866. Ispravlen po l-e Iulia 1866 goda (St Petersburg, 1866).

Spisok chinam Pravitel'stvuiushchago Senata, Departamenta Ministerstva Iustitsii i sudebnykh mest, obrazovannykh na osnovanii sudebnykh ustavov 20-go noiabria 1864 goda (St Petersburg, 1870).

Spisok chinam vedomstva Ministerstva iustitsii (St Petersburg, 1884, 1890, 1900, 1910).

Sudebnaia reforma [35 vols. that correspond to *Delo o preobrazovanii sudebnoi chasti v Rossii* noted in F. B. Kaiser, *Die Russische Justizreform von 1864: Zur Geschichte der Russischen Justiz von Katharina II bis 1916* (Leiden, 1972); vols. are separately subtitled] (HLL).

Sudebnye Ustavy 20 noiabria 1864 goda, s izlozheniem razsuzhdenii, na koikh oni osnovany. Chast' pervaia, Ustav Grazhdanskago Sudoproizvodstva, Chast' vtoraia, Ustav Ugolovnago Sudoproizvodstva and Chast' tret'ia, Uchrezhdenie Sudebnykh Ustanovlenii (St Petersburg, 1866).

Sudebnye Ustavy 20 noiabria 1864 g. za piat'desiat let (Petrograd, 1914), 2 vols. and supplementary appendix.

Svod Zakonov Rossiiskoi Imperii (various edns., St Petersburg, 1832, 1842, 1857, thereafter by separate vol. to 1914).

—— *Prodolzheniia* (annual supplement, various edns.).

Svod zamechanii na proekt knigi chetvertoi grazhdanskago ulozheniia o nasledstvennom prave (St Petersburg, 1904).

Svod zamechanii na proekt knigi tretei grazhdanskago ulozheniia o votchinnom prave (St Petersburg, 1903).

Svod zamechanii na proekt knigi vtoroi grazhdanskago ulozheniia o semeistvennom prave (St Petersburg, 1903).

Trudy kommisii sostavleniia zakonov. tom ii, *Proekt Grazhdanskago Ulozheniia* (2nd end., St Petersburg, 1822).

Tsypkin, P. S., *Zakon 12 marta 1914 goda o nekotorykh izmeneniiakh i dopolneniiakh deistvuiushchikh uzakonenii o lichnykh i imushchestvennykh pravakh zamuzhnikh zhenshchin i ob otnosheniiakh suprugov mezhdu soboiu i k detiam* (St Petersburg, 1914).

Vsepoddanneishii otchet Ober-Prokurora Sviateishago Sinoda po vedomstvu Pravoslavnago ispovedeniia (St Petersburg, 1886–1916) [published earlier as *Izvlechenie iz otcheta Ober Prokurora Sviateishago Sinoda* (1841–1852), —— *po vedomstvu dukhovnykh del* (1853–8), —— *po vedomstvu Pravoslavnago ispovedaniia* (1859–61), and *Izvlechenie iz Vsepoddanneishago otcheta Ober-Prokurora Sviateishago Sinoda po vedomstvu Pravoslavnago ispovedaniia* (1866–83)].

Zagorovskii, A. I., *O vnebrachnykh detiakh po novomu zakonu (3 iiunia 1902 g.) v sviazi s postanovleniiami o nikh zapadnoevropeiskikh grazhdanskikh kodeksov* (Odessa, 1903).

Zamechaniia o nedostatkakh deistvuiushchikh grazhdanskikh zakonov. Izdanie redaktsionnoi kommisii po sostavleniiu grazhdanskago ulozheniia (St Petersburg, 1891).

Zhurnal soedinennykh departamentov zakonov i grazhdanskikh del Gosudarstvennago Soveta o preobrazovanii sudebnoi chasti v Rossii (St Petersburg, n.d.) (HLL).

Zhurnaly redaktsionnoi kommisii, vysochaishe uchrezhdennoi dlia sostavleniia proekta grazhdanskago ulozheniia. Proekt knigi II (semeistvennoe pravo) (Zasedaniia Kommisii s 29 sentiabria 1899 g. po 19 ianvaria 1901 g.) (St Petersburg, 1903) (HLL).

—— *Proekt o nasledovanii. (Zasedaniia Kommisii s 10 noiabria 1889 g. po 11 aprelia 1890 g.)* (St. Petersburg, 1899) (HLL).

Index